Essential Elements for Effectiveness

Optimal Functioning Through Positive Psychology

Juan R. Abascal, Ph.D.
Laurel Brucato, Ph.D.
Dominic Brucato, Ph.D.
Patricia Stephenson, Ph.D.

Seventh Edition

 Pearson

330 Hudson Street, NY NY 10013

Portfolio Manager: Erin Mitchell
Managing Editor: Debbie Coniglio
Development Editor: Jennifer Stevenson
Product Marketing Manager: Chris Brown
Senior Program Manager: Jane Lee Kaddu
Project Coordination, Text Design, and Electronic Page Makeup: Pearson CSC

Cover Designer: Joel Gendron, Lumina Datamatics, Inc.
Cover Photo: Warchi/Getty Images
Manufacturing Buyer: Carol Melville
Printer/Binder: LSC Communications, Inc.
Cover Printer: Phoenix Color/Hagerstown

Acknowledgments of third-party content appear on page 640, which constitute an extension of this copyright page.

Library of Congress Cataloging-in-Publication Data
Names: Abascal, Juan R., author. | Brucato, Laurel, author.
Title: Essential elements for effectiveness : optimal functioning through positive psychology / Juan R. Abascal, Ph.D., Laurel Brucato, Ph.D., Patricia Stephenson, Ph.D., Dominic Brucato, Ph.D.
Description: Seventh Edition. | Hoboken : Pearson, [2018] | Revised edition of Essential elements for effectiveness, [2015]
Identifiers: LCCN 2018005502 | ISBN 9780135199213
Subjects: LCSH: Success. | Success--Psychological aspects. | Self-help techniques. | Self-management (Psychology) | Conduct of life.
Classification: LCC BF637.S8 .A193 2018 | DDC 158--dc23 LC record available at https://lccn.loc .gov/2018005502

1 18

Loose-leaf Edition:
ISBN 10:   0-135-19921-2
ISBN 13: 978-0-135-19921-3

Revel Access Card:
ISBN 10:   0-135-18335-9
ISBN 13: 978-0-135-18335-9
www.pearsonhighered.com

Contents

CV 10.23.2018 2154

About the Authors

Juan R. Abascal, Ph.D., a graduate of Rutgers, the State University, and Kent State University, is a professor of psychology at Miami Dade College. He has been awarded an Endowed Teaching Chair and received the NISOD Excellence in Teaching Award. Dr. Abascal has also been honored with the Service Learning Professor of the Year Award. As a graduate of the Salzburg International Education Institute, he has been involved in the Global Education Initiative as well as the Earth Ethics Institute. He has also served the college as a department chairperson, Associate Dean, Academic Dean, and Associate Provost for Academic Affairs. A clinical psychologist by training, Dr. Abascal has conducted numerous personal effectiveness and stress mastery seminars and workshops with people from all walks of life, from the lay person to the professional health care provider. In conjunction with two of the other authors, he co-founded MindWorks, Int., Inc. a stress management center and comprehensive private practice of clinical psychology. In his clinical practice, Dr. Abascal specializes in helping individuals suffering from anxiety disorders and couples experiencing marital distress. He is committed to the principle that any individual willing to follow a step-by-step process can learn to function optimally and achieve joy in their lives.

Laurel Brucato, Ph.D., a graduate of the University of Illinois and Kent State University, is a clinical psychologist in private practice at MindWorks, Int., Inc., the Stress Management Center she co-founded in 1988. Dr. Brucato views herself as an eclectic positive psychologist who endeavors to help individuals develop and enhance their strengths to work toward optimal functioning, and to overcome their particular problems in living. In her clinical practice Dr. Brucato specializes in the treatment of anxiety and phobic disorders, obsessive compulsive disorders, depression, sexual dysfunctions, marital problems. She has also taught at Miami Dade College as an adjunct professor, as well as conducted numerous training workshops on stress mastery and assertiveness.

Dominic Brucato, Ph.D., a graduate of the University of Notre Dame and Kent State University, is a clinical psychologist and psychology professor at Miami Dade College. He has been the recipient of an Endowed Teaching Chair and the Service Learning Professor of the Year Award. He is also a Core Council Member of the Earth Ethics Institute and is involved with the Global Education Initiative. Along with his wife, Dr. Laurel Brucato, and Dr. Abascal, he co-founded MindWorks, Int., Inc., a stress management center and psychology practice. Dr. Brucato divides his time between teaching and his clinical practice. He specializes in teaching courses aimed at helping students reach optimal functioning in their academic and personal lives. A dynamic speaker, Dr. Brucato has conducted numerous stress mastery and effectiveness workshops dedicated to helping people from all walks of life achieve their full potential.

Patricia Stephenson, Ph.D., a graduate of the University of Florida and Florida State University, is a Professor Emeritus of psychology at Miami Dade College. Dr. Stephenson has been a counselor, director, and Associate Dean prior to returning to her first love—teaching. She is a two time recipient of an Endowed Teaching Award. She received a national award for contributions to staff and organizational development, and has served as a consultant to faculty groups writing curriculum, groups seeking conflict resolution, and training seminars for faculty staff and administration. As a health care professional, she is also an avid promoter of wellness lifestyles. She has presented numerous workshops for students, faculty, and health care practitioners on stress management, wellness, assertiveness and self-development. She is devoted to the teaching/learning process and helping individuals grow into their personal and professional promise.

Preface

Hey you! Yes, you. We *are* talking to you. At least that's what we would really like to establish with you - a dialogue. Now you might ask yourself: "What do you mean . . . a dialogue? To dialogue takes two people; all I have is me and this book!" But that's not true. You have your classmates, your professor, your friends, your family, *and* this book. We sincerely hope that you take the principles and ideas contained within its pages and discuss them. Talk about them. Consider their validity. And most importantly, try them out in your own life.

You see, the material you encounter in this book will best serve you if you use it. We recognize that using it will likely require some changes on your part. And we all know that changing is not always easy. Dialogue about that too. With others for support, explore ways in which what you are learning can have an impact in your life. Expect it to happen, and you might be pleasantly surprised.

So, let's begin. To make the most out of this book, we suggest you take a moment to think about what motivated you to pick it up. Why are you reading it? Even if your initial response is that it was required for the course, think . . . is there something else you want to get, other than a good grade, from reading this book? If you were able to change something as a result of your experience with this book, what would that be? What would be different about you? How would you look, feel, and act differently? Take a moment now to think about these questions.

There is a story about a group of scientists who were walking along the countryside when they saw a field of fruit-bearing trees. A local inhabitant told them that the fruit was called "Mango" by the natives of this land. This kind of fruit was unknown to them and they wanted to learn all they could about it. Half of the scientists went into one side of the field and began measuring the mangoes' weight and their size. They noted the color and the shape and recorded their findings. These scientists now *knew about* mangoes. The other half of the scientists went into the field; each took down a mango from the tree and tasted it. These scientists *knew* mangoes.

Did you do what we suggested in the first paragraph? Did you take a moment to think about what you wanted to get from using this book? If you did, you are like the scientists who ate the mangoes. Continue tasting what we have to offer and we can promise that you will notice a significant positive difference in your life. But if you didn't, your tendency might be to read this book much like the scientists who measured and weighed the mangoes. With that approach, this book might provide you with some interesting facts and general knowledge, but it is doubtful that it would create any significant changes in your life. The material discussed in this book will work for you only if you use it; only if you *do it*. Merely knowing about it is not enough. So if you have not considered the questions posed earlier, we invite you to go back and think about what you want to get, how you want to be different, and notice the results *after* you've tasted the mangoes. This way, you will not just know a lot *about* effectiveness when you are done. Instead, you will know how to *be* effective.

Acknowledgments

The authors would like to thank all of the faculty members who have used our book for their invaluable feedback and encouragement in the development of this edition. Your comments and your anecdotes about students have been inspiring.

We would also like to acknowledge and thank the many students who have not merely read, but used this book in their lives and shared their experiences with us.

Section One
Personal Effectiveness

This applied Positive Psychology textbook has been organized into three umbrella sections, recognizing the fact that optimal functioning occurs within three broad domains: (1) your personal life, (2) your interpersonal relationships, and (3) your work life. Effectiveness in each of these wide-ranging areas depends upon mastering core attitudes, behaviors and habits which are presented in this volume in a building block approach. Since success in relationships depends, at least in part, on developing habits of effectiveness in our personal life, we have begun with this domain. Likewise, in large part, effectiveness at work hinges on interpersonal effectiveness, hence the order of presentation. This first domain, that of Personal Effectiveness, covers a wide range of topics spread over eight chapters. These include how to change our paradigms, how we adopt effective mindsets, how we balance our self-esteem, how to motivate ourselves for and sustain achievement, how to master stress and adopt a healthy lifestyle as well as how to create life satisfaction. Lastly, we address how to find meaning and purpose in our life and the process of setting goals based on our purpose.

Chapter 1: A Reality Check
Chapter 2: Making Positive Choices
Chapter 3: Learning to Accept Yourself
Chapter 4: Pursuing Accomplishment Through Character
　　　　　Development
Chapter 5: Understanding Stress
Chapter 6: Developing Wellness Skills
Chapter 7: Experiencing Positive Emotions
Chapter 8: Creating a Meaningful Vision

Chapter 1
A Reality Check

Learning Objectives

After reading this chapter, you should be able to:

1.1   Explain how the processes of sensation and perception shape our understanding of external reality.

1.2   Describe how paradigms (frames of reference) help us to categorize and interpret our experiences.

1.3   Explain the role of paradigm shifts in the history of science and your everyday life.

1.4   Identify the key elements of Positive Psychology and how they relate to effectiveness.

1.5   Explain the relationship between reframing and paradigm shifts.

1.6   Describe neuroplasticity and how to maximize it.

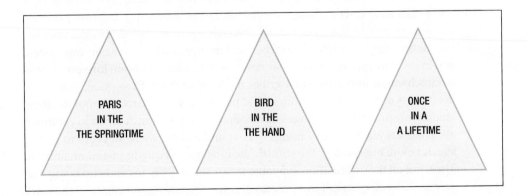

PARIS
IN THE
THE SPRINGTIME

BIRD
IN THE
THE HAND

ONCE
IN A
A LIFETIME

What do you think you just read within the three triangles above? Are you sure? Why don't you go back and read them again just to make sure and come back to this point. * Are you still seeing "Paris in the springtime", "Bird in the hand", and "Once in a lifetime"? After all, you certainly know how to read five little words. If you are so sure, would you be willing to bet your car on this? What about betting your next year's entire income? When we present this to our students in class, some of them are not willing to bet anything because they figure that something is up if the professor is setting the stakes so high and willing to wager at the same level. A small minority are not willing to bet because they recognize that it does not say what the majority of their classmates think it says. But the overwhelming majority of students are willing to bet their most prized possessions. Because after all, they can certainly trust what they see! They certainly *can* read three simple five word sentences. What about you? Did you see the double "the" and the double "a"? At what point did you see it? When you first read it, or when we invited you to reread it, or even after that? You know why? Because we really don't see what is there; *we see what we think is there*. And, believe it or not, this doesn't happen just with clever, little, five word, optical illusions like we presented above, this happens in every area of your life. Every time you face a situation, what you perceive is dependent as much upon your perspective as it is upon external reality. It turns out that reality, as we see it, is a movie generated by our brains. Because we don't realize this, we are far too confident that the stuff appearing in the movie is actually "out there" in the world when, in fact, it is not.

1.1 Sensation vs. Perception

Explain how the processes of sensation and perception shape our understanding of external reality.

To better understand how this is so, let's consider an important distinction within the field of psychology; the difference between *sensation* and *perception*. **Sensation** involves the process of receiving stimuli from our surroundings, such as light waves or sound waves. These then activate the receptors in our sensory organs, our eyes or ears in this case. Finally, through a process called transduction, the signals are translated into electrochemical impulses within our nervous system and brain. **Perception**, on the other hand, occurs when our brain interprets those electrochemical impulses and ascribes meaning to them. Perception, you see, is the process of attempting to understand the stimulation we receive. But the sheer amount of stimuli that impinges upon our senses is too much for us to capture it all. There are just too many things to hear and feel out there. In order to understand, before interpreting the stimuli, we must necessarily limit and organize it. Thus, not all the information available to our sensory organs ends up being perceived. Psychologists call this process of sensory analysis that begins at the entry level and works up as *bottom-up* processing.

A great example is **selective attention**, the fact that we focus our consciousness on only a partial aspect of all that we are capable of experiencing.

To illustrate this, consider the results of a famous experiment wherein subjects watched a short, one-minute scene of three men wearing white shirts passing a basketball, which was superimposed on a scene of three men wearing black shirts engaged in the same activity. The subjects were then asked to count the number of times the men wearing the black shirts passed the ball. About half-way through the video, a woman carrying an open umbrella slowly walked across the screen. The subjects, focused on the passes thrown by the men in black, totally failed to register the appearance of the woman. When they were subsequently shown the scene with their attention drawn to that specific aspect, they were extremely surprised to see the woman (Neisser, 1979, and Becklen & Servone, 1983).

In addition, we build our perceptions not just on the sensations traveling "up" to our brain, but also on our experiences and expectations coming down, in more of a top-down approach. Not surprisingly, psychologists call this *top-down* processing. In a classic experiment, psychologists Bruner and Postman (1949) cleverly demonstrated the fact that what we see does not always correspond to what is really there. These researchers created a standard, North American deck of playing cards except that some of the suit symbols were color reversed. For example, the nine of diamonds had black-colored diamonds instead of red. These special cards were shuffled into an ordinary deck, and then were displayed one at a time to subjects who were asked to identify them as fast as possible. At first the cards were shown very briefly, too fast for accurate identification. Then the display time was gradually increased until all the cards could be identified. The interesting thing is that while all the cards were eventually identified with great confidence on behalf of the participants, none of the subjects noticed that there was anything peculiar about any of the cards! Subjects identified the red six of spades as either a six of spades or a six of hearts, but were not aware that anything was amiss. When the display times were lengthened even more, subjects hesitated and got confused, making comments such as, "this is a six of spades but there's something wrong," but still had difficulty determining what was out of the ordinary. Subjects were eventually able to identify the cards as being the wrong color only when display times were greatly lengthened.

This result illustrates **selective perception**, the fact that we see what we expect to see, and not necessarily what is there to see. Neuroscience sheds light on how this happens at a neuronal level. When we perceive something a whole *network of neurons* in our brain is activated, not just a single brain cell. This allows us to recognize something even if a cell is damaged. This is called **distributed processing** which enables our brains to be very efficient in processing information. Distributed processing also accounts for the fact your brain can construct images even when no information is coming to your eyes, merely by firing a network. In fact, the brain structures used to imagine something are the same as those that process visual stimuli when you actually see it (Farah, 2000). That is one reason why it has been estimated that as much as 60% of vision is imagination.

The world that ends up being represented in our head, then, has been filtered by the stimuli we select to attend to, the way we organize that stimuli, as well as our expectations and past experiences. On top of that, our brains literally guess what we are seeing. To protect you from being inundated with information processing, your brain makes forecasts about what it is seeing, and changes these predictions only when it makes an error, a process called **predictive coding**. For example, did you know that for all humans there is an actual hole in the retina resulting in a blind spot? However, you don't actually see this black hole in your visual field, despite the hole in your retina. Your brain mentally fills in this void with its best guess of what should be there, much like how your cell phone tries to predict what you are texting. In our everyday life, sensation and perception blend into one continuous process and we are not aware of the distinction just described. The reality we perceive is nonetheless created by it.

Questions

1. The fact that we focus our consciousness on only a partial aspect of all that is in front of us is called _____.

   A. sensation

   B. perception

   C. selective attention

   D. transduction

2. _____ occurs when our brain interprets sensations and ascribes meaning to them.

   A. Predictive coding

   B. Selective attention

   C. Distributed processing

   D. Perception

3. The fact that we see what we expect to see and not necessarily what is there is called _____.

   A. perception

   B. selective perception

   C. distributed processing

   D. sensation

1.2 The Concept of Frames

Describe how paradigms (frames of reference) help us to categorize and interpret our experiences.

How you view any event or situation in your life is greatly influenced by your expectations, your beliefs, and your pre-conceived notions. This "way of seeing things" has been called by different terms that mean the same thing. Thomas Kuhn (1962) referred to it as a **paradigm**, in his landmark book, *The Structure of Scientific Revolutions*. Others have called it a perspective or a mind map or a **schema**. We prefer to call it a "frame." Have you ever had an unframed print, painting, or photo which you later got framed? Can you remember when you first saw your picture with its new frame? Didn't it look clearer somehow, more in focus? It was finished now. Can you recall the sense of satisfaction you experienced when you put it on display and stood back? Each and every one of us is adept at developing **frames of reference** or paradigms to enable us to organize and understand our world, our perceptions, our experiences. In every situation in which you engage, you eventually put a frame of reference around it in order to understand it, to make sense out of it. Most of the time this happens instantly and you are not even aware of it.

So how do frames help us? When you are "confused" about something, it takes longer to sort the experience into a frame of reference. Indeed, that is one definition of confusion: the inability to make sense of something or *place it within a frame*. Once we have developed a frame of reference, it is ready to help us more quickly interpret our experience the next time we encounter it or a similar one. Our brains are hardwired, genetically programmed, to create frames of reference to organize our experiences. Without this inherent ability to construct frames the world would be a very perplexing and unpredictable place. We would have to figure out each experience again and again if we didn't have frames in place to help us make sense out of our world.

Experiences are made up of multiple perceptions, sensations and bits of data which we need to categorize. For instance, imagine this situation. You are home alone and have just crawled into bed and it is really late. It is very dark and quiet. As you are just about to fall asleep you suddenly hear something moving near your front door. Then you hear a loud, scraping sound. You worry, "Is someone trying to pick the front door lock? What should I do if they break in?" You feel confused, threatened, and fearful. Sensing danger, you wonder what you should do next . . . should you call the police? Cautiously you creep over near a front window and silently peek out. There he is! You see a huge possum on your front porch clumsily moving around. Instantaneously your frame changes, and at the same moment, your thoughts, feelings, and your behaviors shift as well. You no longer think you are in danger; you now feel relieved, beginning to relax. You yell and make a banging noise on the door which scares him off, and you head back to bed. Think how powerful your frames are in determining your thoughts, your emotions, and your behavior. The very moment your perspective of the situation changed, so too did your whole being!

Figure 1.1 The Nine Dot Problem

You are fortunate that your brain is predisposed to develop frames of reference that were shaped by your learning history, including what you learned from your parents, your peers, in school, your place of worship, from the media and our culture. Some frames of reference remain in flux, but most become fixed. In fact, the more a frame of reference is used, and the more successful it is in helping you to derive meaning from your experiences, the more firmly your brain stores this frame. You tend to forget that it is only a paradigm, a frame, a habitual way of viewing things. The ability to recognize that you are operating within a frame, and shift that frame when appropriate, enhances your flexibility of thought and ability to solve problems. So how well can you do this? Try this problem now. **Connect the nine dots using only four straight lines and not lifting your pen off the paper.** By the way, use a pencil for we guarantee you will need to erase!

Were you able to solve the problem? If you are like most people you will find that it takes you five lines to be able to connect all the dots without lifting your pencil or bending the lines. Is this problem impossible to solve? It is only if you stay within the parameters and limitations of your current frame. We suggest you try going outside the box. When you look at the nine dots, what do you see? If you had to give those dots a name, other than "nine dots", what would you call it? Most people would call it a square or a box. Change that frame. As long as you hold onto the paradigm that this is a square and act accordingly, you will be unable to solve the problem. Go ahead and try it again, this time allowing yourself to go beyond the square. Were you successful? If not, here's another hint. Can you see it as a sort of an arrow? Adopting this frame of reference might help. If all else fails, go to the end of the chapter for the solution to the nine dot problem.

In another exercise designed to give you practice with shifting your frame of reference, look at the optical illusions presented on the next page. These illustrations represent what psychologists refer to as **ambiguous figures**. In the real world, we are faced with ambiguous stimuli and sensations all the time. The recognition that your perceptions are not reality, but just your perceptions, can facilitate the development of flexibility of thought, improved problem solving, and ultimately your effectiveness as a human being.

Figure 1.2 Is the Book Looking towards you . . . Or Away From You?

Figure 1.3 Woman in Vanity . . . Or Skull?

Hint: Move the book a bit farther away from you to see the skull or the woman looking at the mirror.

Figure 1.4 Man Playing Horn . . . or Woman Sillhouette?

Figure 1.5 A Rabbit . . . Or A Duck?

Hint: The duck is looking to the left, the rabbit is looking to the right.

Figure 1.6 Old Woman . . . Or Young Girl?

Hint: The old woman's nose is the young girl's nose and chin.

Figure 1.7 A Vase . . . or Two Faces?

Questions

1. Humans are adept at developing _____ to help us organize and understand our world.

    A. websites

    B. encyclopedias

    C. alternative facts

    D. paradigms

2. The ability to create frames of reference _____.

    A. is unnecessary

    B. is hardwired into our brain

    C. leads to confusion

    D. leads to criminal behavior

3. When we are unable to place something within a frame of reference, we are _____.

    A. in danger

    B. lucky

    C. confused

    D. happy

1.3 Paradigm Shifts and the History of Science

Explain the role of paradigm shifts in the history of science and your everyday life.

Paradigms have also played a major role in the history of science. As Thomas Kuhn observed, most major scientific discoveries are preceded by a **paradigm shift** a change in the overriding theoretical framework that governs a scientific discipline. Kuhn described in great detail how almost every significant breakthrough in the field of scientific endeavor is first a break with tradition, a break with old ways of thinking, a change of old paradigms. For example, in the field of astronomy a paradigm shift occurred after a long, hard fought struggle that spanned centuries until scientists finally accepted the fact that the earth revolved around the sun, instead of the earth being the center of the universe. Similarly, germ theory revolutionized medicine, but was initially resisted by those who found it incomprehensible that there could be infectious agents that could not be seen with the naked eye. Indeed, the reason we invented such tools as the microscope is that we believed in the possibility of extremely small, unseen creatures like germs.

In the *Structure of Scientific Revolutions,* Kuhn observes that the history of scientific advancement is a result of paradigm shifts. What Kuhn refers to as "normal science" proceeds by building a foundation of research and data based upon proving and expanding existing theoretical paradigms. But invariably anomalous results begin to turn up, findings which cannot be understood or accounted for by the overriding paradigm. Often these anomalies are ignored or discounted. Scientists who reveal or publicize these seemingly bizarre results are dismissed, and often even discredited within their profession. New theories or paradigms which attempt to explain the anomalies by expanding or changing the existing paradigm are often treated as heresy. Inherent in this is a struggle between the old guard of a discipline (who believe that they have the truth) and the mavericks who dare to challenge the accepted paradigm. It is no wonder that successful challenges to existing paradigms often come from outside the discipline, developed by individuals with a fresh perspective or different viewpoint. Eventually, the mass of anomalies builds to the point where the discipline must become open to a new paradigm in order to stay viable. Thus a scientific revolution occurs when the paradigm shifts. This may occur suddenly, but typically, given the resistance of the old guard, this is a more gradual process. Two or more paradigms may coexist for a while with separate adherents, but eventually the paradigm with greater predictive value will win out. But Kuhn was primarily describing the process of change within the natural sciences. The process of change in the social sciences tends to be more incremental and appears to be more a process of gradual paradigm shift or paradigm expansion.

A good example of a gradual paradigm expansion exists within the field of psychology. Early in the 1900's Sigmund Freud posited his theory of psychosexual development. Initially this appeared to explain the development of mental disorders and it provided a framework for the treatment of emotional difficulties. It was the first global theory of how personality was formed and it described both normal and abnormal behavior. This new paradigm stimulated the development of a new treatment modality, that of talk therapy, and it provided avenues for new research. But then holes began to appear in the theory. Psychoanalytic theory was a cumbersome model for explaining many emotional problems and psychoanalysis as a treatment often failed. Psychoanalytic theory had great explanatory value, but little if any predictive value. Competing models were developed.

Learning theory explained behavior in terms of conditioning and reinforcement (i.e. rewards and punishment). These theorists were called Behaviorists since they believed that behavior was not a result of repressed psychosexual impulses, as Freud believed, but was driven by the consequences that followed the behavior. At around the same time, humanistic thought came into prominence. The humanists held man to be not quite as dark as Freud postulated, driven by sexual and aggressive impulses. Instead, they professed that humans are driven to continually improve themselves, to move towards self-actualization.

Each of these perspectives was a reflection and a natural outgrowth of the population studied. For example, Freud's patients were primarily neurotic females living in a highly repressive Victorian society. Behavior theories stemmed primarily from laboratory research (often with animals) such as the pioneering work of Ivan Pavlov on classical conditioning, and B.F. Skinner on operant conditioning. Humanistic theories evolved from studying the best society had to offer as evidenced by Carl Rogers' research with college students, and Abraham Maslow's work with highly successful, self-actualized individuals. In fact, Maslow initially studied gorillas, but they were the most dominant gorillas in the pack. With such varying experiences influencing their observations, no wonder such different paradigms emerged. For many years, perhaps even up until the present, these different frames coexisted which led to continual debate about what was truth in psychology. Currently, the majority of psychologists would agree that one of the best and well researched approaches for explaining and predicting human behavior is the Cognitive-Behavioral model. This is especially true when it comes to understanding psychopathology and abnormal behavior. Freud's original paradigm, while not completely discarded, has been greatly expanded and refined. So, to quote Kuhn:

> . . . the historian of science may be tempted to exclaim that when paradigms change, the world changes with them. Led by a new paradigm, scientists adopt new instruments and look in new places. Even more important, during revolutions scientists see new and different things when looking with familiar instruments in places they have looked before. It is rather as if the professional community had been suddenly transported to another planet where familiar objects are seen in a different light and are joined by unfamiliar ones as well. Of course, nothing of quite that sort does occur: there is no geographical transplantation; outside the laboratory everyday affairs usually continue as before. Nevertheless, paradigm changes do cause scientists to see the world of their research-engagement differently. In so far as their only recourse to that world is through what they see and do, we may want to say that after a revolution scientists are responding to a different world (p. 111).

Questions

1. Scientific development is facilitated by _____.
   A. the old guard
   B. selective perception
   C. irrational thinking
   D. paradigm shifts

2. Paradigm shifts _____.

   A. are a primary cause of mental illness

   B. are typically met with resistance by the old guard

   C. do not exist

   D. typically happen very easily

3. Paradigm shifts in the field of psychology have _____.

   A. never occurred because the field has not changed since its inception

   B. been rapid and frequent

   C. typically happened gradually

   D. been irrelevant

1.4 Welcome to Positive Psychology

Identify the key elements of Positive Psychology and how they relate to effectiveness.

The paradigm governing psychology continues to shift and expand, most recently incorporating theory and research in the burgeoning field of **Positive Psychology** which is based upon the growing awareness that research and application in psychology has been incomplete, focusing primarily on understanding and fixing psychological problems. The ratio of journal articles about depression compared to happiness was approximately 100 to 1. There is a new emphasis on understanding and facilitating those healthy aspects of human functioning that make us effective in our lives due to the recognition that mental health is far more than the absence of mental illness. This expansion of the existing paradigm was named Positive Psychology in 1998 by Martin Seligman, the past president of the APA (American Psychological Association), who borrowed the term from an earlier work by Maslow in 1950.

As Martin Seligman (2002) tells it, the epiphany that led to Positive Psychology was set in motion by none other than his daughter Nikki when she was only five years old. According to Seligman, he used to be quite the "grouch." He was an overly serious guy who was very task-oriented and had little time for idle chit-chat, even with his family. One day Seligman was working in his garden and little Nikki was helping him, but she was being playful in that wonderful way young children have, as she was laughing, dancing, and tossing weeds in the air. Seligman got irritated and yelled angrily at her. Little Nikki decided at that time to give her daddy some constructive criticism, so she walked up to him and said,

> *Daddy, do you remember before my fifth birthday? From when I was three until when I was five, I was a whiner. I whined every day. On my fifth birthday, I decided I wasn't going to whine any more. That was the hardest thing I've ever done. And if I can stop whining, you can stop being such a grouch.* (p. 28)

At that moment Seligman had two life changing realizations. First of all, he realized what a curmudgeon he had become, and he vowed to change. But more importantly, he realized that raising his daughter, or any child for that matter, was not about correcting shortcomings, but about nurturing strengths. This was the ideological breakthrough that led to the development of Positive Psychology. Christopher Peterson (2006) talks about this watershed insight:

> *Psychology as it existed had little to say about these remarkable strengths . . . In Nikki's case these strengths included a precocious will to improve herself and the ability to challenge her grumpy father to find that same will within himself . . . To describe anyone in terms of the weaknesses and shortcomings they do or do not have is to ignore half of the human condition—the good half, obviously, that makes life worth living. And yes the garden was eventually weeded, and yes, Seligman became less of a grouch.* (p. 26)

1.4.1 Positive Psychology and Effectiveness

If Positive Psychology is concerned with the study of optimal human functioning, then what does this really mean? Optimal functioning is really just another way of talking about being an effective human being, by being successful in your personal life, in your relationships and in your career. You could say that the guiding questions of the Positive Psychology movement are: (1) What is it that makes individuals emotionally healthy, happy and effective? (2) What combination of skills, attributes, attitudes, talents and behaviors leads to positive emotions, mental health, and effective functioning? So when thinking about effectiveness, it becomes impossible to separate this from all we can learn from the field of Positive Psychology, as they have literally become one and the same. Positive Psychology also deals with many other fundamental questions about the meaning of life including such things as what is true happiness, whether virtue is its own reward, and what constitutes the good life, along with many other questions that will be addressed later in this text. The invaluable lessons from this domain are highly relevant to the study of what makes for an effective human being, as well as to the development of skills and attitudes necessary to function successfully in the world.

Positive Psychology is actually an umbrella term, the purpose of which was to bring together isolated lines of theory and research under one unified heading. These isolated topics were all avenues of psychological research and theory relating to what makes life worth living and how we enhance optimal human functioning. The seeds of Positive Psychology were sown well before 1998, in the Humanistic Psychology movement as conceptualized by Carl Rogers (1951) and Abraham Maslow (1970), in studies of giftedness (Winner, 2000), in conceptions of multiple intelligence (Gardner, 1983), in primary prevention programs based on wellness concepts, and in the human potential movement that was popular in the 1970s and 1980s.

1.4.2 Paradigm Evolution within Positive Psychology

The early conceptual underpinnings of Positive Psychology were built upon three main pillars:

1. The study of positive emotions and how to develop them more fully.

2. The study of character, of positive traits which include strengths and virtues.

3. The study of positive institutions which facilitate character building.

By implication the three are connected, although they certainly can function independently; positive institutions facilitate the development of positive traits which in turn help to promote positive experiences and emotions. However, Seligman (2011) in *Flourish*, has refined and updated his original theorizing. Initially, he proposed that the goal of positive psychology was to increase life satisfaction. Now he advises that the primary topic for positive psychology is **well-being** and the goal of positive psychology is to increase **flourishing** in our own lives and on the planet. In order to do this, positive psychology must focus on measuring flourishing and determining what factors facilitate its development. "Flourishing" is his term for optimal human functioning. According to Seligman, well-being theory is composed of five elements summarized under the acronym PERMA. The five elements of PERMA are:

P Positive Emotions – a wide range of emotions from contentment to bliss

E Engagement – being totally absorbed in an endeavor

R Relationships – having positive, healthy relationships with significant others

M Meaning – having a sense of meaning and purpose in your life, often involving belonging to or serving something bigger than the self

A Accomplishment – your ability to achieve your goals

Each of these five elements has three distinct properties:

1. It contributes to well-being.

2. It is pursued for its own sake.

3. It can be defined and measured independently of the other elements.

In a similar vein, Huppert and So (2009) measured flourishing in over 43,000 adults across 23 European nations. As a result of their findings they defined flourishing as having the three core features of positive emotions, engagement and meaning along with at least three of six "additional features" which consist of: self esteem; optimism; resilience; vitality; self-determination; and positive relationships.

So the field of psychology has expanded to include the study of effectiveness and flourishing, but inevitably there is an old guard that resists this paradigm expansion by insinuating that it is not scientific enough. These critics of Positive Psychology have dismissed it as "Happiology," or the superficial study of happiness when nothing could be further from the truth. While a study of positive emotions, including happiness, is part of the relevant topics we will cover, the real intent of Positive Psychology is to help you discover what it means to live an effective and meaningful life.

1.4.3 Paradigm Shifts in Everyday Life

You too may have a built-in resistance to changing your own personal paradigms regarding your everyday beliefs. There is an "old guard" within each of us that wants to hang on to the old and familiar. And what compounds the problem is that most of what we perceive supports our original frame. Remember selective perception, the tendency to perceive that which we expect to be there? You see, when we frame something, we tend to see only that which lies within the frame. Phenomena outside of it tend to be ignored or labeled anomalies. More often than not, we need to see things differently in order to discover the truth that it is so. Or as we often tell our students, if not the truth, then a whole new pack of lies to be considered until a new, more useful pack comes along. For example, as Mark Twain in his witty and clever manner noted,

> When I was a boy of fourteen, my father was so ignorant I could hardly stand to have the old man around. But when I got to be twenty-one, I was astonished at how much he had learned in seven years.

After a few moments of reflection, or after considering several examples, most people realize that they too experience these everyday shifts in perception. Sometimes they are trivial and sometimes they are profound. As noted earlier, you may have a good laugh after discovering that you are only the victim of an aggressive possum and not the target of a home invasion. Or you may find that your anger over a slow driver impeding your progress subsides when you finally pass her and realize that she is older than your grandmother. Most of us have had the experience of disliking someone, perhaps even intensely, at first meeting and then becoming very good friends later on when we got to know that person. First impressions are not always accurate. Our paradigms about people can change significantly as we get to know and better understand them. Sometimes the shifts are quite dramatic. On 9/11 many people went from frustration to immense gratitude when traffic problems prevented them from getting to their jobs at the World Trade Center or to their plane flights that were subsequently hijacked by terrorists. As the Dalai Lama said, "Sometimes not getting what you want is a wonderful stroke of luck."

Life will shift our perspectives without asking. What is worth asking is, how can we shift perspectives deliberately when we want our lives to be different? Effective individuals appreciate the observation of Einstein who noted that, "the significant problems we face today cannot be solved at the same level of thinking we were at when we created them." In order to solve them you are required to experience a paradigm shift, or a reframe. In his 1991 book, *The Seven Habits of Highly Effective People*, Steven Covey emphasizes that effective people are adept at questioning their frames and recognizing that "the way we see the problem is the problem." Thus, what we are after here is helping you build your skills at changing the way you think.

The Global Perspective
Spaceship Earth

Where do you live? Most of us learned our address and phone number at a very young age just in case we got lost. As we grew, we were introduced to the importance of geography and colored many maps as we learned the names and boundaries of states, cities, continents, and countries. Your family may have owned a globe where you could see the whole world turn on its axis. Just as we have discovered a truer notion of our place in the solar system, galaxy, and universe, we are realizing a truer picture of our own planet. When the astronauts began to embark on journeys orbiting our world, virtually all were struck by the vision of this beautiful blue planet as seen from space. There were no lines, no boundaries demarcating one country from the next. No latitude or longitude lines could be seen. The Atlantic Ocean did not have huge letters floating on it so that it could be clearly identified. In Buckminster Fuller's (1970) words, the astronauts had the profound realization that while they were traveling in a spaceship themselves, they had just left the spaceship that all of us are traveling on, Earth.

Effectiveness, however you define it, requires an inhabitable, sustainable world in which to be effective. All of us are traveling together on this **Spaceship Earth**. If the air is no longer fit to breathe, everyone's breathing will be affected. If the land can no longer support food production, everyone will eventually starve, some sooner than others. Modern humans have emerged in approximately the last 100,000 thousand years. For the vast majority of that time we functioned as hunter-gatherers. We took what we needed to sustain ourselves and moved on to let Earth naturally renew itself. Only 10,000 years ago we discovered agriculture and our population began its geometric expansion. Humankind unfortunately has been laboring under a very convincing yet false belief that we now call the "*fallacy of the commons*." For so long it seemed that we could fish, harvest trees, drill wells for water and oil without limit, and the planet was so large and abundant that there were no apparent consequences. Our best science now reveals that as untrue (Hartmann, 2004; Uhl, 2003). We are affecting the Earth, all of it. These changes that our choices are bringing about have no respect for borders.

James Lovelock (1979) in *Gaia: A New Look at Life* has proposed the Gaia hypothesis which posits that the Earth is not just the third rock from the sun with living organisms on it, but that Earth itself is alive and regulates itself to support the life on it. Humans and the choices they make are part of this process. How might your choices regarding the life you want to live be affected if your paradigm shifted and you saw the fate of yourself, your loved ones, and all of life inextricably linked as passengers on the same spaceship?

Questions

1. The emphasis on studying healthy aspects of human functioning, on effectiveness, and on mental health has been brought together under the heading of _____.

    A. experimental psychology

    B. social psychology

    C. positive physiology

    D. positive psychology

2. Which of the following is an element in PERMA?

   A. Mental Illness

   B. Accomplishment

   C. Religion

   D. Assertiveness

3. What interferes with our ability to shift the everyday paradigms in our daily life?

   A. predictive coding

   B. the old guard within us

   C. thinking outside the box

   D. open-mindedness

1.5 Reframing

Explain the relationship between reframing and paradigm shifts.

There is an oft-repeated story of a Chinese farmer that goes something like this...

A farmer and his only son were busily plowing their fields when their horse broke free from its harness and ran off into the nearby hills. When their fellow villagers heard of their plight they began to commiserate, "Oh, what terrible luck! How unfortunate! What will you do?" To which the farmer responded, "Good luck, bad luck...who knows?" Several days later the farmer's horse returned with two other horses in tow. His fellow villagers were astonished as they exclaimed "What wonderful luck! You lose your only horse and end up with three!" To which the farmer responded, "Good luck, bad luck...who knows?" Several days later the farmer's son was attempting to break one of the horses so as to put it into service on his land. The son was thrown from the horse and broke his arm. All the villagers were united in their opinion that this was indeed bad luck. The farmer as usual responded, "Good luck, bad luck ... who knows?" The very next week the Imperial Army marched through their village conscripting all the able-bodied young men into the service. The farmer's son was spared due to his broken arm. The villagers were once again impressed with this man's extraordinary good luck and told him so. And he replied, "Good luck, bad luck....who knows?"

This story illustrates what we call **reframing**, the process of actively changing perspectives to create paradigm shifts. Because the farmer was able to see things differently (i.e. think about them differently than his fellow villagers) he was able to respond differently, and experience an emotional calmness and equanimity that evaded those around him. Reframing allows us to be creative, increase joy, reduce suffering, and solve problems. Ultimately, all the changes we will suggest that you make are changes in perspective supported by your actions. As with most things, this is easier said than done. However, be assured it is definitely easier on you to learn to do it than to not do it. The primary obstacle to making this change is habit. Imagine riding in a cart on a dirt road for years always going to the same destination. After a while you don't need to steer or choose a direction. The wheels have worn grooves that simply and automatically take you to the same place time after time. If you see a new direction that you would like to pursue, that cart will still more easily go in the direction of the old path. Going down a new path requires a deliberate effort to lift the cart out of the grooves of the old path and onto the new. That old guard in you will want to keep things as they are. Within your brain something very similar happens where the equivalent of grooves are cut within the networks of frequently used neurons which access our paradigms. The first time you are presented with something, multiple neurons within the network might be involved. But by the sixth time, it has become much more efficient with most of the work accomplished by only a few neurons (Kalanit, Henson, and Martin, 2006). Yet this efficiency has a downside, as it creates limitations on our perceptions. Reframing requires a reconfiguration of the well-traveled network. This shift can be consciously initiated, but it requires deliberately engaging our frontal cortex by directing our attention and imagination in a different direction (Farah, 2000). Change takes time and effort. Sometimes it is relatively easy and sometimes it is challenging. It is almost always possible.

> *An adventure is only an inconvenience rightly considered.*
> *An inconvenience is only an adventure wrongly considered.*
>
> G.K. Chesterton

Consider these two differing viewpoints on the craft of acting. Actor Alec Baldwin was asking fellow actor Gene Wilder whether he preferred acting in the movies or acting on the stage in a theater. Wilder replied that he preferred movies because "They [the audience] can't come and get you." Baldwin replied that he liked the theater better because when he saw the audience he thought, "Look! They all came to see me." These are obviously radically different ways to view the same situation and they result in totally different experiences all based on the reality they create.

Reframing in its most basic form is simply asking the question: "Is there another way of looking at this?" There always is. Please understand that this whole book is a suggestion to reframe. Shifting to various perspectives on your personal journey will maximize the possibility of a life well lived or at least a life that is lived in the most enjoyable possible way. Since we are at the beginning of this long journey together, we are going to suggest two general strategies for reframing. Bring these as you explore the world and your story unfolding before you.

1.5.1 The Importance of Humor

An older gentleman approached his doctor with a problem. "Every morning at eight a.m. I have a regular bowel movement," he complained. His doctor was somewhat perplexed and responded, "That doesn't seem to be a problem to me.

Most of my patients would be thrilled to have a regular bowel movement at eight a.m." The patient replied, "The problem is that I don't wake up and get out of bed until nine a.m.!"

Humor is the most familiar way in which reframing is used. We are led to believe a situation is one way and then suddenly we see it differently through an amusing lens. This contrast leads to the experience of laughter. Whenever you can bring humor to your perceptions, your emotions can shift and your effectiveness is potentially increased. Lefcourt (2005) summarized much of the research data on humor and noted clear evidence that it can moderate the effects of stress, lessen depression, enhance immune system functioning, reduce the use of pain killers, and "be a positive asset in the survival and recovery from illness." There is even research documenting that laughter is conducive to creative thinking for problem solving, as well as for changing frames of reference in general. In one study (Isen,1991) psychologists found that subjects who watched a highly amusing video were much better at solving a complex puzzle where the solution required creative thinking about combining or using familiar objects in unusual ways. Subjects who only watched a neutral video were more prone to lapse into **functional fixedness**, wherein they got locked into thinking about using objects only in the most conventional or familiar ways, therefore they had far more difficulty solving the puzzle. The researchers concluded that laughter was instrumental in promoting flexibility of thought; that it literally seems to help people to think more expansively and associate more easily, making connections that might otherwise go unnoticed. This strongly implies that one way to help someone think through a problem is to tell them a joke.

Often our most interesting and funny tales are our descriptions of harrowing or embarrassing moments from our past, told from the safety of the present moment. As we step outside of the experience and see ourselves in it, we see it differently and we can therefore feel differently. You need strategies for modifying your feelings and emotions so that you can choose an effective response. Being able to laugh at yourself is one of the best. This is a simple strategy for changing your point of view and provoking humor. Imagine that your life is being videotaped and consider what this difficult moment might look like to your viewers. One of the authors discovered this strategy accidentally while moving a very heavy sofa with several friends.

The sofa was so awkward and heavy that everyone had to stop periodically to rest and readjust their grip. While we were doing this, I was intermittently warning all my friends to be careful not to set this large object on their feet. At that very moment I proceeded to lower the sofa onto my own foot! (And I realized that, indeed, it really was a very heavy sofa!) Just as my mouth was opening to ask for help, I mentally shifted to an outsider's view of my situation and started laughing hysterically. I had become Jerry Lewis or one of the Three Stooges, and I simply could not stop laughing long enough to speak. Luckily, my friends, also laughing now, realized I was pointing at my foot and removed the couch.

While we still recommend being careful with heavy objects, this incident demonstrates the power of shifting your point of view. The pain and upset would have been far more intense had our colleague not been caught up in the hilarity of the moment. Perhaps even more importantly being able to laugh at oneself not only keeps us humble but gives us an endless and always available source of amusement.

It is important to note the difference between the self-deprecating humor that we are referring to above and hostile humor which disparages others. Janes and Olson (2000) found that hostile humor is intimidating to people who merely observe it even though it was directed at someone else. These observers tend to become more sensitive to rejection and more afraid in general. The bottom line here is that the authors believe that hostile humor can lead to the social isolation of people who use it. So, while laughing at ourselves and with others can be a wonderful way to increase our sense of well-being and community, laughing at others is a far different matter. When we laugh at others, we risk, at the very least, incurring their anger or alienation. More than that, we risk becoming insensitive to the needs of others, and we fail to recognize our fundamental interdependence on other humans and forms of life. This brings us to the second important frame that we believe is fundamental on your journey to the good life, compassion.

1.5.2 Compassion: Opening Your Heart by Stepping into Their Shoes

One of the authors was educated largely in Catholic schools. To this day he considers it a mixed blessing because much of what he was taught, excessive guilt for instance, had to be overcome. However, one teaching from fourth grade always stuck with him. The phrase he was taught was, "There but for the grace of God go I." Whenever he saw someone in difficult circumstances, whether it was sadness, illness, disability, embarrassment, pain, or humiliation, he was urged to remember that under the right circumstances it could easily have been him. The message was to be grateful and be willing to help if you can. It could have been you. This, in essence, suggests a strategy for compassion. In humor we can step outside of ourselves and see ourselves. In compassion, we step into another's shoes and see through their eyes and feel what it is like to be them.

How often do we have conflict in our lives exactly because we failed to step into the other's shoes? There is a famous poem about six blind men in India who get into a heated argument about the nature of elephants. It seems that each of them approached the elephant at a different place and from a different angle, and each decided that he knew the true nature of the elephant. One decided it was like a wall because he had encountered the side of the animal. Another believed it was like a snake because he had grabbed the trunk. The others concluded that an elephant was really like a tree, a fan, a rope and a spear because they happened to approach from another angle. The poem concluded that they argued all night

Figure 1.8 What part of the elephant am I grabbing?

long about who was right and who was wrong. How much easier their evening would have been had they only taken the time to step into one another's places and feel what the elephant felt like from a different point of approach. Next time you find yourself in conflict with a significant other ask yourself, "What part of the elephant am I grabbing?"

There is a beautiful story from the Talmudic teaching tradition that illustrates the wisdom of compassion. The story is called *The Sorrows Tree*. The Sorrows Tree is the place where all souls go after they die. They go to the tree to hang the burden of sorrows that they carried in that lifetime on a branch of the tree. The magic of the tree is that as you hang your sorrows up you get to see and feel the sorrows that all the other souls have left. You are then asked to choose a new batch of sorrows from the tree for the next lifetime that you will lead. Once each soul gets to really know what it was like to feel another's pain, they invariably seek out their old bundle of sorrows since they don't seem so terrible after all.

Now we are not suggesting that many among us have not suffered extraordinary, greater than average difficulties, but we are suggesting that if you only knew what it was *really* like to be inside someone else's skin, you would feel and act differently. We can also come to know the gifts that have been received by those who have overcome great sorrow. Some losses are so great that the individuals who endure them become almost fearless in their approach to the remainder of their lives. What else can truly harm them if they survived that?

Be willing to shift perspectives. Learn not to take yourself so seriously by stepping outside of yourself. Learn to take life seriously by stepping into another's shoes.

Questions

1. Reframing involves _____.
   A. always looking on the bright side of things
   B. scientific progress in physics
   C. putting a new frame on an old painting
   D. significantly shifting how you look at things or view a problem

2. The process of reframing can be summarized by asking which question?
   A. What should I do next?
   B. Why am I confused?
   C. Is there another way of looking at this?
   D. What is in it for me?

3. When you get locked into thinking about things in the most conventional or familiar way it is termed _____.
   A. reframing
   B. functional fixedness
   C. selective attention
   D. PERMA

1.6 The Map Is Not the Territory – Neuroplasticity and the Brain

Describe neuroplasticity and how to maximize it.

Reality is an illusion, albeit a very persistent one.

Albert Einstein

So we invite you to always view your perceptions as just that: your perceptions; nothing more, nothing less. Your perceptions are like maps you use to get around in your world. Remember that a map is not the territory (Bandler and Grinder, 1975). It is just one representation of a territory. And some maps are more useful than others, depending on the circumstances. If you want to drive from Atlanta to Washington, D.C., you will need a good road map. A topographical map of the southeastern United States will be useless. On the other hand, if you want to fly a jet plane from Atlanta to Washington, D.C., a good road map will not help you, but a topographical map which helps you identify landmarks will come in very handy. The same is true of your perceptions. Given that we each have a unique set of glasses which color our perceptions, it makes sense to wear the pair that will be most useful in a given situation. Be open to the possibility that the solution is found in a reframe. Actively seek reframes and you will find that the more you do, the easier it becomes. This is the result of what has been called brain plasticity or **neuroplasticity** the capacity of the brain to change its internal structure by reorganizing neural pathways, connections and functions based on new experiences. In addition, an area of the human brain is capable of growing new neurons in a process called **neurogenesis**.

It was once believed that as we aged, the brain's networks became fixed. In the past two decades, however, an enormous amount of research has revealed that the brain never stops changing and adjusting. For instance, London taxi drivers have a larger **hippocampus**, a structure in the brain responsible for memory and new learning, than London bus drivers (Maguire, Woollett, & Spiers, 2006). It is not a coincidence that, for the taxi drivers, this new growth (neurogenesis) occurs in the region of the hippocampus specialized in acquiring and using complex spatial information in order to navigate efficiently. Taxi drivers have to navigate around London whereas bus drivers follow a limited set of routes.

The same example of brain plasticity is also evident in the brains of bilinguals (Mechelli, Crinion, Noppeney, O'Doherty, 2004). People who speak two languages have a larger left inferior parietal cortex than those who only speak one language. It appears that learning a language facilitates these functional changes and then in turn, the changes facilitate the learning of the new language. Not surprisingly, once you have learned two languages, it becomes easier to learn three, four, or more. Another example of the malleability of the brain is the difference between musicians' brains as compared to those of non-musicians (Gaser and Schlaug, 2003). The investigators compared professional musicians (who practice at least one hour per day) to amateur musicians and non-musicians. They found that gray matter (cortex) volume was highest in professional musicians, intermediate in amateur musicians, and lowest in non-musicians in several brain areas involved in playing music: motor regions, anterior superior parietal areas and inferior temporal areas.

Finally, Draganski and colleagues (2006) recently showed that extensive learning of abstract information can also trigger changes in the brain. They imaged the brains of German medical students three months before their medical exam and right after the exam and compared them to brains of students not studying for the exam at that time. Medical students' brains showed learning-induced changes in regions of the parietal cortex as well as in the posterior hippocampus. These regions of the brain are known to be involved in memory retrieval and learning (Michelon, 2008).

It appears that intense, repeated or prolonged mental/behavioral activity, especially if done consciously and deliberately, creates an enduring imprint in your neural structure much like the before-mentioned grooves on a well-traveled road. Neuroscientists are fond of saying, "Neurons that fire together wire together." That is, your repeated mental states affect your neural circuitry whereby your mind is literally sculpting and building your brain. This is referred to as *experience-dependent neuroplasticity*. As we learn and revise our perceptions, we actually modify the internal structure of the preexisting **neurons** in our brain, particularly at the **synapses**, the spaces where one neuron communicates with another. We also increase the number of synapses between neurons, thereby increasing our ability to create new frames. In addition, there is a new branch of biology, **epigenetics**, which examines the bridge between nature and nurture whereby your environment and your choices influence the expression of your genes and even the genetic code you pass to later generations (Suomi,1999).

Thus, the really ground-breaking news is that we can literally mold our brains by choosing to engage in patterns of thought and behavior (Hanson, 2014). For example, let's say you decided to practice breath awareness meditation on a regular basis. As a result your insula, a part of your cerebral cortex believed to be involved in consciousness, will be activated by this focused attention and will trigger a cascade of changes, some occurring rapidly and some over time. New synapses quickly form and more receptor sites are born within existing synapses, leading to greater synaptic communication. Unused synapses begin to atrophy (weaken) in a process known as **neural Darwinism** (i.e. *the survival of the busiest*). Various genes begin to be expressed due to the increased neuronal activity and your cortex will thicken. In the same way that your muscles are enlarged and strengthened by lifting weights, repeated patterns of mental and/or physical activity build your neural structure. A variety of studies on mindfulness meditation have validated this, wherein meditators demonstrated increased gray matter (a thicker cortex) in three key brain regions including the areas controlling attention in the prefrontal cortex (Lazar and colleagues, 2005), the insula (Holzel, 2008) and the hippocampus (Luders & colleagues, 2009).

Ultimately, you have the opportunity to build your brain to become healthier and more effective due to its enormous plasticity. With enough effort, skill and time you really can shift your brain to overcome the effects of adversity and maximize your strengths. Neuroplasticity can occur quickly at any age, it can develop slowly over your lifespan, and/or it can be expressed over generations through evolution. Furthermore, your experiences can go beyond merely modifying your neurons and synapses, but literally touch down into your genes and affect how they operate, that is, whether they switch on or off via the process of epigenetics. For example, if you choose to regularly practice relaxation, this will promote the activity of genes responsible for lowering your stress level and facilitating calmness (Dusek & colleagues, 2008), ultimately improving your resilience. We will address how to accomplish this in great detail in Chapter 6.

Do you know that exercising or stimulating your brain is highly recommended as part of a brain-healthy lifestyle? As neuroplasticity is becoming more apparent in cognitive science, an increasing amount of evidence has surfaced to validate the idea of "use it or lose it." When you exercise or stimulate your brain through new or merely unfamiliar activities, you can trigger changes in the brain, such as the increased connections between neurons described earlier. These changes contribute to an expansion in what psychologists call **brain reserve**. Research suggests that the more brain reserve, the more resistant the brain is to age or disease-related damages. A great example of this is what has been referred to as The Nun Study, a longitudinal study of 678 Catholic sisters 75 to 107 years of age belonging to the School Sisters of Notre Dame. Callahan, McHorney, & Mulrow (2003) presented case studies of various nuns, some of whom were over 100 years old but evidenced no cognitive deterioration, and some who had dementia and clinically significant Alzheimer's disease. When examining convent archives, they discovered that those sisters who were more intellectually engaged and had more intellectual pursuits, i.e., those who used their brains more, appeared healthier and functioned better cognitively than sisters who had fewer intellectual pursuits. It was the latter sisters who were more likely to show clinical symptoms of Alzheimer's. So it appears that using your brain protects you against dementia. What was equally fascinating was that when postmortem neuropathologic evaluations were performed, they found that the brains of the healthy sisters actually exhibited the same or more of the plaques typical of Alzheimer's than those of the afflicted! So their intellectual endeavors did not prevent the Alzheimer's from developing, rather, it led to the build-up of more brain reserve so the disease did not affect these sisters!

The experimental evidence is by now compelling that learning a new skill produces structural changes in the brain. The new skill could be learning a new language, a musical instrument, human anatomy, a city map, or even a seemingly frivolous activity, such as juggling. Using a sophisticated whole-brain imaging technique to detect changes in gray matter, researchers demonstrated that mastering how to juggle led to a 3 to 4 percent increase in the size of gray matter, the processing portion of your brain tissue. Young adults were randomly assigned to either a juggling group who had three months to show that they could juggle three balls for at least 60 seconds, or a control group that continued with life as usual. Baseline MRIs revealed no significant difference between the two groups prior to the experiment. Only the jugglers evidenced the increase in gray matter after three months. Then, after not practicing for three months, repeat brain scans showed a decrease of 1 to 2 percent from the size they had attained when they were practicing juggling every day (Draganski & colleagues, 2004). A similar study, published in the *Journal of Neuroscience*, using individuals with an average age of sixty rather than young adults, demonstrated that older brains also have the flexibility to grow. Although the older adults did not learn to juggle as well as the younger adults, those that did learn showed similar increases in gray matter (Boyke & colleagues, 2008).

These increases are not limited to our gray matter. Even the white matter, the area of the brain where neuronal communication primarily occurs, shows an increase as a result of learning to juggle. A group of researchers from the University of Oxford, again using young adults, a matched control group, and pre/post measurements, demonstrated that jugglers grew more white matter in the parietal lobe, an area involved in connecting what we see to how we move. No

Figure 1.9 The Nine Dot Solution

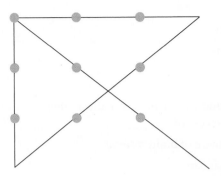

change was apparent in the brain of the non-jugglers. What is perhaps even more revealing is that the growth was evident in all of the jugglers, irrespective of how well they could juggle (Scholz & colleagues, 2009). So it is apparent that it is the learning process itself that is important for brain development, not how well you perform. The brain, like a muscle, needs to be exercised, but it appears that it also wants to be challenged to learn something new.

Thus, the ability to flex your brain is one avenue to creative thinking. What is creative thinking, if not the ability to look for innovative solutions to the problems at hand? Speaking of solutions, how successful were you in solving the problem presented to you earlier in the chapter?

Obviously, to solve this problem you had to go beyond the nine dots, beyond the originally preconceived square which you likely perceived. Your paradigm that this was a square led you to use the corner dots as the edges, which effectively inhibited you from solving this problem. Is this just another clever riddle? Or does it show us that we are predetermined to see things in a particular or familiar way, and what we see dictates how we interact with that reality (in this case how we attempt to solve the problem)? Learning to think "out of the box" is one of the cornerstones of creativity, which in many ways is all about shifting your frame of reference.

Questions

1. The capacity of the brain to change its internal structure based on new experience is _____.

   A. neurogenesis

   B. neuroplasticity

   C. epigenetics

   D. neural Darwinism

2. The structure in the brain responsible for memory and new learning is the
_____.

   A. synapses

   B. frontal cortex

   C. hippocampus

   D. gray matter

3. Your behavior and experiences can affect whether your genes switch on or off due to the process of _____.

   A. the development of brain reserve

   B. neural Darwinism

   C. neurogenesis

   D. epigenetics

Summary

This chapter covered a wide range of topics which all deal with how we perceive and interpret our reality. We began by elucidating the difference between sensation and perception, while emphasizing that our perceptions are dependent as much upon our individual perspectives as by external reality, determined by processes such as selective attention, selective perception, and predictive coding. We are all hardwired to develop frames of reference, termed paradigms, which enable us to organize and understand our world. These paradigms are greatly influenced by our expectations, beliefs, and pre-conceived notions shaped by our learning history, including what we learned from parents, peers, school, and religion as well as from the media and culture at large.

When our paradigms change, whether gradual or suddenly, this is termed a paradigm shift. Most major scientific discoveries in science are preceded by a paradigm shift, which is a change in the overriding theoretical framework undergirding that scientific discipline. But such shifts are typically resisted, often vehemently, by an old guard that clings to the status quo. The same can be true for our personal, everyday paradigms as each of us can harbor an internal old guard that is resistant to change, even in the face of mounting evidence to the contrary. In the field of psychology (where historically paradigm shifts have happened gradually) a new paradigm, that of Positive Psychology emerged which focuses on the study of mental health and effective functioning rather than mental illness. One effective way of facilitating paradigm shifts is by utilizing reframing strategies.

The last section of the chapter contains an overview of neuroscience with an emphasis on neuroplasticity, the capacity of our brain to change and forge expanded neural connections based on new experiences. Actively engaging in reframing can facilitate neuroplasticity which helps build brain reserve. Ultimately, you can build your brain to become healthier and more effective with any activity (mental or physical) which stimulates or exercises your brain.

Positive Psychology Exercise

1. Is there a situation where you are habitually stuck because you are totally unwilling to part with your point of view about it? We guarantee that if you think hard enough you will find that the answer to this question (for everyone) is typically yes. Can you think of a particular instance? Practice shifting your perspective on your issue using reframing. If you are at a loss for how to proceed, then experiment with reframing a past mistake or failure as a valuable learning experience. Think about how your life might have improved or been enriched today, either directly or indirectly, as a result of this experience. You may have to dig deep to adopt this perspective, or to see connections between past mistakes and current successes, but if you persist you will be rewarded.

Key Terms

Ambiguous Figures	Neural Darwinism	Predictive Coding
Brain Reserve	Neurogenesis	Reframing
Distributed Processing	Neurons	Schema
Epigenetics	Neuroplasticity	Selective Attention
Flourishing	Paradigm	Selective Perception
Frames of Reference	Paradigm Shift	Sensation
Functional Fixedness	Positive Psychology	Synapse
Hippocampus	Perception	Well-being

Shared Writing

In the same vein as the wise words of the Dalai Lama, there is an old quote, "When God closes a door, he opens a window." Think of a time when an important door closed for you. What windows opened? Write about your experience.

Chapter 1 Questions

1. _____ involves receiving stimuli from our environment while _____ involves interpreting these stimuli and giving them meaning.

   A. Selective perception; predictive coding

   B. Sensation; perception

   C. Perception; sensation

   D. Selective attention; transduction

2. When the brain makes forecasts about what it is seeing and changes these predictions only when it makes an error, it is engaging in a process called _____.

   A. distributed processing

   B. transduction

   C. predictive coding

   D. selective perception

3. It is estimated that as much as _____ of vision is imagination.

   A. 20%

   B. 40%

   C. 60%

   D. 80%

4. Major scientific discoveries are usually preceded by a _____.

   A. natural disaster

   B. feud between rival scientists

   C. prophetic dream

   D. paradigm shift

5. Frames of reference _____.

   A. cause us to be confused

   B. help us understand and organize our world

   C. are constantly in flux

   D. are useless

6. Flexibility in thinking is a component of _____.

   A. the old guard

   B. effectiveness and creativity

   C. the high-level practice of yoga

   D. functional fixedness

7. Positive psychology involves the study of _____.

   A. mental illness

   B. mental and emotional health

   C. the negative effects of positive thinking

   D. statistics that prohibit inclusion of negative numbers

8. Which of the following is an example of reframing?

   A. detaching and compartmentalizing emotional upset

   B. engaging in denial

   C. putting a new frame on an old painting

   D. seeing the humor in a difficult situation

9. Reframing involves _____.

   A. making up alternative facts

   B. suppressing your thoughts

   C. shifting how you look at something

   D. asking others what they think about something

10. The brain is capable of growing new neurons in a process known as _____.

    A. brain reserve

    B. neural Darwinism

    C. neuroplasticity

    D. neurogenesis

Chapter 2
Making Positive Choices

	Learning Objectives

After reading this chapter, you should be able to:

2.1 Describe the concept of soft determinism and how it relates to positive psychology.

2.2 Explain the ways in which the paradigm of proactivity guides the behavior of effective individuals.

2.3 Define the concept of self-efficacy and list some of the ways it can be increased.

2.4 Identify strategies for identifying and replacing irrational beliefs.

2.5 Identify some practical ways to develop an optimistic outlook and lead a more effective life.

Have you ever wondered, at some time in your life, "Why am I the way that I am?" One of the authors recalls a question frequently asked of him at the start of his graduate career while in training to become a psychologist:

> *'What made you choose to become a psychologist?' people would ask me. My traditional retort was, 'because I'm screwed up and I want to figure myself out'. I guess that I was searching for the truth about myself. Along the way I discovered that I was not as screwed up as I feared I was, the "I'm OK, You're OK" school of thought as proposed in the book with the same title by Thomas Harris (1967). And later I concluded that maybe I was a bit screwed up, but that wasn't so bad, the "I'm not OK, You're not OK, and that's OK" school of thought proposed by Sheldon Kopp (1972), in his book If You Meet the Buddha on the Road, Kill Him! But most importantly I realized that there was no one truth, since the truth was dependent upon the frame of reference, or school of thought that I*

adopted. Early in my career, while enveloped in the Freudian mystique, I blamed my parents for my troubles and felt that I was the victim of, at times, a traumatic childhood. When studying Behavioral theories I concluded that I was the product of an unusual reinforcement and conditioning history. But the Humanists and the Cognitive- Behaviorists helped me realize I had some choices in the matter of who I was, and who I would ultimately become. I realized I was who I was, not because of what had happened to me, but because of the choices I had made in response to what had happened in my life. Lately, I have come to be intrigued by the positive psychologists who suggest that I am what I am by what I choose to focus on. I can entertain misery and wallow in it, or wonder what awaits me in the happiness and acceptance camp. In my life, I attempt to choose the latter.

2.1 Determinism vs. Free Will

Describe the concept of soft determinism and how it relates to positive psychology.

The history of science reveals that the various scientific disciplines developed, in part, in order to determine the causes of events. Meticulous observations and measurements led scientists to the conclusion that everything which occurs in nature has a cause. Theories of causation were postulated and then tested by scientific experimentation. This belief in cause and effect relationships has been termed **determinism**.

As psychology matured as a science, social scientists, in turn, began to posit that human behavior may also be the product of causal relationships, and therefore determined. That is, if nature encompasses all of humanity, then human behavior must also be the result of various determining factors. Determinists espouse the view that all human actions are caused by something, even if we are oblivious to these causative factors. Strict determinists go so far as to imply that free choice does not exist, that all our actions and decisions are the product of outside determining variables over which we have no control. At the other end of the spectrum we find the **Free Will** camp. According to this point of view humans can and do typically ignore so-called determining factors, such as genetics or environmental influences, and freely choose how and when to act.

Psychological theories of personality and behavior can be placed on a continuum between determinism, the belief that who we are is largely governed by outside forces, and free will, which obviously assumes that who we are is a result of the choices we make.

There are three main deterministic theories. The first of these are the biologically based theories which postulate that we are almost exclusively a product of our genetic heritage. Proponents of these theories claim that all of our behavior, both normal and abnormal, can be traced back to particular configurations of our genetic makeup. Support for these theories comes from the obvious fact that abilities, talents, and certain emotional and physical disorders clearly run in families.

Figure 2.1

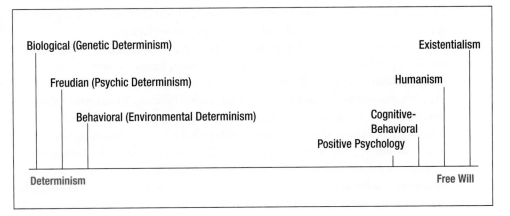

For example, it is evident that singing ability is passed down from generation to generation. Just look at the late, great reggae artist, Bob Marley, and his son Ziggy Marley, or Julio Iglesias and his son, Enrique Iglesias, or Nat King Cole and his daughter Natalie Cole, or Judy Garland and her daughter Liza Minnelli, or in acting ability where actor Michael Douglas followed in his father Kirk's footsteps. Or consider athletics where sons often follow in their father's footsteps like quarterbacks Eli and Peyton Manning and their quarterback father Archie Manning, or basketball superstar Stephen Curry and his father Dell Curry. As another example, let's take the rather severe emotional disorder known as **schizophrenia**. Individuals suffering from this malady have difficulty differentiating traditional reality from their own internal fantasies or fears. Schizophrenic individuals are prone to **"psychotic episodes"** where they lose contact with reality, and suffer from **hallucinations** (seeing or hearing things that aren't really there), and/or **delusional thinking** (believing in ideas that are not reality based, like those involving fears of persecution). Research clearly shows a strong genetic component to this disorder (Mirsky & Quinn, 1988). The **concordance rate** (the probability that two individuals display the same trait or characteristic) of schizophrenia is much higher for identical twins (who have the same genetic makeup) than for fraternal twins (whose genetic makeup is the same as any sibling), or siblings in general. All of these, however, were much higher than for non related individuals raised in the same environment (Gottesmann, 1991; Cannon et. al, 1998). So theories of genetic determinism espouse a view of reality that "my grandparents did it to me. I am who I am because of my genes."

A second set of deterministic theories are those of psychic determinism which postulate that you are who you are because of how you were raised. The most famous of these is Freud's (1924) **Psychoanalytic Theory**. Proponents of this theory believe that your personality is determined by your early experiences, and that by the time you reach six years old, it is pretty well set. So such things as the tenure of your toilet training or your mother's style of feeding you have a profound influence on your later development. This theory says "my parents did it to me. I am who I am because of the way they brought me up."

The third set of deterministic theories, known as **Behaviorism**, postulates that we are a product of our conditioning and learning histories, and of our current reinforcement schedules. There is a wealth of data that the aforementioned factors greatly influence the behavior of both animals and humans. In order to ensure that psychology be accepted as a "science," Behavioral theorists argued that the only unit worthy of study was overt, observable behavior. According to theorists such as B.F. Skinner (1953), and Ivan Pavlov (1927), it is our overall environment that shapes our personality and behavior. Thus, you became a good student because you were rewarded for academic achievement. Or you learned how to be fearful because you copied the behavior of significant others who modeled being afraid. These theories say, "my environment (parents, teachers, bosses, coaches, siblings, peers, etc.) did it to me. I am who I am because of the pressures they exerted and the rewards they provided."

But are these theories based on reality? Is this really all there is to human behavior? Are we just essentially victims of our genes, our upbringing, and our environment? The proponents of the Free Will theories would argue that these deterministic paradigms only tell a part of the story. They are accurate maps of a portion of the territory, but fail to include a key component of the human existence. The fact is, we believe that while you are certainly influenced by all of these factors, human beings are ultimately free to choose. Perhaps the earliest of these theories is based on the European philosophy of **Existentialism**, as popularized by Jean-Paul Sartre and Albert Camus. These philosophical theories, when translated into psychological thought, basically posited that although, undoubtedly, life throws waves at you that are outside of your control, how you ride those waves is up to you. You could choose to be drowned by the rising waters, or you could learn to tread water, or you could master surfing.

Here in America this view was developed further by the **Humanists**, such as Abraham Maslow (1970) and Carl Rogers (1959). They too hypothesized that our personalities and our behavior were not so much a product of our conditioning and our conditions, but of the choices we made in response to those. They were much more optimistic than the existentialists by promoting a belief that if anything occurred naturally, it was human beings striving towards self-actualization, towards becoming all that we can be. These humanistic theories developed partly in reaction to the strictly deterministic Freudian view which dominated psychology and psychotherapy practice at the time.

Cognitive-Behaviorists, such as Albert Ellis, Aaron Beck, and Martin Seligman pointed out that when studying humans, we should not focus solely on the study of overt behavior, as the strict Behaviorists would have it, but must take into account "covert behavior," our thoughts, the internal self-talk that preceded the behaviors. Steven Hayes and colleagues (1999) along with Russ Harris (2009, 2011), proponents of Acceptance and Commitment Therapy (**ACT**), similarly emphasize the role of covert behaviors (thoughts, emotions and images) along with the choices at our disposal for coping and behaving effectively. The strict Behaviorist model is an S - R (stimulus - response) model. Simply stated this cause and effect model holds that all behavior is controlled by the stimulus which precedes it. For example, you walk into your house and your spouse or parent screams at you for being late (the stimulus), and as a consequence of this you get angry and yell back (the response). This model was based on research with animals, which appear to be more stimulus bound. But for humans a more descriptive model is that of S - O - R (stimulus - organism - response). A stimulus impinges upon you, but before you respond, you have a thought about that stimulus, you imbue it with meaning. It is *that thought* that leads to your particular response. To go back to our earlier example, after you've been screamed at, if your first thought is, "how dare you?" or "that jerk, she/he is always picking on me," you are likely to respond in kind. However, if your first thought is "he/she must have been really worried about me," you are much more likely to respond with an apology. You see, it was not the screaming that led to your response, but what you said to yourself about the screaming. It is here, between the stimulus and the response that choice resides. To quote Steven Covey (1991), "Between stimulus and response humans have the greatest freedom, the freedom to choose that response." The difficulty lies in the fact that our thoughts tend to be automatic and rather telegraphic, and we are generally not aware of them. But more on this later in this chapter.

Human history is replete with examples of individuals who, when faced with extraordinarily difficult situations, stimuli which would overwhelm most of us, exercised this freedom to choose their responses. Take, for example, the incredible life story of Nelson Mandela (1918–2013), the first black president of South Africa and the driving force behind the dismantling of apartheid. Mandela spent 27 years in prison after being convicted of treason for advocating resistance to the racist government. He was confined to a tiny prison cell without a bed or plumbing and forced to do hard labor in a quarry. As a black political prisoner he received fewer privileges and far more meager rations compared to other inmates. He was routinely subjected to harsh punishments for even slight offenses. However, he refused to allow prison to rule his life. His goal while in prison was not to be bound by the routines and proscriptions of prison life, but to make his own world within the prison walls. Despite such deplorable circumstances, while confined Mandela earned a law degree from the University of London and mentored his fellow prisoners. He smuggled out political statements to encourage change through nonviolent resistance and he wrote his autobiography *Long Walk to Freedom* (1999). He never allowed his own mistreatment to affect his goal of creating racial equality and harmony while emphasizing restraint against retaliation. After being freed from prison in 1994, he led negotiations with the government and various South African political organizations to end apartheid and establish a multiracial government. In 1994 Mandela became the first black president of South Africa and established a government based on majority rule while prohibiting discrimination against minorities, including whites. His bold agenda involved improving race relations, discouraging blacks from retaliating against whites, and rebuilding the international image of South Africa. He established the Truth and Reconciliation Commission to promote both public accountability of wrongdoing by the government along with forgiveness from the people at large. To help facilitate improved relations between the races, he successfully encouraged all Afrikaners to rally around their popular rugby team, a strategy that helped ease racial tensions. For a different kind of example, we recommend that you *choose* to view the movie *Life is Beautiful*, the 1998 Academy Award winner for best foreign film, which provides a perfect example of our freedom to choose our actions even when faced with intolerable conditions. Lest you think that this is just a romanticized version of a possible response to the tragedy which was the Holocaust, we urge you to read Victor Frankl's (1959) autobiographical account of his time in a concentration camp, as described in his book *Man's Search for Meaning*.

If we take an objective look at the body of knowledge and data amassed in psychology over the last hundred years, the inescapable conclusion is that human behavior can best be understood as lying somewhere in the middle of the free will vs. determinism continuum. There is conclusive research evidence that certain emotional disorders (such as schizophrenia and bipolar disorder) have a strong genetic component, in the same way that inherited predispositions towards diabetes or heart disease run in some families. Likewise, we cannot ignore the overwhelming evidence that we are strongly affected by environmental factors ranging from our past experiences, our learning history (including what we have learned through operant and classical conditioning as well as observational learning), to our current situation. Could it be that our belief in free will is just a fantasy? Do we harbor an illusion of free choice because at any given moment we are bombarded with so many determining variables that we are unable to perceive them or sort them out? Most psychologists have come to the conclusion that human behavior is affected by a combination of determining forces along with each individual's inherent ability to choose, to set and pursue goals, and to decide to change the path set by determining factors. Not all humans rise to this challenge, however, but the capability to do so exists nonetheless. This mixed viewpoint has come to be known as *soft determinism*.

Where does positive psychology fit on this continuum, you may wonder? Positive psychology is not just one theoretical framework or orientation but an umbrella orientation that subsumes aspects of many theories that pertain to human flourishing. So in this regard it incorporates much of Humanistic psychology, aspects of the Cognitive-Behavioral approach, even aspects of the Psychoanalytic/Psychodynamic models (see attachment theory in Chapter 11), as well as recognizing the genetic/biological link involved in both positive emotions and our signature strengths (which we will elucidate in later chapters). But while positive psychology acknowledges the role of genetics, it puts its focus on what we can do about our situation, placing it more squarely on the free will end of the continuum. Research in neuroplasticity and epigenetics, as presented in Chapter 1, shows that when you change your choices and thereby your behaviors, you can change your genetic expression. Even more surprising, when you change your own genetic expression, your future generations profit from the choices you make today.

Questions

1. Theories of personality and behavior fall somewhere on a continuum between _____ and _____.

   A. internal; external

   B. determinism; free will

   C. operant conditioning; classical conditioning

   D. liberal; conservative

2. The _____ theory of personality claims that you are who you are because of your learning and reinforcement history.

   A. Biological

   B. Psychoanalytic (Freudian)

   C. Behaviorist

   D. Humanistic

3. The _____ theory of personality claims that you are who you are because of your early upbringing.

   A. Biological

   B. Behaviorist

   C. Humanistic

   D. Psychoanalytic

2.2 Proactivity

Explain the ways in which the paradigm of proactivity guides the behavior of effective individuals.

This freedom of choice, referred to in the current literature as **"proactivity,"** is an important paradigm guiding the behavior of effective individuals. We have found that a good way to begin to understand the nature of proactivity is to consider your first responses to the word *responsibility*. What first comes to mind when you hear this word? If you are like most of our students you think of things such as paying your bills, doing your homework, picking up the kids, cleaning the house, cooking dinner, washing your clothes or your car, and so on. These are things you feel you should be doing. The image that frequently comes to mind is that of a large ball and chain attached to your ankle, which drags you down and limits your freedom. But, proactivity involves placing a different frame around the concept of responsibility, as aptly described by Covey (1991) in his seminal book, *The Seven Habits of Highly Effective People*:

> *While the word proactivity is now fairly common in management literature, it is a word you won't find in most dictionaries. It is more than merely taking initiative. It means that as human beings, we are responsible for our own lives. Our behavior is a function of our decisions, not our conditions. We can subordinate feelings to values. We have the initiative and the responsibility to make things happen. Look at the word responsibility—'response - ability'— the ability to choose your response. Highly proactive people recognize that responsibility. They do not blame circumstances, conditions, or conditioning for their behavior. Their behavior is a product of their own conscious choice, based on values, rather than a product of their conditions based on feelings. (pgs. 70–71)*

2.2.1 Locus of Control

The concept of proactivity has also been previously referred to, by psychologist Julian Rotter (1966), as an internal locus of control. **Locus of control** is on a continuum ranging from external to internal. Individuals with an **external locus of control** see themselves as victims, buffeted and abused by external events over which they have no control. Individuals with an **internal locus of control** believe that they are responsible for the ultimate outcomes in their life. They do not wait for fate to lead them in a direction, rather they endeavor to take active control over their own life. For Covey, an internal locus of control is "proactivity," while an external locus of control is "reactivity." Reactive persons are at the mercy of forces beyond their control. Have you ever heard someone say, "It's raining outside, how can I be happy?" or, "It's Monday so I don't have any energy." For these people their mood or their energy level is determined by the weather or the day of the week. Proactive people, while certainly influenced by their environment, recognize that they are response-able to choose their responses to these conditions. If you are curious to see where you fall on the continuum of locus of control, we suggest you take the time to complete the following inventory.

Student Locus of Control Inventory

Check True if you agree with a statement; check False if you do not agree.

TRUE	FALSE	
——	——	1. If I can do the work, I can get a good grade in any course no matter how good or bad the instructor may be.
——	——	2. If the teacher isn't a good speaker or doesn't keep me interested, I probably won't do well in the class.
——	——	3. I believe that I have the power to control what happens to me.
——	——	4. I believe that I have very little control over what happens to me.
——	——	5. When I make a mistake, it's usually my fault.
——	——	6. When I make a mistake, it's usually because someone didn't make clear to me what I was supposed to do.
——	——	7. My grades are the result of how much studying I do.
——	——	8. My grades don't seem to be affected by the amount of studying that I do.
——	——	9. I can adapt easily to a change of plans or events.
——	——	10. Adapting to change has always been difficult for me. I like things to be as predictable and orderly as possible.
——	——	11. When I fail a test, it's either because I didn't study or I didn't understand the material.
——	——	12. When I fail a test, it's either because the test was unfair or the instructor did not cover the material sufficiently.
——	——	13. I usually don't need anyone to push me or make me study.
——	——	14. I can't seem to make myself study.
——	——	15. I am a self-motivated person.
——	——	16. I need someone to motivate me.

If you selected "true" to mostly odd-numbered statements, then you tend towards having an internal locus of control. We congratulate you! The rest of this chapter will help you refine and polish skills to make you an even more proactive individual. On the other hand, if you found yourself endorsing more even-numbered statements, then we suggest you consider the possibility that your locus of control is more external. If effectiveness is your goal, then we strongly recommend that you take the ideas and strategies presented in the rest of this chapter and incorporate them into your behavior. Remember, as we discussed in the preface of this text, it is not enough to know about mangoes, you must be willing to taste them.

Students with an internal locus of control recognize the connection between the effort they put forth and the grades they receive. These students tend to be self-motivated and optimistic. They believe in themselves and that they can do whatever they set out to accomplish. They welcome challenges and are not afraid of change. If a student with an internal locus of control fails a test, he does not blame the teacher or the test questions. He takes responsibility for the failure, and attempts to determine what action is needed to avoid this in the future. When these students make mistakes, they endeavor to figure out what they did wrong or what they did not understand. These students don't believe that their grades are a function of luck or fate. When things go wrong, they look to see what they can do to put things right.

Students who have an external locus of control cannot see a connection between the effort they put forth in a course and the grades they receive. If they do poorly on a test or in a course, these students may focus their blame on the teacher in their belief that the tests were too hard or the grading standards too stiff. These students tend to be pessimists who need someone to motivate them and give them a push to succeed. They believe that many of the things they want in life are out of reach or that other people are holding them back. They may be afraid of change and prefer to follow familiar routines. When they make mistakes, they blame others for being unfair or for not giving them the right information. They see themselves as victims in the drama that is their lives. When something goes wrong, they may feel there is nothing they can do about it. They forget that the way they see the problem is the problem.

Research in Positive Psychology has helped to illuminate the connection between effectiveness and locus of control. Studies (Myers, 2004; Burger, 2004) demonstrate that individuals with an internal locus of control are more likely to do the following:

- Succeed academically
- Cope better with stress
- Experience higher levels of job satisfaction
- Be happier with their lives
- Work more diligently towards long term goals
- Be more independent
- Deal more directly with marital problems
- Be more persuasive
- Successfully stop smoking
- Wear seat belts
- Use birth control (rather than depend on fate or luck for protection)

In general, people with an internal locus of control take charge in many areas of their lives and accept responsibility for the outcomes of their actions (Larson & Buss, 2002). In addition, internally oriented individuals are more disposed towards working for social and political change or causes (Levenson, 1981). In sharp contrast, those with an external locus of control are more likely to suffer from anxiety and/or depression. They tend to avoid challenges and give up when faced with obstacles or setbacks.

2.2.2 Three Ways to Increase Proactivity

Perhaps we have convinced you that being proactive is a skill worth cultivating. You might ask, "OK, but how do I go about doing that?" We have found that a useful method for increasing proactivity involves focusing on three key areas: (1) your thoughts; (2) your language; and (3) your actions. We believe that all things are created three times. First, when you think about it; second, by how you speak about it; and lastly, when you take some action to make it happen. Creating the reality of becoming a proactive individual involves a sustained focus on all three areas.

FOCUSING ON YOUR THOUGHTS   Reactive individuals tend to be worriers. If a worrier was conscious of the direction of his or her thoughts, he or she would discover that the focus is mostly on the bad things that could possibly happen. We are not suggesting that you should not plan for the possibility of negative outcomes, but to spend most of your time on this is clearly counterproductive. This is particularly the case if you consider that *fully 80% of what we worry about never happens!* Yet the effects on our emotional and physical health, as well as our productivity, are similar to what might have occurred if the feared event had actually happened. This topic will be dealt with in more detail in Chapters 5 and 6. Are you a worrier? Proactive people make a conscious effort to give more time for considering what might go right and how to make it go right. In other words, they are more likely to be considered optimists.

FOCUSING ON YOUR LANGUAGE   Have you ever heard yourself saying things like "he made me angry," or "I couldn't make it to class, I was just too tired to get up on time?" If you have said things like this, and who among us has not, realize that you are speaking reactively. You were giving your freedom to choose away and giving someone else control of your emotions in the first example, or letting circumstances (i.e. apparent fatigue) determine what you could or could not do in the second example. Proactive individuals realize that they are ultimately in control of their feelings and emotions, and speak in a way that creates and reinforces this reality. So instead of "he made me so mad," they might say, "I am angry about what so and so did." We hope the difference between these two is clear. When you say, "I am angry about what he did," *you* are in control of your response. Please don't think that this is merely semantics. Our language is one of civilized man's prominent ways of defining reality. How we speak has a profound impact on how we view the world.

FOCUSING ON YOUR ACTIONS   Increasing your proactive actions simply requires adopting two habits: (1) making promises and keeping them; and (2) setting small goals and working to achieve them. Proactive individuals are keenly aware of the power of their word. Unfortunately, the authors have noticed that many people fail to grasp or heed this important concept. So people say things like "I'll call you," after running into someone they haven't seen in a while, when, even at the time, they know they are highly unlikely to follow through. Or many students promise themselves that they will study for that test in plenty of time, only to, at best, end up cramming desperately at the last minute. Such behavior has the unfortunate consequence, not just that others stop believing in what you say, but more importantly, that you stop believing in yourself. We recognize that it might not be possible to keep your promises 100% of the time. You can, however, own up to it. Be willing to acknowledge the lapse and seek ways of amending it.

Many people can't wait to be successful so they can do just what they feel like doing. It is this thought, however, that can interfere with ever achieving success in the first place. The bottom line is that *effective people do the things that ineffective people don't feel like doing.* They don't feel like doing those things either, necessarily, but they want to do them out of the strength of their purpose. We strongly believe that there is a big difference between wanting and feeling. Feeling is merely a momentary desire ("I don't feel like getting out of bed"); wanting encompasses not just the present but the future consequences of the present behavior. A proactive individual acknowledges his present feeling ("I feel tired"), but decides to get out of bed because he wants the results of this action, like doing well in class, or keeping his promise. Now at this point you might be thinking, "This is all well and good, but it is easier said than done." You are absolutely right. As is often remarked, "Talk is cheap." But the bottom line can be simply stated as, "To be effective you must be willing to do what is necessary." Perhaps even more proactively stated, "You want to be willing to do what is necessary." So what about you? What do you choose?

Questions

1. Students who take responsibility for their performance if they fail a test have a(n) _____ locus of control, while students who blame the teacher if they do poorly have a(n) _____ locus of control.
   - **A.** pessimistic, optimistic
   - **B.** internal; external
   - **C.** external; internal
   - **D.** reactive; proactive

2. Proactivity is a characteristic typical of _____ individuals.
   - **A.** pessimistic
   - **B.** ineffective
   - **C.** irresponsible
   - **D.** effective

3. In order to increase proactivity, you need to focus on your _____.
   - **A.** thoughts, language, and actions
   - **B.** do's, don'ts, and manners
   - **C.** friends, family, and social media postings
   - **D.** values, morals, and behaviors

2.3 Self-Efficacy

Define the concept of self-efficacy and list some of the ways it can be increased.

In the Positive Psychology literature this whole notion of proactivity and locus of control is approached somewhat differently or more broadly, with what is termed **"self-efficacy,"** a perception of perceived competence. This is one of the most heavily researched areas in positive psychology and it is an outgrowth of Albert Bandura's Social Cognitive theory. So what is self-efficacy and how does it differ, if at all, from proactivity and locus of control? Bandura (1997) defined self-efficacy as "your belief in your capability to produce a desired effect by your own actions." In a similar vein, Maddux (2005) characterized self-efficacy as "what I believe I can do with my skills under certain conditions." The bottom line is that self-efficacy is all about believing that you can accomplish what you want, if you do what is necessary in order to reach a desired goal, after you first examine what is required of you in order to reach that goal. In a sense, self- efficacy represents a marriage between an internal locus of control, that is, the belief that you can control your destiny, and proactive behavior defined as making the appropriate choices and taking the necessary action steps for success. Self-efficacy in many ways appears to be a dimension of effectiveness with both a cognitive component (locus of control) and a behavioral component (proactivity).

Snyder and Lopez (2007) explain that the self-efficacy model flows from Bandura's Social Cognitive theory where humans learn by modeling or copying other humans; therefore self-efficacy is a learned pattern of thinking and behaving rather than a genetically determined pattern. That is, we actively shape our lives rather than passively react to our environment (Bandura, 1986). That's the good news. You have a choice to think and behave in ways that are self-efficacious.

There are three main components to Social Cognitive theory: (1) humans can create powerful symbolic cognitive models of their experiences; (2) humans can then compare their own actions to those of their symbolic models and make course corrections if necessary; and (3) there is an interaction between those cognitive models and the environment which further shapes our personalities. In simpler terms, we can watch how someone acts in order to successfully achieve a goal, and make a mental map (i.e. model) of that and learn from it. We can then choose to copy such successful behaviors based on our mental map (i.e. modeling) which then causes interactions between our cognitions, behaviors and the environment further shaping our behavior and our personalities. These "interactions" typically revolve around whether our efforts worked out or not. If not, we continue to modify our behavior until we obtain some success or reach the desired goal.

To obtain a measure of your own level of self-efficacy, fill out the inventory on the next page developed by Fibel and Hale (1978), which assesses your expectancy of success.

The Expectancy for Success Scale—A Measure of Self-Efficacy

Indicate the degree to which each item applies to you by circling the appropriate number, according to this key.

1 = highly improbable

2 = improbable

3 = equally improbable and probable, not sure

4 = probable

5 = highly probable

In the Future I Expect that I Will:

1. Find that people don't seem to understand what I'm trying to say	1	2	3	4	5
2. Be discouraged about my ability to gain the respect of others	1	2	3	4	5
3. Be a good parent	1	2	3	4	5
4. Be unable to accomplish my goals	1	2	3	4	5
5. Find my efforts to change situations I don't like are ineffective	1	2	3	4	5
6. Not be very good at learning new skills	1	2	3	4	5
7. Carry through my responsibilities successfully	1	2	3	4	5
8. Have a stressful marital relationship	1	2	3	4	5
9. Deal poorly with emergency situations	1	2	3	4	5
10. Discover that the good in life outweighs the bad	1	2	3	4	5
11. Handle unexpected problems successfully	1	2	3	4	5
12. Get the promotions I deserve	1	2	3	4	5
13. Succeed in the projects I undertake	1	2	3	4	5
14. Not make any significant contributions to society	1	2	3	4	5
15. Discover that my life is not getting much better	1	2	3	4	5
16. Be listened to when I speak	1	2	3	4	5
17. Discover that my plans don't work out too well	1	2	3	4	5
18. Find that no matter how hard I try, things just don't turn out the way I would like	1	2	3	4	5
19. Handle myself well in whatever situation I'm in	1	2	3	4	5
20. Be successful in my endeavors in the long run	1	2	3	4	5
21. Be very successful working out my personal life	1	2	3	4	5
22. Experience many failures in my life	1	2	3	4	5
23. Make a good first impression on people I meet for the first time	1	2	3	4	5
24. Attain the career goals I have set for myself	1	2	3	4	5
25. Be able to solve my own problems	1	2	3	4	5
26. Succeed at most things I try	1	2	3	4	5
27. Have difficulty dealing with my superiors	1	2	3	4	5
28. Have problems working with others	1	2	3	4	5
29. Be a good judge of what it takes to get ahead	1	2	3	4	5
30. Achieve recognition in my profession	1	2	3	4	5

Scoring: In order to calculate your total score for this inventory, first reverse the scores for the following items: 1, 2, 4, 6, 7, 8, 14, 15, 17, 18, 24, 27, and 28. That is, change a 1 to 5, a 2 to a 4, leave a 3 alone, change a 4 to a 2 and 5 to a 1. Then add up all of the scores.

The range of total scores can vary from 30 to 150. The higher your score, the greater your expectancy for success in the future, and according to Bandura's social learning and self-efficacy theory, the more motivated you will be to apply yourself in facing difficult challenges in your life. The researchers who developed this inventory (Fibel & Hale, 1978) administered this test to undergraduate students taking psychology courses and found that women's scores ranged from 65 to 143 and men's scored ranged from 81 to 138. The average score for each gender was 112 (112.32 for women and 112.15 for men).

2.3.1 The Practical Impact of Self-Efficacy

Research in self-efficacy has varied depending on whether researchers measured self-efficacy in specific situations, an approach favored by Bandura, or whether they looked at a more overall (global) measure. There are a variety of questionnaires that measure self-efficacy, some from a global standpoint and others from a much more situation specific context. Snyder and Lopez (2007) summarized Bandura's (1997) research with situation specific measures of self-efficacy. They concluded that high levels of self-efficacy are associated with:

1. better academic performance
2. lower anxiety
3. higher pain tolerance
4. following diet and exercise regimens
5. more political participation
6. good dental hygiene
7. sticking with smoking cessation programs

Bandura pointed out that high levels of self-efficacy play a protective role in helping individuals cope with psychological problems. By virtue of what he termed enablement factors, people make choices to structure their environments in ways that increase the likelihood of positive outcomes. It is reasonable to assert that this would apply more to a global level of self-efficacy. Research supporting this comes from Maddux (1995), who demonstrated that self-efficacy is associated with successful coping with a variety of psychological problems, and DiClemente, Fairhurst and Piotrowski (1995), who found that it was an important variable in overcoming eating disorders.

Self-efficacy also plays an important role in maintaining physical health, as individuals with high levels are far more likely to engage in healthy behaviors, to eliminate unhealthy ones, and to live healthy lifestyles in terms of diet, exercise, avoidance of tobacco products, etc. Furthermore, high self-efficacy enables such individuals to maintain this lifestyle over time. This may be due to the same enablement factors which offer a protective role with psychological problems, but in this case operating within the realm of physical health. Ultimately it comes down to making wise choices and believing you have the power to control the outcomes in your life. Many of the methods utilized for helping people to adopt healthier lifestyles often focus on building self-efficacy in order to accomplish this. Increasing self-efficacy does appear to improve physical health, whether the focus is on resistance to infection (O'Leary and Brown, 1995), levels of neurotransmitters in the brain that affect mood, or endorphin levels for decreasing pain (Bandura, 1977).

2.3.2 How to Increase Your Self-Efficacy

Bandura (1997) explained that self-efficacy develops when individuals have opportunities to:

- Experience success in similar situations and call upon those positive memories.
- Watch others who have succeeded and copy them (modeling).
- Imagine or visualize behaving effectively to reach a desired goal.
- Be reassured or persuaded by others who are trusted or have special expertise.
- Pair positive emotions with arousal to heighten their sense of competence.

Therefore, it follows that if you want to enhance your personal level of self-efficacy, it would be useful to practice the following suggestions . . .

- Recall in vivid detail success experiences you have had. Remember the steps you took to get there and the behaviors that led to those positive outcomes.
- Observe other people who you know are effective and successful in various situations. Pay exquisite attention to how they behave; watch what they do that works in detail and try to make a mental map or cognitive model of their behaviors. Anyone is fair game to watch including friends, relatives, teachers, mentors, co-workers, even people you read about or see on TV. But be careful with the latter; and make sure you are watching a realistic model. Don't pick a superhero or a glamorous movie star to model yourself after because you will be setting yourself up to follow an unrealistic standard.
- Imagine yourself stepping into the picture, performing those same behaviors effectively and reaching your desired goal.
- Accept reassurance, praise and advice from those you trust or who have knowledge/expertise you do not possess. This will enhance your expectations for success.
- Maintain your sense of humor and learn to relax (See Chapter 6). This will create comfortable physiological sensations and a calm demeanor which will then help to boost your level of confidence in your abilities.

Questions

1. The Self-Efficacy model is derived from which learning theory?

   A. operant conditioning

   B. observational learning or modeling

   C. classical conditioning

   D. locus of control

2. If you want to enhance your personal level of self-efficacy it would be useful to _____.

   A. avoid copying the behavior of others to preserve your individuality

   B. recall failure experiences you have had in vivid detail

   C. learn how to manipulate people

   D. watch others who are successful and study how they behave

3. High levels of self-efficacy _____.

   A. are not compatible with proactivity

   B. play a protective role in physical and psychological health

   C. are associated with an external locus of control

   D. require that you never study nor copy the successful behaviors of others.

2.4 Dealing with Irrational Self-Talk

Identify strategies for identifying and replacing irrational beliefs.

To make the process of becoming proactive a doable enterprise, we thought it would be helpful for you to learn some specific strategies for modifying the way you think and the way you talk in a more proactive direction. A powerful way humans undermine their effectiveness is by doing what Albert Ellis (1975) called **catastrophizing** when you give yourself messages that a situation is too awful or overwhelming to bear or that the worst is about to happen. These messages, also termed **self-talk** by Ellis or **automatic thoughts** by Aaron Beck (1970), refer to the running commentary that goes on in your head during the course of the day. Most of it is mundane and benign, but problems will arise when your perceptions are influenced by automatic thoughts reflecting irrational beliefs. Many studies have documented the link between irrational beliefs and anxiety (Bonner & Rich, 1991). These typically fall into two general categories: (1) beliefs that the world, someone, or something should be different; and (2) beliefs that your perceptions reflect reality rather than your subjective impressions of reality. Many times these irrational beliefs operate on a subconscious level, yet guide your emotional reactions nonetheless.

Self-talk tends to be circular in nature. Figure 2.2 illustrates this cycle. It begins with events in the environment, events that have no valence until you are there to interpret them or ascribe meaning to them. Next, we have your sensory impressions of the event (your perceptions and sensory input). This is followed by your cognitions and interpretations of your perception of events (your self-talk about the event). This may include irrational ideas or self-statements. The next step is the reaction of your emotional and physical system, not so much to the events themselves, but to your interpretations (self-talk) about the events. These physical/emotional reactions then feed back into your self-talk. For example, if you are feeling disappointed or depressed because of how you have interpreted an event, this sadness will then further influence your self-talk, predisposing you to further negative cognitions. And the cycle goes on. Negative thoughts create unhappiness, and depression stimulates further pessimistic thinking.

At the root of all irrational thinking is the assumption that things are done to you, rather than recognizing that events happen in the world. Going back to the S-O-R (Stimulus - Organism - Response) model presented earlier: you experience those events (**S**); engage in self-talk about those events (**O**); and then experience an emotion (**R**) resulting from your self-talk. **S** does not cause **R**, rather it is **O** that causes **R**. If your self-talk is irrational and unrealistic, you will create negative emotions. The two common forms of irrational self-talk are: (1) statements that catastrophize; and (2) statements that revolve around absolutes. Catastrophic thinking involves expecting the worst and/or giving nightmarish interpretations of your experience (i.e. being a worrier). Thus, a momentary chest pain becomes

---

Figure 2.2

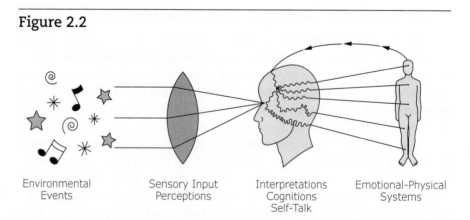

| Environmental Events | Sensory Input Perceptions | Interpretations Cognitions Self-Talk | Emotional-Physical Systems |

a heart attack, your boss's bad mood means you are going to get fired, if you do poorly on a test you assume that you will fail the course. The emotions that follow such expectations are very unpleasant, but you are responding to your own description of the world. Irrational self-statements involving absolutes typically include words such as "should, must, ought, always and never." Here you assume that if things are not a certain way, or if you do not conform to some standard, it is disastrous. Any deviation from that particular value or standard must be bad.

2.4.1 Cognitive Restructuring

A potent strategy for refuting irrational beliefs and changing your self-talk involves the use of **cognitive restructuring techniques**. The most basic technique consists of three steps.

STEP ONE: Attempt to identify the irrational belief that is underlying your reaction. Once you have uncovered this belief you may immediately notice the absurdity of it. Common irrational beliefs include:

1. Everyone needs to like you. It is awful if someone dislikes you.
2. You must be competent and perfect in all that you undertake.
3. Mistakes are sure proof that you are a failure.
4. You should never hurt anyone or refuse a request/favor.
5. It is horrible if things don't turn out the way you want.
6. You are helpless and have no control over your feelings or experiences.
7. You will be rejected if you don't go to great lengths to please others.
8. There is a perfect love and a perfect relationship.
9. You shouldn't have to feel pain. Life should always be fair.
10. Your worth as a human being depends on how much you achieve and produce.

STEP TWO: Examine and challenge the irrational belief with your rational mind. Notice how so many of the irrational beliefs revolve around a "should," or a "must," or the idea that it is catastrophic if something doesn't turn out in a particular way. Challenging irrationalities can be facilitated by asking yourself the following questions:

1. Is there any reason to think that this belief is true?
2. Is there evidence that this belief might not be true?
3. If I reject this belief, what is the worst that could happen to me?
4. If I reject this belief, what good things might happen as a result?

STEP THREE: Substitute a new, rational belief in place of the old, irrational idea. Initially this may seem artificial, a bit phony. But replacing the negative thoughts that led to painful emotional responses with more positive and rational alternatives is a good start, even if you don't completely believe it at first. In time you will start to believe your rational thoughts, particularly after you experience improvements in your situation reflecting the change in you. The changes in your thinking patterns will become natural and comfortable after a while. As you practice reappraising your thoughts in this fashion, your brain is also establishing new habits. It was demonstrated in an fMRI study that successful cognitive restructuring reduced activity in the amygdala, the brain structure responsible for triggering your fear responses. Simultaneously, activity is increasing in the left frontal cortex, the area from which our thought processes originate (Ochsner and colleagues, 2002). Therefore, this area of your brain that thinks is literally calming the area of your brain that reacts with arousal. Thus, with practice, it will get easier and easier to reframe reality and to view things from a more positive viewpoint. Cognitive restructuring does not imply that you should repress your thoughts. It is a process of acknowledging those thoughts and feelings that are reactive in nature, then examining/challenging them, and finally replacing them with more rational thoughts when appropriate. For example, the rational statements below can be substituted for each of the irrational thoughts above. These are not the only options. We invite you to create your own rational alternatives if the following choices below do not fit for you. Notice that these rational statements utilize elements of reframing. Oftentimes, the process of thinking rationally involves the process of reframing, of learning to view a situation from a different, more rational, perspective.

1. It is impossible to be well liked by everyone. No one achieves that. It certainly isn't the end of the world if _____ (insert the name of the person or persons in question) doesn't like me. And, who knows, next month the situation could be totally different.

2. It is impossible to be good at everything. Besides, if I did succeed at being extremely competent in everything I did, many people would no doubt resent me.

3. Everyone makes mistakes. Mistakes can be learning experiences that lead to eventual success. "Failure" is just another word, not an enduring part of my character.

4. _____ will surely survive if I don't do things his/her way.

5. It is unfortunate if things don't turn out the way I would like, but it is hardly the end of the world and I can handle it. By this time next year I will no doubt be completely indifferent to this whole situation.

6. I *always* have a choice over how I respond to situations.

7. If I don't go out of my way to please someone there is a chance I might get rejected, but it certainly is not guaranteed. And, if I need to go to great lengths to please in order for that person to like me, then that individual is not someone that I care to have as a friend. I want to be liked and appreciated for who I am, not for what I can do for someone.

8. There are no perfect relationships. I will focus on making this a healthy, honest, enjoyable relationship and learn to accept the inevitable disappointments and imperfections that come up in all relationships.

9. Life isn't always fair. Feeling pain is a part of being human. If I had never experienced sadness or despair I would not know what it means to be happy and content.

10. My worth as a human being is much more dependent on my capacity to be fully alive, feeling everything it means to be human, the good with the bad. My worth depends more on how I am in relation to the people who are important to me.

David Goodman (1974), in his book *Emotional Well-Being through Rational Behavior Training*, offers six rules or guidelines for rational thinking. You may find these rules to be quite useful for guiding you to think rationally and challenge your irrational beliefs.

1. **It does not do anything to me.**
   That is, the situation does not make you anxious or afraid. The things you say to yourself are what produce the negative emotions you may feel at any given moment. In the same vein, no one can make you feel anything. How you feel is always your choice. Other people may provide provocation, but ultimately, you always choose how you feel in response.

2. **Everything is exactly the way it should be.**
   The conditions for things or people to be otherwise do not exist. To say things should be different is tantamount to believing in magic. Things are the way they are because of a long series of causal events. To say things should be different is to throw out causality.

3. **All humans are fallible creatures.**
   This is an inescapable truth. If you have not set reasonable quotas of failure for yourself and others, you increase the prospects for your disappointment and unhappiness.

4. **It takes two to have a conflict.**
   Before pointing your finger in blame, consider the 30% rule. Any party to a conflict is contributing at least 30% of the fuel to keep an argument going.

5. **The original cause is lost in antiquity.**

   It is a waste of your time to try to discover who did what first. It is often impossible to find the original cause of chronic painful emotions, as such dilemmas are usually extremely complicated, and often the product of multiple interactions. The best strategy is to make decisions to change your behavior now.

6. **We feel the way we think.**

   To again quote Covey, "The way you see the problem is the problem." And what you say to yourself determines your feelings.

2.4.2 What if Cognitive Restructuring Fails to Work?

Although cognitive restructuring offers a useful and reassuring way to offset negative irrational thoughts and worries, the fact remains that this does not always succeed in damping down these thoughts, particularly in the long run as these same or similar cognitions and related feelings often bubble up again and again over time. Recall in Chapter 1 from our discussion of paradigm shifts, that in the field of psychology changes tend to be gradual with theories and approaches building upon each other. A gradual paradigm shift within Positive Psychology has led to an approach (ACT) designed to enable you to develop the psychological flexibility to cope effectively with difficult thoughts, ideas, emotions, or images when the exercise of cognitive restructuring or other forms of optimistic thinking falls short. ACT is an acronym.

A   Accept your thoughts and feelings

C   Choose your values

T   Take action

ACT is an empirically supported set of methods designed to enhance flourishing and functioning effectively in the world. It represents a combination of cognitive behavioral methods, NLP (NeuroLinguistic Programming which deals with the appropriate sequencing of thoughts, feelings, and actions) and behavioral activation (i.e. doing what you want based on your values rather than what you feel like doing) strategies utilizing a variety of cognitive and mindfulness techniques. A comprehensive overview of this approach is presented in Chapter 8.

2.4.3 Correlation ≠ Causation

Irrational thinking takes other forms as well. In our attempts to make sense of our world we often make a common error in thinking by assuming that if things occur together or are associated in some way, that one must therefore cause the other. In statistical terms, when two variables tend to be reliably associated with one another, this is called a **correlation**. The greater the degree of association, the higher the correlation will be. When a correlation is present, it could be that one variable does cause or influence the other (such as in the relationship between height and weight), but this is not necessarily the case. It may be that some other factor or variable is actually influencing or causing the correlation. For example, let's take the common characterization of the bespectacled intellectual (i.e. the high IQ kid with the thick glasses). There is a reason for this stereotype. A correlation does exist between myopia (nearsightedness) and intelligence, as individuals with higher IQ's are more likely to be nearsighted. But what does this mean? Is it that being myopic somehow magically makes you smart? Or does having a high IQ somehow harm your vision (maybe from reading too many books!)? We are sure you would agree that both of these positions are totally absurd. Rather, this correlation is the byproduct of other genetic variables which are beyond the scope of this book to discuss.

Some of the studies and research cited throughout this text are correlational in nature. We advise you to be very wary of inferring any causation from the results of correlational research. Disclaimers to this nature will pop up periodically in reference to these correlational studies. It is only through controlled experimentation that we can get valid information about causation.

When combating irrational thinking, remember that just because two things occur together, that alone does not offer proof that one has caused the other. A prime example of the folly of inferring causation from correlation can be found in the field of psychology. For decades it was widely thought that childhood schizophrenia was caused by the "schizophrenogenic mother," a parent who was cold, aloof and gave a child inconsistent and confusing messages. Although a correlation does exist between parenting styles and the incidence of schizophrenia, we now know that this disorder is primarily a function of a genetic, biochemical disturbance in the brain, and is not caused by cold parents. It is actually more likely that the so-called schizophrenogenic parenting style could have been in reaction to raising an emotionally troubled child, rather than the cause of it.

It is also relevant at this point to alert you to be aware of the very human tendency to perceive a correlation or relationship between things that really does not exist. We call this an illusory or **spurious correlation**. If we believe there is a relationship between variables, we will likely (and nonconsciously) use selective perception to detect and recall only those circumstances which confirm our belief. This is one way stereotypes and racial prejudices get ingrained. All of us fall prey to perceiving spurious correlations and using selective perception to reinforce these mistaken notions. Being aware of this tendency can help you combat this form of irrational thinking. Remind yourself that incidents that superficially appear to confirm your beliefs could just be nothing other than random coincidences.

The Global Perspective
Achieving Global Citizenship

What does it mean to be a global citizen? Consider the concept of citizenship. For many immigrants, citizenship evokes reminders of what they are not. Of the rights and privileges, along with the responsibilities, they wish to attain. It reminds them of separateness. Since we are all human beings existing on this planet, global citizenship is the reality for all of us. Rather than separateness, it is the recognition of our interconnectedness. It is the acknowledgement that, in this no longer so large sandbox we call Earth, our actions on one corner of the box invariably affect the other three corners. A global citizen "places emphasis on individual choice, in a collective setting, for the greater good." Reckmeyer, William J., *Developing Global Citizenship—Leadership for the 21st Century* (2005).

It is important, however, not to confuse interconnectedness with homogeneity. A global paradigm does not imply working towards making us all the same. On the contrary, it acknowledges our individuality and autonomy and celebrates our diversity. The power of our cultural, religious, ethnic, gender, racial, you-name-it, diversity is that it provides a rich and valuable pool of differing paradigms. As you learned last chapter, changes in perspective account for most of the greatest discoveries of our scientific era. What better to promote paradigm-shifting than numerous paradigms from which to choose and an attitude that says let's look for solutions that benefit all?

Going back to Reckmeyer's definition, global citizens value individual choice. They value what Positive Psychology describes as autonomy, not in the sense of being selfish or detached, but instead being able to be conscious of their freedom to choose. In other words, global citizens are proactive. They are aware that their life is a product of their decisions, not their conditions. And global citizens also understand that the freedom to choose must be exercised in a context which acknowledges their obligations to others as well as to themselves. It is

our greatest gift that we want to be connected with others as much as we want to be free (Deci, 1995; Ryan & Deci, 2000).

Global citizenship, then, is caring about the common good as well as our own and making choices that reflect that concern. It is about being aware of our interconnections. But it is also about choosing to be aware of our disconnections. Did you know that in 1900, the top 25% of the population enjoyed 7 times as many resources as the bottom 25%? By the year 2000, the bottom 25% had improved their lot tenfold. That is, one hundred years later, they are 10 times better than they were. However, the top 25% improved their fortune by more than 100 times, as evidenced by the following table:

Year	1900	2000
Top 25% of population	7	730
Bottom 25% of population	1	10

So the disparity between the haves and have-nots has grown. Where it used to be 7 to 1, it is now 73 to 1. And whereas in 1900 the have-nots were certainly aware that the haves were much better off, they did not have the evidence presented daily in their living rooms by television, nor heavily marketed by the media and its advertisers as something to covet.

Ultimately, however, global citizenship is about taking action. About making choices that reflect the reality that is our interconnection. It doesn't start by changing the world, but by changing ourselves. The choice is ours. How mindful are you of conserving resources such as water and energy? How well informed are you about international affairs? How tolerant are you of others' perspectives? How well do you listen? How open are you to considering other views, even when you initially disagree? What behaviors could you change that would bring you closer to global citizenship?

Questions

1. Irrational self-talk typically involves statements that _____ and statements that involve _____.

   A. are proactive; reactivity

   B. catastrophize; absolutes

   C. disparage; judgments

   D. are dishonest; wishful thinking

2. A potent, healthy strategy for defusing irrational thoughts involves _____.

   A. exploring correlations

   B. denial and suppression

   C. repeating positive affirmations to yourself

   D. cognitive restructuring

3. Correlation _____.

   A. does not exist in the real world

   B. is always spurious

   C. does not necessarily equal causation

   D. is proof of causation

2.5 Keys to Effectiveness: The Power of Positive Thinking

Identify some practical ways to develop an optimistic outlook and lead a more effective life.

> *A pessimist sees the difficulty in every opportunitiy; an optimist sees the opportunity in every difficulty.*

> Winston Churchill

Effective individuals develop the habit of perceiving and interpreting potential problems in ways that give their life meaning and a sense of control. That is, they look for reasons to be happy and satisfied with life, imperfect as it is. They have become adept at turning lemons into lemonade and finding the proverbial silver lining in the cloud. Therefore, effective individuals are optimists and are typically more satisfied with life in general. In other words, they are happier. But it is a far cry from recommending that you adopt an optimistic outlook and develop an internal locus of control to actually achieving all of this. Martin Seligman, who spearheaded the field of positive psychology, contributed three groundbreaking books, *Learned Optimism* (1991), *Authentic Happiness* (2002), and *Flourish* (2011), where he offers valuable lessons for developing an optimistic life outlook and leading an effective, satisfying life.

2.5.1 Optimism

Given that effective individuals are optimists, we recommend that you consciously choose to adopt optimistic perceptions. Why? Because that particular map of the world will be the most useful for helping you achieve your goals. Optimists are not necessarily unrealistic, or unwilling to accept or face negative circumstances, rather they choose to focus on what is right, rather than bemoaning all that is wrong. It is a matter of focus. They look for evidence that life is good and that they are doing all right. When misfortune strikes, as it does in everyone's lives at some point, optimists recover more quickly because they find lessons in adversity that continue to give their lives meaning. But it is also essential that you differentiate between "flexible" or "realistic" optimism (Seligman, 1990; Schneider, 2001) and wishful thinking. Flexible optimists are people who are filled with hope but who keep their eyes open. They distinguish between what they can and cannot control and focus on the former. Optimists work on acceptance of that which is uncontrollable, while pessimists are far more likely to engage in denial about unfortunate circumstances (Carver & Scheier, 1999). Optimists simply refuse to let go of their positive expectations. Just as irrational or negative self-statements can create depression, anxiety, or other negative emotions, positive or optimistic self-statements can create and reinforce effectiveness and happiness.

In Seligman's theory of learned optimism, an optimist answers the question, "why did that bad thing happen to me?" with attributions that are *external*, *variable* and *specific*, unlike the pessimist who views negative events as being a product of *internal*, *stable* and *global* actions on his or her part. So it is an **explanatory style**, a perspective one has in dealing with the world. In simpler terms, an optimist would explain a bad event as: (1) taking into account the role of other people and the environment as causal agents (an external attribution); (2) less likely to happen again (variable) and; (3) representing just one area of life or performance and not others (a specific domain).

We encourage you to test your own level of optimism by completing the following survey developed by Scheier, Carver & Bridges (1994).

Life Orientation Test (LOT): How Optimistic are You?

Use the following scale to respond to each question.

0 = strongly disagree   1 = disagree   2 = neutral   3 = agree   4 = strongly agree

_____1. In uncertain times, I usually expect the best.

_____2. If something can go wrong for me, it will.

_____3. I am always optimistic about my future.

_____4. I hardly ever expect things to go my way.

_____5. I rarely count on good things happening to me.

_____6. Overall, I expect more good things to happen to me than bad things.

_____ **TOTAL SCORE**

To determine your score, reverse the numbers you placed in answer to statements 2, 4 and 5 by changing 0 to 4, 1 to 3, 3 to 1 and 4 to 0, with 2 remaining at 2. Leave the remaining numbers in front of the rest of the statements unchanged. Then add up all of the updated numbers in front of all items to compute your total score. The score range is from 0 to 24 and the higher your score the more optimistic your outlook. The average score is between 14 and 15. Scores above 15 reflect higher levels of optimism.

2.5.2 The Benefits of an Optimistic Life Outlook

Research indicates that your level of optimism vs. **pessimism** is a powerful determining factor in your physical and emotional health. Indeed, a review of the research on happiness has consistently identified four traits manifested by happy people: (1) optimism; (2) good self esteem; (3) an internal locus of control; and (4) extroversion (Myers and Diener, 1995). Given that these were correlational studies, it is unclear whether these four personality dimensions lead to happiness or the reverse, but in any event, it is surely safe to conclude that these characteristics help to maintain happiness. The same group of researchers who developed the previous survey found that high LOT scores were highly correlated with a sense of self-mastery and self-esteem and negatively correlated with depression and anxiety. Pessimism has been associated with high stress levels, depression, psychosomatic problems, higher levels of physical illness, and even premature death (Peterson, Seligman and colleagues, 1998). Likewise, where a person falls on the optimism-pessimism continuum is related to health in the future and how quickly that individual will recover from serious illness (Scheier & Carver, 1993). Optimistic new mothers are less likely to experience post-partum depression (Carver & Gaines, 1987). Optimistic individuals are better able to weather major surgery, independent of the severity of their condition. This relationship has been demonstrated with heart bypass surgery (Fitzgerald, Tenner, Affleck & Pransky, 1993) and breast cancer surgery (Carver and colleagues, 1993), where LOT scores predicted both short and long term post-surgical emotional resilience.

Research with other measures of optimism other than the LOT questionnaire has yielded similar results and broader findings as well, indicating that those with optimistic as opposed to pessimistic explanatory styles displayed the following . . .

- More effective coping with life stressors (Nolen-Hoeksema, 2000)
- For men, greater overall health decades later predicted by optimism scores in college (Peterson, Seligman & Valliant, 1988)
- More productivity at work (Seligman & Schulman, 1986)
- Greater physical health (Peterson, 2000)
- Better outcomes for cardiovascular disease based on a meta-analysis of 83 studies (Rasmussen, Scheier, & Greenhouse, 2009)
- Lower vulnerability to depression (Abramson, Alloy & colleagues, 2000)
- More satisfaction in interpersonal relationships (Fincham, 2000)
- Superior athletic performance (Seligman, Nolen-Hoeksema, Thornton & Thornton, 1990)
- Stronger academic performance (Peterson & Barrett, 1987; Seligman 1998b)

Referring to the last point about stronger academic success, you might also be surprised to learn that optimism is actually a better predictor of college academic success than standard measures such as SAT scores or high school GPAs! That was exactly what researchers at the University of Pennsylvania found when they measured the optimism levels of 500 incoming college freshmen, and then compared that to their later college grades. A strikingly similar result was obtained at the University of Kansas when freshmen were administered measures of their level of "hope" (a major factor in optimism). Again, hope was a better predictor of freshmen grades than the usual standard measures. These researchers concluded that the students' emotional attitudes were the critical factor in academic success. Aspinwall & Taylor (1992) found that optimistic college students handled the challenges of college more successfully and reported less stress, depression, and loneliness than pessimistic students.

2.5.3 Impact of Optimism on History

Psychologist Chris Peterson, along with Marty Seligman and other researchers, devised an intriguing method for determining whether an individual is an optimist or a pessimist by analyzing recorded comments or writing samples based on language usage. This method can be used after the fact to analyze the explanatory style of historical figures and then compare it with outcomes years later, to see whether optimists really do tend to succeed more than pessimists. This approach, the Content Analysis of Verbal Explanations (or CAVE approach), has been utilized in many studies to demonstrate the power of positive thinking. Seligman, an avid baseball fan, decided to use his CAVE method to predict the outcome of the 1986 baseball season based on statements made by players and managers of all the major league baseball teams in 1985. In an enormous undertaking, he and others analyzed all of the recorded comments printed in all of the hometown newspapers sports pages. In particular, they compared two evenly matched teams (regarding talent and potential for the 1986 season), the N.Y. Mets and the St. Louis Cardinals. From the CAVE analysis, it was determined that the Mets were by far the more optimistic team in 1985, especially compared to the Cardinals. In 1986 the Mets went on to win the World Series while the Cardinals finished below .500. The 1985 CAVE rating for the other major league teams, based on their optimism scores, also predicted how they finished in the standings in 1986. Seligman was so impressed with these results that he found it difficult to believe, so he redid the study in 1986 to predict for the 1987 season and got similarly impressive results. The more optimistic the team based on CAVE analysis of players and managers comments, the better they performed the following season.

Optimism appears to affect another type of competition as well: in the political arena. The professed optimism of candidates for political office often has a profound impact on their electability. A research project headed by Harold Zullow (Zullow, Oettingen, Peterson & Seligman, 1988) explored whether the optimism displayed by a presidential candidate in his acceptance speech at the nominating convention would influence the election outcome. That is, would the more optimistic candidates be more likely to win? The results indicated that in presidential elections from 1900 through 1984 the more optimistic candidate won 18 out of the 22 elections! After 1984 that relationship began to break down. Why? The campaigns found out about this finding regarding optimism and began to go all out to exceed each other in appearing to be optimistic. To quote Peterson (2006) . . .

> Our attempts to distinguish presidential candidates based on their professed optimism has since been a total failure (e.g. Peterson & Lee, 2000). Each loudly proclaims himself to be an optimist and certainly more of an optimist than his opponent. Each says the sorts of things in speeches that end up being scored by us as hopeful. Again, I wonder if the results of our earlier study had anything to do with this new way of campaigning. Regardless the conclusion it follows that, all things being equal, U.S. voters prefer an optimist over a pessimist as their leader, a conclusion consistent with the results of many other studies of every-day people leading their lives (Peterson, Maier & Seligman, 1993, p. 110)

2.5.4 Optimism and Effectiveness

Why do optimism and hope improve effectiveness? And just how does this work, you may be wondering? First of all, when you believe that something is possible, you are more likely to take action. Optimism provides motivation. Secondly, optimism spurs perseverance in the face of obstacles; optimists are more likely to carry on because of their belief in eventual success. Seligman explains that pessimists tend to view problems as permanent (lasting forever), global (affecting everything), and internal (a result of personal incompetence or faults). This particular framework leads to feelings of helplessness, so why even bother to do anything. This refers back to his pioneering work on **learned helplessness** (Maier & Seligman, 1976; Peterson, Maier & Seligman, 1993). which is defined as the belief that nothing you can do will alter your circumstances or outcomes, therefore you totally give up. On the other hand, optimists are more likely to view their troubles as temporary, specific (applying only to one area of life), and external (due to factors other than personal incompetence). *In other words, pessimism is paralyzing while optimism is energizing.* So it comes as no surprise that optimism is associated with greater success and effectiveness whether you are a college student, an insurance salesman (Seligman & Schulman, 1986), or in any other endeavor.

There is a whole school of metaphysical thought that presumes that you create your own reality with your thoughts. If this is indeed true, then by adopting an optimistic world view you are maximizing your chances for success, happiness, and getting what you want. What have you got to lose by trying? Some of you may answer, "If I expect a positive outcome and it does not happen, then I will be disappointed." You would be a subscriber to the "don't expect anything and you will never be disappointed" philosophy of life. But if you are really honest with yourself, you will admit that even if you truly expect nothing, there's still a small part of you that hopes, and if what you hope for fails to materialize, you still end up disappointed. The problem with expecting nothing is that you might not do what is necessary to get what you want in life. There is an old saying, "If you want your ship to come in, you must go to the dock." The problem with being a pessimist is that you might not bother to go to the dock. Optimists go to the dock and find ways to enjoy their time there whether their ship comes in or not.

Some may argue that it is a lot easier to be an optimist if you are one of those people who just happen to be lucky. Well, believe it or not, whether or not you are "lucky" or "unlucky" may have more to do with whether you are an optimist or a pessimist than with random chance. Professor Richard Wiseman claims that he can tell whether you are lucky or unlucky merely by handing you a newspaper and asking you to count how many photographs are in the paper! Some people finish this task in a few seconds, while others take several minutes. The difference has nothing to do with counting speed. Rather, the secret lies on the second page of the newspaper where Wiseman inserted a not-so-hidden message in **HUGE** one inch block letters. The message is:

Stop Counting–There Are 43 Photographs in this Newspaper

Surprisingly, many people are so caught up in counting photos that they miss the headline completely – they simply fail to notice it. The headline is not a trick as there really are exactly 43 pictures in the paper. Wiseman teaches that those who notice the announcement on page two right away and stop counting tend to be "lucky" individuals who are open to random opportunities and seize them. Those who don't spot the message are more likely to be unlucky individuals who may miss out on good fortune just because they fail to see opportunities on their horizons. This brings us back to our discussion of selective attention in the first chapter. People who are more laid back and cope well with stress (who tend to have an internal locus of control) are typically more open to life's possibilities-like giant newspaper headlines unexpectedly giving you the right answer. On the other hand, unlucky people are more uptight and tend to be closed off, sometimes to potentially useful information.

To test yourself take a quick look at this domain name sometimes used by stress researchers: www.opportunityisnowhere.com. What do you see? Many people see a discouraging message that opportunity is nowhere. But other individuals see the opposite message – opportunity is now here! Lucky people perceive more of the world around them so they are more likely to see the hidden words – they are able to step out of selective attention to get a more holistic view of their environment. Wiseman (2003) writes in his book, *The Luck Factor*, "It is not that they expect to find certain opportunities, but rather that they notice them when they come across them."

Wiseman's study of lucky people led him to conclude that some people really do have all the luck, but it is a byproduct of their mindset. Lucky individuals appear to have four characteristics in common.

1. A heightened awareness of the world around them—they notice and seize upon openings that others simply miss.

2. An optimistic outlook—perseverance in the face of obstacles or failure due to a belief that things will eventually work out if you hang in there.

3. A willingness to listen to their intuition – trusting their gut feelings.

4. The special ability to turn bad luck into good fortune. This plays a vital role in survival situations. Wiseman recounted the work of Siebert (1996) who investigated what he called the "survivor personality," that is, individuals who managed to survive natural disasters or other calamities (e.g. plane crashes) where many others perished. Siebert believes that life's best survivors not only cope well, they often turn potential disasters into lucky developments.

2.5.5 How to Become an Optimist

Seligman offers a variety of suggestions for channeling your thinking in an optimistic direction. Many of the cognitive techniques for doing this are similar and/or identical to the cognitive restructuring methods for defusing irrational thinking. This is not surprising because in many instances pessimism is just one form of irrational thinking. Optimism is not about being unjustifiably positive about the world, but rather about learning to challenge negative thinking. Learning to think optimistically involves learning to dispute pessimistic thoughts. Seligman recommends the following four strategies for defusing negativity.

1. LOOK FOR EVIDENCE   The most convincing way of combating a negative belief is to show that it does not fit the facts, that it is clearly incorrect. Since pessimism is usually either an overreaction or dead wrong, the facts will typically be on the side of a more optimistic viewpoint. This does not mean that we are recommending that you naively repeat positive affirmations to yourself in the hope they will somehow change your life. Most educated people are too scientifically minded or skeptical to blindly believe a positive affirmation without some confirmation that it could be true. *Just repeating positive thoughts to yourself is not a guarantee of success or happiness. Rather, it is how you deal with your negativity that determines whether optimism or pessimism will rule.* In general, negative beliefs that accompany or follow adversity are almost always untrue.

Seligman offers a very useful tip for disputing pessimistic thoughts. He suggests that you challenge your negative thoughts by treating them as if they were uttered by another person whose mission in life was to undermine you, make you miserable, or push you to give up on your goals. You already, no doubt, have developed skills for arguing with others whose ideas, opinions, or accusations about you are unfounded. But chances are that you are not as adept at challenging the accusations that you launch at yourself. Just because it is you putting yourself down does not make it true. Your negative self-statements can be just as off-base as those of a jealous rival. For example, let's say you fail an important exam. Common negative thoughts include assuming that you are stupid, or that you can't cut it in college, or that you are destined to flunk out so why try at all. This is another example of catastrophizing, of picking the worst possible alternative from all the possibilities. One of the most effective techniques is to look for evidence pointing to the distortions in your disastrous explanation of events or catastrophic expectations of what will occur. Evidence to the contrary might include the fact that you got a B on a test last week—that failing one test does not necessarily mean that you will fail every test or flunk out in general. Our professors in graduate school continually reminded us to *never generalize from one piece of data.* You could also remind yourself that even smart people can have a bad day and do poorly at times.

2. GENERATE OTHER ALTERNATIVES   Most things that happen in life have multiple causes rather than just one cause. Most things that will happen in your life are a product of interactions among many factors. It is useful to keep this truism in mind. Pessimists make a habit of latching onto one cause and one cause only, and typically it is the worst of all the possible causes. They usually pick the cause that it is the most *permanent, pervasive* and *personal.* Challenging this typically has reality on its side. To effectively challenge your negative thoughts look for all the possible alternatives. What else could have caused the situation? What else could happen as a result? Focus on what is *changeable,* what is *specific* and what is *nonpersonal.* Returning to our failed exam example, you could focus on the fact that you didn't study hard enough (a condition that is changeable), that the exam was unusually hard (a specific instance that may not repeat in the future), and that the rest of the students also fared poorly (a nonpersonal explanation for your poor grade). You may have to work hard to generate alternatives, and you may not be thoroughly convinced that they are accurate. But the process of searching for alternatives (reframing) trains you to think differently, and oftentimes you will come up with an alternative that makes a lot more sense than your worst-case scenario. But you have to look for the alternatives to get to that place. Latching onto the worst possible alternative and stopping there is a surefire recipe for undermining your effectiveness.

3. REALISTICALLY ASSESS THE IMPLICATIONS   What do you do if the facts are not on your side, if your negative belief turns out to be true? In that case you need to use a technique called decatastrophizing. Ask yourself what the implications are if your belief is true. Generate a variety of alternatives. Challenge the most negative alternatives by asking yourself just how likely those implications really are. For example, let's say that you haven't just failed an exam, but that you are actually in danger of flunking out of college altogether. What does this mean? Is it a catastrophe which guarantees that you will never get a good job, that you will be a failure in life? The answer, of course, is no. Having a college degree certainly helps, but with the right attitude and willingness to do what is necessary, anyone can succeed, even without a college degree. This is not to say that flunking out is a good thing, but it is also *not the end of the world*. Other people have gone on to success without making it through college. For example, look at Bill Gates of Microsoft fame! Even if you flunk out of college, this does not preclude you from coming back at a later time and being successful. And, in addition, you need to remind yourself that flunking out is not a foregone conclusion. You have some choice in the matter depending on how seriously you take your studies from this point forward.

4. EVALUATE USEFULNESS   Occasionally there are situations where the consequences of holding a belief are potentially more problematic than the belief itself, true or not. You need to evaluate whether the belief is potentially dangerous. For example, if you truly believe that you are stupid, even if you are not a rocket scientist, the damage to your self-esteem could be heavy. There are other instances when the best strategy is to distract yourself from a belief rather than taking time to challenge it. This is the case when negative thoughts interfere with your performance. Engaging in negative thinking or the evaluation of such is not useful in a situation where you need to perform now. Distracting yourself and focusing on the task at hand is the most useful response.

2.5.6 The Limits of Optimism

At this point you may be wondering whether optimism has limits, or whether a person can be overly optimistic to an unrealistic degree? Of course the answer is yes. An unbounded optimism not tied to reality can and will have costs and could be dangerous. For example, Weinstein (1989) reflected on how people often underestimate their personal risk for illness, accidents or mishaps, sometimes carrying an unrealistic aura of invulnerability. When asked to estimate their risk for such mishaps, most individuals rate themselves as below average in risk for most maladies in comparison to their peers. This, "it won't happen to me" mindset is very pervasive and sometimes leads people to neglect their health, postpone eliminating bad habits (such as quitting smoking), or overlook safety precautions that make accidents more likely. Just about every one of us has fallen prey to this false sense of safety at some point. Yes, even you! Unrelenting optimism that avoids caution and conservation of resources can prevent you from contingency planning or coping adequately with setbacks. Peterson and Park (1998) found that although optimists are more likely to achieve positive outcomes as a result of their positive expectations, they are also likely to underestimate the likelihood of future bad events (Peterson and deAvila, 1995). There are lessons to be drawn here. For example, just because you believe in yourself and your ability to get a good job and earn a good living doesn't mean you should spend every penny in your savings, if you are fortunate enough to have money saved at this time.

Even when optimism is reality based, you still should be careful not to be blinded with over-confidence to the point where you do not plan adequately for success. Believing that you will succeed in college will help you immensely to reach your goal, but that does not mean that you do not need to study. Belief in your ability alone will not get the job done. That is where self-efficacy comes in, as *optimism without self-efficacy is a recipe for ineffectiveness.*

2.5.7 The Optimism Bias: How Evolution Has Shaped Brain Functioning

Tali Sharot (2011) in her book, *The Optimism Bias: A Tour of the Irrationally Positive Brain*, observes that "most of us have this tendency to overestimate the likelihood of good events happening to us and underestimate the likelihood that bad events will come crashing down." This belief that the future will most likely be better than either the past or present is referred to as the **optimism bias**. For a common example, even though divorce rates for first marriages hover around 50% and exceed 70% for second and third marriages, very few newlyweds expect their union to dissolve.

Sharot argues that optimism serves a vital evolutionary purpose, having evolved as a necessary counterbalance to foresight. Early humans developed the ability to imagine what could transpire in the future so that they could then create plans to influence future outcomes. Yet this skill came with an enormous downside. That is, this ability to visualize our future came with the awareness that we are all going to die. How did our ancestors keep that awareness of future mortality from overwhelming them? Why didn't they just despair, give up and do nothing because they knew they were going to die anyhow (and perhaps even soon as their life expectancy was far shorter)? One way this ability to envision the future could evolve and not be overly disheartening and disabling is if it emerged alongside an irrational optimism wherein knowledge of the inevitability of death was offset by the ability to conceive of a bright future.

Sharot and her colleagues (2011) conducted brain scans of subjects instructed to ponder both negative and positive information about the general probabilities of various events, including data on the probability of developing cancer, Alzheimer's, or heart disease, or being a robbery victim over the course of a lifetime. The subjects were asked to estimate the likelihood that they would experience such negative events in their life both before and after receiving the information on typical probabilities. The results revealed that our brains assimilate positive information quickly and easily which enhances optimism, but we are far less adept at processing negative information. It appears that when presented with information about negative future possibilities, denial sets in for most people. After receiving data about the probability of negative events, subjects revised their estimates of the chance of such negative outcomes in their lives only slightly, assuming that this negative information (the base rate data) did not pertain to them personally. For instance, although 30% of all people will manifest some type of cancer over their lifetimes, few subjects believed that they had a 30% chance of developing a malignancy. This discrepancy between what you expect and what can actually happen is referred to as a **prediction error**.

The brain scans of these same subjects revealed that different, albeit corresponding portions of our brain process good and bad news. A section of the left frontal lobe, the left inferior frontal gyrus, was strongly activated when subjects contemplated good news. Bad news, however, was processed within the right frontal lobe in the right inferior frontal gyrus. But the processing in this region appears to be less effective. Indeed, the more optimistic an individual, the less this brain region was activated by bad news.

Our brains have been wired in this way, with the right inferior frontal gyrus being harder to activate, because from an evolutionary standpoint, positive expectations increase the odds of survival (Sharot, 2012). Those who give up in times of hardship or crisis are far less likely to live. Those who expect to survive and do everything possible to make that happen are more likely to live on and pass along their optimistic genes to future generations.

2.5.8 Is It Possible to Be High on Both Optimism and Pessimism?

Optimism is not simply the absence of pessimism. Optimism and pessimism are typically thought to be mutually exclusive, but surprisingly there is ample evidence that they are not! Some individuals expect both good and bad outcomes to be plentiful. Other people compartmentalize and are very optimistic in some situations and very pessimistic in other circumstances. This ability to be simultaneously optimistic and pessimistic is often observed in Eastern cultures and in Asian Americans, and is addressed in the following sections. Realistic optimists recognize that bad outcomes are possible and at times probable, even though they expect to weather the difficult circumstances, and survive and thrive, nonetheless. So it is not that realistic optimists expect that nothing bad will ever befall them; they just believe that they have the wherewithal to cope with life's vicissitudes and surmount obstacles.

The Global Perspective
Growing Inequality

Earlier you learned about the growing gap between the haves and have-nots in our world. But that growing inequality is not solely apparent when comparing so called third-world countries with those of the industrialized West. It is happening right here in America. Following the Great Recession of 2008–2009 many American families were worse off than they were just forty years ago. Jobs were lost, home values plummeted, and savings, including those meant for retirement, got depleted for many middle class Americans. Yet even given the Great Recession, the US Economy is much larger than it was in 1980. But if the average American is not better off, who is? It appears that the increase in wealth has been enjoyed primarily by the very rich. Back in 1980, the bottom 50% of Americans took home approximately 21% of all income in the country, which was almost double the amount (11%) earned by the top 1% of wage-earners. According to the 2018 World Inequality Report, those percentages have reversed with the bottom 50% earning only 13% of take home pay while the top 1% garners over 20% of the country's income. Therefore, in the last forty years the U.S. economy has redistributed over eight points of national income from the bottom 50% up to the top 1% (Ingraham, 2017). The latest data reveals that by 2007 the top 1% of earners in America received 23% of the nation's total income. By comparison, in 1980 they enjoyed only 8% of the total. That means that in less than 30 years the gap between the 1% and the rest of the 99% has tripled in size! (Wilkinson & Picket, 2010) It is this growing inequality that has spurred movements such as Occupy Wall Street.

A similar trend is evident when comparing CEOs of major American corporations with their average workers. During the 1950s and 1960s, the top administrators in major American companies earned about 25 to 30 times the salary of a typical worker. By 1980, the difference had increased to 40. Just a decade later it had swollen to 100. By 2007, just before the Great Recession, the gap had bulged so that the CEOs were making about 350 times what the typical worker earned. To make the comparison a bit more vivid, in the 1950's if a typical worker made, say, $20,000 a year, his top boss was making $500,000. By 2007, if that typical worker was earning the same $20,000, his chief was bringing in 7 million dollars. To make matters worse, from 1980 to 2014 the bottom 20% in the U.S. saw their incomes increase only by an average of 4% while the top 10% saw their income more than double over the same 34-year period. At the very top of the income distribution, these gains were even more extreme with the top 1% nearly tripling their income and the top .001% experiencing incomes gains of over 600 percent. These trends are even more remarkable when compared with wealthy nations in western Europe where the bottom 50% earn approximately 22% of the income in those economies, while the top 1% take in 12% of available income. It appears that the income situation in western Europe today closely resembles the situation in the U.S. nearly 40 years ago.

But is this growing gap inherently negative? It appears that at least in our perception of fairness it is. Research has evidenced that people would rather take a cut in pay as long as everyone else was taking a similar cut, than get a raise in pay if others were getting an even higher raise. Imagine you received a totally unexpected inheritance of one million dollars. You are really surprised as you were not aware that your parents had amassed that much savings. You call your sister to discuss this, mentioning how surprised you are that your parents left you that much money and she excitedly responds, "Yes, I was blown away, ten million dollars!" How would you feel? What would you think?

What about society in general? Does the growing inequality lead to negative consequences? In their book, *The Spirit Level*, Richard Wilkinson and Kate Pickett (2009) present persuasive evidence that income inequalities are at the core of a wide range of health and social problems in society. They affect the level of trust among members, the percentage of mental illness, life expectancy and infant mortality, obesity, children's educational performance, teenage births, homicides, imprisonment rates, and social mobility.

Let's consider social mobility as an example. In the United States having the right parents increases your chances of ending up middle to upper middle class by a factor of three to four. In countries where the gap has not ballooned as it has here, including Canada, Australia, the Nordic nations and even Germany and France, the ability to climb up the economic ladder is much more favorable. While 42% of American men with fathers in the bottom fifth of the earning curve remain there, only 25% of Danes and Swedes do and only 30% of Britons do. Isabel Hawkins, co-director of the Brookings Institution's Center on Children and Families described it aptly when she said, "When the rungs on the ladder are further apart, it's harder to climb up them" (2009). Based on the data they present, Wilkinson and Pickett show that greater equality benefits not just the poor, but all occupational levels.

> Having come to the end of what higher material living standards can offer us, we are the first generation to have to find other ways of improving the real quality of life. The evidence shows that reducing inequality is the best way of improving the quality of the social environment, and so the real quality of life, for all of us . . . this includes the better-off.

What do you think?

2.5.9 Defensive Pessimism

In most cases an optimistic outlook will maximize your chances for success. However, it turns out that things are a bit more complicated than that. This is where the strategy of **defensive pessimism** comes into play. For certain types of people in certain situations, a strategic type of pessimism may actually prove to be more effective! Defensive pessimism can be defined as a strategy that anticipates a negative outcome and then takes steps to avoid that outcome. This is based on the work of psychologist Julie Norem (2001) and presented in her fascinating book, *The Positive Power of Negative Thinking: Using Defensive Pessimism to Harness Anxiety and Perform at Your Peak.* The most intriguing thing about her work is that she has demonstrated through a series of controlled experiments that defensive pessimists are just as successful as what she terms strategic optimists, but both groups do worse if their normal strategies for effective performance are disrupted. That is, if you interfere with a defensive pessimist's ability to perform last-minute worrying and over-preparation to counteract such ruminations, then her performance will suffer as a result. By the same token, if you prevent an optimist from spending her last moments relaxing before an anxiety-provoking task, then her performance will also diminish.

Norem's signature contribution was to distinguish between defensive pessimism and **dispositional pessimism**, as well as to articulate the role of anxiety in this process. Defensive pessimists are those who are anxious about outcomes in their future. They tend to plan to diminish the anxiety generated by all their "*what if*" questions and worries. Many times their over-preparation comes in very handy, which tends to reinforce it. On the other hand, dispositional pessimists are negative thinkers in general, based on their thoughts about the past, and they are the subjects of most negative thinking studies. With regard to the role of anxiety, Norem took into consideration the fact that people tend to vary widely in their baseline anxiety levels, as well as their susceptibility to spikes or reactivity in their anxiety levels.

According to Norem's research, she estimates that approximately 25–30% of Americans consistently utilize defensive pessimism as a coping mechanism, while 30% consistently use strategic optimism. The other 40–45% vacillate, making use of both. Nationality and culture also influence which predominates. In America, optimism is favored as a cultural ideal while in Asia defensive pessimism is more the norm and the ideal.

Her research (Norem & Cantor, 1986) demonstrated that for anxious individuals who routinely used defensive pessimism, disrupting this pattern or instilling more positive expectations actually hindered their performance. The bottom line is that for those people, worrying and preparing (even to point of over-reparation) constitutes a more effective approach in terms of later performance. In one study, the defensive pessimists' typically low expectations for success on a test were artificially manipulated by giving them false feedback to lead them to believe that they would score really well. Norem hypothesized that the group led to have higher expectations would become complacent and abandon their typical success strategies. True to her predictions, the group with inflated expectations performed worse than a defensive pessimist group whose expectations had not been modified.

In another experiment, defensive pessimists and optimists engaged in a dart throwing activity and were divided into three groups. Group 1 engaged in a coping imagery exercise where they imagined something going wrong (impaling someone with a dart) and how to prevent this mishap. Group 2 visualized themselves throwing darts perfectly (mastery) and Group 3 did a relaxation exercise. True to form, the defensive pessimists performed best after engaging in coping imagery and performed worst after relaxing. The reverse was true for the optimists, who performed best after relaxing (their preferred strategy) and worst after visualizing the worst case scenarios and how to fix them.

In yet another exploration of how worry helps or hinders defensive pessimists, Norem devised an experiment where she provoked anxiety in subjects prior to a performance task, but prevented them from engaging in their usual coping strategy of worrying and preparing by distracting them with busywork. The outcome was that those who were distracted from worrying performed significantly worse than those who were allowed to engage in defensive pessimistic mechanisms.

"Worries, Norem concluded, are exactly what defensive pessimists need on their minds. Trusting in their abilities by setting high expectations or distracting themselves by 'thinking good thoughts' or staying busy can hinder their performance" (Stewart, 2002). Although defensive pessimists report higher anxiety levels prior to performance situations than optimists because of their worries, afterwards they report equally successful outcomes as their optimistic peers. So it seems that the road to success or effective performance is just different for those with higher anxiety levels. The question arises as to what would happen if defensive pessimists learned other methods for lowering anxiety (such as methods explicated in Chapter 6), but that is a question for future research.

Norem's work, while superficially contradicting many of the findings and claims of positive psychology, can be reconciled within the positive psychology framework. Defensive pessimism certainly fits within positive psychology because it can lead to better performance and personal growth (Paul, 2011). Norem herself argues that defensive pessimists have been inappropriately associated with other negative thinkers. Because defensive pessimists report high anxiety levels and appear to be pessimistic on the surface, they tend to be lumped in with dispositional pessimists, those who have an overall pessimistic explanatory style in general. Defensive pessimists typically are not dispositional pessimists, according to Norem. She claims that when anxiety is statistically factored out of the pessimism studies, the defensive pessimists turn out to be no more pessimistic than the strategic optimists.

Thus defensive pessimism is an effective coping mechanism for individuals who tend to be of moderate to high anxiety. It is a strategy that is not recommended for individuals who are not prone to anxiety. But we can begin to see here where realistic or strategic optimism, self-efficacy (which contains an optimism component) and defensive pessimism lie on a continuum of sorts. Which alternative to pick depends on your personality makeup, anxiety level, and the reality of the situation that you may face. But in any event, Norem's work helps to bring a broader dimension to this discussion.

2.5.10 The Ehrenreich Error

Despite the plethora of scientific evidence for the beneficial effects of optimism on physical health, emotional well-being, performance and even luck, not all scientists are enamored of the value of an optimistic paradigm. One notable critic, Barbara Ehrenreich (2009), argues that what is needed is not optimism but realism, and she goes on to assert that optimism can be down right harmful. For example, she blames the "tyranny of positive thinking" and the nation's "reckless optimism" for the poor decisions leading up to the war in Iraq and the economic crash. For the latter, the unwise choices made by lenders and individuals were due to unrealistically rosy expectations that housing prices would never plummet. She asserts that individuals with serious illnesses (Ehrenreich herself is a breast cancer survivor) need to accept the reality of their illness. She complains that optimism just sugar coats the situation and promotes denial. However, when drawing those conclusions she cherry-picked the research literature on optimism, citing only those studies where an optimistic outlook was not helpful.

In what he refers to as the *"Ehrenreich error,"* Seligman (2011) demolishes her argument by pointing out that she confuses optimism that does not influence reality with optimism that can influence reality. To understand this point we must momentarily digress to distinguish between two types of reality. **Nonreflexive reality** is not influenced by the thoughts, expectations, desires or wishes of humans. For example, our weather on a given day is an independent reality. If a hurricane is coming your way, your expectations will not influence the path of the storm, and if it is forecast to come in your direction you are well advised to heed reality, prepare or evacuate if necessary. **Reflexive reality**, on the other hand, is influenced by and sometimes even directly determined by our beliefs, perceptions and expectations. Self-fulfilling prophecies are a great example of this. For instance, if you want to ask your boss for a raise, if you truly believe that you deserve it and can make a strong case, your chances of success are much greater than if you think it is a long shot. Your demeanor in asking for the raise, based on your expectations, will affect your outcome. To quote Seligman:

> . . . *In the case of whether there will be a total eclipse of the sun viewable from Philadelphia next year, my hopes have no influence. However, in the case of future price of stocks, investors' optimism and pessimism strongly influence the market. Enhrenreich . . . ignores the enormous number of reflexive realities in which what a person thinks and feels goes on to influence the future. The science of positive psychology is entirely about such reflexive realities. (pg. 235–236)*

Ehrenreich assumes that all reality is nonreflexive, therefore optimism is useless at best and delusional at worst. Flexible or realistic optimism takes into account that our outlook does not affect every aspect of reality and in some cases the best approach is cold eyed realism without denial. However, how one chooses to deal with the aftermath of any nonreflexive situation (like the weather, or injuries sustained from an accident, or a cancer diagnosis) ultimately becomes a reflexive reality where optimism is proven to facilitate coping, healing and success. Indeed, research (Geers and colleagues, 2005; Jaksic and colleagues, 2013) has demonstrated that optimistic individuals are likely to experience stronger placebo effects and/or to benefit more from actual treatments. Is this because optimists are naive? No, this is because optimism primes one's physiology to be more responsive to healing approaches.

2.5.11 Balancing Optimism and Pessimism

Annie Paul (2011) reports that as positive psychology matures, it is moving away from a one-size fits-all optimism. The key is to use optimism and pessimism strategically to match your mind-set to the demands of the situation. If you are job hunting, for example, it will behoove you to be as optimistic as possible, as that will definitely increase the likelihood that you will be hired (Kaniel, Massey, & Robinson, 2010). Nevertheless, be wary of overconfidence when you have been successful before and have a realistic expectation of a repeat performance. Utilizing defensive pessimism in this situation, that is, imagining what could go wrong and developing contingency plans, could help you avoid potential pitfalls. Paul reminds us that those who excel in using defensive pessimism are often very dynamic, successful individuals. In the same vein, in some situations (when bad news is likely to be delivered), bracing yourself for a potential negative outcome (i.e. expecting the worst) can have the positive psychological effect of helping you cope better because you are not blindsided. Even Seligman, while still advocating optimism, warns us to link positive thinking with reality testing, to rigorously check the results of our efforts to prevent overly positive expectations from leading us astray.

2.5.12 Cross-Cultural Considerations

Non-Western cultures may not necessarily share the same perspectives or explanatory styles (such as optimism) or express them in the same way as in the United States. And we must be careful about over-generalizing results based on research—with subjects often overwhelmingly from a Caucasian American background—which may not generalize to other cultures beyond our shores or even to other cultures or subcultures within our country.

For example, there has been research comparing optimism in Western and Eastern cultures. Lee and Seligman (1997) found that Asian Americans and Caucasian Americans had similar levels of optimism but mainland Chinese students studying here were less optimistic. Chang (1996a) found that Asian Americans were not less optimistic but were more pessimistic, but their higher levels of pessimism were also associated with greater levels of problem solving. This appears to be a function of what Norem refers to as defensive pessimism. So according to Chang (2001a), "what works for Asians relative to Caucasian Americans simply might be different, not necessarily more effective." We cannot assume that Western-based measures and theories will always translate or apply to Eastern cultures.

Questions

1. Defensive pessimists need to _____ and _____ in order to perform their best.

    A. sleep; exercise

    B. whine; complain

    C. calm down; detach

    D. worry; plan

2. The belief that the future will most likely be better than the past or the present is referred to as _____.

    A. the negativity bias

    B. defensive pessimism

    C. the optimism bias

    D. proactivity

3. The Ehrenreich Error confuses _____ reality with _____ reality.

   A. objective; subjective

   B. reflexive; non-reflexive

   C. internal; external

   D. optimistic; pessimistic

Summary

This chapter provided a capsule review of the major theoretical frameworks within the field of psychology with regard to where each falls on the continuum of determinism vs. free will. This laid the foundation for an exploration of proactivity, the paradigm that our behavior is ultimately the product of our choices, not our conditions, while also recognizing the myriad of external and internal factors that impinge upon our ability to choose. The concept of locus of control (a research based way of conceptualizing the cognitive component of proactivity) was introduced with the focus on how to develop an internal locus of control. The Self-Efficacy model, based on Bandura's observational learning theory, was presented as a way to combine a cognitive component (locus of control) with a behavioral component (proactivity) to facilitate your belief that you can accomplish what you desire providing that you do that which is necessary to do so. This was followed by a series of steps for achieving self-efficacy using observational learning and visualization strategies.

Since proactivity, locus of control and self-efficacy are all a function of our internal self-talk, an extended explanation of dealing with irrational self-talk provided a step by step method, that of cognitive restructuring, for refuting irrational thoughts that block self-efficacy. This was followed by an in-depth discussion of all the facets of optimism including its benefits, proven techniques for increasing positive thinking, as well as the limits of optimism. Alternatives to positive thinking, such as defensive pessimism, were reviewed in recognition that a straight optimistic approach is not the best fit for every individual.

Positive Psychology Exercises

1. The next time you find yourself feeling anxious or depressed, look deeper into yourself, and determine whether there are any irrational thoughts fueling your feelings. Look at the list of irrational thoughts and check whether any of your unconscious cognitions are a close match. If so, follow the three step cognitive restructuring technique to counteract those irrational messages.

2. Identify that area of your life about which you are most pessimistic. Experiment with the techniques presented for thinking optimistically and notice how you are able to shift your perceptions or expectations in a more optimistic direction.

3. Think of a situation where it would behoove you to adopt a mindset of defensive pessimism in order to cope in the most effective fashion.

Key Terms

ACT
Behaviorism
Catastrophizing
Cognitive-Behaviorism
Concordance Rates
Cognitive Restructuring
Correlation
Dispositional Pessimism
Delusional Thinking
Determinism
Defensive Pessimism
Existentialism

Explanatory style
External Locus of Control
Free Will
Global Citizen
Hallucinations
Humanism
Internal Locus of Control
Learned Helplessness
Locus of Control
Non-reflexive reality
Optimism
Optimism Bias

Pessimism
Prediction errors
Proactivity
Psychoanalytic Theory
Psychological Flexibility
Psychotic Episode
Reflexive reality
Schizophrenia
Self-Efficacy
Self–Talk
Spurious Correlation

Shared Writing

Write about how the optimism bias operates in your own life. Where are you taking unnecessary risks?

Chapter 2 Questions

1. The combination of an internal locus of control and proactivity can produce a high level of _____.

   A. reactivity

   B. self-efficacy

   C. irrational self-talk

   D. defensive pessimism

2. Deterministic theories hold that _____.

   A. free will is an illusion

   B. if you are determined, you will succeed

   C. heredity is not important

   D. our choices determine everything

3. Spurious correlations are often perceived because we unconsciously use _____ to reinforce our pre-conceived beliefs or stereotypes.

   A. cognitive restructuring

   B. irrational self-talk

   C. proactivity

   D. selective attention

4. Optimism is an explanatory style which uses attributions that are _____.

   A. internal, permanent, and global

   B. external, temporary, and specific

   C. realistic, rational, and permanent

   D. unrealistic, irrational, and temporary

5. A reliable relationship between variables is termed _____.

   A. locus of control

   B. a prediction error

   C. a correlation

   D. self-efficacy

6. The four traits manifested by happy people include: (1) extroversion; (2) healthy self-esteem; (3) an internal locus of control and (4) _____.

   A. reactivity

   B. pessimism

   C. learned helplessness

   D. optimism

7. Luck is a function of _____.

   A. random chance

   B. pessimistic mindset

   C. optimism plus certain personality characteristics

   D. inheriting money from your relatives

8. The discrepancy between what you expect and what can actually happen is called _____.

   A. a spurious correlation

   B. a prediction error

   C. external locus of control

   D. learned helplessness

9. From an evolutionary standpoint, humans are hardwired to be optimistic because _____.

   A. of neuroplasticity

   B. defensive pessimism is dangerous

   C. ignorance is bliss

   D. it increases our odds of survival

10. Optimism and pessimism _____.

    A. have been experimentally disproven

    B. are mutually exclusive and cannot occur together

    C. can co-exist within the same person

    D. have no relationship to effectiveness

Chapter 3
Learning to Accept Yourself

After reading this chapter, you should be able to:

3.1 Define the concept of self-esteem and explain its relationship to personal effectiveness.

3.2 Identify the various influences on our self-esteem.

3.3 Describe the various steps and strategies used to facilitate a healthy level of self-esteem.

3.4 Identify the core virtues of good character, their corresponding signature strengths, and how they relate to self-esteem.

How is **self-esteem** relevant to effectiveness? At least in the Western World, studies suggest that effective individuals have learned to value themselves, to have what psychologists refer to as "healthy" or "positive" self-esteem or self-regard. There are numerous examples evidencing that in our part of the world, people with "low" or "negative" self-esteem have a significantly greater chance of feeling dissatisfied with their lives and suffering from poor mental and physical health, along with troubled relationships and school failure (Antonucci & Jackson, 1983; Dawes, 1994; Diener, 1984; Leary, 1983; Taylor & Brown 1988). Those with low self-esteem are at an increased risk of developing eating disorders, depression, and committing suicide (Emler, 2001). Additionally, studies have demonstrated that self-esteem is positively correlated with values and behaviors such as self-direction, achievement, and personal competence (Feather, 1991). But what is this thing we call self-esteem?

3.1 The Concept of Self-Esteem

Define the concept of self-esteem and explain its relationship to personal effectiveness.

Historically, self-esteem has referred to the relationship you have with yourself, the degree to which you regard yourself in a positive or negative light. It is a measure of how much you value yourself and feel useful and necessary in the world. It is different from your **self-concept**, which is your paradigm about yourself and is reflected in how you might describe yourself. In contrast, your self-esteem refers to how you judge and evaluate yourself based on this paradigm. J. D. Brown (2007) defined self-esteem as the feelings of affection you have for yourself, further describing positive self-esteem as a general fondness or love for oneself. People with healthy self-esteem maintain a basic sense of self-acceptance even when they feel bad due to failure or rejection. They seem to possess an internal safety net that helps them keep disappointments in perspective. Seligman (1995) believes that self-esteem is a measure of how well you are doing in life. Commonly, self-esteem seems to refer to your global evaluation of yourself, and according to Carl Rogers (1959), it results from the discrepancy between your **ideal self** (the person you feel you should be) and your **real self** (the person you feel you actually are).

More recently, however, self-esteem has been defined as a socially constructed emotion, not much different than fear, anger, or joy (Hewitt, 2005). As such, the researchers argue that self-esteem can vary according to the person's mood at the time, and that it is difficult to envision self-esteem as a stable characteristic over time.

Nonetheless, while most psychologists would agree that there is certainly a broad measure of self-esteem, that is, the degree to which you like yourself in general, the fact is that self-esteem also fluctuates depending on how you regard yourself in specific areas. For example, you might have healthy self-esteem and confidence in yourself as an athlete, but low self-esteem as a scholar. Studies have identified several key areas which help determine self-esteem, including physical appearance, scholastic ability, work performance, popularity and social skills, and athletic ability (Fleming & Courtney, 1984). The importance that you place on each of these areas will determine the weight they carry in influencing your global sense of self-esteem. For example, if you overemphasize the importance of physical appearance and you believe that you are unattractive, your self-esteem will clearly be negatively affected.

Why is having positive self-regard so important to your effectiveness? Because in our culture, when you have faith in yourself, it enhances your ability to do your best, which in turn improves your performance and further reinforces your good feelings about yourself. Baumeister (1996), in his review of the research on self-esteem, concluded that people with healthy self-esteem are generally happier and tend to show perseverance in the face of failure. They don't let apparent obstacles or failed attempts dissuade them from their goals. As aptly described by Brehm (1998),

> *When your self esteem is strong, mountains become molehills. A positive self-regard attracts others; when you are happier with yourself, you are happier with life and a pleasure to be with. A healthy self-esteem is essential to clear communication. When you value yourself, you value your thoughts and feelings and can express them more clearly to others. A positive self-esteem allows you to give more of yourself and enjoy other people. Best of all, a positive self-regard gives you freedom, the freedom to try new things, to make the most of opportunities, to be the best you can be, and get the most out of life. (p. 277)*

On the other hand, low self-esteem is a circular, self-defeating process where your negative feelings about yourself result in negative attitudes in general. These negative attitudes then become a driving force in your negative behaviors. Such negative behaviors then promote negative feelings, and so on. Thus the person with low self-esteem becomes a psychological prisoner of his or her own poor self-image. The Neo-Freudian theorist, Alfred Adler (1928), described individuals with chronically low self-esteem as having an "**inferiority complex.**" Figure 3.1 illustrates both the positive cycle described above by Brehm and the contrasting negative vicious cycle.

Lastly, having healthy self-esteem greatly facilitates your ability to cope with stress (Aspinwall & Taylor, 1992). When you have positive self-regard it is much easier to be an optimist, to view life's difficulties as opportunities for growth and self-discovery rather than as problems.

A word of caution here: Don't make the mistake of confusing positive self-esteem with being conceited or self-centered. Some people are afraid to hold themselves in positive regard because they fear it will make them seem stuck-up.

Figure 3.1

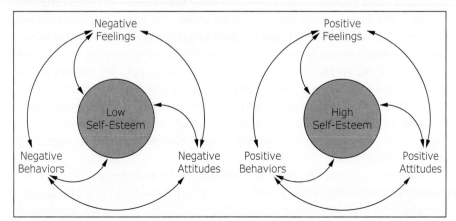

Keep in mind; people who are conceited or stuck up are often braggarts. If you truly have healthy self-esteem you will not need to broadcast it. There is an old saying which sums this up perfectly: "when you have arrived, you don't need to shout." That is, people with healthy self-esteem don't need to boast about themselves or their achievements. They can recognize their strengths and accept compliments *and* criticisms. It is likely that those who feel the need to brag are actually trying to compensate for low self-esteem.

3.1.1 The Downside of High Self-Esteem

Although self-esteem is correlated with effectiveness in our culture, don't make the mistake of assuming that having positive self-esteem necessarily leads to effectiveness. Remember the difference between correlation and causation we mentioned earlier. Various investigators have demonstrated that there are times when a positive evaluation of the self is counterproductive. For example, a study investigating the relationship between self-perceptions that are positively biased and aggression found that the two were positively correlated. The investigators found when studying children in third, fourth, and fifth grades that the higher their self-appraisal, the more the children's peers felt they were both overtly and relationally aggressive (David & Kristner, 2006).

Similarly, there are people who exhibit inordinately high self-esteem. They have an unrealistic self-appraisal termed the "superiority complex," which is equally problematic. Oftentimes these individuals have antisocial personalities or characteristics, or are overly narcissistic (i.e. extremely self-centered). These people tend to see themselves as above or superior to others and act out of that belief. For example, many (but not all) psychopathic individuals have extremely high self-esteem based on a grandiose, inflated self-image. This distortion of self-image leads psychopaths to harbor unrealistic expectations of what the world owes them, and can contribute to disordered, selfish, and even cruel behavior. Studies support the fact that people with an overly high evaluation of themselves might be a threat to others as they are more likely to be racist, violent and criminal (Emler, 2001). These people see themselves as separate from their environment and have little regard for the impact of their behavior on others. They fail to recognize our interconnectedness, the fact that in essence, we are neither superior nor inferior to others. As Hewitt (2005) described, "when people talk of self-esteem, they are expressing the importance of the affective link [emotional connection] between themselves and others; when they experience self-esteem, they are living this connection." "True self-esteem and true humility arise out of that realization" (Tolle, 2005). Self-esteem and humility may seem contradictory, but in truth, they are one and the same.

Although positive self-esteem is considered to be important for healthy emotional functioning it has a darker side which has often been overlooked. Unrealistically high self-esteem inhibits effectiveness. In fact, at times, an elevated positive evaluation might lead to feelings of entitlement, the belief that you deserve things, such as a good grade in a class, the latest clothing fashion, or a particularly hot car, regardless of your actions or the circumstances. This sense of entitlement is often accompanied by a belief that if you try your hardest, you should always be rewarded. These individuals seem to confuse the fact that trying to do something is not the same as doing it, and that often in life you can either have success or the excuses for not having achieved it, but not both.

Pursuing high self-esteem for its own sake can leave you feeling dissatisfied and empty. Why? Even when we achieve goals that we assume will allow us to feel good about ourselves permanently, those feelings are typically temporary as no matter what you achieve, there are always those who are more accomplished. Self-esteem that is contingent solely on success or beauty is very fragile as it is easily damaged by setbacks. Even very successful individuals sometimes fail or fall short.

Although having positive self-esteem has its benefits such as increased happiness and perseverance (Baumeister, 2003), it can also be detrimental to well-being. Crocker and Carnavale (2013) have elucidated a variety of other drawbacks of high self-esteem. For example, very high self-esteem can lead to an unrealistically positive self-appraisal such that one can become blind to one's faults. Individuals with high self-esteem who are unaware of their shortcoming may get very defensive when on the receiving end of negative feedback, blaming the messenger rather than looking within to see whether there is validity to the complaint and then owning up to mistakes. If this becomes a pattern then interpersonal relationships can be damaged. Another potential cost of having high self-esteem based on achievement is that it could lead to an avoidance of failure rather than reaching for success, leading to stagnation rather than growth. The pursuit of self-esteem can also undermine intrinsic motivation, that internal interest in or desire to do something purely for its own sake. Engaging in an activity merely to look good or more accomplished in the eyes of others can take the joy out of the journey. When the motivation is external, the pressure and sense of obligation can mute the satisfaction that comes from hard work. In addition, those pursuing external validation make everything about themselves due to their preoccupation with their worth, therefore personal relationships often suffer as a result.

3.1.2 Positive Self-Esteem Is Not Necessarily a Universal Experience

So, while in our culture successful individuals tend to have a positive self-concept, having healthy self-esteem is not necessarily indicative of being a successful individual. But is the desire for positive self-esteem a universal experience? Do successful people typically experience positive self-esteem everywhere on the globe? You might have noticed that as we spoke about the importance of self-esteem as it relates to effectiveness, we kept qualifying it with "in our culture." There is some evidence that the motivation to have positive self-regard is not necessarily a cross-cultural reality. For example, Asian cultures do not seem to relate feeling good about the self with effectiveness (Heine, Lehman, Markus, & Kitayama, 1999).

In contrast, there is evidence that self-critical and self-improving orientations might be more related to being successful among Japanese and other Asian cultures. Some researchers have theorized that this difference between Western and Asian cultures is grounded on the fact that while Western cultures, and particularly North America, tend to stress the importance of the individual, Asian cultures are more focused on the importance of the collective. Thus, how one feels about the self is just not as important as how others feel about you. "Japanese tend to be motivated to gain the esteem of others rather than dwell on their own self-evaluations" (Kuwayama, 1992, Spence, 1985). Not surprisingly, while it is clear that in our culture there is a tendency to seek to enhance our self-esteem, for the Japanese their goal is to enhance their sense of belongingness (Heine, Lehman, Markus, & Kitayama, 1999).

Perhaps, as social psychologists Romin Tafarodi and William Swann suggest, a universal concept of self-esteem should include two factors: 1) self-liking, which they describe as a sense of social worth and 2) self-competence, a sense of personal efficacy (Tafarodi & Swann, Jr., 1995). When so defined, it again becomes evident that in collectivist societies such as the Chinese, the development of self-liking or social worth is emphasized much more strongly than the development of self-competency or personal efficacy. The inverse is true in individualistic societies such as the United States. Therefore, perhaps rather than talking about high self-esteem, we should focus on healthy or optimal self-esteem.

3.1.3 The Question of Self-Worth

So self-esteem is based on your appraisal of your **self-worth**. But what is your self-worth based on? When we ask this of students in our classes, they typically respond with answers such as their achievements, caring for others, physical appearance, intellectual attributes, financial success, and even the extent of their material possessions (i.e., whether they drive a "hot car" or have fashionable clothes). Jennifer Crocker and Connie Wolfe (2001) examined possible sources of self-esteem, calling these "contingencies" of self-worth – the areas of life in which people believe that success means they are worthwhile and failure means they are worthless. These investigators identified seven possible domains in which people may invest their self-esteem. They labeled these: (1) family support; (2) competition; (3) appearance; (4) God's love; (5) academic competence; (6) virtue; and (7) others' approval. This is by no means an exhaustive list. The list merely reflects some of the more common domains that people identify as important to their self-esteem. We are sure you can think of other factors that might be important in determining the way we feel about ourselves.

Crocker and Wolfe (2001) argue that major problems such as depression, drug abuse, and aggression may be linked not so much to our general level of self-esteem, but rather to the source of our self-esteem. In a study of 600 college freshmen (Crocker, Luhtanen, & Bouvrette, 2001), self-esteem based on appearance was linked to more hours per week grooming, shopping, and partying. Self-esteem rooted in God's love positively correlated to spending more time in religious activities, such as praying and going to church or synagogue, and less time partying. Self-esteem based on academic competence was associated with greater success in gaining admission to graduate school. Not surprisingly, research upholds that if we base our self-esteem on physical appearance, our susceptibility to eating disorders increases. By the same token, people whose self-esteem is based on approval by others are especially susceptible to anger and hostility when others challenge them.

People who are unable to feel good about themselves on the basis of one source may shift to another. Out of frustration, they may even reject one source altogether and this rejection may lead to less than effective lives. For instance, the high dropout rate among African-American college students may be the consequence of rejecting academic performance as a source of self-worth after numerous frustrating attempts to succeed in an environment that assumes they are academically inferior (Steele, 1997).

Research suggests that having multiple sources or contingencies of self-worth is more effective than only having one or just a few. People with various sources of self-worth are less likely to be overwhelmed by negative life events affecting one source. If feeling inadequate in one area of life, they can shift their attention to other important areas where things are going well.

Yet perhaps what is most effective is to have self-esteem that is "non-contingent." Our students are often startled by our suggestion that *your self-worth is based on nothing*. It is a given. It is your birthright. Ideally, your self-esteem should be based on recognition of your inherent sense of worth as a human being independent of your achievements and attributes. You are worthy because you are a unique individual with your own special potentials. Research consistently suggests that contingent self-esteem is too often accompanied by anxiety, hostility, defensiveness, and the risk of depression. Edward Deci and Richard Ryan (1995) compared contingent self-esteem with what they labeled "true" or non-contingent self-esteem. The latter, they claimed, is more stable and securely based in a solid sense of self. People with such non-contingent self-esteem are pleased when they succeed and disappointed when they fail, but their sense of self-worth is not at risk in the process. They have learned that it is not that "you can do it," but that "it's all right if you can't do it; it doesn't mean you are a bad person" (Brown, 1998). Too often we define our self-worth based on our performance or accomplishments. While your achievements are an integral part of who you are, and will undoubtedly contribute to your self-esteem, you will be doing yourself a great disservice if you define your worth solely on the basis of this dimension. You are worthy because you are human. It helps to believe that you are basically good, kind, caring, and worthy of being loved despite your faults or temporary failings. This is, of course, only a frame, but a very useful one, one that will lead to healthy self-esteem and greatly enhance your effectiveness as a human being. To quote the well-known author and motivational speaker Tony Robbins (1986), "I used to have to achieve to feel happy, now I happily achieve."

If you are curious about your level of self-esteem, we invite you to complete this questionnaire. Be honest and answer the questions to reflect how you really feel about yourself.

Self-Esteem Self-Assessment

Answer the following questions by assigning each one the appropriate number from the following scale:
1 = strongly agree   2 = agree   3 = disagree   4 = strongly disagree

_____   1.   I feel that I am a person of worth, at least on an equal basis with others.

_____   2.   I feel that I have a number of good qualities.

_____   3.   All in all, I am inclined to feel I am a failure.

_____   4.   I am able to do things as well as most other people.

_____   5.   I feel I do not have much to be proud of.

_____   6.   I take a positive attitude toward myself.

_____   7.   On the whole, I am satisfied with myself.

_____   8.   I wish I could have more respect for myself.

_____   9.   I certainly feel useless at times.

_____   10.   At times I think I am no good at all.

_____   **TOTAL SCORE** (Read directions below before adding)

Scoring: **On questions 3, 5, 8, 9, and 10 convert your numbered answers as follows: Change 1 to 4; change 4 to 1; change 2 to 3; change 3 to 2. Now total your responses. The lower your score the higher your self-esteem.**

> **10–15 Healthy Self-Esteem**
>
> **16–20 Good Self-Esteem**
>
> **21–30 Moderately Low Self-Esteem**
>
> **31–40 Very Poor Self-Esteem**

So how did you do? Where do you lie on the continuum of negative to positive self-esteem? Now that you have an added measure of your level of perceived self worth, let's look at the characteristics of individuals with healthy vs. low self-esteem listed in Table 3.1.

3.1.4 The Pathological Critic

How is it that we sabotage our self-esteem? Each of us has an inner voice, which evaluates and judges our actions and ourselves. The nature of this inner voice reflects the quality of your relationship with yourself. Psychologist Eugene Sagan coined the term "**pathological critic**" to describe what he saw as a negative inner voice that attacks and judges you. Although it is true that for most people their inner voice tends to be critical, this is clearly not necessary or particularly effective. Perhaps a more appropriate metaphor would be that of a misguided critic or

TABLE 3.1 Characteristics of People with Healthy and Low Self-Esteem

Healthy Self-Esteem	Low Self-Esteem
• Believe that they are worthwhile and valuable.	• Believe that their worth is based on their accomplishments or the opinions of others.
• Sees demanding goals as a challenge.	• Is highly critical of self and others. • More likely to be prejudiced.
• Recognizes the strengths and achievements of self and others.	• Doubt their personal power.
• Acknowledges their personal power without being manipulative.	• Likely to be hero worshipers. • Resistant to change.
• Takes responsibility for their own actions without blaming or making excuses.	• Fearful of taking risks that may lead to failure.
• Able to take risks. Is not afraid of failure.	• View failure or rejection as evidence of their lack of self-worth.
• Do not view failure or rejection as a reflection upon their self-worth.	• Discounts praise from others.
• Accepts compliments.	• Show an inability to accept constructive criticism.
• Accepts and values constructive criticism.	• Give themselves negative internal messages.
• Generous with their praise for others.	• Tend to be highly competitive.
• Is able to give themselves positive self messages.	• Feel a need to win to prove themselves.
• Do not feel the need to continually prove themselves.	• May resort to workaholism to prove their worth.
• Is able to communicate their needs and wants effectively.	• Have difficulty communicating their needs.
• Is able to develop satisfying interpersonal relationships.	• Are likely to remain in unsatisfying relationships.
• Recognizes the value of all experiences.	• Tend to value appearances over substance.
• Is capable of working well as a team member.	• Inability to make decisions and take action without clearly defined rules.
• Have trust in themselves.	• Doubt themselves.
• Seeks balance in their life.	• Lack balance in their lives.
• See the value in continued personal growth and self exploration.	• Are threatened by personal growth experiences.
• Surround themselves with people who validate them.	• Often attract people who denigrate them.
• Are seldom controlled by guilt.	• Are guilt ridden.
• Are optimistic about themselves, others and the world.	• Are pessimistic about themselves, others, and the world.
• Value the power of their word.	• Typically don't live up to their word.
• Are proactive.	• Are reactive.
• Accept all of their feelings as natural, human and a part of life.	• Consider negative emotions as further proof of their lack of worth.
• Are good losers.	• Are poor losers.
• Are not afraid to be different or take an unpopular stand.	• Resort to fadism to be included in the "in crowd."

coach. The intention behind this inner coach's behavior and communications is always positive, i.e. it is always trying to help you do that which it believes is best for you. However, the way that it goes about this frequently accomplishes just the opposite of what it is trying to do. Our goal is not to help you get rid of this coach altogether, but to train it in using methods which are more aligned with assisting you to improve your self-esteem, to value yourself more positively.

To illustrate this point, we ask that you entertain the notion that change or growth in the human being occurs in a similar fashion as that of the task of toilet training a child. Initially, the child does not even recognize that she is not to relieve herself in her clothes. After some training, she knows what is expected, but cannot translate this into appropriate anticipatory behaviors. Thus she can only report to us once she has already messed her clothes. Later on she can recognize it as it is happening, and thus can change her behavior midstream (pun intended). After a while she can anticipate the need to defecate or urinate and can go and do it in the toilet. Now, we know that toilet training occurs quickest and most effectively if we acknowledge and reinforce (reward) the child every step of the way, for indeed this is clearly a process of step-by-step learning. If we want to make toilet training difficult and lengthy, then we need to criticize and demean the child for the mistakes she makes. The same holds true for how we deal with ourselves. If we criticize and demean ourselves, we get stuck repeating the same behavior or mistakes over and over again, and as an added bonus we lower our self-esteem. But if we approach ourselves as we would someone we respect, admire and love, then we find we feel better about ourselves and can notice changes in ways which promote our growth.

Questions

1. Your _____ refers to your paradigm about yourself, whereas your _____ refers to the degree to which you regard yourself in a favorable or unfavorable light.

   A. self-esteem; ideal self

   B. ideal self; real self

   C. self-concept; self-esteem

   D. self-esteem; self-concept

2. Chronically low self-esteem leads to a(n) _____.

   A. superiority complex

   B. inferiority complex

   C. self-concept

   D. ideal self

3. Your self-esteem results from the discrepancy between _____ _____.

   A. your real self and your ideal self

   B. your self-concept and your self-worth

   C. your inferiority complex and your real self

   D. your real self and your self-concept

3.2 The Roots of Self-Esteem

Identify the various influences on our self-esteem.

Self-esteem has its roots both in genetics and in learning (i.e. environmental effects). Studies of identical twins reared apart, as well as studies comparing the personalities of adopted children with their biological and adoptive parents, clearly reveal that our adult personalities are influenced by our genetic makeup (Lykken, and colleagues, 1992; Plomin and colleagues, 1994; Bergemen and colleagues, 1993). Identical twins reared apart are more like each other in such **traits** as shyness, well-being, intelligence, anger, neuroticism, and depression (traits which would influence our self-esteem), than fraternal twins reared together. Similarly, adopted children are more similar as adults to their biological parents than to their adoptive parents, with regard to these traits. Thus, there is little doubt that your genetic makeup does contribute to your level of self-esteem. Remember that people with healthy self-esteem retain an innate sense of self-acceptance even when saddened by rejection or failure. Those with low self-esteem lack this internal safety net. When they fail at something or experience rejection, they plummet much lower. And they tend to perceive rejection and failure even when it does not exist. Jonathon D. Brown, one of social psychology's most frequently cited authors, believes that we all have a basic level of self-esteem that is set during our childhood interactions with parents. He believes that the solid safety net of basic self-esteem grows out of a secure attachment to a parent (Brown, 2007). As you will see in more detail in Chapter 11 when we discuss attachment theory, it might be that a corrective relationship wherein you are loved and valued for more than your accomplishments or characteristics is the best way of achieving an optimal level of self-esteem.

By the same token, your interactions with those around you are also a major contributing factor to how you evaluate yourself. Many people and events in your life combine to shape your self-esteem from the moment of your birth. Infants can sense whether people respond to them with acceptance and love, contempt, or indifference, which helps lay the early groundwork for self-esteem (Pelham & Swann, 1989). Your self-esteem is influenced by your parents, siblings, relatives, schoolteachers, peers, bosses, co-workers, etc. Although many of these individuals may no longer be involved in your life, what you learned from them may still wield a dramatic impact on your self-perceptions. The foundation for self-esteem appears to be laid very early in life, and it is believed that some children have poor self-esteem even prior to starting school.

3.2.1 Parental Influences

For most of us, our parents are the most significant influence in shaping our self-esteem, particularly early in life. In most cases, they were our major source of love, security and need fulfillment. If you were fortunate enough to have been raised by parents who cherished you and treated you as a valued human being, worthy of love, you will probably enjoy positive self-esteem in your later life. However, if your parents were too preoccupied with their own troubles, or with work, to give you the attention and love you deserved, the development of healthy self-esteem, while not impossible, would certainly be more difficult.

Many theorists have speculated on how parental behavior influences the self-esteem of children. Carl Rogers (1951) observed that children develop positive self-esteem when parents show them **unconditional positive regard**, which refers to their acceptance of them as having intrinsic merit regardless of their behavior at the moment. Unconditional positive regard involves a consistent expression of love and esteem for the child as a person. When parents show children **conditional positive regard**, that is, they judge the child's value and deliver their love based on the acceptability of the child's behavior, children develop **conditions of worth**, meaning that they only think they are worthwhile or lovable if they behave in certain ways or meet certain standards. Karen Horney (1956) suggested that parents often unknowingly diminish their children's self-esteem by being erratic, domineering, overprotective, demanding, critical, overindulgent, partial to other siblings, or indifferent. Harry Stack Sullivan (1953) noted that when children are treated badly they can develop what he described as **the malevolent attitude**—the belief that one is surrounded by enemies. As a result of this attitude the child comes to view him or herself as someone who is detestable and will always be treated poorly, and moreover, who does not deserve to be treated well.

Returning to our coach metaphor, it is safe to say that for most of you, your original coaches did the best they could and most likely had your best intentions in mind; however, their teaching styles may not have always been healthy. If your coach was overly critical, that took a toll on your self-esteem. Perhaps even more crucial, many of them may have failed to differentiate between you and your behavior when correcting or disciplining you. Have you ever heard, "You are a bad boy," or "You are so lazy," or "How stupid could you possibly be?" These statements are directed at the self and teach you to evaluate yourself negatively. Had your coaches been able to differentiate between you and your behavior, they may have made comments like "I don't like it when you act that way," or "That behavior is unacceptable," or "I get angry when you do . . . " In addition, your level of self-esteem is also a byproduct of how you saw your coaches treat themselves, that is, what they modeled for you. If they were overly self-critical you may have learned to adopt this particular style. The bottom line is that how you treat yourself, or more specifically, how you coach yourself, typically resembles how you were coached.

PARENTING STYLES   At this point you may be wondering what kind of parenting is likely to maximize the opportunities for the healthy development of self-esteem in the child. To answer this we first need to consider what have been termed parenting styles. Diana Baumrind (1991) identified three basic parenting styles that impact on child development: (1) **authoritarian parenting**; (2) **authoritative parenting**; and (3) laissez-faire (permissive) parenting. Other theorists (Maccoby and Martin, 1983) further differentiated permissive parenting into two subgroups: (1) **permissive-indifferent** and (2) **permissive-indulgent.** Authoritarian parents have a restrictive, punitive style of parenting focusing on following rules and assuming that the child is incompetent. Permissive-indifferent parents are uninvolved in their child's life. They are not particularly harsh or punitive, but basically treat the child as if he/she is not particularly important. Permissive-indulgent parents are very involved in the child's life and often very loving, but they fail to set limits or provide meaningful controls over the child's behavior. They may be very indulgent without requiring the child to earn any of the rewards, thus the child may end up quite spoiled. Authoritative parents are warm and nurturing while at the same time setting meaningful limits and controls for the child. These parents are very involved in the lives of their children.

It may seem rather obvious to you that the authoritative parenting style should be the most effective for fostering self-esteem in the child. You are correct if you have made this assumption, and it useful to know that research backs this up as well, according to Bolt (2004). The classic research of Coopersmith (1967, 1975) demonstrated this by studying the self-esteem patterns of fifth and sixth grade boys. The boys with healthy self-esteem typically came from homes where their parents were strict, but not harsh. Their parents were affectionate, accepting, very involved in their son's activities, and used consistent, reasonable discipline for enforcing clear-cut limits. Boys with low self-esteem came from families where the parents were in some ways more permissive, but were quite harsh when discipline was enforced. These parents were far less involved in their sons' lives, often oblivious to misbehavior until it reached a critical point where the parents might overreact. The parents of the boys with positive self-esteem were more demanding of their sons in terms of achievement and meeting standards, but their involvement in their sons' lives communicated a deep caring and value for the child. Coopersmith also found that once self-esteem was established it remained relatively consistent across the school years.

But is this always the case? You may be interested to know that other researchers have found that some children develop healthy self-esteem even though they were raised in very dysfunctional environments. For example, Emmy Werner (cited in Hamburg, 1994) conducted a longitudinal study of 700 children from dysfunctional homes, where parenting styles were far from ideal. Some of the children in this study had positive self-esteem despite inadequate parental influences. These resilient children all appeared to have four characteristics in common: (1) they took an active approach to problem solving, believing they could find solutions; (2) they found positive ways of reframing their experiences, even the bad ones; (3) they were adept at getting positive attention from others; and (4) they were optimists. How did this happen? We are not certain from the research, but somehow these children had learned to be more proactive, perhaps on their own, or perhaps out of their proclivity to attract positive people into their lives (i.e. teachers, coaches, etc.) to serve as mentors, and perhaps some were genetically predisposed to higher levels of self-esteem.

Let us also make clear that when we talk about the different parenting styles, we are oversimplifying a very dynamic and complex relationship. No parents are always authoritative or always authoritarian or always permissive. Their behavior towards their children varies depending on a multitude of factors including level of stress, difficulties at work, and hours of sleep. Since parenting is not one-way, but an interaction, the parents' behaviors are also influenced by the behavior of their children. A particular behavior pattern, which might have produced the desired results with one child, might result in quite different and often surprising reactions from a sibling. Each child is different, and as such, parents must, by necessity, behave differently with each child.

3.2.2 Other Important Influences

Obviously, parents are not the only agents who influence self-esteem. Teachers can often have a deep impact on the development of a child's self-esteem, particularly in the early years. A highly critical teacher can certainly inflict damage on a child's self image, especially if it involves being ridiculed in front of the class. On the other hand, a good teacher, one who encourages and praises a child's progress, can help repair the faltering self-esteem of a child who is very unsure of her abilities. Certainly peer influences are paramount as well. The agony of being rejected by peers, ostracized on the playground in elementary school, left out of the cliques in middle school, not being invited to parties, or picked for sports teams in P. E. class, can each take a heavy toll.

But the development of our self-esteem is not only dependent upon what we have learned from others or how others treated us. It is also a byproduct of what we learn from experiencing life independently. Failure experiences can certainly undermine self-image, whether this occurs in childhood or in adulthood. Given that our level of self-esteem represents an ongoing process, events in adulthood can either enhance or detract from our perceived level of self-worth. So if you enjoy success at work and/or in your relationships, you will likely experience enhanced self-esteem. If you are losing jobs or failing to gain advancement at work, or you are suffering disappointments in love, you may experience diminished self-esteem.

Questions

1. Which type of parenting creates the most opportunities for the development of healthy self-esteem?

   A. authoritarian parenting

   B. laissez-faire parenting

   C. permissive-indifferent parenting

   D. authoritative parenting

2. According to Carl Rogers, children develop positive self-esteem when parents show them _____.

   A. the malevolent attitude

   B. conditional positive regard

   C. unconditional positive regard

   D. conditions of worth

3. Which of the following statements applies to self-esteem?

   A. Your self-esteem is purely a function of your genetics.

   B. Children can develop healthy self-esteem even if raised in dysfunctional environments.

   C. Permissive-indulgent parents never spoil their children.

   D. Authoritative parenting produces low levels of self-esteem in children.

3.3 How to Boost Your Self-Esteem

Describe the various steps and strategies used to facilitate a healthy level of self-esteem.

If your self-esteem is a measure of how you evaluate yourself, then let's return for a moment to two previously mentioned concepts which are central to your level of self-esteem, that of your real self and your ideal self. Your real self, your evaluation of yourself regarding various characteristics and attributes is, for most people, regularly compared to your ideal self, the desired state of being which you seek to achieve. Many people hold their ideal self to be something they *should* be and then feel disappointed with themselves when they fail to reach this goal. What many people forget is that the ideal self is just that, an IDEAL. It serves as a guiding light in your continual process of growth rather than a grade you need to achieve. The person with healthy self-esteem realizes that their real self is in an everlasting process of change, moving towards their ideal self but never reaching it. This is what Carl Rogers (1951) described as "The Process of Becoming."

   The first step in learning to improve your self-esteem is to realize that your current level of self-esteem is, ultimately, your choice. This is, of course, not to say that the myriad of past and present influences on your level of self-esteem, both positive and negative, as well as your genetic makeup, did not influence how you feel about yourself. Your genes and your experiences *influenced* your self-image, but they do not determine it. You can choose to work towards developing a satisfying level of self-esteem. The task of enhancing and then maintaining positive self-esteem is a life long process of personal growth in which we all proceed slowly, step by step. This is made challenging by the fact that the world is often a far less than ideal place to live. Disappointments occur, things change, and events will not always go your way. You will inevitably make mistakes, and you will not succeed at everything you attempt. Your self-esteem can be a casualty in this process unless you have learned how to nurture yourself. What follows are strategies and guidelines for building a nurturing relationship with yourself that will allow you to truly appreciate who you are, in bad times as well as good times.

3.3.1 Uncovering Irrational Beliefs

To begin, we suggest you examine your paradigm regarding the qualities you believe a person worthy of optimal self esteem must possess. Could some of your beliefs be based on unrealistic expectations or irrational thoughts? As described in Chapter 2, it is important that you take a look at any irrational thoughts which may be influencing the frame by which you evaluate yourself. Albert Ellis and others have described how irrational beliefs affect the way we feel about ourselves. Irrational beliefs, which impact on self-esteem, typically take the form of what we should and should not do and be. These *shoulds* are generated by parental, cultural, and peer expectations, as well as by your need to feel loved, to belong, and to feel safe and good about yourself. What gives these shoulds their power is your belief that they represent the truth. This is the *tyranny of the shoulds*: the absolute nature of beliefs, this unbending sense of right and wrong. If you don't live up to your shoulds, you then judge yourself to be a bad, unworthy person and your self-esteem goes out the window.

The following is a list of some of the most common irrational beliefs people hold about themselves. Look through this list carefully. Do any of these statements fit you, even occasionally? This exercise will help you identify your irrational beliefs and give you insight about thoughts, which stand in the way of your self-esteem.

Common Pathological Shoulds Questionnaire

1. _____ I should be the epitome of generosity and unselfishness.

2. _____ I should be the perfect lover, friend, parent, teacher, student, spouse, and so on.

3. _____ I should be able to endure any hardship with equanimity.

4. _____ I should be able to find a quick solution to every problem.

5. _____ I should never feel hurt. I should always feel happy and serene.

6. _____ I should be completely competent.

7. _____ I should know, understand, and foresee everything.

8. _____ I should never feel certain emotions such as anger or jealousy.

9. _____ I should love my children equally.

10. _____ I should never make mistakes.

11. _____ My emotions should be constant—once I feel love, I should always feel the same.

12. _____ I should be totally self-reliant.

13. _____ I should never be tired or sick.

14. _____ I should never be afraid.

15. _____ I should always be busy; to relax is to waste my time and my life.

16. _____ I should have achievements that bring me status, wealth, or power.

17. _____ I should always put others first; it is better that I feel pain than cause anyone else to feel pain.

18. _____ I should be unfailingly kind.

19. _____ I should never feel sexually attracted to _____.

20. _____ I should care for everyone who cares for me.

21. _____ I should make enough money so that my family can afford _____.

22. _____ I should be able to protect my children from all pain.

23. _____ I should not take time just for my own pleasure.

24. _____ I should be more like other people.

3.3.2 Overcoming the Tyranny of the Shoulds

How many of the above items did you endorse? Even if only a few, recognize that the pathological critic feeds and thrives on these shoulds. What image comes to mind when you hear statements such as: "You should be successful," "You should always be considerate of others," or "You should never get angry?" For most people the image that comes up is that of a parent or authority figure pointing their finger and scolding them, telling them what they should or should not do, or think, or feel. To increase your self-esteem, we encourage you to *stop shoulding on yourself.* You have the right to question any and all of these shoulds. When you recognize that your behavior is being guided by "a should," ask yourself, "Should according to whom?" Are these your choices, or are you merely parroting some often heard messages that you have gotten from others? If the latter is so, realize that you are being reactive, literally giving away your power to that internalized authority figure. You would be proactive if you can say with certainty that these are values that you truly want for yourself, and *you* decide to set them as the standards by which you live. The irrational beliefs which undermine your self-esteem, the *tyranny of the shoulds*, are a subset of the irrational beliefs discussed in Chapter 2. Remember that many of us were taught unrealistic beliefs such as those. That is why we have such terrible feelings when someone does not like us or when we fail. In spite of their prevalence, though, these beliefs are irratio-nal. They are based on the premise that our self-worth is solely determined by the approval of others and by continual striving for perfection. We urge you to challenge the frames by which you are judging yourself using the techniques of cognitive restructuring discussed earlier.

According to Ellis and Harper (1961), the negative self-statements used by the pathological critic, which are generated by these irrational beliefs, must be replaced by positive self-statements. Following the four step framework for challenging irrational beliefs presented earlier in Chapter 2, question your shoulds. You will find that by replacing these with more rational self statements, your self-esteem will steadily climb. For example:

> It is definitely nice to have people like and approve of me, but even without that, I can still accept and love myself.
>
> Doing things well is satisfying, but it is human to err.
>
> It is healthy for me to relax at times. It is important to recharge my batteries.
>
> Not all problems lend themselves to quick solutions.
>
> It is part of the human experience to occasionally feel emotions such as anger, sadness, jealousy and hurt.

One of the most salient differences between individuals with positive self-esteem vs. individuals with low self-esteem is in the nature and content of their self-talk. People with healthy self-esteem do not continually barrage themselves with negative messages or observations about themselves. This does not mean that they are unaware of their faults or that they discount constructive criticism, but rather that they tend to give positive, self-affirming messages to themselves. For example, a person with positive self-esteem who is required to give a speech but is nervous about the upcoming performance would prepare himself by recalling other successful public speaking experiences, and by reassuring himself that he knows the material. A person with low self-esteem in the exact same situation would likely remember only uncomfortable public speaking experiences, and tell himself that he was going to do poorly, or make a fool of himself.

Research has shown that people with low self-esteem can successfully change irrational negative beliefs about themselves. Individuals with low self-esteem tend to attribute their failures to internal causes (weaknesses and shortcomings), reflecting doubts about their self-worth. However, when these individuals succeed they tend to attribute their success to external sources such as luck. Brockner and Guare (1983) hypothesized that by inducing people with low self-esteem to ascribe their failures to possible external causes (factors beyond their control), and their successes to internal causes (ability and effort), self-esteem could be modified. In addition, they theorized that people with low self-esteem could be encouraged to try harder, thereby maximizing their chances for success, which could further elevate their self-esteem. Does this sound familiar? It harkens back to the lessons on developing an optimistic outlook.

In their study, college students were divided into two groups based on low and positive self-esteem. All students were then given an unsolvable task so that each student experienced failure. Following this initial failure experience each student was given a task that was solvable. Prior to the second task, some subjects in both groups were told that their previous failure stemmed from external causes (e.g. the task could not be solved). Other subjects in both groups were led to believe that their previous failure was due mostly to internal causes. And the remaining subjects in both groups were given no information regarding possible causes of the initial failure. The results indicated that students with low self-esteem were able to accept that failure may be due to external causes. But more importantly, the students with low self-esteem who were led to believe that the initial failure was not their fault, performed the best of any group on the second task! So a positive cycle had been set in motion. Now, this does not imply that it is wise to teach people with low self-esteem to always attribute all failures to external causes; that certainly would not be proactive. But the process of challenging irrational, perfectionist beliefs can assist individuals with low self-esteem to evaluate themselves more realistically and fairly.

ELIMINATING COGNITIVE DISTORTIONS Irrational beliefs are also fueled by **cognitive distortions**, which refer to the tendency to look for verification to support your existing opinion of yourself. In other words, via selective perception we tend to pay attention to that which supports what we already believe about ourselves. Epstein (1992) pointed out that individuals with low self-esteem are prone to look for evidence of where they fall short rather than appreciating their achievements. If your self-esteem is low and you are focusing only on where you come up short, return to the guidelines for facilitating optimism covered in Chapter 2. Using the method of looking for alternative evidence, challenge your cognitive distortions. If you look for contrary evidence, it is quite likely that you will find it.

3.3.3 Alternative Ways of Framing Mistakes

"I have not failed 10,000 times,
I have successfully found 10,000 ways that will not work."

Thomas Edison

Most people think of a mistake as something they did wrong. But this is simply not the case. A more appropriate definition is that a mistake is any behavior which you do or fail to do which later, as you reflect about it, you wish you had not done or had done differently. The key word here is LATER. At the time you behaved or did not behave in a particular fashion, you did the best that you possibly could. All decisions are made on the basis of insufficient information, for none of us has the power to foretell the future. "Mistake" is a label which you apply later on, when you wish you had done something else based on 20/20 hindsight. The issue here is awareness. At the time you did or did not do something, you were functioning with a certain degree of awareness. By the time you labeled something a mistake, you had more information and were more aware of the consequences. Within that awareness you always behave in a way that you believe will best meet your needs. If you want not to repeat the same mistakes, we suggest you focus on expanding your awareness, that is, gathering more data before acting, or learning to anticipate the consequences of actions, rather than just resolving to never make the same mistake again. Unless you expand your awareness, it is almost guaranteed that you will repeat the same mistakes. In addition, the more you berate yourself for having made them, the greater the probability that you will make them again.

Thus a mistake becomes a mistake only after some time has passed. The length of time is not important. What is important is that at the time you did it, you did the best you could. It makes no sense to criticize yourself about it. Thinking about mistakes in this fashion allows you to see them in a different light or to reframe them. To further this new perspective, consider that a strong case can be made that mistakes serve as invaluable teachers. They provide you with information about what works and what does not work. When you were a toddler learning how to walk, you needed to fall in order to learn your balance. Had you been afraid of making mistakes, you would still be crawling! This is true for everything in your life. Mistakes are an absolutely necessary part of the learning process. Rather than fearing them you need to welcome them. It might help to think that the more mistakes you make, the more you are learning. Ultimately, there is no such thing as mistakes, only feedback. If you set perfectionistic standards for yourself, you rob yourself of the ability to accept yourself as a fallible but worthwhile human being.

Another way to view mistakes is to think of them as warnings. If you get a poor grade on a test, that could be a warning that you need to study more or change your study habits. It is only when you think that you need to be perfect that mistakes become an indictment rather than a warning.

Yet another way to throw a different frame around mistakes is by realizing that if you are going to behave in a spontaneous fashion, you will most certainly make some mistakes. Without the willingness to make mistakes, you can only act in totally predetermined ways in familiar situations. How boring! You would also kill your self-expression, since to say what you feel or what you think does not always have predictable results, i.e. you risk making a mistake. If you don't allow yourself to say the wrong thing, then you are never free enough to say the right thing.

In his book *Building Self-Esteem*, Glenn Schiraldi (1993) recommends utilizing a particular technique for maintaining your self-esteem in the face of mistakes. This technique is called "Nevertheless," which helps you to acknowledge your mistakes while simultaneously affirming your basic self-worth. People with low self-esteem typically are likely to engage in "because...therefore" thinking, reflected in such statements as, "because of _____, therefore I am no good." You can replace this with "even though _____, nevertheless." So for example, instead of saying, "because I did poorly on this test, therefore I am stupid," you could say, "even though I did poorly on this test, nevertheless I am capable of doing much better if I study harder."

We hope by now you may be beginning to see mistakes in a different light, perhaps as friends rather than enemies. Some people believe that all mistakes are to be avoided, that intelligent, competent people somehow don't make them. That is nonsense. A much wiser position is to allow for a quota for mistakes, for without them you would not be human.

3.3.4 The Pursuit of Self-Compassion Rather than Self-Esteem

In a thought-provoking article entitled *Letting Go of Self-Esteem*, Jennifer Crocker and Jessica Carnavale (2013) argue that, ironically, a far more effective way to bolster self-esteem involves thinking less about yourself. Adopting a compassionate attitude towards yourself and others in addition to removing the focus on your self-worth sets the stage for positive self-esteem. Individuals with compassion towards themselves treat themselves as kindly as they would a close friend, with patience, tolerance for imperfection, and a nonjudgmental mindset. This requires that you defuse negative self-talk. Self-compassion enables you to accept the inevitable setbacks in life as part of the universal human experience. To quote the authors:

> By focusing on others, having self-compassion or adopting a distanced view of yourself, you can work toward your goals without constant self-evaluation and self-criticism. If we were to design a new self-esteem movement, it would teach people to reduce focus on the worth of the self altogether because any action designed to enhance self-esteem is destined to have, at best, temporary benefits and most likely will fail because such actions are motivated by a toxic preoccupation with self-judgment. (pg. 33)

Questions

1. To overcome the *tyranny of the shoulds*, _____.

   A. deliberately violate your own rules for yourself

   B. use cognitive restructuring to challenge these irrational expectations

   C. obey your pathological critic

   D. frequently repeat positive affirmations to yourself

2. One of the most important differences between individuals with healthy self-esteem and those with low self-esteem is _____.

   A. their bank account balance

   B. whether they are happily married or in a satisfying relationship

   C. whether they are physically attractive

   D. in the nature and content of their self-talk

3. Which of the following facilitates the development of healthy self-esteem?

   A. the *tyranny of the shoulds*

   B. the pathological critic

   C. conditions of worth in your upbringing

   D. unconditional positive regard in your upbringing

The Global Perspective
The Power of Service

One of the most encouraging developments on college campuses throughout the United States has been the explosion of **service-learning**. The American Association of Community Colleges defines service-learning as "the combination of community service and classroom instruction, with a focus on critical, reflective thinking as well as personal and civic responsibility." But use of service learning as a teaching strategy is not limited to our nation. Some countries such as Nigeria, China, Ghana, Canada, France, and Germany have well-established national service programs similar to the federal AmeriCorps programs in the U.S. (Gottlieb and Robinson, 2002). A growing body of research makes evident the power of service learning in teaching students to be more involved citizens. Studies out of UCLA revealed that participating in service learning while in college significantly improved students' civic responsibility, academic development, and overall life skill development (Astin and Sax 1998; Astin and colleagues, 2000). Other studies support the fact that students who partake of service-learning through their classes subsequently demonstrate greater citizenship, social responsibility, cooperation, and leadership (Andersen, 1998; Putnam, 2000). Similarly, another research project showed that students who performed community service were more aware of the need to become involved in the policy process, felt a greater connection to the community, and were better able to view situations from other's perspectives (Eyler, Giles, and Braxton, 1997).

For many of the students, the experience was a powerful one as reported by Gottlieb and Robinson (2002):

"My idea of citizenship and civil society has changed as a result of my [service learning] experience. I now feel like it is my duty to give back to the community by becoming an involved citizen. Because of this wonderful experience, I now see the positive effects service learning has on society."

(Service learning student at Miami Dade College).

Research in Positive Psychology has clearly demonstrated the link between service and positive self-esteem. The "*feel good/do good effect*" is in fact now a well-established psychological principle. People who feel good about themselves are more helpful. But the reverse is also true, what we may call the "*do good/feel good effect*." People who help others feel better about themselves. In fact, they feel better, in general. A survey of over 1700 women who frequently participated in pro-social activities, reported that they experienced a "high" while helping and a sense of "calm" following the experience (Batson, 1991). It seems it is true that it is better to give than to receive. Indeed, giving support and assistance is a better predictor of longevity than receiving it (Brown and colleagues, 2003). Individuals who engage in service to others are half as likely to die within a specified time period, than those who receive help from others, when other variables related to mortality, such as age, gender, smoking and drinking were factored out. It seems that focusing beyond the self allows us to expand our view of ourselves to include our interconnectedness. When we become genuinely invested in others or in a task larger than ourselves, we find more meaning and evaluate ourselves more positively. As Mother Theresa counseled "nothing makes you happier than when you really reach out in mercy to someone who is badly hurt" (Myers, 1992). Does your campus offer opportunities for service? Have you participated in any service efforts, either through your school or on your own? Describe your experiences.

3.4 Enhancing Your Self-Esteem: Core Virtues and Signature Strengths

Identify the core virtues of good character, their corresponding signature strengths, and how they relate to self-esteem.

Earlier in the chapter we mentioned how a measure of self-esteem that is relevant worldwide might need to include two factors: (1) your perception of how other members of your community appraise you; and (2) your own sense of personal efficacy and worth. Positive psychology suggests an approach to enhancing self-esteem which encompasses both of these factors. This involves the study of **character**—the development of **virtues** and their corresponding **signature strengths.**

Consideration of the role of character in human development was virtually ignored once Behaviorism became the dominant paradigm in psychology in the second half of the twentieth century. The indirect study of character was relegated to one corner of scientific psychology – the study of personality. The direct study of character was abandoned because of the bias that science should only describe behavior, rather than recommend certain behaviors, and also because character was viewed as a value-laden construct tied to Victorian morality and therefore non-scientific and unworthy of study.

Positive psychology resurrected the study of character by enlisting a distinguished panel of mental health professionals to create a system designed to be the opposite of the DSM (Diagnostic and Statistical Manual of Mental Disorders), which classifies and describes mental illnesses, to catalogue the components of mental health. They began this process by setting three criteria for strengths, which are as follows:

- They are valued in almost every culture.
- They are valued in their own right, not just a means to other ends.
- They are malleable, changeable by choice and exercise of will.

After surveying writings spanning over 3000 years covering virtually every major religious, philosophical and cultural tradition, they discovered that all endorsed and agreed upon these six core virtues which encompass good character.

- **WISDOM AND KNOWLEDGE**
- **COURAGE**
- **HUMANITY AND LOVE**
- **JUSTICE**
- **TEMPERANCE**
- **SPIRITUALITY AND TRANSCENDENCE**

These broad areas comprising the six core virtues can be further subdivided into what Seligman (2002; 2005) refers to as "signature strengths," which are traits and behaviors that you can develop by exercising proactive choice. These strengths are not the same as talents. Talents are typically inborn (such as musical or artistic abilities, athletic virtuosity). You can choose to develop your talent or capitalize on it, but it is innate, a genetic gift of sorts that you may or may not cultivate with practice, training or dedication. In other words, you either have a talent or you do not. You can learn to play a musical instrument competently, but you can't learn to be a talented musician. On the other hand, strengths based on virtue can be built, even from scratch, with enough dedication, persistence, practice or access to good teaching if you choose to do so. You cannot waste nor squander a strength as you can with talent. This is because the development of signature strengths is based upon decisions, the choice as to whether to acquire it in the first place, where and how to utilize it, and whether to keep developing it. Signature strengths also have the following hallmarks:

- A sense that this represents the real you, the core of who you are (eudemonia).
- A feeling of excitement while displaying it, particularly at first.
- A rapid learning curve as the strength is displayed, especially in the beginning.
- A strong desire to find new ways to demonstrate it.
- A feeling of empowerment, as if it would be hard to stop you from practicing it.
- A sense of invigoration rather than exhaustion while using the strength.
- The pursuit and creation of projects that provide opportunities to use the strength.
- Experiencing positive emotions while using it.
- At times having flow experiences when exercising the strength.

Before we talk in more depth about these signature strengths, it is important to clarify the link between the development of character and self-esteem. When you develop good character, which is manifested through developing and using your strengths, it can have a significant, real world positive effect upon your self-esteem. For example, if you find a wallet with ID that is loaded with cash and you return it with all funds untouched to its rightful owner, or you alert a store cashier that you were given too much change and return the balance, you deserve to feel pride that you did the right thing. You know that despite any inner temptations to pocket the money, you put forth the effort to behave honestly. If you are fair to yourself, you will feel good about you. When you behave honestly, kindly, wisely, fairly, prudently, which are all matters of choice; you provide a plethora of opportunities to feel good about yourself and enhance your self-evaluation. Learning to challenge negative self-statements and silence the pathological critic can help you stave off self-imposed assaults on your self-esteem, but developing your character is also guaranteed to directly improve your estimation of yourself.

A strength is more than a solitary act (of kindness for example); it is a **trait** which can be defined as a psychological characteristic exemplified by consistent behaviors across time, place and situations. Strengths are valued in their own right and typically produce good consequences or outcomes. But strengths are displayed for their own sake (i.e. because it is the integral way to behave), whatever the outcome. Strengths represent what every parent wishes for in their newborn children. When you display a signature strength, no one is diminished and everyone has the capacity to be inspired or elevated. When you engage in your signature strengths you can feel pride, satisfaction, joy, harmony, fulfillment, etc., and your self-esteem benefits as a result. Seligman (2002) identifies the following twenty-four signature strengths, which make up the six core virtues.

3.4.1 Wisdom and Knowledge—*Cognitive Strengths involving the acquisition and use of knowledge*

1. CURIOSITY   This incorporates your hunger for new experiences and your openness to and flexibility about matters that do not necessarily fit your preconceived notions about the world. You are tolerant of uncertainty and ambiguity. In other words, you make the choice to be open to exploring new and unfamiliar paradigms.

2. LOVE OF LEARNING   You value knowledge and learning for its own sake, whether in school or on your own. You are open to the opportunities to learn even in mundane situations and you go out of your way to educate yourself, to read, visit museums, travel, and explore.

3. JUDGMENT/CRITICAL THINKING/OPEN-MINDEDNESS   This embodies the choice to examine things from all sides, to resist jumping to conclusions based on preconceived notions, looking at all the data and relying on solid evidence from which to draw conclusions and make decisions. You are open to changing your mind. Critical thinking involves choosing to use objectivity and rationality to process information, rather than falling prey to selective attention and only focusing on facts that confirm your old paradigm. You choose to avoid black and white thinking and open yourself to the gray areas.

4. CREATIVITY   This strength is not at all limited to the fine arts. It encompasses your willingness to think out of the box, to use your ingenuity, originality, common sense and street smarts. You are open to finding unconventional ways or methods of doing something or approaching a problem.

5. EMOTIONAL INTELLIGENCE - EQ   This important and broad concept involves your knowledge of yourself and others and takes into account how well you deal with people. In Chapter 9 we explore this construct in depth and delve into methods for enhancing your EQ.

6. PERSPECTIVE   The authors agree with Seligman's (2002) conclusion that perspective is the "most mature strength in this category, the closest to wisdom itself." To have perspective, you must have the life experience and emotional distance to be able to deduce and see the higher level meaning and purpose in things. Typically this takes many years to achieve, although we all know people who are wise beyond their years (the proverbial "old souls") because they have a perspective that belies their youth. When you have perspective, others will often seek your advice and help because your way of looking at the world is useful, beneficial, reassuring, and makes sense. When you have perspective, you are an expert in understanding life.

3.4.2 Courage—*Emotional Strengths involving the exercise of will to accomplish goals in the face of external or internal opposition*

7. BRAVERY AND VALOR   You choose to face your fears squarely, despite fear. You do not run away from threats, pain, difficulties, or challenges, including having the guts to take controversial or unpopular positions (either intellectually or emotionally) that may expose you to ridicule, yet you stand firm in your beliefs. The concept of valor has broadened from physical or battlefield courage to moral and psychological courage. Nelson Mandela and Rosa Parks exemplify moral courage. Psychological courage refers to the optimism needed to face serious illness, natural disaster, or catastrophic loss.

8. PERSEVERANCE AND INDUSTRIOUSNESS   Effective individuals finish what they start. This persistence is not about obsessively pursuing unrealistic goals or being perfectionistic, but diligently following through and doing what is necessary, even if inconvenient or unpleasant. It involves flexibility and taking pride in your work.

9. HONESTY/INTEGRITY/GENUINENESS   The cornerstone of what we mean by integrity involves being honest, telling the truth even if it is not in your best interest to do so. Yet it is more than simply telling the truth. It is also about presenting yourself in an authentic and genuine fashion, about being open and sincere in words, deeds, and commitments. It is about making the choice to keep your word and live by your principles – to walk the talk.

3.4.3 Humanity—*Interpersonal Strengths involving tending and befriending others*

10. KINDNESS AND GENEROSITY   You choose to treat people well and live by the Golden Rule. You are generous in spirit as well as materially in that you are willing to give of yourself and your time to help others, do favors, be a true friend, or a listening ear. You enjoy doing good deeds for others even if you hardly know them. We are reminded of ordinary people who snuck into New Orleans to help rescue the Hurricane Katrina survivors. Three college students from Duke University drove non-stop from North Carolina to New Orleans with the intention of helping total strangers in any way they could. When denied entry to the city of New Orleans, they stole press passes to sneak in and they personally drove two carloads of stranded disaster victims to the Houston Astrodome shelter. True kindness and generosity requires an acknowledgement of the worth of the other person and is fueled by empathy and compassion. Just as with the other strengths, anyone can choose to be kind, compassionate, and generous. That gift of yourself to others ultimately comes back to you by bolstering how you regard yourself.

11. LOVING AND ALLOWING YOURSELF TO BE LOVED   The capacity to love and receive love may represent the ultimate fulfillment in life and relates to our purpose on the planet. This is choosing to open yourself up to intimacy beyond what is traditionally considered romance.

3.4.4 Justice—*Civic Strengths that support healthy community life*

12. CITIZENSHIP/DUTY/TEAMWORK/LOYALTY   This cluster of strengths is often manifested in civic activities and reflects how you relate to groups such as your family, community, country, and the globe. It is about making a commitment to being a responsible and loyal team player, doing your share of the work and contributing to the success of the whole. It is also about thinking of yourself as a global citizen and how you can contribute to the health of our planet. But this does not imply blind obedience or deference to authority. Sometimes being a good citizen or team member means that you must challenge or resist authority that is harmful or not in the best humane interests of the group.

13. FAIRNESS AND EQUITY   You choose to set aside your personal feelings or biases to make the most impartial and even-handed decisions or judgments possible. You choose to use overriding moral principles of fairness to guide you in your dealings with others, whether family, friends or strangers. To do this you must choose to look at what is fair for all involved. It also involves looking for win-win solutions whenever possible (refer to Chapter 9 for an in depth discussion of Win-Win).

14. LEADERSHIP   While it is certainly true that some people are born leaders, leadership skills can be learned (refer to Chapter 12). Effective leaders have learned how to organize others, resolve conflicts and facilitate harmony, motivate others to get things done, and set a good example. Effective leaders are fair and impartial. A good leader learns lessons from history in general, and the history of the group in particular. A good leader takes responsibility for his or her mistakes as well as the errors of the group, exemplifying former President Harry S. Truman's famous motto, "The buck stops here."

3.4.5 Temperance—*Self-Regulatory Strengths that protect against excess*

15. SELF-CONTROL   You develop the ability to hold back on your needs, wants, desires and impulses until the appropriate time. That is, you know how to wait, or how to defer gratification (for more on this see Chapter 4). Positive psychologist Roy Baumeister (2007) believes that self-control is the most important of the signature strengths.

16. CAUTION AND DISCRETION   You choose to think before you speak or act to minimize doing or saying something you may later regret. When possible you proceed carefully and get as much information as you can before choosing a course of action. You choose to make the effort to take a far sighted view in matters of importance. You can recognize when the pursuit of short term rewards will sabotage long term goals and you decide to resist immediate gratification.

17. HUMILITY AND MODESTY   You can choose to be proud of yourself, yet humble, allowing your accomplishments to speak for themselves or your good character to be readily apparent. You do not put yourself above others or act in a condescending way. You choose to behave in an unpretentious fashion.

3.4.6 Transcendence—*Metaphysical Strengths that forge connections to the larger universe and provide meaning*

18. APPRECIATION OF BEAUTY AND EXCELLENCE   You bring a sense of awe and wonder to the table as you relish the beauty, skill and excellence in all facets of life, whether in nature, art, science, everyday matters, or the first words or steps of your own child. Not only do you stop to smell the roses, you take the time to admire their color, design, and relationship to the landscape.

19. GRATITUDE   You choose to adopt an "attitude of gratitude." You choose not to take things for granted and you take the time to give thanks. Refer to Chapter 7 for an in depth discussion of the effects of gratitude.

20. OPTIMISM AND HOPE   Given our emphasis on this in Chapter 2, we won't belabor the point except to remind you that you have a choice whether to be hopeful and optimistic. Choosing to do so enhances your overall effectiveness, can improve your interpersonal relationships, and ultimately helps boost your self-esteem because you believe in yourself and your ability to create positive outcomes.

21. SPIRITUALITY   You have made the effort to adopt a strong, coherent guiding set of beliefs about the meaning and purpose of life and your role in the universe. You know where you fit in within the larger scheme of things. Your spiritual beliefs and values guide your actions and provide comfort for you.

Your spirituality may be based on the organized religious beliefs and traditions in which you were raised or chose to adopt, or it may come from more secular sources. What is important is that you have a philosophy of life that is meaningful for you and provides a sense of purpose. See Chapter 8 for a more in depth discussion of the role of spirituality in effectiveness.

22. FORGIVENESS AND MERCY You have learned how to forgive and give others a second chance. You choose to allow mercy, not revenge, guide you down the oftentimes rocky road to forgiveness. Refer to the end of Chapter 9 for guidance on how to be more forgiving in your own life.

23. HUMOR AND PLAYFULNESS You love to laugh and make others laugh. You choose to see the absurdity and silliness around you and revel in it. You choose not to take yourself so seriously and know how to kick back and have fun. Refer back to Chapter 1 for tips on how to enhance a humorous world view.

24. ENTHUSIASM/ZEST/PASSION You are full of life and embody "joie de vivre" (zest for life). When you do something of import to you, you throw yourself into it wholeheartedly and, as such, your enthusiasm can rub off on others. You give yourself permission to feel things intensely. You risk giving up detachment for a chance at deeper fulfillment and enjoyment of life.

3.4.7 Identifying Your Signature Strengths

Which of these signature strengths do you already possess? Which would you like to develop? Fill out the "Signature Strengths Inventory," adapted from one developed by Seligman (2011), to help you identify your own signature strengths. After identifying your particular strengths, we suggest that you utilize those strengths to help develop those areas you feel are in need of improvement.

Typically you will have five or fewer scores of nine or ten and these represent your highest strengths, according to your self-report observations of yourself. You will also have several scores in the four to six range and these represent your weaknesses. It may be interesting to have a significant other fill out this inventory about you, to get a sense of whether your perception of your strengths matches that of others.

3.4.8 A Cautionary Note: When Virtue
Becomes Vice

In a thought-provoking article (Loftus, 2013) the author cautioned us that if virtue is carried to an extreme it can become a vice. She reminds us that strengths, like traits, are often on a continuum and each can hold the seed of its own destruction. For example, an overabundance of self-control can become over-inhibition. An unhealthy level of perseverance can lead to not knowing when it is healthy to stop. An unrelenting passion or zest can turn into obsession. The lesson here is that to maximize our strengths, we also need to find balance.

Signature Strengths Inventory

Respond to the following descriptive statements using the scale below. Circle your answers.
5 = Very much like me   4 = Like me   3 = Neutral   2 = Unlike me   1 = Very much unlike me

a.) I am always curious about the world.	5 4 3 2 1
b.) I rarely get bored.	5 4 3 2 1

1. Total these two to get your **Curiosity Score** _____

a.) I am thrilled when I learn something new.	5 4 3 2 1
b.) I often go out of my way to visit museums.	5 4 3 2 1

2. Total these two to get your **Love of Learning Score** _____

a.) When the topic calls for it, I can be a highly rational thinker.	5 4 3 2 1
b.) I rarely tend to make snap judgments.	5 4 3 2 1

3. Total these two to get your **Judgment Score** _____

a.) I like to think of new ways to do things.	5 4 3 2 1
b.) I am more imaginative than most of my friends.	5 4 3 2 1

4. Total these two to get your **Ingenuity Score** _____

a.) No matter what the social situation, I am able to fit in.	5 4 3 2 1
b.) I am very good at sensing what other people are feeling.	5 4 3 2 1

5. Total these two to get your **Social Intelligence Score** _____

a.) I am always able to look at things and see the big picture.	5 4 3 2 1
b.) Others often come to me for advice.	5 4 3 2 1

6. Total these two to get your **Perspective Score** _____

a.) I have taken frequent stands in the face of strong opposition.	5 4 3 2 1
b.) Pain and disappointment rarely get the better of me.	5 4 3 2 1

7. Total these two to get your **Valor Score** _____

a.) I always finish what I start.	5 4 3 2 1
b.) I rarely get sidetracked when I work.	5 4 3 2 1

8. Total these two to get your **Perseverance Score** _____

a.) I always keep my promises.	5 4 3 2 1
b.) My friends tell me I'm down to earth.	5 4 3 2 1

9. Total these two to get your **Integrity Score** _____

a.) I have voluntarily helped a neighbor in the last month.	5 4 3 2 1
b.) I get as excited about good fortune of others as I do about my own.	5 4 3 2 1

10. Total these two to get your **Kindness Score** _____

a.) There are people who care as much about my feelings and well-being as their own.	5 4 3 2 1
b.) I have no trouble accepting love from others.	5 4 3 2 1

11. Total these two to get your **Being Loved Score** _____

a.) I work at my best when I am part of a group.	5 4 3 2 1
b.) I am willing to sacrifice my self-interest for the benefit of groups I am in.	5 4 3 2 1

12. Total these two to get your **Citizenship Score** _____

a.) I treat all people equally, regardless of who they might be.	5	4	3	2	1
b.) If I don't like someone, I am still able to treat him or her fairly.	5	4	3	2	1

13. Total these two to get your **Fairness Score** _____

a.) I can always get people to do things together without nagging them.	5	4	3	2	1
b.) I am very good at planning group activities.	5	4	3	2	1

14. Total these two to get your **Leadership Score** _____

a.) I control my emotions.	5	4	3	2	1
b.) I am typically able to stay on a diet.	5	4	3	2	1

15. Total these two to get your **Self-Control Score** _____

a.) I avoid activities that are physically dangerous.	5	4	3	2	1
b.) I rarely make poor choices in friendships and relationships.	5	4	3	2	1

16. Total these two to get your **Prudence Score** _____

a.) I change the subject when people pay me compliments.	5	4	3	2	1
b.) I very rarely brag about my accomplishments.	5	4	3	2	1

17. Total these two to get your **Humility Score** _____

a.) I always say thank you, even for little things.	5	4	3	2	1
b.) I often stop and count my blessings.	5	4	3	2	1

18. Total these two to get your **Gratitude Score** _____

a.) In the last month I have been thrilled by excellence in the arts, sports, science or math.	5	4	3	2	1
b.) I have created something of beauty in the last year.	5	4	3	2	1

19. Total these two to get your **Appreciation of Beauty Score** _____

a.) I always look on the bright side.	5	4	3	2	1
b.) I typically have a well-thought-out plan for what I want to do.	5	4	3	2	1

20. Total these two to get your **Optimism Score** _____

a.) My life has a strong purpose.	5	4	3	2	1
b.) I have a calling in life.	5	4	3	2	1

21. Total these two to get your **Spirituality Score** _____

a.) I always let bygones be bygones.	5	4	3	2	1
b.) I never try to get even.	5	4	3	2	1

22. Total these two to get your **Forgiveness Score** _____

a.) I always mix work and play as much as possible.	5	4	3	2	1
b.) I often say funny things.	5	4	3	2	1

23. Total these two to get your **Humor Score** _____

a.) I throw myself into everything I do.	5	4	3	2	1
b.) I rarely mope around.	5	4	3	2	1

24. Total these two to get your **Zest Score** _____

Record your scores on the following page.

(Continued)

Scoring

Wisdom and Knowledge

1. Curiosity _____
2. Love of Learning _____
3. Judgment _____
4. Ingenuity _____
5. Social Intelligence _____
6. Perspective _____

Courage

7. Valor _____
8. Perseverance _____
9. Integrity _____

Humanity and Love

10. Kindness _____
11. Zest _____

Justice

12. Citizenship _____
13. Fairness _____
14. Leadership _____

Temperance

15. Self-Control _____
16. Prudence _____
17. Humility _____

Transcendence

18. Gratitude _____
19. Appreciation of Beauty _____
20. Optimism/Hope _____
21. Spirituality _____
22. Forgiveness _____
23. Humor _____
24. Zest _____

3.4.9 Developing Your Signature Strengths More Fully

Remember that in most cases, developing the traits or characteristics comprising signature strengths just involves a conscious choice or decision to do so, even if it may be hard, inconvenient or awkward at first. Unlike talents, the genetic basis for character is limited. There are no genes or chromosomes for kindness, or honesty, or open-mindedness. *Rather these are behaviors that you have direct control over. As your signature strengths build and expand, so too will your self-esteem. You will learn to respect and value yourself more deeply, as will others around you, because you have character. That is invaluable.* Here are some suggestions for how to develop your strengths offered by Lynn Johnson (2008). Remember that the more energy and emphasis you put into practicing these suggestions, the more dramatic the effect will be in your life.

1. **Curiosity and Interest in the World**

   a. Ask questions of people.

   b. Discover new places.

   c. Explore the stacks in a library; browse widely, or pick an interesting looking book each day and spend twenty minutes skimming it.

    d. Eat something new that you never otherwise would have tried.

    e. Go to a meeting or hear a speaker.

2. **Love of Learning**

    a. Discover one new place in town everyday.

    b. Read a newspaper other than your usual.

    c. Ask a question of someone you admire.

    d. Go to an online search engine like Ask.com and ask a question and explore sites you never otherwise would have discovered.

    e. Read a book about something you've always found intriguing but never found the time to learn more about.

3. **Judgment, Critical Thinking and Open-Mindedness**

    a. Go to a multi-cultural group or event.

    b. Play devil's advocate and discuss an issue from the side opposite to your personal views.

    c. Take a colleague out to lunch who is different from you in some way.

    d. Go to a different church or religious event or political gathering.

    e. Every day pick something you believe strongly, and think about how you might be wrong. Ask yourself how you would know if you were wrong.

4. **Creativity, Ingenuity and Originality**

    a. Keep a journal. Work on a picture or poem.

    b. Submit a piece to a literary magazine or newspaper.

    c. Decorate a room in your home or your workspace.

    d. Pick one object in your room and devise a use for it rather than its intended one.

    e. Find a new word everyday (perhaps at dictionary.com) and use it creatively.

5. **Emotional/Social Intelligence**

    a. Meet one new person each day by approaching them.

    b. Go into a social situation where you would normally feel uncomfortable and try to fit in.

    c. Whenever you talk with someone, try to figure out what his or her motives and concerns are.

    d. By being friendly, include a person who is all alone in your group.

6. Perspective (Wisdom)

a. Get a quote a day online.

b. Give advice to an upset friend.

c. Think of the wisest person you know. Try to live each day as that person would live.

d. Look up prominent people in history and learn their views on important issues of their day, and/or find a significant quotation that they said.

7. Valor

a. Speak up in groups or volunteer to speak publicly (if you don't normally).

b. Go against peer pressure or social norms.

c. Stand up for someone even if you disagree with him/her.

d. Ask someone to spend time with you.

e. Introduce yourself to a stranger.

f. Speak up for an unpopular idea (if you believe in it).

8. Industry, Diligence, and Perseverance

a. Finish work ahead of time.

b. Notice your thoughts about stopping a task, and ignore them. Focus on the task at hand.

c. At work, resist daydreaming and distractions.

d. Plan ahead—use a calendar for appointments and meetings.

e. Set a high goal (i.e. for exercise or studying) and stick to it.

f. When you wake up in the morning, make a list of things that you want to get done that day that could be put off until the next day. Make sure to get them done that day.

9. Honesty, Authenticity, and Genuineness

a. Refrain from telling small white lies to friends (including insincere compliments). If you do tell one, admit it and apologize right away.

b. Monitor yourself and make a list of every time you tell a lie, even if it is a small one. Try to make your daily list shorter every day.

c. At the end of each day, identify something you did that was attempting to impress people, or put on a show. Resolve not to do it again.

10. **Zest, Enthusiasm, and Energy**

    a. Go out of your way to become more involved in an organization to which you already belong.

    b. Take up a greater interest in other's work, i.e. volunteer to help them in a project.

    c. While eating or drinking something, concentrate on the taste and sensations. Try to really savor and appreciate every aspect of that food or drink.

    d. Get a good night's sleep and eat a good breakfast, to give yourself more energy during the day.

    e. Do something physically vigorous in the morning (e.g., jogging, push-ups). Note carefully how you feel ten minutes later, an hour later.

11. **Kindness and Generosity**

    a. Leave a huge tip for a small check.

    b. Do a random act of kindness every day (a simple small favor). Make it anonymous if possible.

    c. Ask a friend how their day was and actually listen to the answer before telling them about your own day.

    d. Send an e-card to a different friend each day.

    e. Pay the whole tab when you are out with friends.

12. **Capacity to Love and Be Loved**

    a. Tell spouse/boyfriend/girlfriend/sibling/parent that you love them.

    b. Send a loved one a card or e-card to say that you were thinking about him/her.

    c. Give loved ones a big hug and a kiss.

    d. Show great enthusiasm when a friend achieves something.

    e. Write a nice note where someone you love will find it sometime during the day.

13. **Citizenship and Teamwork**

    a. Volunteer at a school.

    b. Take on added responsibility within an organization in which you are already a part.

    c. Pick up litter that you see on the ground, in your neighborhood or other places.

    d. Organize a neighborhood dinner.

    e. Organize a volunteer group in you neighborhood.

14. Fairness, Equity, and Justice

    a. Allow someone to speak their peace while keeping an open mind by not passing judgment.

    b. Stay impartial in an argument between friends despite your beliefs (be the mediator).

    c. Notice when you treat someone based on a stereotype or pre-conception; resolve not to do it again.

15. Leadership

    a. Organize something special for your friends one evening.

    b. Organize a study group, book club, or a volunteer group in your neighborhood.

16. Modesty

    a. Don't talk about yourself at all for a full day.

    b. Dress and act modestly, so as to not attract attention to yourself.

    c. Compliment someone you know who is better than you in some way.

17. Self Control and Self-Regulation

    a. Set aside a designated amount of time and work on a work project in a quiet, private place.

    b. Exercise four days a week (if you don't already do so).

    c. Clean or organize your living space. Everyday, make sure that you pick up whatever mess you made during the day.

    d. Leave something uneaten on your plate that you usually regret eating afterwards.

    e. When something upsets you, acknowledge it and instead choose to focus on the good things in your life.

    f. Make a resolution to not gossip. Stop yourself whenever you find yourself doing it.

18. Caution, Prudence, and Discretion

    a. During a conversation, think twice before saying anything. Weigh the probable effect of your words on others.

    b. Before you decide to do something important, reflect on it for a moment and consider if you want to live with its consequences.

19. **Forgiveness and Mercy**

    a. Think of someone that you found very hard to forgive. Try to see the situation from their perspective.

    b. Actively seek to forgive others.

    c. When someone does something you don't understand, try to imagine his or her intentions for their actions.

20. **Appreciation of Beauty and Excellence**

    a. Go to a museum and pick out a piece of artwork or a display that has aesthetic value and touches you because of its beauty.

    b. Write down your thoughts about a piece of art, or something beautiful that you see.

    c. Take a walk with a friend and comment on something pretty that you see.

    d. Keep a journal and every night record something you saw during the day that struck you as extremely beautiful or skillful.

21. **Gratitude**

    a. Keep a journal and each night make a list of three things you are grateful for in life.

    b. Every day thank someone for something that you might otherwise take for granted (e.g., thanking the janitor who cleans your office).

    c. Keep a record of the number of times you say "thank you" in a day. Try to double the times within the first week.

    d. Send someone a "thank you" e-greeting.

22. **Hope, Optimism, and Future-Mindedness**

    a. Keep a journal and every night, record a decision you made that day that will impact your life in the long run.

    b. When you are in a bad situation, turn it around to see the bright side to it.

    c. Notice your negative thoughts. Counter them with positive thoughts.

    d. Reaffirm to yourself that you can and will succeed at whatever you decide.

23. **Spirituality and Sense of Purpose and Faith**

    a. For a few minutes a day, relax and think about the purpose of life and how you fit in it.

    b. Explore different religions. You can do this by going to a library, looking on the Internet, or asking your friends about their religions.

    c. Spend time each day in meditation or prayer.

    d. Invest in a book of affirmations or optimistic quotes. Read a few every day.

24. Humor and Playfulness

a. Every day, make someone smile or laugh.

b. Learn a joke and tell it to your friends.

c. Watch a funny movie or TV show.

d. Read the comics.

e. Learn a magic trick and perform it for your friends.

Questions

1. Signature strengths refer to _____.

A. your talents

B. traits and behaviors that you can develop by exercising proactive choice

C. negative aspects of your character

D. areas to ignore so you can focus on improving your weaknesses

2. The positive psychology approach to enhancing your self-esteem involves:

A. focusing on and improving your weaknesses

B. dwelling on your mistakes

C. developing and using your signature strengths

D. ignoring your faults

3. Which of the following applies to signature strengths?

A. Signature strengths are genetically based talents.

B. Kindness and generosity are not signature strengths.

C. Virtue overdone can turn into vice.

D. Artistic or musical talents are signature strengths of character.

Summary

This chapter elucidated the concept of self-esteem and defined it as the discrepancy between your real self and your ideal self. Self-esteem differs from our self-concept which is your paradigm about yourself reflected in how you would describe yourself, whereas self-esteem refers to how you judge and evaluate yourself based on this paradigm. The roots of self-esteem were explored with an emphasis on different parenting styles and how they can affect and mold later self-esteem. The authoritative parenting style was identified as being the one most likely to foster healthy self-esteem in a child. Special emphasis was placed on the development of a healthy level of self-esteem rather than very high self-esteem which can be associated with a superiority complex, narcissism, and whole host of other negative behaviors and attributes.

Various methods of enhancing self-esteem were explored including developing self-compassion, cognitive restructuring for refuting irrational expectations about yourself (the tyranny of the shoulds) and using reframing techniques such as framing mistakes differently.

Lastly, the chapter explored a key component of positive psychology - that of character development as reflected in the six Core Virtues further subdivided into the twenty-four Signature Strengths. The strengths represent traits and behaviors that can be developed by exercising proactive choice rather that being a result of inborn talents. The link between character and self-esteem was explored, emphasizing that developing and using your personal signature strengths has a significant real world, positive effect upon your self-esteem. The chapter concluded with suggestions for developing your signature strengths more fully.

Positive Psychology Exercises

1. **Deliberately Making Mistakes:** While this exercise may not seem logical, following through with it will prove to be invaluable in terms of building your self-esteem. What we want you to do is to experientially give yourself permission to make mistakes. The most effective way of achieving this is for you to go out and deliberately make a mistake. We want you to think of a relatively harmless, innocuous mistake you can make, preferably one that is humorous, and to plan it out and set a date to do it. It could be something as silly and mundane as wearing two different color *sucks* or putting your make-up on wrong. Be creative and let yourself play. By the way, did you catch our mistake above?

2. **Looking at Yourself Through the Eyes of Someone Who Loves You:** Think of someone who you believe really loves and values you for who you are. Imagine that person standing in front of you as vividly as you can. Look at them looking at you with that expression which lets you know how much they appreciate you. Now imagine in your mind's eye that you can look at yourself through their eyes. Seeing, perhaps for the first time, what someone who loves you sees as they look at you. Watching and listening closely to your own gestures, words, looks, as perceived by someone who loves you. Can you recognize qualities and attributes which were perhaps viewed as faults by your own eyes? Allow yourself to perceive what it is about you that this person cherishes. Now describe yourself as you know this person would, highlighting your endearing qualities and traits, using the positive adjectives you know this person would use.

Key Terms

Authoritarian Parenting
Authoritative Parenting
Character
Cognitive Distortions
Conditional Positive Regard
Conditions of Worth
Ideal Self
Inferiority Complex

Malevolent Attitude
Pathological Critic
Permissive-Indifferent
    Parenting
Permissive-Indulgent Parenting
Real Self
Self-Concept
Self-Esteem

Self-Worth
Service Learning
Signature Strengths
Traits
Unconditional Positive Regard
Virtues

Shared Writing

Set aside a time to use one of your strengths in a new or creative way. For example, if appreciation of beauty is one of your strengths, you could deliberately take a different route home from work that passes through an attractive area, even if it takes you longer to get home. Write about your experience.

Chapter 3 Questions

1. Self-esteem is _____.

    A. your paradigm about yourself

    B. a measure of how much you value yourself

    C. a measure of how popular you are

    D. an indication of how financially successful you are

2. According to Carl Rogers, your ideal self is _____.

    A. the person you actually are

    B. the person you want to be

    C. a global citizen

    D. the person your parents want you to be

3. Regarding self-esteem, it is best to have _____.

    A. one strong source or contingency of self-worth

    B. your primary source of self-worth revolves around your physical appearance

    C. a minimum of three and a maximum of five sources or contingencies of self-worth

    D. multiple sources or contingencies of self-worth

4. One of the best ways to enhance your self-esteem is _____.

    A. to develop self-compassion

    B. make more money

    C. get a make-over or lose weight

    D. brag about yourself

5. The inner voice which evaluates and judges our actions and ourselves has been called:

   A. the inferiority complex

   B. the ideal self

   C. the pathological critic

   D. the superiority complex

6. The most potent and effective self-esteem is that which is _____.

   A. contingent upon your accomplishments

   B. contingent upon your appearance

   C. contingent upon your material possessions

   D. non-contingent

7. Mistakes are _____.

   A. feedback—a valuable part of the learning process

   B. always avoidable

   C. proof that your real self and your ideal self will never come close to a match

   D. a result of the pathological critic

8. Which of the following is useful for boosting your self-esteem?

   A. obeying the *tyranny of the shoulds*

   B. using selective perception to support your existing beliefs about yourself

   C. using reframing techniques, especially regarding alternative ways of viewing mistakes

   D. vowing to accept all that your pathological critic has to say

9. Healthy self-esteem is associated with _____.

   A. rejecting constructive criticism

   B. fear of risk taking

   C. being conceited

   D. being able to accept constructive criticism

10. Permissive-indifferent parents _____.

    A. are uninvolved in their child's life

    B. are very involved in their child's life while failing to set limits or provide meaningful controls over their child's behavior

    C. are warm and nurturing and set appropriate limits for their children

    D. have a restrictive, punitive style of parenting focusing on following rules

Chapter 4
Pursuing Accomplishment Through Character Development

 ## Learning Objectives

After reading this chapter, you should be able to:

4.1 Explain the roles of character vs. intelligence/talent relative to success.

4.2 Explain how the seven key character strengths affect the ability to achieve and accomplish goals.

4.3 Describe strategies used to increase self-motivation.

4.4 Identify eight effective strategies for using time wisely.

4.5 Explain how dividing your tasks into quadrants can lead to effective use of time.

4.6 Understand the causes of procrastination and methods for overcoming the habit.

4.7 Recall tips for improving academic effectiveness.

One vital aspect of optimal human functioning is being able to accomplish your goals – achieving success whether in your job, your academic pursuits, or in your personal life. We begin this chapter by asking this question: "What leads to success?" According to Paul Tough (2012) in his thought provoking book *How Children Succeed: Grit, Curiosity and the Hidden Power of Character,* for the better part of the

20th century, both psychology and education were barking up the wrong tree in their mission to help individuals acquire the tools for achievement, particularly when it came to either academic or occupational success. The single-minded focus was on training academic and cognitive skills in efforts to boost IQ and achievement levels so individuals could succeed in life. This was based on the *cognitive hypothesis* which held that success in life was based on IQ and talent, both of which are largely fixed early in life. Now we are not in any way saying that education or helping individuals improve academic or cognitive skills is useless. Nor do we deny the effects of environmental factors such as lack of opportunity due to poverty, discrimination or racism. Rather, our message is that when it comes to the factors which lead to success, other things besides cognitive skills might play an even more important role.

4.1 What Leads to Success?

Explain the roles of character vs. intelligence/talent relative to success

Consider these facts. When you compare the IQs of high school dropouts with the IQs of people who graduated from high school and also with those who got their GEDs, it turns out that those who passed the GED are just as smart (in terms of IQ and achievement) as high school graduates and significantly smarter than high school dropouts. Therefore, you could assume that they are just as prepared to succeed as the high school graduates in terms of important future outcomes such as maintaining employment, finishing college, divorce rates, tendencies toward substance abuse, and so forth. As it turns out, when you look at the statistics for such future outcomes, the GED holders do no better than the high school dropouts despite the fact that as a group they are considerably smarter and have much better academic skills (Heckman & Rubinstein, 2001). Should we conclude from this that getting a GED is a waste of time? Obviously, the answer is no. What we need to look at is the psychological traits that enabled those who graduated from high school, whatever their IQ or achievement level, to make it through school. Traits such as the ability to persist at a boring task, to plan, to think ahead, to follow through, and to wait for your rewards (which psychologists call deferring gratification) turn out to be invaluable in college, in the workplace and for life in general. These are non-cognitive skills which, believe it or not, contribute far more to success than the intellectual skills we often make the focus of our efforts whether in terms of self-improvement or in helping others to succeed (Tough, 2012).

Consider another fact. The U.S. ranks 8th in the world in college enrollment rate, a respectable rank. But in terms of college completion, that percentage of students who go on to finish their degrees, the U.S. is second to last! We used to lead the world in producing college graduates and now we are the leaders in churning out college dropouts (Tough, 2012). If you consider that the value of a college degree is now at its peak in terms of impact on later income (a typical American college graduate can expect to earn almost twice as much over the course of a lifetime than a typical high school graduate), it makes this dropout rate even more puzzling. Why is this happening? We used to think that this was the result of poor academic preparation or a greater influx of low IQ students into higher education, a variation on the cognitive hypothesis. However, it turns out that whether a student graduates from college doesn't have as much to do with how smart he or she is. It has to do with certain character traits that involve self-control, motivation, perseverance and time management skills which predict who will succeed in college, in the workplace, and in life overall. Bearing this in mind, there are invaluable lessons from the realm of Positive Psychology that can assist you in developing those skills and attitudes which are necessary to function successfully.

4.1.1 Positive Psychology and the Study of Character

Recall that Martin Seligman, a founder of positive psychology, advises that the primary topic for positive psychology is the study of well-being and the primary goal of positive psychology is to help you achieve optimal human functioning, which he refers to as flourishing. In review recall that, according to Seligman, flourishing is composed of five elements summarized under the acronym *PERMA* which includes:

P Positive Emotions – a wide range of emotions from contentment to bliss

E Engagement – being totally absorbed in an endeavor

R Relationships – having positive, healthy relationships with significant others

M Meaning – having a sense of meaning and purpose in your life, which often involves belonging to or serving something bigger than the self

A Accomplishment – your ability to achieve your goals

For you to fully flourish, it would be helpful to have high levels of all five elements of PERMA operating in your life. However, most people typically place unequal emphasis on each of these aspects and may even ignore one or more. Is it possible to flourish without an emphasis on all five? According to positive psychologists, the answer is yes. Indeed, many people may make up for a lack of good relationships with an emphasis on accomplishment, or compensate for a lack of accomplishment with an emphasis on good relationships, or a strong sense of meaning or purpose. Nevertheless, if you are employed in a demanding job or occupation, or involved as a student in an academic environment, it is very difficult to flourish without developing the motivation and skills for accomplishment (the A in PERMA). To this end, this chapter explores lessons and applications derived from positive psychology geared toward enabling you to accomplish the goals on your personal path towards flourishing.

It turns out that character is vitally important to flourishing. As explained in Chapter 3, during the second half of the twentieth century the field of psychology virtually abandoned the direct study of character due to the bias that science should only describe rather than recommend certain behaviors. In addition, character was viewed as too tied to morality, therefore non-scientific and unworthy of study. Positive psychology reversed this long-standing trend. We will emphasize what positive psychology offers regarding the study of character reflected in our strengths and virtues, and how that relates to accomplishment. Specifically, how can each of us motivate ourselves towards achievement? Then how can we follow through to do what is necessary to make that a reality?

Questions

1. Success is primarily a function of _____.

    A. intelligence

    B. luck

    C. being born into the right family

    D. character

2. _____ is an important aspect of flourishing as summarized by PERMA.

    A. Wealth

    B. Cognitive ability

    C. Accomplishment

    D. Religion

3. Positive Psychology resurrected the study of _____ in psychology.

    A. character

    B. talents

    C. epigenetics

    D. genetics

4.2 The Seven Key Character Strengths for Accomplishment

Explain how the seven key character strengths affect the ability to achieve and accomplish goals.

In this chapter we will be using the terms accomplishment and achievement interchangeably. In our culture there is a tendency to confuse accomplishment with talent, with high IQ, or athletic ability, or artistic or musical gifts. Talent is helpful for success, but not necessary. Skill is essential for success, but skill can be developed without talent. Beyond sheer intelligence and talent, character plays a major role. If one is long on smarts or talent, but short on signature strengths denoting character, then accomplishment is much harder to realize or sustain. Most people know someone gifted with high intelligence or great talent who squandered it because of a lack of character. The study of character and signature strengths provides a roadmap for enhancing your ability to achieve and accomplish your goals.

In the early years of psychology there was an emphasis on character; however, in the twentieth century this changed to a focus on the environmental variables which shape behavior. This emphasis on the environmental causes of low accomplishment tended to either ignore or minimize the role of individual responsibility or choice in lack of achievement. Psychology was centered on pathology and weakness and tended to attribute poor achievement only to external factors such as parenting or poverty. On the other hand, accomplished individuals from all walks of life were given personal credit for their achievements rather than ascribing their success solely to the effects of a fortunate environment. The end result of this was a paradigm where individuals were products of and driven primarily by the effects of their past. Positive psychology takes a different view on this, emphasizing that individuals can also be driven by hopes for their futures. This is not to deny that people are sometimes victims of very difficult or traumatic circumstances and deserve our help in any way possible. But often, people are responsible for their own actions, and their poor choices can stem from their character, or lack thereof. Positive psychology advocates improving difficult circumstances along with shaping character which entails enhancing strengths and ameliorating weaknesses.

While all signature strengths are important in their own regard, there are particular character strengths which are associated with accomplishment (Tough, 2012). The conclusions from a wealth of studies in positive psychology identify seven key signature strengths which are essential to achievement, with each contributing in a different way. These seven include:

Self-control

Perseverance/Grit

Emotional Intelligence/EQ

Zest/passion/energy

Gratitude

Optimism

Curiosity

4.2.1 Motivation and Volition

Before we embark upon a discussion of each of these seven key strengths, it is important to point out that the mechanics of achievement fall into two separate dimensions, that of **motivation** (the desire for a goal) and **volition** (the ability to do what is necessary to achieve the goal). Each of these is necessary to achieve long term goals but neither is sufficient alone. For a common example, you might be very motivated to lose weight, but unless you have the volition, the self-control and willpower to monitor your eating and activity levels, your motivation alone will not get you very far. In fact, high motivation with lack of volition just produces frustration. On the other hand, if you have lots of volition but no desire to work toward a goal, you will be stymied by lack of direction. Consider the example of an individual who works as a housekeeper and has become an expert in cleaning and organizing. However, her own house is a mess because by the time she arrives home her motivation to clean has disappeared despite her high skill level. Therefore, to maximize accomplishment both motivation and volition must be addressed. Referring back to the seven key strengths, several relate directly to motivation for accomplishment. Zest, curiosity, optimism and gratitude and some aspects of EQ or Emotional Intelligence (EQ will be covered in detail in Chapter 9) enable us to create and enhance our motivations. However, volition requires self-control, perseverance and aspects of EQ and zest/energy. Chapter 2 focused intensively on optimism. Chapter 8 will introduce you to the visualization techniques which can be powerful tools for enhancing motivation and helping you achieve your goals. This chapter will emphasize methods for improving volition with a focus on self-control and perseverance.

4.2.2 Self-Control and Accomplishment

Many positive psychologists have come to the conclusion that to become effective, especially when accomplishment is involved, **self-control** is perhaps the most important signature strength to cultivate. Why? Self-control, to a great extent, involves the ability to **defer gratification**, to wait for your rewards. You may wonder why this is so important. Just so you don't underestimate the profound impact of being able to defer gratification, consider the results of this landmark study. Researchers Walter Mischel and Phillip K. Peake (1990) offered four year olds at a preschool at Stanford University a simple choice. They could receive and eat one marshmallow at the start of class, or they could get two marshmallows if they waited until the end of class. A long term follow-up study of these same children later after high school graduation revealed that those who opted to wait for two marshmallows were far more successful and effective in their lives, in general, than those who had grabbed for one marshmallow now. The implications of these results were discussed at length by positive psychologist, Daniel Goleman, in his landmark 1995 book *Emotional Intelligence*, where he stated:

> The emotional and social difference between the grab-the–marshmallow preschoolers and their gratification delaying peers was dramatic. Those who had resisted temptation at four were now, as adolescents, more socially competent, personally effective, self-assertive and better able to cope with the frustrations of life. They were less likely to go to pieces, freeze or regress under stress, or become rattled and disorganized when

pressured; they embraced challenges and pursued them instead of giving up even in the face of difficulties; they were self-reliant and confident, trustworthy and dependable; and they took initiative and plunged into projects. And, more than a decade later, they were still able to delay gratification in pursuit of their goals (p. 81).

Thus, one of the key building blocks of effectiveness is the ability to use self-control to wait for your rewards, to delay gratification. Various studies of self control, such as the marshmallow research, underscore the importance of this for academic and job success. For example, there have been numerous studies demonstrating that individuals measuring high in self-control were more successful, especially with college academic achievement (Tangney and Baumeister, 2000). The bottom line is that to receive future rewards you often need to undertake present discomfort. The authors of this text wonder whether the proliferation of technology has undermined our ability to defer gratification, due to the fact that we are becoming more accustomed to instant rewards at the touch of a keystroke or a swipe of our cell phones.

4.2.3 Perseverance: The Role of Effort in Achievement

In order to put in sustained effort you often have to defer gratification, especially if the task is one involving long term as opposed to quick, short-term rewards, such as writing a term paper. But you also have to be able to persevere, especially if the going gets rough. Putting in sustained effort is vital for accomplishment, whether in your job, your academic pursuits, or even in the quality of your interpersonal relationships. Consider the following equation which represents the invaluable role of character in accomplishment.

$$\text{Achievement} = \text{Skill} \times \text{Effort}$$

Assuming that opportunities for accomplishment are kept constant, achievement can be represented as the multiplicative product of skill (defined as intelligence, talent and/or competence) and effort. Therefore, a high level of effort can compensate for a low level of skill and vice versa, but if either is zero then achievement will be nil. Thus, no matter how skilled you are in any area, if you put in no effort you will accomplish nothing. If your skill level is high, greater effort will reap even greater rewards. This applies whether we are talking about academics, sports, your job, the arts, playing computer games or chess, or any area where you care to achieve. Sustained effort, it turns out, is all about character.

One aspect of effort for accomplishment involves your willingness to practice. *Never underestimate the value of practice in achievement.* For example, if we are talking about highly accomplished individuals, there is a wealth of evidence that high level expertise is not a function of genius, but rather flows from the amount of time and energy spent in deliberate practice (Ericsson & Ward, 2007). The fact of the matter is that most geniuses throughout history worked extraordinarily hard

(Dweck, 1999). In many cases genius is more made than born. Famous geniuses such as Einstein, Darwin, and Tolstoy were not considered to be exceptional children. Even musical geniuses, while obviously gifted with talent, typically put in thousands of hours of practice while they were very young. For example, Mozart is well known for having composed symphonies as a child, but his early works were not noteworthy or particularly original, as compared to his later compositions which were an outgrowth of all of his hard work. Scientists who research creativity have developed the *ten year rule*, that is, no truly great creative contributions come without at least a decade of intense effort. Along these same lines, Malcolm Gladwell (2008) in his fascinating book, *Outliers*, insists that in order to achieve true mastery in a discipline, one has to put in *about 10,000 hours of practice*. According to Gladwell, it takes the brain that long to assimilate all that it needs to learn in order to achieve true mastery, whatever your level of talent.

If we refer back to the research on neuroplasticity, this makes perfect sense. Your brain evolves and changes depending on how you habitually use it. Individuals who practice regularly really do change their brains in the long run! Therefore, if you want to achieve world class status, whether you are playing a musical instrument, training for the Olympics or any sport, playing chess, writing, or anything else, you have to put in your 10,000 hours which often ends up taking about 10 years (the ten year rule). Think about it: have you ever known anyone who was really good and really successful at something (job, hobby, sport, relationship) who did not put in extensive time and effort? This takes perseverance.

Ultimately, to maximize your ability to achieve you have to utilize self-discipline, exercise self-control, and persevere. This is where putting in your 10,000 hours is vital if you want to achieve mastery. This applies whether in your job, playing the violin, or perfecting your jump shot. It takes perseverance and self-control to put in those 10,000 hours. That's why positive psychologists consider these traits to be, by far, the most important of all when considering accomplishment. If you already possess these signature strengths then you are poised to achieve. However, if self-discipline and self-control are not your strengths, consider implementing the specific exercises at the end of Chapter 3 to further develop these areas.

4.2.4 The Power of Grit: Passion + Perseverance

If you have a very high level of self-discipline, characterized by both high persistence and an extraordinary passion to complete a goal, you may display what is referred to as **GRIT**. This is the marriage between the signature strengths of passion/zest and perseverance. Self-discipline underlies achievement, but grittiness often underlies extraordinary accomplishment. This level of exceptional achievement is rare. Grit is a "never-give-up" form of self-discipline where very high effort is the byproduct of the signature strength of extreme persistence. It follows that the more grit you display, the greater your effort (i.e. the time and energy spent on a task), and all that effort multiplies your progress towards your goal.

To determine your personal level of grit, fill out the following inventory developed by positive psychologist Angela Duckworth (2009), a protégé of Seligman and the guru of grit.

The Grit Scale

Respond to the following statements using the following scale.

1 = not like me at all   2 = not much like me   3 = Somewhat like me
4 = Mostly like me   5 = Very much like me

1. ____ New ideas and projects sometimes distract me from old ones.

2. ____ Setbacks do not discourage me.

3. ____ I have been obsessed with a certain idea or project for a short time but later lost interest.

4. ____ I am a hard worker.

5. ____ I often set a goal but later choose to pursue a different one.

6. ____ I have difficulty maintaining my focus on projects that take more than a few months to complete.

7. ____ I finish whatever I begin.

8. ____ I am diligent.

SCORE ____
Scoring: 1. Add your score on statements 2, 4, 7 and 8.
2. Add items 1, 3, 5 and 6 and subtract that total from 24.
3. Add the two steps together and divide by 8.
Low Grit: Below 3.03 for males; below 3.13 for females
Medium Grit: Between 3.04 and 3.74 for males; between 3.26 and 3.78 for females
High Grit: Above 3.75 for males; above 3.79 for females
Superior Grit: Above 4.21 for males; above 4.25 for females

Duckworth (2007) demonstrated through research that grit is not related to IQ. Her research further indicated that students with high grit scores but low SAT scores achieved high GPAs. Grit turned out to be a major factor in who survived until the final rounds at the National Spelling Bee. Furthermore, although the military has their own complex evaluation system to determine who has the right stuff to survive the demands of West Point, it turns out that the Grit Scale is a better predictor of which cadets made it through the grueling basic training than the military's own system. The bottom line is this: You may not have control over how much natural ability you bring to a task, but how much effort you put in is always up to you. Making the choice to put in maximal effort involves persistence and self-control. If you expend really extraordinary effort, you can even achieve grittiness.

4.2.5 Overcoming Blocks to Accomplishment

As individuals we all have our own idiosyncratic ways of putting roadblocks in our paths towards achievement, some of us more than others. For some of us the blocks relate to motivation; for others the obstacles relate to volition. It is impossible, within the confines of this textbook or this course, to review every conceivable block to effectiveness when it comes to accomplishment. But by addressing four general areas, we are likely to hit upon themes or difficulties that are relevant for each of you. In general, when it comes to accomplishment the most common ways to make it harder for yourself involve:

1. Low motivation
2. Failure to use your time wisely (i.e. poor time management skills)
3. Failure to prioritize
4. Procrastination

What follows are tips, techniques, reframes and frameworks to help you overcome such stumbling blocks on your personal road to accomplishment.

Questions

1. The most important signature strength for accomplishment is _____.
   A. gratitude
   B. curiosity
   C. bravery
   D. self-control

2. Achievement = _____ × _____
   A. Luck; Effort
   B. Skill; Effort
   C. IO; EQ
   D. Optimism; Curiosity

3. The mechanics of achievement involve both _____ and _____, both of which are necessary but neither of which is sufficient.
   A. talent; skill
   B. motivation; volition
   C. high IQ; motivation
   D. grit; sweat equity

4.3 How to Enhance Self-Motivation: The Role of Visualization

Describe strategies used to increase self-motivation.

To work on the first obstacle to achievement, that of low motivation, skip ahead to the lessons in Chapter 8 on visualization and goal setting. Practice those visualization techniques and apply them to your goals. Experience how this can facilitate your motivation. However, there is yet another strategy which can be applied to enhance both motivation and volition utilizing a combination of visualization and cognitive strategies developed by NYU psychologist Gabriele Oettingen and colleagues (2012, 2014). This method is called *Mental Contrasting with Implementation Intentions* or *MCII*. Oettingen discovered that people tend to use three strategies for goal setting and two of these often don't work very well for helping people to accomplish their goals. The first strategy, which she calls "indulging," involves vividly imagining the future outcome you would like to achieve and all the good things that can accompany it, akin to the kind of visualization promulgated by *The Secret*. While indulging is fun, it often does not lead to actual achievement because it is typically disconnected from the effort component. The second strategy is "dwelling," where individuals focus almost exclusively on all of the obstacles that could potentially get in the way of accomplishing their goals. Needless to say, this does not work very well either as people just get discouraged and give up.

The third strategy involving mental contrasting uses both indulging and dwelling together in strategic combination, once sufficient motivation exists. This is similar to the defensive pessimism strategy discussed previously in Chapter 2. MCII involves visualizing a positive outcome while simultaneously concentrating on potential obstacles in the path (for example, you could visualize getting high grades this semester in all of your classes while simultaneously acknowledging that your tendency to procrastinate and prioritize TV-watching and Facebook could jeopardize achieving this goal). Oettingen advises that MCII be used primarily when high motivation or expectation of success exists, as it facilitates increased commitment toward your goals and energy to complete goal-directed behaviors. The next step is to create a series of implementation intentions which are specific plans in the form of *if/then statements* that link obstacles with ways to overcome them. For example, if the desired outcome is an A on a test, then make a statement to yourself such as "*If* I am distracted by TV after school, *then* I will wait to watch my programs until after I finish studying for my exam." Research has demonstrated the effectiveness of this MCII method in a variety of situations, such as improving academic performance (Gollwitzer, Oettingen & colleagues, 2011), assisting high school students to practice more diligently for the SAT (Duckworth, Oettingen & colleagues, 2011), helping dieters eat healthier foods (Adriaanse & colleagues, 2010; Johannessen, Oettingen & colleagues, 2012), prompting more exercise (Kappes, Singmann & Oettingen, 2012), enabling chronic back pain patients to achieve greater mobility (Duckworth, Oettingen & colleagues, 2012), and quitting smoking (Oettingen, Mayer & Thorpe, 2010).

In her book *Rethinking Positive Thinking: Inside the New Science of Motivation* (2014), Oettingen provides a useful acronym for the MCII process that she labels WOOP. This breaks down the key aspects of the mental contrasting technique into a four step WOOP process consisting of **W**ish, **O**utcome, **O**bstacle and **P**lan. Moreover, WOOP is also available as a WOOP app for most smart phones and tablets enabling you to record/save your wishes and goals, to share these with your friends, and to observe and chart your progress. This app offers information about the important steps to get into and through college and provides support for taking the necessary steps for reaching your goals.

Two of the authors of this text have devised a way to expand the effectiveness of WOOP for situations where initial motivation is low and/or to minimize the discouragement that can flow from the focus on obstacles. They propose adding a step to the beginning of the process whereby an individual pulls up a memory of a previous success experience, using vivid visualization, to lay a foundation of expectation for success. This is especially useful if the success remembrance is in any way similar or related to the WISH step. The revised version then becomes SWOOP, a five-step process consisting of **S**uccess, **W**ish, **O**utcome, **O**bstacle, **P**lan.

Why does WOOP or SWOOP work? Basically MCII helps you to set rules for yourself. In terms of how our brains operate, there is a neurobiological reason why rules work (Kessler, 2009), whether you are using them to avoid junk food, to structure study time, or to tackle a daunting project at your workplace. When you are making rules for yourself you are utilizing your prefrontal cortex, the site of the all-important **executive functions** of your brain which include planning, judgment, focusing, screening out distractions, organizing, using and integrating new information, and inhibiting thoughts and actions. This helps tame the more impulsive, short term reward driven parts of your brain. Rules are not necessarily the same as willpower. Rules can become habits which, if followed over time, can substitute for willpower. By making a rule for yourself, you can sidestep the painful internal conflict between your desires and your determination to resist temptation. Rules give us a structure to prepare for encounters with temptation and allow us to redirect our attention elsewhere. If you follow a rule long enough it becomes a habit. Effective habits and character ultimately become the same thing. William James said that our nervous system is analogous to a sheet of paper which is folded over and over again until it develops a crease, which then becomes your default option. If your creases (habits) are in the direction of self-control and perseverance, this becomes a reliable part of your character. Developing new habits is facilitated by practicing the new behaviors regularly. Remember this important tip: Your brain will adopt a new habit more readily if you practice once a day for fourteen straight days than if you practice once a week for fourteen straight weeks (Atkinson, 2014).

Questions

1. The various forms of MCII utilize _____ and _____ together in strategic combination.

    A. self-control; self-indulgence

    B. indulgence; dwelling

    C. IQ; EQ

    D. motivation; volition

2. Why do MCII or SWOOP work?

    A. They automatically enhance your motivation.

    B. They automatically improve your volition.

    C. They help you set rules for yourself and activate the executive functions of your brain.

    D. They deactivate your self-control.

3. The full SWOOP strategy for enhancing motivation involves:

    A. visualizing success, goals, and plans to overcome obstacles

    B. visualizing success

    C. goal setting

    D. dwelling on obstacles and making plans

4.4 Managing Yourself in Time: How to Use Your Time Wisely

Identify eight effective strategies for using time wisely.

When we think about effective people, what typically comes to mind are individuals who are accomplished and productive, who not only do most things competently, but who do them in a timely manner. Effective people respect deadlines and usually finish tasks on time, sometimes with time to spare. But effectiveness is much more than just producing a lot of work. The quest for optimal functioning requires organization as well as creativity. Effective people are typically well organized, and have learned to juggle multiple responsibilities, projects, and tasks while still making time for relaxation, enjoyment and personal relationships. Success in our current world usually requires an ability to see the big picture followed by a sustained focus on the critical details for getting it done. What enables effective individuals to develop and maintain competence and maximize their chances for success is that they are adept at culling out what is important, and then they use their time wisely.

Indeed, the ability to use time wisely is typically a hallmark of effective individuals. Please notice that we are not talking about time management, but rather about *managing yourself in time.* We often hear people talk about needing to "make more time," as if we all didn't get just 24 hours in a day. The key is to manage yourself and the decisions you make regarding how to use the resource that is time. To do that you need to be wary of the common tendency to confuse efficiency with effectiveness. While effective individuals are typically well organized and they may be efficient, an over-emphasis on efficiency will actually diminish your effectiveness.

Have you ever spent a day, at work or at home, where you were busy almost nonstop, but by the day's end you felt as though you had accomplished nothing? Perhaps this was because you put your focus on doing busywork, trivial jobs that were easy, or tasks requested by others, but which were of low relevance to your own agenda. Perhaps you felt you had accomplished little because nothing was finished, or because you were immersed in multiple tasks in a disorganized fashion, flitting back and forth and never really making any headway on any. Every one of us has had at least one day like this, but if you find yourself fitting this pattern on a regular basis, it is time to look at how you manage yourself in time and experiment with more effective strategies. Even if you are adept at utilizing time, you may find at least a few tips or tools here that will refine or add to your skills.

4.4.1 Eight Strategies for Success

If you follow these central strategies for everyday success, you will increase your productivity and your effectiveness, and as a side benefit, you will lower your stress level.

FOCUS FIRST ON HIGH PRIORITY ITEMS   Think in terms of the Pareto principle, a concept from economics, which is also called the 80/20 rule. The Pareto principle teaches that 80% of the benefit comes from doing 20% of the work. Figure out the most important and beneficial 20%, and make that your priority to tackle first. Completing the important 20% often expedites completion of the remaining 80% of the work.

How do you determine what is or should be a high priority? How do you know what is really important? This is not always that obvious. Tasks, jobs, or things you have to do are rarely either important or unimportant. Importance lies on a continuum ranging from low to high. Covey (1991) recommends that you determine importance based on how closely an activity is tied to your life goals and desired results as defined by your "personal mission statement" which will be explained in Chapter 8. Time management expert Dru Scott (1980) advises completing "marginal matters," the hundreds of relatively trivial but time-consuming tasks (i.e., washing dishes, looking through email, running errands, or updating your files), last. Many people try to get these little tasks out of the way first to make time to focus on the important stuff. But too often these small, marginal tasks end up consuming your whole day, and before you know it, nothing of lasting value is accomplished. Give these tasks the lowest priority. That does not mean that you ignore them. After all, these tasks do have their place in the scheme of things. Just do them last when possible.

GROUP RELATED TASKS AND DO THEM TOGETHER   It is common sense that when you group similar jobs together you can accomplish them faster than if you did each one separately. For example, if you have three errands to run, it is certainly more efficient to do all in one trip rather than take the time to drive your car three different times.

GET ORGANIZED   Lack of organization contributes to ineffectiveness. When you approach your work in a disorganized fashion, tasks generally take longer to accomplish, and the finished product often is not as good. Experiment with the following tips for improving your organization.

   a. Things To Do Lists
   Making a list of Things to Do on a daily or weekly basis is an excellent way of getting yourself organized and helping yourself to remember tasks that are easily forgotten. Post your list in a prominent place (like the bathroom mirror or the refrigerator door) where you will likely see it often, or keep it in your phone to refer to regularly. Scratching finished items off your list becomes rewarding, leading to a sense of relief and accomplishment each time an item is crossed off.

   b. Create a Realistic Schedule
   Things to Do lists are very useful, but they have their limits. Avoid getting caught in the trap of spending all your time on marginal items to scratch off your list while ignoring important, difficult and time-consuming tasks. Without some sort of schedule, you can create stress by wasting time, working inefficiently, and missing opportunities because you didn't plan ahead. But over-scheduling yourself is stressful as well. There is an art to creating a workable daily, weekly and monthly schedule. Start by compiling a list of all you want and need to accomplish over a certain time period, say a month. Begin your daily schedule by arranging time for any scheduled appointments or meetings. Next, block out chunks of at least an hour for high priority projects that require sustained work over time. The earlier in the day you can get to these, the better. Then build in time for other required tasks. Complete your schedule with the routine, quick or easy, marginal tasks that need to be completed that day. Make your schedule flexible. Build in time for interruptions, unexpected events, problem solving, and travel time, as well as for breaks and relaxation. If you can't finish everything, and this may occur often, postpone the lowest priority items. Following a schedule will not guarantee that you always get everything done that day, but if you have made progress on your high priority goals, you will feel more in control. Engaging in this type of planning may seem time-consuming at first, but it will increase your time in the long run.

c. Get Rid of Unnecessary Papers

Is your desk at work or at home piled high with stacks of papers waiting for your attention? Do you feel overwhelmed just looking at the paper piles? If so, follow these guidelines. Handle each piece of paper only once, if possible. Each time you handle a piece of paper do something to move it along (i.e. pay that bill, toss out junk mail, file that important paper, fill out that form). Most importantly, when in doubt, THROW IT OUT. If you don't, it is likely to just sit there on your desk, collecting dust and adding to your pile. Once you have made sufficient headway on clearing the pile, keep your desk cleared of everything except the highest priority items.

BREAK IT INTO DOABLE CHUNKS   Many tasks, particularly if complicated or time-consuming, can appear overwhelming, leading to avoidance, delays, or disorganization. We can't emphasize enough how helpful it can be to break big jobs into workable steps. Taking time to initially subdivide the project into steps, then listing and ordering those steps, will save you time later on. It will help you to proceed more smoothly, and often with less frustration. Approaching the task in an organized fashion minimizes chances of forgetting an important step, allowing you to feel a sense of completion as each step is finished. Remember, a skyscraper may look huge, but it was built one brick at a time.

DEVELOP AND USE TIMETABLES   We humans are much more likely to begin and to complete something when we have committed to a deadline. Deadlines bring home the reality that we have to get moving. If you do not have a deadline from an external source such as a boss or a teacher, set your own target date or time for completion. After breaking the task or assignment into doable chunks, estimate how much time each chunk will reasonably take to finish. Then give each chunk its own target date or time for completion. Doing this gives you an opportunity to plan accordingly, leaving yourself ample time for task completion. This will help you to avoid the stress of last minute rushes, or settling for slip-shod work if you run out of time.

For example, if you are a student facing a big assignment, such as a term paper that is due in two weeks, you could chunk the job in a format such as the following:

1. Get relevant articles and books from the library.	2 hours
2. Do Internet search.	2 hours
3. Read through sources and pick out relevant information.	4 hours
4. Organize report into 3 sections.	1 hour
5. Write introductory paragraph.	1/2 hour
6. Write section one.	2 hours
7. Write section two.	2 hours
8. Write section three.	1 hour
9. Edit and Proof read report.	1 hour

You would next assign each chunk to a date and time of day to work on it within your school or work schedule. You have nine chunks to be divided over fourteen days. The four-hour preparatory chunk (reading through source material) could be sub-divided into two two-hour chunks scheduled for consecutive days for continuity. This schedule takes a large intimidating job and makes it doable.

FOCUS ON ONE THING AT A TIME   It often helps if you focus on one task at a time. People with problems managing themselves in time often flit from one project to another, or try to do several things simultaneously. The end result is often delays, mistakes and disorganization which waste rather than save time. Uninterrupted concentration on a task, when possible, produces a better product in less time. Arrange your work space to minimize distractions. This does not mean that you can only do one thing at a time. It is certainly possible to type your term paper while your clothes spin in the dryer. The key here is *not to try to do two or more things that require concentration or focus at the same time.*

FINISH IT FULLY   Effective individuals finish what they start. This involves utilizing the signature strengths of perseverance and industriousness. No matter how much work you may do in the course of a day, if you don't finish anything, you may end up feeling frustrated and your effectiveness is diluted. You will be far better off with three finished projects as opposed to six half-finished jobs. Finishing will boost your personal satisfaction and motivation, lower your stress level, and enhance your ability to concentrate because you have fewer tasks with which to be concerned. That is, you only have three tasks to finish rather than six. Finishing tasks on a regular basis has a large impact on how others view you as well, whether you are perceived as effective, dependable, and successful. Starting many tasks or projects and leaving them unfinished wastes time and energy, contributes to disorganization, and also makes mistakes or careless errors more likely. Although attempting to focus on one task at a time sets the stage for task completion, we certainly realize that in the real world this is not always possible. At work phones ring, colleagues interrupt you with pressing concerns, meetings must be attended, or equipment breaks down. But when possible we recommend that you opt for task completion rather than switching to another task that is neither pressing nor vitally important.

DO IT WHEN YOU THINK OF IT   Oftentimes it is just the sheer volume of tasks which makes you want to delay. By doing the task immediately, if possible, you can avoid the inefficiency involved in relocating the necessary materials, which saves time and effort. You also prevent yourself from forgetting to handle it.

4.4.2 Common Time Wasters and Effective Antidotes

There are always a myriad of potential time wasting or time consuming influences, both internal and external, which can interfere with accomplishment. Which of the following obstacles apply to you? Consider how you might put these suggestions to good use to creatively turn potential time wasters into opportunities for getting something done.

INFORMATION OVERLOAD SABOTAGES DECISION-MAKING   Your ability to make decisions can be significantly slowed or stymied altogether by **information overload**. Do you feel that you always have to do exhaustive research in order to make the best decisions? Do you then find that because of the abundance of available information, the more data you acquire, the more confused you become? The science of decision-making has demonstrated that too much information can paralyze you, or lead to poor choices on your part which is referred to as *decision fatigue* by East and Tinker (2015). The easy availability of information online contributes to this dilemma. Research has shown that many decisions benefit from letting the issue percolate. Opening yourself to a steady stream of new information interferes with that process. Why? Incoming information presents you with choices. Do you attend to it, ignore it, or reply to it? Decision science shows us that there is a tipping point; when you have too many choices or too much information, you are apt to postpone a decision or make an unwise choice. Although many people desire to accumulate more information to assist with decision-making, past a certain point this actually becomes "debilitating" according to Sheena Iyengar (2010) in her book *The Art of Choosing.*

The more data you have to juggle, the harder the decision, particularly when information is complex and/or the stakes are high. The reason for this has to do with the capacity of our brain's working memory, which can typically hold an average of seven items at one time. Therein lies the beauty of seven-digit phone numbers. Anything beyond seven items represents an overload and is much harder to remember in its entirety. Furthermore, if you exceed this limit your focus is lost and judgment likely falters. According to JoAnne Cantor (2009) in her book *Conquer Cyber Overload*, when overloaded our brains struggle to figure out what to discard, which inhibits decision-making.

Research reveals the important finding that some of our best decisions are made through nonconscious processes rather than just rational analysis. It can be harder to reach a decision if you expose yourself to a constant barrage of new data because you are not giving your nonconscious, intuitive mind the time to make the connections that lead to a wise judgment. Taking a break allows your brain to subconsciously integrate new information into existing knowledge to guide you. That is why the notion of "sleeping on it" is a good idea. How can you shield yourself from the effects of information overload?

1. Recognize that you need to set a limit on how much data you gather to avoid exceeding your tipping point. Focus on gathering data for one to three criteria that you determine are most important for your decision. For example, let's say you want to buy a used car. The possibilities are endless. You could narrow your search by emphasizing three criteria with built in limits: (1) your budget; (2) make of car (i.e. only consider Hondas); and (3) mileage on the vehicle.

2. Deliberately take breaks to allow your unconscious mind to process the information.

3. Don't be afraid to make snap judgments regarding inconsequential, everyday matters. If nothing of any significance is riding on your decision, then just pick because either way it will not matter very much. Whether you pick chocolate or vanilla ice cream does not really matter.

4. Restrict your intake of digital messages. Gold (2017) reports a study at FSU where researchers interrupted students with texts or calls during a task and found a 25% increase in error rate compared to when students completed the task uninterrupted. Deal with tasks like emails and text messages (part of the ongoing barrage of information) in batches rather than piecemeal all day long.

5. Lastly, when you start to feel overloaded, take that as a cue to stop searching because you probably have more than enough data from which to reach your decision.

WORRYING Do you spend a lot of time worrying about all you have to do or would like to do rather than doing it? Rumination can be a major time waster as it is neither a productive nor rewarding use of your time. But trying not to worry is destined to fail. Telling yourself not to worry is the equivalent of commanding yourself, "Don't think about pink elephants." What happens? Of course, the first thing you think of is a pink elephant! The key is not to try to stop worrying, but rather to schedule it, to literally set up a time devoted exclusively to worry at a convenient time. Effective individuals worry just like everyone else; they just limit the distraction of nonproductive worry by scheduling it. To this end, try the following exercise.

Positive Psychology Exercise
The Worry Appointment

If frequent worrying is an issue for you, set up a fifteen minute period to worry to your heart's content. Avoid scheduling your worry time right before or at bedtime as this could disturb winding down for sleep. If you do not worry on a daily basis but have difficulty letting go of worries when they pop up, schedule a weekly half hour worry appointment. Scheduling such worry times helps put your mind to rest. Then if fears or obsessive concerns enter your mind, remind yourself that you will definitely consider this later at your worry time. Sometimes we worry for fear that we will forget to handle something unless we remind ourselves with worries. The value of scheduling worry time is that it makes it easier to let go of those concerns because you know that you will get to them later, freeing you to focus elsewhere. Many people find that once they begin their worry time, some concerns have already evaporated and others can be dismissed quickly. You may end up finishing your worrying appointment even before your time is up.

ATTEMPTING TO DO THINGS PERFECTLY   Don't try to do things perfectly, just focus on doing them well. Striving for perfection can lead to fear of failure, procrastination, or difficulty finishing due to delays until it is "perfect." Effective individuals strive for excellence—not perfection. In most cases an 80% job is all that is necessary to accomplish the task appropriately. Does that inter-office memo really have to be perfect every time? Is it really the end of the world if there is some dust on top of the TV? There are some rare tasks worth doing as close to perfect as you can, and those should relate closely to your high priorities. Abandoning the need for perfection on unimportant tasks will save you valuable time and energy that you can invest in what is really important.

WORKING AGAINST YOUR BODY RHYTHMS   Sometimes we slow ourselves down or lower our effectiveness by failing to heed the rhythms of our bodies. If you are a morning person, have you ever tried to finish an important report late at night to meet a deadline? Remember how hard it was to stay awake and focused? If you are a night owl, can you recall how difficult it can be to try to effectively plan your day at the crack of dawn? Pay attention to your body rhythms. Schedule difficult, challenging tasks for the times when you are most alert and energetic. If you are a morning person, do the difficult, energy-consuming tasks early in the day. If you are a night person, save the challenging projects for the evening. Save the easy, routine tasks for times when your energy is at low ebb, which is mid-afternoon for many people.

FAILING TO RECHARGE YOUR BATTERIES   Effective individuals work hard, play hard and know when to relax. Rest and relaxation are essential to keeping your energy level up so you can be productive. Working until you burn out will only slow you down and limit your effectiveness. Take short breaks to refresh and revitalize, particularly if you notice your concentration faltering. Sometimes engaging in a **power nap**, shutting your eyes for about twenty minutes and reclining in your chair, is all you need to perk up. Nadja Sayej (2016) reported on the installation of power nap pods on college campuses such as the University of Miami to enable students to refresh themselves. Or take a five minute walk around your workplace and step outside for some fresh air. Likewise, all work and no play is a sure way to maximize stress. Make time for relaxing activities and fun. Don't be afraid to occasionally take a day off to recharge and revitalize. We refer to this as a "mental health day," a day off to prevent getting sick while increasing your energy for work.

FEELING THAT YOU ARE RESPONSIBLE FOR EVERYTHING   Is your motto, "If you want it done right, then do it yourself?" If so, you may often find yourself bogged down by insignificant tasks that you could easily delegate. Delegating tasks to others at work or at home is an investment that could really pay large dividends of time later on. What if others don't do those tasks perfectly or as well as you can? If there are no major consequences, then don't sweat it. Give feedback for improvement and put your focus on the important aspects of your own work. Remember, *perfection for the sake of perfection is a total waste of time.*

If you are in a situation where you have no one to whom you can reasonably delegate any of your tasks, consider that effective individuals can say "No" to low priority items or requests from others which distract them from completing work that is really important. Remember that spreading yourself too thin detracts from your effectiveness.

GETTING STUCK WAITING   One of the most notorious wastes of time is getting stuck waiting; whether at the doctor's office, a checkout line, or stuck in traffic, these common, insidious little delays add up. They rob you of time that could be better spent accomplishing something or enjoyed in a relaxing or pleasurable pursuit. Have you ever wished to find an extra hour in your day? Using waiting time constructively or reducing it can help you to find that magical "25th hour" in your day.

Sometimes it is possible to reduce or eliminate waiting time. For example, you could call ahead to your physician's office before a scheduled appointment to check whether the doctor is on time, or as is usually the case, behind schedule, and then adjust the time you leave accordingly. Or you could choose to purchase groceries when the supermarket is not crowded.

Waiting may be a fact of life but wasting time while stuck waiting is not. If you anticipate that you will need to wait, come prepared. Small chunks of time often offer great opportunities to complete quick, routine tasks. For example, while waiting at the dentist's office, use that fifteen or twenty minutes to pay bills, read your email, or answer a text message. If you are at work and are waiting on someone else, switch to other tasks rather than watching the clock in frustration. When waiting at the offices of others, bring portable work with you that you could do while waiting. Laptops and cellular phones are the perfect tools for this situation. One of the authors actually spent a significant amount of time writing this chapter while in the waiting room during her daughter's orthodontist visit. Remember, found time is like found money.

Questions

1. Which of the following suggestions will help you manage your time wisely?
   A. Ignore your body rhythms
   B. Finish trivial busywork first to clear time to focus on important tasks
   C. Break a large project into doable chunks to decrease feeling overwhelmed
   D. Spread your focus and multitask as much as possible

2. Information overload _____.

    A. facilitates efficiency

    B. facilitates effectiveness

    C. helps decision making

    D. impedes decision making

3. Effective time managers _____.

    A. always strive for perfection

    B. schedule tasks to correspond to their personal body rhythms

    C. give the highest priority to tasks deemed important to others

    D. do not bother making lists of things to do

4.5 Enhancing Volition: Prioritizing for Accomplishment

Explain how dividing your tasks into quadrants can lead to effective use of time.

Time is our most precious commodity and none of us really know how much we have. Yet we do know it is a limited amount. How we spend our time should take into account what we truly want. As Covey, Merrill and Merrill describe in *First Things First* (1994), you need to ask, "Am I doing the right things?" before "Am I doing things right?" The system popularized by the late Steven Covey approaches this issue from a different perspective than traditional systems of managing your time. He recommends that you organize your schedule around priorities rather than prioritize your schedule. The first step is to consider what is really important in your life, which you can use as your guide to determine current and future priorities. Covey recommends dividing your work tasks and projects into four categories (or quadrants) as illustrated on the next page.

    The two aspects that define any activity are its urgency and its importance. Things which are urgent, such as a ringing phone, demand to be attended to immediately, or at least very soon. Urgent matters are often popular or important to others, but they may or may not be important for you. Covey further recommends that you define importance based on how closely an activity is tied to your goals and desired results. Urgent activities call for a quick reaction. Tasks that are important but not urgent typically require more initiative and proactivity. If you have not defined your goals and therefore are unclear as to what is important to you, it is very easy to be swallowed up by urgency. That is why it is so important to develop your personal mission statement and attempt to live by it. Chapter 8 contains instructions for developing your personal mission statement.

Quadrant I Urgent and Important	Quadrant II Non-Urgent but Important
Crises	Proactive activities
Pressing problems	Long-range planning
Projects with deadlines	Networking
Some meetings	Relationship building
Some preparations	Prevention/Maintenance

Quadrant III Urgent but Not Important	Quadrant IV Neither Urgent nor Important
Interruptions	Busywork, trivia
Some phone calls	Some phone calls
Some meetings	Some mail/junk mail
Some reports/some mail	Pleasant activities
Many pressing matters	

Quadrant I tasks, both urgent and important, typically take the form of crises or problems which require immediate attention. Although we all have some Q I activities in our work lives, many people are consumed with Q I work and are beset with problems all day long. While the demands of any quadrant could potentially be stressful, clearly it is Q I activities that contain the greatest potential for raising your stress level. It is not surprising that individuals mired in Q I are more prone to burnout. And the more time spent in Q I, the more it expands, because you are not taking the time to be proactive and prevent future problems. When overly immersed in Q I work, the tendency is to escape to the more mindless, easy Quadrant IV activities. While that might provide a temporary breather, it does little to set the stage for a meaningful decrease in Q I and its inherent stress.

When people spend a lot of time in Quadrant III activities, urgent but not important, it is usually because they assume that these tasks are really important and lie in Q I. This is based on being influenced by the expectations of others, because the matter is urgent or important for them. That does not necessarily mean that it need be urgent or important for you unless it fits with your goals. Quadrant IV activities are often pleasant and offer an opportunity to take a break. Be wary of spending the majority of your time in Q III or Q IV, for that leads to irresponsibility. Successful, effective people minimize time spent in

Q III or Q IV, saving that for mini-breaks, because urgent or not, they are not important.

The key to effective personal/time management is to maximize time spent on Q II activities which are important but not urgent. This involves work which is proactive and preventative such as long term planning, preparation, networking and building business relationships, establishing long term goals, and preventative maintenance, along with maintaining your health and personal relationships. These are all things we want to do, and know we should do, but tend to put off because they are not deadline driven. But it is only by engaging in Q II activities that you can shrink the stressful Q I, by preventing crises and problems in the first place, thereby increasing your effectiveness. This is all about exercising the signature strength of caution and discretion by thinking ahead, deferring gratification and engaging in long term planning for your future.

Initially, the way to spend more time on Q II activities is to subtract time from Q III and IV. Increasing your emphasis on Q II requires proactivity, that you make it a priority to attend to important tasks that relate to your life goals, even if these tasks are not deadline driven or urgent. Obviously you cannot ignore Q I, but it will begin to diminish once you increase your Q II proactivity. In order to lessen time spent in Q III and IV, you have to learn to say "No" to some activities, even if important or urgent to others, or to delegate. This may require that you strengthen your assertive skills which we will address in Chapter 10. A ringing phone is a typical example of a Q III situation. It urgently demands that you interrupt your work to answer and respond, but often the calls are only important to the caller. The perfect example of this is telephone solicitation. Our method for handing such calls is short and sweet. We diplomatically state, "Sorry, we don't accept telephone solicitation," and hang-up immediately.

The focus here is on determining what is really important to you, on what you want to accomplish and what type of person you want to be. This helps to address the gap that many people perceive between the way they spend their time and what is really important to them. Too often we fall into the trap of focusing on our schedule, which can lead to perceiving other people and relationships as interruptions or barriers to efficiency. It is impossible, not to mention unwise and unfulfilling, to be efficient with people. You can be efficient with things, with writing reports, housecleaning, or errands, but being in relationship with other people is not about cutting corners, delegating intimacy to others, or setting limits on conversation. If a significant other is upset and needs to spend some quality time with you, scheduling a ten minute appointment to fit him or her into your schedule isn't the way to proceed. The advantage of this system is that it focuses more on results and on your relationships.

The Global Perspective
The Time Is Now

The lessons gleaned from Covey's time management quadrants are especially relevant when we consider the best approach to many global problems. That is, the only way to prevent many QI crises is by focusing on QII long term planning and prevention. Are humans utilizing the resources of the planet in a way that is not sustainable? By this we mean, are we are meeting our present needs for food, water, energy, and various manufactured goods in such a way that future generations will be unable to meet their needs?

> On a planetary scale, humans now exceed the earth's carrying capacity. We are drawing down natural stocks of water in Earth's aquifers, soil in Earth's agricultural lands, timber resources in Earth's forests, and fish in Earth's oceans. We are also exceeding the "capacity" of Earth's atmosphere to absorb our wastes as evidenced by ozone thinning, acid precipitation, and climate change. Slowly but surely these overdrawn natural capital accounts will come due.
>
> Developing Ecological Consciousness by Christopher Uhl pg. 147

Most of these changes are not readily visible to the untrained or inexperienced eye. In this country we still have ready access to drinkable water and energy. But in many places in the world hours a day are spent just gathering wood and water to survive another day. Thus, what might seem to us to be long term considerations that are important but not urgent are in reality important and urgent elsewhere. Since we are so interconnected, the crisis affecting the poorest among us really will affect all of us eventually. In Jared Diamond's (2005) book, *Collapse*, he notes that the difference between civilizations that failed and those that weathered environmental crises was the ability to realize the causes of the crisis and then take proactive action.

So, it appears that we cannot continue on as we have been or we risk everything, not necessarily for ourselves but for our children and our grandchildren. But we cannot live only in a crisis mode. Thus we are brought to a further consideration of time and values. How will we use the time we have and to what end to reduce crises with which we have to cope? While we worry about whether or not there is a viable future for humans on the planet, could it be that our preoccupation with progress and acquiring wealth and possessions has taken us away from the most important time – NOW. Might we need new priorities? However, it is our inability to stop and engage our senses in the present moment that prevents us from remembering what is most important in life. Until we can come to some agreement as human beings about what our priorities are, we cannot enact a coherent plan.

Taking time to slow down, to meditate, contemplate, and appreciate is how we can discover our personal priorities. Talking to people from other countries and cultures and cultivating an understanding of what they value is the beginning of finding a common ground and purpose. A global citizen values establishing a dialogue with others. These are all activities that are extremely important, but not necessarily urgent. However, the failure to do them will no doubt make them important and urgent activities.

There is no lack of individuals who feel that the only way humans will change their ways is when they face a severe crisis. Perhaps, they are right. What do you believe? When you take the time to be silent and fully immerse yourself in this moment, what do you want for yourself and your children?

Questions

1. Covey recommends ordering your work tasks based on _____ and
   _____.

   A. importance; unimportance
   B. urgency; non-urgency
   C. urgency; importance
   D. size; goals

2. Covey's time management system involves organizing your schedule around
   _____.

   A. efficiency
   B. your priorities
   C. your bosses' priorities
   D. what will get you a raise

3. In order to maximize time spent in QII activities, you must be _____.

   A. a perfectionist
   B. hard-working
   C. proactive and assertive
   D. focused on finishing busywork

4.6 Enhancing Volition: Overcoming Procrastination

Understand the causes of procrastination and methods for overcoming the habit.

For many people one of the most notorious enemies of optimal functioning and accomplishment is **procrastination**. "Never do today what you can put off until tomorrow" is the motto of the procrastinator. We all procrastinate at least some of the time, to one degree or another. It becomes a major problem in your work, academic, or personal life when important tasks or responsibilities are left undone or are completed in a slipshod manner because inadequate time was left to complete the task properly. Gura (2008) estimated that 15 to 20% of American adults routinely put off activities that should be accomplished in a timely manner. Steel (2007) conducted a meta-analysis which indicated that a whopping 80 to 95% of college students, whose lifestyles often mix packed academic schedules with social distractions and/or work obligations, are plagued with procrastination issues.

Whether putting off the start of a term paper until tomorrow because it creates anxiety or delaying a task like cleaning your room because it is boring or overwhelming, procrastination provides a convenient escape from anticipated unpleasantness. Procrastination lowers anxiety in the short run due to the relief you feel from task avoidance. But it greatly increases your stress in the long run as tasks pile up or time runs short. Meanwhile, you are sabotaging your effectiveness the longer you delay. Researchers Diane Tice and Roy Baumeister (1997) examined procrastination among college students and adults and found that those who delayed seemed to benefit in the short run from their laissez-faire, casual attitude, but this advantage was very short-lived. They found that procrastinators had higher levels of stress, poorer physical health, and lower academic achievement. When it came to the quality of specific academic assignments, procrastinators typically spent a lot less time and produced inferior work. In addition, procrastination often carries other penalties as well, in terms of finances, career advancement and relationships. According to Gura (2008):

> Experts estimate that 40% of people have experienced a financial loss because of procrastination, in some cases severe. In 2002 Americans overpaid $473 million in taxes as a result of rushing and consequent errors. And American's dearth of retirement savings can be attributed, in part, to people putting off putting away cash . . . In 2006 psychologist Fuschia Sirois . . . reported in a study of 254 adults that procrastinators had higher stress levels and more acute health problems than did individuals who completed jobs in a timely manner. (Scientific American Mind, p. 28–29)

Is procrastination a problem for you? Take a moment to complete the following scale to see how you compare to other undergraduate students.

The Procrastination Scale

For each statement, use this scale to indicate whether or not this is characteristic of you.
1 = *That's not me for sure* 2 = *That's not my tendency* 3 = *That's my tendency* 4 = *That's me for sure*

— — 1. I needlessly delay finishing jobs, even when they are important.

— — 2. I postpone starting on things I don't like to do.

— — 3. When I have a deadline, I wait until the last minute.

— — 4. I delay making tough decisions.

— — 5. I keep putting off improving my work habits.

— — 6. I manage to find an excuse for not doing something.

— — 7. I put the necessary time into even boring tasks, like studying.

— — 8. I am an incurable time waster.

— — 9. I am a time waster now, and I can't seem to do anything about it.

— — 10. When something is too tough to tackle, I believe in postponing it.

— — 11. I promise myself I'll do something and then I drag my feet.

—— 12. Whenever I make a plan of action, I follow it.

—— 13. Even though I hate myself if I don't get started, it doesn't get me going.

—— 14. I always finish important jobs with time to spare.

—— 15. I get stuck in neutral even though I know how important it is to get started.

—— 16. Putting something off until tomorrow is not the way I do it.

To obtain you total score, first reverse your responses for items 7, 12, 14, and 16 (where 4 = 1, 3 = 2, 2 = 3, 1 = 4). Then add up the numbers for all 16 items. Scores range from a low of 16 to a high of 64, with higher scores reflecting a greater tendency to procrastinate. The average score for college undergraduates is approximately 40, at the midpoint of the scale. How does your score compare?

4.6.1 Why Do We Procrastinate?

Tice and Baumeister (1997) remind us that procrastination, like other self-defeating behaviors, is fueled by short term benefits with many long term costs. The main cause for procrastination is **low frustration tolerance** (Ellis & Knaus, 1977). You need to accept the fact that to receive future rewards you often need to undertake present discomfort. In essence, you need to be able to defer gratification. In the positive psychology literature the ability to defer gratification is referred to as self-control. A wealth of studies of **self-control**, such as the marshmallow research, underscore the importance of this for academic and job success.

Low frustration tolerance is based on the irrational notion that present pain or discomfort is "too hard to bear." This belief that you cannot stand present pain for future gain enables you to continue your delay tactics. This can be a very debilitating cycle. Again, everything hinges upon what you tell yourself about the "onerous task." In order to overcome procrastination you need to begin by utilizing cognitive restructuring to identify your irrational thoughts and then replace them with thoughts that promote productivity. If your frustration tolerance is adequate, you will take the temporary discomfort in stride and conclude that, indeed, the task may be aversive, boring or anxiety provoking, but "So what?" Where was it decreed that you have to like everything you do? After all, the task will not go on forever, particularly if you start now. If you tell yourself that it may be unpleasant, but so are many things that you easily survive, it will help you to persevere. If you remind yourself that there actually may be aspects to the task that could intrigue or benefit you, it can give you the wherewithal to get started.

For example, if you are avoiding beginning and/or completing a certain project at work or school, it is likely that you are thinking (on either a conscious or unconscious level) one or more of the following irrational and ridiculous thoughts: (1) that you will be totally miserable the whole time you are working on this task; (2) that you cannot possibly bear the torture of this duty; (3) that it is entirely unfair and sadistic for your boss or professor to foist such a terrible assignment upon you; (4) that you cannot possibly enjoy any part of this project; (5) that you are destined to fail horribly at this task; or (6) that if you rebel you will get a hero's acclaim down the road. In place of these self sabotaging statements you can choose to substitute the following: (1) that you can choose not to be miserable; (2) that you certainly won't die from working on this task so of course you can stand it (no doubt you have endured much worse); (3) your boss or professor's goal is not to ruin your life; (4) perhaps some aspect of the work could prove reasonably interesting; (5) there is no guarantee that you will fail, and it is not the end of the world if you don't succeed in everything; and (6) the one you hurt the most by delaying is yourself.

Many people believe that if they wait until they feel more like doing the avoided task, they will be able to finally get moving. Actually, the reverse is more often true and certainly more effective because if you wait around for your feelings to change, you could wait forever. But if you change your behavior, your feelings will change to match your new actions. This reflects the important psychological tenet: *attitude change follows behavior change*. When you behave differently you tend to feel differently, as emotions tend to shift to fall in line with your actions. Therefore, acting in a timely, efficient, and productive manner, even when you don't feel like it, helps to create the motivation to continue working and can lead to increased task enjoyment. At the very least you can enjoy the fact that you have finished the task and it no longer hangs over you.

Some people delay because of a misguided belief that they work best under pressure, that they even need that rush of a last minute deadline to get started. Some even believe that it is only through procrastination that one can finally get enough adrenalin pumping to have a true "flow experience." If you are someone who believes that you do your best work under pressure, then we hate to burst your bubble, but there is quite a bit of evidence to the contrary. According to Lee (2005), as cited in Gura (2008), procrastination does not facilitate flow. Lee surveyed 262 students and found that procrastinators tended to have less, not more, flow experiences.

4.6.2 Six Steps to Overcoming Procrastination

The following six steps provide tried and true, research-based approaches for enabling you to overcome your tendency to procrastinate ranging from how to get yourself over the hump to begin (often the hardest part), how to sustain your progress when stymied and how to ensure you will finish.

THE BITS AND PIECES APPROACH One of the best antidotes to procrastination is to break tasks or projects down into doable chunks. Are you prone to letting tasks pile up until you feel overwhelmed? You might feel as though you need to accomplish an entire task all at once, and this can become an overwhelming undertaking. Giving yourself permission to do just one small piece can get you started and provide the necessary momentum for completion of the whole project over time. By using the bits and pieces approach you can whittle down unfinished tasks and finish parts of projects, and eventually the entire project. Once you start a small part of a task and get into the swing of it, you might discover that you feel like finishing the whole thing, especially if it goes faster or smoother than you had anticipated. Or you can use your energy to switch over to another avoided task which may prove to be easier once you have built up positive momentum from the former, especially if the tasks are related.

Peter Gollwitzer (1999) encourages procrastinators to create what he terms implementation plans, which involve approaching complicated tasks by converting doable chunks into short term goals. For example, when revising this chapter for a recent edition of this text, the author devised a set of sequential goals with each representing a doable chunk or step. The goals were as follows: (1) conduct an internet search to find new research and applications; (2) review the chapter and decide what to delete; (3) rewrite the beginning of the chapter based on a new theoretical approach; (4) add relevant new research, techniques and theory; and (5) proof read the chapter. Each step took several hours.

Gollwitzer recommends using an implementation plan to get started because such a plan tells you when, where and how to start by linking a specific situation to a specific response, such as, "When situation x arises, I will perform response y." Gollwitzer and Veronica Brandstatter (1997) asked college students to identify two projects they hoped to complete during their holiday break, an easy one and a complicated one. With regard to the difficult projects, two thirds of those who formulated implementation plans had finished their projects. Almost all of those who did not make plans did not finish their projects. The presence of a plan for the easy projects was not related to task completion. Thus, such plans are especially useful for difficult or complicated tasks, especially if you tend to procrastinate. Owens and colleagues (2008), as cited in Gura (2008), demonstrated that procrastinators at Hofstra University who formed implementations plans were eight times more likely to follow through than subjects who had not formed such a plan.

GETTING ORGANIZED   Lack of organization contributes to procrastination, for when you approach your work in a disorganized fashion, tasks feel more overwhelming and generally take longer to accomplish. Follow the suggestions from earlier in the chapter regarding:

   a. *Make a To-Do list.*

   b. *Create a realistic schedule.*

Smart scheduling can also thwart procrastination. Dan Ariely (2008) in his book *Predictably Irrational* recounted an instance where, when teaching at MIT, he asked students in an education class to set their own deadlines for three papers due that semester. Ariely set penalties for papers turned in after the self-imposed deadlines. Despite the penalties, 70% of the students chose to set their deadlines spaced out over the semester rather than clustering all the due dates at the end. In other words, they chose not to procrastinate. Those who chose to space out the deadlines performed better in the class, on average, than the students who left all their work for the end of the semester. According to Ariely, by imposing the staggered deadlines those students became better performers.

c. *Do it when you think of it.*

d. *Modify your work environment.*

Your work environment can be conducive to getting down to business or it can promote procrastination depending on how you arrange your work space. Remove as many distractions as possible from your work sphere. Take an hour to clean up your desk or work space. Throw out all unnecessary papers or paraphernalia.

e. *Block off escape routes.*

Put your cell phone on silent, close your door, turn off the TV, pull down your window shades. Arrange your work station so you have all the materials you need to get started. That way you avoid getting up, and possibly getting distracted, to get various items.

THE FIVE-MINUTE METHOD   You can use this technique to start a wave of positive momentum. Pick that task or project that you have been delaying starting and agree to start and work on it for just five minutes. At the end of this time period you can stop or you can ask yourself whether you are willing to invest another five minutes. Do this as a non-demand procedure and follow your sincere inclinations. You do not have to work beyond the first interval, but if you are like most people, once you have gotten past the first five minutes you will probably find that you can easily continue, as getting started is often the hardest part. So you can work for another five minutes, and perhaps another, and before long you are working steadily. Many people find that once they get started it is far less onerous or aversive than anticipated. Once a significant amount has been done, the drive for completion kicks in as you want to get the task finished and behind you. Likewise, when you complete one task it is often easier to switch over to other long postponed activities (particularly if related to the first task) due to the build up of positive momentum.

Timothy Pychyl (2000) advises procrastinators to "just get started." He explains that the anticipation of the task typically is far worse than the actual task itself. To demonstrate this fact, he gave 45 students pagers and checked in with his subjects 40 times over the course of five days to inquire about their moods and how often they were putting off a task that had a deadline associated with it. He found that when his subjects actually got down to doing the task that they had been avoiding, their perceptions of the task changed significantly. Frequently they reported that they actually enjoyed working on the task.

DON'T WAIT FOR INSPIRATION

Genius is 1% inspiration and 99% perspiration.

Thomas Edison

People who procrastinate when faced with a creative endeavor often delay, waiting for that moment of "inspiration" to overtake them before they begin.

Oftentimes the best strategy is just to begin and allow motivation to build later. Instead of putting off your project, use probability theory to help you begin. When you begin a project, with or without any particular inspiration, you stand a good chance of perhaps stumbling into a streak of spontaneous brilliance and producing extremely good work. Or at the very least, you increase your chances of getting good ideas for that task or future projects. The more you produce, the greater the probability that some of it will be very good.

But what if your work or creation fails to live up to your high standards? It is perfectly okay if some of what you turn out is not very good. Do you really think that every canvas turned out by Picasso was ready to hang in the Louvre? And do you honestly believe that Mozart never wrote a sour note, or that your favorite author hasn't deleted or revised file after file? As consumers or admirers of artwork or books we see only the finished products which usually have been refined countless times. Successful artists, musicians, and writers thrive by giving themselves permission to make mistakes and produce a certain amount of garbage in the process of doing good work. Remember that you need to put in your 10,000 hours. Playing the probabilities also gives you the opportunity to hone your skills through experience from practice. If your work requires creative projects, or if you are an artist, musician or writer who is not currently inspired, forcing yourself to work at the very least will improve your level of craftsmanship. So, when inspiration does come you will be far better prepared to perform.

REWARD YOURSELF   All human behavior is motivated by reward or by the expectation of reward in the future. A reward is anything that feels good, be it money, praise, awards, a new car, a vacation, or a back rub. Humans can often sustain unrewarded behaviors for long periods of time as long as there is some hope for reward down the line. Procrastination persists because it is reinforced by the immediate reward of relief from task avoidance. Tasks that you dread and delay may often have rewards associated with them, but typically they are in the future or you need to wade through discomfort first to get those rewards. Even though procrastination carries with it many long term punishments, the short term rewards motivate you to keep delaying. To counterbalance the rewarding aspects of procrastination, it is also important to find ways to make the "dreaded task" rewarding in the short run.

One reward strategy involves utilizing the **Premack Principle**, postulated by David Premack (1959). This principle states that if two behaviors differ in their likelihood of occurrence, the less likely behavior can be reinforced by using the more likely behavior as a reward. In layman's terms, this capitalizes on the fact that any enjoyable activity can be used as a reward or incentive for working on a task you tend to put off. Here you give yourself permission to engage in rewarding activities contingent upon doing the tasks you tend to put off. For example, you could record a favorite TV show or movie and indulge in watching it after a concentrated period of effort.

Sometimes we procrastinate because a task appears boring and/or meaningless. Household chores often fall within this category. However, when your sink is full of dishes or you run out of clean clothes to wear, your quality of life suffers. A useful strategy to motivate yourself to complete tedious chores involves using reframing to create a cognitive reward for yourself, enabling you to upgrade your view of yourself. That is, link that mundane task to another more general attribute that is important to you, such as being responsible, conscientious, considerate, or well groomed.

VIEWING MISTAKES AS FEEDBACK   Perhaps you procrastinate for fear of making a mistake or doing something poorly. However, it is quite irrational to think that leaving yourself even less time to complete something will make you less likely to make mistakes. And where is it written that it is catastrophic or even necessarily bad to make a mistake? Mistakes are feedback, nothing more and nothing less. Both forms of feedback, correct and incorrect, are equally vital for the learning process. Without both we learn more slowly.

Research reveals a strong link between procrastination and perfectionism (Flett, Blankstein, Hewitt & Koledin, 1992). Perfectionism goes hand in hand with fear of failure. If you maintain a perfectionistic attitude you will be more prone to stall until you can do it right, or you avoid doing it because you fear that you can never do it right. So what if you do it and part of it is wrong? Is the world going to come to an end? If you delay, that is the equivalent of doing it wrong anyhow. At least, if you go ahead and complete it, you stand a chance of getting part or all of it right. Striving for excellence is not the same as holding out for perfection.

You cannot achieve excellence without making mistakes along the way or risking making other errors. In short, making mistakes is an essential part of improving yourself. What is necessary is to adopt a healthy attitude about being in error. It means learning to laugh at yourself and not take yourself so seriously all the time. The vast majority of errors are harmless and ultimately can be humorous or neutral if reframed to the proper perspective. Think about the life stories of great men and women. Almost invariably, they are stories of failures that were converted into learning experiences which then led to success. For example, were you aware that Abraham Lincoln lost eight elections, failed in business, went bankrupt and suffered a nervous breakdown before he was elected president? There was a guy who didn't let failure get in the way of his success. His numerous failures built his character and made for a fascinating life story.

Questions

1. The main cause of procrastination is _____.

   A. depression

   B. self-control

   C. low frustration tolerance

   D. grit

2. All of the following strategies are helpful for overcoming procrastination except _____.

    A. Covey's Time Management Matrix

    B. the bits and pieces approach

    C. the five-minute method

    D. getting organized

3. What will help you get started if you tend to procrastinate?

    A. Wait for inspiration.

    B. Criticize yourself for mistakes.

    C. Hold out for perfection.

    D. Use the five-minute method.

4.7 The Effective Student

Recall tips for improving academic effectiveness.

The fact that you are reading this book and/or taking this course indicates that you are a student—if not in school per se, than at least a student of your own life, interested in learning how to function more effectively. Whether you are a full time or a part time student, whether you are fresh from high school or returning to college after years in the workplace, it pays to master the techniques and strategies that can enable you to achieve academic success. The ability to manage your time wisely and stay on task will serve you well in this context. A comprehensive review or an in–depth exploration of the myriad ways to develop and improve your study habits is certainly beyond the scope of this text, but in the pages that follow we will offer you a sampling of tips that we have found to be the most crucial for promoting academic effectiveness. These tips fall into three broad categories: (1) improving your memory; (2) mastering a good study method; and (3) learning test-taking strategies, including overcoming **test anxiety** and developing test-taking sophistication.

4.7.1 Improving Memory Retention

While there are many gimmicks and so-called herbal panaceas for supercharging your memory, the fact remains that you first have to learn something, and often learn it well, before you can expect to remember it. There are no magic substitutes or reliable short cuts for the memory enhancement steps outlined below, but if you follow these strategies, we guarantee significant improvement in your retention skills.

1. **Pay attention.** If you are not paying adequate attention, information will never be properly encoded and thus never transferred into either your working memory or long term memory. This is why popular sleep learning

products rarely work, such as tapes to learn a foreign language while you sleep. It's likely that you can remember a time when you went to class but were so distracted or preoccupied with other matters that you were clueless as to what was presented. Just showing up is not enough.

2. **Organize the material.** Create an organizational structure that makes sense to you. One way to do this is to rewrite your lecture notes in outline form while it is still relatively fresh in your mind, or outline a chapter in your textbook. To the extent that you can make information meaningful to you by relating it to other concepts or experiences with which you are familiar, it will be much easier to remember. This occurs because it promotes the kinds of associations which facilitate memory retrieval.

3. **Use rehearsal.** Contrary to popular belief, over-learning aids in retention because repetition is the key to memory. *Repeat to remember and remember to repeat* is a useful mantra for studying (Medina, 2008). Brain pathways that ultimately establish long-term memories are created through the repetition of the material you are attempting to learn. Review of material works best within ninety minutes of its initial presentation. Quite literally, new connections beginning to sprout from neurons in your brain begin to retract if not stimulated within this short time period. (Medina, 2008). The more you rehearse new information, the stronger your ability to retrieve and recall it. But this does not mean that you should just reread the same material over and over; rather, what is more effective is to paraphrase the information by putting it in your own words, or even better, attempting to explain it to another person by making a connection to an event in your own life. This is known as **elaborative rehearsal**, which has been shown to really facilitate memory (Gardiner & colleagues, 1994).

4. **Minimize rote memorization.** The rote method, where you attempt to just memorize information without any organization, has only limited utility. As stated above, we tend to remember that which is meaningful to us, so rote memorization is only helpful if and when you create a meaningful structure and attempt to commit that to memory.

5. **Write it down.** Taking notes in class or writing about material you are attempting to learn, particularly if you paraphrase, is a powerful tool for transferring information into long term memory. This is also important for remembering day to day, practical information as discussed earlier in this chapter. That is why Things to Do lists, reminder lists, and appointment calendars are so helpful. Among researchers in the field of memory enhancement, these are the most frequently used memory aids.

6. **Use memory aids when appropriate.** These techniques, called **mnemonics**, are very helpful, particularly for remembering strings or lists of information. These systems work by making material more meaningful by adding a structure, such as making it into a song or rhyme, or linking it with other entrenched memories like the letters of the alphabet. A good example of a simple mnemonic is the made up, catchy word **PERMA,** which we use to help us remember the five domains of flourishing.

7. **Reduce interference and distractions.** One of the biggest factors causing you to forget is the role of interference. Competing information, both related and unrelated, that you learned before and after you study, can interfere with memory retrieval. When new learning interferes with previous learning, this is **retroactive interference**. When old learning inhibits retention of new material, this is **proactive interference**. Smart timing of studying can minimize interference factors. For example, studying just prior to going to sleep helps to prevent interference. Be careful not to study similar topics within the same study interval. Confusion between topics can lead to retroactive and/or proactive interference. Limit background distractions while studying, because this can also create interference and disrupt later recall. Save watching TV or listening to music for your study breaks, or for a reward for staying on task for a specified work period. There can be some individual variability, however, as some people concentrate better with some background noise or music.

8. **Sleep on it.** As mentioned above, going to sleep immediately after studying minimizes interference with new learning because you are limiting your mental activity after studying. There is also evidence that sleep allows for the consolidation of newly learned material.

9. **Distribute learning sessions.** Avoid cramming by spreading your study periods over spaced time intervals. Data indicates that two or three shorter study periods interspersed with breaks are usually more effective than one long, unbroken, exhausting study session. When studying more than one subject, be sure to take breaks between subjects so as to reduce the potential for both retroactive and proactive interference effects. To further inhibit interference, make sure that you engage in activities unrelated to your studying during your breaks. Kick back and have some fun! But if you must study several subjects in one day, try to vary the topics as much as possible, again to decrease the potential for interference. Retroactive and proactive interference are more likely to develop in the middle of a long study session. By taking breaks you restrict that middle ground which breeds interference effects.

10. **Exercise.** Research appears to indicate that physical exercise facilitates memory in humans as well as animals (Samorajski, Delaney, Durham, Ordy, Johnson & Dunlop, 1988). The reasons for this are still unclear, but researchers believe that increased levels of oxygen and brain nutrients stimulated by exercise are responsible for the boost in memory acuity. *What is good for your heart is good for your brain!*

11. **Test yourself.** Periodically obtain self-feedback about what you have and have not retained by testing yourself. There are numerous ways to do this, including end of chapter questions, practice exams, listing the important points you have learned from memory, and crosschecking this with your notes. Keep in mind that just because you felt that you understood the material presented in class or in your textbook, this does not guarantee that you will remember it the next day without practicing the steps outlined above.

12. **Be aware of the influence of learning contexts.** It helps with information retrieval if you can learn the material in a situation similar to the one requiring recall of that same information. This applies to the physical environment in which you are learning, such as the room, the seating arrangement, or the lighting, as well as to your emotional state. In other words, if you study in the library, and it is very similar to your classroom, then it is easier to remember. And did you know that interference can be reduced just by studying two different subjects in two different rooms (Higbee, 1988)? One of the authors has noticed that students who choose to sit in the same seat in their classrooms perform better academically.

4.7.2 An Effective Study Method – The SQ4R

There is a particular study strategy that we recommend for approaching this textbook. Actually, we advocate that you use this method for studying in general. Many educators laud a study system known by the acronym of the **SQ4R** (Robinson, 1970). If you use this technique for studying any textbook or course, you will find that it will greatly enhance your understanding and retention of course material. The SQ4R method consists of the following:

- **Survey:** Before beginning the book, thoroughly survey the Table of Contents to get the big picture of what is covered. Then before reading each chapter, look over the chapter headings, tables and graphs to get an overview of the information covered in that particular section.

- **Question:** Before reading each chapter in full, turn the headings and sub-headings into questions.

- **Read:** Carefully read the chapter and find answers to the questions that you previously created based on the headings.

- **Recite:** Paraphrase what you have learned. To reiterate, putting material into your own words greatly enhances your ability to understand and retain information. One helpful hint for doing this is to explain the material to yourself as if you were attempting to explain it to a friend or younger sibling.

- **Review:** After each chapter, go over the material carefully, including answering the end of chapter questions and making sure you know the definitions to all key terms.

- **Reflect:** Think about what you just read and imagine how you can connect it to your life. How is this material relevant for you? This is called **deep processing**.

4.7.3 The Art of Taking Tests

In your role as a student you are inevitably faced with the onerous task of taking tests, often multiple exams in each course you take. Unlike in high school, in college your test scores may determine most if not all of your grades in many classes. One of the most frequent student complaints centers around an inability to do well on tests despite adequate preparation. Meanwhile, other students breeze through tests, getting high grades with minimal preparation. Is this just a function of the *survival of the smartest?* No, not at all. Psychologists have long recognized that certain students possess a set of skills along with an emotional equilibrium that contributes to passing and doing well on tests. Of course, adequate preparation lays the solid foundation, but test-taking skills can confer an added edge. These test-taking skills fall into two main categories.

MASTERING TEST ANXIETY   Upcoming in Chapter 5 you will learn about the Yerkes-Dodson law, the fact that you are more likely to perform well when you are moderately aroused. In test-taking terms this means that having some anxiety before an exam is actually a good thing, because it heightens your mental alertness and acuity. But very high anxiety levels can interfere with performance, particularly on difficult tasks such as a hard or confusing exam (for many people this means math!). Have you ever failed or done poorly on a test for which you thought that you were well prepared? Have you ever been so anxious about a test that you totally blanked out, unable to think straight or recall information you knew well just hours before? If you suspect that test anxiety is a problem for you, fill out the following brief self test to check this out.

Measuring Test Anxiety

Read the following statements and rate how they apply to you, using the following scale.
0 = Never   1 = Sometimes   2 = Often   3 = Always

_____1. I do not feel that I study properly for tests.

_____2. I typically begin to feel nervous several days before a test.

_____3. My nervousness increases on the day of the test.

_____4. I believe that I will do poorly on tests.

_____5. If I do not know an answer, I begin to panic.

_____6. I get confused when taking rests.

_____7. Even if I have prepared adequately, I feel unsure of my answers.

_____8. I forget information that I have studied.

_____9. While I'm taking a test, I tell myself that I do not know the answers.

_____ **Your Score**

Interpretation:
A score of 12 or higher indicates you suffer from test anxiety. The higher your score beyond 12, the more debilitating your test anxiety will be. If all or even most of these statements frequently apply to you, pay particular attention to and follow the guidelines in the next section.

If your test anxiety level is high, there are a variety of techniques that can enable you to reduce your anxiety prior to and during test-taking. *Remember, the goal here is not to be completely cool, calm and collected, but to get your anxiety down to that moderate, manageable level which will enhance your performance.*

Practice Active Relaxation – In Chapter 6 we will introduce you to a variety of relaxation techniques that can be used in this context. To help calm yourself, engage in diaphragmatic breathing at least six to ten times prior to the test and use it during the test if you need to relax yourself. Put your emphasis on a slow exhalation as that is vital for quick relaxation. To further help yourself unwind, do a quick Progressive Muscle Relaxation sequence just prior to your exam. You needn't go through the whole sequence if pressed for time or not in a setting conducive to the technique. Just focus on tensing and relaxing the muscles in your shoulders, neck and head.

Use Cognitive Restructuring – Following the instructions for cognitive restructuring, identify your irrational thoughts and fears regarding the test. Challenge your assumptions about failure and humiliation. Substitute rational, reassuring messages reminding yourself of past test-taking successes, and about how well prepared you will be (based on heeding the study tips in the last few pages, of course!).

Visualize Success – Using the teachings on visualization in Chapter 8 as your guide, first vividly imagine yourself in a relaxing scene. Pick a scene that you typically associate with calmness and tranquility and put yourself there in your mind's eye. Once you are feeling mellow, then fantasize that you are about to start the test. Imagine yourself remaining tranquil, reading each exam question thoroughly and calmly, recognizing that you do know the right answer, and then envisage yourself getting fully absorbed with putting down your answers. Allow yourself to recall previous times of test-taking success. Clearly remember those scenes and that sense of flowing with the exam. Visualizations of this type will boost your self-confidence and help you to relax during the test. Remember that being able to vividly imagine a realistic scene makes it far more likely that you can realize that goal.

TESTWISENESS   Developing **testwiseness**, which is also called test sophistication, involves learning strategies for guessing that can help increase the likelihood of picking the right answer, particularly on multiple choice exams. Many studies have demonstrated that these methods can be learned and that utilizing them improves test performance (McClain, 1987). McClain's work also revealed that A students often try to come up with the correct answer prior to reading the answer alternatives and high test scorers as a rule carefully read and consider each test question and answer alternative. But being testwise is much more than just using tricks to improve guesswork. It involves:

- Using your time during exams wisely
- Mastering strategies to minimize your errors

- Applying deductive reasoning by proceeding from the general to the specific
- Recognizing clues inherent in the tests which point to the right answers

We must stress, however, that *learning these strategies is not a substitute for studying.* Don't fool yourself into thinking that you can go into a test totally unprepared, armed only with this system, and walk out with a good grade. These strategies can enhance your performance to elevate a C performance to a B, or a B to an A, but no amount of cleverness in test-taking can replace studying and learning the subject matter.

Testwiseness involves recognizing that many multiple choice tests have built-in flaws within the questions that can help you determine or deduce the right answer, or at the very least, help you eliminate certain alternatives. The common flaws are as follows:

1. Information in earlier or later questions can reveal the right answer. If you are stumped, skip a question for the time being because information that turns up in later questions may hold the key or clues to the correct answer.

2. Alternatives that are highly implausible or improbable are likely to be incorrect and should be rejected. Options that contain flippant or overly judgmental words or phrases often fall into this category.

3. If two answers are equivalent or basically the same then neither can be correct, and both can be eliminated. On the flip side, if two answers are contradictory, then one is likely to be the correct option.

4. Correct answers are likely to be more detailed, longer and specific. When in doubt, pick the most detailed option.

5. Beware of all-inclusive words. Incorrect answers are far more likely to include words such as always, never, every time, everyone, etc. Alternative words such as sometimes, some, or may are more likely to appear in correct answers.

6. Look for the greatest similarity in terminology between the question and the answers. The answer most similar to the question is more likely to be correct.

7. Be aware of grammatical inconsistencies between questions and answers like changes in verb tense or singular to plural nouns. Exclude answers which contain such inconsistencies and pick the options which match grammatically.

8. When questions have answer alternatives that include dates or numbers that are ordered, avoid picking the first or the last. The correct answer is usually somewhere in the middle rather than at the extremes.

9. Don't be afraid to change your answer. A myth has been perpetrated that your first guess has the greatest chance of being right. This is not necessarily the case. Several studies have demonstrated that regarding answer changes during tests, wrong to right changes outnumber right to wrong changes (Benjamin, Cavell & Shallenberger, 1987).

Questions

1. _____ refers to approaching test questions in a way that facilitates picking the right answer.
   A. Cheating
   B. Testwiseness
   C. Efficiency
   D. Elaborate rehearsal

2. When new learning inhibits previous learning, this is referred to as _____.
   A. elaborate rehearsal
   B. rote memorization
   C. retroactive interference
   D. proactive interference

3. Which of the following methods for studying and retention should you avoid?
   A. the SQ4R
   B. distributed learning sessions
   C. elaborative rehearsal
   D. rote memorization

Summary

Accomplishment is one of the important components of flourishing, represented by the A in PERMA. The key to accomplishment involves your willingness to put in the necessary effort to develop the skills required for success in any endeavor. The harder the task and the lower your skill level, the more effort you need to put forth. True mastery in an area requires at least 10,000 hours of regular practice. The ability to sustain such effort is directly tied to your character – to a variety of signature strengths. Positive psychologists have identified seven key signature strengths that promote achievement with **self-control** as the most important for facilitating accomplishment. Exceptional accomplishment is possible if you develop **Grit** – the combination of both extraordinary perseverance and passion. In general, your ability to succeed and accomplish your goals is enhanced when you can maintain your motivation, wisely set priorities, manage yourself effectively in time, and overcome temptations to procrastinate. Self-control is vital for all of these.

In order to achieve you must have both **motivation** and **volition**. Strategies for enhancing both were covered in this chapter including MCII and SWOOP. A variety of suggestions for managing yourself wisely in time were covered along with an in-depth review of Covey's Time Management Matrix for how to organize your schedule around your priorities, taking into consideration the urgency and importance of various tasks. The causes of **procrastination**, one of the most common obstacles to achievement, were explored and various strategies for overcoming this were presented.

The last section of this chapter dealt with how to become an effective student. Academic achievement is enhanced by learning proven strategies for effective studying and retention, along with developing test taking skills. Ultimately, managing yourself wisely for accomplishment is about making choices for your life. Effective individuals are adept at balancing – knowing when to be organized, productive, and efficient, and when to rest and have fun.

Positive Psychology Exercises

1. Pick two or three of the myriad suggestions for managing yourself in time that appeal the most to you, or are the most relevant for your particular situation. Commit to experiment with using them for a two week period. Pay careful attention to the effects in your life.

2. If you have never experimented with using the SQ4R study method, try using it to prepare for next upcoming exam and evaluate whether it was useful for you.

Key Terms

Accomplishment	Mnemonics	Self-control
Deep Processing	Motivation	SQ4R
Defer Gratification	Pareto Principle (80/20 Rule)	SWOOP
Elaborative Rehearsal	Power Nap	Test Anxiety
Executive Functions	Premack Principle	Testwiseness
Grit	Proactive Interference	Volition
Information Overload	Procrastination	
Low Frustration Tolerance	Retroactive Interference	

Shared Writing

What obstacles to accomplishment are you aware of operating in your own life? Do you have issues with motivation, volition, or both? After you identify your personal challenge, which of the various suggestions, tips, and methods presented in this chapter do you think would be most helpful for you? Write about your thoughts on this matter.

Chapter 4 Questions

1. Self-control involves the ability to
   _____.

   a. successfully use denial and repression

   b. master motivational strategies

   c. defer gratification

   d. utilize your EQ

2. GRIT = _____ + _____

   a. motivation; volition

   b. IQ; EQ

   c. passion; procrastination

   d. passion; perseverance

3. Never underestimate the value of
   _____ for achievement.

   a. practice

   b. luck

   c. procrastination

   d. perfectionism

4. _____ strategies are useful for
   enhancing motivation.

   a. Organizing

   b. Studying

   c. Self-control

   d. Visualization

5. Setting a limit on _____ facilitates
   decision making.

   a. information overload

   b. TV time

   c. Facebook

   d. homework

6. The Pareto Principle teaches that _____ of the
   benefit comes from doing _____ of the work.

   a. 20%; 80%

   b. 80%; 20%

   c. 50%; 50%

   d. 95%; 5%

7. Quadrant II (QII) activities are _____.

   a. urgent and important

   b. non-urgent but important

   c. urgent but not important

   d. neither urgent nor important

8. Quadrant IV (QIV) activities are _____.

   a. urgent and important

   b. non-urgent but important

   c. urgent but not important

   d. neither urgent nor important

9. Which of the following is recommended to
   facilitate studying and retention?

   a. long, unbroken study sessions

   b. rote memorization

   c. utilize the SQ4R

   d. pulling an all-nighter before a test as
      sleeping leads to forgetting the material

10. True mastery in an area typically requires
    _____.

    a. at least 10,000 hours of practice

    b. at least 12,000 hours of practice

    c. at least 15,000 hours of practice

    d. at least 20,000 hours of practice

Chapter 5
Understanding Stress

Learning Objectives

After reading this chapter, you should be able to:

5.1 Differentiate between positive and negative stress.

5.2 Understand the connections between stress and illness.

5.3 Describe the effects of stress on physical, psychological, and occupational functioning.

5.4 Recognize the causes and effects of the body's fight or flight response.

5.5 Understand the role of the placebo effect in stress and illness.

5.6 Describe how the connection between the mind and body can affect the immune system and healing.

Effective individuals have learned how to become *masters* over **stress**. Mastering stress is an essential element in maintaining a healthy lifestyle, which is fundamental to wellness. The study of factors that contribute to high level wellness comprises an important aspect of positive psychology. This chapter and the next will prepare you to master the stress in your life by first giving you a thorough understanding of how stress affects you, and then teaching you a variety of strategies and techniques for modifying your thinking and your physiology in ways that will allow you to develop resistance to and mastery over stress. The following chapter will also explore the concept of wellness in a more comprehensive fashion.

5.1 The Definition of Stress

Differentiate between positive and negative stress.

What is stress? When we ask students, employees, and employers this question, they typically respond that it is tension, nervousness, headaches, having deadlines to meet, etc. Basically what we hear is a list outlining the effects of stress or specific causes of stress. The official definition of stress is that *stress is anything that requires an adaptive response on the part of the organism*. But what does that mean? It means that anything that requires you to respond, to make a change or an adjustment, is stressful. So, when people say they want to get rid of stress, the reality is that this is impossible. That is not to say that you cannot reduce the amount of change or responsibilities you have in your life. Indeed, this is at times recommended as a way of minimizing your stress level. But we want you to understand that even if you went and hid out on a mountaintop in order to escape the rat race, you would probably eventually get bored and boredom itself is stressful. See, the fact is, *stress is an inescapable part of modern life.*

That is not necessarily as bad as it may sound. One of the best-known experts on stress, a Canadian scientist by the name of Hans Selye, was quoted as saying that "stress is the spice of life." Just as spice can make your food tasteful and come alive, stress can give your life meaning and excitement. This depends, of course, on the amount and type of spice you use. We all know that the wrong spice, or too much spice, can make you sick to your stomach. Selye (1956) differentiates between these two types of stress, referring to positive stress as **"Eustress"** and negative stress as **"Distress."** So stress is not all bad. We all need an optimal level of change and stress in our lives to keep things interesting. And that level varies from person to person.

Given the pejorative connotations given to stress, it is easy to forget that an appropriate level of stress in your life is often helpful. Stress can help motivate you to perform and meet the challenges you will face. The physiological and psychological aspects of the arousal produced by stress can be useful, and unless you are routinely overloaded and aroused, stress may not necessarily harm you (Kobasa, 1982). It may surprise you to find out that you need an optimal level of stress and arousal in order to perform at your best. This fact was established many years ago by pioneering psychologists Yerkes and Dodson (1908), who demonstrated that performance on a given task improves as physiological arousal increases until some optimal point, after which performance declines as arousal continues to climb. This optimal level of arousal varies with the type of task. The more complex the task for an individual, the less arousal can be tolerated before performance suffers. In layman's terms, when you are totally cool, calm and collected in a performance situation, you may not have the required motivation or edge necessary to perform at your best. If, on the other hand, you are panic-stricken or you are a nervous wreck, your high arousal level will interfere with your performance. *Many tasks are best performed with moderate levels of arousal.* This relationship is known as the Yerkes-Dodson Law. This is useful to remember next time you have to speak before a class or group or are in any type of performance situation. There is a misconception that you should be "super cool." This is not necessarily true, for you will actually perform better if you are moderately aroused—that is, stressed. What does this have to do with **stress mastery**? If you are under-aroused you will experience the stress of boredom. If you are over-aroused you will experience anxiety. If you can find your optimal level where you are stimulated and performing at your best, you can experience satisfaction and master stress. This is best illustrated in the following graph which demonstrates peak performance under conditions of moderate arousal.

Figure 5.1

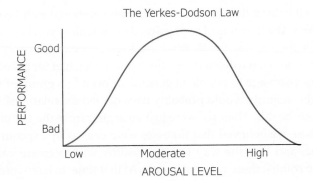

The Yerkes-Dodson Law

Questions

1. _____ is anything that requires an adaptive response on the part of an organism.

   A. Arousal

   B. Boredom

   C. Stress

   D. Eustress

2. The Yerkes-Dodson law demonstrates that many tasks are best performed with _____ levels of arousal.

   A. moderate

   B. low

   C. high

   D. subatomic

3. Stress is _____.

    A. an avoidable part of modern life

    B. an inescapable part of modern life

    C. anything that requires a maladaptive response

    D. always damaging to you

5.2 Stress and Illness

Understand the connections between stress and illness.

Do you believe that stress can make you sick? If you are like most people, you would answer with a resounding "YES!" When we ask people this question in our classes, all believe that stress can affect their emotional well-being, and the majority realize that it can lead to physical illness. Unless you have been living off-planet for the last few years, you have had some exposure to the fact that stress can and does have deleterious effects. However, had we asked this question just fifty years ago to people in general, or even to a group of health professionals, the majority would probably have denied the relationship between stress and our health. Then we were just emerging from the era of infectious diseases where we believed that illnesses were caused by exposure to germs and bacteria, and that the way to keep healthy was to create vaccines and medicines to combat these external agents. At that time, to have considered the notion that stress could lead to illness would have been *avant garde* thinking.

Then Thomas Holmes, M.D., a professor at the University of Washington School of Medicine, began doing research on the effect of changes on our physical and emotional well being. Remember that change is stressful because it requires an adaptive response on our part. Together with Richard Rahe, Holmes developed a questionnaire measuring life changes and set out to study whether there was a relationship between the number, seriousness, and pervasiveness of changes and our frequency of illness (Holmes & Rahe, 1967). Using army personnel because they were a captive audience and their progress could be followed easily, they demonstrated that the questionnaire could help them predict with remarkable accuracy those soldiers who would get ill within the next two years and those who would remain healthy. We suggest that you complete and score the Holmes-Rahe Life Readjustment Scale to determine your own level of stress as measured by this inventory.

Life Readjustment Scale Part A

Instructions: Think back on each possible life event listed below and decide if it happened to you within the last year. If the event did happen, check the box next to it.

	Check here if event happened to you.	Mean Value (Use for scoring later)
1. A lot more or a lot less trouble with your boss.	___	___
2. A major change in sleeping habits (sleeping a lot more or less, or change of sleep habits).	___	___
3. A major change in eating habits (a lot more or a lot less food intake, or very different meal hours or surroundings).	___	___
4. A revision of personal habits (dress, manners, associations, etc.).	___	___
5. Major change in your social activities (clubs, dancing, movies, visiting, etc.).	___	___
6. A major change in your usual type and/or amount of recreation.	___	___
7. A major change in church activities (a lot more or less than usual).	___	___
8. A major change in number of family get-togethers.	___	___
9. A major change in financial state (for better or for worse).	___	___
10. In-law troubles.	___	___
11. A major change in the number of arguments with your spouse.	___	___
12. Sexual difficulties.	___	___

Life Readjustment Scale Part B

Instructions: In the space provided, indicate the number of times that each applicable event happened to you within the last two years.

	Number of times	×	Mean Value	Your Score
13. Major personal injury or illness.	___		___	___
14. Death of close family member (not spouse).	___		___	___
15. Death of a spouse.	___		___	___
16. Death of a close friend.	___		___	___
17. Gaining a new family member (through birth, adoption, oldster moving in, etc.).	___		___	___
18. Major change in the health or behavior of a family member.	___		___	___
19. Change in residence.	___		___	___
20. Detention in jail or other institution.	___		___	___
21. Minor violations of the law (traffic tickets, jaywalking, disturbing the peace, etc.).	___		___	___
22. Major business readjustment (merger, reorganization, bankruptcy, etc.).	___		___	___
23. Marriage.	___		___	___
24. Divorce.	___		___	___

(Continued)

	Number of times	×	Mean Value	Your Score
25. Marital separation from spouse.	___		___	___
26. Outstanding personal achievement.	___		___	___
27. Son or daughter leaving home (marriage, attending college, etc.).	___		___	___
28. Retirement from work.	___		___	___
29. Major change in working hours or conditions.	___		___	___
30. Major change in responsibilities at work (promotion, demotion, lateral transfer).	___		___	___
31. Being fired from work.	___		___	___
32. Major change in living conditions (building a new home, remodeling, deterioration of home or neighborhood).	___		___	___
33. Spouse beginning or ceasing work outside the home.	___		___	___
34. Taking on a mortgage greater than $25,000 (purchasing a home, business, etc.).	___		___	___
35. Taking on a mortgage or loan of less than $25,000 (making a large purchase).	___		___	___
36. Foreclosure on a mortgage or loan.	___		___	___
37. Vacation.	___		___	___
38. Changing to a new school.	___		___	___
39. Changing to a different line of work.	___		___	___
40. Beginning or ceasing formal schooling.	___		___	___
41. Marital reconciliation with mate.	___		___	___
42. Pregnancy.	___		___	___
YOUR TOTAL SCORE	___		___	___

Scoring

The "Mean values" for each life event are listed below. Write in the mean values for those events that happened to you. For items in Part B, multiply the mean value by the number of times an event happened, and enter the result in "Your Score." Add up the mean values in Part A and scores in Part B to get your total score.

Life Event	Mean Value	Life Event	Mean Value
1	23	22	39
2	16	23	50
3	15	24	73
4	24	25	65
5	19	26	28
6	18	27	29
7	19	28	45
8	15	29	20

Life Event	Mean Value	Life Event	Mean Value
9	38	30	29
10	29	31	47
11	35	32	25
12	39	33	26
13	53	34	31
14	63	35	17
15	100	36	30
16	37	37	13
17	39	38	20
18	44	39	36
19	20	40	26
20	63	41	45
21	11	42	40

Interpreting Your Results

The more change you have, the more likely you are to get sick. Of those people with a score of over 300 for the past year, almost 80% get sick in the near future; with a score of 200 to 299, about 50% get sick in the near future; and with a score of 150–199, only about 30% get sick. A score of less than 150 indicates that you have a low chance of getting ill. So the higher your score, the harder you should work to stay well. Stress can be cumulative. Events from two years ago may still affect you now. If you think this applies to you, repeat this test for the events of the preceding year and compare your scores.

While this questionnaire succeeds in establishing the relationship between life changes and illness, it fails to take into account individual differences in our abilities to cope with the changes and demands of our lives. We will address this point in greater detail in the next chapter.

Questions

1. The Life Readjustment Scale is based on research showing _____.

   A. the relationship between the frequency and severity of life changes and the likelihood of getting ill

   B. that our stress level will automatically increase as we get older

   C. that college students have the most stress

   D. that change is not stressful

2. Of those people with a score of over 300 on the Life Readjustment Scale, almost _____ got sick in the near future.

   A. 30%

   B. 50%

   C. 80%

   D. 10%

3. According to the Life Readjustment Scale, _____ is the life event with the highest mean value of stress.

   A. getting arrested

   B. retirement from work

   C. the death of a spouse

   D. taking on a mortgage

5.3 Negative Effects of Stress

Describe the effects of stress on physical, psychological, and occupational functioning.

So what are the negative effects of stress? What can happen when stress overloads your coping resources, when your skills are inadequate to deal with the demands placed on you by circumstances? *Stress negatively affects your physical, psychological and occupational functioning in a variety of ways.*

5.3.1 Physical Consequences

The relationship between stress and your health is not simple or straightforward. Stress will not automatically cause you to become physically ill. The impact of stress on your health is mediated by a variety of personality variables, as well as your genetic makeup and environment. But physically, it is clear that when you are under prolonged stress your immune system can be weakened, creating vulnerability to illness and bodily system breakdown. Chronic high levels of stress hormones, known as **glucocorticoids,** are known to weaken immune functioning (Brehm, 1998), leading to an increased susceptibility to diseases, including cancer and heart disease. Glucocorticoids are adrenal secretions associated with the primitive survival circuitry of the brain/body. They quickly turn cells into energy to mobilize the body to deal with danger, much like a desperate person might burn the furniture to keep from freezing in a frigid night. Cells of the hippocampus, the area in charge of memory and meaning, and those of the cardiovascular system are most vulnerable to the destructive effects of glucocorticoids. A recent meta-analysis (an analysis of multiple studies including over 18,900 subjects within 293 independent experiments) conducted by Segerstrom and Miller (2004) provided powerful confirmation of the fact that stress alters immunity. The major findings of this study were three-fold: (1) short term stress actually "revs up" the immune system in an adaptive way to prepare individuals to cope with injury or infection; (2) chronic or long term stress causes excessive wear and tear leading to eventual systemic break down; and (3) the immune systems of individuals who are older or already sick are more prone to stress-related damage. Furthermore, as illustrated by the list below, stress can create a wide assortment of psychosomatic problems in which the weakest link in your system of organs, muscles and glands is affected. For some individuals the heart is affected, for others the stomach or the pancreas; thus, some develop heart disease, others ulcers or diabetes.

- Approximately 75–90% of all visits to doctor's offices are for stress-related disorders.

- Since 2007 the American Psychological Association (APA) has conducted an annual "Stress in America" survey to draw attention to the physical and emotional ramifications of stress. The 2013 online survey included 1,950 participants. According to the survey results, 72% of Americans reported stress-related physical symptoms, with 37% enduring fatigue, 32% suffering from headaches, 24% reporting upset stomachs, 24% experiencing muscular tension, 17% noting stress-induced changes in appetite and 11% reporting lower libido (sexual energy). These percentages reflect a small decline from previous years, perhaps due to the improvement in the economy and concomitant decrease in financial stress. The 2013 survey indicated that 80% of respondents reported stress levels equal to or greater than in 2012, while 72% report that their stress level has stayed the same or increased over the last five years. The number of Americans in 2013 reporting extreme stress (20%), defined as an 8 or over on a 10 point scale, is only slightly lower than in previous years. Compare this with the 2016 survey where 31% of Americans claimed an increase in stress over the past year with 71% reporting at least one stress related symptom. This rose to 80% in early 2017 with 34% complaining of stress related headaches.

- The 2013 survey listed the following top causes of stress in order of magnitude: (1) job pressure; (2) financial issues; (3) health; (4) relationships; (5) poor nutrition; (6) media overload (a new genre of stressor); and (7) sleep deprivation. Since 2007, participants have consistently rated work and financial pressures as the biggest stressors. According to the same survey conducted in January 2017 (covering 2016), the top causes of stress (finances, work, and the economy) remained the same, but for the first time since the 2007 inception of this survey, a new and statistically significant increase in reported stress was noted due to the appearance of a brand new source of stress: the increasing concern about the results of the 2016 presidential election. More than half of Americans (57%) reported that the current overly polarized political environment poses a significant source of stress for them. Two thirds (66%) are very worried about the direction and future of our nation while 49% indicate that the election outcome has been a marked source of personal stress.

- There is an increased risk of cardiovascular diseases, such as heart disease and stroke, when individuals report high levels of job stress (Brydon, Magid, & Steptoe, 2006). In a study of 17,415 middle-aged American women, Slopen and colleagues (2010) found an 88% increased risk of heart attacks in women enduring high levels of workplace stress. Likewise, in a study of 12,116 females nurses in Denmark, Allsoe & colleagues (2010) found that high levels of workplace pressure led to a 40% increased risk of cardiovascular disease. This is further supported in a Swedish study of 7000 men (Rosengren & colleagues, 1990) where men who reported the highest levels of stress were 50% more likely to have a heart attack in the next eight years than men who were less stressed. On the other hand, losing a job more than doubled the risk of heart attacks in a 10 year study of middle aged U.S. workers (Gallo & colleagues, 2006).

- Most heart attacks occur around 9:00 a.m. on Monday mornings (Elliot, 2001).

- Hypertension (high blood pressure), a stress-related disorder, afflicts at least 35.7 million people in the U.S. (National Ambulatory Medical Care Survey, 2006), with some estimates going as high as 80 million. The stress hormone **cortisol**, unleashed by the adrenal glands in times of stress, is linked to increases in free fatty acids in the bloodstream, which contribute to the buildup of plaque in the lining of blood vessels and the subsequent narrowing of these pathways. These processes combine to produce hypertension, atherosclerosis and coronary heart disease.

- Cholesterol levels in the bloodstream rise during periods of stress (Mattiasson, Lindgarde, Nilsson, & Theorell, 1990).

- According to *The Crohn's Disease and Ulcerative Colitis Fact Book* (1983), chronic diarrhea (irritable bowel syndrome) may have a causal relationship to emotional factors and stress. This is not the case for inflammatory bowel disease.

- Ulcers, spastic colon and similar gastro-intestinal disorders are the direct result of elevated acidity brought on by the release of cortisol. These disorders are classified as **psychophysiological disorders**, illnesses that are triggered and exacerbated by stress. With any of these disorders the most severe symptoms often do not manifest until after the stressor has diminished or ended. Ulcers are a good example of this. Sapolsky (1994) noted that the stomach is more vulnerable to ulceration after a long period of stress is over.

- About 18% of women and 6% of men are stricken with migraine headaches. Estimates of the frequency of tension headaches in the American population vary from 30 to 80%. Stress is one of the many factors that trigger headaches of all types (Elkind, 2004).

- It has been estimated that 70 million visits a year to doctor's offices are due to pain complaints (Koch, 1986). Estimates of the number of adult Americans suffering from chronic pain are as high as one-fifth of the population (Joranson & Leitman, 1994). Negative emotions and stress can aggravate pain and cause acute pain to develop into chronic pain. The stress hormone ACTH can impede endorphin production. **Endorphins** are our body's natural painkillers. Inability to produce endorphins leads to increased pain and discomfort.

- Research indicates that stress even plays a significant role in the development of osteoporosis in women due to increased levels of stress hormones (Kumano, 2005).

- Psychological factors such as stress are clearly implicated as a factor in what is known as nocturnal **bruxism** or teeth grinding at night (Carvalho, Cury, & Garcia, 2008).

- Periods of elevated stress are "linked to the onset and worsening of rheumatoid arthritis" (Nakazawa, 2008). The hormone prolactin, released by the pituitary gland in response to stress, triggers joint swelling.

- A study by Deinzer and colleagues (2000) revealed that during college exam week students possess lower levels of salivary immunoglobulin, a defense against respiratory infections. This suppression of immune response was observed to last up to two weeks after the stressful period ended. In addition, students' acne worsens during times of high stress (Chiu, Chon, & Kimball, 2003).

- A study showed that people ranking high on a test of perceived stress were more likely to develop colds when intentionally infected with a virus (Cohen, Tyrell, & Smith, 1991). These same authors repeated this study in 1993 and replicated these findings.

- Most dentists report an association between stress and gum disease, known as gingivitis (Brehm, 1998).

- Although stress does not cause people to catch AIDS, research indicates that HIV+ men who experience stressful events, such as the loss of a partner, develop full blown AIDs quicker and decline faster (Bower & colleagues, 1998; Leserman & colleagues, 1999).

- It is unclear whether there is a link between stress and cancer. Stress does not create cancer; however, it may weaken the body's defenses against malignant cells (Antoni & Lutgendorf, 2007), thus increasing vulnerability to tumor growth. In a large Swedish study, individuals with a history of workplace stress developed colon cancer at a rate more than five times greater than that of their non-stressed peers, who were matched in terms of age, smoking and drinking patterns and physical characteristics (Courtney & colleagues, 1993). Steptoe & colleagues (2010) found people to be at an increased risk of cancer within a year following bereavement. However, other studies failed to demonstrate any link between stress and cancer in humans (Coyne & colleagues, 2010; Petticrew & colleagues, 1999 and 2002).

5.3.2 Psychological Consequences

It is not surprising that stress is also a key factor in the development of emotional difficulties and behavioral problems. Can you remember a time when you felt there were too many demands placed on you? What was that like for you? Did it affect your ability to relax and enjoy life? Stress clearly influences our psychological well-being in a host of different ways as elucidated below:

- Stress is a major factor in the development of anxiety, phobias, panic attacks, depression, post traumatic stress disorder, obsessions, compulsions and all major psychiatric disorders. The 2013 APA Stress in America survey found that 67% of the participants reported experiencing psychological symptoms related to stress. Thirty seven percent of the subjects reported anxiety and feeling overwhelmed, 41% had issues with anger or irritability, 36% had depressive symptoms, 30% admitted wanting to cry frequently and 37% experienced fatigue on a regular basis. Levels of anxiety and depression decreased slightly (to 33% and 32% respectively) according to the survey conducted in January 2017.

- According to the World Health Organization (WHO), depression, often a stress-related disorder, is the number one cause of disability worldwide. The most current statistics from WHO estimate at least 120 million people worldwide suffering from depression.

- It has been demonstrated that stress alters serotonin pathways. Imbalances in serotonin levels have been linked to depression and in some cases aggression. According to the APA, approximately 19 million American adults are afflicted with depression.

- The National Institute of Mental Health (NIMH) reports that 19 million American adults have anxiety disorders, including approximately 2.4 million manifesting panic disorder.

- According to the National Institute on Alcohol Abuse and Alcoholism, an estimated 14 million Americans are alcoholic. Relief of stress and anxiety is one of the primary motives for the use and abuse of alcohol. Repeated use for that purpose is viewed as an important factor in the development of habituation and addiction. Millions more use and/or abuse drugs, both illegal and prescription medications, to cope with stress. The 2007 APA survey found that 39% of the participants admitted to drinking and 19% to smoking cigarettes far more regularly during periods of high stress.

- Fifty-five percent of all marriages end in divorce. According to the APA survey, stress causes more than half of Americans (54%) to fight with people close to them. Twenty-five percent of survey participants reported that they became alienated from a friend or family member because of stress, and 8% cited stress as a major factor in a divorce or separation. Experts report that stress is a major contributing factor to relationship conflicts and the rising incidence of divorce. For example, in one longitudinal study (Kiecolt-Glaser and colleagues, 2002), couples who divorced after 10 years of marriage displayed 34% higher levels of stress hormones at the *beginning* of the study than those whose marriages remained intact.

- Chronic stress can create long term changes in the brain by decreasing the number of neurons that assist with information processing (Chetty & colleagues, 2014). Researchers have found a connection between the stress hormone cortisol and short term memory loss in older adults. The mechanism of action here is that cortisol reduced the synaptic connections in the prefrontal cortex which help us to store and recall information (Anderson and Radley, 2014).

- Current information technology has created a new and potent source of stress, namely that of data stress. This leads to information overload (IO) or infoxication which inhibits and can even paralyze decision making because of the overabundance of available information, particularly online (see Chapter 4 for tips on how to deal with information overload). More information has been created in the last decade than in the history of humankind, and we simply cannot handle all of it. Psychologist Daniel Levitian (2014) contrasts a trip to the grocery store in 1976 when there might have been approximately 9000 products from which to choose, compared to over 40,000 at the same store today. Although the average person needs at most 150 products at any one outing, we now have to wade through or ignore at least 39,850 things just to get what we need.

5.3.3 Consequences in the Workplace

At times of stress, how well can you concentrate on the task at hand? Do you find thoughts, preoccupations, and fears interfering with your ability to function? The ability to concentrate is significantly affected by stress. It is no wonder that an inability to cope with life stressors leads to lowered productivity and an increased frequency of mistakes on the job. In addition, you are more likely to miss work due to both emotional and physical illness. As the following list demonstrates, this leads to major financial losses for business, industry and employees.

- According to the 2013 Work Stress Survey conducted by the Harris Institute, 83% of American workers reported being stressed out at work, up from 73% in 2012. Common stressors included unreasonable workloads, low pay, fear of layoffs, lack of advancement opportunities, conflict with co-workers, long commutes and poor work/life balance. The pressure for constant availability in this wired age of email and smart phones came up as a big factor. The cause of work stress varied by earnings with low wage employees stressed out by financial concerns and highly paid workers burnt out by heavy workloads.

- People are more accident prone during periods of stress (Williams & colleagues, 1993). According to the American Institute of Stress (AIS) statistics, 60–80% of accidents on the job are stress-related. Industrial accidents account for 2 million disabling injuries per year, more than 15,000 deaths, and 3 billion dollars annually in lost productivity. Peterson (1984) reviewed research studies linking stress to work-related accidents and concluded that high stress levels are an important risk factor. Raymond & Moser (1995) implicated stress as a major risk factor in aviation accidents associated with pilot error. Murphy (1987) hypothesized a *stress-accident model* whereby stress symptoms such as anxiety have a detrimental effect on workers' capabilities, such as attention and reaction time, which leads to increased accident risk. That is, transient unsafe behaviors due to stress create disorganization and lead to more mistakes and accidents.

- As reported by AIS, according to a survey of 800,000 workers in over 300 companies, the number of employees calling in sick because of stress tripled from 1996 to 2000. An estimated 1 million workers are absent every day due to stress. Unanticipated absenteeism is estimated to cost American companies over $600 per worker/year with the price tag for large companies exceeding millions annually! AIS also cites a three year study concluded in 1997 which determined that 60% of employee absences could be traced to psychological problems stemming directly from job stress.

- According to AIS, the Integra Survey (2000) indicated that 19% of respondents had quit a previous position due to the demands of an overly stressful job.

- Stress is eroding the bottom line for business. According to AIS statistics, job stress is estimated to cost U.S. business over $300 billion annually as a result of accidents, absenteeism, employee turnover, diminished productivity, workers comp, insurance, medical and legal costs.

Questions

1. Stress hormones are known as _____.
   - A. endocrine glands
   - B. immunity boosters
   - C. glucocorticoids
   - D. endorphins

2. Ulcers are an example of a _____.
   - A. positive effect of stress
   - B. psychophysiological disorder
   - C. psychological disorder
   - D. genetic gastrointestinal condition

3. Approximately _____ of all visits to doctors' offices are for stress-related disorders.

    A. 100%

    B. 75–90%

    C. 25%

    D. 0%

5.4 The Physiology of Stress

Recognize the causes and effects of the body's fight or flight response.

There is more than sufficient data demonstrating that stress can lead to physical, emotional and behavioral maladjustments. But how does this happen? How is it that changes in our lives lead to ill health? The answer lies in a physiological mechanism known as the **"Fight or Flight response."** The fight or flight response is a survival mechanism present in humans and most animals which prepares us to deal with physical danger. When faced with threat, two almond-shaped structures in our brain called the amygdala, which play a primary role in the processing and memory of emotional reactions, are activated. They send messages to the HPA axis (hypothalamus-pituitary-adrenal axis), which forms the circuitry responsible for connecting the brain and the body. Imagine our ancestors, cavemen and cavewomen, exploring their terrain, perhaps even enjoying the wonders of their prehistoric environment, when suddenly out of the corner of their eyes they spot a saber-toothed tiger, licking his lips in anticipation of a tasty human morsel. The fight or flight reaction would kick in preparing their bodies to either fight or flee from the tiger. It would do this through a series of instantaneous physiological and psychological changes which prepare us to take immediate physical action in the face of danger. These changes and their resulting physical signs are outlined in Tables 5.1 and 5.2.

TABLE 5.1 Signs of Fight or Flight

• Racing thoughts	• Attention span narrows
• Rapid pulse	• Pounding heart
• Gritting of teeth	• Muscular tension
• Can't sit still	• Jaw clenching
• Tremors	• Stomach tightens
• Rapid, shallow breathing	• Perspiration increases
• Serious, concerned expression	• Field of vision narrows
• Numbness	• Cold, clammy hands
• Impulsive behavior	• Gripping emotions
• Inability to concentrate	• Dry mouth

TABLE 5.2 Physiology of the "Fight or Flight" Response

- The breathing rate becomes more intense and rapid, increasing the oxygen supply in the blood.
- Breathing becomes shallower, switching from diaphragmatic to thoracic respiration, shifting the oxygen/carbon dioxide balance.
- Muscles tense in preparation for strenuous action.
- Heart rate speeds up insuring sufficient blood supply to needed areas, especially to the brain for optimized control over conscious functions as well as to major muscles to prepare for taking action.
- Peripheral blood vessels constrict again to send the bulk of the blood supply and the oxygen it carries to needed areas. Blood clotting mechanisms are also activated to protect against injury. This prevents excess bleeding should the person be cut in a struggle.
- Increased heart rate and constriction of peripheral blood vessels cause blood pressure to soar.
- Digestion ceases, so blood may be diverted to muscles and brain.
- Stored sugar and fats pour into the blood stream to provide fuel for quick energy.
- The adrenal gland is activated releasing adrenalin into the system, along with the hormones epinephrine and norepinephrine.
- Triggered by the pituitary gland, the endocrine system steps up hormone production.
- All senses are heightened. Pupils dilate making vision more sensitive. Hearing becomes more acute.
- Electrical resistivity (perspiration/galvanic action) and skin temperature change.
- Perspiration increases and saliva decreases.
- The urethra and anal sphincter muscles (controlling bowel and bladder function) initially loosen, in order to evacuate waste if necessary, but then constrict to prevent waste elimination when running or fighting. So when people say, "I was so scared that I peed in my pants," there is a physiological mechanism underlying this humiliating phenomenon.

In short, fight or flight shows a picture of hyperactivity in your **autonomic nervous system** (ANS). The ANS has two divisions: (1) the **sympathetic** branch which mobilizes your body for action via the fight/flight response; and (2) the **parasympathetic** branch which allows your body to gradually calm down. If we return to the example with the cave dwellers, the Caveperson's body and mind would be on "red alert" in order to deal with the impending danger. This activation would not go on for long, however. If the tiger had his way and caveperson ended up serving as a meal, he would definitely be relaxed as the deceased tend to show no autonomic activity. If, on the other hand, our friend was lucky enough to escape and tell the story to his friends back in the cave, his physiology would return to a state of **homeostasis** or balance when the parasympathetic branch takes over and enables relaxation. After a slight period of recovery, caveperson would be no worse for the wear. Visually, this may be represented as follows in Figure 5.2.

Figure 5.2

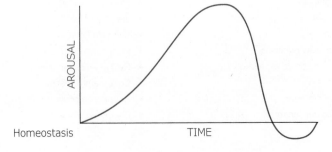

5.4.1 The Downside of the Fight/Flight Reaction

This mechanism is clearly an adaptive response to the presence of physical danger. The problem is that the response is triggered not only by actual physical danger, but by perceived danger. The tigers that chase modern man and woman are not of flesh and blood. They are things like deadlines, unpaid bills, confrontations with others, overload from homework or final exams, rush hour traffic, demands from bosses, professors, parents, spouses or children. All these and many more trigger the fight or flight response in the person of today. But it gets worse, for not only are the tigers the actual events, but also those events remembered and anticipated by us. So not only does the act of asking the boss for a raise lead to increased autonomic activity, but also our anticipation of our meeting, along with the recollection of the event, particularly if we didn't obtain the desired results. The predicament lies in the fact that the fight or flight reaction prepares us to either fight or run away and neither of these responses is particularly useful nor adaptive for dealing with most of the stresses we face in our modern world. To further aggravate the situation, caveperson's stresses had a distinct beginning and a definite ending, whereas the tigers we face today seem to be much more ongoing. No sooner have we begun to recover from fight-flight activation when another event, real or imagined, triggers the response. Thus, we never really have the chance to fully recover and return to homeostatic balance before we are faced with the onslaught of new or old stressors recurring in our environment. This can be expressed visually as follows in Figure 5.3:

Figure 5.3

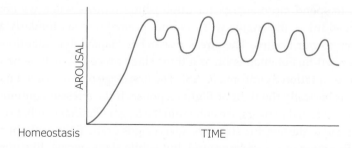

Day after day we are faced with a continuous barrage of stressors. Depending on the context of a situation, we label the physiological arousal generated by the fight/flight reaction differently. If a bear is chasing us in the woods, we label our arousal as "fear." If we are uncertain and worried about an important outcome, we label this arousal as "anxiety." If someone or something really annoys us we label that arousal as "anger." Whatever the label, on a purely physiological level it is still the same fight/flight reaction complete with heightened heart rate, rise in blood pressure and respiratory rate, adrenaline release and so forth. We get some relief at night when we sleep, but even in our sleep we might dream about our stressors, again triggering the fight-flight response, and the next day we awaken with our physiology just a bit above homeostasis, to begin the whole cycle over again. After years of this pattern we forget what relaxation really feels like, as we habituate to a state of autonomic arousal. This state feels relaxed in comparison to full blown fight-flight activation, but in reality it is higher than true homeostasis, which we need to maintain health. This is illustrated in Figure 5.4:

Figure 5.4

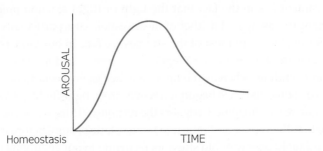

Thus a person under chronic stress is like a car with its idle set too high. Imagine for a moment an automobile whose engine is idling just a little too fast. What would happen to it? For one thing, it would use more gas, just as we tend to spend more energy for diminishing returns when we are under stress. In addition, the engine will wear out prematurely as similarly appears to happen to our bodies. The stress researcher Hans Selye, mentioned earlier, described this phenomenon as a three stage process which he named the **General Adaptation Syndrome (GAS)**. The first stage of GAS, called the *Alarm Reaction*, is basically the fight or flight response. If the stressor continues, as is typical of modern day tigers, we enter into the *Stage of Resistance* where our bodies habituate to the specific stressors. Overt signs of the fight or flight reaction would disappear or go underground, but subtle signs persist, like our neural and glandular systems remaining hyperactive, leaving us over-stimulated and vigilant. The last phase, known as the *Stage of Exhaustion*, occurs when stressors are prolonged despite our best attempts at coping. Just as we have to rest, so must our glandular system rest in order to regain balance. Without rest it wears down and eventually out, resistance deteriorates, and stress-related symptoms resurface. Clearly, if there is no relief, even death is possible (Selye, 1982). See Figure 5.5.

Figure 5.5

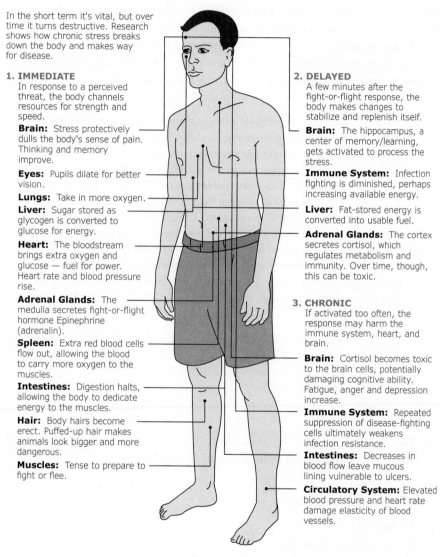

STRESS
THE GENERAL ADAPTATION SYNDROME

In the short term it's vital, but over time it turns destructive. Research shows how chronic stress breaks down the body and makes way for disease.

1. IMMEDIATE
In response to a perceived threat, the body channels resources for strength and speed.

Brain: Stress protectively dulls the body's sense of pain. Thinking and memory improve.

Eyes: Pupils dilate for better vision.

Lungs: Take in more oxygen.

Liver: Sugar stored as glycogen is converted to glucose for energy.

Heart: The bloodstream brings extra oxygen and glucose — fuel for power. Heart rate and blood pressure rise.

Adrenal Glands: The medulla secretes fight-or-flight hormone Epinephrine (adrenalin).

Spleen: Extra red blood cells flow out, allowing the blood to carry more oxygen to the muscles.

Intestines: Digestion halts, allowing the body to dedicate energy to the muscles.

Hair: Body hairs become erect. Puffed-up hair makes animals look bigger and more dangerous.

Muscles: Tense to prepare to fight or flee.

2. DELAYED
A few minutes after the fight-or-flight response, the body makes changes to stabilize and replenish itself.

Brain: The hippocampus, a center of memory/learning, gets activated to process the stress.

Immune System: Infection fighting is diminished, perhaps increasing available energy.

Liver: Fat-stored energy is converted into usable fuel.

Adrenal Glands: The cortex secretes cortisol, which regulates metabolism and immunity. Over time, though, this can be toxic.

3. CHRONIC
If activated too often, the response may harm the immune system, heart, and brain.

Brain: Cortisol becomes toxic to the brain cells, potentially damaging cognitive ability. Fatigue, anger and depression increase.

Immune System: Repeated suppression of disease-fighting cells ultimately weakens infection resistance.

Intestines: Decreases in blood flow leave mucous lining vulnerable to ulcers.

Circulatory System: Elevated blood pressure and heart rate damage elasticity of blood vessels.

5.4.2 Stress Sensitization

To make matters even worse, before the Stage of Exhaustion overtakes us, research indicates that we can become sensitized, or acutely sensitive, to stress. That is, we may respond to stress as we do an allergy. Once that happens, even ordinary stress can trigger a torrent of chemical reactions in both our brains and bodies that besiege us from within, making stress the psychological equivalent of ragweed (Carpi, 1996). Even though at some level we realize that what we are facing are normal, daily hassles, our brains are signaling our bodies to overreact. We may not think we are getting worked up over running late for an appointment, but our brains are responding as though it were a life or death situation. Years of research has demonstrated that people become sensitized to stress and this sensitization actually alters physical patterns in the brain. We may produce too many excitatory chemicals or too few calming ones; either way we are responding inappropriately. According to Carpi:

> The revelation that stress itself alters our ability to cope with stress has produced yet another remarkable finding. Sensitization to stress may occur before we are old enough to prevent it ourselves. . . . studies suggest that animals ranging from rodents to monkeys to humans may experience still undetermined developmental periods during which exposure to extreme stress is more damaging than in later years. 'For example, we have known that losing a parent when you are young is much harder to handle than if your parent dies when you are an adult', says Jean King, Ph.D. of the University of Massachusetts Medical School. What we now believe is that a stress of that magnitude occurring in childhood may rewire your brain's circuitry, throwing the system off kilter, leaving you less able to handle normal, everyday stress. (Psychology Today, Jan./ Feb. 1996 p. 12)

So clearly, stress does not just grab us for a time and then release us. It changes us by altering our bodies and our brains.

Questions

1. The _____ is a survival mechanism present in humans and animals which prepares us to deal with physical danger.

   A. glucose response

   B. endorphin response

   C. fight or flight response

   D. homeostatic response

2. Your body returns to _____ or balance after you relax, following the fight/flight response.

   A. GAS (General Adaptation Syndrome)

   B. the sympathetic nervous system

   C. high arousal

   D. homeostasis

3. The fight/flight response is a result of hyperactivity in your
_____.

    A. autonomic nervous system

    B. central nervous system

    C. peripheral nervous system

    D. hippocampus

5.5 What Is Possible?

Understand the role of the placebo effect in stress and illness.

But enough of this doom and gloom scenario! Are we totally at the mercy of our past and current stressors? Is there nothing we can do? Research in positive psychology and an overwhelming amount of anecdotal evidence support the idea that, just as we have the potential to slowly destroy ourselves, our mind/ body system can also create miraculous beneficial results. What is possible can sometimes border on the unbelievable.

For example, you may have heard the story of Norman Cousins (1981), who wrote about his remarkable recovery from a supposedly incurable disease that leads to spinal deterioration and paralysis in his bestselling book *Anatomy of an Illness.* Cousins was a distinguished author and editor of the *Saturday Review* who, in the mid 1960s, developed a very painful, degenerative, connective tissue disease called ankylosing spondylitis. He became partially paralyzed and was given only months to live. He refused to buy into the gloomy predictions of his physicians, who gave him a 1 in 500 chance of recovery, so he designed a regimen of self-healing based largely on using humor as a stress reducer. He checked out of the hospital, moved into a hotel room, took very large doses of vitamin C, and as part of his regimen he spent several hours daily watching slapstick comedies. Initially he reported that ten minutes of belly laughter had a powerful anesthetic effect, allowing him to sleep at least two hours without painkillers. Laughter also reduced his inflammation, probably by stimulating the release of endorphins. Slowly he regained the use of his limbs and his condition steadily improved over several months. Gradually he resumed his busy life, and ultimately, much to the surprise of his physicians, he went into a complete remission. He returned to his full time work as the editor of the magazine, and wrote the book to tell the story of his recuperation. Clearly the power of optimism in promoting healing was at work in this case.

Fifteen years after his bout with the collagen disease, he suffered a near fatal heart attack. Just as before, he followed a similar regimen for healing himself and gradually improved. He chronicled this recovery in his book *The Healing Heart* (1983). Cousins died in 1990 at the age of 75. He lived many years longer than his doctors had predicted, surviving 10 years after his first heart attack, 16 years after being diagnosed with heart disease, and 26 years after his bout with collagen disease.

5.5.1 The Power of Belief

Or what about the amazing story reported by Ernest Rossi (1986), in his book *The Psychobiology of Mind-Body Healing?* Dr. Rossi recounted the story of Mr. Wright, as told by his personal physician, Dr. Phillip West, over 30 years ago. Mr. Wright suffered from advanced malignancy of the lymph nodes known as lymphosarcoma. His condition was terminal and he had deteriorated to the point where his physician thought death was imminent. He had tumors the size of oranges in his neck, groin, chest, and abdomen. His spleen and liver were grossly enlarged. Copious amounts of fluid were drawn from his chest on a daily basis. He was bedridden and having severe difficulty breathing. All standard cancer treatments of that time, including radiation, had proved useless. Although his doctors had given up hope for his recovery, Mr. Wright maintained an optimistic attitude, for since the onset of his illness he held fast to a belief that a miracle drug would come along to save the day. This expectation was fulfilled when newspapers reported that a newly developed drug, Krebiozen, showed significant promise in the treatment of cancer. This hope was further heightened when he learned that the hospital where he was staying would be included in a research project studying the effectiveness of this new drug. Even though he did not fit the criteria for inclusion in the study because of the advanced nature of his condition, he begged his doctors to include him in the treatment protocol. Against their better judgment his doctors included him in the study, fully expecting that he would die within the week, thus freeing up a supply of Krebiozen for another patient. His response to the drug was nothing short of miraculous! Within several days he went from death's door to walking around the ward, joking with nurses. His tumors were half of their original size. After ten days of Krebiozen treatment, he was discharged from the hospital with his cancer in complete remission. In the meantime, early results of the study indicated that this miracle drug appeared to be ineffective in the treatment of cancer. Unfortunately, Mr. Wright became aware of these initial reports of the lack of effectiveness of the drug, and within a short period of time he completely relapsed.

Clearly, it wasn't the Krebiozen that was responsible for his improvement, but the power of his belief. In order to test this out, his doctors decided to see if they could recreate the previous results. They deliberately lied to him and told him not to believe the discouraging results he had read in the newspapers. They further informed him that Krebiozen was highly effective, and that his relapse occurred because his last doses had deteriorated on the shelf. They further added that he would be receiving double strength dosages from a fresh shipment of the drug which should restore him to health. They then, with great fanfare, proceeded to inject him with saline solution, nothing but a placebo. What do you think happened? Again he made a remarkable recovery, even quicker than the first time. He was discharged from the hospital and remained in complete remission for two months, until reports appeared in the press that Krebiozen had proven to be totally worthless in the treatment of cancer. Mr. Wright quickly relapsed and was readmitted to the hospital, dying two days later.

The Global Perspective
Coping with Stress Around the World

One of the advantages of living in a global society is the availability of choices from around the world. We enjoy a wide array of food, music, dance, film, sports, and literature that have their beginnings in other places. Since stress itself is a universal human experience, it behooves us to consider how other cultures successfully deal with the problem.

For instance, consider this approach to reducing stress and increasing well-being that began in India and is already making inroads into the United States and all over the world. In 1995 Dr. Madan Kataria from Mumbai, India began the practice of laughter yoga. In this practice people gather in groups and simply begin to pretend laughing. In short order the whole group will begin to genuinely laugh and this is carried on for 15 to 20 minutes. Participants feel that their breathing patterns shift to a slower, deeper movement associated with relaxation. They also feel a reduction in stress and an improved sense of humor. An increased resistance to illness is also reported.

Humans have known for a long time that positive emotions seem to promote good health. For instance, in the Bible it is said that a merry heart is like a medicine. But is there scientific evidence to support these anecdotal claims about laughter? Indeed there is.

- Laughter was shown to reduce cortisol levels and increase the production of lymphocytes essentially improving the functioning of the immune system (Berk et. al., 1988).
- The body's first line of defense against respiratory infections is a substance called salivary immunoglobulin A (IgA). Dillon, Minchoff and Baker (1985) found that IgA concentration increased significantly after exposure to a funny video.
- In a study conducted at Indiana State University, laughter led to a significant increase in natural killer cells as compared to control subjects (Bennet, et. al., 2003). Natural killer cells are a special type of white blood cell with the task of attacking cancer cells.

Stress is also impacted by our lifestyle. The island of Okinawa in Japan is home to an exceptional number of very healthy centenarians (people at least 100 years old). The Okinawa Centenarian Study began in 1976 in an attempt to understand the reasons why so many live for so long with outstanding health. Genetics definitely seems to play a role but when Okinawans move to other countries and abandon their traditional lifestyle, their mortality rate increases. The investigators have also isolated other lifestyle variables that they believe contribute to the exceptional well being of these people. For instance, they note that successful aging seems enhanced by the following factors:

- Diet and dietary practices are important. Okinowans eat fewer calories in general due to a cultural practice known as hara hachi bu (eating to a point of 80% fullness). Their diet itself is high in vegetables and fruits, good fats, fiber, and soy proteins and grains which contain high concentrations of estrogenic compounds. These foods tend to confer protection from heart disease and stroke as well as leading to much lower rates of cancer of the breast, prostate, ovaries, and colon.
- Their lifestyle includes regular exercise all through their lifespan and avoidance of smoking which in conjunction with their diet also protects their hearts, their bones, and lowers stress levels.
- They seem to possess an optimistic and easy going approach to life.
- There are also strong social support systems in place. Individuals are involved in their communities and generally have deep spiritual practices.

Thus it is clear that our global family has much to offer that can reduce your stress, improve your health and the quality of your life. What else might you learn by keeping your global antenna tuned to lessons from other lands?

What can be learned from this? You could conclude that the lesson here is that Mr. Wright should have stopped reading the newspaper! But obviously what is evident, and rather amazing, is that it was the power of Mr. Wright's belief that affected his physiology. Doctors would dismiss this as a dramatic example of the **Placebo Effect**. We often hear our colleagues in the health profession refer to similar, if less dramatic, results with their own cases as "just a placebo." To us, the fact that IT'S JUST A PLACEBO! opens up a whole new range of possibilities. Rather than an area to be dismissed, we consider this to be a phenomenon to explore fully. The consensus in the field is that 30% of the effectiveness of any treatment, including drugs, can be accounted for by placebo effects. One highly respected researcher in the area of stress reduction and mind/body connection, Herbert Benson (1997), believes that the placebo effect is responsible for 80% of the success of all treatments!

5.5.2 The Neurobiology of the Placebo Effect

We know that the placebo effect is a real and often robust phenomenon. But how does belief in a treatment create actual changes in health or subjective well-being even in the absence of real treatment? It turns out that our beliefs activate regions in our brain which mimic or induce the same changes as actual treatments. For example, let's consider the placebo response in pain control. MRI studies (Petrovic, 2002; Wager, 2004) demonstrated that placebo pain reduction derives from an expectation signal from the prefrontal cortex that instructs the midbrain to release natural opioids (i.e. painkillers like endorphins) to satisfy our expectation of relief. The placebo effect also involves emotions. Atlas and Wager (2012) reported that robust placebo effects were typically accompanied by changes in brain regions involved with emotional appraisal such as the amygdala, the orbiofrontal cortex, and the insula. This creates what Wager terms *endogenous regulation* which is his term for our ability to reinterpret, or reframe, our situation. In addition to expectations of relief, placebos appear to allow people to reframe the meaning of their pain and develop greater hope that their pain will be short-lived, thus decreasing its emotional significance. Atlas and Wager (2012) further demonstrated that expectations work through a somewhat different pathway than active pain medications. The expectation of pain reduction increased activity in the prefrontal cortex and calmed the amygdala, whereas drugs more directly influenced the pain processing areas of the brain.

Questions

1. When people report feeling better after being given a sugar pill presented as a painkiller, this is _____.

   A. a psychophysiological disorder

   B. a placebo effect

   C. homeostasis

   D. the General Adaptation Syndrome

2. The mind-body connection _____.

    A. is a myth

    B. can make us sick but cannot facilitate healing

    C. has nothing to do with placebo effects

    D. is capable of helping us to heal

3. The placebo effect works because _____.

    A. our beliefs activate regions in the brain that mimic the effects of actual treatments

    B. the sympathetic nervous system takes over

    C. stress sensitization sets in

    D. there is a sucker born every day

5.6 The Mind-Body Connection

Describe how the connection between the mind and body can affect the immune system and healing.

So clearly, just as we have the capacity to do ourselves tremendous harm through our reactions to stress, so too do we have the ability to create dramatic positive outcomes in our lives. The first step is acknowledging this possibility. Our mind and body are not as separate as was once thought. In fact, they are profoundly interconnected and interdependent. As a result of this shift from the old paradigm where mind and body were thought to operate separately, a whole new branch of psychology, called **psychoneuroimmunology** or PNI, has developed over the last forty years. PNI is the study of the relationship between stress, our immune system and health outcomes in order to uncover the workings of the mind-body connection, and discover how to use these mechanisms to fight illness, ranging from AIDS to the common cold.

One facet of PNI research is focused on proving the mind-body connection by establishing a direct physiological link between the body's immune system and the brain. This is based on a theory (Maier and Watkins, 1998) which hypothesizes that the immune system functions as a messenger which signals the brain of injury or impending illness by releasing cytokine proteins which travel to the nervous system and the brain. In response, the brain then releases its own cytokines to prompt the nervous system to discharge a cascade of responses, such as fever and fatigue, which assist the body's healing mechanisms by lowering activity level and thus conserving energy. These researchers question whether depression in humans may have developed as a survival mechanism for saving energy during times of illness.

PNI researchers Margaret Kemeny and her colleagues (2000) at UCLA are exploring a theory which challenges and expands upon Selye's well accepted

G.A.S. model of the stress response. Kemeny and her associates propose that there are actually two potential stress reactions: (1) the classic fight/flight reaction Selye describes; and (2) a withdrawal response where people cut back to conserve energy (by, for example, getting depressed rather than anxious). Kemeny's team is also studying the cognitive aspects of these two reactions. They have found that people respond differently to the same stressful events depending on the meaning given to the stressor. That is, the interpretation given to the stressor helps determine whether a person withdraws or becomes agitated. Our bodies respond not so much to our environment, but to our interpretations of our environment. By now this should be starting to sound very familiar to you, as it once again reflects that the way you view the problem often is the problem. This aspect will be dealt with in much greater detail in the next chapter, which focuses on wellness and stress mastery.

A related theory about alternative stress reactions (Taylor, 2000) posits that women will often respond with "tend and befriend" behaviors rather than fight/flight behaviors. That is, when under stress females will often initiate nurturing behaviors to protect their children and their loved ones, as well as themselves. That is, women often respond to stressful situations by protecting themselves and their young through nurturing behaviors and cleaning up their environment, the "tending" part of the model, and forming alliances with the larger social group, particularly other women, the "befriend" part of the model. Men, in contrast, when stressed tend to respond more with a typical fight/flight pattern, opting to either isolate/withdraw (go out to the garage and work on the car) or fight. For women, talking about stressful issues typically reduces stress levels, while for men, at least initially, withdrawal is needed to lower arousal levels before communication is desired. Taylor and her colleagues presented evidence from human and animal studies that demonstrated that when under stress, females prefer being with others, while males prefer being alone. "It is one of the most robust gender differences in adult human behavior," notes Taylor. It also appears that men and women often respond differently to stress. Women's blood pressure goes up less than men's in reaction to stress, possibly related to the fact that in men the size of the amygdala is typically twice that of women, but women tend to react to a wider range of stressors than men. Women feel stress more often because they take a more holistic view of everyday life (Taylor, 2000).

Does this mean that women do not respond to stress with the fight/flight response? Not necessarily. The fight/flight response seems to be present in women under acute stress. The tend and befriend response then seems to kick in with females, but not typically with males. Female animals may need to protect their young in stressful situations when fleeing too soon would expose their young to danger. Taylor's research suggests that hormones play a role in these differences. Males under stress produce androgens such as testosterone, in addition to stress hormones like cortisol. Females, on the other hand, produce oxytocin which creates a feeling of relaxation, thereby lowering fear and decreasing some aspects of fight/flight arousal. Oxytocin is also a chemical which promotes social bonding.

5.6.1 Your Immune System Can Learn!

Experiments with animals have demonstrated that the immune system is capable of learning by association, or classical conditioning. In one study (Ader & Cohen, 1975), rats were given sweetened water, the equivalent of rat Coca-Cola, which contained a drug which suppressed immune functioning, and not surprisingly, they began to get sick at an abnormally high rate. After a hiatus when no sweetened water was available, it was reintroduced but without the drug. Guess what? The rats started getting ill again, as the flavor of the water created a conditioned response that once again inhibited their immune functioning even though the immunosuppressant drug was absent. In another rodent experiment (Ader & Cohen, 1982), mice were bred to be genetically vulnerable to an autoimmune disease where an overactive immune system literally attacks the body's own tissues. They were then fed a flavored solution which included an immunosuppressant drug, and as a result, it delayed the onset of the disease because their immune systems were suppressed. The researchers then continued giving the mice the flavored solution minus the drug, and the mice continued to resist the disease. Once again the immune system had learned to inhibit itself by association to a taste. In yet another rodent study (Shmeck, 1985), mice were repeatedly exposed to the smell of camphor while simultaneously receiving an injection which enhanced "natural killer" (NK) cells. NK cells, a type of white blood cell, are vitally important to immune functioning because they kill germs. Later on, when these mice were exposed to the smell of camphor without the injection, their NK activity increased once again.

This, of course, raises the intriguing question of whether we can modify our immune systems by what we learn. The answer appears to be an enthusiastic yes. An exhaustive review of all the PNI research is beyond the scope of this text; however, consider the following two unpublished studies cited by Rossi (1986). Barbara Peavey (1982) investigated the effects of a relaxation training program on the immune functioning of her subjects. In particular, she looked at the neutrophil counts for these subjects. Neutrophils are blood cells that comprise approximately two-thirds of our body's white blood cells, a significant aspect of our immune system. Anything that boosts neutrophils amplifies resistance to illness. Although the subject's neutrophil counts did not increase, these cells were found to function significantly more effectively following the relaxation training. Schneider, Smith, & Witcher (1984) carried out an even more creative study designed to facilitate neutrophil activity using subjects' imagery to boost immune functioning. Students were given information about how white blood cells function, and then shown microscopic slides of actual neutrophils, pictures which they could then incorporate into their imagery training. They were then trained in relaxation and imagery techniques. The subjects practiced imagining modifying their neutrophil levels and also drew pictures to accompany their imagery. After six sessions it was found that subjects could reliably and significantly increase or decrease the number of circulating neutrophils in their bloodstream. So when it comes to our own bodies, there really is such a thing as mind over matter in some instances.

5.6.2 More Research Evidence for the Mind-Body Connection

The Harvard Mental Health Letter (April, 2002) reviewed a variety of PNI studies which demonstrated a link between stress levels and vulnerability to illness on the human level. For example, researchers have demonstrated that NK cells decreased in medical students preparing for exams, but those students who were calmer and had slower heart rates exhibited less immune suppression. Similarly, another study showed that unhappily married women had lower numbers of certain immune cells than happily married women. Individuals caring for relatives with Alzheimer's disease, which is a very stressful task, have also been shown to have higher than average cortisol levels and lower levels of antibody response to influenza vaccines. In a 1991 English study, the stress levels of 420 subjects were evaluated immediately following an administration of nose drops containing a cold virus. These subjects were then quarantined for nine days, and those reporting the highest levels of stress were more likely to catch the cold. In a similar study (Cohen and colleagues, 1998) at the University of Pittsburgh, 276 healthy adults were given cold virus nose drops. Those under the most stress manifested the most severe cold symptoms, but mainly when their stress levels were affected by serious problems such as troubled marriages or unemployment. In another study, 1900 subjects were monitored for one year and were required to keep a diary of life events and their emotional reactions. Periodically they were examined for bacteria in throat cultures and antibodies to viruses in their blood. The results showed that stressful events were four times more likely to precede rather than follow incidents of illness.

With regard to healing from injuries, one study found that biopsy wounds healed more slowly in women who were under high levels of emotional stress. In another experiment, students' wounds healed slower if inflicted just before an examination rather than just before vacation (Kiecolt-Glaser & colleagues, 1998). Slow healing has also been reported in people caring for relatives with Alzheimer's disease.

Social stress appears to be even more damaging than physical stress for animals as well as humans. Our poor friends the rodents were once again tortured in the next study where one group of mice was put into a cage with highly aggressive mice. Another group of mice were kept in tiny cages without food or water for long periods of time. Then both groups were exposed to a bacterial toxin. The mice who were socially stressed were twice as likely to die as the mice who were just physically stressed.

For humans, isolation often inhibits immune functioning. Some studies have reported lower NK cell activity in separated and divorced men compared to married men. Medical students who are lonely have been found to have lower NK activity than non-lonely med students. In a year-long study of people caring for spouses with Alzheimer's, decreases in immune functioning were greatest in those who had the weakest social networks and the least outside help. In general, good social support is strongly correlated with stronger immune functioning in the elderly, even after factoring out variables such as emotional health, health habits, and stress levels. In the University of Pittsburgh study mentioned previously, social support was correlated with resistance to the cold virus, that is, those with the weakest social networks were four times more susceptible to the cold that those with the strongest ties.

There have even been a few studies of the effects of traumatic stress on our immune functioning. According to one report, four months after Hurricane Andrew, Miami residents in the most heavily damaged neighborhoods demonstrated reduced activity in four out of five immune indicators. Similar results were found in a study after the Los Angeles earthquake. Weakened immune functioning has been reported among women who are victims of physical abuse. Another article suggested that men with a history of Post Traumatic Stress Disorder (PTSD), even though recovered, showed weakened immune functioning, which may indicate a long-lasting suppression of their immune systems.

The Harvard Mental Health Letter (April, 2002), which summarized these findings, concluded that . . .

> Animal experiments suggest that the nervous system responds differently to acute and chronic stress. The acute stress reaction is often a healthy response to a challenge. But chronic stress may cause the feedback controls to fail, turning the emergency response into a condition that persists when it no longer has any use. Stress hormones and sympathetic activity remain at a high level, suppressing immune function and possibly promoting illness. The immune system of people who are under chronic stress may also respond abnormally to acute stress. (p. 5)

5.6.3 The Healing Power of the Mind

What really matters is whether our minds can influence our immune systems to prevent or lower the risk of illness or injury, and also promote healing. At this point you may have several questions such as, "How can I cope better with stress?" Or you may want to ask, "How can I get the mind-body connection to work for me?" We now know enough of the necessary steps to harness this power. What remains is to learn and then practice these steps. If you follow the techniques and suggestions outlined in the next chapter and also in chapter 8, in the section on using visualization techniques to promote healing, we promise that you will reap significant benefits. But let us caution you that knowing the steps is not enough; it is only in the doing that solutions are found. The following chapter on wellness will enumerate specific techniques for mastering stress and staying healthy.

Questions

1. Your immune system can learn to _____.
   - **A.** inhibit itself
   - **B.** make you lose weight
   - **C.** turn off the fight/flight response
   - **D.** read and write

2. _____ stress is even more damaging than physical stress.
   - **A.** Neurotic
   - **B.** Acute
   - **C.** Cognitive
   - **D.** Social

3. PNI research has demonstrated that _____.
   - **A.** your immune system is incapable of learning
   - **B.** people respond differently to the same stressful event depending on how they interpret the stressor
   - **C.** men and women react identically to stress both behaviorally and physiologically
   - **D.** when under stress our resistance to the common cold increases

Summary

In this chapter, stress was defined as anything that requires an adaptive response on the part of an organism. The relationship between stress and illness was explored in-depth based on research demonstrating the association between the frequency, intensity, and pervasiveness of change in your life and the likelihood you will get ill. Stress affects our psychological, physical, and occupational functioning in a myriad of ways. Common manifestations of stress in all three arenas were explicated. This was followed by an in-depth explanation of the physiology of stress including the fight/flight response, the three stages of GAS (the General Adaptation Syndrome) as well as **stress sensitization**. Differences in the stress responses between the genders were also reviewed. The fact that the fight/flight response can be triggered as easily by perceived stress as by actual physical danger was emphasized.

It is abundantly clear that our mind-body system can wreak havoc on our health, especially due to chronic stress or chronic perceived stress, but this mind-body connection can also create miraculously beneficial results. The last section of this chapter included a deep dive into all that is possible with the mind-body connection, ranging from how to harness the healing power of mind, to the phenomenon of the placebo effect, the neurobiology of this effect along with research into psychoneuroimmunology (PNI), and the applications for our ability to heal ourselves.

Positive Psychology Exercise

1. Be aware of the relationship between stress and the fight or flight response in your own life. Next time you are feeling anxious or shaky, note what is triggering this reaction. Is it actual danger or more likely just perceived danger? Conversely, the next time you are faced with a stressor, pay attention to how your body reacts. Awareness of increased arousal or fight/flight activation is the first step in learning to calm yourself, which is addressed in the next chapter.

Key Terms

Autonomic Nervous System
Bruxism
Cortisol
Distress
Endorphins
Eustress
Fight/Flight Response

General Adaptation Syndrome
  (GAS)
Glucocorticoids
Homeostasis
Parasympathetic
Placebo Effect
Psychoneuroimmunology

Psychophysiological Disorders
Stress
Stress Mastery
Stress Sensitization
Sympathetic

Shared Writing

What are the biggest sources of stress in your life? What effects do you notice in your psychological, physical, and/or occupational functioning as a result? Write about your observations of the causes and effects of stress for you.

Chapter 5 Questions

1. Prolonged stress _____
   _____.

   A. improves your psychological functioning but damages your health

   B. negatively affects your physical, psychological, and occupational functioning

   C. enhances workplace productivity

   D. affects your physical health but has no impact on your occupational functioning

2. A new source of stress comes from
_____.

   A. the results of the 2016 presidential election

   B. improvements in the economy

   C. information underload

   D. monogamy

3. Which of the following is a sign of fight/flight arousal?

   A. slow, relaxed breathing

   B. decreasing heart rate and blood pressure

   C. a release of adrenalin

   D. loose muscles

4. The fight or flight response _____
_____.

   A. can lead to hyperventilation

   B. can lead to slow, deep breathing

   C. inhibits the production of cortisol

   D. is the same as homeostasis

5. The first stage of GAS, the alarm stage, is
_____.

   A. homeostasis

   B. exhaustion

   C. the fight/flight response

   D. stress resistance

6. _____ is possible if there is no relief from the 3rd stage of GAS, the stage of exhaustion.

   A. Sleep

   B. Homeostasis

   C. Stress sensitization

   D. Death

7. A theory about alternative stress reactions posits that women will often respond with _____ and _____ behaviors rather than fight/flight reactions.

   A. bait; switch

   B. tend; befriend

   C. whining; complaining

   D. meet; greet

8. The two branches of the autonomic nervous system are _____.

   A. central and motor

   B. sensory and perceptual

   C. unsympathetic and psychological

   D. sympathetic and parasympathetic

9. When your body responds to stress as it would to an allergy, this is
_____.

   A. stress sensitization

   B. homeostasis

   C. the placebo effect

   D. the General Adaptation Syndrome (GAS)

10. _____ is the study of the relationship between stress, our immune system, and health outcomes.

   A. The Yerkes-Dodson law

   B. The GAS

   C. Psychoneuroimmunology

   D. Stress sensitization

Chapter 6
Developing Wellness Skills

Learning Objectives

After reading this chapter, you should be able to:

6.1 Describe the various components that make up the concept of wellness.

6.2 Explain how the use of active relaxation techniques increases our ability to master stress.

6.3 Explain how awareness of our thoughts and feelings allows us to have more control over them.

6.4 Identify the three stress hardiness attitudes that help make individuals more resistant to the negative effects of stress.

6.5 Recognize the goals and guidelines of progressive muscle relaxation.

6.6 Describe the benefits and techniques of regular meditative practice.

6.7 Explain how various types of muscle stretching can be used to reverse the effects of negative stress.

6.8 Recognize the various ways in which adopting healthy lifestyle practices affects your ability to master stress.

Wellness as a term was introduced decades ago when a forward thinking physician began writing about well-being as an integration of the mind, body and spirit and encompassing many components of human functioning (Davis, 1961). Today **wellness** as a term has caught on, but to many it is associated primarily with physical fitness. We see "Wellness Centers" in communities and on campuses that are

Wellness Wheel

actually gyms with exercise equipment and machines. This reinforces the connection between wellness and exercise rather than suggesting a more comprehensive meaning of the term. The wellness concept we are referring to in this text is indeed more multi-dimensional.

As the literature and practice of wellness has expanded over the decades, numerous models have emerged that illustrate the components of well-being. Drawing from many of the various schemas, we have included those elements most prominent in other models into our own wellness wheel.

This current chapter will build further understanding of stress mastery and offer specific strategies for stress reduction through relaxation and meditation practices. **Exercise** is examined here as it relates to minimizing stress, as well as other benefits that being active engenders. The importance of **Nutrition** and its significance for wellness is reviewed. Pointers for attaining **Financial Competence** are also offered. Finally, the power of **Social Support** to sustain and enrich our sense of well-being is also addressed. The remaining components of our wellness wheel are addressed in other chapters to follow. So, welcome to the world of wellness. Further skill building through the concepts presented here will propel you onward in your quest for excellence.

6.1 What Is Wellness?

Describe the various components that make up the concept of wellness.

Wellness, or the state of being well, is a lot more than just feeling that you are not ill. By the same token, mental health is not the same as an absence of mental

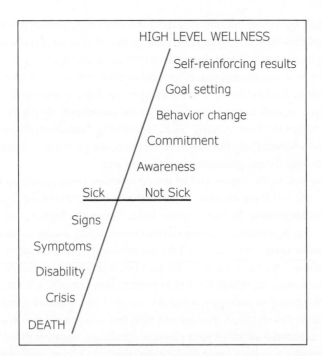

HIGH LEVEL WELLNESS

Self-reinforcing results

Goal setting

Behavior change

Commitment

Awareness

Sick / Not Sick

Signs

Symptoms

Disability

Crisis

DEATH

illness. Mental health reflects the presence of PERMA: of having positive emotions; a sense of meaning and purpose in life; good relationships; accomplishment; and engagement, all the elements of flourishing. John Travis (1981), a physician, has developed a model of progression that amply illustrates the path to wellness.

If you asked most people what "wellness" means, they would probably answer that it means you're not sick. However, considering wellness as only being "not sick" is too limiting. Most of us would probably say at this moment that we are not sick, yet we could be a long way from a high level of wellness. Examine the model above depicting the differences in being sick or not sick. Look first at the downward progression of being sick. It starts with signs and symptoms, the origin or cause of which can be physical, cognitive or emotional. For example, you could experience physical changes such as fatigue, a headache, or shortness of breath on exertion. Cognitively, you could be confused, unfocused, having memory lapses, or unable to organize ideas or derive solutions. Emotionally, you could be overly anxious, frightened, sad, or engulfed in anger. Any of these signs and symptoms reflect that something is not right, and you may say to yourself, "There's a problem here."

If you don't recognize the problem, or don't do something to reverse the symptoms, you will probably slip further downward to serious dysfunction, even to the point of being disabled. For example, physically your fatigue could reflect a severe lack of red blood cells (anemia) leading to very low energy, perhaps even an inability to ambulate. Cognitively, you may not be able to keep up with projects or assignments. Emotionally you may not be able to maintain normal relationships or may exhibit behavior that is negative or destructive to yourself and others. You may not need a wheelchair, need someone else to think for you, or be in a straight jacket, however, you are still disabled from functioning productively and may spend time in bed sleeping and resting, not able to meet daily tasks like attending work or classes. If you do nothing to reverse being disabled, you may plunge further to acute illness, reaching a crisis state where the status of your survival is critical. And yet again, if something is not done to reverse the crisis, it means that you can sink to the lowest point in the paradigm...death. So we note that there are stages or steps to being "sick." Most of us have been through some of these stages so we are quite familiar with this process; however, we may be less informed regarding the progression of being "not sick."

When you look at the higher end of the continuum, progressing up the "not sick" side, you see that there are also stages on the wellness side of the continuum, beginning with **awareness**. To move up the ladder toward a higher state of wellness, the first step is recognizing your current state. Being aware is the starting point. As someone once said, "You can't fix something if you don't know it's broken." For example, let's suppose you find that because you have gained weight, your clothes no longer fit, which has led to pummeling yourself with self-deprecating thoughts. Being so unhappy, what do you do? You comfort yourself with chocolate cake. In this situation, you are not sick, but you are not that well either. However, if you become aware of your physical condition, negative thoughts, and destructive behavior, you have taken the first step toward a higher level of wellness.

Now you have the opportunity to make positive choices to take better care of yourself. Choosing to change your body composition, restructuring your thinking to positive self-talk, and modifying how you reward yourself will result in *commitment*. This makes you want to continue in proactive behavior that leads to a healthier you. Actually taking the steps to develop and follow a meaningful weight loss program is what we mean by self-efficacy.

As you can see in this model, the road to wellness involves specific stages from awareness, to commitment, to *behavior change*. The next step is to set specific goals, such as changing your nutrition and exercise patterns. Achieving these goals requires engaging in the desired positive behavior. Significant progress toward these goals becomes a natural reinforcer to continue the newly acquired behavior. Now that your clothes are a size smaller and fit great, you are more optimistic, and you feel terrific about yourself; the "new you" solidifies your continuing positive behavior. This is the way we move from awareness to a *high level of wellness*. May your journey up the line bring you to a heightened state of well-being!

Questions

1. What is Wellness?

   A. exercising regularly and being physically fit

   B. the opposite to being sick

   C. the absence of mental illness

   D. a lot more than just feeling you are not ill

2. All of the following are components of wellness, except_____.

   A. stress mastery

   B. nutrition

   C. genetics

   D. relationships

3. What is the first rung on the ladder towards high level wellness?

   A. goal setting

   B. awareness

   C. wealth

   D. good nutrition

6.2 Mastering Stress Through Active Relaxation

Explain how the use of active relaxation techniques increases our ability to master stress.

Mastering stress on the path to high level wellness is a life-long process. If you choose to incorporate the concepts and techniques presented in this chapter into the daily fabric of your life, your capacity to cope with and thrive from stress will flourish. Clearly, to deal with stress effectively, you must pay attention to both your body and your mind. Deepak Chopra (1993) in *Ageless Body, Timeless Mind* summarizes research which showed that meditators tended to age slower than non-meditators, a rather dramatic finding. During meditation one focuses on quieting both the body and the mind through the act of fixing on a single thought, image, or visualization.

Truth be told, the distinction between body and mind is really an artificial one, as we discussed in the previous chapter. We now know that body and mind are really one, an intricately interrelated system where thoughts give rise to our physical reactions and, in turn, our physical reactions trigger our various thoughts. But for the purpose of training, of learning how to begin moving toward stress mastery, it is useful to talk about addressing your body first. It is very difficult to change the way you think if your body is simultaneously sending messages of danger. Addressing the body is best accomplished by learning **active relaxation**.

Most people confuse inactivity with relaxation. You might say, "I do relax. I go home and sit down in front of the TV, watch my favorite programs, and let the stress of the day melt away." But the fact is that you just do not get the same beneficial biochemical and physiological changes from watching TV, a passive activity, as you do when practicing active relaxation. EEG research monitoring

---

TABLE 6.1 Potential Benefits of Practicing Active Relaxation Skills

- Decreased anxiety and muscular tension
- Decreased cortisol (stress hormone) levels
- Decreased heart rate and blood pressure
- Decreased respiratory rate
- Boosts serotonin levels (related to improved mood and arousal levels)
- Improves sleep
- Increase in alpha brainwaves indicating a restful state
- Boosts immune functioning
- Greater stability in blood sugar levels
- Increase in salivation and improved digestion
- Greater activation of the parasympathetic (calming) branch of the ANS

the brainwave activity of subjects watching TV compared to subjects engaged in active relaxation demonstrated that practicing relaxation reliably led subjects' brains to shift into alpha brain wave patterns (indicating a relaxed state), while TV viewing led to negligible changes in brainwave patterns (Benson, 2000). You see, **passive relaxation**, like watching TV, is not nearly as effective for reducing stress. What is needed is relaxation aimed at reducing the fight/flight response and thereby restoring balance or homeostasis within your autonomic nervous system (ANS). The **sympathetic** (fight or flight) branch and the **parasympathetic** (rest and digest) branch of the ANS interact with each other like the two ends of a seesaw; that is, when one goes up the other goes down. So raising parasympathetic activation through active relaxation lowers the arousal which you typically experience as anxiety. Active relaxation involves becoming aware of your body and your physiological reactions so that you may consciously reduce your level of arousal.

In the latest edition of his classic book *The Relaxation Response*, Herbert Benson (2000) indicated that regular practice of active relaxation can have beneficial effects on a wide variety of psychological, physiological and psychosomatic symptoms and health issues such as those listed in Tables 6.1 and 6.2.

TABLE 6.2 Conditions Potentially Helped by Regular Elicitation of the Relaxation Response

Agoraphobia	Eczema	Pain in general
Angina Pectoris	Emphysema	Panic attacks
Anxiety	Epilepsy	Phobias
Arthritis	Fibromyalgia	Post surgical recovery
Asthma	Hypertension	Pre menstrual syndrome-PMS
Back pain	Infertility	Psoriasis
Childbirth	Insomnia	Raynauds
Crohns & Colitis	Irritable Bowel Syndrome	Stress and burnout
Depression	Menopause	Skin problems
Diabetes	Migraines	Tension Headaches

6.2.1 The Magic of Diaphragmatic Breathing

Any journey which you undertake begins with a first step. The key to any practice of active relaxation is to relearn proper breathing patterns. Breathing slowly, deeply, and regularly is the easiest and most accessible relaxation technique (Loehr & Migdow, 1986). Most of the time, you are no doubt oblivious to your breathing patterns. Let's first begin by discovering where you are now. Sit with your back supported, your feet flat on the floor and your eyes closed. Put one hand on your chest, and the other on your diaphragm, the muscle right above your stomach, as you focus on your breathing. Notice the pattern and rhythm of your breath as you breathe in and out. Then take a few deep breaths, noticing as you breathe in and out which hand moves more. Does the hand on your chest move up and down, with the shoulders rising and falling, as you breathe? Or is it the hand on your abdomen that does most of the movement? Take a few moments to do that now.

So what happened? Which hand moved more as you breathed deeply? We notice in our classes and workshops that for the majority of students and participants, it is the hand on the chest that evidences more movement. If you have ever seen a baby breathing while she is at rest or asleep, you may have noticed that it is the stomach that moves up and down, while the baby's chest remains relatively still and quiet. This is called **diaphragmatic breathing** and it is a natural antidote to stress. Diaphragmatic breathing involves deep, slow, rhythmic breaths.

Pay attention to what happens to your breathing the next time you feel stressed. You may notice that your breathing becomes quicker, more shallow and irregular. Some people even hold their breath or begin to hyperventilate when under significant stress. What happens to many adults is that after years of frequently activating the fight/flight response, the fast, shallow, upper chest breathing characteristic of this physiological reaction becomes a habit. This breathing is ineffectual, disrupting the proper balance of carbon dioxide and oxygen in your blood stream and thereby creating a continual, if not full blown, over-activation response. There is an optimal balance of oxygen and carbon dioxide that needs to be maintained in your bloodstream for you to remain calm. When you breathe in air, your blood cells receive oxygen and release carbon dioxide (CO_2). CO_2 is a waste product that is carried back through your body and exhaled. **Hyperventilation** a rapid, shallow type of over-breathing, reduces the level of carbon dioxide and calcium in the blood. This causes the blood vessels in the brain to constrict, leading to physical symptoms including dizziness, numbness, headache and/or muscle tension, even tremors. These symptoms can be frightening and tend to cause considerable psychological distress along with increased panic and anxiety. That is why hyperventilation is so counterproductive. The more quickly you breathe, the worse you feel.

6.2.2 Practicing Diaphragmatic Breathing

Retraining yourself is, in most cases, a rather simple procedure. What is required is just about five minutes a day of conscious focusing on your breathing. You can do this by practicing the following technique, once a day, for three weeks. Three weeks are generally required to bring tone to the diaphragm muscle. We have discovered that a few minutes prior to going to sleep is a good time to practice for many people. Others prefer to take five minutes when they return home from either work or school. It is important for you to discover which time is best for you.

Find a quiet place where you are unlikely to be disturbed. Recline and put one hand on your diaphragm and one hand on your chest. Focus on allowing the hand on your diaphragm to rise as you breathe in, as if your stomach were a balloon filling with air. Then watch it go back down as you breathe out and the balloon deflates. It is very important that you put emphasis on exhaling very slowly. One way to train yourself to slow down your exhalation is to exhale through a regular size (not super-sized) straw. Notice the rhythm of the rising and falling of your abdomen as you inhale and exhale. Focus on the particular feelings and sensations you experience in your diaphragm as the breath comes all the way into your lungs and then completely empties from your lungs. Do this for about five minutes, gently focusing your attention on your breath.

If you find yourself having difficulty initially lifting your abdomen as you breathe, try imagining that you are putting on a tight pair of jeans, when they come out fresh from the drier. You would let all the air out of your lungs first, as if you wanted to touch your spine with your bellybutton, then slowly inflate the balloon as you let the air come all the way into your lungs.

Yet another technique that has proven successful for many people is to use a heavy book placed on top of your stomach as you practice your breathing exercises. You could watch the rising and falling of the book as you breathe in and out. This method has the added advantage of providing a weight against which the diaphragm is rising and falling, thereby conditioning the muscle much quicker. Most people find that with just a little attention and practice they can return to that slow, diaphragmatic breathing they knew as a child.

We cannot emphasize enough how important this first step is. Without shifting your breath to a calm, relaxed, diaphragmatic pattern, it will be very difficult to start your journey on the path towards stress mastery. The type of breathing you employ is the key to unlocking the magic. We know it sounds simple, but it is nonetheless true.

Take as an example people suffering from panic attacks, a disorder in which intense anxiety (often accompanied by hyperventilation) is experienced at various times, often causing the individual to withdraw and increasingly restrict their activities in the hope of preventing the attacks. In the extreme, these individuals develop a condition known as "agoraphobia" where they become house bound as a way of coping with the fear of the attacks reoccurring. Developing appropriate diaphragmatic breathing patterns has been identified as essential in learning to overcome the panic.

Focusing on your breathing helps to keep you in the present moment. Your worries, anxieties and stress occur when you focus on either the past (i.e. mistakes you have made or things you wish would have happened differently), or you focus on the future (i.e. worrying about what is going to happen and how you will be able to survive). But the past has already happened; there is little you can do to alter that except change your attitude or perception about what occurred. And the future is yet to come. You can only affect it by working in the present, the here and now. Breathing helps you exist in the now in a way which increases your effectiveness.

Most spiritual traditions recognize the importance of the breath. It is often considered our direct link to God or a Higher Power. The word "inspiration" has a double meaning, being used both to describe breathing as well as being infused with spirit and motivation. Alterations in breathing can create dramatic effects on our consciousness. Holotropic breathing, an alteration in breathing in which controlled hyperventilation is employed, for example, has been shown to create dramatic shifts in consciousness in the practitioners, akin, if somewhat less intense, to those experienced when using hallucinogens. So breathing is clearly a powerful tool; one that can create numerous changes in our bodies, and in our experience of ourselves and our world.

Once you can breathe comfortably using your diaphragm as you think consciously about it, it becomes important to be able to generalize that response to your daily life. One easy way to do this is to set up a number of reminders in your everyday environment. For example, you could take a few brightly colored, small Post-It Notes (3–5) and put them in different places around your home and work environment. We suggest that you resist the temptation to place these on the foreheads of people who are a source of stress to you. However, feel free to use your imagination. Each time you see a Post-It, stop for a second, take one or two breaths using your diaphragm, and then go on with your activity. Or you could set a reminder alarm on your cell phone. This will allow you, with minimal effort, to remind yourself to breathe this way at different times during the day. In just a short time you will be pleasantly surprised, as you focus on your breathing, to discover that you are automatically breathing deep, diaphragmatic breaths.

Another way to ensure that you generalize the correct breathing response to a variety of situations is by using a higher order classical conditioning principle, called the Premack Principle (Premack, 1959). This principle states that when a new behavior is paired, and thus eventually associated with a behavior which is frequently emitted, the new behavior becomes conditioned. This means that you will learn how to breathe correctly faster and better if you do it at the same time that you are doing things which you do frequently, like answering the phone, going to the bathroom, or stopping at red lights.

Another obvious way, and indeed, the first building block, is to remember to breathe from your abdomen whenever you feel yourself becoming stressed. This will help interrupt the automatic cognitive and behavioral strategies you may be using now, which merely lead to an escalation of the stress response. Remembering to breathe in these situations allows you a pause which opens up the possibility of thinking or behaving differently, thereby using stress rather than being used by it.

We should caution you, however, that it is not wise to use only situations when you are feeling stressed as reminders to practice your breathing. You will clearly find it more difficult initially to successfully focus on appropriate breathing at these times. Until you have learned and feel comfortable with abdominal breathing, you need to practice in situations which are less demanding and in which the fight/flight response is not fully activated.

You need only do the most basic breathing awareness exercises to achieve a much more relaxed state of body and mind. As long as your breathing is becoming slower, quieter, and deeper, you are moving in the right direction. Quite frankly, the hardest part is remembering to remember to be aware of your breathing and then to practice. But the fact remains that wherever you are, you still have to breathe, so you might as well practice doing it properly in a manner that will help keep you calm yet alert.

6.2.3 Cultivating Awareness

By now you have become more aware of your breathing. You can notice just how you are breathing. Are you using your diaphragm or your chest? Are you breathing deeply and slowly, with a comfortable rhythm? Or is your breath fast and chaotic? In any situation, if you notice you are engaged in unhealthy, stress-producing breathing, this awareness allows you the opportunity to shift the pattern to a more appropriate one.

Can you do this? If you can't, we strongly urge you to continue your practice. Without the ability to breathe appropriately, it will be difficult for you to master stress. If you can, we congratulate you! You have taken the first and most fundamental step towards stress mastery. It is important that you now remember to do this throughout your day, in a variety of settings; that you think about it at work and at home; that you notice your breathing as you are going to sleep, and shortly after you wake up. It is essential that you remember to remember to notice your breathing. The more you do this, the more you are cultivating awareness. You are replacing your automatic behavior with conscious behavior.

Questions

1. Many people confuse _____ with relaxation.
   A. inactivity
   B. exercising
   C. passivity
   D. sleep

2. The _____ branch of the Autonomic Nervous System (ANS) increases arousal while the _____ branch lowers arousal.

   A. parasympathetic; sympathetic

   B. sympathetic; parasympathetic

   C. physical; psychological

   D. central; motor

3. A simple, healthy, natural antidote to stress involves_____.

   A. hyperventilation

   B. tensing your muscles

   C. drinking a 6 pack of beer

   D. diaphragmatic breathing

6.3 The Value of Self-Awareness

Explain how awareness of our thoughts and feelings allows us to have more control over them.

You see, all human beings have the ability to be aware, not just of our breathing, but of a multitude of things that make up who we are. Let us demonstrate what we mean. Imagine, in your mind's eye, that a part of you can float out of your body, floating up to a particular corner of the room, so that you can see yourself, from that perspective, sitting over there reading this book. What would it be like to do this, what would it feel like? How would you describe the particular sensations that the "you" who is sitting there is experiencing right now? Focus in on a particular part of your body and become aware of your experience there. Perhaps you can be aware of pressure, or temperature, or perhaps some other sensation. It's not important what the specific sensation is, just your ability to notice it. How about your overall mood? How would you characterize that? What can you say about your thoughts? Are you thinking about what you are reading right now, and yet perhaps at the same time wondering what's the point of all this? As you answer these questions, make sure you get back into your body. We certainly wouldn't want you to remain floating around the room somewhere while you continue reading this chapter.

6.3.1 The Witnessing Stance

By doing what you just did, answering the questions we just asked, you have demonstrated your ability for **self-awareness**. All human beings share the ability to be aware of ourselves. The fact that we can do this, that we can stand apart from our feelings and our thoughts, suggests that we can have some control over them.

Ram Dass (1990), formerly known as Richard Alpert, a Harvard psychologist who studied extensively in India and is renowned for integrating both Eastern and Western techniques, describes our ability to stand apart from ourselves, to view ourselves from the outside, as assuming the **witnessing stance**. Whenever you are involved in the many experiences that make up your life, you have the choice to be a witness to your own life. This shift in perspective provides you with the possibility that you can change the particular situation. The fact is (as we addressed in Chapter 2) that you cannot always change situations (i.e. external stressors or events) you are faced with, but you can always change your reaction towards the stressor. Assuming the witnessing stance allows you to do this. Remember that, as we mentioned earlier, what inappropriately triggers your fight/flight response and therefore your stress is not actual physical danger. Not many of you have guns pointed at your head, at least not on a daily basis. What triggers your stress response is your perception of danger. And whether you perceive something as dangerous or not depends on the meaning you give the particular situation. Fortunately or unfortunately, human beings are the kind of beings that give meaning to everything. And what we say, especially to ourselves, about a situation or event determines our attitude towards it. Assuming an observer perspective allows you to get a glimpse of the meaning you are ascribing and therefore provides you an opportunity to change your attitude.

Psychologists also have other labels to describe the processes involved in becoming self-aware. The term **metacognition** refers to becoming aware of your thought processes, and **metamood** to becoming aware of your emotions. The process of assuming the witnessing stance allows you to step back from your experience, to go "meta," where you hover somewhere above the main flow, aware of what is happening rather than being immersed and therefore lost in it, which facilitates getting a better perspective. This refers to the difference between being furious and having the thought, "I'm feeling anger." But this subtle shift in mental activity is the first step in gaining some control. Becoming aware of your underlying thoughts and emotions is essential to developing emotional self-control. Certainly, there is a big gap between being aware of a feeling and being able to change it, but the two often go hand in hand. That is, if you recognize that you are in a rotten mood, typically you will want to get out of it. Self-awareness appears to have a greater impact on intense negative feelings. The recognition of what it is you are feeling gives that slight bit of distance that sets in motion an awareness of alternatives, such as the option to attempt to let go of the feeling.

6.3.2 Attitude Is Everything!

Research has revealed that the attitude you have at the beginning of a task determines the outcome of that task more than any other single factor (Seligman, 1991). For example, if you are optimistic and believe you will be able to succeed at a particular undertaking, and you approach the endeavor with a sense of excitement and joyful expectation, your chances of achieving success are much higher than if you face the task with dread and apprehension. Self-fulfilling prophecies can be positive or negative, depending on your expectations. So your attitude is more important than any other possible factor, both external and internal. This is clearly true when it comes to stress and whether we thrive from it or are buried by it.

Remember Thomas Holmes and his research showing that there was a relationship between the number, severity, and pervasiveness of life changes and our physical and emotional health? We mentioned that this series of studies did not take into account individual differences in abilities to cope with the changes and demands. This research only focused on the effects of external events or stressors. A psychologist by the name of Suzanne Kobasa (1979) decided to focus her research interests on individual differences in coping skills. What makes some people capable of handling enormous amounts of change and demands without suffering the devastating physical and emotional consequences predicted by the Holmes research? Kobasa studied individuals whose lives seemed so filled with stressors that, according to Holmes, they should have been growing massive tumors on the sides of their heads. Yet these folks were successful in their endeavors and seemed to be suffering no apparent negative consequences from their demanding lifestyles.

Questions

1. Adopting the *witnessing stance* enables you to _____.
    A. testify at trial
    B. detach and compartmentalize
    C. develop self-awareness
    D. accurately observe those around you

2. _____ refers to becoming aware of your thought processes.
    A. Meta-mood
    B. Metacognition
    C. Metamorphosis
    D. Metamucil

3. Hyperventilation _____.
    A. reduces the amount of CO_2 and calcium in your blood leading to increased arousal
    B. increases the amount of CO_2 in your blood thus reducing arousal
    C. is characterized by slow, deep breathing
    D. is not associated with panic attacks

6.4 Stress Hardiness Attitudes

Identify the three stress hardiness attitudes that help make individuals more resistant to the negative effects of stress.

Kobasa discovered three attitudes which these people all shared and which appeared to make them resistant to the negative effects of stress. She called these three attitudes the **Stress Hardiness** attitudes because individuals who possess them appear to be "stress hardy," i.e. capable of dealing effectively with stressors. These three attitudes are **control**, **commitment**, and **challenge**. These attitudes are also referred to as the *three Cs of stress hardiness* (Kobasa, 1979).

6.4.1 Control

Let's take a look at the first, the attitude of **control**. Stress hardy individuals believe that they are in control of their lives, rather than stressors having control over them. They recognize that they have resources and options that allow them to influence events in their lives. Although stress hardy individuals recognize that they may not always have direct control over the actual onset or occurrence of an event, they certainly have control over their own response to the stressor. And this is not only true of humans, but also true of such higher life forms as rats. For example (Weiss, 1971), let's say you placed two rats in cages capable of delivering an electroshock to their unsuspecting paws. (Psychologists do, indeed, do this and other perhaps less kindly things to these animals. That is why our standing as a profession is rather low in the rodent community!) Using what is known in experimental psychology as a "yoked research design," both rats are then shocked simultaneously at various intervals. One rat has a lever available in its cage which if pressed will discontinue the shock. The second rat has no such escape opportunity. When the first rat presses the lever, it stops the shock for both rats. This ensures that both rats are exposed to the same level and intensity of the shock, but only the first rat has control over discontinuing the stressful event. Can you guess what happens? The first rat, the one with control, is minimally if at all affected by the series of shocks. The second "helpless" rat, on the other hand, suffers negatively, developing multiple psychosomatic symptoms such as ulcers.

These differences in stress response are maintained even when the escape lever is removed and replaced merely by a light which precedes the shock. In this design, the first rat had no means of escape, but was warned that a shock was imminent. Although the rat could do no more than dance around the cage, the effects of the stressor were somehow reduced perhaps because the rat knew it was going to be dancing around and was, therefore, more prepared to do so. Thus, our sense of control is also affected by the extent to which we can anticipate and prepare for the onset of stressors and change. Involvement in exercise is a perfect example of this. We know that physical exercise is stressful. Yet it is stress over which we have control because we typically can choose when to begin and when to end our exercise routine. Stress researchers conclude that it is this sense of control which is at least partially responsible for the beneficial effects of repeated exercise (Brehm, 1998).

So, stress hardy individuals refuse to see themselves as victims, buffeted and abused by external occurrences over which they have no control. Persons exhibiting this attitude see themselves as active players in their own lives. They possess what was discussed in Chapter 2 as an internal locus of control; for such individuals believe that they are responsible for the ultimate outcomes in their lives. They do not wait for fate to lead them in directions; rather they endeavor to take active control over their own life. This is the same attitude described by Covey as proactivity.

6.4.2 Commitment

The second attitude characteristic of stress hardy individuals identified by Kobasa involves **commitment**. It is not merely persistently working toward a goal, it is an attitude which expresses a real *joie de vivre*, a zest for life. Commitment involves believing that what you do is of value and importance. Individuals exhibiting this attitude seem to possess an almost romantic relationship to their own life and the pursuits they choose. When they awaken they don't start their day with, "Oh God, I wonder what could go wrong today? What horrible ambush can life have planned for me?" Instead they wake up expectant of the possible surprises and wonderful experiences the day has in store for them. They have an optimistic outlook. Stressors are viewed as potentially interesting and meaningful. Commitment is the opposite of alienation and is characterized by involvement.

It is not surprising that research has linked how one answers two simple questions with the likelihood of developing heart disease. The two questions are: *Are you happy?* And, *do you like your job?* If you answer yes to both of these, your chances of developing heart disease are much lower. Clearly the reverse is true when the answer is no. We are not implying here that overall life/job dissatisfaction causes heart disease. Obviously there are many other factors operating in the development of cardiovascular problems. But your attitude towards your life is one important contributing factor. What is your attitude when you first open your eyes in the morning? We suggest you begin with an *attitude of gratitude* which we will discuss in detail in the next chapter. One that says, "thank you. I'm glad I'm alive. I wonder what adventures and experiences this day has for me." You see, happiness is not a condition, but a decision. You can choose to focus on all that can make you miserable. If you do, you will get results fitting this attitude. Or you can choose to count your blessings, to be thankful for all you have, and all you still have coming. To quote the great comedienne Gilda Radner shortly before her untimely death, "Happiness is not about getting what you want, but about appreciating what you have."

6.4.3 Challenge

The third and final attitude discovered by Kobasa to be typical of stress hardy individuals is that of **challenge**. This attitude can perhaps be best explained by considering the concept of *crisis*. The Chinese write this word using two characters as illustrated below:

The first character is the symbol for danger; the second is the symbol for opportunity. Think about that, what a wonderful way to describe a crisis. Not a catastrophe, or a problem, but a *dangerous opportunity*. Individuals exhibiting the attitude of challenge focus not so much on the danger aspect of the crisis, but on the opportunities available as a result. Every crisis, no matter what, has inherent opportunities. Those who cope well look for these opportunities and capitalize on them. Those who cope poorly get paralyzed by the inherent danger. To quote Don Juan, from Castaneda's *The Teachings of Don Juan (1998)*:

> The basic difference between a warrior and an ordinary man is that a warrior sees everything as a challenge. While an ordinary man sees everything as either a blessing or a curse.

Or to quote another colorful literary character, Zorba, from the movie *Zorba the Greek*.

> Life is trouble, only death is not. To be alive is to undo your belt and go looking for trouble.

6.4.4 Hardiness and Stress Resistance

Take a moment and fill out the Stress Hardiness Inventory. Research has documented an association between high hardiness scores and lower rates of physical illness among white collar male executives and women in various occupations (Rhodewalt & Zone, 1989), blue collar workers (Manning, Williams, & Wolfe, 1988), college students (Roth and colleagues., 1989), and adolescents (Sheppard & Kashani, 1991). Hardiness is also associated with psychological health. Stress hardy individuals report lower anxiety levels, less depression, greater job satisfaction and lower levels of tension at work. In other studies, hardy subjects were shown to have stronger physical tolerance for stress. When exposed to a stressor they have a lower increase in diastolic blood pressure (Contrada, 1989) and a smaller increase in heart rate (Lawler & Schmied, 1987).

Stress Hardiness Self-Assessment Inventory

Use this scale to indicate how much you agree or disagree with the statements below:

0 = Strongly disagree   **1 = Mildly disagree**   **2 = Mildly agree**   **3 = Strongly agree**

_____ **A.** Trying my best at work and school makes a difference.

_____ **B.** Trusting to fate is sometimes all I can do in a relationship.

_____ **C.** I often wake up eager to start on the day's projects.

_____ **D.** Thinking of myself as a free person leads to great frustration and difficulty.

_____ **E.** I would be willing to sacrifice financial security in my work if something really challenging came along.

_____ **F.** It bothers me when I have to deviate from the routine or schedule I've set for myself.

_____ **G.** An average citizen can have an impact on politics.

_____ **H.** Without the right breaks, it is hard to be successful in my field.

_____ **I.** I know why I am doing what I'm doing at work or school.

_____ **J.** Getting close to people puts me at risk of being obligated to them.

_____ **K.** Encountering new situations is an important priority in my life.

_____ **L.** I really don't mind when I have nothing to do.

To get your scores for control, commitment and challenge, write the number of your answer, from 0 to 3, above the letter of each question. Then add and subtract as shown below. Then add up the column of scores for control, commitment and challenge.

(A + G = _____) − (B + H = _____) = _____ Control
(C + I = _____) − (D + J = _____) = _____ Commitment
(E + K = _____) − (F + L = _____) = _____ Challenge
_____ Total Hardiness Score

Score	Interpretation
10–18	Hardy personality
0–9	Moderate hardiness
Below 0	Low hardiness

One interesting study (Allred & Smith, 1989) demonstrated that male college students who scored low on hardiness experienced high levels of tension before the onset of a stressor (i.e. as they waited and anticipated), while those scoring high on hardiness measures displayed higher arousal only during exposure to the stressor. It appeared that the hardy subjects got aroused only when they needed an adrenalin surge to confront the stressor more effectively, while the others spent valuable energy worrying. Hardy individuals do get physiologically aroused but at the right time and to the right level.

Strong resistance to stress is associated with optimism, and clearly the ability to think positively is a defining characteristic of the stress hardy. Stress resistant people are more likely to use problem-focused coping measures, positive thinking, and support-seeking strategies when faced with stress (Cohen & Edwards, 1989; Holt, Fine & Tollefson,1987; Nowack, 1989). Those scoring low on measures of hardiness tend to respond passively to stress, whether with avoidance or maladaptive behaviors. Hardy individuals are much more likely to take care of their health, which helps to boost their stress resistance. A strong sense of personal control over one's life is associated with better health habits, such as exercise and good nutrition, and lower likelihood of abusing alcohol, drugs or nicotine, or of aggressive acting out when under stress.

THE THREE CS IN ACTION The authors had an opportunity to witness, first-hand, how stress hardiness attitudes affected the ability of literally thousands of people to cope with a monumental crisis. Being based in Miami, Florida, we, along with thousands of other people, back in 1992 experienced Hurricane Andrew, one of the strongest and most destructive storms ever to ravage the mainland U.S.A. prior to Hurricane Katrina. The scale of property destruction and disruption of normal life for months afterward was extensive. Just about everyone in the hurricane zone (including the authors) suffered severe damage to their homes, businesses, cars, and personal property. Rebuilding took years and normal routines were totally disrupted for at least six months for most. As psychologists we paid close attention to how individuals coped with the aftermath of the storm and we found that three distinct styles emerged: (1) The Whiners-individuals who spent months bemoaning their plight and all the inconveniences, hassles, and property losses they suffered; (2) The Stiff Upper Lip Crowd—individuals who were very upset but focused on cleaning up and rebuilding, and didn't spend an inordinate amount of time complaining, but internally they focused primarily on how awful it all was; (3) The Adventurers—individuals who did not deny the reality of the damage but who focused on how interesting, how exciting, what an adventure it all was. These people relished rebuilding their homes with insurance money. They delighted in the sense of camaraderie and community that developed between neighbors who found themselves in the same boat, who previously had barely spoken to one another. Needless to say, the latter group experienced far fewer emotional disturbances and physical illnesses than the other two groups. They believed that they could *control* their destiny, even in the face of incredible ruin. They were *committed* to making the rebuilding process as joyful as possible. And they viewed the crisis as a *challenge* and opportunity to recreate their living situation and make new friends. For them, the hurricane became an epic, fascinating story to share with friends rather than merely a tragic event.

Clearly, you should be able to perceive the wisdom in Covey's oft-quoted phrase, "The way you see the problem is the problem." Ultimately, whether something is stressful or not depends on the way you look at the situation. Remember, it is not the world out there that makes you a victim, it is your perception of the circumstances and events which lead you to be either defeated by stress or to survive and thrive from the challenges and opportunities presented to you. You may not have control over all that happens to you, but you certainly always have control over the meaning you give to the events in your life. There is an old saying, "When God closes a door, He opens a window." Remember this as you face apparent hardships in your life. Always look for the windows; we guarantee that they will be there, no matter what the circumstances.

PROBLEM-FOCUSED VS. EMOTION-FOCUSED COPING STRATEGIES Other factors influence how individuals choose to cope with stress as well. Richard Lazarus (1966, 1991) emphasized the role of how an individual appraises a stressful situation in determining both the impact of the stressor, and in the choice of the appropriate method of coping. Coping strategies can be partitioned into two broad categories where **Problem-focused coping** refers to attempts to deal with the stressor head-on to remove or defuse its effects, and **Emotion-focused coping** is a more indirect method, where attempts are made to moderate one's own emotional response to the stressor. For example, a broken down car would call for problem-focused coping (i.e. get the car repaired a.s.a.p.), while a broken heart would require emotion-focused coping. Lazarus pointed out that there is no one preferred strategy of coping, as different stressors or stressful events demand different coping styles. The effective individual appraises events in ways that allow for the choice of the most appropriate coping strategy given the particular stressor. Emotion-focused coping strategies for dealing with stress include relaxation techniques such as diaphragmatic breathing, progressive relaxation and meditation along with cognitive restructuring methods.

6.4.5 The Biology of Stress Hardiness

What is actually happening on a physiological level to promote health in individuals who display the 3 Cs? Let us begin this discussion by focusing on the effects of hardiness on cardiovascular disease (CVD). We know that optimism, an essential component of hardiness, is strongly associated with cardiovascular health and mortality rate. In one longitudinal study with over 97,000 women (Tindle & colleagues, 2009), optimists had 30% fewer coronary deaths than pessimists. This brings up the question of whether the real culprit was depression, since dysthymia is correlated with pessimism. However, not all pessimists are depressed. Indeed, this study controlled for levels of depression as well as other risk factors and found that optimism was the crucial factor. In yet another study, 120 men who suffered one heart attack were studied over $8^1/_2$ years, and within that time frame half of them had died of a second heart attack. The usual risk factors such as blood pressure, cholesterol levels, or amount of damage from the first attack were not predictive of who would die of a second heart attack. The only reliable predictor turned out to be levels of optimism vs. pessimism. Fifteen of the sixteen most pessimistic patients died, but only five of the sixteen most optimistic men lost their lives to a second coronary event (Buchanan & Seligman, 1995). Optimism was also shown to be strongly associated with fewer deaths from all causes, including CVD, in a large Dutch study (Giltay & colleagues, 2004).

One potential biological explanation for the protective effects of optimism on cardiovascular functioning has to do with the repercussions of stress on our bodies. Due to their mindset, pessimists tend to give up, which increases their stress levels. The opposite typically occurs for optimists, who cope better and report lower stress levels. Ongoing or episodic stress triggers the production of the stress hormone cortisol along with other circulatory responses (such as higher blood pressure and heart rate) that can weaken the lining of blood vessels or worsen existing damage. This is part of what causes atherosclerosis, the hardening of the arteries and plaque deposits in the vessel walls. Another factor in CVD is inflammation. Research suggests that heart disease can develop when chronic stress triggers persistent inflammation (Matthews, 2005; Miller & Blackwell, 2006). Stress is known to elicit higher production of particular neurotransmitters known as catecholamines along with cortisol. Both of these can provoke the inflammatory processes which exacerbate atherosclerosis. Individuals exposed to ongoing stress, such as children raised in abusive homes, are more prone to inflammatory responses (Dickerson & colleagues, 2009; Miller & Chen, 2010).

Yet another CVD risk factor is the possibility of forming blood clots which could get lodged in an arterial wall and lead to a heart attack or stroke. Women who score low in feelings of mastery (the sense of control over the environment) were shown to have higher degrees of calcification (plaque buildup) in their aortas, the major artery of the heart (Matthews & colleagues, 2006). The mechanism for this may relate to the production of fibrinogen, a substance produced by the liver, which promotes clotting. Excess fibrinogen makes the blood thicker which can lead to the formation of blood clots within the circulatory system. Research (Steptoe, Wardle, & Marnot, 2005) has shown that those who display higher levels of positive emotions produce less fibrinogen when under stress than those with low levels of positive emotions.

Optimists are much less vulnerable to all types of disease, in general. What mechanisms enable optimists, who are likely to be more stress hardy, to stay healthy? Due to the fact that optimists believe that they have control over their health, that their actions matter, they are more likely to make healthy lifestyle choices. They are also more likely to follow medical advice because they expect it to make a difference. For example, after the early warnings about the dangers of cigarette smoking, it was the optimists who were more likely to quit (Vaillant, 2003). Pessimists revert to learned helplessness, making poor lifestyle choices because they do not believe they have any control over their health.

Optimism appears to facilitate immune functioning, thereby improving resistance to illness. In one study (Kamen-Siegel, Rodin, Seligman & Dwyer, 1991), the blood drawn from optimists contained significantly more infection fighting cells (T lymphocytes) than for pessimists. In the previous chapter we mentioned a series of studies demonstrating that subjects exposed to a cold virus were more likely to become ill if they were under stress. In a later series of studies by some of the same researchers (Cohen & colleagues, 2003; 2006), the relationship between positive emotions and susceptibility to cold and flu viruses was analyzed. They found that subjects displaying high levels of positive emotions developed fewer colds and were less likely to catch the flu. The biological mechanism for this appears to be the production of the protein interleukin 6, which causes inflammation. Inflammation is the culprit that leads to a host of bodily dysfunctions including susceptibility to illness. The greater the subjects' levels of positive emotion, the lower their interleukin 6 production and, therefore, the less the inflammation (Doyle, Gentile & Cohen, 2006).

Based on all of this data, Seligman (2011) asserted that "optimism is robustly associated with cardiovascular health and pessimism with cardiovascular risk." In addition, he concluded that positive emotions protect us by boosting immune functioning, while negative emotions increase our risk of getting sick. In summarizing the literature he concludes that "well-being is associated with less risk for death from all causes." The one exception where this cannot be stated conclusively is with regard to cancer. While optimism may lower cancer risk, the research results supporting this are inconsistent.

The Global Perspective
The Effects of Ikigai on CVD

The lower rate of CVD in Japan has often been linked to a healthier diet rich in seafood and vegetables. But another factor appears to be at work, relating to a cultural trait combining optimism with a strong sense of meaning and purpose in life (the M in PERMA). This is the Japanese concept of **ikigai** which can be translated as "something to live for." Three Japanese studies all point to high ikigai levels being associated with lowered cardiovascular risk. In one study (Sone & colleagues, 2008) the death rate from CVD for individuals with very low ikigai was 160% higher than for individuals with high ikigai! How would you rate your own concept of ikigai? Would you say you have high or low ikigai?

6.4.6 Resiliency: The Key to Post-Traumatic Growth

Stress hardiness refers to the ability to be resistant to the negative effects of stress. But what about when the stress is of the truly catastrophic variety, like a traumatic injury, sudden death of a loved one, a natural disaster, or being a victim of violent crime? The ability to bounce back from severe trauma or loss is referred to as **resilience**. It can also be defined as the capacity to adapt successfully in the presence of risk and adversity (Meichenbaum, 2012). A resilient individual may bend but will not break when confronted with adversity, enabling that person to recover. Resilience involves the ability to regulate and constructively harness the biological and psychological aspects of the stress response, which is essential to maintaining physical and emotional health. Those with resilience do not avoid stress, but rather learn to tame and master it even when trauma is involved. These are the individuals who may display what has come to be known as **post-traumatic growth**. In Donald Meichenbaum's (2012) *The Roadmap to Resilience* (a handbook for returning military personnel and their families), he concludes that the research evidence on resilience indicates that individuals with a history of moderate exposure to adversity tended to actually have lower levels of distress, less impairment and higher well-being than individuals with no exposure to hardship. According to Meichenbaum, this exposure to highly stressful life events can have an "inoculating effect" which better prepares people to handle future stress and strife. This exposure to adversity can create a psychological "toughness" which accords a protective effect, especially when such exposure is time-limited with the opportunity for recovery. This toughness can then stretch across a variety of situations. Furthermore, such resilience is more common than you may think and, according to Masten (2001), it is not a product of rare or extraordinary ability, but rather is a capacity inherent in normal, everyday coping skills. Meichenbaum reminds us that "following a natural catastrophe or traumatic event no one walks away unscathed by such events, but neither do most survivors succumb in the aftermath to despair. Most show remarkable levels of resilience. Following exposure to traumatic events, 70% of individuals evidence resilience."

Dean Becker (2002), founder of a resilience training firm, links resilience to life success. Since setbacks, obstacles and stress are part of life, those who react effectively get the farthest. Like most characteristics, resilience is a product of inborn traits (genetics) and environmental factors that affect the ability to adapt to extreme stress. The good news is that anyone can boost their level of resilience by working to develop the mental attitudes and physical habits that facilitate positive adaptation to stress and trauma. Some environmental/situational factors may be beyond our power to change, however, with practice you can learn to think and act in ways that greatly enhance resilience. In their book *Resilience: The Science of Mastering Life's Greatest Challenges*, authors Steven Southwich and Dennis Charney (2012) identify a variety of methods for building resilience:

1. Utilize cognitive restructuring to reframe the meaning of an adverse event so it is perceived as less negative. To facilitate this the following questions can be useful:

   - Is there a less destructive way to view this situation?
   - Am I catastrophizing or exaggerating the potential negative impact or effects?
   - What can I learn from this trauma?
   - Is it possible to grow stronger from this?

2. Practice realistic optimism to help boost positive emotions.

3. Engage in regular physical exercise.

4. Practice mindfulness meditation.

5. Incorporate **stress inoculation**. This involves gradually increasing the difficulty levels of challenges you face to allow yourself to acclimate to progressively higher levels of stress. This principle of graded exposure to stress can apply to a broad range of activities designed to increase physical, emotional and cognitive resilience. It is important that these progressively greater exposures be outside your comfort zone, but not so intense as to be overwhelming or potentially harmful.

6. Make ample use of your support system.

7. Learn from role models who you view as exemplifying resilience. Using what we know about the power of observational learning (based on Bandura's work on modeling), observe the attitudes and behaviors of resilient individuals and attempt to imitate those aspects which can work for you.

6.4.7 Can Hardiness Be Taught? The Penn Resiliency Program

Martin Seligman and his research team put together a training program for children through young adults geared to develop the skills for resilience. The major goal of the Penn Resiliency Program (PRP) is to increase the ability of students to cope with common daily problems or stressors. There have been over 3,000 participants in the PRP ranging in ages from 8 to 22. Over the last two decades more than twenty separate studies have evaluated the effectiveness of this program. Seligman (2011) claims that it is "the most widely researched depression prevention program in the world." PRP develops participants' coping abilities by teaching realistic optimism, assertiveness, relaxation techniques, and decision-making, among other skills. The widely diverse subject population is representative of multiple racial, ethnic and socioeconomic backgrounds, as well as urban and rural settings in the U.S., Europe, China and Australia.

A meta-analysis of all of the PRP studies revealed that the training significantly reduced or prevented symptoms of depression compared to the control groups, and these results endured for at least two years afterward (Brunwasser & Gillham, 2008). The meta-analysis also demonstrated that PRP significantly increased optimism and well-being levels while reducing hopelessness, the precipitant of learned helplessness. PRP reduces and prevents severe levels of depression (Gillham, Reivich, Jacox, & Seligman, 1995) and anxiety (Gillham, Hamilton, Freres, Patton & Gallup, 2006). In addition, conduct problems were reduced (Cutuli, Chaplin, Gillham, Reivich & Seligman, 2006). Lastly, students who went through PRP were healthier; they got sick less often while exercising more and eating better than the controls (Seligman, 2011). These results were consistent for children of all racial and ethnic backgrounds (Brunwasser & Gillham, 2008). Clearly PRP succeeded in building stress hardiness skills for the participants.

Buchanan, Gardenswartz & Seligman (1999) took PRP one step further by singling out and training college freshmen identified as at high risk for depression based on their highly pessimistic explanatory style as assessed by questionnaire responses. These pessimistic freshmen were randomly assigned either into a no intervention control group or an eight week "stress management seminar" which consisted of the PRP. The results were identical to those obtained with the children and adolescents. The group that received the training was significantly more optimistic and physically healthier than the controls. They got sick less often and had better health habits.

6.4.8 Acquiring Body Wisdom: The Warrior Stance

If you have been applying what you have learned thus far, your breathing will be becoming slower, deeper, and quieter. Your awareness will be keener as you notice that you can observe and stand apart from your attitudes and emotions. It is from this very place that all systems of personal change and development begin. Now that you have gotten your feet wet, it is time to dive a little deeper and focus your new tools more intently on both body and mind.

This section will focus on acquiring what we call **body wisdom**. Usually we think of wisdom as having an awful lot to do with the things we say and think. For many it is a measure of how many facts they know or how intelligent they are. Body wisdom, however, is not about how thoughts affect your body but about how your body affects your thoughts. We maintain that the body is intelligent, wise if you will, and that this wisdom can be tapped to improve your health, well-being, and performance.

Midway through graduate school one of the authors made a personal discovery which has guided his work as a therapist, trainer, and student ever since. The story illustrates the central premise of this concept.

> *It was the most difficult emotional period I had ever experienced in my life. I was a novice psychotherapist facing the pressures of a new job, a new relationship, physical illness, and the most difficult examinations of my academic life. My symptoms were classic: difficulty eating and sleeping, obsessive thoughts, a lack of energy and feelings of hopelessness. Since I had never experienced anything like this before, I had no clear idea how to get better. The difficulties lingered for months, even after many of the problems had been resolved. It certainly didn't make sense to me that it just kept going on and on. It was as if my emotional life was going downhill and all I could do was watch. I was alternately frightened, sad, and bewildered by my inability to feel the way I used to feel, joyful and engaged in life. Finally, one afternoon as I sat alone in my office, particularly exasperated, I asked myself the key question. How did I act when I felt better? I was, as they say, sick and tired of being sick and tired. Thinking alone had not really changed anything for me. I knew I used to be different and I began to focus on acting that way again. Quite literally I decided to change my posture, the*

speed of my walk, the tilt of my head, the expression on my face. I walked out of my office in character, whistling a happier tune in my head, and asked the first person I saw how he was feeling. I played this part the remainder of the day and I noticed that I felt better. I decided to continue playing the role for a while longer and soon forgot that I was playing the role. I simply began to be the way I was with one important difference: I now knew there was a way out of the darkness. I knew I would never be quite that lost again. This was the beginning of a series of physical and mental practices that have served me very well over the years. My body had led me out of the wilderness the way a horse carries an injured rider back to the stable.

Shakespeare once wrote, "If you lack the virtue, act the virtue." Today we say, "Fake it, til you make it." What we are suggesting is that there is a stressed stance as well. If you act stressed, holding your body in the manner characteristic of the fight or flight response, you will feel stressed, even if there is no particular reason to be stressed. Luckily, there is an antidote for this and that is to discover what we call the **warrior's stance**.

At first blush the notion of a warrior's stance leading to a more peaceful, less stressed existence may seem like an oxymoron. Why not a monk's stance or a gardener's stance? However, since life, business, and relationships are often presented in terms of struggles, battles, conflicts, and competitions, we might find it useful to examine this metaphor more carefully. Contrary to popular belief, successful warriors are ultimately peaceful individuals whose primary battles are fought internally. They display a relaxed and balanced posture. This enables them to have exceptional reaction times and full freedom of movement. This capacity for relaxed balance also begets a fluidity of response that allows them to pull an opponent who pushes them or push one who pulls. It is a capacity to literally flow around obstacles. Anyone who has gone white water rafting has been given the wise counsel to let the river carry you to a safe place when you have been thrown from the boat. To resist overpowering force is to risk being thrown into the rocks. A warrior knows that it is best to stay relaxed and alert and float feet first so you can be aware of genuine routes of escape.

A warrior cultivates fearlessness. This does not mean recklessness. It simply speaks to the survival value of being able to notice the body's response to a threat and, by the force of the regular practice of a discipline, still maintain the ability to choose a course of action. This grace under fire is often the difference between life and death in survival situations. Fear is a process that necessitates that we step out of the moment and contemplate the past or future. However, an intense focus in the here and now is the best way to keep fear at bay. The easiest way to maintain this present focus is to cultivate the breathing and relaxed posture of the warrior. A warrior does not seek out or create conflict. Their preference is to walk away. But once engaged in battle, they are fully committed to their chosen course of action.

This is truly a critical piece of information for individuals who have attempted to change their lives by changing the content of their thoughts through endless affirmations. In our experience, "nice thoughts" have very little impact on someone's long term well-being if their body is wracked with tension and stress-related hormones. You must actively change your physiology if you hope to contend successfully with stress. Consider a parallel from the study of communication. Research estimates (Mehrabian, 1971) that only 7% of the meaning of any communication is actually in the words themselves. The remaining 93% of the meaning is communicated by our body language and the tone and tempo of our speech. In a similar vein, if we wish to communicate to ourselves the value of a more relaxed stance, we will need more than words. We need to speak to our bodies in a way that they will understand.

However, in the realm of relationships, the behavior most of us need to cultivate is listening. This is no less true of our relationship with our body. The disorders that are brought on by chronic, excessive muscle tension begin as mere brief episodes of tension. We may grit our teeth in anger and still maintain some residual tension even after the cause of our anger is gone. Over time this can develop into bruxism, the grinding and gnashing of the teeth while sleeping. We may tighten our neck and shoulder muscles in response to fear or anxiety and again retain excess tension even after the threat has disappeared. This is how tension headaches begin. Why exactly does this occur?

You might say that in each of the cases above someone failed to listen to his or her body. Now the body's usual response is to continue communicating in its language of rising tension. Ultimately, when we are stricken with a stress-related illness, the body is now screaming, "Why didn't you listen when I was whispering?" This is the primary aphorism of this chapter: **IF YOU LISTEN TO YOUR BODY WHEN IT WHISPERS, YOU WON'T HAVE TO LISTEN TO IT SCREAM.**

Once again we return to the issue of awareness. To listen to the whispers of tension we must be aware of what it means to be truly relaxed. In point of fact, most people simply do not know what it means to be relaxed. We have seen many individuals claim that they are relaxed only to be shown otherwise when they are monitored by biofeedback equipment. As noted earlier, breathing is the starting point of your relaxation practice. But to go deeper into relaxation requires an additional practice and we would like to introduce that to you next.

Questions

1. Stress hardy individuals possess attitudes of _____, _____, and _____.

    A. internal; external; subdural locus of control

    B. control; commitment; challenge

    C. optimism; defensive pessimism; self-esteem

    D. wellness; fitness; mindfulness

2. Which of the following characterizations applies to stress hardy individuals?

    A. They have an internal locus of control.

    B. They have an external locus of control.

    C. They focus on all the problems inherent in adversity.

    D. They tend to be pessimistic.

3. Adopting the *warriors' stance* helps you to acquire_____.

    A. wealth and power

    B. self-awareness

    C. sexual satisfaction

    D. body wisdom

6.5 Progressive Muscle Relaxation

Recognize the goals and guidelines of progressive muscle relaxation.

In 1929 the book *Progressive Relaxation* by Edmund Jacobson, a Chicago physician, was published. He theorized that physical tension leads to mental tension which further exacerbates physical tension. Therefore, learning to relax your body should promote mental relaxation and lowered stress levels. This technique has been used very effectively to treat a wide variety of stress-related disorders (Seaward, 1997). The theory of its use is simple, that is, if you induce a feeling of deep relaxation in your body you simply cannot be feeling stressed. As your body experiences a return to homeostasis, your body's natural inclination towards healing and health is activated and enabled.

    While we will present a formal protocol which you can follow to implement **Progressive Relaxation**, it is most important that you understand the principles and guidelines that will allow you to succeed as long as you commit to regular practice for several weeks. The reward for this short term commitment is that you will be able to reduce the time needed to reach a relaxed state from 25 minutes down to 5 to 7 minutes. Before you begin you may find the following guidelines to be helpful:

- Prepare a convenient time and place, and practice regularly. Remove distractions.

- Set up a regular practice schedule. Several times weekly is recommended until you have mastered the technique. You can then use it on an as-needed basis.

- Be comfortable. Wear loose fitting clothing. Recline on your bed, sofa or in a cozy recliner chair. Some people place a rolled towel under their knees and lower back to maintain a comfortable spinal alignment.

- Avoid falling asleep, unless you are using this procedure to facilitate sleep.

- Don't try too hard. Paradoxically, if you try too hard to relax it will only increase your level of tension.

- Allow yourself to "let go." Sometimes people fear letting go, for it is equated with losing control. The only thing you have to lose here is unhealthy muscle tension. Learning to relax increases your control, but first you have to let go and allow this to happen.

- If you find your mind wandering, gently bring your focus back to your breathing and to this technique without scolding yourself or passing judgment.

- Finish your relaxation practice by coming back slowly. At the end of your practice session, slowly bring your attention back to your surroundings, gently stretch your muscles, and open closed eyes. If you are lying down, roll over slowly onto your side, pause, and then sit up. When your muscles are deeply relaxed, you do not want to contract them suddenly. Coming back slowly allows your relaxed state to linger for hours.

One goal of this procedure is to help you become aware of the difference between feelings of muscle contraction vs. muscle relaxation. Begin by taking a few moments to scan your body for tension and to focus your attention on any physical sensations. The basic method in Progressive Relaxation is to first carefully tense a particular muscle or group of muscles. This is to further develop your *awareness* of that part of your body, specifically when that part is tense. It is important that you contract the muscle only to a low level of tension. Be particularly careful not to over-tense any muscle or muscle group where you are prone to experience muscle spasms. Contracting a muscle as hard as you can only leaves you more tense and does not cultivate relaxation. Tense each muscle group for up to 5 to 7 seconds, and then release the muscle and focus your awareness on how the muscles feel as they relax for the next 20 to 30 seconds. Allow yourself to focus on any sensations of warmth and heaviness. As you continue from muscle to muscle, slowly but surely the sensation of warmth and heaviness begins to spread throughout your body. It can help to talk to yourself during this process with self-instructions such as the following:

> *Clench your right hand into a fist. Tighten your fist and study the tension as you do so. Become aware of the tension and discomfort in your hand and forearm as you tense. Now let go of the tension and let your hand go limp. Pay careful attention to the feelings of relaxation spreading in your hand as the tension drains away. Notice the difference between the comfortable sensations of relaxation in your hand now, compared to the uncomfortable feelings of tension. Let go more and more, letting the muscles in your hand and forearm grow more and more deeply and fully relaxed.*

The typical sequence of movements would be as follows:

TABLE 6.3 Progressive Relaxation Sequence

1.	HANDS AND FOREARMS	Clench fists—left then right; bend hands backward at wrist, left and then right
2.	BICEPS	Flex by bending elbows and bringing hands up to your shoulders
3.	TRICEPS	Straighten arms and push down against the chair or floor.
4.	FOREHEAD	Wrinkle forehead
5.	EYES	Squeeze tightly shut
6.	JAW	Press teeth together then let jaw drop
7.	TONGUE	Press into roof of mouth
8.	LIPS	Press together
9.	HEAD AND NECK	Push head back; bend head forward—touch chin to chest
10.	SHOULDERS	Shrug and try to touch ears
11.	CHEST	Take three deep breaths—hold each several seconds
12.	BACK	Arch
13.	ABDOMEN	Suck stomach in; make it hard as if it was going to be hit
14.	THIGHS	Tense thigh muscles—stretch legs out
15.	ANKLES AND CALVES	Point toes toward face; point toes downward

After you have gotten familiar with this sequence of movements, there are a number of techniques for coordinating your breathing, language, and imagination to creatively deepen and enrich your experience.

- Experiment with coordinating your breathing with the tensing and relaxing of each muscle group. Inhale and briefly hold your breath as you tense the muscle group. Exhale as you let go. Be aware of the sounds of the breath as you relax as well as the feelings of relaxation. Over time the hissing of the slow release of breath will become associated with relaxation and speed up the process of letting go.

- Some people prefer to visualize their breath as light that carries warmth and relaxation to their muscles. In this scenario, as you tense a muscle and inhale you are pulling light to the muscle group. As you exhale you expel darkness and tension from the muscles. Gradually you build an image of your body filled with light. If another set of colors feels better to you feel free to experiment. For instance, some people like to use the color blue to symbolize relaxation and red to indicate tension. Once you have reached a relaxed state you can really embrace your relaxation experience by imagining a scene that is pleasant to you, such as lying on a beach or walking in the woods.

- There is also a time-honored method known as **Autogenic Training** in which one literally talks oneself into relaxation. This is done by repeating certain phrases over and over while focusing your attention on a particular muscle group. For instance, if after going through a Progressive Relaxation exercise, you still feel residual tension in a body part, then you would repeat to yourself, "My (name the part, i.e. arm, hands, thighs) feel warm and heavy." Or you could say to yourself, "My (arms) feel loose and relaxed." In fact, this method of systematically repeating relaxing phrases over and over again can be used on its own to induce relaxation. It can, however, be terminally boring, so be certain to tailor your program to your needs and interests. Create a routine that interests you and you will increase the likelihood of following through and mastering this skill.

One main goal of Progressive Relaxation training is to help you achieve **differential relaxation** throughout your day. Accomplishing this means you are able to contract only those muscles which are necessary to accomplish the task at hand, while keeping all other muscles relaxed (McGuigan, 1984). For example, there is no need to clench your jaw, stiffen your shoulders, or squeeze the steering wheel while driving. But your arm and leg muscles will certainly need to contract in order to operate a car.

Barbara Brehm (1998) extols the virtues of relaxation techniques such as progressive muscle relaxation for people who she characterizes as "hot reactors." These are individuals who startle easily, who get stressed out easily, and who tend to overreact physically to stress. Such relaxation techniques are essential for people with stress-related psychophysiological disorders or illnesses. Many people report that daily relaxation practice is an effective antidote for stress-related illness (Matheny and colleagues, 1986). Muscle relaxation techniques are being prescribed by physicians and psychologists for the treatment of stress-related disorders such as headaches (Sorbi &Tellegen, 1986), heart disease (Ornish, 1990), gastrointestinal problems and insomnia (Hellman and colleagues, 1990), muscular pain due to muscle tension (Kabat-Zinn, 1990), and anxiety disorders (Sachs, 1991). The technique is also useful for helping individuals cope with academic stress (Rajendran & Kaliappan, 1990) and workplace stress (Stanton, 1991). Progressive muscle relaxation has been used successfully with all types of people of all ages to lower baseline tension and stress levels (Brehm, 1998).

Questions

1. _____ relaxation exercises are an effective method for reducing and/or eliminating muscular tension.

   A. Passive

   B. Regressive

   C. Progressive

   D. Natural

2. One goal of Progressive Relaxation is to help you achieve_____.

    A. posttraumatic growth

    B. enlightenment

    C. differential relaxation

    D. autogenic training

3. Progressive relaxation exercises are especially helpful for_____.

    A. stress-related physical disorders

    B. cold reactors

    C. counteracting poor nutrition

    D. loneliness

6.6 Meditation

Describe the benefits and techniques of regular meditative practice.

One of the most powerful and efficient methods for reducing stress is to include regular meditative practice in your life. At Herbert Benson's Mind/Body Medical Institute, participants experience the "relaxation response" by repeating a word or sound that can be anything from reciting a Hail Mary to chanting "Ommm" silently while exhaling. Benson reports that such meditative practice leads to a calm state of mind, slower breathing, and lower blood pressure. Richard Davidson at the University of Wisconsin's Center for Mindfulness demonstrated that regular meditative practice positively affects our brains (Davidson, R. & Kabat-Zinn, 2003). Davidson took brain images of 25 participants, all of whom worked at a biotech firm, who meditated six days a week for eight weeks straight. The results showed increased activation in a part of the brain associated with decreased arousal and increased positive emotion, along with suppression of the amygdala, the fear and anxiety center of our brains. According to Atkinson (2014), mindfulness meditation produces growth in brain areas involved in mood regulation, attentiveness and empathy. Atkinson reviewed nineteen studies which demonstrated that practicing mindfulness meditation regularly for as short as eight weeks created changes in the brain conducive to facilitating focus, attention, and optimism along with anxiety reduction.

    There is no shortage of reading material regarding the value of meditative practice (Goleman, 1977; Kabat-Zinn, 1990; Ram Dass, 1990). Nor is there any lack of scientific research demonstrating that the practice of **meditation** indeed works to reduce and relieve pain (Kabat-Zinn, 1990), to lower blood pressure and the advance of atherosclerosis (Benson, 1984; Ornish, 1992) and to facilitate healing in general. Deep relaxation, euphoria, and heightened awareness can also be byproducts of meditative practice (Wallace & Benson, 1972; Kabat-Zinn, 1994;

Alexander and colleagues, 1993). People who regularly meditate report less stress, anxiety, depression, and hostility than non-meditators. However, while meditation has these many benefits, they are ultimately not the point of the practice. All meditation methods are like roads leading to Rome. There are lots of ways to get there. In this case Rome is the ability to maintain a focused awareness in the present moment. It is to be in each and every moment without being preoccupied with thoughts of the past or the future. It is to realize that you are much more than you think you are. That realization depends upon recognizing that you are more than your thoughts. Meditative practice is designed to break you out of your habitual patterns of perceiving and thinking about the world and who you are. While practical results abound in terms of improved concentration, relaxation, health, and awareness, it is ultimately a spiritual journey of discovery. *Every* religious tradition has some practice within it which can be considered meditative.

6.6.1 Attitudes for Mindfulness Meditation

Before we embark on a discussion of technique it is important to consider the attitudes that you want to bring to whatever practice you begin. In his book *Full Catastrophe Living*, Jon Kabat-Zinn (1990) suggests cultivating the following attitudes as part of the practice of meditation, particularly the practice of mindfulness.

1. **Non-Judging**

   As you begin a meditative practice you can be sure that you will immediately discover that you are making judgments about every aspect of your experience: "This is good." "This is bad." "Who cares about that?" These judgments create feelings and often stress. When you notice this kind of thinking arising, remind yourself to suspend judgment and just notice whatever comes up including the tendency to judge.

2. **Patience**

   Suffice it to say that things emerge in their own time. You cannot make a butterfly emerge from its cocoon sooner than necessary without damaging the butterfly. You can generally recognize impatience when you decide that there is something missing in this moment, a kind of judgment. All these practices take time and you make progress by accepting each moment of practice as being just where you need to be for now, simply because it is now.

3. **Beginners Mind**

   To quote Kabat-Zinn, "We tend to take the ordinary for granted and fail to grasp the extraordinariness of the ordinary." To see things with the wonder of a child seeing things for the first time is to practice **beginners mind**. So often we don't really see, hear, or feel what is here, but instead react to our memories of similar moments, but not this moment. How many times have you walked in a familiar place and suddenly seen something that you never noticed before and realized it had always been there? That is all too typical of our perceptions. We often see those closest to us as we remember them and not as they are now. Experiment with this. Look at someone familiar to you and see them as they are now. Look at how they may have changed.

4. **Trust**

This is a most crucial point. Just as there is no shortage of texts about meditation, there is no shortage of teachers and gurus either, and not all necessarily have your well-being or best interests at the top of their agenda. Ultimately you must learn to trust your own internal guidance and intuition. Everyone makes mistakes along the way. The best teachers will strive to help you develop this trust in yourself. You are not here to imitate others and follow their orders and ideas about who you should be. You are here to become more fully yourself.

5. **Non-Striving**

This is very similar to a recommendation for a "passive attitude" that Herbert Benson (1976) makes in his landmark text *The Relaxation Response*. Most everybody begins meditation because they want something. The promise of meditation is that you will get something, but not if you try too hard. You simply need to do the technique and not worry whether it is working. If you notice that you are unable to let go of a preoccupation with certain thoughts, simply notice this instead of striving to rid yourself of these thoughts, and then return to your technique.

6. **Acceptance**

Kabat-Zinn again summarizes this attitude beautifully. Although he does not talk directly about effectiveness per se, the relevance of adopting this attitude to the cultivation of personal effectiveness should be obvious.

> *Acceptance does not mean that you have to like everything or that you have to take a passive attitude toward everything and abandon your principles and values. It does not mean that you are satisfied with things as they are or that you are resigned to tolerating things as they 'have to be.' It does not mean that you should stop trying to break free of your own self-destructive habits or to give up on your desire to change and grow, or that you should tolerate injustice, for instance, or avoid getting involved in changing the world around you because it is the way it is and therefore hopeless. Acceptance as we are speaking of it simply means that you have come around to a willingness to see things as they are. This attitude sets the stage for acting appropriately in your life, no matter what is happening. You are much more likely to know what to do and have the inner conviction to act when you have a clear picture of what is actually happening than when your vision is clouded by your mind's self-serving judgments and desires or its fears and prejudices. (p. 38–39)*

7. **Letting Go**

If you know how to fall asleep, you know how to let go. If you have ever had insomnia you also know how difficult letting go can sometimes be. You cannot will yourself to fall asleep. Paradoxically, sleep comes when you let go and stop trying to fall asleep. Letting go means that it is important not to try to hold on to any aspect of our experience but simply to notice it and let it go. When we want to hold on to certain thoughts, this can tell us a lot about what may be causing difficulty in our lives. There are things to discover in the practice of meditation that go beyond the power of words to say. No one of us is ultimately any better or worse or less capable of discovering the beauty of their existence. However, you do need to practice something to move you down the road toward Rome. What follows is a discussion of basic techniques to get you started.

6.6.2 The Practice of Meditation

Meditation can be divided into techniques which emphasize focused concentration on a word, phrase, sound, image, physical movement or posture, or on techniques which emphasize the cultivation of mindfulness or awareness in each present moment.

FOCUSED CONCENTRATION   To begin the practice, it is best to find a quiet place and to sit in a comfortable position with an erect spine. You could do this practice lying down or in a recliner, but very often the tendency is to then fall asleep and not cultivate concentration and awareness. So for that reason, we recommend that you do your practice in an upright sitting position. You next need to choose a mental device, i.e. something upon which to focus your concentration. Some people choose to focus on their breath, the sound and feel of the process of the breath moving in and out of their body. Some focus on the word *in* as they breathe in and *out* as they breathe out. Other people simply choose a word or phrase to focus on such as *relax* or *peace*. Still others choose a sound with resonance which is referred to as a **mantra**. A common example of a mantra is the sound "Ommmm" which is repeated over and over again in the mind. An important point to note here is that there is data that suggests that focal points which have some spiritual significance or deep meaning for the meditator have led to more clinical improvement and more disciplined practice (Benson, 1984).

Once you have chosen your focal point, simply sit and bring your attention to it. To use breathing as an example, you would bring your attention to the in and out movement of the breath and, if you like, repeat in your mind the word *in* on the inhalation and *out* on the exhalation. That is basically it in terms of technique. What you will initially and over time experience may vary considerably. One thing is certain: You will find your mind wandering everywhere and that is fine. When this occurs, notice that you are thinking and label it as thinking. Then return to the in and out of your breathing. Do not try to stop thinking because that is just doing more thinking. Notice your thoughts and let them go. You may want to think of your thoughts as bubbles rising before your eyes. Let them float by and return to noticing your breath. With continued practice and cultivation of the proper attitudes you will begin to notice the differences in your life.

If you were to practice chanting, or **Tai Chi** (a moving meditation), or **Qi Gong** (a focus on the movement of energy) or any other discipline, the challenge and ultimate results tend to be quite similar. All roads lead to increased awareness and that is to be treasured above and beyond any specific path. These paths take you toward awareness by way of concentration. That is, as you gain the ability to concentrate you are able to stay more aware and involved in the moment, and you are less distracted by the meanderings of your thoughts.

6.6.3 Mindfulness

Mindfulness is the cultivation of awareness by practicing awareness. Virtually any activity, whether eating, walking, lovemaking, driving, bathing, etc. can become the vehicle for your practice. You can even consider the breathing meditation above as a kind of mindfulness practice. Attention brought to the breath over time generally results in slower, quieter, deeper breathing, i.e. relaxation.

Perhaps mindfully eating is the best place to get a feel for how unaware we are and how practicing mindfulness can increase awareness and lead to very practical results. How many times have you sat down to a meal and ate without truly tasting more than the first bite or two? Do you eat while reading or watching TV? Do you eat when you are not really feeling hungry? No, this is not a chapter on dieting, but a lack of mindfulness of all of the processes involved in eating can certainly lead to gaining weight. Try this mindfulness experiment when you have some quiet, uninterrupted time to enjoy a meal.

Positive Psychology Exercise

Mindfulness Meditation

Set your plate down and simply look at your food. Attend to the colors, shapes, and textures. Notice the aromas or perhaps steam rising up from the dish. Also at this moment attend to your own body. Is your mouth salivating? What is your tongue doing? Is your stomach growling? Do you find it difficult to be patient while doing this exercise? What are your thoughts like? Does this seem pointless to you? Do you wonder if you are doing this correctly?

As you prepare to take your first bite, notice your intention to pick up your utensil. Feel your arm, hand, and fingers move to grasp the fork or spoon. Feel the utensil in your hand. Are you breathing or holding your breath? Feel the additional weight of the food on your fork. Notice your arm rising, your mouth opening. Now taste the food. Notice the actual action of chewing and the change in taste as the food moves around your mouth. Be aware of the impulse to swallow. Keep chewing. Swallow. Feel the food go down your esophagus. Perhaps feel one bite heavier. Set your silverware down with full awareness. Are you breathing? Begin again.

What did you become aware of in this process?

How satisfying can a single bite of food be?

Do you think you would eat more or less if you ate mindfully?

Did the food really taste good? Did you taste something different from what you expected?

How might your experience change if you were blind or had a head cold?

(Continued)

This same intensity can be brought to observing any process including your own thinking. To bring this discussion full circle, there is incredible value in observing your thoughts because that is how you create the world of your experience. As we said at the very beginning of this text, you create your reality. Meditation allows you to see how you have been doing it. If you take the responsibility and make the commitment to practice, you can reshape your life. If you are creating your reality with your thoughts, words, and images, why not be proactive and deliberately choose to create a reality by consciously employing thoughts, words and images that promote your effectiveness.

Questions

1. Which of the following attitudes is helpful for the practice of mindfulness meditation?

   A. control

   B. commitment

   C. challenge

   D. beginners mind

2. Mindfulness is _____.

   A. being careful to mind your manners

   B. being mindful of the needs of others

   C. the cultivation of awareness by practicing awareness

   D. only achieved if you try as hard as you can

3. Tai Chi and Qi Gong are _____.

   A. moving meditations

   B. dance routines

   C. ancient Native American shamanic rituals

   D. illegal in the U.S.

6.7 Other Active Relaxation Methods

Explain how various types of muscle stretching can be used to reverse the effects of negative stress.

As noted earlier, an intrinsic part of the fight/flight response is muscle tension. When muscles tighten they also shorten. One way to reverse the fight/flight response is to lengthen your muscles. This is accomplished quite simply by stretching the muscles. Our goal here is not to provide a comprehensive manual on stretching exercises, but we would like to mention some guidelines for stretching intuitively.

6.7.1 Intuitive Stretching

As you cultivate body awareness and relaxation you will notice an urge to stretch your body in various ways. Many people notice that yawning is accompanied by an almost instinctual urge to lean back and extend one's arms. We are very aware of the need to stretch after sitting in a car or at a desk for a prolonged period of time. Anyone who has dogs or cats can watch them stretch when they awaken or when they anticipate that they will go for a walk. The point we are making is that while we would suggest that it is a good idea to read a manual on stretching or to take a yoga class to learn a specific routine, your body is actually a very good guide to this procedure if you will pay attention to it. After all, someone figured this stuff out without referring to a textbook. Nor has anyone found the family dog curled up in front of the fireplace with an autographed copy of *The Autobiography of a Yogi*. This information is inside of you. These are guidelines for intuitive stretching:

- Set up a comfortable environment for your practice. This might include soft music.
- It is always easier to stretch muscles when they are warm. Thus, some light exercise like walking until you begin to break a sweat is recommended. Another alternative would be to stretch after or while in a hot shower.
- Stretch on a firm padded surface such as an exercise mat.
- Pay attention to what you are doing. It should not hurt when you stretch. Pain is a sure signal that you are doing something with too much intensity or in a direction that your body was not meant to accommodate. Progress in stretching will come rapidly, within weeks, but it is accomplished in small, incremental steps. Stretch and move your body until you feel a solid pull on the muscles and maintain that position as long as you feel comfortable. Return to your original position slowly.
- Move slowly, and do not bounce into any stretch.
- Do not hold your breath while stretching, but keep your breath flowing. Breathe in through your nose and exhale slowly through your mouth. Visualize or sense your breath carrying oxygen to the areas being stretched. See and sense them loosening.
- Rest for a short time after each stretch.
- At the end of your stretching period, take time to cool down and relax. An excellent time to do a breathing meditation or Progressive Relaxation is following stretching.

- While it is optimal to do a set stretch routine on a daily basis, do not limit your stretching to only one time or place. There are many moments throughout the day, at your desk, stopped in your car, etc., where you can relieve the stress and tension in certain muscle groups with a quick stretch.

- The muscles that support the head and neck are also intensely involved in the fight/flight response, as primates (including humans) tend to pull their shoulders up to protect their necks and appear bigger when threatened. Over time chronic tension in these muscles leads to tension headaches. Pay particular attention to these muscles in your stretching routine.

The ancient tradition of yoga also offers many stress mastery and wellness benefits (Patel, 1984). Many relaxation techniques are ultimately outgrowths of yoga practice. **Hatha yoga** is a branch of yoga that emphasizes physical postures and stretches that incorporate breath control and focused, meditative concentration. Although stress mastery is one enormous benefit of yoga practice, its primary purpose is to enable the practitioner to attain spiritual enlightenment. Proper practice of Hatha yoga typically requires coaching and guidance. Most communities offer yoga classes.

6.7.2 Massage

Let us not ignore the healing power of touch as a powerful stress reducer. A wonderfully enjoyable way of reducing physical tension, lowering your stress level, and getting deeply relaxed is to treat yourself to a massage. As reported in an article in Newsweek magazine in June, 1999, Tiffany Field, director of the University of Miami's Touch Research Institute, exposed 60 schoolchildren who had been traumatized by Hurricane Andrew to half hour massages twice a week for one month. The levels of the stress hormone cortisol, an important indicator of stress, decreased significantly for the kids who received the massages compared with a control group who only watched a relaxing video. Overall, the stress levels for the control group did not change at all. If you cannot afford to get professional massage, offer to swap a good massage with a friend, family member, or significant other. You can then give the gift of relaxation as well as receive it.

6.7.3 Rocking for Relaxation

Research has validated every mother's intuition that rocking is relaxing (Bayer & colleagues, 2011). That is why mothers instinctively rock their babies back and forth to soothe them or lull them into sleep. It turns out that this works for people of all ages. This is why many people like to sit in a rocking chair, or on a porch swing, or gently rock in a hammock. It seems that the rocking motions from the 10:00 to the 2:00 position on the clock are the most soothing, helping to lower arousal. Consider the results of the Bayer & colleagues (2011) study where the effects of rocking on sleep in a dozen adult men were examined. None of the subjects had insomnia and all were well rested at the start of the study. The researchers created a special bed that mimicked the rocking motions of a hammock. Each man was required to take two 45 minute naps, one with rocking and one without rocking. During the experimental nap the bed rocked back and forth, and in the control nap the bed remained still. Subjects' brain activity was measured by an EEG. The findings revealed that:

- All subjects fell asleep quicker when rocking.
- 75% of subjects reported the rocking nap as "more pleasant."
- Rocking naps led to quicker progression into deeper sleep as indicated by EEG readings.
- Brainwave activity associated with deeper, more restful and continuous sleep was recorded during the rocking nap as compared to the control nap.

Next time you are feeling stressed or having trouble falling asleep, allow yourself to rock.

Questions

1. An intrinsic part of the fight/flight response is _____, which can be alleviated by_____.
   A. depression; taking an antidepressant
   B. muscle tension; weight lifting
   C. muscle tension; intuitive stretching
   D. homeostasis; massage

2. Hatha Yoga is _____.
   A. a Western method of physical therapy for rehabbing torn muscles
   B. the modernized version of Tai Chi
   C. an ancient form of stretching that reduces stress and can lead to spiritual enlightenment
   D. a method to improve your sexual performance

3. Rocking _____.
   A. only works for babies
   B. is an effective way to relax for most people
   C. should only be used for autistic children
   D. is not an effective relaxation technique

6.8 Staying Healthy

Recognize the various ways in which adopting healthy lifestyle practices affects your ability to master stress.

Given the mind-body connection, it naturally follows that what is good for your body will be good for your mind and vice versa. Another important aspect of mastering your stress involves adopting a healthy lifestyle. A new branch of psychology called health psychology was developed in the 1970s to study the psychological factors that cause or contribute to illness and to promote behaviors that foster wellness. In particular, there is a focus on **psychosomatic illness**.

An unhealthy lifestyle, characterized by lack of exercise, poor diet, cigarette smoking, and alcohol or drug abuse will definitely impact your stress and wellness levels, and eventually even your mortality. One study (Powell, Spain, Christenson & Mollenkamp, 1986) found that at least half of premature deaths in the U.S. were a direct result of such unhealthy behaviors. The 1979 U.S. Surgeon General's report reached this same conclusion and went on to state that seven of the ten leading causes of death in the U.S. (such as from heart attacks, stroke, etc.) could be significantly reduced by adopting the following six lifestyle modifications:

- **improving diet**
- **quitting smoking**
- **getting regular physical exercise**
- **eliminating substance abuse**
- **practicing stress reduction techniques**
- **properly following medication regimens (especially for hypertension)**

Breslow (1983) found that when people adopted these healthy lifestyle behaviors, mortality rates declined significantly over a nine year period. In addition, this study showed that older people derived an even greater benefit from adoption of healthy behaviors than younger individuals, and the effect of lifestyle in general appeared more crucial to the health of males as compared to females.

6.8.1 The Importance of Exercise

By far, one of the simplest and most effective methods of mastering stress to enhance wellness is to engage in regular exercise. Your body immediately reacts to stress by gearing up to respond physically to a stressor. Given that the original evolutionary purpose for the "fight or flight response" was to enable humans to fight or to flee physical danger, it follows that the natural outlet for built up physiological arousal is some type of vigorous physical activity or exertion. Exercise releases pent up muscular tension, allowing your body to return to equilibrium.

Throughout most of human history our ancestors got plenty of exercise while taking care of basic living tasks like searching/hunting for food, walking from one place to another, chopping wood for fires, etc. Currently, the advent of modern conveniences such as the automobile, elevator, supermarket, or washing machine greatly reduces the need for physical activity to accomplish basic tasks. It has gotten to the point where we don't even have to move to change the channel on the TV, thanks to the ever-present remote control! Consequently, if you don't make a point of exercising you are probably leading a sedentary lifestyle, unless you are involved in a job or profession involving physical labor or physically exerting activities. But the vast majority of us have sedentary occupations, sitting behind a desk, barely flexing our arm muscles to type at our computers. The majority of college students are trained for and hold sedentary jobs after graduation. Leisure activities often involve sedentary pursuits as well. Thus, even though the tempo of modern life and the rate of change is accelerating (further adding to our stress), our activity levels are falling. And this comes at a time when our need for regular exercise to bolster coping resources and wellness is increasing.

A comprehensive exercise program to improve your well-being has three major types of exercise: (1) **aerobic exercise** that conditions your cardiovascular system; (2) **strength training** that builds, strengthens and maintains muscle capacity and balance; and (3) **flexibility exercises** that maintain healthy joints, good posture, body alignment and the capacity to move the body in its full range of motion. The Department of Health and Human Services has recommended at least one hour and 15 minutes a week of intense aerobic activity (e.g. jogging or swimming) or substituting that with twice as much (2 hours and 30 minutes) moderate exercise, such as brisk walking, combined with two periods of muscle strengthening or stretching (Southwick & Charney, 2013).

While aerobic conditioning for your heart and vascular system can be achieved by continuous exercise, the best results are often achieved with **interval training**. Interval training consists of alternating bursts of speed or high intensity activity for a set amount of time or distance followed by a longer period of rest by either walking or jogging depending on your fitness level. For example, this could involve running fast for 30 seconds to one minute, followed by three minutes of walking. Interval training ups the ante on traditional cardiovascular work where you continuously move at the same rate. Interval training is the quickest way to increase your stroke volume, which refers to the amount of blood pumped by your heart per heartbeat. Interval cardiovascular training increases the blood flow to your heart, enabling your heart rate to slow over time, your oxygen usage to improve, and your blood to flow cleaner and faster. Thus you are improving your stroke volume. The more blood is pumped per beat, the less your heart has to work. The less your heart has to work during exercise, the healthier it becomes. The jump in your heart rate during interval training followed by an abrupt decrease forces your body to work hard to burn fat but still allows for sufficient recovery time. Engaging in interval training enables you to get the same or better benefit from shorter, more intense workouts, facilitates weight loss, lowers cholesterol, and helps combat boredom due to lack of variety in the workout routine.

However, do not discount the benefits of moderate exercise. A study at the Cooper Center for Research examined three groups: Low, Moderate, and High Fitness to compare the rate of deaths in each group. The low group included basically unfit, sedentary persons who did not exercise, the moderately fit group exercised 150 minutes a week, and the highly fit group included extreme exercisers who spent many hours a week in cardiovascular training. At the conclusion of the study, the results indicated that the number of deaths in the moderate exercise group was 50% less than in the low fitness group. The participants in the moderate group walked on a treadmill for 150 minutes a week, in other words, 30 minutes a day/5 days a week, something most of us could do easily on a treadmill or in our neighborhood. The high fitness group had slightly fewer deaths than the moderate group. However, the dramatic finding in this study was that there were half as many deaths in the moderate exercise group as in the sedentary low fitness group. The lesson here is that you don't have to run a marathon to be fit! Moderate regular exercise can prolong your life. Dr. Church (2006), the physician who conducted this study, says his three favorite exercises are: (1) *walking*; (2) *walking*; and (3) *walking*! If you are starting an exercise regimen, it is important to get a doctor's approval before beginning.

OTHER BENEFITS OF EXERCISE   Is there proof that exercise improves our wellness by helping us to cope with stress? Research clearly indicates that exercise is an effective stress reducer. Indeed, many studies have found that one of the most reliable differences between individuals with high vs. low levels of stress resistance was exercise and activity level (Brown, 1991; Kobasa, Maddi, & Puccetti, 1982; Roth & Holmes, 1987, just to name a few). In one study, McGilley and Holmes (1989), found that individuals who exercised regularly had lower cardiovascular and subjective responses to psychological stress than individuals who were not physically fit. Studies have also been done linking regular aerobic exercise to reductions in depression (McCann and Holmes, 1984), anxiety (Long, 1984) and improvements in self-esteem (Sonstroem, 1984). Speisman and colleagues (2013) have provided evidence for a mechanism of action explaining how exercise facilitates emotional well-being. They demonstrated in animal studies that exercise increased neurogenesis in the hippocampus, which is known to be associated with resilience to depression. Neuroscientists Jorge Ruas and colleagues (2014) showed that the changes in muscles as a result of exercise helped rid the body of a particular stress-induced amino acid called kynurenine, which has been associated with mental illness.

Remember, as discussed previously, the amount and intensity of exercise necessary to produce stress mastery and other wellness effects need not be overly extensive. Regular exercise, even of only moderate intensity, literally provides a dress rehearsal for dealing with stress (Brehm, 1998). Why is this the case? Because the way your body responds to exercise is very similar to the way your body reacts to stress. During exercise your heart rate increases, blood pressure rises, respiration quickens, stress hormones are released, and muscles tense to perform the activity. Does this sound familiar? Therefore, engaging in regular exercise gives your body practice in experiencing stress, allowing you to develop more strength and stamina to cope. If you recall our previous discussion of the Stress Hardiness attitude of control, exercise gives you practice with controlling the onset and the end point of the stress response. Exercise promotes resilience through a variety of neurobiological mechanisms such as the suppression of the stress hormone cortisol. Working out also appears to activate genes for the production of certain proteins such as BDNF (brain derived neurotrophic factor), which promotes the growth and repair of neurons damaged by stress. Kramer and colleagues (2011) found that moderate intensity aerobic exercise performed regularly (three times weekly for a year) led to an increase in the size of the hippocampus for participants. Recall that the hippocampus is a region of the brain involved in stress regulation and memory. This growth in the hippocampus was associated with increases in BDNF levels along with improved memory, which suggested that regular exercise can protect neurons in this vital area of the brain and thus may be instrumental in recovery from adverse circumstances. Exercise provides a perfect medium for stress inoculation to promote resilience as you can gradually increase the intensity and length of your workouts.

It appears that the stress-reducing effects of exercise are both short and long term. Many people find a single exercise session to be an excellent way of releasing tension. Proponents of regular exercise, who exercise at least three times weekly, typically report lowered levels of tension overall, even on days when they are less active (Holmes & Roth, 1988). So clearly, exercise has powerful positive effects on both our psychological and physical well-being. These are some of the most notable benefits that are possible from engaging in regular exercise:

TABLE 6.4 The Cumulative Benefits of Regular Exercise

- Improved sense of well-being, decreases in depression.
- Lowered anxiety and muscular tension.
- Greater ability to handle domestic and job-related stress.
- Increased endorphin production.
- Decreased production of stress hormones such as adrenalin and cortisol.
- Improvements in concentration and productivity.
- Quicker recovery from acute stress.
- Decreased fatigue; more energy and stamina.
- Reduction in blood pressure and resting heart rate.
- Improved cardiopulmonary functioning. Lower risk of heart disease.
- More restful sleep.
- Fewer physical complaints in general. Boosts in immune functioning.
- Better self-image and more self-confidence.
- A more attractive physique.

There is also evidence that fitness can help compensate for obesity (Lee, Sui & Blair, 2009) in terms of mortality rates. Researchers compared the death rates for all causes between both fit and unfit obese individuals with that of normal weight individuals who were fit and unfit. Factors such as age, smoking and pre-existing health conditions were kept constant between the groups. The death rate for fit but overweight individuals was significantly below that of unfit persons. The results indicated that those who were fat but fit had almost half the risk of death as the fat and unfit. Meanwhile, individuals who were obese but fit were only slightly more at risk for death that those who were thin and fit (Sui & colleagues, 2007). The stark conclusion appears to be that your fitness level is much more important than what you weigh. Ultimately, inactivity is the biggest problem. If you are fit, even if overweight or moderately obese, your risk of mortality is much lower. If you are unfit, your risk of death is much higher whether you are thin or not. To enhance your fitness level, consider the suggestion in the following exercise.

Positive Psychology Exercise

10,000 daily steps

The 2008 Surgeon General's report made clear-cut recommendations emphasizing that adults need to take 10,000 steps daily to maintain fitness. If you average below 5,000 steps daily, you are in that dangerous couch potato zone that puts you at undue risk for death. One way to check whether you are sufficiently active, that is, getting in an average of 10,000 daily steps, would be to utilize a pedometer. Many cellular phones have a pedometer app. This allows you to check your activity level and take corrective action if you are too sedentary. For example, you could choose to take a walk after dinner if you are well below the recommended step goal on any given day.

6.8.2 The Role of Proper Nutrition

The average American diet is a direct reflection of our lifestyle; everyone is busy, in a rush, looking for the fastest, easiest, cheapest way to procure food. Cooking at home has given way to eating out. Not only have we lost nutrition, but we no longer have the family connections of dinner conversations. This results in a pattern that includes skipped breakfast and "drive through" meals or visits to the vending machines for daily food choices. The outcome of this pattern is an epidemic of obesity, diabetes, malnutrition, and diminished wellness. This in turn leads to increased stress and diminished stress resistance which further complicates the cycle.

The old adage, "You are what you eat," is more true than you might imagine. Why is this? Because how well or how poorly you eat has a direct relationship to your level of wellness, including your ability to handle stress. Your body needs 40 to 60 nutrients to stay healthy. When you are under stress your need for all nutrients increases, especially for B vitamins (which help combat stress) and calcium. Calcium is especially important because it counteracts the lactic acid buildup created by muscular tension. If your diet is deficient in milk and leafy vegetables, your ability to reduce high levels of lactic acid related to stress will be impaired along with your bones and other systems. This will leave you feeling more fatigued, anxious and irritable than if your diet is more balanced. You also need to realize that certain foods provide the biochemical building blocks for the neurotransmitters (brain chemicals) that affect mood and behavior, and consequently your ability to handle stress and interact positively in relationships. For example, your body synthesizes the neurotransmitter **serotonin** from the amino acid tryptophan, which is found in certain high carbohydrate foods such as bread, potatoes and pasta. Healthy levels of serotonin help you to stay relaxed, sleep well and have less sensitivity to pain. That is why we tend to crave carbohydrate rich foods when we are in a bad mood in order to get a temporary lift. And it is also important to know that protein rich foods tend to improve concentration and alertness, particularly if you have them for breakfast. Missing breakfast altogether can deprive your brain of essential nutrients needed for effective functioning throughout your day. You can learn to make changes in your diet that will help you to cope more effectively, increase your productivity, and heighten your wellness level by heeding the following seven steps to good nutrition.

1. **Eat a Variety of Foods** including proteins, fruits and vegetables and other complex carbohydrates, as well as healthy fats found in coconut oil or olive oil. Avoid simple carbohydrates such as sugar, high fructose corn syrup, white flour and white rice.

2. **Eat More Whole Foods**—foods that are in their natural state, i.e. not with coatings removed, colors changed, or additives or preservatives included.

3. **Drink Caffeine in moderation** (no more than 1 or 2 cups) or not at all.

4. **Drink Alcohol in moderation** (no more than 1 drink/day for women, 2 drinks/day for men) or not at all.

5. **Take Vitamin and Mineral Supplements** remembering that these do not absorb as well as getting vitamins and minerals from food eaten.

6. **Eat Small, Frequent, Calm Meals**.

7. **Maintain a Healthy Weight**—Body Mass Index or BMI = (weight in pounds/height in inches^2) $\times$ 703. Values between 18.5 — 24.5 are within the healthy weight range.

The Global Perspective
Sustainable Food Choices

All of the Global Perspectives in the text represent aspects of the interconnections between all of life. There is no subject more central to this discussion than food and nutrition. And there is no topic wrapped in more controversy than nutrition. What is the best way to eat for your personal health and for the health

(Continued)

of Earth? Well, it all depends upon whom you ask and what is their stake in the answer. Over the years we have been urged by various experts to eat or not eat, supplement or not supplement, virtually everything that you can eat. The current paradigm shift in nutrition is bringing us full circle to an acceptance of the importance of protein sources, including meat, and fat in the diet. It is still important to eat your vegetables but the most controversial food stuffs are now carbohydrates, especially simple carbohydrates like sugar, starches, grains and white flour found in most processed foods. It seems that a closer look at the scientific data suggests that the rise in diabetes, obesity and heart disease is correlated with the removal of fat from our diet and the subsequent replacement of the fat with sugars and other simple carbohydrates (Diamond, 2014). This is a field in great flux and it requires keeping an open mind regarding what is optimal nutrition for the human omnivore. We must consider not only the health aspects of our diet but also where we stand in terms of which parts of life we are willing to consume. Whether we like it or not, life feeds on other life.

What is less controversial now is that while meat and fat in our diet are not unhealthy in themselves, the way cattle are raised and fed in factory farms is decidedly unhealthy for humans and the planet. Thus, we must also consider whether poor food choices lead to unintended consequences, not only in terms of our own health, but taking into consideration what will also threaten the well-being of humanity by poisoning the environment, depleting drinkable water supplies, and accelerating climate change. Consider the following facts cited on www.earthsave.org.

- As noted earlier, the aquifers, which supply drinkable water, are being rapidly depleted. The main drain on these aquifers is the irrigation of crops that are used to feed cattle. Not only could 10 people be fed with the grain used to produce meat for one person, but it takes atleast 2500 gallons of water to produce a pound of beef!
- Livestock waste is a primary source of water pollution. Natural processes to disperse sewage are overwhelmed by the enormous quantities of waste produced by the factory farming

of animals. For example, consider that the drinking water of 65% California's population is threatened by pollution from dairy cow manure!

- Cattle also pass gas, lots of gas! Cattle are actually the source of 1/5th of the world's methane, which is 21 times more powerful than CO_2 in the acceleration of global warming.
- Huge tracts of rainforest are destroyed every year to create grazing land for more cattle. Rainforests are not only a great source of biodiversity but also reabsorb carbon dioxide from the atmosphere. Many scientists believe this is a critical facet of long term control of global warming.
- In order to minimize the disease caused by the crowded conditions of factory farming, the animals are fed huge quantities of antibiotics. Due to this overuse of antibiotics, we now have disease organisms that are resistant to virtually all antibiotics and, therefore, extremely hazardous to human health.
- Last but not least, modern agriculture has grown extremely dependent upon pesticide use. These pesticides accumulate in the animals that eat the grains that are treated with these chemicals. Thus, the higher you eat on the food chain (meaning the more meat you eat), the greater your exposure to these toxic chemicals. As you may have guessed, these toxins also end up polluting the ground water through the animal waste and by being absorbed in the soil during application. These chemicals are implicated as possible causes of Parkinson's disease and suspected as causes of cancer and other disorders. This is one of many reasons for the movement towards growing food organically without pesticides.

After considering all this you may be wondering, *"How can I make a difference in my own health and the sustainability of my environment?"* It seems that something as simple as what you choose to eat today has enormous consequences not only for your health and well-being but also for the health and well-being of everyone else and the earth itself. Eating for good health means investing more time, more thought, and (to eat naturally) perhaps a bit more money. Again you are faced with choices, the results of which have consequences for sustaining your life and that of your planet. What kinds of choices might you make to make a difference in your own health and the sustainability of the environment?

6.8.3 The Stress-Reducing Benefits of Contact with Nature

Time spent outdoors in nature may be one of the best and most accessible natural stress-busters readily available to us. Whether hiking in the mountains, walking in the woods, swimming in the ocean, strolling in your neighborhood park, or directly watching wildlife, interacting with nature has a significant positive effect on humans. According to Ben Hirshberg (2012) in his review of research on the beneficial effects of being in nature, "The sounds, smells and sights of the great outdoors appear to have an amazing stress-reducing capacity. Research backs up this folk wisdom, showing that spending time with nature can decrease feelings of depression, increase self-esteem, and decrease tense feelings." Hirshberg described a study that compared the mental state of depressed subjects who walked outdoors in a park compared to those who walked inside a shopping mall. The results indicated that 71% of the outdoor walkers reported a decrease in depression, while only 22% of the mall walkers reported an improvement in mood. In the same study, 71% of the outdoor walkers reported feeling less tense compared to only 50% of the mall walkers. The outdoor walkers also reported a significantly greater boost in self-esteem following the walk. Likewise, Shanahan and colleagues (2016) found that 10% of people with hypertension could get their blood pressure under control and reduce depression if they spent a minimum of 30 minutes in a park weekly.

Japanese researchers (Park, Miyazaki & colleagues, 2010; Hansen and colleagues, 2017) have touted the benefits of *shinrin-yoku* or *forest bathing*. This practice employs a mindfulness approach to embracing nature by using all five senses when outdoors, actively touching and smelling plants, listening to birds and animals while watching the natural display in the here and now. The researchers demonstrated that individuals who spent 40 minutes walking and forest bathing in a cedar forest had significantly lower levels of the stress hormone cortisol than control group subjects who spent 40 minutes walking in a lab. Psychologist Roger Ulrich (1984) conducted a famous study showing that hospitalized patients with a view of the natural world had quicker surgical recovery times than those with a view of a brick wall from their hospital room window. A 2016 study (Janus & colleagues) spanning 44 cities found that when people live in urban areas with more green spaces (e.g. parks) they are more likely to report better health, higher energy, and a greater sense of purpose. So, why not combine the stress reducing effects of exercise with nature and experience the additive effects? A new type of intervention, called *ecotherapy*, uses activities in nature to promote emotional and physical well-being.

6.8.4 Enhancing Financial Competence

The next area on our wellness wheel relates to your ability to manage your finances. An extensive primer on financial management is beyond the scope of this text, but we will offer you the most salient pointers. It is important to have thoughts, feelings and behaviors regarding money that are positive for your well-being. How we treat our money is a statement about how we value ourselves. There is a connection between *net worth* and *self-worth*. Although most of us have never had a course in personal finance, it is important that we take control of our financial destiny. To be financially competent means that you have knowledge and skills in the areas that follow (Orman, 2007, 2010).

CHECKING AND SAVINGS ACCOUNTS

- Know how to develop and follow a budget, use your bank statements, balance your checkbook and find free checking.
- Have a savings account, make monthly payments into it for your financial security, and know how to find the best interest rate.
- Build a savings account that alone would cover your living expenses for at least six months as your financial safety net.

CREDIT CARDS AND CREDIT SCORES

- Have only a few credit cards and check your statement carefully every month.
- Be aware of fees and avoid extra fees and high interest rates.
- Pay your total statement balance off each month. If you are only paying the minimum, it may take months, or years, to pay it off.
- Understand what a credit score is and what events can change it. Obtain and review your score every year.
- Remember that a credit card *used* is money *borrowed*.

GROWING YOUR MONEY—INVESTING FOR LATER

- Invest your money to guard it from losing buying power through inflation. **Inflation** is the rise of the costs of goods and services that, over time, erodes the value of your funds.
- Go on-line and search *inflation* or *inflation rate* to find numerous calculators that estimate changed values due to inflation.
- Do not rely on Social Security as your sole financial support in your later years. To estimate your benefits, go to www.socialsecurity.gov/ planners/ calculators.htm.
- Additionally, you must contribute to a personal retirement fund such as an IRA or 401K.

PROTECTING YOURSELF AND YOUR ASSETS—LEGAL DOCUMENTS AND INSURANCE

- Have a revocable living trust that has an incapacity clause and ownership of your assets; also have a will.

- Purchase protection for you and your family through life, health, home, personal property, and other appropriate insurance.

To learn more about how to implement the actions discussed here, seek more detailed information on personal finance. Go to *mappingyourfuture.org* and download the free "12-Step Guide to Financial Success" (2009). Be sure to also use College materials and programs available to you for furthering your financial competence.

6.8.5 Social Support and Wellness

Remember Kobasa's three Cs of Stress Hardiness? Her colleague Salvatore Maddi posited that there is actually a fourth C, that of **connection** (Maddi and Kobasa, 1984). Having meaningful connections to others has often proven to be the crucial factor for individuals who bounce back from and resist stress. Creating and maintaining a supportive, caring social network goes a long way to enhancing your level of stress hardiness. Being in a committed relationship, having close family ties, friendships, and other avenues for social support, such as involvement in religious or spiritual activities, community-based clubs or interest groups, or volunteer work, has been shown to contribute significantly to health and happiness (Seligman, 2002). Cacioppo & colleagues (2002) found that those who are lonely are far less healthy than those who are sociable.

Perhaps the most striking example of the salutary effect of social support on health was documented by Bruhn and Wolf (1979, 1993) based on their epidemiological research in the small town of Roseto, Pennsylvania. Roseto is a city populated almost exclusively with descendants of Italian immigrants who came to the U.S. in the late 1800s from a town of the same name in Italy. Inhabitants of Roseto enjoy an extremely low rate of heart disease, virtually half that of the U.S. in general, or of surrounding towns or counties in Pennsylvania. The researchers systematically ruled out diet, exercise and genetics as contributing factors in the health of Roseto's population. Their diet was not overly healthful; in fact, many had abandoned their healthy Mediterranean cooking style (olive oil based), and ate too much fat. They did not exercise any more than people in nearby towns with similar topographies. Close relatives from the same gene pool who had moved away from Roseto began to develop cardiovascular disease at the same rate as nonresidents, which ruled out genetics. The researchers realized that what made Roseto special was the incredible level of social support and connection that existed in the town, the close friendships and kinship, multigenerational family units, extensive civic organizations for a small town, and neighbors helping and supporting one another. This provided a layer of protection that appeared to insulate the inhabitants from many of the detrimental effects of stress. Not only was their rate of cardiovascular disease much lower, there were no suicides reported, no substance abuse, and very little crime uncovered by the researchers.

Not all of us are lucky enough to live in a supportive community like Roseto. For many individuals, loneliness is synonymous with stress and perhaps a lack of healthy relationships. Consider the following facts regarding the connection between social support and wellness.

- People who are in stable relationships and have a strong social network are typically happier (Seligman, 2002).

- Married men tend to live longer than single men (Seligman, 2002).

- Cancer patients who join positively oriented support groups are more likely to go into remission and typically live longer (Seligman, 2002).

- Those who are lonely are more at risk for heart disease. Dean Ornish (2005), the cardiologist who pioneered the well known, state-of-the-art lifestyle regimen for those with cardiovascular disease, described three studies to illustrate this point. In the first, individuals who felt high levels of love and support in their lives had significantly less coronary artery blockages. In the second, researchers from Case Western Reserve University studied 10,000 married men and found that those who felt loved by their wives had less angina (chest pain). In the last study, from Duke University, individuals with heart disease who were single and lacked confidants were three times as likely to have died after five years.

- Holt-Lunstad & colleagues (2010) conducted a meta-analytic review of 148 previous studies of the relationship between social interaction and health. The results were clear cut. Individuals with active social lives were 50% less likely to die than their nonsocial peers. In addition, low levels of social interaction had greater negative effects than either obesity or a sedentary lifestyle in terms of health outcomes. *The negative health effect of low levels of social interaction was equivalent to smoking $3/4$ of a pack of cigarettes daily!* The section on friendship in Chapter 11 explores the benefits of having friends in more depth.

- The more social connections you have, the greater your ability to fight infection. Cohen & colleagues (1997) demonstrated that subjects who reported having the most extensive social networks were four times less likely to develop a cold after receiving nasal drops containing a cold virus than those reporting the fewest friends. Other factors which could have explained these findings were controlled.

- Uchino (2006) reported that close friendships have protective effects on our cardiovascular system, especially in times of stress. His study indicated that the blood pressure of women exposed to a stressful situation (involving performance anxiety) did not rise nearly as much when a close friend was nearby to give encouragement, as compared to when subjects were accompanied by a friend who was less supportive.

High stress levels have long been identified as one of the major factors in the development of cardiovascular disease. The availability of a strong social support network appears to have a powerful impact on our ability to cope with stress (Grambling & Auerback, 1998). Numerous studies have linked strong social support networks to superior ability to cope with stress and higher levels of wellness (Andrew, Tennant, Hewson, & Schonell, 1979; Auerback, Mastelli, & Mercuri, 1983; Gore, 1978). But again, perception plays a key role in whether such support will offer protection from stress. It is the recognition of the availability of the support, rather than the actual amount of it, that is more closely related to stress mastery (Cohen & Will, 1985; Sarason, Sarason & Pierce, 1990). That is, if you dismiss the support available to you from family or friends, it will not have a beneficial effect.

Dr. Ornish's program focuses on a healthy diet and exercise, but he places equal emphasis on stress reduction though social support groups, yoga and meditation to help prevent further heart attacks. The following quote from Ornish in *Newsweek magazine* (10/03/05) makes an eloquent case for the importance of relationships, social support, and altruism to our wellness.

> *Medicine today focuses primarily on drugs and surgery, genes and germs, microbes and molecules. Yet love and intimacy are at the root of what makes us sick and what makes us well. If a new medication had the same impact, failure to prescribe it would be malpractice. Connections with other people affect not only the quality of our lives but also our survival. Study after study finds that people who feel lonely are many times more likely to get cardiovascular disease than those who have a strong sense of connection and community. I'm not aware of any other factor in medicine . . . that has a greater impact on our quality of life, incidence of illness, and premature death . . .*
>
> *. . . Instead of viewing the time we spend with friends and family as luxuries, we can see that these relationships are among the most powerful determinants of our well-being and survival. We are hard-wired to help each other. Science is documenting the healing values of love, intimacy, community, compassion, forgiveness, altruism and service-values that are part of almost all spiritual traditions as well as many secular ones. (p. 56)*

6.8.6 The Role of Proactivity in Stress Mastery: An Ounce of Prevention

Harvard stress researcher Robert Epstein (2011) offers a different perspective about what to emphasize in a comprehensive stress mastery program. He concluded that recent research implied that there are four broad and trainable skill sets or *competencies* which individuals can use to master stress effectively, including:

1. **Source Management** – reducing or eliminating sources of stress or stressful stimuli

2. **Relaxation Techniques** – active relaxation practices covered in this chapter

3. **Thought Management** – including reframing and cognitive restructuring techniques

4. **Prevention** – planning and conducting your life in order to avoid known stressors

Prevention and Source Management are proactive strategies aimed at helping you to avoid or minimize stress altogether or mitigate the effects of such before the fact. Relaxation techniques can either be proactive, by lowering your baseline arousal level to better prepare you to cope with stress, or reactive by helping you to lower fight/flight arousal after you are stressed. Thought Management is typically reactive as it enables you to cognitively frame existing stress in a way that helps lower your arousal level.

Epstein (2011) conducted a study utilizing a survey similar to the one included at the end of this chapter, which measures stress mastery competence across these four general areas. His results indicated that prevention, planning to avoid stressors before they can affect you, was the most helpful competency in terms of predicting happiness and life success. The second most important competency was source management, which includes practices such as organizing your space, scheduling your time effectively and delegating tasks, all preventative measures. The least predictive of life satisfaction was Thought Management, almost always a reactive approach, which fared worse than relaxation techniques. The clear conclusion is that proactive methods are ultimately the most important to your quality of life. Knowing how to manage your existing stress is vital, but in the long run you will flourish best if you can maximize your ability to avoid situations and stressors that affect you in the first place. Epstein offers six strategies for prevention:

- **Seek and Defuse** – take a few minutes each day to identify stressors in your life, large and small, and attempt to figure out how to eliminate or reduce them. This could involve biting the bullet and finally buying that new piece of equipment to replace the one that keeps breaking down and frustrating you. Or it could involve taking a lower paying job closer to home to eliminate that awful commute.

- **Commit to the Positive** – avoid self-destructive coping behaviors (i.e. drinking, over-eating) and replace with healthy ones (i.e. regular exercise, meditation, yoga class).

- **Organize Yourself** – including organizing your space and making lists of things to do. Chapter 4 deals with this in detail.

- **Immunize Yourself** – practice active relaxation skills and thought management daily to foster resilience.

- **Make a Daily Plan and Schedule** (See Chapter 4).

- **Make a Long Term Plan.** Refer to the section in Chapter 8 on establishing your personal mission statement.

Overall, the results of Epstein's study demonstrated that over half of the large sample had poor stress mastery skills. The better the stress mastery skills, the higher the overall levels of happiness reported by the subjects. This is correlational data; nonetheless, a statistical analysis of the results suggested that approximately 25% of life satisfaction is related to, and perhaps even the direct result of, our ability to manage the stress in our daily lives. Likewise, there were strong correlations between the level of stress mastery competency and personal/professional success among the research participants. Epstein concluded that developing stress mastery skills is very beneficial, but the greatest benefits accrue from preventing stress before it begins.

Assess Your Stress Mastery Competence

The following survey represents an abbreviated version of the Epstein Stress Management Inventory (ESMI-i). To get a rough measure of your competence within and across the four broad areas, check the items that apply to you. If you are honestly able to check three or four items in a category, you are probably reasonably competent in that domain. To determine your overall score add up all check marks across categories. If you scored under 12, you definitely need to put in more work on your stress mastery skills. Visit http://MyStressManagementSkills.com to take the full version of the test.

Competency 1

Manages Sources of Stress

__ I have adequate shelf and drawer space to serve my needs.

__ I consistently put important tasks ahead of unimportant tasks.

__ I try to schedule appointments and meetings so that they won't overlap.

__ I have no trouble keeping my work area organized.

Competency 2

Manages Thoughts

__ I regularly examine and try to correct any irrational beliefs I might have.

__ I'm aware that my thinking is sometimes unclear or irrational.

__ I keep myself calm by being selective about what I pay attention to in my environment.

__ I often reinterpret events to reduce the stress I'm feeling.

Competency 3

Practices Relaxation Techniques

__ I schedule some relaxation time every day.

__ I sometimes visualize soothing scenes to to relax.

__ I sometimes use special breathing techniques to help me relax.

__ I sometimes tense and relax my muscles as a way of fighting stress.

Competency 4

Prevents Stress from Occurring

__ I try to fight stress before it starts.

__ I keep an up-to-date list of things I'm supposed to do.

__ I spend a few minutes each morning planning my day.

__ I have a clear picture of how I'd like my life to proceed over the next few years.

Questions

1. According to experts, adults are recommended to take _____ to maintain fitness.

   A. multiple naps throughout the day

   B. hot baths in the forest

   C. 10,000 daily steps

   D. all protein out of their diet

2. The inhabitants of Roseto, Pennsylvania had significantly lower levels of cardiovascular disease than average Americans due to_____.

   A. exceptionally heathy eating habits

   B. exceptionally high levels of social support within the community

   C. exceptionally high levels of exercise due to the hilly terrain

   D. the regular practice of forest bathing

3. The best results for cardiovascular conditioning are achieved with_____.

   A. strength training

   B. flexibility exercises

   C. eating a lot of carbohydrates

   D. interval training

Summary

In this chapter we have outlined how to achieve high level wellness including in-depth explorations of wellness dimensions such as stress mastery, exercise, nutrition, finances, and social support. A special emphasis has been placed on stress mastery because stress is such a pervasive and powerful force in our culture. There are a myriad of approaches to mastering stress. Therefore, this chapter offers a step-by-step primer on how to practice an array of proven **active relaxation** techniques, such as **diaphragmatic breathing, progressive muscle relaxation, mindfulness meditation,** and stretching. Emphasis was placed on developing **self-awareness** via the **witnessing stance** and **body wisdom** via the **warrior's stance** to help you to cultivate **stress hardiness**. Stress hardy individuals manifest three valuable attitudes summarized as the 3 C's – **control, commitment, and challenge.** Development of these attitudes promotes **resiliency.** A fourth C has been added – that of **connection** – which refers to the importance of social support to wellness and stress mastery. Lastly, the role of proactivity for preventing stress in the first place was explored.

Review the wellness wheel at the beginning of the chapter and choose one area on which to focus. Pick the one that you think might be the easiest to begin your journey of self-improvement. When you have made good progress on that dimension, move on to another. Mastering one area of wellness is motivating—and will inspire you to continue on to adopt other new behavior patterns that help generate a high level of wellness. Go forth...keep progressing upward...and be well!

Positive Psychology Exercises

1. The next time you are feeling stressed or anxious, or anticipate that this will be the case, take the time to focus on your breathing. It is likely that you will note more rapid, shallow respiration. Take several deep, slow, diaphragmatic breaths to center yourself, and notice the difference this makes. As suggested earlier in the chapter, practice this relaxed breathing pattern at non-stressful times to ensure mastery of the technique for when you really need it.

2. If you are feeling tense, or suffering from a tension headache, neck or shoulder soreness or stiffness, or back pain, practice Progressive Relaxation exercises. Relieving the tension in various muscle groups will go a long way towards improving how you feel. Remember, pain can be reduced up to 40% just by relaxation alone! In fact, much of the effectiveness of painkillers comes from the fact that these medications relax you. Better yet, practice Progressive Relaxation as part of your regular routine and you will find that the frequency and severity of stress-related aches and pains will decrease sharply by preventing cramping.

Key Terms

Active Relaxation
Aerobic Exercise
Autogenic Training
Awareness
Beginner's Mind
Body Wisdom
Challenge
Commitment
Connection
Control
Diaphragmatic Breathing
Differential Relaxation
Emotion-focused Coping
Exercise
Financial Competence

Flexibility Exercises
Hatha Yoga
Hyperventilation
Inflation
Interval Training
Mantra
Meditation
Metacognition
Metamood
Mindfulness
Nutrition
Parasympathetic
Passive Relaxation
Post Traumatic Growth
Problem-focused Coping

Progressive Relaxation
Psychosomatic Illness
Qi Gong
Resilience
Self Awareness
Serotonin
Social Support
Strength Training
Stress Hardiness
Sympathetic
Tai Chi
Warrior's Stance
Wellness
Witnessing Stance

Shared Writing

Which area on the wellness wheel is most in need of your attention? Which recommendations for living a heathy lifestyle seem most relevant for you? Write about your thoughts.

Chapter 6 Questions

1. High level _____ is about achieving a state of physical and emotional health based on living a healthy lifestyle.

    A. competence

    B. effectiveness

    C. wellness

    D. worthiness

2. _____ relaxation techniques are aimed at decreasing fight or flight arousal and restoring balance or homeostasis.

    A. Passive

    B. Active

    C. Flexible

    D. Vigorous

3. All of the following are active relaxation techniques, except_____.

    A. mindfulness meditation

    B. progressive muscle relaxation

    C. playing video games

    D. diaphragmatic breathing

4. Adopting the _____ stance makes it easier to be objective about a situation, which helps you to choose the most effective response.

    A. wellness

    B. warrior

    C. witnessing

    D. watching

5. If you are feeling stressed out and over-whelmed by a full schedule of classes and work, dropping a class to lighten your load would be an example of _____.

    A. passive-relaxation

    B. active-relaxation

    C. emotion-focused coping

    D. problem-focused coping

6. Emotion-focused coping refers to attempts to _____.

    A. deal with the stressor directly to remove it or defuse its effects

    B. change the way you perceive the stressor

    C. change your emotional response to the stressor

    D. distract yourself from the stressor

7. _____ refers to the graded exposure to stressors designed to increase resilience.

    A. Stress sensitization

    B. Stress inoculation

    C. Body wisdom

    D. Stress hardiness

8. The ability to bounce back from severe trauma or loss is called _____.

    A. beginners mind

    B. PTSD

    C. stress sensitization

    D. resiliency

9. Having a good network of _____ in place is vital to wellness.

    A. personal trainers

    B. social support

    C. money managers

    D. massage therapists

10. The neurotransmitter _____, which helps keep us calm, is synthesized from amino acids found in certain carbohydrates.

    A. adrenalin

    B. endorphin

    C. tryptophan

    D. serotonin

Chapter 7
Experiencing Positive Emotions

∨ Learning Objectives

After reading this chapter, you should be able to:

7.1 Describe the connection between positive emotions and effectiveness.

7.2 Identify the elements that help us to define happiness.

7.3 Identify common misconceptions about what makes us happy and the mechanism which often causes happiness to be transient.

7.4 Describe actions and mindsets that can increase happiness about your past and future, as well as in the present moment.

7.5 Differentiate among a variety of expert suggestions for enhancing happiness.

When it comes to flourishing as human beings, what often takes center stage is our ability to feel **positive emotions**. In particular, to be able to know what it is to be happy and to experience an enduring sense of well-being. For many of us, this is a dream, a goal that is never quite fulfilled, or a peak moment that is short-lived, evanescent, or gone with the wind. One of the core elements of flourishing is the study of positive emotions (the P in PERMA) and how to develop them more fully. This mission purports not only to understand how and why individuals experience the range of positive emotions, but also to enable positive psychologists to guide individuals like you to maximize your ability to find and develop happiness, and all the other positive emotions available to you in your life. Although the right to the "pursuit of happiness" is guaranteed to all Americans by the Declaration of Independence, the scientific study of such had been meager until the advent of positive psychology.

If we consider the lessons of the previous chapters as we embark upon an exploration of positive emotions, it raises many interesting questions. Do positive attitudes such as optimism generate positive emotions? Or do positive emotions generate positive attitudes? Or is it a little bit of both? Are some people naturally happier than others? Are some people born smiling with a perpetually sunny disposition, while others are born with a more melancholic bent? And if this is so, is there anything we can do to offset or affect this in a positive direction? Is your level of happiness related to how satisfied you will be with your life later on? Is your level of happiness related to how effective you will be in your personal life, in your relationships, or in your career? These are complex questions, but research and data in positive psychology are beginning to provide us with some intriguing and helpful answers.

For example, were you aware that there are two very different kinds of smiles? One type of smile is referred to as a "**Duchenne smile**" (named after its discoverer, Guillame Duchenne) which is a full face smile where not only your mouth turns up, but the corners of your eyes crinkle, as well. That is, you smile with your eyes as well as with your mouth. It is that kind of authentic, from the heart smile that is hard to fake. It can often be infectious, coming across as warm, friendly, and inviting to others. The other smile, with the mouth only, does not involve the eyes. It is often perceived as an insincere, polite, or half-hearted smile. Researchers Lee Anne Harker and Dacher Keltner (2001) analyzed 114 female high school yearbook photos from 1958 and 1960 and rated these photos on the degree to which the subjects displayed a Duchenne smile on a scale of one to ten. These particular women were chosen because they had already been subjects in a long term longitudinal study of life events (Helson, 1967); therefore mounds of data had been previously collected on them including marital status, marital satisfaction and overall happiness levels. The extent to which the women displayed the Duchenne smile in their high school photos strongly predicted their marital and life satisfaction decades later. Interestingly, their level of physical attractiveness was not related to how satisfied they were later on, either in their marriages or in their lives, nor was it related to the extent of their Duchenne ratings (Argyle, 2001). Was there something about how those with that special smile viewed the world that enabled them to maintain a sense of well-being? Were those with Duchenne smiles just so pleasant to be around that they drew positive people and events toward themselves, like magnets? A striking example of this is the famous smile of Academy Award-winning actress Julia Roberts. Could that explain why so many people enjoy seeing Julia Roberts on the silver screen? Former president Barack Obama is also well known for his inviting Duchenne smile. Did that contribute to his astronomical rise in the political sphere?

7.1 The Role of Positive Emotions

Describe the connection between positive emotions and effectiveness.

Why address the importance of happiness in a book about effectiveness? Barbara Fredrickson's (1998) theory about the function of positive emotions sheds light on this. In her book *Positivity* (2009), Frederickson lists the ten most frequent positive emotions including joy, gratitude, amusement, serenity, hope, pride, interest, inspiration, awe and love. In a nutshell, Fredrickson posits that positive emotions serve an indispensable evolutionary purpose. Fredrickson put forth the broaden and build theoretical framework to explain the wide-ranging, beneficial effects of positive emotions on humankind. Fredrickson points out that while negative emotions serve the important purpose of alerting us to danger, positive emotions let us know when we are safe. Positive emotions let us know when the coast is clear to engage in activities geared for the future. Therefore, we are free to **"broaden and build"** upon our existing skills, because we don't need to focus on fighting for survival in the present moment. Thus the evolutionary reward for positive emotions is in the future, pushing our adaptation in ways that enhance our abilities and our knowledge.

Fredrickson has helped to validate her theories with a variety of research studies which flesh out aspects of her theoretical perspective. For example, Fredrickson and Branigan (2005) exposed college student subjects to short film clips designed to induce different emotional states such as anger, anxiety or opposite emotions such as amusement or contentment. The subjects were then given a visual processing task requiring them to match visual stimuli. These same subjects could choose between a higher order, global (big picture) strategy or a lower order (small details) strategy to approach the task. The subjects who spent time watching a video that elicited positive feelings were significantly more likely to utilize the global, big picture approach to problem solving. This is typical of Fredrickson's experimental findings, which demonstrate that positive emotions lead to broader attention, greater working memory, enhanced verbal fluency and increased open-mindedness, all of which facilitate problem solving, learning and adaptability; therefore, positively influencing effectiveness.

Fredrickson (2000) also experimentally demonstrated that joyful emotions led to expanded concepts of what people would be willing to do at a given moment in time, eliciting a "broadening" of their behavioral repertoires. Negative emotions had the opposite effect, effectively shutting down ideas and actions, and therefore constricting what individuals were willing to do. Joy also makes it more likely that we will behave in positive or caring ways towards others and build good relationships. From an evolutionary standpoint, joy was also very important because it induced playfulness (Frijda, 1994). Play has always been adaptive in the acquisition of resources and the development of skill sets, especially for youngsters.

Fredrickson also expanded her theory to encompass what she termed an **undoing** component. She proposed that positive emotions can literally function as an antidote to undo the physiological effects of negative emotions. This was demonstrated in two studies (Fredrickson, Mancuso, Branigan & Tugade, 2000 and Tugade & Fredrickson, 2004). In these experiments subjects were given an anxiety-provoking task (told to hurriedly prepare a speech that they would later have to present and be rated upon) while hooked up to a variety of psychophysiological monitors to measure their arousal levels. Then each subject was shown one of four different videos. Two of the films elicited positive emotions, one film invoked sadness, and the last one was neutral. The undoing hypothesis was supported as the subjects who watched either of the positive videos produced significantly more rapid reductions in arousal (i.e. faster cardiovascular recovery) back to a normal state than those who watched the neutral video or the sad video. Clearly, the positive emotional state created by the videos offset or undid the anxiety created by the difficult task.

Fredrickson's work is especially important because of its relevance beyond the research lab or the theories taught in a classroom. These results match what we all know from common sense about what works well for coping in real life stressful situations. We all know how keeping your sense of humor and maintaining an optimistic outlook, even in the face of difficulty, are invaluable.

Given the potential for positive emotions to undo the damage from negative emotional states, Fredrickson and Losada (2005) further theorized that optimal mental health or flourishing is associated with positive emotions. They even came up with an equation which they say reflects and predicts human flourishing based on extensive data collected on undergraduate participants who provided mental health data for research purposes. The research team determined that there is a ratio of approximately 2.9 to 1 positive to negative emotions as the "magic ratio" which predicts human flourishing. And this certainly makes sense. When happy, our intellectual, physical, and social resources expand, and can build reserves to draw upon in times of stress. Interpersonal relationships are more likely to flourish in a positive emotional climate, improving the likelihood of propagation, and therefore the survival of our species. Happy people are more empathic and helpful to others which can also promote survival. Unlike negative emotions which tend to constrict our thinking, positive emotions promote flexibility, tolerance, creativity and openness to new perspectives. A variety of experiments on functional fixedness, as described in Chapter 1, validated that people are more creative and quicker when solving problems after a positive emotional state has been established. Estrada, Isen and Young (1997) also provided evidence that positive emotions can help boost decision-making skills by maximizing openness to problem solving options. This was demonstrated in a well known study with physicians who were divided into two groups. One group of doctors received a gift which contained a bag of candy while the other group of doctors did not receive a gift. Although the doctors were not permitted to eat the candy, the gift recipients displayed superior reasoning and decision-making compared to the doctors who didn't receive any candy. The candy group did not jump to conclusions and were more cautious, even though they arrived at correct diagnoses sooner. Theoretically, the positive feelings engendered from receiving the gift, even though it had not been consumed, enabled those physicians to function more skillfully on that day. These results suggest that you should bring a candy bar with you at your next doctor appointment to maximize the care you receive! All kidding aside, when in a good mood we typically think more clearly and use better judgment. Thus positive emotion has survival value and also clearly facilitates our effectiveness. This text will offer you many paths toward a more effective life, as obviously there are many avenues to becoming all that you can be. Learning to maximize your positive emotions is an enjoyable and essential road that you do not want to miss. To quote Seligman (2002):

> *"[P]ositive psychology takes seriously the bright hope that if you find yourself stuck in the parking lot of life, with few and only ephemeral pleasures, with minimal gratifications, and without meaning, there is a road out. This road takes you through the countryside of pleasure and gratification, up into the high country of strength and virtue, and finally to the peaks of lasting fulfillment, meaning and purpose. (p. xii)*

Positive emotions contribute not only to the propagation of our species, but to longevity as well. A long term study of the happiness and longevity of nuns (who all live a very similar lifestyle in terms of living circumstances, diet, medical care, and social support) showed that the best predictor of health and long life was the amount of positive emotions expressed in their writings over the years. A full 90% of the most cheerful nuns lived to be at least age 85, while only 34% of the least cheerful sisters made it into old age (Danner, Snowdon & Friesen, 2001). The researchers painstakingly ruled out all other factors in accounting for this remarkable result. Even more remarkable was the fact that the happiest nuns outlived the least happy by an average of ten years! To put that into context, consider the fact that non-smokers outlive smokers an average of seven years, a considerable difference of time, but still three years less than the effect of happiness. Does this mean that happiness is a more potent variable in longevity than abstinence from tobacco products?

> *"So, what can you tell from a personal statement? If you focus on the happiness expressed, you can tell whether someone will have a long life . . . We can suspect that these effects were not wrought by magic but rather by their mundane day-to-day activities, with the happy women slowly building good lives one smile and one word at a time . . . I will conclude that happiness is not just a feeling in the moment but an important influence on the future."(Peterson, 2006, p. 77)*

Another study (Abel & Kruger, 2010) found a relationship between the Duchenne smile and longevity. The researchers examined old issues of the Baseball Register, analyzing photos of 230 players. They found that on average, the guys with big smiles lived 4.9 years longer than the players with partial smiles, and a full 7 years longer than the men with serious facial expressions.

Positive emotions and emotional style are related to many aspects of health including susceptibility to the common cold (Cohen, 2003). These researchers discovered that those who scored low on positive emotional style were three times more likely to catch a cold than those who scored high after the subjects were administered a shot of rhinovirus.

Happiness pays other major physical and emotional dividends as well. When compared to unhappy people, happy individuals are more productive at work and have higher incomes, are more tolerant, creative, decisive, persistent, empathic, and have more friends and better marriages (Seligman, 2002).

Questions

1. Positive emotions _____.
   A. are rarely displayed by individuals who display a Duchenne smile
   B. have served the evolutionary purpose of signaling safety
   C. are distracting and limit our effectiveness
   D. tend to increase our level of stress

2. The _____ and _____ theory explains the wide range of beneficial effects of positive emotions on humankind.
   A. doing; undoing
   B. optimism; pessimism
   C. broaden; build
   D. generosity; selfishness

3. Frederickson proposed an _____ component whereby positive emotions can function as an antidote to the physiological effects of negative emotions.
   A. undoing
   B. unwrapping
   C. undulating
   D. umbrella

7.2 How Should We Define Happiness?

Identify the elements that help us to define happiness.

Okay, it is clear that happiness is good. You are healthier, live longer and are more productive, among other things. But what exactly is happiness? Seligman takes great pains to distinguish the study of what he terms "**authentic happiness**" from **hedonism**. The most useful definition, one that is agreed upon by positive psychologists, neuroscientists, and even Buddhist monks is more akin to satisfaction or contentment rather than happiness in the form of jumping for joy or floating on cloud nine. It contains depth and deliberation. It encompasses living a meaningful life, utilizing your skills and talents, and involves taking the time to live your life with purpose. It is maximized when you feel part of a community. It is enhanced when you are able to confront irritations and crises with grace. It involves a willingness to learn, stretch and grow, which can sometimes cause temporary discomfort. It is far more than temporary exhilaration or even sensual pleasure, although such feelings often accompany living each day to its fullest.

As you embark on your personal journey to maximize positive emotions, take a few moments to complete the Authentic Happiness Inventory, on the next pages, adapted from a questionnaire developed by Christopher Peterson, to determine your current level of happiness.

Authentic Happiness Inventory

Please read each group of statements carefully. Then pick the one statement in each group that best describes the way you have been feeling this past week, including today. Be sure to read all of the statements in each group before making your choice. Select the one that best applies.

A. 1. I feel that I am extraordinarily successful.

2. As I look back on my life, all I see are victories.

3. I feel like I have succeeded more than most people.

4. I do not feel like a winner.

5. I feel like a failure.

B. 1. I am usually in an unbelievably great mood.

2. I am usually in a great mood.

3. I am usually in a good mood.

4. I am usually in a neutral mood.

5. I am usually in a bad mood.

C. 1. When working, I am totally oblivious to outside events.

2. When working, I rarely notice what is going on around me.

3. When working, I attend more to my work than what is going on around me.

4. When working, I attend as much to what is going on around me as to my work.

5. When working, I attend more to what is going on around me than to my work.

D. 1. I have a very clear idea about the purpose or meaning of my life.

2. I have a pretty good idea about the purpose or meaning of my life.

3. I have a hint about my purpose in life.

4. I do not know the purpose or meaning of my life.

5. My life does not have any purpose or meaning.

E. 1. I always get what I want.

2. I usually get what I want.

3. Somewhat more often than not, I get what I want.

4. Sometimes I get what I want sometimes not.

5. I rarely get what I want.

F. 1. My life is filled with joy.

2. I have much more joy than sorrow in my life.

3. I have more joy than sorrow in my life.

4. I have neither sorrow nor joy in my life.

5. I have sorrow in my life.

G. 1. Most of the time I feel fascinated by what I am doing.

2. Most of the time I feel quite interested in what I am doing.

3. Most of the time I feel interested in what I am doing.

4. Most of the time I feel neither bored nor interested in what I am doing.

5. Most of the time I feel bored.

(Continued)

H. 1. By objective standards, I do amazingly well.
2. By objective standards, I do quite well.
3. By objective standards, I do rather well.
4. By objective standards, I do neither well nor poorly.
5. By objective standards, I do poorly.

I. 1. I am extraordinarily proud of myself.
2. I am very proud of myself.
3. I am proud of myself.
4. I am not ashamed of myself.
5. I am ashamed of myself.

J. 1. My existence has a lasting, large and positive impact on the world.
2. My existence makes the world a better place.
3. My existence has a small but positive effect on the world.
4. My existence neither helps not hurts the world.
5. In the grand scheme of things, my existence may hurt the world.

K. 1. I do really well at whatever I am doing.
2. I do well at most things I am doing.
3. I do well at some things I am doing.
4. I do okay at most things I am doing.
5. I do not do most things very well.

L. 1. I have so much enthusiasm that I feel I can do most anything.
2. I feel enthusiastic doing almost everything.
3. I have a good amount of enthusiasm.
4. My enthusiasm level is neither high nor low.
5. I have little or no enthusiasm.

M. 1. I truly love my work.
2. I really love my work.
3. For the most part, I like my work.
4. I feel neutral about my work.
5. I do not like my work (paid or unpaid)

N. 1. I feel extraordinarily optimistic about the future.
2. I feel quite optimistic about the future.

3. I am somewhat optimistic about my future.
4. I am neither optimistic nor pessimistic about the future.
5. I am pessimistic about the future.

O. 1. I have accomplished a great deal more in my life than most people.
2. I have accomplished more in life than most people.
3. I have accomplished somewhat more in life than most people.
4. I have accomplished no more in life than most people.
5. I have accomplished little in life.

P. 1. I feel close to everyone in the world.
2. I feel close to most people, even if I do not know them well.
3. I feel close to friends and family members.
4. I feel neither close to nor cut off from other people.
5. I feel cut off from other people.

Q. 1. Time passes so quickly during all of the things that I do that I don't notice it.
2. Time passes quickly during all of the things that I do.
3. Time passes quickly during most of the things that I do.
4. Time passes quickly during some things that I do, and slowly for other things.
5. Time passes slowly during most of the things that I do.

R. 1. I could not be any happier with myself.
2. I am happy with myself.
3. I am neither happy nor unhappy with myself.
4. I am neutral.
5. I am unhappy with myself.

S. 1. My skills are always challenged by the situations I encounter.
2. My skills are often challenged by the situations I encounter.

3. My skills are sometimes challenged by the situations I encounter.

4. My skills are occasionally challenged by the situations I encounter.

5. My skills are never challenged by the situations I encounter.

T. 1. I spend practically every moment every day doing things that are important.

2. I spend most of my time every day doing things that are important.

3. I spend some of my time every day doing things that are important.

4. I spend a lot of time doing things that are neither important nor unimportant.

5. I spend all of my time doing things that are unimportant.

U. 1. If I were keeping score in life, I would be far ahead.

2. If I were keeping score in life, I would be ahead.

3. If I were keeping score in life, I would be somewhat ahead.

4. If I were keeping score in life, I would be about even.

5. If I were keeping score in life, I would be behind.

V. 1. My life is filled with pleasure.

2. I experience much more pleasure than pain.

3. I experience more pleasure than pain.

4. I experience pain and pleasure in equal amounts.

5. I experience more pain than pleasure.

W. 1. I like my daily routine so much that I almost never take breaks from it.

2. I like my daily routine so much that I rarely take breaks from it.

3. I like my daily routine but I take breaks.

4. I feel neutral about my daily routine.

5. I do not enjoy my daily routine.

X. 1. My life is a wonderful one.

2. My life is a very good one.

3. My life is a good one.

4. My life is an OK one.

5. My life is a bad one.

Results:

Add up the numbers associated with each of your answers. Once you have tabulated this total then divide the total score by 24 to get your Happiness Score.

Scores between 3.0 and 2.5 indicate moderate happiness and contentment.

If you scored under 2.5 you are generally happy and often very happy.

If you scored under 2.0 you are extremely happy. (If your score is between 1.0 and 1.5 you may not have been realistic in your assessment – everyone has some issues in life.)

Scores between 3.0 and 4.0 indicate that you have some dissatisfaction in your life.

If you scored above 4.0 you are not happy with your life and may be depressed.

Questions

1. The definition of "authentic happiness" that is generally agreed upon by most people studying the concept is most similar to the concept of _____.

   A. satisfaction

   B. longevity

   C. floating on a cloud

   D. jumping for joy

2. What tends to maximize the experience of authentic happiness?

   A. feeling part of a community

   B. momentary successes

   C. religious ceremonies

   D. wishful thinking

3. Seligman distinguishes authentic happiness from _____.

   A. curiosity

   B. hedonism

   C. melancholy

   D. pessimism

7.3 Misconceptions About What Leads to Happiness

Identify common misconceptions about what makes us happy and the mechanism which often causes happiness to be transient.

Many misconceptions about what leads to happiness are unfortunately ingrained in our culture. Before we help you embark on your personal journey to greater happiness, fulfillment, and effectiveness, it will be useful to correct the mistaken notions most of us hold about what will really make us happy. For example, were you aware that . . .

- Wealth, and all the possessions it can buy, has a surprisingly low correlation with levels of happiness. Believe it or not, the wealthy are only slightly happier than the poor! While pay raises can temporarily boost job satisfaction, average salaries do not correlate with happiness. One study, cited in *The Week* (Dec. 5th, 2008), found that the happiness benefits of money peaked at the modest income of $20,000! In a national sample of Americans (Aknin, Norton & Dunn, 2009), individuals expected their life satisfaction and happiness to double if their incomes increased from $25,000 up to $55,000. Double the money, double the happiness, or so they assumed. In reality, the data revealed that people making $55,000 yearly were only 9% more satisfied than those earning $25,000. Even the super rich, such as multi-millionaires, are only slightly happier than the typical middle class American. Globally, income levels have surprisingly meager influence on whether people enjoy themselves, smile or laugh on a given day (Diener, and colleagues, 2010). Kahneman and Deaton (2010) demonstrated that for U.S. residents, once incomes exceeded $75,000 yearly for a family of four, higher earnings had virtually zero impact on day-to-day feelings of happiness. Although U.S. residents who are poverty-stricken tend to be unhappy, once people have the basic necessities, more money does not buy nor build happiness. This brings to mind the bumper sticker which opines, "He who dies with the most toys is still dead."

- There appears to be no reliable correlation between physical attractiveness, despite any advantages that beauty may provide, and happiness.
- Physical health also does not reliably predict happiness.
- IQ and educational level are not reliably correlated with happiness.

Take a moment and consider statistics showing that, according to survey research, people in the U.S. are no happier than their counterparts were 50 years ago. This is true despite the fact that, by all objective measures, life has improved for most Americans in terms of standard of living and health over the last half century. Even the poor have vastly more material goods than their counterparts of 50 years ago, although they still may be quite poor relative to others. We have far more abundant material goods that provide safety and comfort, life expectancy is longer, information is much more readily available, transportation is more easily accessible, and literacy rates are higher. Yet despite all this, our self-reported happiness levels have not kept pace with the increase in health, wealth and education. This phenomenon has been called the **progress paradox** by George Easterbrook (2003).

Surveys have shown that most people would actually be happier making less money, but on one condition: that everyone else made even less (Solnick and Hemenway, 1998). In fact, most people prefer that scenario to one in which their income rises but everyone else's income increases more. In other words, it's not how much we have that counts; it's how much we have compared to the Joneses! This could explain why people in more egalitarian societies generally report higher levels of life satisfaction. Scandinavian countries with large social safety nets consistently score the highest on the happiness scales. Inhabitants of Costa Rica, a relatively poor Central American country compared to the U.S., also post very high happiness scores compared to our country. The Costa Rican national motto, *"Pura Vida"* or "living well" may offer a clue to the attitudes of the typical Costa Rican. In June of 2012, Costa Rica exceeded the U.S. and Western Europe for the second time as the happiest nation in a study of 151 countries with regard to level of well-being and progress not tied to GNP (i.e. economic indicators). Costa Rica ranked first on the Happy Planet Index created and measured by the

New Economic Foundation, a British research center which studies and promotes global well-being along with sustainable development.

7.3.1 The Hedonic Treadmill

Why is it that riches, beauty, health, or education (or any combination of such) do not reliably lead to lasting happiness? There are two main explanatory factors for this, one lying in genetics and the other in adaptation, the latter of which has been referred to as the "**hedonic treadmill.**" The first factor, your genetic makeup, reflects the fact that to a certain extent your level of positive emotion is genetically inherited. That is, each of us has a personal, genetically determined set point for happiness to which we tend to revert after the passage of time. Consider the fact that studies of major lottery winners revealed that although these lucky individuals may at first experience elation, followed by several months of increased happiness, after a year or so they were no happier than a matched control group, similar in all ways but minus a lottery windfall (Brickman, Coates & Janoff-Bulman, 1978). In that study, 22 lottery winners, each of whom received a minimum of $50,000 with some netting over one million during that year, were asked to rate their past, present and future happiness, as well as the pleasure they derived from everyday activities. Believe it or not, the lottery winners were only a wee bit happier than the non-winners in terms of present and future happiness, and they actually found less pleasure in everyday activities than the controls. But the reverse is true as well. Individuals who become paralyzed as a result of spinal cord injuries are typically emotionally traumatized at first (some to the point of becoming suicidal), but after a few years of adjustment their happiness levels are only slightly lower than those who are able-bodied. The same research group (Brickman, Coates, & Janoff-Bulman, 1978) interviewed 29 individuals who had become paralyzed the preceding year due to accidents and compared their happiness levels to the lottery winners. Although their present happiness was lower, as would be expected, their expected future happiness and pleasure in everyday activities was actually higher than the lottery winners! However, although there is strong evidence that happiness levels are partially set by your genetic inheritance, **do not make the mistake of assuming that you are stuck.** Again, happiness set points are only partially determined by your genetic inheritance, and as such there is a wide variety of things you can do to affect your happiness levels, as will be outlined in this and later chapters.

The second factor accounting for the failure of money, beauty, health, or a high IQ to generate long term happiness is the fact that we tend to inevitably adapt to fortunate circumstances and take these for granted. Brickman and Campbell (1971) first introduced this concept of the hedonic treadmill, where we continually adapt to improving circumstances to inevitably return to a point of relative neutrality. Due to the hedonic treadmill our expectations tend to rise as our bank accounts grow, our houses and cars get more expensive and luxurious, and our wardrobe bulges out of our closet. So we tend to need something more or better to recreate the thrill. Likewise, the more we accomplish, the more we expect of ourselves. The more we accumulate or accomplish, or the more attractive we become, we tend to compare ourselves with those who have more, are more successful or more attractive, so we still feel incomplete. We keep running on the treadmill and getting nowhere. The more money we have, the more beautiful we become, the more we strive because what was exciting before is now commonplace. If this treadmill did not exist, individuals with more good things going for them would be happier than those who are less well off, yet this is just not the case. Possessions and accomplishments appear to only raise happiness levels in the short term. But adaptation also works to help us recover from loss and disappointments as well. As an example, recall the spinal cord injured individuals whose baseline happiness returned to their former levels within a couple of years after their injury.

So why does this adaptation occur? Why can't our honeymoon with our beloved last forever? Why does our excitement about the new job, or promotion, or award evaporate? Why does the fascination with the new car, or house, or _____ (you fill in the blank) wear off? One potential reason for this adaptation response has much to do with the survival of the human species. Pleasure can be very distracting, as preoccupying as pain, especially if very intense. The fact that pleasurable experiences tend to be brief and diminish over time allows us to get back to the rest of our lives and not be diverted (Barkow, 1997), which clearly has survival value. Think of what happens to drug addicts if they spend all of their time pursuing their next fix. Or for a healthier example, remember the last time you fell head over heels in love (in the beginning). For many of us, falling in love makes it hard to concentrate, to eat, to sleep, or to work, as all we want to do is think about our beloved, to be with that person, or talk or text with that person, or tell our friends all about that person. Not much of a productive nature gets done in the early stages of being in love. (And this is all well and good – everyone needs to know the joy of this in their lives at least once.) Once you calm down a bit you can begin to accomplish what you need to do in your life, but if you stay madly in love all the time you might never finish anything.

It also appears that people often tend to overestimate how long pleasurable feelings will last. In a series of studies, Gilbert, Wilson and colleagues (1998, 2000, & 2001) examined the expectations and emotional reactions of people before and after significant life events of both a positive and negative nature. The events included romantic break-ups, getting a desired job, being fired from a job, receiving tenure in teaching positions, or failing to get tenure. The results clearly showed that while people correctly predicted that favorable outcomes would boost their happiness levels, they consistently overestimated how long the improvement would last. The same was true for negative outcomes. The subjects correctly predicted that they would be depressed and/or disappointed by that setback, but they consistently overestimated the length of their emotional reaction. So the hedonic treadmill can certainly work in our favor to help us recover from difficult times, often quicker than we anticipate. Most people are more resilient than they realize. When depressed, whatever the reason or source, it is often useful to remind yourself that "this too shall pass."

The other good news is that adaptation does not permanently damage our ability to enjoy a given pleasure. We can come back for more later as long as sufficient time has passed to allow adaptation to subside. What constitutes an adequate waiting period varies widely depending on the person, the pleasurable stimulus and the context of the situation. But as a rule, it is wise to spread your pleasures over time to maximize your satisfaction, whereas cramming them all together leads to adaptation and under-appreciation. Think about overindulged children who get every new toy on the market in a short time frame. They are often easily bored and play with each toy a few times before tossing it aside in pursuit of the next.

7.3.2 The Role of Genetics

In *Authentic Happiness* Seligman introduces an equation to guide you on your journey to happiness:

$$H = S + C + V$$

H refers to your enduring level of happiness, not momentary blips of joy or pleasure, but your overall happiness level over time. **S** refers to your genetic set point which partially accounts for your baseline happiness level. Research has indicated that approximately 50% of most personality traits are genetically determined, but that means that we have much more control over the remaining 50%. **C** reflects the circumstances of your life, some of which you can control and some you can not. **V** represents your internal mind-set, those all-important cognitive, emotional and behavioral factors over which you have voluntary control. One goal of positive psychology is on altering the **V** (voluntary) factors to maximize life satisfaction, which has profound implications for your ability to be effective. According to the research of Lyubomirsky, Sheldon and Schkade (2005), the S (genetic) factor accounts for 50% of your happiness level, the C factor only 10%, and the all important V factor (your internal mind-set) accounts for 40% in their happiness model. In an even more specific breakdown of the genetic determinants of emotional states, Tellegen and his colleagues (1988) estimated that 40% of positive emotionality and 55% of negative emotionality (i.e. such as vulnerability to depression) are genetically based.

Meehl (1975) was one of the first to suggest the possibility that happy people were just born with more of what he called *cerebral joy juice*. He referred to the ability to experience positive emotions as an individual's **hedonic capacity**, and he theorized that it represented individual differences between people which were influenced by genetics as well as environment and learning histories. He further hypothesized that hedonic capacity was linked to the personality trait of **extroversion**, being outgoing and comfortable around other people. Research has supported much of Meehl's theorizing about hedonic capacity, which is now referred to in the positive psychology literature as **positive affectivity**. Watson (2000) confirmed that positive affectivity is more common among extraverts, whether male or female. Those who are high in positive affectivity are more socially active, have more friends and belong to more social organizations. They are more likely to be married, to be satisfied with their marriages, and to be happy with their jobs as well. People high in positive affectivity are also very likely to be low in neuroticism, meaning that they have fewer neurotic (anxiety-based) symptoms. But since these are correlational results, we do not know what causes what. Does positive affectivity lead to personal, marital, and occupational satisfaction, or is it the other way around? The results of the Duchenne smile study suggest that positive affectivity may help produce or create the conditions for later life satisfaction in a variety of areas. It can be said that an extroverted, non-neurotic person has a bit of a head start in achieving happiness. Individuals who are religious or very spiritual also score high on positive affectivity (Clark & Watson, 1999). Here again, we don't know whether positive affectivity leads one to religion, or whether the sense of meaning, comfort and community that religious affiliation provides boosts positive affect. Argyle (1987) stressed the community aspect of religion as being the important linchpin here, as religious individuals rate themselves as being less lonely as compared to the nonreligious.

Twin studies do support the heritability of positive affectivity (Finkel & McCrue, 1997 along with the aforementioned work of Tellegen and his colleagues). But heritable does not mean fixed or unchangeable. Depression is even more heritable than positive affectivity and that is readily changed through psychotherapy and/or ameliorated with psychotropic medications. According to David Watson (2005), one of the world's-leading authorities on positive affectivity, "The genetic and biological data should not induce a fatalistic resignation; we are still free to increase our positive affectivity."

Questions

1. Riches and beauty do not lead to happiness in the long run because of the
   _____.

   A. impermanence of beauty

   B. progress paradox

   C. inevitable health declines

   D. hedonic treadmill

2. Which of the following statements is applicable to your level of happiness?

   A. One-hundred percent of your happiness level is due to your genetic heritage.

   B. The hedonic treadmill helps you recover from loss and disappointment.

   C. People typically underestimate how long positive feelings will last.

   D. An optimistic outlook is unrelated to your happiness level.

3. Positive affectivity tends to be positively related to levels of _____ and negatively related to levels of _____.

    A. extroversion; neuroticism

    B. introversion; optimism

    C. genetics; wealth

    D. religiosity; intelligence

7.4 How to Boost Your Happiness: The "V" Factor

Describe actions and mindsets that can increase happiness about your past and future, as well as in the present moment.

Seligman recommends that you pay much more attention to the role of the V factors in your life rather than spending all your time trying to improve your life circumstances. In terms of the effects of the C factor—the external circumstances of your life—upon your level of happiness, Kasser & Ryan (1993.1996) studied whether the American dream—riches, fame and beauty—really fosters happiness. They found that striving for this actually led to less vitality, lower fulfillment of potential, and physical distress. In stark contrast, the pursuit of self-acceptance, friendship, and being helpful to others was linked with greater psychological well-being. Thus, Seligman makes the following recommendations based on what situations are associated with happiness and which are not. Remember that these relationships are correlational in nature and may or may not reflect causality. To maximize your chances of happiness you should:

- Get married (strongly correlated with happiness)
- Develop a varied social network (strongly correlated with happiness)
- Involve yourself in religion or find meaning through spiritual belief or practice (moderately correlated with happiness)

Seligman further recommends that you do not bother to do the following if you hope to increase your happiness level:

- Make more money. The more materialistic you become, typically the less happy you become.
- Stay healthy. Surprisingly, it is how you view your health rather than your objective health that affects happiness levels.
- Get more education. Although certainly a worthy pursuit, it is not related to happiness levels.
- Attempt to change your race (no correlation with happiness).
- Move to a warmer or sunnier climate (no correlation to happiness).

According to Harvard psychology researcher Daniel Gilbert, as explicated in his book *Stumbling on Happiness* (2006), the single best predictor of happiness is the quality of your interpersonal relationships. Therefore, he concludes that "it is not marriage that makes you happy, but a happy marriage that helps lead to happiness." He further explains that this is why people often experience a surge in happiness when an unhappy marriage is finally dissolved. Gilbert also reported an unpublished study using an iphone sampling where respondents reported feeling happiest when talking, engaging in sexual activity or spending time with friends. Interestingly, respondents did not report feeling happier when resting, explaining that when not actively involved in tasks their minds often wandered to worries or negative thoughts.

Gilbert also found that happiness decreased for both sexes following the birth of the first child. People without children are happier than parents, and parents of young kids are the least happy. The bottom line is that children do not make us happy (dirty diapers and tantrums are typically not much fun), but parents need to believe that children lead to happiness because of all the time and effort involved in raising a child properly. Gilbert reflects that "as a result of that sacrifice we love them all the more. We don't value our children in spite of how difficult they are, we value them because of how difficult they are."

In summary, we offer the following chart to summarize the myriad findings regarding what does and what does not correlate with happiness and life satisfaction and to what extent.

TABLE 7.1 Positive Correlations with Happiness and Life Satisfaction

No Correlation	Moderate Correlation	High Correlation
Age	being married	optimism
Gender	number of friends	gratitude
Education	physical health	being employed
Income level	agreeableness	good self-esteem
Social class	religiosity	high frequency of sexual intercourse
Intelligence	level of leisure activity	extraversion
Ethnicity	internal locus of control	happily married
Physical attractiveness	conscientiousness	many good friends
Having children	open-mindedness	low neuroticism

Surprisingly, research indicates that just the act of imagining living a wealthy lifestyle can make you less likely to engage in the very behaviors that promote happiness, like socializing with friends or helping others (Piff and colleagues, 2012). Vohs, Meade & Goode (2008) demonstrated that wealth contemplation often leads people to prefer solitary activities.

Seligman divides positive emotions into three temporal categories depending on whether they relate to the past, the present, or the future. Positive future-oriented emotions include optimism, hope, and trust. Pleasure, joy, ecstasy, enthusiasm, and calmness reflect positive emotions in the here and now. Past-oriented positive emotions range from satisfaction, pride, contentment and serenity. It is very possible to experience positive emotions in one time dimension, but not the others as these emotions are related but not all-encompassing. Some of your present emotions are instantaneous and not dependent on thought. You don't have to think to experience the pleasure of chocolate melting in your mouth. You don't need to interpret anything to enjoy the feeling of a good massage on tense, sore muscles. But your feelings about the past and the future are totally reliant on your thoughts, your interpretations, and your habitual frames. And here we can put the lessons from Chapter 1 on reframing and in Chapter 2 on cognitive restructuring and optimism to work for us. Developing and enhancing your positive emotions about the future is the best place to start, because those can also affect your present feelings, and potentially can help you interpret your past in the most favorable light.

7.4.1 How to Brighten Your Expectations for Your Future—Flexible Optimism and Hope

In Chapter 2 we discussed the importance of optimism to effectiveness and provided specific steps for enhancing an optimistic outlook. We want to remind you that optimism is a necessary ingredient in happiness. Research in cognitive psychology has shown that just as negative self-statements can create depression, anxiety, or other negative emotions, positive or optimistic self-statements can create and reinforce effectiveness and happiness. Many studies have demonstrated that levels of optimism vs. pessimism are a powerful determining factor in our physical and emotional health. Indeed, a review of the research on happiness has consistently identified optimism as one of the four traits manifested by happy people (Myers and Diener, 1995). In addition, pessimism is often linked to depression in a wide variety of studies.

Optimism refers to beliefs regarding the future, regarding the probability of negative vs. positive outcomes and regarding one's ability to cope in the event of a negative outcome. Optimists believe that they are likely to experience positive outcomes and success, and in the event of a negative outcome, they will be able to cope. Because of this optimists are more likely to persevere in the face of obstacles due to their belief in eventual success. And that is why *optimism is energizing, while pessimism is paralyzing*. If you believe you are going to fail, it is so much easier to give up. But if you believe that you will win, succeed, or eventually prevail, then you find the strength to keep going no matter how difficult the challenge.

Is there experimental evidence that boosting optimism levels will lead to increased happiness? There have been few direct experimental interventions in this regard, but in one notable study with children, Seligman, Revich, Jaycox, and Gillham (1995) identified elementary school children who were at risk for depression and exposed them to optimism training. Using cognitive restructuring techniques and social problem-solving training, the kids were taught to look on the bright side of things. Following the training period, the children exposed to optimism training were significantly less depressed than the control group of kids who did not receive any training, and this effect was even more pronounced at a two year follow-up of the progress of the children.

7.4.2 Finding Happiness in Your Past— Maximizing Satisfaction and Contentment

Your feelings about your past are determined by the nature of your memories, which are heavily colored by your interpretations of past events. Since you can't change your past, you are left with finding ways to influence these interpretations to generate satisfaction and a sense of meaning. There are three main methods of moving your feelings about your past toward greater contentment and satisfaction. The first involves letting go of the paradigm that your past, particularly your childhood, solely determines your future. Are you stuck believing that you are a prisoner of your upbringing, or forever a helpless victim of your past traumas, hurts, or disappointments? The deterministic branches of psychology which ruled the discipline in the mid-1900s promoted extensive research to establish evidence of the destructive effects of bad childhood events (i.e. parental death, abuse, divorce). But upon reviewing a wealth of research, Seligman and others have concluded that the influence of childhood trauma on adult personality can be negligible, despite strong expectations to the contrary on the part of so many researchers. So there you have it. Again, the choice is yours. You have choice over whether you allow a troubled past to define you or to strengthen you.

The second and third strategies for improving happiness about the past involve making a proactive effort to engage in both gratitude and forgiveness. Gratitude works to enhance your appreciation of your past and present, while forgiveness gives you the power to let go of bitterness while potentially allowing you to rewrite the meaning of your personal history in the process.

So cultivate what we call an **attitude of gratitude**. This is far more than counting your blessings, although that is a part of it. Adopting an attitude of gratitude involves noticing, appreciating, and being thankful for the people, events, and even the small benefits of your life. Highly grateful people operate from the framework where everything they have, all that they have experienced, past and present, is a gift. The French novelist Colette was quoted on her deathbed as saying, *"What a wonderful life I've had. I only wish I'd realized it sooner."* Gratitude improves your satisfaction with life because it revivifies your good memories and colors how you interpret them. On top of this, those who are grateful are less at risk for negative emotions such as depression, anxiety, or envy. They are more empathic, forgiving, and helpful to others. Emmons & McCullough (2003) assigned two groups to keep a daily journal. One group kept a journal of all they were grateful for, past and present. The other group kept a journal of hassles and ongoing neutral life events. It is no surprise that happiness levels soared for the former group. Sarah Ban Breathnach (1995), in her book *Simple Abundance,* suggests that you keep such a gratitude journal and record at least five things daily about which you are grateful. These entries need not be major accomplishments or gifts, just simple pleasures that you may often take for granted. For example, one of the authors worked as an intern on a spinal cord injury ward for a year. The most important thing that he drew from that experience was a constant appreciation for having an intact body and being able to walk, something that we regularly take for granted. We recommend that whenever you feel particularly mistreated by life, consider the ramifications of losing one of your senses, or the function of some part of your body. Remember the last time you were ill, or had a toothache or headache, and appreciate just how wonderful normal is.

Researchers have recently identified a very healthy neuropsychological pattern that is associated with gratitude. McCraty (2002) and McCraty & Atkinson (2003) reported a synchronization of alpha brain wave activity (associated with relaxation and positive emotions) and heartbeats after experimental manipulation of appreciation levels in their subjects. McCraty concluded that the gratitude-related human response of appreciation appeared to have a coherent psycho-physiological pattern.

Seligman, Steen, Park & Peterson (2005) asked students in their positive psychology classes to write gratitude letters and found that the senders of those letters felt significantly happier for several weeks afterward. It would be interesting to know what the effect was on the recipients of the letters.

Positive Psychology Exercise

The Letter of Gratitude

Following the model utilized by Seligman and his colleagues in the experiment mentioned above, we encourage you to think about all of the people in your life who have been helpful to you, kind to you or, who have been there for you in one way or another to whom you have never expressed your gratitude in a meaningful way. This could be a friend, relative, parent, teacher, employer, member of the clergy, neighbor, teammate, coach, co-worker, fellow student, etc. It could be anyone. Write a letter of gratitude to that valued person and describe in concrete terms why you are so grateful to him or her. If it is at all possible, deliver the letter in person and allow that individual to read the letter in your presence. If this is not possible, send it by text, fax, regular mail or e-mail, and then call the person afterwards by phone. While doing all of it by text or e-mail might be tempting, a follow-up phone call is preferable to keep it on a more personal level. Following through with this assignment will give you, and most likely the recipient of your letter, a real lift in spirit and mood, even if only temporarily. To make these results last, send a new gratitude letter out every few months to someone whose efforts you truly appreciate.

Positive Psychology Exercise

Three Good Things

A variation on the gratitude journal involves writing down three things that went well at the end of each day. Why three things instead of five or ten? According to the research of Seligman and his colleagues, who varied both the number of good things to be listed and the timing of when to do it, the combination of listing three things at the end of the day (as opposed to the morning) was optimal for boosting happiness levels. To further enhance the benefits you can obtain from this exercise, answer a simple question after each entry of a positive event. The question is, "why did this happen?"

The next strategy has to do with being able to forgive. **Forgiveness** allows you to let go of the energy attached to bad memories without necessarily forgetting what happened. Trying to forget about something is rarely a useful strategy. Sometimes, the more we try to forget, the more we just remember. For example, give this a try. For the next few seconds, whatever you do – *do not think about PINK ELEPHANTS!* Chances are that this did not work. Why? Because in order to not think about pink elephants, you must first conjure up a rosy colored pachyderm, and then try to erase this image. This is a task of elephantine proportions. The fact is that every time we command ourselves to *just forget about it,* the more we remind ourselves. Thus the only viable strategy left is to forgive, which leaves your memories intact (preserving whatever important life lessons you have gleaned), but allows for the hurt and bitterness to dissipate. You can choose to forgive, whatever the circumstances, because ultimately forgiveness is not for others, it is for you. It frees up your energy and allows you to move on and increase your sense of life satisfaction. A far more comprehensive discussion of forgiveness, along with suggested steps to achieving it, will come at the end of Chapter 9.

There are other considerations regarding whether we view our past with positive feelings which have to do with the nature of memory. Realize that when we review pleasant memories from the past, our recollections of pleasure are not necessarily accurate, faithful, blow by blow accounts or summaries of what happened. Rather our memories are influenced by the intensity of the experience, as well as how it ended, a formula referred to as **peak-end theory** by psychologist Daniel Kahneman (1999). Studies have corroborated peak-end theory, which states that evaluations of past experiences reflect an average of the highs and lows, along with an assessment of how it was just before it ended. Another factor often overlooked is how long the experience lasted. Kahneman called this phenomenon **duration neglect** and this also affects how we interpret the positive or negative impact of experiences in our past. The practical lesson here is that it is useful to build in high points and good finales or finishes, if possible, with respect to your experiences so that you will be more likely to remember things in a favorable light. This is a way to ensure that your remembrances of things past will be more positive. This could be a strategy to use, for example, when planning for a vacation. Remember to plan in at least one high note and end with a big adventure so your recollection of your past trip will be maximized as a positive memory.

7.4.3 Finding Happiness in the Present Moment—Pleasures and Gratifications

Happiness in the here and now differs from happiness about your past or future. Present moment happiness falls into two separate categories: (1) the pleasures; and (2) the gratifications. Pleasures are temporary and typically involve enjoyable sensory sensations and minimal, if any, thoughts. This is the territory of joy and thrills, emotions and feelings such as orgasm, ecstasy, comfort, bliss, merriment and excitement. Pleasures are wonderful, part of the spice of life, but they habituate quickly (remember the hedonic treadmill), and as such, are almost always short-lived. Gratifications, on the other hand, represent activities that we find very fulfilling, that we tend to lose ourselves within, that absorb us fully. Gratifications can be anything from hobbies, reading a great book, painting, sculpting, building, fixing, creating, writing, singing, playing a musical instrument, gardening, collecting, anything that enjoyably fills our attention. When we engage in activities we find gratifying, we often lose track of time, our skills are up to challenges we face, and we tap into our strengths. This relates to **engagement**, the E in PERMA. Gratifications are more long-lasting than pleasures because they are far more resistant to habituation, while often leading to self-improvement due to the exercise of our strengths.

While we all enjoy indulging in our own personal pleasures, focusing our lives on the pursuit of continual pleasure is very unlikely to bring about lasting happiness. When we repeatedly encounter the same pleasure-producing stimulus over and over, it arouses less pleasure for us over time. This is adaptation. Because of the hedonic treadmill, you will never be satisfied for long, and will need something more to capture the thrill and escape boredom. When this becomes obsessive, addiction is born. Addictions can be to substances that bring momentary pleasure such as alcohol, drugs, food, or chocolate, or behaviors like compulsive gambling, shopping, or sexual addictions. To counteract this we recommend that you consider spacing your pleasures out over time as the best way to enhance them. Try to find the optimal interval between pleasures that prevents habituation from occurring. For example, if you ride that awesome roller coaster five times every day for a month, it will soon get quite dull. But riding that same coaster one to two times a year will remain a great thrill. Or eating that creamy chocolate sundae can be a great sensual treat, but if you eat three a day for a few days, you will get to the point where you won't even taste it anymore (not to mention the bloat). Adding the element of surprise is another approach that helps ward off habituation. Work to put a little unpredictability into your sensory pleasures.

Seligman (2002) laments how the rat race of modern life combined with our future-mindedness keeps us from appreciating the present moment. Bryant and Veroff recommend **savoring** as a way of maximizing pleasure in the present. They define savoring as the awareness of pleasure that comes from paying deliberate conscious attention to your experience of pleasure. Bryant (2003) found that those who routinely savor, who anticipate positive events and relish them in the moment, are happier and more satisfied with life. Bryant and Veroff distinguish between four kinds of savoring:

1. **Basking** (openly receiving praise and/or congratulations)
2. **Thanksgiving** (being thankful for your blessings)
3. **Marveling** (being filled with awe at the wonder of the moment)
4. **Luxuriating** (indulging your senses)

Other savoring strategies include:

1. **Sharing** – talking about it with others
2. **Memory Building** – make mental pictures or even take a physical souvenir of the experience, if possible, to help you reminisce
3. **Self-Congratulation** – remind yourself of a job well done. Congratulate yourself
4. **Sharpen your perception** – narrow your focus to certain aspects of an experience and block others out
5. **Absorption** – allow yourself to get totally immersed in the pleasure of the moment and shut out other stimuli

Practicing mindfulness is one key avenue for savoring pleasure. Mindfulness can allow you to see the present moment as new, a practice of shifting perspective to see things in a fresh light. This is best achieved through the practice of mindfulness meditation, which allows you to slow down your mind and be open and attentive to the present moment. Refer back to Chapter 6 for a detailed discussion of mindfulness meditation and a guide to the practice of such.

What we are really trying to convey here is that the royal road to happiness is through the gratifications. The "pleasures" are about enjoyable sensory stimulation and emotional experience. The "gratifications" are much more about discovering and using your own strengths and virtues, and becoming totally absorbed in the process. This absorption, this stoppage of time, is called **flow** (Csikszentmihalyi, 1990), a very important concept that we will explore in greater depth in Chapter 14 in reference to the role of flow in your occupational life. Flow is such an important concept in positive psychology because it represents a person working at full capacity. The aftermath of the flow experience is typically invigorating, although joy is not typically felt during the experience, which is often nonemotional. Flow is most likely to occur when there is an optimal balance between a person's skills and the degree of challenge (Moneta & Csikszentmihalyi, 1996). Gratifications produce flow, but pleasures typically do not. While experiencing pleasure you are typically caught up in the good feelings. While engaging in gratifying activities you will often be unaware of feeling – you can literally get out of your head for awhile. And it is precisely this escape aspect, this absorption in something else, that allows the best in you to blossom, ultimately resulting in a far deeper level of happiness over time than the momentary pleasures. Pleasures typically come easy, while gratifications, which involve the effort of using your skills and virtues to meet challenges, offer a deeper, more enduring level of satisfaction.

Be careful to distinguish between activities that truly lead to flow and those that create "junk flow" or "faux flow" such as watching TV shows. Those activities have some aspects of flow as they can be quite interesting and absorbing, but they are not necessarily challenging and do not typically lead to feelings of satisfaction. In this regard, consider the conclusion of 34 years of survey data on how people spend their time, collected from more than 45,000 participants (Robinson and Martin, 2008), where unhappy individuals were found to watch 30% more TV than people who reported being happy. Individuals who described themselves as very happy tended to spend more time in social activities, attending religious services, and reading the newspaper. In contrast, those who described themselves as unhappy tended to spend their free time watching television. Since this was correlational research we cannot make the assumption that watching TV causes unhappiness; rather, it is just as plausible that individuals who are unhappy are unmotivated to go out, and therefore opt for the comfortable fix of TV viewing. Watching TV is easy in that you don't have to go anywhere, get dressed, spend money, expend energy or interact with anyone. But while TV might be entertaining for the moment, it is unlikely to provide the kind of fulfillment or gratification that could shift depression to happiness. Bruno Frey (2007) also concluded that watching TV makes us less happy due to four reasons:

1. TV programs and advertising often focus on material goods or values, prompting us to compare ourselves to more glamorous or affluent individuals thereby priming the hedonic treadmill to operate at a higher speed.

2. TV takes away your time for socializing. In addition, TV often portrays a skewed version of reality replete with more violence, leaving viewers often feeling less safe and/or trusting of others.

3. TV fails to fulfill two of the three fundamental human needs (identified by Deci & Ryan, 2000) for autonomy, competence and relating to others. TV may fulfill the first need (you can be autonomous while watching the tube), but fails to instill any competence or provide social outlets.

4. TV is not challenging enough to create a true flow experience.

Seligman bemoans the fact that our modern culture often encourages preoccupation with momentary pleasures, while neglecting the gratifications. That is, we try to take shortcuts to happiness by pursuing pleasure, based on the inaccurate assumption that pleasures are what happiness is all about. He warns that the reliance on pleasure at the expense of the gratifications is more likely to lead to depression than joy. Therefore, if you ask the question, "How can I be happy?" you must make the distinction between pleasures and gratifications or risk being seduced by pleasures alone. Seligman makes a point to distinguish between the good life (steeped in gratifications) as opposed to the pleasant life (full of pleasures), and clearly he recommends that you pursue the good life. Ultimately, finding a balance between pleasures and gratifications is essential to happiness in the present.

One of the most robust findings in positive psychology is that a deeper sense of satisfaction and happiness in the long run comes from being actively concerned for the welfare of others, rather than from the pursuit of hedonistic pleasures. We will be dealing with this subject in more depth when we discuss altruism in Chapter 11, but Seligman devised another exercise to help you discover this distinction for yourself.

Positive Psychology Exercise
Fun vs. Philanthropy

Make a list of all of the things you like to do, that you consider to be fun, and that are within your ability and budget to easily arrange to do. Then make a list of the things you could personally do to be helpful to others. This could involve volunteer work at a local hospital, offering to mow your neighbor's lawn or babysitting for free, helping a young family member with homework, assisting at an animal shelter, or anything else that would be of service for your community, friends, family or neighbors. Next week pick one fun thing and one helpful activity from your lists and engage in both. Flip a coin to determine which to do first. Spend an equal amount of time on both pursuits. Afterward write a brief reaction paper summarizing your thoughts and feelings about each activity and how it affected you. Pay attention to anything you have learned.

The Global Perspective
Gross National Happiness GNH

After his tiny Buddhist nation was criticized for slow economic growth, the King of Bhutan proposed the concept of Gross National Happiness, the GNH, in 1972 to help identify more appropriate indicators to truly measure the quality of life within nations and organizations. This is based on the radically different paradigm that conventional development concepts such as the GNP (Gross National Product) or Per Capita Income do not really adequately reflect the general well–being of the inhabitants of a nation. While conventional development models stress economic growth as the ultimate objective, the concept of GNH is based on the premise that optimal development within a country occurs when the material, spiritual and positive emotional development occur side by side and reinforce each other. The GNH measure is based on the concept that indices of emotional well-being are more relevant than objective measures like consumption. The government of Bhutan is devoted to pursuing a policy with four pillars: equitable and sustainable economic growth; environmental conservation; cultural preservation; and good government. Med Yones, president of the International Institute of Management, created the first global GNH survey in 2006, incorporating the following seven metrics: (1) economic wellness; (2) environmental wellness; (3) physical wellness; (4) mental wellness; (5) workplace wellness; (6) social wellness; and (7) political

(*Continued*)

wellness. In a recent study using a GNH measure (White, 2007), Bhutan ranked 8th out of 178 countries in subjective well-being even though it is not an economically advanced nation.

In other studies of happiness across the globe, political science professor Ronald Inglehart at the University of Michigan published a paper in *Perspectives in Psychological Science* (July, 2008) in which he refuted the long held assumption that happiness across societies worldwide has remained constant. His research indicated that significant changes in happiness levels have occurred for societies as well as for individuals. The study was based on an analysis of polls conducted by the World Values Survey from 1981 through 2007 covering 88 countries containing 90% of the earth's population. This particular survey measured happiness and overall life satisfaction. Martin Seligman referred to this study as the best he has seen on happiness within the last five years.

The results of this study demonstrated that in the 52 countries that completed all surveys over the 17 year period, 86% of those countries (45 nations in all) experienced a rise in average happiness levels within the population. Happiness levels declined in six countries and stayed constant within one. Even the British are showing interest in happiness research. British Prime Minister Gordon Brown, encouraged by fellow Labor Party member and renowned happiness scholar Richard Layard, has shown interest in using happiness studies to advance "well being" the U.K., as reported in *The Week* (Dec. 5th, 2008).

According to Inglehart, the most likely variables accounting for the increase in happiness levels are improved economic development, democratization, and increased social tolerance. Economic development results in a significant improvement in subjective well-being, particularly for poorer third world nations. But for less impoverished nations, democratization and social tolerance are more salient contributing factors. Why? Democracy allows individuals greater freedom and more choice which helps produce an environment conducive to happiness. "Support for gender equality and tolerance of people who are different from oneself are also strongly linked, not just because tolerant people are happier, but because

living in a tolerant society enhances everyone's freedom" (Inglehart, 2008).

The most recent observations of happiness around the globe were reviewed by Dan Buettner in *Blue Zones of Happiness* (2017). He identified three countries (Costa Rica, Denmark and Singapore) which exemplify three different strands of happiness, referred to as pleasure, purpose, and pride. As mentioned earlier in this chapter, Costa Rica is not only the happiest country in Latin America, but is currently the nation where inhabitants report feeling more positive emotions on a daily basis than anywhere else in the world. In Costa Rica the synergy of breathtaking geographical beauty and caring social policies has led to a healthy blend of strong family ties, universal health care, egalitarian policies, peace, and generosity, creating a climate of good cheer. Meanwhile, Denmark has consistently been first in happiness rankings in Europe for the last forty years due to its role as a society that covers its citizens' basic needs, freeing them to pursue their leisure interests and passions while finding meaningful work. Danes tend to live a purpose-driven life with a focus on both self-fulfillment and community. More than 90% of Danes belong to some type of club or association and more than 40% do volunteer work. The Danish society encourages balance between interesting work and rewarding play. Mihaly Csikszentmihalyi finds Denmark to be a society which is more cognizant of the total needs of a person than most other places, setting up the conditions ripe for flow. Singapore has created a society that fosters accomplishment and rewards ambition. Citizens of Singapore score exceptionally high on measures of life satisfaction, especially relating to pride in achievement. Singapore's society is based on harmony, respect, and hard work. Anyone who works, no matter how mundane or lowly the job, is guaranteed a living wage along with housing and health care subsidies. Given their strong work ethic, denizens of Singapore are skilled at deferring gratification to build toward future rewards and the development, over time, of pride in what they have achieved.

The annual World Happiness Report found that 75% of human happiness is driven by six interlocking factors: (1) strong economic growth; (2) healthy life expectancy; (3) strong social networks; (4) generosity;

(5) trust; and (6) freedom – the freedom to live the life you choose. Clearly, these conditions are rare and do not magically appear but are fostered by cultural values and governments that prize freedom. The happiest places each create breeding grounds for pleasure, purpose, and pride. Support for this conclusion was embedded in the analysis of a report where 500,000 surveys completed by immigrants to Canada over the last forty years. The results demonstrated that within a few years of emigrating, immigrants who came from unhappy homelands began to report increases in positive emotions corresponding to their new Canadian home.

You may be wondering about happiness levels in the U.S., which vary given the enormous diversity of American life, geography, and state cultures. Is there a place in the U.S. which incorporates elements of the natural beauty and day-to-day joy of Costa Rica; the value-driven, financial security, and work ethic of Singapore; and the egalitarian, socially democratic aspects of Denmark? Boulder, Colorado, a college town nestled in a stunning mountainous setting produces the highest level of overall well-being for U.S. residents. According to Dan Witters, a research director with Gallup, "People there live better than residents of any other city for which we have results," referring to Gallup's surveys of over 2,500,000 people since 2008. Boulder is a community whose citizens are mission-driven, committed to physical fitness with a clear vision of the good life, encapsulating the three strands of happiness – pleasure, purpose, and pride as explicated by Buettner. How do you think the United States would score on a measurement of GNH? Based on what you have read about Inglehart's study, what factors do you think would contribute to the score?

Questions

1. Improving happiness about your past involves cultivating an attitude of _____ and practicing _____.

   A. gratitude; forgiveness

   B. indifference; forgetting

   C. optimism; defensive pessimism

   D. peak end; duration neglect

2. _____ are longer lasting than _____ because they are more resistant to habituation and allow us to utilize and build upon our strengths.

   A. Pleasures; gratifications

   B. Gratifications; pleasures

   C. Talents; hobbies

   D. Gratifications; flow

3. _____ is most likely to occur when there is an optimal balance between a person's skills and the degree of challenge.

   A. Savoring

   B. Mindfulness

   C. Pleasure

   D. Flow

7.5 What Do Other Experts Recommend for Boosting Your Happiness?

Differentiate among a variety of expert suggestions for enhancing happiness.

Many books have been written on the subject of enhancing or boosting happiness. There is considerable overlap in terms of the recommendations put forth by many of the better known and respected authorities, psychologists, and philosophers in the field. So you may notice some redundancy in the suggestions put forth by various experts, but that speaks to the fact that these recommendations have been shown, both experimentally and in practice, to help people improve their mood when depressed, discover happiness, and even find their bliss. One expert in the field, David Myers, put forth the following suggestions in his 1993 best selling book, *The Pursuit of Happiness* . . .

1. **Fake it till you make it.** Act as if you were happy. Sometimes you can actually act yourself into a new and better frame of mind. Going through the motions can trigger more positive emotions. This phenomenon was discussed previously in Chapter 6 from a different perspective.

2. Understand that success, wealth or possessions do not lead to enduring happiness. **Remember the hedonic treadmill.**

3. **Seek work and leisure activities that engage and make use of your skills.** This refers to the importance of gratifications and flow experiences to enduring happiness.

4. **Build close relationships** and give them priority in your life.

5. **Engage in regular exercise,** which has been shown to help boost mood and decrease anxiety. Monchon, Norton & Ariely (2008) demonstrated that typically, the more you exercise the happier you are. (To learn more about this refer back to Chapter 6).

6. Learn to be in control of your time. **Don't let time control you.** Learn to set limits and not over commit yourself. (Refer to tips in Chapter 4.)

7. **Get an adequate amount of sleep.** Sleep deprivation is a silent cause of depression. Sleep researchers warn that many of us are sleep deprived (Dement & Vaughan, 1999). Getting an optimal amount of sleep is essential to maintaining your positive emotional equilibrium.

8. **Get in touch with your spirituality.**

9. Focus beyond yourself. Helping others helps you to feel good. This is also called the **Do good, feel good effect.** (Read more about this in the altruism section in Chapter 11).

10. **Keep a gratitude journal.**

Martin Bolt (2004), in a review of the positive psychology literature on the pursuit of happiness, offers the following summary tips for finding your happiness and maintaining it.

- Don't confuse being well-off with well-being.
- Make wise comparisons
- Keep a gratitude journal
- Discover your flow
- Finish what you start and wholly experience it along the way
- Strive for excellence but not perfection
- Find a hobby
- Cultivate family ties and friendships
- Know your neighbors
- Volunteer
- Practice spirituality

Peterson (2006) conceptualizes four possible routes to happiness and opines that individuals need at least one route, with some routes working better than others, to achieve happiness. The four routes he outlines are:

1. hedonism
2. eudemonia
3. engagement
4. victory

Although Peterson does not deny that hedonism, the pursuit of maximal pleasure and minimal pain, is relevant to life satisfaction, he strongly cautions us that hedonism contributes far less to long term happiness than eudonia. What is **eudemonia**? This is a complex concept, going all the way back to the writings of Aristotle, which refers to being true to your inner self. According to the eudemonic view, happiness is about identifying your own signature strengths and virtues and then living your life in accordance with those. This is very much in line with Maslow's (1970) concept of self-actualization, or Carl Rogers, (1951) vision of the fully functioning person, or Ryff and Singer's (1996) ideal of psychological well-being. Peterson implores his readers to favor eudemonic pursuits over hedonistic ones, stating that

> Some of our own recent research suggests that eudemonia can trump pleasure as a predictor of life satisfaction (Huta, Park, Peterson & Seligman, 2005; Peterson, Park & Seligman, 2005b). Using different samples and different methods, we found that those who pursue eudemonic goals and activities are more satisfied than those who pursue pleasure. This finding is robust, occurring across Canada, and other nations. He who dies with the most toys may or may not win, but he will not do so as happily as he who dies after a life of helping others. (p. 79)

It is also very important to note that happiness and well-being are not always synonymous. True psychological well-being occurs when you have both happiness and a sense of meaning and purpose in your life (the eudemonic life), fulfilling the M in PERMA. Or put more simply: **Well-being = Happiness + Meaning**.

The third route, engagement, subsumes the E in PERMA, including activities that Seligman would call gratifications, particularly those that involve flow. The last route, the victory route, has to do with competition. Some people thrive on the pursuit of victory, whether in sports, games, business, the battlefield, or in love. While we can debate the merits of this, for some individuals, engaging in competitive activities provides enormous pleasure and a sense of meaning and purpose in life. For some this fourth route also exemplifies accomplishment, the A in PERMA, for winning is one aspect of achievement.

After several years of teaching positive psychology classes and noticing the powerful effects of prescribed happiness boosting exercises on the satisfaction and mood of their students, several researchers (including Seligman and Peterson) decided to do a controlled study of the effects of such exercises. In the experimental design (Seligman, Steen, Park & Peterson, 2005) participants were required to engage in five separate happiness boosting exercises, each of which took one week to complete. Two of the exercises will be familiar to you as they were discussed in detail earlier in this chapter. The five exercises were as follows:

1. **Gratitude Visit.** Write and deliver a letter of gratitude.
2. **Three Good Things.** Keep a special journal where every day for one week jot down three things that went well that day and describe them in detail.
3. **You at Your Best.** Write a story about an event that brought out the best in you. Review this story every day for a week.
4. **Identifying Your Signature Strengths.**
5. **Using Signature Strengths in a Novel Way.** Once you have identified your personal strengths, figure out unique ways to utilize them during the following week.

The subjects were recruited from the internet and were given pre- and post-measures of happiness and depression in order to determine whether the exercises had any effect (short term and long term) on their mood and life satisfaction. To control for placebo effects (i.e. the possible mood elevating effect of being a participant in a research study), they created a placebo control condition as well. Placebo group subjects, also recruited online, were given a series of writing exercises regarding early childhood memories over a five week period, a plausible task for a psychology experiment. All subjects were randomly assigned to either the placebo control group or the experimental group who had to complete the happiness exercises. Follow-ups were completed at one month and six month intervals to check the happiness levels of the participants at those times.

The results were clear and unequivocal. First of all, the placebo subjects did report increased happiness and decreased depression, but this effect was very short-lived and was not present at the follow-ups. Placebo effects like this are quite common in studies of the effectiveness of techniques, treatments and/or medications, which is why placebo controls are included in the first place—that is, to discriminate real treatment effects from pure placebo effects. The biggest overall boost in happiness resulted from the Gratitude Visit, but this effect evaporated after one month. Long term effects for increased happiness, present at the six month follow-up, were found for the Three Good Things exercise and for Using Signature Strengths in Novel Ways. The subjects who got the greatest benefit in terms of improved happiness were those who continued to practice the techniques beyond the required time periods. The lesson here is that for these techniques to have a lasting effect they must become part of the fabric of your life. But isn't that true about so many things in life? In order for healthy habits that promote well-being to work, whether it involves eating right or exercising, or taking care of your emotional health, you need to follow through. Seligman and his colleagues reported that 60% of the subjects in their study continued to practice the Three Good Things exercise six months later. Of the subjects who were married, some made it a routine in the marriage to share their list with their partner at the end of each day. Going to sleep happy with your partner will certainly increase the likelihood that both of you will wake up happy!

Positive Psychology Exercise

Have a Good Day

This exercise challenges you to systematically figure out what makes a good day for you, a day that would elicit positive emotions (based on variables you have control over), and then, using patterns you discern, to build a structure to increase the number of those good days. Many people have never really considered what makes for a good day in terms of the concrete measurable events of what you did and didn't do that particular day which helped to make it a good day. What are those variables, over which you typically exert a lot of control, that you can choose to include in your life to increase the frequency of good days? There are some things you just can't control. You can't control the weather on a given day, or the behavior of others, or the ups and downs of the stock market or other myriad external factors which may affect you. You do, however, have control over your own behavior and your reactions to those external events. So keep track in detail of what you do during the day, each day, for one month. At the end of each day rate on a 1 to 10 scale how good that day was for you, with a rating of 1 representing awful and a 10 representing one of the best days of your life with gradations in between. Ratings of 7 – 8 would be good days. A 9 would be a great day. Average days would be in the 5 – 6 range. After a month of listing your daily activities in detail and compiling your ratings, look at the pattern of what you were doing on your good days. Were you more productive on the good days? Were you more social? Were you more likely to exercise? How much sleep did you get? Trends and patterns will emerge that you may not have been aware of before. Having a good day is often about a lot more than finding a $20 bill in the street, or getting an A on a paper in class, or a raise at work, although any of those fortuitous events are certainly mood boosters. For example, when this author did this exercise it was abundantly clear that my best days were when I was very productive at work, but also found time to connect with family and/or friends to balance my hard work; when I spent at least 40 minutes exercising; and when I cooked a nice meal for my family, but found someone else to do the dishes! Good days also tended to end with watching a particular late night TV comedy show that spoofed politics and allowed me to go to sleep with a smile on my face.

7.5.1 More on *Fake it till you make it*

Referring back to David Myers' suggestion to *fake it till you make it*, and following in the footsteps of the Have a Good Day exercise mentioned above, it would be useful to mention yet another study which looked at the results of asking people to "act as if" they felt better. Fordyce (1977, 1983) published a series of studies wherein he evaluated a program designed to boost levels of happiness. The program was based on the hypothesis that levels of subjective well-being could be increased if people could learn to imitate the traits and behaviors of happy people, such as keeping busy, being well-organized, spending more time socializing (acting like extroverts), maintaining an optimistic outlook and developing a healthy personality. Fordyce found that this program produced increases in happiness for the group that acted happy, compared with a placebo control group, as well as compared with participants in conditions receiving only partial information. In a follow-up 9 to 25 months after the study, Fordyce discovered that there were lasting effects, as those who learned how to act happy remained much happier than either of the control conditions.

What about the effects of smiling on mood and happiness levels? Can remembering to smile improve your mood? It turns out that the answer is *yes*, thanks to something called the *facial feedback effect*, which has been demonstrated in many experiments with a variety of emotions (Myers, 2013). In one famous study, subjects found cartoons to be more amusing when they were required to hold a pen in their teeth, an action which activates the smiling muscles (Strack & colleagues, 1988). Engaging in a full Duchenne smile allows you to maximize your positive feelings when you are reacting to pleasant or humorous stimuli (Soussignan, 2001). In an ingenious study conducted in Japan (Mori & Mori, 2009), researchers got students to either smile or frown without telling them to do so. They attached the ends of a long rubber band to both sides of the subjects' cheeks with adhesive bandages. One group had to pull the rubber band over their head, raising their cheek muscles into a smile. The other group had to run the rubber band under their chin, pulling their cheek muscles down into a frown. It is important to note that these students did not consciously know that they were either smiling or frowning. How do you think these subjects subsequently responded when asked how they felt? True to the facial feedback effect, students made to frown typically reported feeling sadder while students whose cheeks were pulled upwards into a smile reported feeling happier. In a similar study (Kraft & Pressman, 2012), subjects were made to adopt either neutral, sad or smiling faces by holding chopsticks between their teeth in various positions and then required to engage in a stressful task. The results indicated that smiling during brief stress reduced the intensity of the stress response. These authors suggest that you literally *"grin and bear it,"* that is, if stuck in traffic or exposed to some other stressful situation, deliberately hold your face in a smile for a few moments as this will help you cope. Ultimately, according to Myers (2013):

> . . . *your face is more than a billboard that displays your feelings; it also feeds your feelings. No wonder depressed patients reportedly feel better after*

*between-the-eyebrows Botox injections that paralyze the frowning muscles (Finzi
& Wasserman, 2006). Two months after this treatment, 9 of the 10 non-frowning
patients given this treatment were no longer depressed. (p. 475).*

On a neurological level, it appears that smiling sends a message to the brain
signaling safety, which translates to decreased heart rate and overall stress levels.
Neurotransmitters which facilitate positive emotions such as dopamine, serotonin
and endorphins are released when we smile (Lane, 2000).

Positive Psychology Exercise

Experience the Facial Feedback Effect

Stomp around noisily for awhile while frowning and pay attention to how you feel. Do you notice feelings of
anger coming up? Then look down, slouch your shoulders, shuffle your feet sluggishly and frown. What do
you notice? It's likely that you will get in touch with feelings of sadness as this is how most people hold their
bodies when feeling unhappy. Then, next time you are feeling down remember to *grin and bear it*, force yourself to smile, wave hello to people whether you feel like it or not, and hold your head up high (nonverbal facial
behaviors we engage in when feeling good) and notice whether your mood begins to shift.

7.5.2 Is There Such a Thing as Happy Money?

There is a new twist on the money = happiness debate. Elizabeth Dunn and
Michael Norton, in their highly thought-provoking book *Happy Money: The Science of Smarter Spending* (2013) remind us that while money cannot buy happiness,
how you spend your cash can have a direct effect on your emotional well-being,
particularly if you learn to spend money in ways that enhance your life instead
of just adding to your possessions. The authors reviewed over 17,000 studies on
the relationship between money and happiness, the vast majority of which indicated that increased income failed to lead to increased happiness. They wondered
whether money could potentially augment happiness if people spent their money
differently. According to Dunn and Norton, "Shifting from buying stuff to buying
experiences and from spending on yourself to spending on others can have a dramatic impact on happiness." Kumar, Killingsworth & Gilovich (2014) validated
this in their research on what kinds of fantasies elicited the most positive feelings
from subjects. Fantasies involving attending a concert or going on vacation were
described as more exciting than thinking about purchasing a laptop or clothes
that the subjects were impatient to acquire. In another part of this same study,
subjects reported that thinking about purchasing an experience evoked feelings of
happiness, but imagining buying material goods failed to affect their mood in any
significant way. Dunn and Norton offer five key principles for spending money
(whatever your income) in a way that promotes life satisfaction. These principles
can be expressed as rules including:

RULE #1: BUY EXPERIENCES   Many material things (whether a fancy house, sports car or designer handbag) lead to far less continued happiness than "experiential purchases" such as vacations, attending a concert, play or sporting event, going to an amusement park or eating a great meal. According to the authors, "whether you're spending $2 or $200,000, buying experiences rather than material goods can inoculate you against buyer's remorse." Furthermore, even experiences that are painful or difficult can produce lasting pleasure, hence the joy of running and completing a marathon.

RULE #2: MAKE IT A TREAT   This strategy borrows from the lessons on savoring. Dunn and Norton remind us that limiting our access or exposure to our favorite things helps to "revirginize us" and renew our capacity for pleasure. According to these authors, "If abundance is the enemy of appreciation, scarcity may be our best ally." Knowing that something won't last forever allows for deeper appreciation because we are more likely to savor it. However, they do not endorse complete self-denial, rather they recommend the spacing of pleasures as discussed earlier in this chapter.

RULE #3: BUY TIME   Using your money to outsource your least favorite chores (i.e. hire a maid to clean that toilet) frees you to spend your time having experiences you truly enjoy. After all, what's the point of spending all your time working to make lots of money and then having no time or energy left to enjoy yourself? A series of four studies (Kasser & Sheldon, 2008) demonstrated: (1) that individuals with greater **time affluence**, that is, more free time reported greater happiness even when they valued being busy; and (2) wealthier individuals often feel more rather than less time pressure, which may help explain why increased wealth fails to produce higher levels of happiness due to the concomitant *decrease* in time affluence. Since happiness derives from being in the moment, it becomes much harder to be fully present if you feel pressed for time.

RULE #4: PAY NOW, CONSUME LATER   The authors propose that by paying up front and delaying consumption, you can reap the benefits of anticipation and therefore enjoy consumption more (whether experiences or products) while spending less. Kumar and colleagues (2014) reported that consumers actually enjoy waiting for experiences, which basically whets their appetite. For example, more than half the fun of a vacation is imagining how wonderful it will be. Paying upfront typically has the added benefit of decreasing how much we spend because without the distancing effect that comes with using credit cards (allowing us to avoid confronting the bill until a month later), frugality more easily comes into play. Why? It is far easier to swipe plastic than part with cash. This leads to less debt which also increases happiness in the long run for most individuals.

RULE #5: INVEST IN OTHERS   Spending your money on others instead of or in addition to yourself can provide deep joy, the "do good, feel good effect." Making charitable contributions activates brain areas associated with reward (Harbaugh & colleagues, 2007), which helps explain why people who give money away are often happier than those who spend it mostly on themselves. For example, Dunn & colleagues (2008) gave subjects an envelope filled with cash. One group was instructed to spend it on others and the other group to spend it on themselves. Who do you think was happier at the end of the day? You guessed it! The group instructed to provide for others was significantly happier.

Positive Psychology Exercise
Your Experience of Happy Money

Think about major purchases made over the course of your life where you held expectations that your happiness would increase as a result. Consider one big, special material purchase, like a new car or expensive jewelry. Now recall another purchase that provided you with a special life experience, like a unique vacation or seeing your favorite band in concert. Which of these purchases made you happier over time? Research (Van Bowen & Gilovich, 2012) revealed that 57% of Americans declared that their experiential purchases led to greater happiness whereas only 34% reported greater life satisfaction from the material purchase.

There are other benefits that derive from experiential purchases. Experiences can lead to the stories we most like to share with others and in turn, help define us far better than our possessions. In one study people aged 18–72 indicated their belief that their true, essential self would be far more clearly revealed to a stranger who knew of them only by their experiential purchases as compared to their material acquisitions (Carter & Gilovich, 2012). In another experiment, respondents were asked about regrets regarding past purchases. With regard to experiential purchases, most participants (83%) regretted their *inaction,* that is, having passed up an opportunity for a good experience. But when it came to material purchases, most subjects regretted having bought something that failed to live up to their expectations (Rosenzweig & Gilovich, 2012). This brings us back to the hedonic treadmill. Dunn and Norton remind us that "we are happy with things until we find out that there are better things available. Luckily this tendency may be limited to things. Even the simplest experiences are relatively immune to the detrimental effects of attractive alternatives." Why is this? Because it is very easy to compare things with other similar things, whereas experiences tend to have an apples to oranges dimension that makes such comparisons much harder to draw. Although every individual is singular in terms of the kinds of experiences they would appreciate, you are more likely to derive happiness from an experience if it . . .

- brings you together with others or creates a sense of social connection.
- makes for a memorable story you will enjoy recounting.
- is highly compatible with your sense of who you really are or who you want to be.
- provides a unique opportunity which is hard to compare to other options.

7.5.3 The Role of Curiosity in Happiness

Kashdan and Biswas-Diener (2013) also extol the virtues of new and interesting experiences on happiness by stressing the importance of curiosity in the happy life. According to these authors:

> *"It turns out that activities that lead us to feel uncertainty, discomfort and even a dash of guilt are associated with some of the most memorable and enjoyable experiences of people's lives. Happy people, it seems, engage in a wide range of counterintuitive habits that seem, well, downright unhappy. Truly happy people*

seem to have an intuitive grasp of the fact that sustained happiness is not just about doing things that you like. It also requires growth and adventuring beyond the boundaries of your comfort zone." (pp. 52–53)

Kashdan and Steger (2007) demonstrated that when study participants monitored their daily activities, the more curious they felt on a given day, the more satisfied they felt with life and the more they involved themselves in interesting activities. The happiest people divide their time between engaging in feel-good, pleasant activities along with seeking out experiences that are novel, uncertain, intense or difficult, complicated and perhaps even anxiety-provoking. This author is reminded that the highlight of her recent trip to Costa Rica was the zip line, a simultaneously terrifying and wonderful experience.

In addition to curiosity, these researchers also point to a variety of habits, traits and mindsets of happy people that are worth emulating. For example, happy people . . .

- **Do not sweat the small stuff.** As a result they are more devil-may-care about performance and they eschew perfection. To facilitate this they are far less focused on and critical of small details and more attuned to the bigger picture.

- **Celebrate.** The researchers contend that the happiest people are the ones who are present when things go right for others. They remind us that being a good friend is more than being available in times of trouble, but being willing to sincerely celebrate a friend's achievements or good fortune. (Read more about the importance of this for healthy relationships in Chapter 11.)

- **Practice Flexibility.** Happy people are psychologically flexible. They do not avoid feeling or expressing negative emotions and are able to shift nimbly between pleasure and pain, to modify their behavior to match the demands of a situation. This ability to shift mental states as required by circumstances is a fundamental aspect of well-being.

- **Find Balance.** The happiest people have developed a balance between pleasure and purpose (eudemonia). Kashdan and Biswas-Diener offer this helpful description: "If you want to envision a happy person's stance, imagine one foot rooted in the present with mindful appreciation of what one has—and the other foot reaching toward the future for yet-to-be-uncovered sources of meaning." Happy people are honest with themselves about what does and does not fulfill and energize them, and they allow time for pleasure and gratifications interspersed between activities that give their lives meaning and purpose.

7.5.4 The Role of Neuroplasticity in Developing Positive Emotions

As mentioned earlier, neuroplasticity allows us to gradually reshape the structure of our brains with our thoughts and our actions. However, we must be mindful of the fact that due to the rigors of evolution our brains were primed to be extremely good at learning from bad experiences, as our survival often depended upon this. Our brains evolved to have what is referred to as a **negativity bias** (Hanson, 2013). This negativity bias affects our learning on a nonconscious, emotional level, referred to as our **implicit memory**, which is the neural storehouse for our expectations, attitudes, assumptions, fears, motivations, and moods below the level of conscious awareness. Conscious recollections, on the other hand, tend to reflect a subtle positivity bias wherein we tend to forget or deny negative aspects and accentuate the positive (i.e. how we remember the good old days). So on a nonconscious level, we are just more sensitive and reactive to negative stimuli and as a result negative states are more readily converted into neural structures than are positive stimuli. In a nutshell, we learn faster from pain than pleasure. Therefore, something bad about a person, place or thing is typically more memorable than the good, so we can protect ourselves if necessary. Negative interactions with people usually have a greater impact than positive ones. According to Hanson (2013), if 19 bits of positive feedback are followed by one piece of criticism, most of us will remember that one piece of negative feedback more clearly. Hanson states, "What sticks is the negative 20th." Thus, to ensure our survival as a species we have a hard-wired asymmetry whereby negativity holds the advantage for influencing the vast neural storehouse of implicit memory.

Hanson reminds us that just as our negative experiences can sensitize our brains to react more intensely to negative experiences, routinely intensifying our positive experiences can gradually sensitize our brains to more rapidly convert those positive experiences into neuronal circuitry. Despite our nonconscious negativity bias, we can compensate for this and level the playing field by consciously activating and installing positive experiences (such as practicing gratitude). According to Hanson (2013):

> Any single moment of taking in the good won't change someone's life. But a handful of times each day, day after day, month after month, year after year, will gradually—bit by bit, synapse by synapse—make a big difference. Deciding to reshape one's brain by intentionally taking in the good, one thought or experience at a time, begins with a conscious, willed decision of the mind. (pg. 48)

Hanson (2013) in his book *Hardwiring Happiness: The New Brain Science of Contentment, Calm, and Confidence* offered a four step method to facilitate this process of influencing neural circuitry by turning passing positive experiences into lasting inner strengths. He summarized this method with the acronym HEAL wherein he advises that we . . .

H: *Have an experience.*

E: *Enrich* this experience using any and all of the following five factors which have been shown to enhance learning.

1. *Sustain* it for at least 5–10 seconds.

2. Ramp up the *intensity* of the experience – feel it fully.

3. Engage as many *sensory modalities* as possible including sights, sounds, feelings, tactile sensations, smell, taste and so forth.

4. Look for what is *novel* or unexpected in the experience.

5. Find the *personal relevance* in the experience. How does it matter to you?

A: *Absorb* the enriched experience.

L: *Link* this experience to the existing negative material to reframe it, assuage it or even replace it.

7.5.5 Bias Confusion

Recall that in the optimism section of Chapter 2 we described how humans have an *optimism bias*. This brings up the obvious and rather oxymoronic question: "How can we have both a *negativity bias* and an *optimism bias*?" Both are possible because of the time frames involved and whether we are dealing with conscious vs. nonconscious processes. The negativity bias refers to our brains' predilection to more readily encode into implicit memory negative events from our *past*, as they often make a stronger impression upon us than positive events. The optimism bias refers to the human tendency to consciously underestimate the likelihood of negative events happening in our *future*, even in the face of grim statistics to the contrary. Evolution has programmed us to be hypersensitive to negativity in our past, to enable us to learn how to protect ourselves, and then conversely to optimistically expect to survive in the future so that we do all that is possible to preserve our lives.

7.5.6 Happiness—A Cause or Effect of the Good Life?

We began this chapter with a series of questions as to whether happiness is a cause or an effect of a variety of positive life outcomes. To summarize the research findings, happy individuals are more likely to experience success in many domains of life including:

- Marriage
- Employment
- Income
- Work performance
- Friendships
- Psychological health

Lybormirsky, King & Diener (2005) tackled this chicken or egg problem by conducting a thorough review of two different kinds of happiness studies: (1) longitudinal studies that looked at what variables were correlated with happiness over time;

and (2) experiments that manipulated positive moods to see what caused what. They concluded that happiness is not just a byproduct of living the good life, but also one of its causes. So, as we expected, happiness is both a cause and an effect! For a specific example, happy people are more likely to find and attract a mate. They are typically more outgoing, more optimistic about their prospects for relationships, and more fun to be around. Happy people tend to make a better adjustment to marriage, thus they are more likely to experience marital satisfaction. Then being in a happy marriage leads to greater happiness. It is like a positive cycle where positive emotions beget positive outcomes which beget happiness. The key is to break into the cycle at some point, using any and all of the strategies outlined, if your life circumstances or your genetics have not predisposed you in a cheerful direction.

7.5.7 Could Happiness Be Contagious?

A fascinating study was published online in a British Medical Journal (Christakis and Fowler, 2008) which reported that happiness appears to be contagious, that it spreads among friends, relatives and next-door neighbors like the flu! This study demonstrated that emotions have ripple effects throughout social networks of people, even to the point of affecting people who do not know each other.

Christakis and Fowler conducted a longitudinal study of 4700 subjects followed over a span of 20 years. They found that individuals who were happy or who eventually became happy increased the chances that someone they knew would be happy. Furthermore, this power of happiness spanned yet another degree of separation, boosting the happiness of those in the social circle of that happy person known by the original subject!

According to researcher Nicholas Christakis, a medical sociologist at Harvard, "You would think that your emotional state would depend on your choices and actions and experiences. But it also depends on the choices and actions and experiences of other people, including people to whom you are not directly connected. Happiness is contagious." The even better news is that the researchers found that this effect can linger for as much as a year, and while unhappiness can also rub off, it appears to be far less infectious than happiness.

Although previous research has documented the common experience that one person can lift the spirits of another who is in a bad mood, or, for example, seeing someone laugh often triggers giggles in others, this study is the first to demonstrate happiness spreading across groups, a *social networking effect*, for extended time periods. The researchers reported that when one person in the network became happy, the chances that friends, relatives, a spouse, or next-door neighbors became happy increased anywhere between 8% to 34%. These results do not hold for neighbors down the block beyond those who live next-door. This effect persisted through three degrees of separation (e.g. friends of friends), although it grew progressively weaker with each degree of separation, dropping from 15%, to 10%, to 6% before completely disappearing. These findings provide stunning new evidence of the power of social networks.

7.5.8 Positive Psychology and Social Media: Does Facebook Impair Happiness?

According to researchers at the University of Michigan (Kross & colleagues, 2013), spending a lot of time on Facebook can increase sadness for some people, a phenomenon that has come to be known as *"Facebook depression."* Why is this the case? Many Facebook users reveal only their best moments and their most flattering photos, while posting the high points of their day or week—another method of keeping up with the Joneses. So if you spend a long time gazing at the content and photos of other people's idealized and edited lives (low points often not included), your own reality can seem painfully dull. Kross' research found that the more time users spent on Facebook, the sadder they became, independent of their life circumstances. It's not surprising that the researcher's initial prescription for Facebook despair was "less Facebook." They concluded that face-to-face interactions or phone conversations typically enabled people to feel better.

Not surprisingly, this study attracted a ton of attention as well as negative publicity for Facebook. The researchers decided to look into this matter in more depth since Facebook usage comprises a whole set of activities ranging from browsing to liking, to directly interacting with others. So the researchers went beyond just correlating time spent on Facebook with well-being. They conducted an "intervention" where subjects repeatedly visited the University lab and used their Facebook accounts in a variety of specific ways. What was discovered was that Facebook usage only lowered mood if users were passive, viewing others' pages and perusing the happy moments of others with no direct interaction or contribution of any kind. On the other hand, if users directly interacted with others through messaging, commenting, sharing, or posting status updates, their mood remained stable. Therefore, Facebook need not be a pit of despair if you use it to socialize and communicate directly with others. However, using it as a means to compare yourself to others is a sure-fire recipe for dissatisfaction.

Furthermore, your level of well-being and overall life satisfaction can be predicted from the content of your Facebook posts and tweets. Seligman's Positive Psychology Center is doing just that, as they are engaged in an indirect study of the well-being of large populations by analyzing written expressions on social media (Schwartz, Eichstaedt, Seligman & colleagues, 2013). In this ongoing study, thousands of randomly selected telephone respondents indicate the general area where they reside and then are asked to respond to a life satisfaction (LS) phone survey. These geographically organized LS inventories are then compared with posts/tweets coming from the same areas. Among their preliminary findings:

- Your Facebook posts are predictive of your well-being.
- Twitter language predicts community well-being over and above the effects of income, age, education or gender.
- The types of post or tweets that are predictive of either individual life satisfaction or a high level of life satisfaction within residents of a community

include: words expressing positive emotions, topics including learning, experiences, charitable donations, community activities, ideas, meetings and conferences, building things, spirituality, and especially exercise and outdoor activities such as hiking, camping or boating.

- High individual or community LS was predicted by a higher usage of plural pronouns such as "we" or "our," reflecting a social orientation and focus on relationships which correlates strongly with life satisfaction. Words expressing engagement or enthusiasm such as "excited" or "wonderful" are predictive of high LS.

- Lower individual or community LS was predicted by a higher frequency of words reflecting disengagement (such as "bored, tired, sleepy," swear words, or stress words) and by a higher percentage of singular nouns like "I" or "me," reflecting a less social orientation.

7.5.9 New Trends in Positive Psychology

Like all branches of psychology, positive psychology has continued to evolve. Martin Seligman (2011) has once again spearheaded a shift away from his previous emphasis on attaining authentic happiness and life satisfaction, to a focus on flourishing and its five core elements (PERMA). His original theory postulated that happiness could be subdivided into three different elements: (1) positive emotions; (2) engagement (gratifications and flow); and (3) meaning and purpose. Over time Seligman realized that there were three basic inadequacies in this model. First and foremost, he recognized that happiness is often disproportionally tied to one's mood of the moment. For example, Veenhoven (2006) demonstrated that subjects' moods colored their questionnaire responses to a large extent. He found that up to 70% of self-reports of life satisfaction are heavily determined by mood at the time of assessment, while only 30% of the respondents reported life satisfaction which reflected their subjective judgments of the quality of their lives in general.

Secondly, in a nod to the critics of positive psychology as "Happiology," Seligman recognized that undue emphasis was put on the attainment of positive emotions, with not enough focus on developing engagement and meaning. This is further complicated by the fact that your happiness level is often partially constrained by your genetically determined level of positive affectivity. Seligman himself bemoans the fact that he is relatively low on cerebral joy juice and therefore, he puts more emphasis on engagement and meaning for his personal well-being and life satisfaction.

Lastly, Seligman came to appreciate that his focus on the triumvirate of positive emotions, engagement and meaning was too limited. He recognized that for truly well-rounded flourishing, you also need positive relationships as well as a sense of accomplishment. Adding these dimensions rounds out the concept of well-being and gives each of us many worthwhile options of where to put our energies in our own personal journey toward flourishing.

7.5.10 A Final Note: Pain Is Ultimately Part of Happiness

Just as we could not acknowledge beauty if we had no conception of ugly, nor could we recognize light if we did not experience dark—we cannot truly appreciate happiness unless we have known sadness. It is because of these contrasts that we become aware of our deepest feelings. Real life can be full of disappointments, loss, and inconveniences. Therefore, in any rich and meaningful life there will be a full range of emotions. We can learn from what hurts us; that is, pain often has inherent gifts which help us to grow. This is the phenomenon known as *Post-Traumatic Growth*. We can learn to appreciate life more. We can develop coping skills. Ultimately it is about learning to flourish in spite of pain, emotional or otherwise.

We began this chapter with a series of questions about the nature, pursuit, and effects of positive emotions. It is only fitting that we conclude with another set of questions: Is the pursuit of happiness worthwhile or counterproductive? Can our efforts to create bliss actually prevent us from finding true happiness? This brings us to explore the latest iteration in Positive Psychology which we briefly introduced in Chapter 2 – that of ACT, the Acceptance and Commitment approaches – and how they interface with the study and pursuit of positive emotions. In *The Happiness Trap: How to Stop Struggling and Start Living* (2011), author Russ Harris argues that it is the very pursuit of happiness that prevents us from achieving it. He views this quest as a vicious cycle exemplified by **experiential avoidance**, which is defined as our ongoing attempts to control, avoid, escape, or get rid of unwanted thoughts, feelings, memories, or images even when doing so becomes self-defeating, useless, or costly. According to Harris, the harder we try to get rid of unpleasant feelings, the more we create and perpetuate them.

Harris reminds us that we are not any happier than our ancestors even though they typically led far more difficult and impoverished lives (recall the progress paradox). Why is this so? Remember that the top priority for our ancestors was being hypervigilant to danger to enable them to live and reproduce successfully, what we alluded to previously as the negativity bias. Over time our brains evolved to be increasingly adept at detecting, predicting, and avoiding anything that could hurt us. Therefore, our brains have been gradually hardwired to be on guard as to what could go wrong or what dangers may be lurking. In modern times, this is less about physical dangers and more focused on emotional dangers like loss of prestige, rejection, or financial concerns. In general, as a species we are programmed to worry. It appears that evolution has predisposed us toward psychological suffering, to worry, to be self-critical, to focus on what is missing, to compare ourselves to others, and to imagine scary scenarios about what could go wrong even if highly unlikely. No wonder we humans have such a hard time being happy! Indeed, this hardwired mechanism likely provides the neurological foundation of the hedonic treadmill.

To quote Harris (2011), "Happiness is not just a matter of feeling good. If it were, drug abusers would be the happiest people on the planet." Thus, the more we strive to feel pleasurable emotions via experiential avoidance, the more we are prone to substance abuse or behavioral addictions, and the more likely we are to manifest depression or anxiety. According to Mitch Album in *Tuesdays with Morrie* (1997), "It appears that we do, indeed, learn as much from what hurts us as what loves us." A better route involves the pursuit of gratifications, a process of defining happiness as living a rich, full, and meaningful life, complete with the full range of human emotions including sadness, grief, fear, loneliness, boredom, and even jealousy – feelings we all experience at times. To prevent yourself from falling into the happiness trap, recognize that you cannot avoid nor escape all emotional pain or unpleasant emotions. However, you can learn to handle and withstand these feelings effectively. That is where ACT comes in, which we will explore in greater depth in the next chapter.

Questions

1. Well-being = _____ + _____
   A. gratifications; pleasures
   B. eudemonia; savoring
   C. happiness; meaning
   D. gratitude; pleasure

2. What type of purchases are more likely to lead to long-term happiness?
   A. material purchases
   B. experiential purchases
   C. expensive purchases
   D. buying on credit and taking a long time to pay

3. Which of the following is more likely to decrease rather than increase your happiness level?
   A. keeping a gratitude journal
   B. exercising regularly
   C. watching more TV
   D. getting in touch with your spirituality

Summary

In this chapter we explored the nature of happiness and the factors that contribute to it, recognizing the partial genetic loading on our respective levels of positive affectivity. We reviewed the V (voluntary factors) that contribute to authentic happiness and offered a variety of suggestions for maximizing happiness in the past, present, and future. A multitude of tips from a myriad of experts on how to enhance your positive emotions were covered. Lastly, we questioned whether the very pursuit of happiness prevents us from ever achieving it.

Ultimately, crossing the finish line is not as rewarding as the anticipation of achieving your goal or the pursuit of such. Recognize that often, it is your actions within the journey toward your goals that leads to happiness, rather than the goals themselves. The hedonic treadmill eventually takes it toll on all goals, but not on the journey towards the goal. Easy hedonic pleasures rarely offer the lasting pleasure that mastering a new skill or creating something from scratch will.

Events in our life are almost never as bad or as good as we expect them to be. In general, humans are rotten at predicting our future feelings accurately, especially if our predictions are based on our past memories. Our memory is a very unreliable recording device, to a great extent because the passage of time skews our perceptions of happiness in many ways, either magnifying or minimizing it. The truism, "this too shall pass" holds many lessons for developing positive emotions. That is, when things are good, appreciate them to their fullest because they will not last forever. Conversely, when times are bad you can console yourself with the fact that they too will pass.

Lastly, it is nice to know that learning how to increase your level of positive emotions may have a delightful side effect – you may inadvertently boost the mood of loved ones and others around you, in subtle and indirect ways. Smile and the world smiles with you, especially when you flash a Duchenne smile, a beacon of contagion for joy.

Key Terms

Attitude of Gratitude	Extroversion	Negativity Bias
Authentic Happiness	Flow	Peak-End Theory
Broaden and Build	Forgiveness	Positive Affectivity
Duchenne Smile	Hedonic Capacity	Positive Emotions
Duration Neglect	Hedonic Treadmill	Progress Paradox
Engagement	Hedonism	Savoring
Eudemonia	Implicit Memory	Time Affluence
Experiential Avoidance	Mindfulness	Undoing

Shared Writing

Of all the happiness boosting techniques and strategies mentioned in this chapter, which three were most relevant for you? What produces flow for you? Write about your thoughts.

Chapter 7 Questions

1. The Losada ratio of 2.9 : 1 of positive emotions to negative emotions predicts _____.

   A. human flourishing

   B. your income

   C. the number of close friends you will make in your lifetime

   D. your anxiety level

2. Which of the following has been reliably correlated with happiness?

   A. wealth and possessions

   B. beauty

   C. high intelligence

   D. having many good friends

3. The hedonic treadmill explains the fact that _____.

   A. it's hard to lose weight when you eat while walking on the treadmill

   B. we tend to adapt to fortunate and unfortunate circumstances

   C. it is so hard to sustain an attitude of gratitude

   D. our happiness levels are determined by how many hours of exercise we do

4. Self-reported happiness levels have not kept pace with advances in health, wealth, and education. This phenomenon is termed the _____.

   A. progress paradox

   B. hedonic treadmill

   C. broaden and build hypothesis

   D. negativity bias

5. _____ and _____ are ways to maximize pleasure in the present.

   A. Drinking; driving

   B. Savoring; mindfulness

   C. Optimism; forgiveness

   D. Gratitude; forgetting

6. Living a _____ life involves being happy and having a sense of meaning and purpose in your life.

   A. eudemonic

   B. hedonistic

   C. materialistic

   D. philanthropic

7. Our brains evolved to have a(n) _____ where we are more sensitized to learn from unpleasant experiences. This occurs on a nonconscious, emotional level referred to as _____.

   A. optimism bias; implicit memory

   B. hedonism bias; pleasure principle

   C. negativity bias; implicit memory

   D. genetic bias; positive affectivity

8. Which of the following is likely to decrease your happiness level rather than boost it?

   A. Adopt an attitude of gratitude.

   B. Passively peruse Facebook and compare yourself to others without interacting.

   C. Focus on gratifications rather than pleasures.

   D. Spend money on others rather than yourself.

9. Which of the following statements applies to happiness?

    A. Happiness is neither a cause nor an effect of life outcomes.

    B. Well-being = Beauty + Wealth

    C. Attitude change follows behavior change.

    D. Hedonism produces flow.

10. The harder we try to get rid of unpleasant feelings, the more we create and perpetuate them. This pursuit of happiness can become a counterproductive, vicious cycle exemplified by _____.

    A. experiential avoidance

    B. flow

    C. the pleasure principle

    D. gratifications

Chapter 8
Creating a Meaningful Vision

After reading this chapter, you should be able to:

8.1 Describe some of the guideposts that can help us as we try to define our path in life.

8.2 Explain the roles of connection, compassion, and contribution in spirituality.

8.3 Define the components of a vision quest.

8.4 Describe the elements included in and the importance of a personal mission statement.

8.5 Define the recommended steps to secure your goals once they are clearly defined.

8.6 Define the process of visualization and discuss its various applications.

8.7 Describe how ACT differs from other perspectives on how to achieve well-being.

8.8 Explain the six Core Principles of ACT and how to apply them to deal with unwanted thoughts, feelings, and images.

> *Each path is only one of a million paths. Therefore, you must always keep in mind that a path is only a path. If you feel that you must not follow it, you must not follow it under any circumstances. Any path is only a path. There is no affront to yourself or others in dropping it if that is what your heart tells you to do. But your decision to keep on the path or to leave it must be free of fear or ambition. I warn you! Look at every path closely and deliberately. Try it as many times as you think necessary. Then ask yourself, and yourself alone, one question . . . It is*

this . . . Does this path have a heart? All paths are the same. They lead nowhere. They are paths going through the brush or into the brush. Does this path have a heart is the only question. If it does, then the path is good. If it doesn't, it is of no use. Both paths lead nowhere, but one has a heart and the other doesn't. One makes for a joyful journey; as long as you follow it you will be one with it. The other will make you curse your life. One makes you strong, the other weakens you. (p. 82)

Carlos Castaneda, *The Teachings of Don Juan* (1998)

One of the hallmarks of effective people is that they have a very clear sense of where they are going and how they intend to get there. When we say that effective people know "how" they are getting to their destination, it does not always mean that they know ahead of time what each specific step of their journey will entail. It is a cliché to say that our plans seldom work out as we intend them. But one thing that does seem to be a constant among effective people is that they have a deep awareness of the values that guide their choices at each step. It can be said that they are on a mission based on a vision that emanates from their hearts. As Joseph Campbell recommended, they are following their bliss. Unless you are one of those rare individuals who seem to have always known what you want, you will need to do what has been done from ancient times. You will need to go on a vision quest. But before we discuss the specifics of establishing the path of our lives' endeavors, how can we not consider questions regarding the ultimate meaning and purpose of life?

8.1 The Big Picture

Describe some of the guideposts that can help us as we try to define our path in life.

Have you ever felt helped by unseen hands?

Do you ever feel sorry for the man who has no invisible means of support?

Bill Moyers' questions to Joseph Campbell

To discuss a spiritual perspective in a book about personal effectiveness may impress some as painfully obvious, and others as patently unscientific and unnecessary. After all, we the authors are scientists and as such are obligated to attempt to cite evidence to substantiate our point of view. Traditionally, spiritual matters have been outside the realm of the scientific and relegated to the corridors of faith and speculation, or, at worst, merely the superstitions of those with an unsophisticated grasp of probability theory, placebo effects, and psychopathology. Yet the vast majority of people on our planet hold to some kind of belief system that affects their day-to-day quality of life. These beliefs, unscientific or not, can be sources of great pain, guilt, feelings of inadequacy, hopelessness, confusion, and fear. But they can also be the source of love, compassion, joy, vitality, and a peace that surpasses understanding. A complete treatise on this subject is well beyond the scope of this text, but to leave it unaddressed is to abandon our charge of presenting you with a wide buffet of ideas regarding the process of becoming an "effective individual."

But what if you are scientifically minded? Then you are in great company, because many of the leading scientific minds of our time and the past century realize that, in fact, the most advanced representations and speculations about the nature of reality do not preclude the possibility of a spiritual reality. Furthermore, they do not suggest a reality that is capricious and unlawful. They simply suggest that our most sophisticated attempts at measurement, in the scientific sense, have led us to the realization that consciousness, the activities of our minds, directly affects the "reality" around us. For example, when scientists study the nature of light, they find that it literally behaves as either a wave or a particle, presenting a different appearance when projected on a surface. The really strange thing is that the way in which light behaves appears to depend on what the scientists decide to measure! That is, it depends on their decisions or thoughts. While much of modern Western psychology has been based on extrapolations of work with animals to create models for human experience and treatments for problems, there is no shortage of theories regarding the interface between psychology and spirituality. These various models are grouped under the rubric of what has come to be known as **Transpersonal Psychology**, which explores this overlap between the realms of psychology and spirituality. That is, these models speak to the belief that humans are much more than a bag of skin and bones with a very sophisticated computer animating the machinery. Carl Jung's most important work began after he broke with Freud over Freud's unwillingness to see humans as anything more than advanced, complicated animals driven by sex, aggression, and pleasure-seeking. Jung took a larger view of humankind and explored the possibilities of spiritual experience with concepts like the **collective unconscious** a storehouse of experience to which all of us are connected, and **synchronicity**, which refers to meaningful coincidences and also implies that events in our lives are connected in a way that is beyond our material measuring devices.

Currently, theoreticians like Stanislov Grof (1985, 1988), Ken Wilbur (1979), and Charles Tart (1986) are actively pursuing ideas like the reality of the soul, reincarnation, and the whole realm of paranormal phenomena. The domain of the paranormal includes extra-sensory perception, as manifested by such phenomena as clairvoyance, telepathy, precognition (knowing the future), and telekinesis. There is even an Association for Transpersonal Psychology which was founded in 1972 and a publication called *Journal of Transpersonal Psychology* which addresses these issues as well. Both the American Psychological Association and the British Psychological Society explore these issues within their various divisions. As we proceed through the remainder of this chapter we will cite references, when appropriate, to current theoretical models which bridge what appears to be the gap between the spiritual and the scientific.

> *"We do not know what anything is. The summarization of our existence is Mystery, absolute, unqualified confrontation with what we cannot know. And no matter how sophisticated we become by experience, this will always be true of us." (p. 89)*

Da Free John, *Easy Death* (1983)

We began this book in the preface with a tale of tasting mangoes, our simple premise being that it is one thing to know about mangoes intellectually and quite another to truly taste a mango, savor the experience, and be fully alive in that moment. After all, when we cut through all of the words and rationalizations about mastery and optimal functioning, what we are after is a sense that we are really alive and living an existence that is meaningful to us. Some might refer to this as a spiritual quest. This chapter, too, is full of words and ideas and questions, but if you do not taste them, chew on them, and mull them over then you will have missed the point. Words, while they are wonderful tools, always reduce experience. They aren't the experiences themselves. Joseph Campbell (1988) once related in a lecture that the best things in life cannot be told because they are beyond thought. The next best things are misunderstood, and the next best are those things about which we talk. Consider the words written here as only fingers pointing at the moon. As the ancient expression goes, "focus too much on the fingers and you miss the heavenly splendor above." If you get caught up in the rightness or wrongness of these words you will fall into the trap of being right that we will discuss in Chapter 9, and miss the opportunity to choose happiness. Paraphrasing the words of the mystic Rumi, out there beyond ideas of right-doing and wrong-doing there is a field. We would like to meet you there. We'll bring the mangoes.

As you consider the goals that you want to pursue in your life, you must come to terms with what we believe are fundamental human concerns that we all must confront if we are to truly become masters of living our lives joyfully and effectively. Something that is fundamentally stressful to humans is the experience of having an inadequate map for a territory that they are exploring. Unfortunately or fortunately, depending on your perspective, life lived well will present you with the unexpected and you will be scrambling to find directions and maps to guide you. We would like to humbly offer some landmarks that we hope will help you to find your way, or at least help you learn to enjoy being lost. Remember, maps are never the territory that they represent. You do not eat the menu when you go to a restaurant. We hope these maps are useful. Some may even be true!

This chapter is also about how you face the inevitable choices and decisions that you must make throughout the course of your life. If you avoid making these choices, ultimately they will be made for you. If you want to maximize your effectiveness by enhancing your sense of control, you need to again consider the maps on which you base your decisions. You must determine what is important to you, or your life will not be your own and surely your effectiveness will be undermined.

What follows are simply guideposts, ideas worth considering. When you find yourself struggling to get your bearings, attempting to make some sense out of life and your place in it, remember these things.

8.1.1 Life Is a Mystery.

For one of the authors, who was educated largely in Catholic schools, a very frustrating memory of childhood was being told that the answer to his inquiries about God and life was "It's a mystery." Now, he appreciates the essential truth of that assertion. No matter how many books we read, how much knowledge we acquire, or experiments we conduct, there will always remain that which is elusive, mysterious. Consider building a fire on a moonless night deep in the woods. The larger the fire the more trees we illuminate. However, the amount of darkness that we become aware of expands in direct relationship to the areas of light. Of this you can be sure: nobody knows what's really going on here. Life is ultimately a mystery that won't ever be solved no matter how big you build your bonfires. But you can develop a relationship with life. That relationship begins by humbly acknowledging the depth of the mystery and then setting out to seek answers anyway.

When we suggest building a relationship with the mystery (or God, Goddess, the Fates, or whatever you choose to name it), we mean this literally. In the privacy of your own mind begin to have a conversation with the source of the mystery. Say the things you've always wanted to say. Ask the questions you've always wanted to ask. Now, like most conversations, the real key to success is *listening*. To listen means quietly focusing your attention so as not to be drawn into the meandering of your own mind. It means to be open to signs and synchronicities (meaningful coincidences). Answers may appear in many forms. For example, while standing in a line, you may meet a stranger who just happens to say something particularly meaningful to you at that moment. Unexpected feelings of contentment or joy may flow through you without warning. And it is possible to hear "the still small voice" that is spoken of within metaphysical literature. Meditation is one key skill in quieting the mind. Some suggested readings in this area would be:

The Search for the Beloved	By Jean Houston Ph.D. (1987)
Journey of Awakening	By Ram Dass (1990)
The Meditative Mind	By Daniel Goleman (1988)

8.1.2 Therefore, Life Is Uncertain.

Things change. Get used to it. Be thankful for it. This is the one thing you can be certain of, that things will change. This is true not only in the world of work, but in all aspects of your life. You may ask yourself, "will my life ever calm down, become stable and predictable? Will I ever get caught up?" The answer is yes and then things will change. When things are going badly, things will change. When things are going well, things are going to change. Peace seems to lie in realizing and accepting this fact. It is about reassuring yourself that *when times are bad, that this too shall pass.* Repeating that phrase to yourself is one of the most effective stress reducers. Thus, you can be grateful for the changes you know will carry you out of difficult times and be appreciative for the good times, because all good things will ultimately change or come to an end.

8.1.3 Everything Is Connected.

One of the most profound illusions of our being is the essential solidity of the objects around us. Science, particularly physics, assures us that in spite of appearances, things are more empty space than solid matter. What appears to be solid is really a vibrating group of particles, most of which have no mass. These particles seem to be influenced by the people who try to study them. These particles also retain a relationship with one another over astronomical distances! Furthermore, all beings constantly exchange particles with one another. Chaos theorists (Gleick, 1987) have demonstrated that profound changes can be induced by minor perturbations in a system, meaning that something as minor as a butterfly flapping its wings in one part of the world can lead to a powerful storm somewhere else. The science of ecology demonstrates that change in one part of a system necessarily provokes change across the system. Remember the notion of Spaceship Earth that was discussed in Chapter 1. As global citizens, it is as if we are all swimming in the same pool. You cannot have a "no peeing section" in one part of a swimming pool. We are ultimately not separate from anything. Therefore be careful and consider the actions you take on every level including your thoughts. Whatever you do, you do it to yourself. Do not burn your own house down. This is the fundamental truth that underlies the various versions of the Golden Rule. It makes sense to treat others how you would like to be treated. After all, they are you!

You can reinforce this belief by reading about cutting edge discoveries in science. Paradigms for understanding the mystical/spiritual view of life are becoming more and more accepted and are supported by experimental data. Some reading to whet your appetite includes:

The Holographic Universe	By Michael Talbot (1991)
Recovering the Soul	By Larry Dossey M.D. (1989)
A New Science of Life	By Rupert Sheldrake (1981)
The Conscious Universe	By Dean Radin (1997)

8.1.4 Life Is Trouble.

To again quote Zorba the Greek, "Life is trouble. Only death is not. To be alive is to undo your belt and go looking for trouble." Now before you seek out a bar room brawl, let us suggest that it is the attitude that is important here. Life very often involves dealing with problems. We have a choice. We can whine about them or we can deal with them. We have tried whining. Sometimes even very dedicated whining! It doesn't help. We recommend taking the challenge, jumping into the fray and solving problems. Trouble simply cannot be avoided. Those who have tried to elude it report that it comes looking for you.

Questions

1. What is Transpersonal Psychology?
   A. a subfield within Interpersonal Psychology
   B. the study of groups
   C. the study of the overlap between the realms of psychology and spirituality
   D. the psychology of LGBTQ issues

2. Jung referred to the storehouse of experience to which we are all connected as the _____.
   A. subconscious
   B. Id
   C. Akashic record
   D. collective unconscious

3. Which of the following statements *contradicts* the philosophical underpinnings of Transpersonal Psychology?
   A. You are separate from your environment.
   B. Change in one part of a system provokes change across the system.
   C. One thing you can be certain of is that things will change.
   D. Everything is connected.

8.2 Pathways to Spirituality

Explain the roles of connection, compassion, and contribution in spirituality.

As discussed in the previous chapter, individuals with some sort of spiritual practice in their lives tend to experience greater levels of life satisfaction (O'Hanlon, 2007). Now obviously this is an area of intense debate among individuals, groups and even nations. Not a little blood has been shed over questions of religious faith. People have been willing to die and to kill over spiritual questions. And also, people have taken great solace and joy from their spiritual practices and used them as a basis for providing aid, support and sustenance to the deprived, hungry, and heartbroken among us. Therefore, in a book on personal effectiveness this question of spiritual practice needs to be addressed. Is there a way into that conversation without endorsing a specific practice or tradition? We believe there is.

> *When I say spirituality, I don't necessarily mean religion; I mean whatever it is that helps you feel connected to something that is larger than yourself.*

Dean Ornish, M.D.

In his book *Pathways to Spirituality,* Bill O'Hanlon (2007) has proposed a definition of spirituality that provides a practical approach to integrating this idea into anyone's life without imposing a particular dogma or belief system. That is, even if you consider yourself to be an atheist, this approach can still provide guidelines for bringing more meaning, satisfaction and positive emotions into your life. O'Hanlon's definition states that spirituality has three basic components common to most religious and spiritual practices. He calls them the *"Three Cs" of spirituality* and they are *connection, compassion and contribution* or service.

Connection is quite literally the felt experience of being connected to something larger and more expansive than the you that seems to be completely enclosed within your body. Learning to connect to this larger sense of self beyond your limited personality is an important component of spirituality. For many people this sense of connection is most often experienced when immersed in nature. Displays of the massive power of thunderstorms, or the unobstructed vistas of open seas, or views from mountaintops or the edge of the Grand Canyon can, for moments or more extended periods, allow us to merge into something larger than ourselves and put aside our limited sense of self and feel part of a larger whole. But connecting to nature is not the only pathway to connection. Some other ways to a sense of connection can be experienced as follows:

1. Develop a regular practice of meditation or journaling to connect with your deeper self.

2. Connect to the body by attending completely to sensual experiences, like eating dinner slowly a bite at a time, or getting a massage.

3. Remember to connect to others by spending time with family, close friends, or support groups or 12 step organizations.

4. Many find a connection in the arts. Take time to appreciate the process of creating and consuming art. This can be anything from literature, cinema, and painting to sculpture, theater, dance and photography.

5. Engage in the daily practice of gratitude as discussed in chapter 7.

Compassion refers to our capacity to step into another's shoes and see the world through their eyes. Our ability to do this usually leads to a kinder, gentler, more accepting and trusting way of being in the world. For most parents this sense is natural in regard to their own children. Quite literally, their joy is your joy and their pain, sadness, and loss can be felt as if it is your own. To develop a sense of compassion try the following:

1. Listen deeply to one in need. Mirror their facial expressions and body language. Attempt to see the world through their eyes.

2. Begin the process of forgiveness of one who you feel has wronged you. This is indeed a process as discussed in chapter 9, but it culminates in being able to consider this person who harmed you as someone who has also been damaged. O'Hanlon notes that studies have shown that forgiveness lessens our experience of depression and anxiety.

3. Consider how important it is to learn to forgive one's own self. O'Hanlon passed on this saying: "Lord, help me accept the truth about myself no matter how good it is."

4. Meditate on the importance of the lessons learned from the mistakes we and others make.

Contribution or service is usually a by-product of connection and compassion. When we have a sense of being larger than we thought, we feel the cares and concerns of those around us. We are thus naturally moved to help those others and go beyond our purely personal and often petty motivations. A well-known, reliable experience in relationship to service is the phenomenon of the *"do good, feel good"* effect. Our contributions to others, our giving of our time and efforts to ease another's pain or lighten their load, rewards us with feelings of bliss and gratitude.

As noted in chapter 11, adults engaged in providing service to others are happier with an increased sense of well-being. The elderly who participated in volunteer activities lived longer and experienced improved health (Brown, Nesse, Vinokur, & Smith, 2003). There is no shortage of opportunities and occasions to provide service. Consider the following:

1. Volunteer your time for an organization you believe in.

2. Engage in random acts of kindness.

3. Make an anonymous contribution to a cause you believe to be important.

4. Contemplate these words of Mahatma Gandhi: "The best way to find yourself is to lose yourself in the service of others."

Questions

1. The "Three C's of Spirituality" offered by Bill O'Hanlon are _____, _____, and _____.

   A. control; commitment; challenge

   B. connection; compassion; contribution

   C. compassion; contrition; competition

   D. collaboration; contemplation; compassion

2. Contribution, that is, engaging in service and random acts of kindness can lead to _____.

   A. the feel good, do good effect

   B. bad karma

   C. the do good, feel good effect

   D. good messages from the collective unconscious

3. Which of the following is recommended by Bill O'Hanlan for developing compassion?

   A. Forgive yourself and others.

   B. Keep a mistake journal and dwell on it.

   C. Learn to rely only on yourself.

   D. Detach from the emotions of others.

8.3 The Vision Quest

Define the components of a vision quest.

These musings about the reality of a spiritual domain lead us to ask questions about our lives. The questions you ask go a long way towards shaping the possible answers you will find. Questions like, "What should I do with my life?" have an inherent appeal to look outside of yourself for answers, for validation, for reassurances that you are doing the right thing. Yet all wisdom traditions suggest that it is knowing and trusting yourself, that is looking inside yourself, that leads to the best and most fulfilling answers.

The Sufi mystic Rumi once said, "Start a large, foolish project, like Noah. It makes absolutely no difference what people think of you." If you don't take the time to seek answers, if you don't make the effort to really get to know yourself and what really moves your heart, you risk living somebody else's life. Yes, life is difficult, full of choices, seemingly unfair at times. But life is also beautiful, effortless, and involving when you do the things you love, the things that come easily to you. When you find ways to serve others while doing what you love, success is virtually inevitable. Keeping the big picture in mind, let's move on now to seeking a vision that will inspire you and then composing a mission statement to keep you focused on your vision.

> *Dream lofty dreams, and as you dream, so shall you become.*
>
> *Your vision is the promise of what you shall one day be.*
>
> James Allen

A **vision quest** can be thought of as a search for or recognition of an aspect of your destiny. Not only does it include a strong sense of a place that you are

The Global Perspective
A Global Vision

In this chapter you set about to establish a personal vision to guide your day-to-day choices. What this implies, however, is that there will be a viable world in which your vision can occur. Thom Hartmann (1998) in *The Last Hours of Ancient Sunlight* summarizes a most convincing case that we are utilizing vital resources and affecting the climate in such a way that Earth will be fundamentally altered. For example he notes the following:

- Three-quarters of the world's fisheries have been fished to or beyond their sustainable limits and the oceans have lost over 90% of large predatory fish.
- We are in the midst of a mass extinction of plant and animal species not seen since the time of the dinosaurs. The normal rate of loss of species is approximately 250 species every thousand years. Because of the effects of human development, we are losing anywhere from 17,000 to 100,000 species a year!
- Due to radically ascending damage claims from increasingly erratic and powerful storms, the insurance industry called for a decrease in carbon dioxide emissions. Many scientists warn that global warming is affected by human activity, and the possible consequences might be another ice age.
- "The human need for fresh water will outstrip the entire planet's replenishable supply by 2025— even before we run out of oil."

These changes will not destroy Earth and all of its life. But the human population may be radically reduced or, in the worst case scenario, go the way of the dinosaurs. These conditions are brought about by our current vision of our place on Earth that is based upon questionable assumptions like these cited by Christopher Uhl (2004) in *Developing Ecological Consciousness*.

- Humans are separate from nature.
- Our resource supplies are inexhaustible.
- Humans are only motivated by self-interest.
- Economic growth is more important than environmental protection.

What we might ask ourselves at this point is what vision does Earth have for itself? What vision will provide an environment where humans can continue to exist? Since humans have been gifted with the ability to envision a future, what is our responsibility to life? Is there a way to arrive at a global vision that can find general agreement amongst people?

It is easy to feel overwhelmed at the scale of problems on a global level. After all, what can one person do? However, feeling helpless and small is not a very useful state of mind. Perhaps remembering that we are also a part of the incredible web of interconnections that constitutes life can serve us better. Here is a notion currently being explored that may provide an antidote to feeling small. Rupert Sheldrake (1981) in his book *A New Science of Life* explores the notion of **morphic resonance**. In a nutshell, it implies that all matter and living things are connected and affected by fields that influence not only their structure but also their behaviors. It has been observed, for instance, in a particular species of monkey that when a new behavior has emerged and been adopted by a certain number of monkeys, then all the monkeys acquire this behavior. This occurs even when they have been isolated on another island from the monkeys who originally expressed the new behavior. Thus, there seems to be an interconnection that cannot be explained by traditional science. Sheldrake suggests that these fields function at every level of organization of matter, plants, animals, and societies. The implication for our purposes is that when enough people begin to believe something new, then that idea or possibility becomes a new reality for all people. No one knows what that tipping point may be, but each person who develops their consciousness as a global citizen is helping to move all humanity towards that consciousness.

(Continued)

How might we develop a global vision that inspires us to move toward it? As we discussed in this chapter, the larger goals are reached by taking smaller steps first. Local goals compatible with a global vision are a way to begin this process. A method for establishing positive goals is known as **Appreciative Inquiry** (Hammond, 1998). The focus of this technique is to consider what is right about a situation and ask how more of it can be created. In other words, when you look around, what is wonderful about the world in which you live? How can we bring more of those things into being? This stands in stark contrast to our usual tendency to begin by noticing all the things that are wrong. Some examples of possible questions to help a global vision emerge could be:

- Where has peace broken out between previously warring peoples? What brought this about?

- Where is the air most fit to breathe? How can that be duplicated?
- What cities are easiest to live in with low rates of poverty and crime? What happened there?
- South Africa has gone from apartheid to radically improved racial relations? How was this accomplished?
- Europe was previously besieged by world wars but has now formed the European Union. How did they do this?

For those of you interested in viewing a comprehensive vision of a possible future, we recommend that you read *The Earth Charter*, "a declaration of fundamental principles for building a just, sustainable, and peaceful global society in the 21st century." You can view this document at www.earthcharter.org. What are some steps you personally could take to help develop and move toward a global vision?

---

moving toward, but also an awareness of allies that will help you along the path of your journey. In archaic times shamans, the spiritual guides and healers of their cultures, would direct individuals to undertake ordeals, oftentimes involving strenuous, food-deprived quests after objects or animals. Sometimes these vision quests involved the ingestion of psychedelic substances which can produce an ordeal in their own right. Dreams were also interpreted to assist the seeker in discovering what they really want. The object of all these techniques was to help an individual transcend the limitations of their everyday perceptions, and thus the limits that may have been placed on their own possibilities. Even today, many people report that it was in moments of extraordinary stress and upheaval, often life-threatening, that what they wanted from life became crystal clear and ever after directed their actions.

Now before you close this book out of concern that we are going to recommend that you bungee jump out of a helicopter to determine your heart's desire, relax. There are alternatives available. The good news is that you need to spend more time with your dreams and fantasies. Take quiet time to remember times that have made you smile, warmed your heart, filled you with compassion, excited you, put you at peace. While you are feeling any of these feelings, follow the flight of your thoughts. Your heart is a compass that will point to your path. In this respect it can be said that the successful life requires constant questioning and attending to how you answer those questions, moment to moment, and day to day until you die and get the answers to the ultimate questions. Here are some questions to live with and by. Put them on your mirror or in your notebook, and check them regularly. They can begin to focus you on what is really important to you.

WHO AM I?

WHAT DO I LOVE TO DO?

WHAT IS MY PURPOSE?

HOW CAN I HELP? (Instead of, "What's in it for me?")

WHAT IS LIFE? (A dance, banquet, seasons, game, comedy, etc.)

HAVE I LAUGHED TODAY?

WHAT IS SUCCESS FOR ME?

IS THERE ANOTHER WAY OF LOOKING AT THIS? (Of course there is!)

IS THIS THE DAY I'M GOING TO DIE?

AM I LEADING THE LIFE I WANT TO LIVE?

AM I THE PERSON I WANT TO BE?

DO I KEEP MY WORD? (Especially to myself)

HOW WOULD THE PERSON I'D LIKE TO BE DO THE THINGS I'M ABOUT TO DO?

It has been said that at the end of our lives we will be concerned with the answers to only two questions:

WAS I LOVED?

DID I LOVE WELL?

Positive Psychology Exercise

Wishstorming

Your vision quest can also begin with a *wishing quest,* something you've been playing with since childhood. We all know the stories of three wishes conferred upon some fortunate soul by an enchanted being. We also know that these stories usually end with those so-called fortunate souls making some very bad choices. Subtly, we can be discouraged from the wishing process because we fear that we are not worth it (due to low self-esteem), or that we will just screw it up, or that we will be disappointed if our wishes don't come true. Nonetheless, this is where it begins and we recommend that you start by engaging in a process we call **wishstorming**.

Wishstorming is basically brainstorming about what you would wish for if you had an unlimited supply of wishes. In fact, you *do* have an unlimited supply of wishes. There are no wish police out there making certain that you don't exceed the wish limit. As in brainstorming, you want to let your imagination run free and unrestrained. However, be aware that there will be effort involved in overcoming habits established in our brains and genetics. Because the brain likes to categorize things, it gets comfortable seeing things as it has always seen them. This can put limits on the range of our imaginations since the same brain areas are used for perception and mental imagery (Kosslyn & colleagues, 1995). As a species we are also constrained by a tendency to conform to the larger group's perceptions. The amygdala of the brain responds as if threatened when individuals risk saying that they see things differently than the majority. When people conform, the

(Continued)

activity in the amygdala begins to decrease. Most people would rather conform and restrict their imaginations to how things have always been seen (Berns and colleagues, 2005). Since it is your imagination, give yourself permission to really let go, but be as *specific* as possible when wishing and write your wishes down on paper. In other words, don't just wish for a car. Wish for a specific make, model, and color. Don't just wish for a relationship. Wish for someone with specific qualities. Wish for as many things as you can imagine, one hundred or more. Do this now and you will have taken the best first step towards freeing your imagination and establishing your mission.

8.3.1 A Consultation with the Grim Reaper

"No one on their death bed wishes they had spent more time at the office."

Anonymous

"The question is not whether we will die, but how we will live?"

Joan Borysenko

Wishing is like stretching in that you begin to become more comfortable with your desires. Common sense suggests that you can't go after all your desires simultaneously. And a closer look at your wish list will certainly suggest that some wishes are more of a priority to you than others. One of the ways to begin to narrow and clarify a vision is to make the possibility of your death part of the equation. You began this process in the previous section on the importance of questions. You can also do this in fantasy without risking life and limb. After all, it is true that not one of us is promised any more life beyond this moment.

Leo Buscaglia (1982) suggested that you can begin this process by answering the following question: What would you do if you had six days to live? What activities would you seek to do? Where would you like to visit? Who would you like to see? What would you want to say to them? How would your answers change if you had six months to live rather than six days?

Steven Covey (1991) suggests a slightly different strategy for using the specter of your own death to clarify your goals and values. He recommends an exercise wherein you attend your own funeral, and listen to several individuals eulogize you. These individuals should come from different areas of your life experience. For example, you might listen to a friend speak about you. Alternatively, you could listen to a family member, a wife or husband, a boss, a professor, or a child of yours even if it is yet to be born. Done properly this exercise will help you discover what things are really important to you. We are rather certain that you will realize that you must take into account the importance of relationships in the pursuit of your goals. Success in the presence of failed relationships can hardly be called success at all.

8.3.2 Groundhog Day

By now you may be thinking, "I've had enough already of this death stuff." Is there another way to approach the process? We maintain that there is always another way to look at things. Another strategy is what we call Groundhog Day, named after the movie of the same name. In this film the main character is faced with the dilemma of living the same day over and over again. Initially this is a frightening situation for him, but soon he realizes that he is virtually immortal. He can do whatever he wants each day with no fear of death. In the beginning he indulges himself in all manner of pleasures. However, in time he becomes bored with a purely hedonistic life (remember the hedonic treadmill!) and becomes depressed to the point of wanting to commit suicide. He cannot though, because he cannot die. Thus, he is forced to look deeper inside himself to find that which he really loves to do. Ultimately, the only thing which brings him satisfaction is to help others, and to master various skills, such as playing the piano, sculpture, and French Literature, which bring him joy. He has discovered a truly eudemonic life, a life not merely filled with pleasantries but filled with meaning.

Use your imagination and put yourself in a similar scenario. What would you do with eternity? What warms your heart and excites you? What can you do that leads you to become so absorbed in it that you lose track of time? What would be a part of a perfect day for you? So often we can let the outside world dominate our choices of what to do. We end up doing what we "ought" to do or "should" do. No one else can tell you what you love to do. It is a most personal and crucial decision because life already has enough difficulties even when you are doing what you love to do. When you are doing something that doesn't really reflect your heart's desire, life can become downright miserable.

Questions

1. Effective people consistently look _____ for reassurance that they are doing the right thing.

   A. to others

   B. to experts

   C. within themselves

   D. to psychic readers

2. At the end of our lives we will be concerned with the answers to only two questions, which are: _____.

   A. Was I famous? Was I successful?

   B. Was I loved? Did I love well?

   C. Was I popular? Am I going to heaven?

   D. Did I make enough money? Is my will fair?

3. A vision quest can be thought of as _____.

    A. a search for your destiny

    B. a search for your significant other

    C. meaningful coincidences

    D. a storehouse of experience to which we are all connected

8.4 Your Mission, Should You Choose to Accept It

Describe the elements included in and the importance of a personal mission statement.

A country sets down its fundamental principles in its constitution. When there are questions about how the country should respond to ongoing concerns in the pursuit of its goals, the people turn to this document and seek guidance. A mission statement is similar, akin to your own personal constitution which can function as the basis for making major life decisions as well as everyday decisions. It is a statement of your largest goals based upon your largest beliefs about the mystery of life that we discussed previously. What kind of person do you want to be? What do you value? How important are your family, friends, career, etc? It reflects your uniqueness as a person. Your mission statement can help you exercise your self-efficacy as you choose short and long term goals.

It is important that your personal mission statement takes into consideration all of the major roles you play in your life. This could include your role as a son or daughter, husband or wife, as a parent, or as a family member. It would include your roles in your job or career, and your role as a student, whether you are in school full or part time. It should also include your role in any other pursuit or hobby that takes a reasonable amount of your time and/or interest (i.e. golfer, sculptor, skier, runner, boat owner, guitar player, gardener, etc.). Even though your mission statement addresses each of the major roles you play, be aware that many people feel torn between the various roles which compete for their limited time and attention. Sometimes these goals feel incompatible. This conflict is most often pronounced between work and family roles. Finding your balance is not always easy and goes to the heart of effectiveness. Composing your mission statement with all your vital roles in mind and then committing to live by it can assist you in finding that balance.

One strategy for composing a mission statement is to use the 100th birthday technique which helps you adopt a useful perspective on long range accomplishments. Imagine that you have made it to your 100th birthday and you are still alive, well, and lucid. A newspaper reporter comes to interview you to write the story of your life and asks you to name your most important contributions in terms of accomplishments and roles you have played. How would you answer? Would you want to say that you were a good parent or loving wife/husband, that you made a million dollars, that you wrote a best-seller, climbed Mt. Everest, invented a new household appliance, became a CEO, achieved a black belt, mastered gourmet cooking, broke par when golfing, ran a marathon, wrote or sang a hit song, operated your own successful business, or? Of course, the list is endless, limited only by your interests and imagination. But be realistic. Do not set goals you cannot possibly achieve.

Questions

1. Your personal mission statement _____.

   A. functions as your own personal constitution

   B. is a statement of your day to day, small goals

   C. should not be reflective of your values

   D. needs to be completed if you plan on becoming a missionary

2. Your mission statement should _____.

   A. reflect the kind of person your parents want you to be

   B. ignore the major roles you play in your life

   C. reflect your values

   D. focus on how to best conform to your primary group

3. It is important that your personal mission statement take into consideration _____.

   A. all the major roles you play in your life

   B. the expectations of your parents

   C. the size of your bank account

   D. only a few roles so you can focus better

8.5 Getting Clarity: The Goal of the Goal

Define the recommended steps to secure your goals once they are clearly defined.

By now you should have a list of goals that excite you. But before you can proceed with taking action toward the goals, you must take another action first. You must examine the goals themselves. In *Heart of the Mind,* Connie Rae and Steven Andreas

(1989) recommend a number of steps that will assist you in thinking about your goals in a way that can increase the likelihood of your meeting them. But before we detail these steps, it is worth considering another critical question raised by the Andreases. They suggest that many people choose unrealistic goals, goals that are really impossible to achieve. For example, people might want to live lives free of mistakes or want to be loved by everyone. Their recommendation is to seek out the "goal of the goal" by asking this important question: "What will this goal get for me?" This question enables you to dig deeper into what it is that you really want. Many people have the goal of becoming rich and famous. Yet a moment's glance at tabloid TV or the history of the rich and famous show that this is not a group of very happy people. The more basic issue is: "What do you hope to get by being rich and famous?" If the goal of the goal is to feel worthwhile or loved, then clearly there are other ways to achieve this without pursuing fabulous wealth and fame.

If you are pursuing a specific career, say medicine, because you believe it will secure money and respect, but you really hate studying science, then it would be wise to consider many other options that offer money and respect. You don't have to narrow the doorway to one specific career path. By seeking the goal behind the goal, you broaden the number of options available to you for getting what you want. Thus, it is worth examining your goals carefully to make sure you really want them. Oftentimes what we really want is much more basic and involves feelings of safety, security and self-worth.

8.5.1 Six Steps for Securing Your Goals

Assuming now that you know what you really want, we can move onto the steps the Andreases recommend for securing your goal.

STEP 1: *The goal must be stated in positive terms and in a way that you can achieve it yourself regardless of the behavior of others.*

Rather than saying, "I no longer want to be lonely and overweight," it would be better to say, "I would like to have a healthier lifestyle and spend more time with friends." This way of thinking motivates you instead of reminding you of the aspects of yourself you dislike. It is also critical to set goals that do not depend upon others. For example, if your goal is, "I want my girlfriend to be more affectionate," you have set a goal over which you have only indirect control. This is when it is appropriate to ask what is the goal of the goal. What would getting more affection from her do for you? Would it help you feel confident or more secure? You would probably benefit more from working directly on feelings of self-confidence that would allow you to ask for what you want and move on if it is not forthcoming.

STEP 2: *Make certain you know how you will know that you have reached your goal.*

There are a couple of things to note here. One is that you don't generally achieve your goals in one step. It will take time, and it is good to have small benchmarks along the way that let you know that what you are doing is working. For instance, you may want an A grade in a course you are taking (perhaps even this course). In that case it makes sense to keep track of your grades on all tests and projects along the way. This is realistic evidence that lets you know if you are on the path to success. Sometimes people rely on evidence that does not give them useful feedback. For example, you are not necessarily an effective parent because your children tell you that you are doing a great job. Nor are you an effective employee on the rise in your career because you feel good at the end of the workday. Perhaps you feel great because you spend your time at work catching up on your sleep! Performance evaluations are a better measuring rod. Therefore, take the time to ask how you would know if you are reaching your goals. Then take the time to feel satisfaction at each step along the way.

STEP 3: *Describe your goals as specifically as you can.*

This will be particularly important when we discuss the actual processes of moving towards your goals. Where, when, and with whom you want to reach your goals are critical questions that will help you clarify your goals. If one of your goals is to feel more passion and excitement about your life, do you want to feel that all the time, at every moment? Is passion and excitement what you want to feel at a funeral, or while having lunch with your grandmother? Do you want to feel passion and excitement during a proctological exam? As you prepare to reach your goals, ask yourself what will be the sights, sounds, and feelings that will accompany reaching your goal. For example, "When I hear my professor assign a large term project, I will feel challenged and confident that I can do what is necessary to get the grade I want."

STEP 4: *Are your goals compatible with each other?*

Most of us have more than one goal we want to reach. This step simply asks that you make sure you find a way to reach both goals or once again return to evaluating what you really want. For example, since the women's rights movement, many women are faced with the dilemma of balancing career and motherhood. Now, having a career and being an involved mother are not necessarily incompatible goals, but it requires very clear thought about how they are to be balanced or sequenced in order to support reaching both goals.

STEP 5: *Assess what you already have and what you are going to need in order to reach your goals.*

In other words, what are your skills, your assets? If you want to be a stand-up comedian, you may already possess a wonderful sense of humor and a quick mind. You may need a lot of confidence building, public speaking skills and practice, an ability to withstand criticism so as to grow a thick skin and continue to improve, or even some training regarding how to formulate an act. This kind of thinking allows you to direct your energy in the appropriate directions.

STEP 6: *Make a plan.*

A journey of a thousand miles begins with a single step. It is often useful to work backwards from the place where you want to be to the place where you are now in order to determine your very next step. For example, if you've decided upon a career as an attorney, the step just before entering practice is passing the bar exam. The step before that is completing law school. The step prior to that is getting into law school which requires taking and scoring well on the law boards (LSAT). And of course you need to have a bachelors degree before the law boards results are significant. Obviously we can take this process all the way back to toilet training, as most attorneys do not practice in diapers either. However, the point is that there is a next reasonable step to take and you need to take that step. Working backwards from your goal lays out a path for you to follow.

Questions

1. To determine whether a goal is truly right for you _____.

   A. ask others for their opinion

   B. consult a shaman

   C. assess the goal of the goal

   D. pay attention to your mistakes

2. Which of the following applies to goal setting?

   A. Describe your goal globally rather than specifically.

   B. Avoid setting benchmarks so you don't get discouraged.

   C. Don't be afraid to set incompatible goals. The universe will sort it out.

   D. State your goal in positive terms in a way that does not depend on the behavior of others.

3. What is the purpose of exploring the goal of the goal?

   A. to confuse you

   B. to help you figure out what you really want

   C. to assist you in wishstorming

   D. to gain enlightenment

Positive Psychology Exercise

Compose Your Personal Mission Statement

Really give it some thought based upon all the guidelines for thinking it through. You will find that the time and effort you put into this will be well spent.

8.6 Visualization

Define the process of visualization and discuss its various applications.

As an infant, before you learned to speak, you were able to think, but this rudimentary thinking took the form of images rather than words or phrases, which you had not yet mastered. That is why, for most people, our earliest memories from childhood tend to be fragmented images rather than conversations or events. Indeed, mental imagery is perhaps the most basic way that your mind represents and stores information. And imagery is the primary medium by which your **unconscious mind** operates. Freud (1924) in his psychodynamic theory developed the concept of the unconscious mind to describe that part of the mind containing aspects of our functioning of which we are totally unaware. Freud believed that the mind is like an iceberg which is mostly hidden underwater. He saw our conscious mind as being the part of the iceberg that is above the waterline. But below the surface is the much larger unconscious region containing thoughts, wishes, feelings and memories of which we are largely unaware, but which influence our feelings and behaviors nevertheless. When asleep, as you detach from your conscious mind and waking verbal thought, your unconscious mind emerges and dream images abound. The imagery of the unconscious mind is not confined to just mental pictures; it can represent impressions from any of your senses, i.e. remembered sounds, feelings, aromas, tastes, etc.

Visualization is a time-honored method of deliberately using imagery, visual and otherwise, to alter your feelings, your behavior, and even your physiology. Because of the dominance of imagery in the functioning of your unconscious mind, which has a powerful effect upon your motivation, visualization practice can have a profound effect on your emotions or behavior, over and beyond your conscious efforts to change. Early in the twentieth century, the French pharmacist, Emil Coue (1922), wrote that the power of the imagination exceeds that of the conscious will. That is, you may or may not be able to will the achievement of a specific goal, but repeatedly visualizing attaining that goal greatly increases the probability of success. Mastery of the art and practice of visualization will help propel you down the road to effectiveness.

Covey (1991) also spoke to the importance of this when he exhorted us to "begin with the end in mind." With this he is talking both about the importance of setting goals *and* then being able to visualize the achievement of those goals as necessary prerequisites to effectiveness.

8.6.1 Applications to Sports Performance

In a now classic study (Richardson, 1969), three groups of boys were tested on their ability to make free throws on a basketball court. After the initial assessment they were instructed to spend the next two weeks in one of three ways. One group practiced shooting free throws. Another group did nothing with a basketball for two weeks. The third group was instructed to mentally rehearse shooting the basketball, to visualize themselves shooting and making free throws. All of the groups were then retested. The group that did nothing showed no change in their free throw proficiency. The group that actually practiced with the ball improved 24%. The group that only visualized improved 23%! This is only one of many demonstrations of the power of human beings to achieve extraordinary results by controlling the content of their thoughts.

In a comprehensive treatise called *Peak Performance*, Charles Garfield (1984) documented extensive research done with world class athletes in Russia and the United States. He stated unequivocally that almost all world-class performers are visualizers. In fact, in the realm of the world-class athlete, he cited a study done in the then Soviet Union where different athletic training regimens were compared. Some athletes spent almost 100% of their time in physical training for their event. Others spent between 25%, 50%, and 75% of their time in mental training and rehearsal, i.e. visualization for their event. The results showed that performance results improved as the amount of time devoted to mental practice increased. Garfield also points out that "peak performers are highly motivated by a deep and personal sense of mission which is distinctly different from the highly specific and measurable goals each person may set."

There is little doubt that visualization or imagery works. How, when, where, and under what circumstances it works is being actively studied. Morris and colleagues (2005) summarize the current state of affairs in their text, *Imagery in Sport*.

> *Until a thorough understanding of imagery emerges, systematic research programs that examine one aspect of it in a variety of ways are needed. . . . In particular, we propose that substantial evidence indicates that imagery works in a range of sport contexts. Imagery can enhance learning, performance, confidence, and motivation, reduce stress and anxiety, and facilitate recovery from injury, among other benefits. We need more research on how imagery works, because by understanding the mechanisms we will be able to predict and control its use, even in untested circumstances. (pg. 11)*

8.6.2 Applications for Healing

Cancer researcher O. Carl Simonton (1975), in *Getting Well Again*, reports increased longevity in cancer patients who practice relaxation and visualize their diseases remitting. This process literally involves creating vivid mental images of the disease process, a tumor for instance, and then deliberately imagining that the image is changing. For example, you might imagine a tumor as a black octopus with tentacles reaching into various body parts. You then imagine that your chemotherapy or radiation treatment is acting as a weapon, shrinking the octopus, damaging its arms, changing or fading its color to white, and causing it to eventually disappear. While this treatment approach is still controversial, it is becoming a widely used technique in fighting cancer.

Simonton is far from alone in his faith in the power of belief that is reflected in how one "sees" things. Both Jeanne Achtenberg (1985) and Bernie Siegel (1986) in their respective texts, *Imagery in Healing,* and *Love, Medicine and Miracles*, cited many examples indicating that our beliefs affect our physical health for better or worse. When you believe you will survive and thrive, your probability of doing so increases. If you believe your disease is a death sentence, then unfortunately that becomes true with increasing frequency as well. In fact, Achtenberg achieved a 95% rate of accuracy in predicting who would survive their illness and who would die simply by a careful analysis of patients' drawings of themselves, their cancers, their immune systems, and their treatment.

Anees Shiekh (2005) summarized the current state of the research on the uses of imagery in healing in *Healing Images: The Role of Imagination in Health.* He points out that imagery has been demonstrated to create measurable physiological changes in heart rate, blood pressure, blood flow, sexual response, body chemistry, various ocular effects, electrodermal activity, muscle tension and the immune system. And this is only a partial list! He further noted that the effectiveness of procedures such as biofeedback and hypnosis is clearly related to the capacity of those being treated to become absorbed in imagery. His conclusions are remarkably similar to the findings in the area of sport. Imagery practices work, but much more research is needed to determine which techniques under various circumstances are most effective for different disorders. Exactly how imagery assists the body to heal is the focus of much current theory and research.

The placebo effect, as discussed in Chapter 5, also stands as powerful proof of the role of belief and paradigm in the creation of our reality. In fact, in the realm of metaphysical and spiritual practice it is understood that the eyes are more than simply receptive organs. The root word of eye actually translates as "fountain." That is, the eyes send energy out and thus are involved in creation itself. Pick up virtually any revered text of wisdom teachings and you will find references and specific instructions for controlling and shaping your thoughts and images to manifest the life you desire. This is best summed up by Michael Talbot (1991) in his book *The Holographic Universe.*

> *Paramahansa Yogananda advised people to visualize the future they desired for themselves and charge it with the "energy of concentration." As he put it, "Proper visualization by the exercise of concentration and will power enables us to materialize thoughts, not only as dreams or visions in the mental realm, but also as experiences in the material realm."*
>
> *Indeed, such ideas can be found in a wide range of disparate sources. "We are what we think," said the Buddha. "All that we are arises with our thoughts. With our thoughts we make the world. As a man acts, so does he become. As a man's desire is, so is his destiny," states the Hindu pre-Christian Brihadaranyaka Upanishad. "All things in the world of Nature are not controlled by Fate for the soul has a principle of its own," said the fourth-century Greek philosopher Iamblichus. "Ask and it will be given you . . . If ye have faith, nothing shall be*

impossible unto you," states the Bible. And, "The destiny of a person is connected with those things he himself creates and does," wrote Rabbi Steinsaltz in the kabbalistic Thirteen Petaled Rose. (p. 222)

8.6.3 Possible Explanations for How Visualization Works

How does visualization work? One explanation seems to be based on principles first outlined by Albert Bandura (1977) in his Social Cognitive Learning theory. While this theory has many elements, it relies on thoughts, beliefs, and a principle known as modeling to explain why you behave as you do and how you acquire behaviors and skills. The principle of **modeling** describes the ability of humans to learn how to do something simply by observing others. This is also referred to in the literature as **observational learning**. It works whether the models are live or on a TV screen. It also apparently works when the models are in your imagination. *And* it also works well when the model is a new, improved, and more successful you that is created in your imagination.

Modeling or observational learning may be partially explained by the presence of mirror neurons in the brain (Ramachandran, 2000). Whenever we observe someone performing an action, the same neurons required to perform that action being observed are being triggered in the observer as well. Those neurons firing in the observer are mirror neurons. It is as if we are hard-wired to learn by watching others.

Other speculations as to why visualization works (Morris, Spittle, and Watt, 2005) include that it increases feelings of self-confidence and self-efficacy. It may well work by raising arousal levels to their best level for optimal performance as suggested by the Yerkes Dodson curve relating arousal and performance. Some suggest that visualization enhances motivation. Others believe that visualization practice sends electrical impulses to the actual muscles that are used in the execution of the imagined activity, thereby providing a virtual rehearsal of the actions one is imagining. Truth be told, it is probably a combination of all of these, and there is research data to support each explanation.

8.6.4 The Process of Visualization

Now that a case has been made for the power of visualization, it remains for us to specify how to actually use this capacity in a way that works to your advantage. What follows is a discussion of critical principles in understanding and using this process.

BEGIN BY MASTERING VOLUNTARY RELAXATION SKILLS. This is an absolutely critical element in the use of visualization. Your body is a reflection of your mental state. If you are tense, anxious, fearful, or lack confidence, this is reflected in your musculature. Thus you may verbalize positive thoughts and even conjure up positive images. But if your body is presenting a competing picture of negativity then you are sending mixed messages to yourself and your results will be mixed at best. When you relax completely prior to your visualization practice, you are creating on a blank sheet of paper. There are no competing images to interfere with the process of your learning. You might also think of this process as familiar to recording music in a studio. Recording studios are deliberately soundproofed so that only the music played in the studio is recorded, not the sound of traffic or conversation in the hallway. Relaxation is the moral equivalent of silence in your body, and allows for a clearer recording of the behaviors, skills, and attitudes you wish to acquire.

The techniques discussed in Chapter 6 will allow you to master the act of relaxation. Pay special attention to the discussion of basic meditation technique, which is another pathway to relaxation and the quieting of competing thoughts.

GARBAGE IN, GARBAGE OUT.   Your consciousness is an equal opportunity employer. It really doesn't care if what you visualize is good or bad for you. It just produces results. In this case, what you see is what you get. Consider this analogy. You can think of visualization as being to your mind what food is to your body. Positive images are the equivalent of healthy food and negative images are like feeding yourself junk food. If you recall, earlier we stated the necessity of stating your goals positively. This is to avoid the pitfall of visualizing and manifesting what you *don't* want. For example, one of the authors discovered this principle in a rather embarrassing fashion . . .

> I was waiting at the first tee of the golf course with my father and some of his friends. The first tee is the one place on a golf course where you are being observed by many people. My concern, my absolute preoccupation, was that I did not want to embarrass myself by hitting a terrible shot in front of my father and all of these people. To that end I began saying to myself, "just don't shank the ball," a particularly bad shot. I kept thinking this over and over again until it was my turn to hit. In short order, I stepped up to the ball and shanked it! I got exactly what I didn't want because I had rehearsed it so thoroughly.

VISUALIZATION IS MUCH MORE THAN IMAGES.   You don't necessarily see things when you visualize. This is a crucial point because many people are not aware of the visual aspect of their thoughts. If you ask them to visualize something they panic because they believe that they should be seeing a mental television set with crisp, clear images. For those of you that can do this, that is wonderful. For those of you that cannot, there is no need to worry because *all* of your senses are involved in the visualization process. It is sufficient to have a *sense* of what it would be like if your imagined future or outcome was occurring. In other words, as long as you *know* what your image would look like if you could see, or hear, or feel it, that is good enough for the purposes of creation. In an ideal scenario the outcome that you imagine should be developed as vividly as possible. You should see, hear, and feel your future in as much detail as possible. For instance, if you want to be more assertive in your communications, it would be best not only to hear the words in the appropriate speed and tone of voice, but also to see yourself acting in an assertive fashion. You could also see the people you are speaking to responding appropriately and receptively to your communication. And lastly, you should feel what it would be like to communicate in this way.

Positive Psychology Exercise

Enhancing Your Visualizations

If you have difficulty with making visual images and would like to learn to enhance your ability, try this simple exercise. Just close your eyes and allow yourself to recall your bedroom, or a pleasant experience, either recent or from childhood, or what you ate at your last meal, in as much detail as possible. Pay special attention to the colors, shapes and lighting, as well as any tastes, smells, textures, temperatures, sounds, physical sensations and feelings you experienced. If you are not a strong visualizer that likely means that you tend to store your memories in another **representational system**. We use representational systems to encode information in our brains. There are five primary representational systems relating to each of the five senses: **auditory** (our hearing represented in sounds, words and language); **visual** (our vision represented in mental pictures); **kinesthetic** (our sense of touch represented by feelings and physical sensations); **gustatory** (taste); and **olfactory** (smells). Each person has a dominant representational system, a sense that they favor for encoding and remembering information. Although the visual system is typically dominant, many individuals prefer another representational system for storing memories. If this is the case for you, remember any experience by tuning into whatever sense is most dominant for you, and then imagine any visual images associated with these other sensory images. So, for example, if you are remembering your bedroom, first recall the sensation of lying in your comfortable bed and feeling the softness and warmth of your comforter or bedspread while listening to music or talking on your cell phone. Now connect that with actually seeing what that comforter or bedspread looks like. What color is it? Does it have a pattern? What color are the walls in your room or the floor? Where is your dresser, or your desk? What can you see when you look out of your window? Basically, you can use memories from one sense to bridge into memories from any other sense. Doing this enables you to make your visualizations more vivid by giving them the depth of multiple sensory representations.

USE PARTICIPANT AND OBSERVER IMAGERY. This brings us to another subtle but critical distinction in the visualization process, participant and observer imagery. Consider for a moment that all of the movie special effects you have ever witnessed originated first in someone's imagination; therefore, these are available to you as well. Special effects have different effects on you as you watch them. For example, most likely you have experienced simulation rides (such as those at Disney World or other amusement parks) and their powerful impact on your physiology. You can actually feel as if you are on a roller coaster or an airplane if the ride presents you with the sights and sounds you would experience if you were actually on the plane or coaster. This is what is referred to as participant imagery—you feel as if you are actually participating in the experience. Observer imagery occurs when you see a roller coaster or airplane "out there" or in the distance. The difference in your experience is that you may have feelings about the airplane or coaster but you don't feel as if you are on it, directly experiencing it. It is the difference between watching a mental image of yourself riding the coaster (a third person experience) vs. imagining yourself actually riding it (a first person experience). Depending upon the results that you want, you need to use these two variations appropriately.

Participant imagery involves actually practicing the result you want in your mind. This is how world-class athletes prepare for their events without leaving their rooms. You feel what it is like to be doing what it is you want to be doing. Your muscles are actually experiencing the same electrical impulses that they would during the actual activity. In other words, there really is no difference to your brain between real and imagined. Observer imagery has a different effect. It involves watching yourself in your mind's eye, thus in this context it tends to be more motivating. As you see yourself behaving, looking, and sounding as you would like, you tend to be positively motivated to expend the energy to do what is necessary to achieve the result. Using observer imagery can also be helpful when imagining yourself doing something which is frightening or anxiety-provoking for you. Since you are viewing yourself at a distance when using observer imagery, it can give you more emotional distance, and as a result help allay anxiety. You can then shift to participant imagery once you feel comfortable with your observer images.

THE RECOMMENDED SEQUENCE FOR THE PROCESS OF VISUALIZATION WOULD BE AS FOLLOWS:

a. Decide on your goal, the actions and attitudes you wish to adopt.

b. Think of a model who can do what you want to do.

c. Get into a comfortable position.

d. If possible, make sure that your environment is relatively quiet and free from distractions.

e. Use a relaxation technique to establish a receptive mental state.

f. Begin to imagine or sense your model doing the desired goal or behaviors.

g. Study what the model does, how does he or she look, sound, move, until you can vividly "sense" him or her in your imagination.

h. Substitute yourself for the model. That is, see yourself doing the desired goal and allow yourself to feel motivated (observer imagery).

i. Step into the image and see, hear, and feel what you would feel if you were doing the desired goal (participant imagery).

j. Practice this for 15 minutes daily. For faster results practice 2–3 times daily.

LET GO AND BE PATIENT.   This part is a little trickier. Visualization is effective. You do it all the time effortlessly. When you begin to deliberately direct it, it is often difficult to maintain that effortless quality. After all, you want something and have been taught that you need to try your hardest to get those things you want. Unfortunately, trying hard can be counterproductive because it is associated with tension, which interferes with the visualization process. Also, there is a tendency when embarking on this process to worry whether or not it will work. You may remember other things you wished for and never got. You may find yourself looking for results each day and feeling frustrated that your progress isn't more obvious. All we can say is to continue to practice, relax, and let go. All of the other worry and concern leads to visualizing all of the things you don't want. If you are having difficulty with this, review the lessons from Chapter 2 on maintaining an optimistic perspective. Visualization is similar to gardening. You plant seeds of positive thought through imagery and pluck out the weeds of negative thoughts by refusing to invest your energy in contemplating all the things that can go wrong. When you plant a seed, you don't dig it out of the ground every day to check its progress. Now we are not suggesting that you never plan for the possibility of things not going your way (i.e. engage in defensive pessimism if that style suits you better). Life will definitely surprise you. But when you are exercising the power of visualization it is important to keep your eye on the prize. Obviously, what is required is a mind able to maintain a focus on the present moment. This is also a skill that can be learned and is the primary benefit of the practice of meditation.

8.6.5 A Final Note on Visualization

A story is told of a good and holy man named Saul who had lived a life of love and service to his family and community. Saul began to pray regularly at temple with a particular request of God. After praising and thanking God, Saul reminded God of all of his good works and finished with the statement, "I don't think it's too much to ask that I should win the lottery." This routine went on for several months but Saul failed to win the lottery. Still he persisted until one day a booming voice from behind the altar said, "Saul, do me a favor. Buy a ticket!" Visualization seems like a miraculous process but it requires effort and it ultimately requires that you take action. (Refer back to the SWOOP method in Chapter 4.) You may visualize yourself getting an A in a college course but you will have to register, buy the book, go to class, and study. You may visualize a perfected athletic technique but you will still have to practice on the field of play. The Universe is wondrous and mysterious. So, by all means, expect miracles, but remember to do your part.

Questions

1. Imagery that enables you to feel as if you are in the experience is referred to as _____ imagery.

    A. participant

    B. observer

   C. vivid

   D. sensory

2. Representational systems refer to _____.

   A. learning styles

   B. the five senses

   C. visual cues

   D. categories of visual images

3. Research on applications of visualization for sports performance demonstrates _____.

   A. that visualization does not facilitate performance

   B. that it helps for baseball but not basketball

   C. that it actually hurts performance because it detracts from practice time

   D. that for world class athletes in the U.S. and Russia, performance improvement directly corresponded to the percentage of time spent in mental rehearsal

8.7 Putting It All Together: Using ACT to Enhance Flourishing

Describe how ACT differs from other perspectives on how to achieve well-being.

In this chapter and those preceding, you have been introduced to a wide range of perspectives and techniques for enhancing your strengths, improving your functioning, and coping with the vicissitudes of life. This has included learning to utilize paradigm shifting for enhancing **psychological flexibility**, cognitive restructuring for modifying negative thoughts, mindfulness meditation for relaxation and stress management, and composing your personal mission statement to help clarify your values, along with goal setting and visualization for how to act based on those values. Now we can combine these tools and skills with the insights and techniques of the ACT framework. To reiterate, ACT is an acronym for:

   A   Accept your thoughts and feelings

   C   Choose your values

   T   Take action

ACT is an empirically supported set of tools and techniques which takes a counter intuitive approach to dealing with life satisfaction. The aim of ACT is to create a rich, full, meaningful existence while accepting the inevitable pain in life. ACT accomplishes this by: (1) teaching the psychological skills to handle negative thoughts and emotions effectively to lessen their influence via mindfulness skills; and (2) helping clarify your values to enable meaningful goal setting and goal directed behaviors (Harris, 2009). ACT encourages you to give up on the pursuit of happiness while teaching you how to undermine struggle and avoidance of pain, thereby gaining psychological flexibility defined as the ability to be in the present moment, open to experience, and able to do what matters. The happiness trap as explicated by Harris (2011) is a result of believing in any or all of these four myths.

Myth # 1.   Happiness is the natural state for humans.

Myth # 2.   If you are not happy, you are somehow defective.

Myth # 3.   To live a good life, you must rid yourself of negative thoughts and feelings.

Myth # 4.   You should be able to exert control over what you think and feel.

We are taught from early on that we should be able to control our feelings and thoughts. However, it turns out that we have a lot less control over our thoughts and emotions than experts would have you believe. It's not that you have absolutely no control at all, just less than you would desire. Suppression of unwanted thoughts often leads to a rebound effect where these thoughts increase in frequency and intensity (Wenzloff & Wegner, 2000). This same rebound effect has been noted with emotions (Feldner, Zylensky, Eifert & Spiro, 2003; Wegner, Erber & Zanakos, 1993). Basically, that which you resist persists. Additionally, the amount of control you have is inversely proportional to the intensity of the thoughts or emotions and dependent on your stress level. That is why techniques like optimistic thinking or cognitive restructuring, although useful and effective at times, don't always succeed or only help temporarily for banishing or reducing negative thoughts or feelings. What we do have much more control over is our overt behaviors, but our covert behaviors (those thoughts and feelings) may linger even if we are adept at controlling our outward behaviors. In sum, we can choose our actions but not necessarily our thoughts and feelings. Nevertheless, it is very valuable to develop self-control over your behavior for obvious reasons. To get an idea of the extent to which you firmly accept the belief that you must control your thoughts and feelings, fill out the following questionnaire. For each numbered alternative, pick either option a or b depending on which better describes your beliefs and attitudes.

Belief in Control Questionnaire

1a. _____ I must have good control of my feelings in order to be successful in life.

1b. _____ It is unnecessary for me to control my feelings in order to be successful in life.

2a. _____ Anxiety is bad.

2b. _____ Anxiety is neither good nor bad. It is merely an uncomfortable feeling.

3a. _____ Negative thoughts and feeling will harm you if you don't control or get rid of them.

3b. _____ Negative thoughts and feelings won't harm you even if they feel unpleasant.

4a. _____ I'm afraid of some of my strong feelings.

4b. _____ I'm not afraid of any feelings, no matter how strong.

5a. _____ In order for me to do something important, I have to get rid of all my doubts.

5b. _____ I can do something important, even when doubts are present.

6a. _____ It's important to reduce or get rid of negative thoughts or feelings as quickly as possible.

6b. _____ Trying to reduce or get rid of negative thoughts and feelings frequently causes problems. If I simply allow them to be, then they will change as a natural part of living.

7a. _____ The best method of managing negative thoughts and feelings is to analyze them and then use that knowledge to get rid of them.

7b. _____ The best method of managing negative thoughts and feelings is to acknowledge their presence and let them be, without having to analyze or judge them.

8a. _____ I will become happy and healthy by improving my ability to avoid, reduce, or get rid of negative thoughts and feelings.

8b. _____ I will become happy and healthy by allowing negative thoughts and feelings to come and go of their own accord and by learning to live effectively when they are present.

9a. _____ If I can't suppress or get rid of negative emotions, it's a sign of personal failure or weakness.

9b. _____ The need to control or get rid of a negative emotional reaction is a problem in itself.

10a. _____ Having negative thoughts and feelings is an indication that I am psychologically unhealthy.

10b. _____ Having negative thoughts and feelings means I'm a normal human being.

11a. _____ People who are in control of their lives can generally control how they feel.

11b. _____ People who are in control of their lives do not need to control their feelings.

12a. _____ It is not okay to feel anxious, and I try hard to avoid it.

12b. _____ I don't like anxiety, but it's okay to feel it.

(Continued)

13a. _____ Negative thoughts and feelings are a sign that something is wrong with my life.

13b. _____ Negative thoughts and feelings are an inevitable part of life for everyone.

14a. _____ I have to feel good before I can do something that is important and challenging.

14b. _____ I can do something important and challenging even I am feeling anxious or depressed.

15a. _____ I try to suppress thoughts and feelings that I don't like by just not thinking about them.

15b. _____ I don't try to suppress unwanted, negative thoughts and feelings but let them come and go.

To score your survey count the number of times you selected option "a" or "b." The more you picked option "a," the greater the likelihood that control issues are causing problems or suffering in your life.

Proponents of ACT emphasize that our efforts to reign in our thoughts and feelings often end up exacerbating them. Sometimes our control efforts turn into problems. Common examples of this include being overly possessive and controlling to reduce jealousy and fear of rejection, thereby pushing others to reject you, a self-fulfilling prophecy, or binge eating to sooth your upset over being overweight. We all engage in efforts to control our thoughts and feelings – this is part of the human condition. These strategies we use for control can be categorized using the fight or flight response as our guide, specifically, do we tend to run from our unwanted thoughts/feelings or do we fight them?

Common Control Strategies	
Flight	**Fight**
Hiding/Escaping	Suppression
Distraction	Arguing (including with yourself)
Zoning out/Numbing (including substance abuse)	Taking charge/Self-criticism

Utilizing any of the above strategies is not necessarily unwarranted nor always bad. These coping mechanisms can be effective if three rules are met.

1. You only use them in MODERATION.
2. You only use them if they work and DO NOT have negative consequences.
3. Using them does not contradict your values.

The happiness trap results from engaging in ineffective control strategies which often result in the following unintended consequences:

- Efforts at control take lots of time and energy.
- When control efforts fail, you feel inept or powerless.
- Control strategies that decrease unwanted thoughts and feelings in the short term often lower your quality of life in the long term (e.g. substance abuse).

Positive Psychology Exercise

ACT and the Unintended Consequences of Avoidance

Take a moment to identify the thoughts and feelings you would most like to get rid of and write them down. Now make a list of everything you have done or tried to accomplish this. Go through your list of control strategies one item at a time and ask yourself the following questions:

1. Did this attempt at control work long term?
2. What are the downsides of this (i.e. what did it cost me in time, money, health, energy, relationship issues, etc.)?
3. Did this attempt at control enhance the quality of my life?

   You may find that you have invested loads of time and energy, that you felt better in the short term but not in the long term, and/or the control strategy lowered your quality of life overall.

ACT was designed to facilitate your self-awareness of everything that you do to avoid unpleasant, unwanted thoughts and feelings. ACT is comprised of six Core Principles to help you develop psychological flexibility. The greater your psychological flexibility the better able you will be to handle painful thoughts and feelings enabling you to flourish, to take action to live a rich and meaningful life. We will begin with a brief description of each of these six principles. In the following sections, we will explicate tools and techniques available for mastering each principle. Within the confines of this text we cannot offer comprehensive coverage of the myriad of ACT perspectives and techniques for each core principle. We will offer you a representative sample. If you desire to delve more deeply into this material we suggest you read *The Happiness Trap* (Harris 2011), a down to earth, user-friendly, empirically tested self-help guide to using the plethora of ACT insights and tools in your daily life.

Questions

1. ACT stands for accepting your thoughts and feelings, choosing your values, and _____.

   A. testing yourself

   B. trying new approaches

   C. taking action

   D. talking it out

2. The *happiness trap* results from _____.

   A. believing any or all four myths related to your thoughts and feelings regarding happiness

   B. living in the present moment, rather than looking to the future

    C. not being able to control what we think or feel

    D. not pursuing happiness forcefully enough in your daily life

3. Research on mental suppression of thoughts and feelings illustrates that *that which you resist* _____.

    A. vanishes

    B. persists

    C. enlists

    D. haunts

8.8 The Six Core Principles of ACT

Explain the six Core Principles of ACT and how to apply them to deal with unwanted thoughts, feelings and images.

1. **DEFUSION:** The process of relating to unwanted thoughts or feelings differently, rather than avoiding, suppressing, or denying them so they will have less influence or power over you.

2. **EXPANSION:** Making room for negative thoughts or emotions instead of suppressing them or pushing them away.

3. **CONNECTION:** Connecting fully with the present moment. Being fully engaged in whatever you are doing or experiencing in the here and now rather than worrying about the future or dwelling on the past.

4. **OBSERVING SELF:** Identical to what we have previously referred to as the witnessing stance (see Chapter 6) for developing self-awareness.

5. **VALUES:** Connecting with your core values – an essential step in making your life meaningful.

6. **COMMITTED ACTION:** Acting on your values, that is, walking your talk in a committed fashion.

Principles 1 – 4 draw on the mindfulness skills elucidated in Chapter 6 in the section on mindfulness meditation. Principles 5–6 draw on lessons from earlier in this chapter on developing your personal mission statement based on values, goal-setting, and visualization as well as the information on self-efficacy from Chapter 2.

8.8.1 DEFUSION–Perspectives and Techniques

Thoughts run through our minds constantly, even when we sleep. Each of us has literally hundreds of silly, useless, mundane or unhelpful, negative thoughts daily that we cannot prevent. But we always have a choice about whether to take these thoughts seriously. The fact is you don't have to control your thoughts; you just have to stop letting them control you. Ultimately, our thoughts are nothing but a string of words or phrases in our head. ACT refers to thoughts as "stories" we tell ourselves which can be true (facts) or false, but they typically consist of opinions, expectations, beliefs, ideas, theories, wishes, and goals which are neither true nor false. The focus in ACT is not whether any given thought is true or false, but whether paying attention to it is useful, allowing us to create the life we want to lead. ACT reminds us to discriminate between the story and the event (remember from Chapter 1 that the map is not the territory). We tend to react to our thoughts as if they represent absolute truth. So, if we expect to be rejected, we may act as if this is an unavoidable outcome. This is what is termed **fusion**, defined as the melding of a thought with an event as if they are one in the same. Fusion causes you to respond to your thoughts as if . . .

- They represent reality.
- They are important.
- They are orders to be obeyed.
- They are always wise.
- They can be threats.

Defusion is an acceptance strategy, not a control strategy. The overarching purpose of ACT is not to change or eliminate negative thoughts and feelings, but rather to accept them. You do not have to like the unwanted thoughts or emotions. The goal is to give up struggling with them using mindfulness techniques to just notice them. The objective of defusion is not to get rid of negative thoughts but to see them for what they are – just words. Do not expect these thoughts to magically vanish. Practicing defusion will not necessarily make you feel good or happy, but it will free up your energy so you can focus on more important things, whether pursuing life goals or just having fun. Often, as a byproduct, you do end up feeling better, but only if you do not carry the expectation that this will occur. Defusion does not always work. When your best efforts at defusion fall short, take this as an opportunity to notice the difference between fusion and defusion. Defusion is just like any other skill where you grow more adept with practice. To bypass fusion, it helps to practice defusion whereby you separate the thought from the event by saying to yourself, "I'm having the thought that . . . "

DEFUSION TECHNIQUE #1: NOTICE AND LABEL
Begin with a negative thought in the form of: " I am X." (For example, "I am stupid.")
Focus on this and believe it for 10 seconds.

Take this thought and insert the following phrase before it: "I'm having the thought that I am X." Notice what happens.

Now elongate the phrase by adding: "I notice I am having the thought that . . . " Practice doing this.

Pay attention to how inserting these observational phrases creates some distance from the original negative thought. This allows you to step back from it and see it for what it truly is, just a string of words passing through your mind. You can use this technique for any negative or upsetting thought.

When you are fused, your thoughts seem to be very important and true. Practicing defusion allows you to begin to recognize that negative thoughts are just words, only stories in your head that are not necessarily true, wise or important, nor orders to be obeyed or threats to be feared. Using this technique does not guarantee that these thoughts will vanish, but getting distance reduces the power they have over you. The goal here is not to get rid of the thought but rather to let it go. This psychological distance enables you to cope far better with any negative, unwanted thoughts. As a byproduct, such thoughts may become less frequent and intense now that their power is reduced. However, this is just a bonus, not the goal of using the technique.

DEFUSION TECHNIQUE #2: MUSICAL THOUGHTS

Take a negative, unwanted thought and sing it to yourself in your head to the tune of Happy Birthday or Take Me Out to the Ballgame or any other silly, common song you know. Then replay the same thought in your mind without a tune. Now sing it yourself again to the tune of Jingle Bells. Then replay the thought again without music. It is likely that you are not taking it quite so seriously as before. You have not fought the thought, challenged it, or tried to replace it with a positive thought. But by putting it to music, it is far easier to see it for what it really is, just a series of words playing in your mind, like song lyrics. You are gradually becoming desensitized to the power of the thought.

DEFUSION TECHNIQUE #3: NAME YOUR STORIES

Identify a typical negative story about your life or yourself like "Nobody likes me" or "I'm a loser" and then label it accordingly. So, the former becomes the "No one likes me story" and the latter becomes the "I'm a loser story." This allows you to recognize it as just a story. The story will come and go but recognizing it as a story helps reduce its power. You can use this for any story you carry in your head that troubles you. Pay attention to what is really going on around you rather than your story about it.

At this point you may be wondering, "But what if my negative thought or story is really true?" ACT points out that attempting to determine the veracity of a thought is a waste of time. Rather, you need to ask the more relevant question, "Is this thought helpful?" If the answer is "yes," then by all means pay attention to it. If it's not helpful, then defuse it with any of the defusion techniques. You may further wonder how to ascertain whether a particular thought is helpful. The following questions can help you make that determination:

- Does this thought help me be who I want to be?
- Does this thought help me build relationships I value?
- Does this thought enable me to connect with my true values?
- Does this thought help me create a full, meaningful life?

If the answer to any of these questions is yes, then it's likely the thought, albeit negative, is helpful and merits your attention.

DEFUSION OF UNWANTED IMAGES, MEMORIES, OR JUDGMENTS

Variations on the defusion techniques explained previously can be used to help defuse unpleasant images, unwanted memories (often a combo of painful images and thoughts), or judgments (a subset of thoughts). Manuals on ACT offer a wide variety of other defusion techniques as well.

It is useful to recognize that images are nothing more than a series of pictures floating through your mind. You can label them, "I'm seeing a picture of X," or "I'm viewing a movie of X." Using your visualization skills, you can pretend that the painful image is on a TV screen in your mind's eye broadcast either as a movie or a still picture. This makes it possible for you to adjust the color, change the location, vary the speed, or you can run it backwards, or upside down, or play it in black and white. You can throw in any special effect you can imagine, just like in the movies. The key is not to resist or avoid the image but to see it for what it is – just a picture or movie in your mind. The same is true for memories. You can label it, "I'm having the memory of X." Or you can focus on the thought embedded in the memory and label that, or hone in on the images involved in the memory and label those. Likewise, you can do the same for judgments. You can notice that, "I am having a judgment about X."

8.8.2 EXPANSION Techniques–Making Room for Your Feelings

It is importance to recognize that emotions are like the weather, always present and constantly changing. Likewise, you have moods which change gradually over time and feelings which are more discrete episodes and sensations. Emotions are neither good nor bad but represent a stream of constantly changing sensations and urges passing through your body, just like the thoughts that pass by in your mind. For the most part, emotions cannot harm you unless they are chronic. If you accept your emotions instead of struggling with them, they will ebb and flow on their own, receding on their own schedule. The expansion principle is based on the premise that we need to make room for all our feelings. The goal here is to observe your emotions rather than analyze them. Mindfulness practice combined with diaphragmatic breathing are the perfect vehicles to allow for expansion, no matter what the feeling.

THE FIVE STEPS OF EXPANSION

1. Body awareness – Notice what sensations you have in your body and where.
2. Observe your feeling (i.e. "I notice I am having the feeling of X.").
3. Breathe into these sensations and/or feelings.
4. Make room for them.
5. Let those feelings be there.

Sometimes our feelings can be overwhelming. How can expansion work to help us cope when our pain, anger, anxiety, sadness etc. is too much to handle, even in small doses? If this is the case, then you need to start small. Pick only a mild sensation associated with the feeling and start there, expanding enough to allow for that sensation and breathing into it. So, if you are experiencing unbearable anxiety, start with observing the butterflies that may be fluttering in your stomach, or the shaking in your legs and focus just on that.

A subset of feelings worth addressing is urges. Urges are the overwhelming desire or impulse to act in a certain way or to have something. With any urge, you have two choices: act on it or not. To enable yourself to make a choice ask yourself, "If I act on this urge, will I be acting like the person I want to be?" Follow this up with, "Will acting on the urge help take my life in the direction I want?" If the answers are "yes," then follow the urge. If the answers are "no," then take action more in line with your values. But how do you resist this urge, this irresistible feeling, even when you know you shouldn't give in to it? To assist you in resisting an unhealthy urge, use the following five step expansion technique called Urge Surfing.

URGE SURFING

1. Observe the urge – Notice where you feel it in your body.

2. Acknowledge your urge to do X.

3. Breathe and make room for it.

4. Watch the urge rise, crest, and then fall. Rank the intensity of the urge from 1 to 10 and notice how it changes over time. Trust that if you give it time and space, it will always rise and fall.

5. Take action according to your values that will enhance your life in the long term.

8.8.3 CONNECTION Techniques–Being in the Here and Now

Developing connection makes full use of the practice of mindfulness which is the conscious awareness of the here and now with an attitude of interest, openness, and receptivity. ACT relies on the practical application of mindfulness skills to enable you to make important life changes. It is not about enlightenment or religion. Finding connection involves using your observer self (the ACT version of the witnessing stance described in Chapter 6) to enable you to be in the present moment. To do so, you are encouraged to conduct a running commentary in your mind, an ongoing factual, non-judgmental description of what you observe taking place from moment to moment. Doing this helps you stay in the here and now. The observer self is not judgmental. It is like a camera attached to you recording what is happening in the present moment. During this process, it is likely that judgments will pop up as part of your running observations. Let those judgments come and go without buying into them. Simply acknowledge them as judgments. The goal is to use factual descriptions in place of judgments on a moment to moment basis. To hone your mindfulness skills, we suggest a variety of introductory practice exercises.

- Be aware of your breathing.
- Be aware of sensations in your body.
- Be aware of the sounds around you.
- Notice five things that you can see, hear, or feel using all your senses.
- Connect with an aspect of your morning routine.
- Connect with one pleasant, values-driven activity each day; it need not be important or life altering.
- Connect with a useful chore you don't like.
- Connect with your experience of reading this book.
- Connect with a task you have been avoiding.

8.8.4 The OBSERVING SELF

This core principle enables you to practice defusion on a deeper level by activating your observer self to notice that you are noticing. This provides one more layer of increased distance to facilitate defusion. Accessing your observer self is not hard. Just choose anything of which you are currently aware. It could be a sight, a sound, a smell, a thought, a sensation, a movement, even a pain. Then focus on it, label it and as you are noticing it be aware that you are noticing it. So, you start with, "I am noticing that I hear X outside." Then this progresses to "I am noticing that I am noticing that I hear X outside."

8.8.5 Identifying your VALUES

It is important to discriminate between your values and your goals. Values represent the ongoing direction that guides your choices. It is a process that never ends. Goals represent desired outcomes that can be completed. Your goals may be derived from your values but typically are discrete benchmarks that you achieve (or not) and can be short term or long term. Connecting with your values and acting on these provides satisfaction in the here and now. Your values help you find the meaning and purpose in your life, an essential aspect of flourishing. It is much easier to endure any difficult thoughts or emotions you may experience when you have meaning and purpose in your life. Victor Frankl, in *Man's Search for Meaning* (1959), observed that those who managed to survive the longest in the Nazi concentration camps were not necessarily the strongest physically or the healthiest, but rather those who were most connected with their purpose in life. This gave them the reason, the will to live and endure all the suffering.

If you need help in defining or clarifying your values, refer back to your personal mission statement and think about the goal of your goals. The goal of your goals usually reflects a value. Another useful exercise involves imagining that you are 80 years old and looking back over your life. Ask yourself the following questions which may help clarify what you really value vs. what you are actually doing.

- I have spent too much time worrying about _____?
- I have spent too little time doing things like _____?
- If I could turn back the clock, what I would do differently is _____?

8.8.6 Taking COMMITTED ACTION

Now it is time to take action based upon your values. This involves goal setting, using visualization to motivate yourself and imagining taking effective action no matter how you are feeling. Inevitably, obstacles will arise that block or impede the path toward your goals whether from external sources or self-imposed blocks. To deal with external obstacles, employ the five step SWOOP process (see Chapter 4) to assist you in taking action towards your value based goals. But many times, those obstacles are the ones we generate ourselves. Self-induced obstacles often take the form of FEAR, literally and as an acronym for

F	Fusion
E	Excessive Expectations
A	Avoidance of discomfort
R	Retreat from Values

The antidote to FEAR is DARE, the acronym for:

D	Defusion
A	Acceptance of Discomfort
R	Realistic Goals
E	Embracing Values

Use the defusion techniques to deal with self-imposed obstacles based on fusion with your thoughts or feelings. Excessive expectations typically are a result of goals that are too big or based on an unrealistic timeframe. Or you may lack the necessary skills or resources to achieve the goal, or you expect perfection. Breaking your goals into doable chunks (see the time management section in Chapter 4) helps to prevent feelings of overwhelm. The more you avoid discomfort the harder it is to make important changes or take committed action. Use the expansion techniques to accept and make room for the discomfort of stepping out of your comfort zone. Remind yourself of your values regularly. Do not get so caught up in pursuing your goal that you lose sight of the values that underscore it.

The most common self-imposed obstacles are the reasons we give ourselves for why we cannot take action, all the excuses we have for not following through on things we know we want to do. Recognize that these reasons or excuses are just negative thoughts, a string of words in your head which are not literal truth nor commands you must obey. Defuse these excuses by noticing them and saying to yourself, "I'm having the thought that I can't do this because ----." Or you could notice the excuse and label it as "reason giving." Or you can name the story associated with the reason (i.e. "This is my I can't do this because I might fail story.") As you practice noticing, labeling, singing, or any other defusion exercise, the power of the excuse will begin to fade as you get distance from it. This allows you to recognize that it is just a string of words which you are not bound to follow, freeing you to finally take committed action.

Questions

1. All of the following are Core Principles of ACT except _____.

   A. defusion

   B. expansion

   C. fusion

   D. connection

2. ACT encourages you to _____.

   A. give up on the pursuit of happiness

   B. try harder to be happy

   C. separate your values and your goals

   D. fuse with your thoughts and feelings

3. The core principles of ACT build on _____.

   A. the practice of mindfulness

   B. the fight/flight reaction

   C. the pursuit of happiness

   D. ignoring your values

Summary

In this chapter, the overarching theme relates to the M in PERMA, having a sense of Meaning and purpose in your life, which often involves belonging to or serving something bigger than yourself. To that end, we reviewed aspects of **Transpersonal Psychology** which explores the overlap between the realms of psychology and spirituality, while offering some helpful, nondenominational, spiritual guidelines which you can apply however you choose to worship. Bill O'Hanlan's three C's of spirituality, that of connection, compassion, and contribution were explored along with suggestions as to how to utilize mindfulness, gratitude, forgiveness, and service to achieve these ends.

The process of connecting to your values using **wishstorming**, your personal mission statement and exploring the goal of your goals was connected with the six steps for securing your goals. This was followed by an in-depth discussion of how **visualization** aids in achieving our goals, including its applications to healing and sports performance along with a step by step primer in how to successfully visualize. Lastly, all these skills and perspectives were combined in the ACT approach, designed to enable you to develop the psychological flexibility to cope effectively with difficult thoughts, feelings, or images while facilitating taking committed action based on your values.

Key Terms

Auditory
Appreciative Inquiry
Collective Unconscious
Defusion
Fusion
Gustatory
Kinesthetic

Modeling
Morphic Resonance
Observational Learning
Olfactory
Psychological Flexibility
Representational Systems
Synchronicity

Transpersonal Psychology
Unconscious Mind
Vision Quest
Visual
Visualization
Wishstorming

Shared Writing

Pick one of your primary aspirational goals and ask yourself, "What is the goal of that goal?" Are there other, more realistic ways to achieve the value underlying your goal? If not, what is your step-by-step plan for achieving your goal?

Chapter 8 Questions

1. A possible alternate title for Chapter 8 could have been _____.

    A. Focus on Performance

    B. Follow the Path With the Heart

    C. Life Is Easy, Only Death Is Not

    D. Breathe In and Out

2. Considering your own death_____.

    A. should be avoided

    B. is too scary to contemplate

    C. should motivate you to plan your funeral arrangements

    D. can help you clarify your goals and values

3. The notion that all matter and living things are connected and affected by fields that influence their structure and behavior is termed _____ by Rupert Sheldrake.

    A. Transpersonal Psychology

    B. morphic resonance

    C. appreciative inquiry

    D. paranormal phenomena

4. _____ is a useful technique where you consider what is right about a situation and ask how it can be recreated.

   A. Morphic resonance

   B. Appreciative inquiry

   C. Transpersonal inquiry

   D. Wishstorming

5. When developing a step-by-step plan to reach your goal it is helpful to _____.

   A. wishstorm

   B. only focus on the goal of the goal

   C. be a perfectionist

   D. work backwards

6. Which of the following statements applies to the process of visualization?

   A. Relaxation is irrelevant to the visualization process.

   B. Athletes who practice their sport with mental rehearsal typically find it to be a waste of time.

   C. Both participant and observer imagery are useful in the visualization process.

   D. It is a myth that visualization practice can facilitate either healing or sports performance.

7. When you imagine watching yourself having an experience, this is called _____.

   A. observer imagery

   B. participant imagery

C. witnessing stance

D. observer self

8. The success of visualization is hypothesized to be a result of which part of the brain?

   A. the amygdala

   B. the hippocampus

   C. the frontal cortex

   D. mirror neurons

9. Which of the following guidelines is useful for the successful practice of visualization?

   A. Use only observer imagery.

   B. Use only visual imagery and ignore the distractions of other sensory systems.

   C. Start by relaxing.

   D. Push yourself and try as hard as you can.

10. ACT _____.

    A. aims to help you to avoid feeling emotional pain or thinking negative thoughts

    B. emphasizes that your efforts to reign in your negative thoughts and feelings often end up making them worse

    C. is a method for goal setting

    D. is a new type of visualization technique

Section Two

Interpersonal Effectiveness

Men and women are social animals. It is close to impossible to function effectively on Planet Earth without having the skills to get along with other people, or at least the people we choose to befriend, to live with, to love, to work with. The three chapters in this section focus on the development of key attitudes, behaviors and habits that foster healthy interpersonal functioning on our part thus facilitating healthy interpersonal relationships. Beginning with a thorough exploration of what it means to be emotionally intelligent and how to further develop this, this section further provides a primer on handling anger, specific guidelines for improving interpersonal communications, both on a receptive and expressive level, along with multiple strategies for how to improve relationships of all types.

Chapter 9
Developing Your Emotional Intelligence

Learning Objectives

After reading this chapter, you should be able to:

9.1 Describe the history and different domains of the concept of emotional intelligence.

9.2 Differentiate between the terms independent, interdependent, and co-dependent.

9.3 Explain the importance of a win-win paradigm to the concept of interpersonal effectiveness.

9.4 Recognize the benefits and challenges of putting ourselves into the shoes of others.

9.5 Describe the nature of anger and effective methods for managing anger constructively.

9.6 Define the process of forgiveness.

This textbook has spent a lot of time talking about effectiveness and flourishing. But what do we really mean by this? To define it as success in school, or in a career, or in terms of income level, is of course, far too narrow a definition to be meaningful. In general, effectiveness refers to competency in skills for living in your personal life, in your relationships, and in your chosen occupation, hence the overall organization of this book to address those three broad areas. This book has been designed to foster the development of building blocks for optimal functioning. Acquisition of various skills build in a cumulative fashion which will become evident as you read further.

9.1 The Concept of Emotional Intelligence

Describe the history and different domains of the concept of emotional intelligence.

In his groundbreaking 1995 book, *Emotional Intelligence*, psychologist Daniel Goleman summarizes a body of theory and research emphasizing the fundamental role of **emotional intelligence** in effectiveness and life success. Goleman reminds us that high intelligence (as measured by IQ tests, SAT tests, G.P.A.s, etc.) is a very poor predictor of who will succeed and/or be effective in life. In fact, Goleman refers to the **EQ**, or the emotional quotient as the counterpart to the IQ. So the good news here is that you don't need to be a rocket scientist to be an effective human being. But why is it that, among individuals with relatively equal potential in terms of levels of intelligence, education and opportunity, only certain ones excel while others flounder? For example, a longitudinal study (Valliant, 1977) was conducted with a sample of Harvard graduates from the 1940s, following them over several decades of life. Back in the 1940s there was much greater variability in admission testing scores for Harvard enrollees than exists today. Those with the highest SAT scores actually tended to be less successful than their lower scoring counterparts with regard to career success, income and even more importantly, in their interpersonal lives, as measured by marital satisfaction and quality of social life. In a similar vein, an ongoing study of valedictorians and salutatorians graduating from high schools in Illinois in 1981, as reported in the Chicago Tribune on May 29th, 1992, revealed that while this group continued to achieve academically in college, they did not necessarily excel later on in their careers. Ten years after high school graduation, only 25% of this group had risen to the higher levels of their chosen professions. Another study (Felsman & Valliant, 1987), conducted with hundreds of boys who grew up in a slum in Massachusetts, many of whom had low IQs, found that IQ level was not a good predictor of employment stability. The researchers concluded that other factors such as frustration tolerance, ability to control emotions, and to get along well with others were far more important.

Goleman concludes that IQ contributes at most about 20% to the factors leading to success in life. The other 80% is due to other factors. Goleman makes the convincing case that many of these other characteristics comprise that set of attitudes, skills and behaviors that we have come to know as emotional intelligence. So what exactly is this "emotional intelligence?" It includes such skills as being able to motivate yourself and persevere in the face of frustration, to delay gratification, to control your emotions and impulses, that is, think before you act, to empathize with others and to think positively. (Remember the seven key strengths essential for accomplishment?) Psychologists are discovering that EQ is just as important, if not more powerful than IQ in contributing to your effectiveness. And while IQ is a relatively stable attribute, your EQ can be modified and improved far more readily.

Gardner (1983) was one of the first to attack the notion of an overall IQ, preferring to break intelligence into a wide spectrum of intellectual abilities. Initially he posited seven types of intelligence, with the first two representing the traditional academically-based abilities of verbal and mathematical aptitude. Along with this he described spatial intelligence (relating to artistic abilities), kinesthetic intelligence (related to athletic ability), musical intelligence, and two levels of emotional intelligence characterized by leadership skills and people skills. Later Gardner subdivided emotional intelligence into four components: (1) leadership skills; (2) the ability to make friends and nurture relationships; (3) the ability to resolve conflicts; and (4) emotional perceptiveness. He emphasized the role of what he termed intrapersonal intelligence, that is, knowing and understanding yourself and your emotional reactions, and interpersonal intelligence, the ability to read and understand other people along with how to work cooperatively with them. Goleman takes this one step further and divides emotional intelligence into five domains. Notice the similarity between these and what you have learned so far in this text. The five domains are as follows:

1. **Self-Awareness**—the ability to know your own emotions. This involves being able to adopt the witnessing stance so as to master self-understanding and insight into your own needs and feelings. Knowing and understanding your feelings gives you more information for wise decision-making.

2. **Managing your emotions**—the ability to master stress, control anger, overcome depression and anxiety all contribute to resiliency, allowing you to bounce back from life's inevitable setbacks. The lessons gleaned from previous chapters are relevant here, along with the section on managing anger in the later part of this chapter.

3. **Self-motivation**—the ability to persevere, to delay gratification and wait for your rewards (i.e. remember the marshmallow study!), and to stay focused and on task is essential in most life endeavors, particularly those that involve long term goals. Recall how to manage yourself in time. In particular, the section on overcoming procrastination is very applicable here.

4. **Perceptiveness**— the ability to perceive and correctly identify the emotions of others along with skill at recognizing the impact of your behavior on others. The cornerstone of this is the ability to empathize with others, to literally be able to put yourself in the shoes of another person. This chapter and the next will help you acquire and sharpen these important skills.

5. **Handling relationships**—skill in relating to others and managing their emotions. It involves listening skills, conversational skills, being able to resolve conflicts, and knowing how to be appropriately assertive. It also subsumes the ability to establish rapport with others along with leadership skills. The next few chapters will develop and hone your abilities in these areas.

Take a moment to complete the following **Multifactor Emotional Intelligence Scale** (Salovey, Mayer and Carusok 2002) to get a rough estimate of your own EQ level.

Measure Your EQ

The MultiFactor Emotional Intelligence Scale

Indicate the extent to which each item applies to you using the following scale

1 = strongly disagree   2 = disagree   3 = neither agree nor disagree

4 = agree   5 = strongly agree

1. ____ I know when to speak about my personal problems to others.
2. ____ When I am faced with obstacles, I remember times I faced similar obstacles and overcame them.
3. ____ I expect that I will do well on most things I try.
4. ____ Other people find it easy to confide in me.
5. ____ I find it hard to understand the nonverbal messages of other people.
6. ____ Some of the major events of my life have led me to reevaluate what is important and not important.
7. ____ When my mood changes, I see new possibilities.
8. ____ Emotions are some of the things that make my life worth living.
9. ____ I am aware of my emotions as I experience them.
10. ____ I expect good things to happen.
11. ____ I like to share my emotions with others.
12. ____ When I experience a positive emotion, I know how to make it last.
13. ____ I arrange events others enjoy.
14. ____ I seek out activities that make me happy.
15. ____ I am aware of the nonverbal messages I send to others.
16. ____ I present myself in a way that makes a good impression on others.
17. ____ When I am in a positive mood, solving problems is easy for me.
18. ____ By looking at their facial expressions, I recognize the emotions people are experiencing.
19. ____ I know why my emotions change.
20. ____ When I am in a positive mood, I am able to come up with new ideas.
21. ____ I have control over my emotions.
22. ____ I easily recognize my emotions as I experience them.
23. ____ I motivate myself by imagining a good outcome to tasks I take on.
24. ____ I compliment others when they have done something well.
25. ____ I am aware of the nonverbal messages other people send.
26. ____ When another person tells me about an important event in his or her life, I almost feel as though I have experienced this event myself.
27. ____ When I feel a change in emotions, I tend to come up with new ideas.

28. ____ When I am faced with a challenge, I give up because I believe I will fail.

29. ____ I know what other people are feeling just by looking at them.

30. ____ I help other people feel better when they are down.

31. ____ I use good moods to help myself keep trying in the face of obstacles.

32. ____ I can tell how people are feeling by listening to the tone of their voice.

33. ____ It is difficult for me to understand why people feel the way they do.

To compute your total EQ score, first reverse the numbers that you have placed in response to items 5, 28, and 33 (1 = 5, 2 = 4, 3 = 3, 4 = 2, 5 = 1), and then total the numbers in front of all 33 items. Total scores range from 33 to 165 with higher scores suggesting greater EQ. The mean score for males is 125 and 131 for females as reported by the developers of this scale, therefore scores above the mean are indicative of above average emotional intelligence.

When the researchers used this scale in studies they found that higher EQ levels were linked to . . .

- Higher levels of prosocial behavior and lower aggression levels in both college and high school students
- Lower substance abuse in adolescents
- More effective leadership skills in the workplace
- More effective performance in handling consumer complaints in the workplace
- Greater levels of optimism
- Lower levels of depression
- Lower levels of impulsiveness
- Higher first year academic achievement (but unrelated to SAT or ACT scores, reiterating the findings mentioned earlier in this section)

Questions

1. EQ is composed of all of the following, except _____.

   A. self-awareness

   B. managing your emotions

   C. IQ

   D. handling relationships

2. Which of the following describes perceptiveness?

   A. the ability to perceive and correctly identify the emotions of others

   B. focusing on the words of others and ignoring nonverbal behaviors

    C. focusing only on yourself

    D. being popular and charismatic

3. Which of the following contributes most to effectiveness?

    A. IQ

    B. EQ

    C. luck

    D. wealth

9.2 Effectiveness in Relationships

Differentiate between the terms independent, interdependent, and co-dependent.

When you were a child, you were dependent on your parents for all your basic needs. You needed them to feed you, look after your safety, educate you, and generally make sure that you survived. You even needed them to wipe your behind! As you grew and matured you became increasingly less dependent on others for meeting your basic needs, but you still remained dependent financially and emotionally. The United States has traditionally been described as a highly individualistic society where independence is highly valued. If you are like most Americans, your goal is to become independent. Indeed, independence has been glorified by our culture and by the media. History books pay homage to the rugged individualists who helped tame and expand our country from coast to coast. These were individuals who depended primarily on themselves and the land for their survival. Popular culture lionizes heroes who personify the qualities of independence and courage. The current drive to own a car (no pun intended) is partly an outgrowth of this need for independence, the ability to rely on yourself to get where you want to go.

9.2.1 From Independence to Interdependence

In the previous chapters we have explored what we believe to be the essential elements of personal effectiveness. If you practice these and incorporate them into your life you will find yourself becoming a truly independent person, someone who recognizes that his life is his own responsibility, who sets a direction for his life and then can make things happen. But truly effective people realize that independence, while certainly a worthy goal, is not the end of the road. You see, we really are not islands unto ourselves. Personal effectiveness is not enough. To be genuinely effective, you have to learn to become interdependent. **Interdependence** is the relationship that ensues when two or more independent individuals decide to come together to achieve a common goal. They recognize that by working together they can achieve much more than the mere sum of their individual accomplishments. This has been referred to in the literature as **synergy**. Healthy marriages are characterized by interdependence, resulting from two spouses working as a team to satisfy mutual interests, such as paying the bills, raising the children, or cleaning the house. In fact, interdependent relationships, whether in a marriage, a business partnership, or a friendship are typified by mutual respect and a workable division of labor.

Unfortunately, many individuals in our society go from being dependent to being **co-dependent**. Co-dependent individuals depend on each other because deep inside they feel they could not survive on their own. Rather than give support to each other's growth, they seek to create situations which assure them that they will not be left alone. That is, they seek to make the other person dependent on them, just as they are dependent on the other person. The classic example is that of an alcoholic husband and his co-dependent wife. Although she professes that she wants her husband to stop drinking, she dutifully buys his six packs so that he won't be angry at her. While co-dependency can masquerade as interdependence, the difference lies in that true interdependence can only be achieved after you have successfully become independent. Figure 9.1 visually represents the continuum from dependence to interdependence with co-dependence as an offshoot which bypasses independence.

Figure 9.1

Dependence — Independence — Interdependence
Co-dependence

While we are saying that the road to interdependence, that is, interpersonal effectiveness, goes through independence, we are not implying that you must be perfectly independent. Becoming independent and interdependent is an ongoing, life-long process. This is not a static goal that you achieve, but rather one which you continually move towards.

Questions

1. _____ happens when two individuals work together and achieve more than the sum of their individual contributions.

    A. Interdependence

    B. Co-dependence

    C. Independence

    D. Synergy

2. _____ is the type of relationship that ensues when two or more independent individuals decide to come together to achieve a common goal.

    A. Dependence

    B. Co-dependence

    C. Interdependence

    D. Synergistic

3. A person who enables or supports the problems of a significant other out of fear of angering that person is said to be _____.

    A. independent

    B. dependent

    C. interdependent

    D. co-dependent

9.3 The Win-Win Frame

Explain the importance of a win-win paradigm to the concept of interpersonal effectiveness.

Just as personal effectiveness requires adopting a frame of proactivity, interpersonal effectiveness begins by embracing the paradigm of win-win. To be interdependent, and therefore interpersonally effective, you must set out looking for **win-win outcomes**. According to Adler and Towne (1993), when you approach an interaction within the framework of win-win. . . .

> the goal is to find a solution that satisfies the needs of everyone involved. Not only do the parties avoid trying to win at the other's expense, but they also believe that by working together it is possible to find a solution that goes beyond a mere compromise and allows everyone to reach their goals. (p. 395)

This might be obvious, but we are here to tell you that it is easier said than done. We often introduce this concept to our students by engaging in a simple demonstration. We ask for two volunteers to come up in front of the class and arm wrestle with each other. The rules are that each time one participant pins the other, he receives a dollar as a reward. We tell them that they have one minute to get as many pins as possible. What would you do if you were one of those students? What typically happens is that the two struggle against one another, trying with all their might to pin the other whom they perceive as their opponent. As a result, very few pins are recorded and very little money is earned. If they approached the task with a win-win outlook, they would quickly realize that the way to maximize earnings is to offer no resistance, and merely take turns quickly pinning one another. With this frame of mind they could conceivably pin each other as often as once per second and each walk away with a bulging wallet.

9.3.1 Win-Lose or Lose-Win Outcomes

The model that has been ingrained in almost all of us is one of competition, not cooperation, leading to **win-lose outcomes** where (hopefully) you win and they lose, or **lose-win outcomes** where you lose and the other person wins. Think about it. Sports are based on win-lose. Card games and board games are also based on win-lose. Similarly our educational system is based on a win-lose paradigm where students are compared to each other, with some coming out on top with As and Bs, and others winding up on the bottom with Ds and Fs. Admissions to most universities and access to scholarships and grants are dependent on how you stack up against your fellow students on various measures. So it is not surprising that we hang a frame of win-lose when approaching most situations, even when such a frame does not yield the most effective results. We often fail to realize that other frameworks even exist.

If you are playing tennis, or chess, basketball, or any other competitive event, we recommend that you still put your focus on beating your opponent. After all, it would get really boring to shoot hoops if you let each other score without playing defense. However, we strongly recommend extreme caution in trying to win in the arena of interpersonal relationships, whether at home or at work. If someone asked you who was winning at your marriage or at your relationship, we hope you would recognize the absurdity of this question. Yet most often, spouses with troubled marriages enter marital counseling with the hope that the psychotherapist will choose their side and explain to their partner how wrong they are. You see, they are hoping the psychologist will declare them the winner and their partner the loser. Perhaps this helps to explain why over fifty percent of marriages end up in divorce. It is explained rather early on in the process of marital therapy that in interdependent relationships if you are both not winning, you both end up losing in the long run.

9.3.2 Lose-Lose Outcomes

A **lose-lose** outlook is one which assumes that none of the participants can get what they want and neither side is satisfied with the outcome. It's hard to imagine how anyone could deliberately go for a lose-lose outcome, yet this is a fairly common way of failing to resolve conflict. Since both parties have their focus solely on winning, they fail to realize that as a result of their struggle they often both end up losers. Perfect examples of this on the global scene are the many wars which have been waged throughout history. On an interpersonal level most of us have witnessed battles of pride where both parties dig in their heels and end up losing in order to save face.

9.3.3 Other Possible Outcomes

Covey, who taught us to "Think Win-Win" in his popular *Seven Habits* book (1991), also lists two other possible outcomes. One alternative is to go for **Win** without concern for whether the other party loses or wins. Here the outcome for the other party is irrelevant. You don't necessarily want to defeat the other person, your only concern is whether your needs get met. Another possibility is what Covey refers to as **Win-Win or No Deal**. Here each party agrees that if they cannot find a solution that is mutually beneficial then there is no deal. They would then walk away agreeing to disagree. This is more common in the context of a business deal where parties negotiate and discover that a mutually beneficial arrangement is not possible so they agree not to enter into the deal. This is a far better outcome than if the parties entered into a business relationship, deal, or contract which later turned out poorly, and led to disillusionment and conflict.

9.3.4 Win-Win Outcomes

Good relationships embody the ability to compromise, to find ways that allow each party to get some of what they need. Great relationships embody the ability to synergize. That is, they find ways for both parties to collaborate and create means that allow for the needs of each to be met. In other words, they find a way for everyone to win. As Covey has said, "this requires courage and consideration." Courage helps us stand up for what we need. Consideration allows us to honor the fact that others feel their needs as deeply as we feel ours. Consider this story for a moment...

> *Two young girls are fighting over a single remaining orange. Both simply insist that they need it. In a win-lose relationship one of the children will end up with the orange, and one will end up with nothing but bad feelings and a desire to win the next time. In a good relationship they will cut the orange in half and share it. They will compromise and this is better than one of them losing. Neither, however, is completely satisfied. In a great relationship they speak to one another about why they want the orange. As it turns out, one of them needs the peel for a recipe and the other simply wants some orange juice. Both can have everything they want because they had the courage to speak up for themselves and the consideration to listen.*

It is also important to note that the value of win-win solutions is deeply ingrained in our evolutionary history and brain structure. All primates seem to have an inherent negative reaction to what they perceive as unfair treatment. When capuchin monkeys are subjected to witnessing another monkey get a treat while they get none, their interest in continuing to interact with the researchers plummets (Brosnan and de Waal, 2003). Humans are no different. When subjected to unfair conditions while playing a game, an area of the brain, the anterior insula, increases in activation. This part of the brain also reacts when we taste something disgusting, and the more active it is the less we are interested in cooperation. We seem to have a deep attraction to fairness and win-win solutions that probably can be traced to how vital cooperation was and is to our survival (Sanfey & colleagues, 2003).

BARRIERS TO WIN-WIN   It is obvious that win-win resolutions to conflict are superior to win-lose and lose-lose solutions. Why is it then that win-win outcomes are rare? There are three basic obstacles to win-win solutions with the first being that often people are oblivious to the possibility of a win-win solution. As mentioned beforehand in the arm wrestling example, we are all socialized to be competitive and to mistakenly define winning as defeating our opponent.

A bigger barrier that prevents many people from seeking win-win solutions is anger or resentment. Disagreements and conflicts are often emotional affairs where people get so caught up in their emotions, in their need to be right, to win, or come out on top, that they reflexively resort to a combative approach without stopping to consider other alternatives. The latter part of this chapter deals with handling anger. Learning to work through negative emotions constructively will help put you in the frame of mind necessary to think clearly and be open to win-win possibilities.

Lastly, win-win outcomes are unusual because they require the cooperation of the other person as well. No matter how creative and open you are to generating a win-win outcome, it can be difficult to do so if the other person's primary agenda is to defeat you. In this case the challenge is to persuade the other to see how a spirit of cooperation is in his or her best interests as well as yours.

The Global Perspective
Reducing the Gap—A Global Win-Win

At the Seattle Special Olympics, nine contestants, all physically or mentally disabled, assembled at the starting line for the 100-yard dash. At the gun, they all started out, not exactly in a dash, but with a relish to run the race to the finish and win. All, that is, except one little boy who stumbled on the asphalt, tumbled over a couple of times, and began to cry. The other eight heard the boy's agonizing lament and despite their desire to cross the finish line first, slowed down and looked back. Then, to the surprise of most of the spectators, they all turned around and returned. Every one of them rushed to lend aid to their competitor. One girl with Down's syndrome bent down and kissed him and said, "This will make it better." Then all nine linked arms and walked together to the finish line. Not a soul in the stadium remained sitting as the sound of awe and appreciation erupted. The cheering and clapping went on for several minutes. Why did the crowd react with such emotion? Because these young people that we call "retarded" were showing

their deep understanding of the reality of life. What matters in this life is more than winning for us. What matters in this life is helping others win, even if it means slowing down and changing our course.

In Chapter 2, you learned that the disparity between the haves and the have-nots has grown to a staggering 73 to 1 ratio. In fact, a more accurate description of the economic reality of the world today would be to divide it into the haves, have-nots, and have-lots. Truth be told, the poverty rate on our planet remains untamed. A recent United Nations report revealed that about 40 percent of the world's people struggle to survive on less than two dollars a day! That means 2.5 billion people in a world housing about 6 billion people must make due with less than what we typically pay daily for watching cable television. At the 2005 United Nations general meeting, Sri Lankan President Chandrika Kumaratunga said "it is unconscionable" to let 6 million children die from malnutrition before their fifth birthdays and to have more

(Continued)

than 50 percent of Africa's people suffer from diseases caused by contaminated drinking water. At the same meeting of world leaders, Peruvian President Alejandro Toledo warned, "poverty and exclusion conspire against peace, security, and democracy."

"I am what I am because of what we all are," an old South African proverb wisely reminds us. As you learned in this chapter, the paradigm of interpersonal effectiveness is "win-win." As global citizens, we must extend this paradigm beyond our family, community, or nation, to include our whole human family. What would win-win look like on a global scale? From an economic perspective, most experts agree that it would mean reducing the gap between the have-lots and have-nots. Thomas P. M. Barnett (2003) in his book, *The Pentagon's New Map – War and Peace in the Twenty-First Century*, argues that to ensure domestic security the new paradigm for defense of the United States must include bridging the divide between what he describes as the Functional Core nations and the Non-Integrating Gap nations - namely, the Caribbean Rim, Africa, the Balkans, The Caucasus, Central Asia, the Middle East, Southwest Asia, and much of Southeast Asia.

Yet for this to truly be win-win, the bridge between the Core and the Gap must not be built at the expense of the environment, for to do so would be to enter into a win-lose with our children and grandchildren. The world's snowcaps are changing drastically. Greenhouse gases are increasing. Our rainforests are being depleted. The River of Grass, our Everglades, is drying up. We cannot develop the Gap without regard to dwindling resources and increasing pollution. Instead, we must practice what the World Commission on Environment and Development described as **Sustainable Development**. Sustainable Development is development that meets the needs of the present without compromising the ability of future generations to meet their own needs (World Commission on Environment and Development, 1987, p. 43). Sustainable Development makes sense not just environmentally, but economically as well. As a prime example, consider the country of Haiti, where a shortsighted vision led to the depletion of their forests and natural resources and a population that is mired in poverty and squalor. We cannot afford to indulge in what has been called the "fallacy of the commons." Countries cannot make use of our shared resources, our "commons," such as our oceans, our energy sources, our very air, as if they were unending. As global citizens we must be good stewards of our planet. Describe what win-win would look like on a global scale.

MENTAL SETS ESSENTIAL FOR WIN-WIN   Effective individuals operate from a model of looking for win-win solutions to disagreements or conflicts, whenever possible. As stated before, not all situations lend themselves to win-win outcomes, but in the arena of interpersonal relationships, most conflicts can be approached from a standpoint of cooperation. There are three mental sets that you will need to incorporate into your way of thinking that are prerequisites to generating win-win options and win-win solutions.

1. MAKING DEPOSITS INTO THE EMOTIONAL BANK ACCOUNT   In order for win-win to be possible, both parties need to trust one another. But how do you build trust? Covey (1991) coined the concept of an **emotional bank account** which we hold with each other just by virtue of being in a relationship. We continually make withdrawals from and deposits into this bank account. The amount of trust experienced in a relationship is directly proportional to the balance in this account. Consider a romantic relationship. When you first meet the person, you make numerous deposits into the emotional bank account. You are attentive and complementary, you listen because you really want to get to know the other person. You call them often, spend time with them, and maybe exchange gifts. Perhaps you might even put the object of your desire up on a pedestal. But as so often happens after the novelty wears off, you begin to take the other person for granted. You stop making as many deliberate deposits. There is a tendency to assume that the balance will stay static. After all, you have made many deposits. You forget that you make withdrawals just because you have different needs or because you may, at times, act in an insensitive fashion. As time passes, all the little withdrawals add up, and you no longer have funds in the account. That is when the relationship gets into trouble.

Our ongoing relationships, like marriage, parenthood, or business partnerships, require frequent, ongoing deposits. Old deposits evaporate if you don't replenish them. If you run into an old friend that you haven't seen for years, it is often possible to pick up right where you left off because your earlier deposits are still there and there have been no withdrawals. But with people that you interact with regularly, more frequent investment is necessary. Remember, you are likely oblivious to some of your withdrawals. In fact, recent research in positive psychology indicates that for relationships (other than marriage) to thrive, a ratio of least 3 to 1 positive to negative interactions must exist (Gottman, 1994). Covey recommends six types of deposits that help build the fund in your emotional bank account with another:

- **Understand the Individual**—In order to make deposits, you must first know what the other considers a deposit. You can only do this by learning to really listen to learn about a person's needs or interests. Remember that what may be a deposit for you may be meaningless or even a withdrawal for someone else.

- **Attend to the Little Things**—Oftentimes it is the little things that count the most. Small insensitive things that you do or forget to do add up to be large withdrawals. On the other hand, those small niceties or favors that you do for another are often the purest proof that you care. In fact, frequent small deposits typically lead to larger balances than the occasional huge deposit. *In relationships, the little things are the big things.*

- **Keep Your Commitments**—Remember the power of your word. Keeping your promises constitutes a major deposit and is an essential element of trust. Breaking your promises, particularly if this happens regularly, constitutes a major withdrawal.

- **Clarify Your Expectations**—You can create many problems and potential withdrawals by assuming that your expectations are self-evident and understood by the other person. *Keep in mind, other people are not mind readers.* It is a major deposit to make your expectations explicit and clear right from the beginning.

- **Show Personal Integrity**—Integrity embodies many things, all of which are essential for trust to develop. Integrity is more than just being honest or keeping your word. It is also about being loyal and fair. One of the best ways you can show that you are loyal and fair is by acting this way towards those who are *not* present. If you are two-faced and criticize or gossip about others behind their back, those present can't help but wonder if you will do the same to them.

- **Apologize Sincerely When You Make a Withdrawal**—Those with integrity admit when they have been wrong and apologize from the heart. It takes courage and healthy self-esteem to do this. A genuine apology will typically constitute a major emotional bank account deposit into any relationship.

2. GIVING UP BEING RIGHT   When relating to others, one of the strongest barriers to cooperation is our incredibly strong need to be right. It seems that human beings are the kind of beings who just need to be right. And this seems to be the case only with humans. Think about it, animals clearly do not display this tendency. For example, if a stray dog was used to frequenting a certain restaurant to feast on leftovers and steak bones in the garbage, and then suddenly the restaurant discontinued the practice of having easily accessible leftovers, the dog would no doubt return several times to check it out, but he would then roam elsewhere in search of a good meal. Doggy is able to forget about being right. He just switches his behavior to something else that works. Animals don't care about being right; they just want to be happy. People, on the other hand, are a different story. If a group of people was used to eating a certain favored dish in a restaurant and it was taken off the menu, they would first complain bitterly. If the restaurant did not capitulate, they then might form a committee to investigate the problem further. They might decide to picket the restaurant or call for a boycott. Perhaps they would even sue the restaurant for denying them their constitutional right to their favorite meal. But all the time they were being right they would be hungry!

Interpersonally effective individuals realize that always needing to be right does not lead to satisfying relationships. Instead they operate from the premise that they would rather be happy than right. We suggest that when involved in interpersonal struggles, you ask yourself the question: Would I rather be right or happy? You see, being happy often requires giving up the need to be right. Please understand that giving up being right does not necessarily imply that you are wrong. It just means that you switch your focus from winning the argument or disagreement to accepting that there are probably valid aspects to each viewpoint. Remember the lessons from Chapter 1? There is no substitute for your willingness to experiment with different pairs of glasses and notice what happens when you do. In other words, there is no right way to see things. Of all the possible ways of looking at the world, the one most guaranteed to impede your effectiveness and create conflict is the one that insists that your way of seeing things is the right way.

Giving up trying to always be right is a really hard thing to do. Why? We all love being right. Right? We've been taught since our youngest days to do the "right thing" according to the authority figures that surround us. We are rewarded for it. We feel good about ourselves for doing it. We try to figure out what the right thing is because we want to succeed, to win. Our culture worships winning.

We remember the winners and display their names prominently in our stadiums, magazines and commercials. Winners generally make a lot of money. The losers don't get the endorsements, the high praise. When you win you typically feel good about yourself. Losing often hurts. And losing can be stressful and threatening to your self-esteem. The key is to remember that in the long run, in interpersonal relations, if all parties involved do not win, then you all lose.

3. STEPPING INTO THE SHOES OF THE OTHER   But practically speaking, how do you give up the need to be right, to win in your personal relationships? When we are trying to be right, by definition we see the other as wrong in their point of view, in their way of thinking. In order to go for a win-win solution to a problem

The Global Perspective
The Elephant in the Room

What if what unites us is more than we realize, and what divides us is less than we fear?

Let's Talk America

There is a famous poem about six blind men in India who get into a heated argument about the nature of elephants. It seems that each of them approached the elephant at a different place and from a different angle, and each decided that he knew the true nature of the elephant. One decided it was like a wall because he had encountered the side of the animal. Another believed it was like a snake because he had grabbed the trunk. The others concluded that an elephant was really like a tree, a fan, a rope and a spear because they happened to approach from another angle. The poem concluded that they argued all night long about who was right and who was wrong. This poem is really a short hand summary of politics and competing cultures. Everyone is prone to believing that their point of view is *the truth, the right way*. We tend to seek out others who agree with us and read and listen to sources of information that assure us that we are right and the others are wrong. Via selective perception, we are more prone to notice facts or data that support our beliefs, while we ignore or are oblivious to that which may contradict our views. We don't stop there either. We often make the other evil, stupid, corrupt, sinister, unholy and/or dangerous. We assume we know what they are really like and what

they really want, and therefore real communication is unnecessary. After all, we already know *the truth*.

This polarized way of thinking is dangerous. It has conflict built into it and ignores some obvious facts of our existence on Earth. Fact one: No one knows or can even speak to the full depth of the mystery of our existence. Fact two: We all come from the same beginnings, and all aspects of life on this planet are interconnected and interdependent. Fact three: We don't perceive the absolute truth but instead view the world through frames that we have assimilated through immersion in our families and culture.

Here is the bottom line. We must move beyond seeing one another in rigid categories. Labeling each other as liberal/conservative, pro-choice/pro-life, right/left, infidel/faithful, American/anti-American, and then pretending to listen to one another when we have really already decided what the other is about, will not solve the problems that we face. We must communicate, especially with those we think are so different from us. The next time you are in a conflict with someone, ask yourself, "Which part of the elephant am I grabbing?" When we take the time to really look through each other's eyes, we get a clearer picture of the world on which we all must ride. Think of a recent conflict you'd had with someone. How might asking, "Which part of the elephant am I grabbing?" have helped you resolve the situation?

it helps to be able to step into the other person's shoes and experience the world through their eyes. To accomplish this we suggest that you use the skills of visualization and imagination that we have discussed earlier. Start the process by doing your relaxing breathing, and then begin to allow a sense of the other to form in your mind. See that person in detail. Notice the facial expressions. Pay attention to the language communicated through the body, the nonverbal communications. Hear not only the words spoken by the person, but the tone, tempo and volume of their speech. Speculate about what that individual might be feeling. As you do this, imagine that you can step into his body and look out of his eyes. Hear yourself saying the words and thinking the thoughts that person might be thinking until you can feel what he is feeling. Do this until you can feel his sense of being right. Then step back into your own body and notice if you feel any differences. Could he possibly feel as strongly as you do? Is it possible that his position has merit as well? Remember, the idea is not necessarily to give up your position and adopt his, though that might happen. The idea is to move yourself to a place where you can work towards both of you meeting your needs, where both of you can win. Allowing yourself to feel, think and experience the other person's viewpoint is a powerful way of facilitating the process of win-win.

9.3.5 When Not to Try for Win-Win

Given that not every situation will lend itself to a win-win outcome, despite your best intentions, how do you know beforehand whether to approach a conflict from a win-win standpoint? Adler and Towne (1993) offer some guidelines to help you tailor your approach. They recommend that you:

1. Consider giving in to the other person and accepting a lose-win outcome when...

   - you discover that you are in the wrong.
   - the issue is very important to other person and of minimal importance to you.
   - other people need to learn a valuable lesson by making a mistake.
   - the long term cost of winning outweighs the short term gains of such.

2. Consider a compromise when...

   - sufficient time does not exist to forge a win-win solution.
   - the issue is not important enough to spend time in further negotiation.
   - the other person is definitely not open to a win-win outcome.

3. Consider competing and going for a win-lose outcome when...

   - the issue is very important to you, the other person is certain to take advantage of you if you approach the situation in a noncompetitive fashion, and you are really not concerned with establishing a long term relationship.

4. Consider cooperation and trying for a win-win outcome when...

- the issue is too vital to settle for a compromise.
- a long term relationship between you and the other is at stake or in jeopardy.
- the other person is willing to cooperate.

CONFLICT RESOLUTION When conflicts or disagreements erupt between friends, lovers, spouses or relatives, typically the problem is approached in an informal fashion. Ideally, all parties express their positions and needs, possible options and solutions are discussed, and eventually a consensus is forged. Giving up being right and a willingness to step into the shoes of the other allows the creation of a climate conducive for effective problem-solving, as well as the possibility of a win-win outcome. We recommend that all parties agree to a time and place for a discussion, preferably when everyone is relatively calm. When conflict or disagreement exists between people who do not have emotional bonds with each other, the steps to effecting what has come to be called in the literature as "conflict resolution" tend to become more formalized. The rules for resolving conflicts in formalized settings such as in business, or the workplace, or in mediation situations such as a divorce are covered in Chapter 14.

Questions

1. A key component of interpersonal effectiveness involves looking for
_____ outcomes.
   A. win-lose
   B. win-win
   C. lose-lose
   D. synergistic

2. For win-win outcomes to be possible trust must be built. What is a good way to build that trust?
   A. Ignore the little things and only focus on big things.
   B. Hide your expectations.
   C. Make deposits in the emotional bank account of the other.
   D. Insist that you are right.

3. When should you abandon looking for a win-win outcome?
   A. when the issue is of vital importance to you and the other party
   B. when a long-term relationship between you and the other is in jeopardy
   C. when the other is willing to cooperate
   D. when other people need to learn a valuable lesson by making a mistake

9.4 Empathy

Recognize the benefits and challenges of putting ourselves into the shoes of others.

In the previous sections we expounded upon the importance of looking for win-win solutions for resolving conflicts. We explained that in order to do this it was often helpful, and sometimes even vital to step into the shoes of the other. It is this that enables us to have **empathy**. According to Martin Bolt (2004) in *Pursuing Human Strengths*:

> . . . *philosophers and psychologists have claimed that empathy is the bedrock of human morality . . . but compassion is more than a rule. In many respects, it is the most natural thing in the world. Most of us come hard wired for empathy. Newborns cry in response to the sound of another infant's cry. In hospital nurseries, one newborn's distress can evoke a chorus of crying. Rudimentary forms of compassion and helping—for example, offering a toy to a distraught sibling—can be observed in children before their second birthday.* (pgs. 57–58)

The term empathy was first used by psychologist Edward Bradford Titchener back in 1909 in reference to the tendency of observers to project themselves inside the scene of a painting. Modern conceptions of this term refer to our ability to imagine how the world looks through the eyes of another. As we see what they see, we can also begin to feel what they feel. Our heart begins to resonate with the heart of the other and we feel the emotional impact of the other person's experience. Batson and his colleagues (2005) define empathy as "an other oriented emotional response elicited by and congruent with the perceived welfare of someone else." Empathy is closely linked to compassion, a term derived from the Latin *cum passio*, which means "to suffer alongside the other."

Science has recently discovered the existence of **mirror neurons** in our brains which seem to explain, in part, our capacity for empathy and our ability to learn through observation. Mirror neurons may provide the neurological basis for the empathic response. These neurons have the ability to fire in the exact pattern that they would have to fire in order to execute the behavior that is being observed. In other words, as you watch a friend juggle, eat soup, or scratch his ear, the same areas in your brain that would juggle, eat, or scratch are also stimulated. Rizzolatti and Craighero (2004) recounted how mirror neurons were first discovered in animals. But they have now been directly observed in humans (Ramachandran, 2000). We appear to be literally hardwired to be empathic. When former President Bill Clinton said, "I feel your pain," he was not just playing politics. He was speaking to a deep truth about humanity's interconnectedness. We all have the ability and are even compelled by our biology to be empathic. To differing degrees, we all, unless we have a lack of these neurons, feel each other's pain; but we also feel all the other emotions as well. It has even been speculated that a deficiency in the network of mirror neurons may underlie some disorders such as autism, which is, in part, characterized by an inability to emotionally connect with others (Oberman and colleagues, 2006).

It has been empirically demonstrated that stepping into the shoes of the other leads to empathy. Stotland (1969) conducted a study where subjects watched a patient undergo what they were led to believe was a painful medical procedure. One group of observers was instructed to imagine how the patient felt during the painful treatment. The other group of observers was instructed to merely watch the patient's movements. Not surprisingly, the group instructed to step into the patient's shoes manifested greater psychophysiological arousal and reported stronger empathic feelings than the other group.

To get a sense of your own level of empathy, fill out the following Empathy Self-Assessment, designed by Mark Davis (1980).

Empathy Self-Assessment

For each item, indicate the degree to which the statement is self–descriptive using the following scale.

0	1	2	3	4
Does not Describe me well				**Describes me very well**

___ 1. Before criticizing somebody, I try to imagine how I would feel if I were in their place.

___ 2. If I'm sure I'm right about something, I don't waste much time listening to other people's arguments.

___ 3. I try to understand my friends better by imagining how things look from their perspective.

___ 4. I believe there are two sides to every question and try to look at them both.

___ 5. I sometimes find it difficult to see things from the "other guy's" point of view.

___ 6. I try to look at everybody's side of a disagreement before I make a decision.

___ 7. When I'm upset with someone, I usually try to put myself in his or her shoes for a while.

___ 8. When I see someone being taken advantage of, I feel kind of protective toward him or her.

___ 9. When I see someone being treated unfairly, I sometimes don't feel very much pity for him or her.

___ 10. I often have tender, concerned feelings for people less fortunate than I am.

___ 11. I would describe myself as a pretty soft-hearted person.

___ 12. Sometimes I don't feel very sorry for other people when they are having problems.

___ 13. Other people's misfortunes do not usually disturb me a great deal.

___ 14. I am often quite touched by things that I see happen.

___ Total Score

Items 1 through 14 assess one's ability to step outside the self and assume another's perspective. In scoring your responses, first reverse the number before statements 2, 5, 9, 12 and 13 (i.e. 0 = 4, 1 = 3, 2 = 2, 3 = 1, 4 = 0). Then add the numbers in front of all items to obtain a total score. Average scores are 28 to 30; higher scores indicate a greater capacity for being empathic towards others, for being able to shift your perspective.

9.4.1 Benefits of Empathy

If you have the ability to empathize with others, it brings with it a vast array of potential benefits to you as an individual, as well as to those in relationship with you, or who come within your sphere of influence. Since empathy enables you to have more compassion for others, you will be less likely to be totally self-absorbed, which frees you to be more responsive or helpful to others. This, in turn, gives you increased opportunities to live your life with a greater sense of meaning and purpose. Batson, Ahmed, Lishner & Tsang (2005) reviewed over 25 studies and concluded that empathy clearly leads to the altruistic motivation to be helpful. Thus, when you are empathic you will be more likely to be responsive to the people in your life and they will theoretically benefit. For example, Schroeder, Penner, Dovidio, & Piliavan (1995) reported on a series of studies which demonstrated a strong relationship between scores on the Empathy Self-Assessment and prosocial action, whether it involved volunteering at the Special Olympics or responding to an unexpected request for help. Unger and Thumuluri (1997) found that among 400 adults with heavy involvement in charitable organizations, all were high scorers on empathic measures.

When we see other people in distress, particularly strangers, this often makes us feel uncomfortable and we may want to try to avoid this by finding a way out of the situation. But having empathy for the affected party can lead to a response of helping rather than leaving the scene. For example, Batson and colleagues (1981) conducted a study where they had subjects watch a young woman called "Elaine" receive what appeared to be a series of painful electric shocks. They then instilled empathy in some of the subjects by informing them about how similar they were to Elaine in many ways. Elaine then told the subjects a story about a childhood accident that made her exceptionally sensitive to the pain of electric shocks. At that point the researchers gave all subjects the option of taking Elaine's place and receiving the rest of the shocks that she was due to receive. Some of the subjects were told that they could leave at that time (i.e. escape was possible), while others had to stay and watch Elaine's next shock session. Those who felt empathy for Elaine chose to take her place whether they could have escaped or not. Those without empathic concern for her were far more likely to choose to leave and avoid the discomfort of watching Elaine in pain.

The ability to empathize with others and to convert this into being helpful has been linked to happiness, as was discussed in Chapter 7. Rimland (1982) noted that people devoted primarily to making themselves happy, who we might deem as rather selfish, tend to be far less happy than those who are committed to making others happy. The Global Perspective in Chapter 7 titled the "Power of Service" discussed what has come to be called the *do good, feel good effect*, referring to how psychological and physical well-being are enhanced as a result of helping others due to empathy-induced altruism. In that same section we also cited a study which indicated that compassion, empathy, and helping others appear to contribute to longevity, allowing us to speculate that perhaps it really is better to give than to receive, after all! Cialdini speculated in a *USA Today* feature (Elias, 2002) that this "helper's high" may boost the immune system and lower the output of stress hormones. If this is the case it may help account for the increased longevity of the givers. Refer to Chapter 11 for a more in-depth discussion of altruism.

9.4.2 Blocks to Empathy

The very human tendency to make what we call "snap judgments" is one inherent stumbling block to the development of empathy. As we discussed in depth in Chapter 1, our perceptions are often automatic, based on ingrained, habitual frames of reference, and are not always accurate. Optical illusions dramatically demonstrate for us that things are not always what they seem to be. In the same way, our first impressions of people are not always right. In fact, because first impressions are often based solely on superficial bits of information and sensory data, without any real knowledge of a person's history or any sense of context of their behavior in a given situation, our initial judgments are often widely off the mark. Recognizing this helps to sensitize us to the danger of relying on snap judgments. You will continue to make snap judgments, of course. To do so is only human nature because the demands and pressures of daily life often force us to make quick assessments. But it is important to be open to new information and to be willing to revise your initial impressions. Oftentimes a prerequisite to empathy is a willingness to resist making such snap judgments.

Why is it that people often rush to judgment so quickly? Psychologist Melvin Lerner (1980) suggests that most people hold a deep-seated belief that our world is a just place where people typically get what they deserve. That is, that evil is eventually punished and good is eventually recognized and rewarded; that hard work will be compensated and laziness will ultimately backfire. Furthermore, Lerner holds that people care about justice for themselves and for others and this can motivate them to help others in distress, to some extent in order to validate their worldview that this really is a just world, after all. But conversely, this can also lead people to sometimes find reasons to rationalize injustice, to naively believe that those who are treated well must therefore always be good, and those who are punished must therefore, by definition, always be bad. For example, after World War II, British solders escorted German civilians through a Nazi concentration camp to educate them about the horror. One German remarked that the victims of Nazi atrocities must have been "awful criminals" to have received such abusive treatment at the hands of the Nazis.

One way to prevent a rush to judgment and foster empathy is to heighten awareness of the similarities between people. Individuals who helped to rescue Jews in Nazi-occupied Europe often indicated that it was their perception of common human kinship—a sense of connection to people from diverse backgrounds— that motivated them to take great risks to save the lives of others, some of whom were complete strangers. Those who were rescuers focused on their similarities to others, while non-rescuers tended to focus on how they were different from others. Daloz, Keen, Keen & Parks (1997), in cataloguing the lives of over 100 humanitarians, found that they shared in common the experience of befriending someone whom they had previously thought was very different from them. This experience radically shifted their paradigm about who is and is not one of us.

9.4.3 Cultivating Empathy

How can you learn to become more empathic, to more easily slip your feet into the shoes of others, whether loved ones, friends, or complete strangers in need of help? How do we facilitate the development of social compassion in ourselves and in our children? Research and practice in positive psychology offer the following steps and suggestions:

1. **Practice what is termed *reflective or active listening.*** An in-depth discussion of these techniques is presented in the next chapter in the section on listening skills. Learning to really listen will greatly facilitate your ability to be empathic and compassionate.

2. **Utilize reframing to counteract snap judgments about people.** For example, what other factors could account for a person's attitude or behavior, other than your first assumption?

3. **Engage in *random acts of kindness.*** As we have reiterated over and over, *attitude change follows behavior change.* Acting in a compassionate manner will elicit feelings of compassion. To set the stage for this mindset, watch the movie *Pay it Forward.*

4. **Pay attention to the similarities** between yourself and people from other backgrounds, nationalities, races, or religious faiths. Too often we focus on the differences, which typically promotes detachment. Empathy and compassion are cultivated by appreciating our kinship with our fellow human beings, by seeing ourselves as fellow travelers on Spaceship Earth. All of us at some point in our lives will deal with illness, with the death of a loved one, or the threat of our own death, with the break-up of a valued relationship, or a loss of prestige in some way. All of us are vulnerable to loss, emotional pain, or to suffering, and we share this in common with all our counterparts on this planet. Awareness of this lifts the walls that divide us, and allows empathy to flow.

5. **Engage in community service.** In your role as a student, involve yourself in service learning programs which will give you an opportunity to provide help or service to those in need, while cultivating your empathic side and challenging your pre-conceived notions. In your role as a private citizen, volunteer in your community. Or provide some *pro bono* services at your place of business, if that can be arranged.

6. **Open your heart.** Many times we are touched by heart-rending or heart-warming stories depicted in films, TV, books, the internet, or even in newspaper or magazine articles. Movies, in particular, often allow us to delve into the experience of another person, to see out of their eyes and feel what they

might feel; to really identify with that character. Such experiences can often lead to dramatic shifts in thinking or in our ability to understand the point of view of another person or group who previously had been alien to us. Likewise, we can be educated about the plight of people who are victimized, marginalized or oppressed.

7. **Try on the shoes of the other.** It isn't always possible to "walk a mile in another person's shoes" to understand their experience. But sometimes you will have opportunities, if only briefly, to assume some responsibilities of another. Doing so can help you understand or empathize with that person and their particular struggles in life. For example, a student confided in one of the authors that she was irritated by her mother's complaints about how much work it was to take care of the numerous, beloved family pets. The student had a hard time comprehending why this was such a big deal to her mother, because everyone in the household just adored all the pooches and pussycats. When her mom went on vacation and the task of doggy and kitty sitting (with all the feeding, cleaning and grooming that accompanied this job) fell to her, she suddenly understood what her mom was talking about. After that, when her mom complained, she commiserated with her and offered to help more with the animals rather than rolling her eyes and tuning her out as she did before.

8. **Raise your children to be helpful.** Martin Bolt (2004) offers these suggestions for raising empathic children.

   - Model empathy for your children. Be an empathic parent to teach your children how to relate to others in a compassionate fashion. Establish a warm and nurturing relationship with your kids. Follow the guidelines for authoritative parenting discussed in Chapter 3.

   - Express your own feelings in an appropriate way and show compassion/empathy towards others in front of your children.

   - Tune into your child's emotions. Ask your kids about their feelings and teach them how to express, describe, and label what they are feeling. Doing this will help them to build their own emotional vocabularies.

   - Explain the reasons for things to your children to deepen their understanding of emotional issues. This fosters emotional, as well as intellectual, insight.

   - Encourage your kids to do volunteer work or community service. Many communities require students to do community service as a high school graduation requirement. If you engage in community service activities, your kids will be more likely to follow your lead.

   - Teach your children to value empathy and compassion as desirable traits to possess, as valuable as honesty, or intelligence, or athletic prowess, or creativity, or any of the other talents or character strengths that we attempt to instill in our children.

Questions

1. _____ in the brain provide the neurological basis for the empathic response.

   A. Mirror neurons

   B. Motor neurons

   C. Synaptic pathways

   D. Epigenetic triggers

2. Which of the following is a block to empathy?

   A. stepping into the shoes of another

   B. noticing similarities to another

   C. making snap judgments

   D. opening your heart

3. To cultivate empathy, _____.

   A. trust your snap judgments

   B. step into the shoes of another

   C. attend to how others are different from you

   D. talk about yourself

9.5 The Nature of Anger

Describe the nature of anger and effective methods for managing anger constructively.

As mentioned previously, one of the biggest barriers to a win-win outlook is your anger. Anger motivates you to want to win, to defeat others whom you view as opponents or adversaries. Effective individuals have learned to cope with anger, to work it through and manage it constructively rather than destructively. This is essential to adopting a win-win framework. But how do you do this? To answer this question, you first need to understand the nature of anger.

Have you experienced times when you were quick to anger, as if your fuse had become significantly shorter? Unless you are a yogi master and have achieved perfect balance and enlightenment, of course you have. All of us have had periods when we were more irritable and less tolerant. Have you noticed that there is a direct relationship between these periods and the level of stress in your life? Undoubtedly, a very common response to stress is anger and irritability. But why? Remember, stress is your body and mind's response to perceived threat. If you consider that for our ancestors "threat" typically took the form of attacks by animals or other tribes, then anger was an adaptive reaction which mobilized them to take defensive action. Therefore, anger had survival value because typically, for our forebears, the appropriate response was to physically fight for their lives. But in today's world physical confrontations are no longer useful in most situations. Yet, you are left with this holdover emotional baggage of anger. Verbal expression of this anger, particularly if not modulated, is certainly not much more adaptive, either in your personal life or in your work environment.

Violent, unrestrained expression of anger has been at the forefront of national headlines and at the core of many of the most serious problems faced by today's society. The 9/11 attacks on the World Trade Center and the Pentagon and the plethora of mass shootings focused everyone's attention on the profoundly tragic consequences of violence, while highlighting the need to understand the underpinnings of anger and to develop methods to prevent future bloodshed. Meanwhile, we all struggle to understand why adolescents and college students have engaged in school slaughters over the last few decades, and why adults bring firearms to work and shoot co-workers and innocent bystanders. Has our world become more violent, or is it the ever-present media coverage which gives this impression? By the same token, is domestic abuse, of both children and spouses, on the rise? Or is domestic violence just more routinely reported and publicized? Either way it is clear that violence is a serious problem with which we must all contend, so as to avoid either becoming a victim or a perpetrator of such. Learning to co-exist is of paramount importance, and the prevention of violence first involves learning to handle anger.

But anger is a basic human emotion that we all experience from time to time, sometimes to the level where we can lose control of our behavior and/or resort to aggression. According to a study by Averill (1983), most people report being angry, at least to the point of getting mildly annoyed, several times weekly. Researcher Diane Tice (1993) found that anger is the emotion that people have the hardest time controlling. Making it even harder is the fact that for some, anger can be energizing or even exhilarating at times, leading to something akin to a rage addiction in certain individuals.

Many theorists have attempted to explain the root causes of anger and aggression. An early theory, the **frustration-aggression hypothesis** (Dollard, Miller, Doob, Mowrer, & Sears, 1939), focused on the role of frustration as a result of being blocked from reaching a goal as a primary factor. Most psychologists readily acknowledge the role of frustration in the development of anger, but agree that other variables are equally important. Freud postulated that humans have an inborn aggressive drive which contributes to personality formation. Furthermore, Freud recommended pursuing an emotional release, which he called **catharsis**, by venting or acting out anger. This, as you will read more about later, is not advisable. There is also some evidence that testosterone levels are related to levels of aggression, but this is based on correlational studies so causation cannot be conclusively inferred.

Currently there is a greater emphasis on the role of learning histories as the primary factor in the etiology of anger. That is, an individual will exhibit anger and hostile behaviors to the extent that anger has been rewarded and modeled (Cantor, 1999). Likewise, to the extent that anger was punished and inhibition of such was modeled, an individual will display the ability to control anger and restrain aggression. Research indicates that merely observing violence can trigger heightened aggression (Bandura, 1965; Lemish, 1998). As a result, there is a lot of controversy today over the role of observational learning or modeling on the expression of anger, particularly in children. Consequently, the debate rages over the extent to which children should be allowed to watch violent movies or TV programs or play violent video games. There is research which suggests that long term viewing of violent TV shows can cause children, particularly boys, to behave more aggressively. One study found that eight year old boys who preferred violent programs were more aggressive at that age, as well as at age eighteen, as compared to a group of boys who preferred less violent entertainment (Lefkowitz, Eron, Walder, & Huesmann, 1977). But because this was correlational research, again it is unclear whether this was a cause or an effect. That is, was their preference a function of a more violent disposition, or did watching violent shows create more violent kids? Bushman & Phillips (2001) concluded that "the fact that TV violence does not noticeably increase violence in everybody does not mean that TV does not increase violence in anybody." That is, highly aggressive individuals are likely to be drawn to violent media, and after watching violent movies their aggression levels will be heightened (Black & Bevan, 1992). Regarding the effects of video games, the best evidence was summarized by Craig Anderson & colleagues (2010) who conducted a meta-analysis of 400 studies with over 130,000 participants. They concluded that playing violent video games did increase aggression. Furthermore, this finding applied to children and young adults in North America, Japan and Western Europe.

When is anger likely to lead to violence? There is no foolproof method for predicting who will become aggressive and when violence will occur, but there are factors (Capaldi & Patterson, 1996) which are associated with the likelihood that an individual will engage in violent expression of anger, including:

- a previous history of violent behavior
- having been physically abused in childhood
- having witnessed violence in the home as a child
- a history of harming animals as a child
- heavy exposure to violent TV programs or video games
- absence of remorse over hurting others
- family history of mental illness or violence
- brain damage (which can interfere with the brain's inhibitory mechanisms)

ROAD RAGE One common situation where many individuals experience anger, often to irrational levels, is while they are driving. Does this ever happen to you? This common phenomenon, dubbed **road rage**, is on the rise, reportedly increasing by 7% yearly since 1990. A leading researcher in this area, Jerry Deffenbacher (1994), surveyed 1500 college drivers and identified the following six situations likely to trigger road rage emotions and behaviors:

- hostile gestures from other drivers
- other drivers breaking traffic laws
- the presence of a police car
- another driver driving too slowly
- driver discourtesy such as being cut off or slow driving in the passing lane
- traffic jams or obstructions

Everyone feels aggravation on the road sometimes, but for some individuals, driving to work every day is a never-ending exercise in fury. To determine whether you have a problem with road rage, fill out the following questionnaire which will compare you with other college students. High scorers are three times more likely to experience road rage than low scorers. You are prone to experience road rage if you are likely to personalize the mistakes or behaviors of other drivers, to view these incidents as personal affronts.

Road Rage Scale

This test describes common, potentially anger provoking situations that occur during driving. Imagine that each of the situations described is actually happening to you while driving. Then rate the amount of anger that would be provoked in each situation using the following rating scale:

1 Not at all **2 A little** **3 Some** **4 Much** **5 Very much**

_____ 1. Someone makes an obscene gesture toward you about your driving.

_____ 2. You pass a radar speed trap.

_____ 3. Someone runs a red light or stop sign.

_____ 4. Someone honks at you about your driving.

_____ 5. Someone is weaving in and out of traffic.

_____ 6. A police officer pulls you over.

_____ 7. You are driving behind a large truck and cannot see around it.

_____ 8. A bicyclist is riding in the middle of the lane and slowing traffic.

_____ 9. Someone is slow in parking and holding up traffic.

_____ 10. A truck kicks up sand or gravel on the car you are riding in.

_____ 11. Someone speeds up when you try to pass them.

_____ 12. A slow vehicle on a mountain road will not pull over and let people by.

_____ 13. Someone backs right out in front of you without looking.   (Continued)

_____ 14. You are stuck in a traffic jam.

_____ **Total Score**

Interpretation: The higher your score the more likely you are easily provoked and angered while driving. Compare your level of driving anger with that of other college students on the chart below. The percentile tells the percentage of students who scored at or below your level.

Score	Percentile		Score	Percentile		Score	Percentile
21	0		41	25		52	72
26	1		42	28		54	79
30	3		43	32		56	86
32	5		45	40		57	89
35	10		47	50		59	93
38	17		49	60		60	95
40	22		50	64		64+	99

9.5.1 The Physiology of Anger

So what can you do about learning to control your anger and modulate your expression of it? First, it is important that you understand the physiology of anger. Goleman (1995) offers an illuminating explanation of why certain individuals sometimes "go off the deep end" and respond impulsively and explosively with anger. He refers to such outbursts as **emotional hijacking** and explains this in terms of brain circuitry as outlined in the work of LeDoux (1992). Our brains have two basic neural response systems, one governed by a brain structure called the **amygdala**, a center in our primitive brain, and the other controlled by the **prefrontal cortex**, the thinking brain or seat of higher reasoning and planning, responsible for the before-mentioned executive functions. By the way, the prefrontal cortex is the last part of the brain to develop. Its axons do not fully complete the process of myelination until age 25 or later. When a myelin layer is completed, the speed at which impulses travel along the myelinated fiber is greatly enhanced. This is also the first part of the brain affected by alcohol. It is especially vulnerable to substances, like alcohol, which dampen its ability to inhibit your behavior. This is why you are more likely to lose your temper under the influence of alcohol. Emotional explosions, particularly anger, occur when the amygdala perceives what it thinks is an emergency and bypasses the prefrontal cortex. In an instant the amygdala triggers the fight/flight response before the cortex has a chance to process any information, let alone determine how to respond appropriately. And if the prefrontal cortex has not yet fully developed (i.e. myelinated), it is even less capable of exercising restraint.

This capacity to act before you think does have survival value for it gives you the potential to react instantaneously in an emergency so as to avert danger, when taking the time to evaluate the situation might waste precious seconds and endanger your life. The problem is that, for some people, this cortical bypass occurs in many situations where it is not only unnecessary but harmful. Here the brain interprets danger not just from physical threats but also from symbolic threats to our dignity and self-esteem, but the failure to activate the prefrontal cortex typically results in behaviors we later regret. This direct amygdala circuit accounts for those instances when our emotions totally overwhelm our rational minds.

The work of psychologist Dolf Zillman (1989) is also relevant here. In a series of studies Zillman demonstrated how rage reactions develop. Typically, once the fight/flight reaction is activated even mildly, the body remains in a state of heightened arousal, or edginess, for awhile. Then, if later stimuli should mobilize the amygdala and trigger an emotional hijacking, the subsequent emotional response, whether it takes the form of anger or anxiety, is of especially great intensity. This cumulative reaction helps explain why people sometimes greatly overreact to what appears to be only mild provocation.

Physiologically, anger is arousal. When you are angry the fight/flight response has been activated, preparing your body to either fight or flee. Clearly, anger helps you if you need to fight. The problem is that when we are stressed we tend to look around to see what is making us angry. That is, we tend to externalize the sources of our anger and/or stress. We assume that something out there is causing our arousal. This is true, not just with humans, but with our animal cousins as well. For example, imagine a lab rat in a box whose floor is covered with an electric grid. If that rat is alone and we shock it, the rat will jump, look for an escape route, and will manifest clear signs of arousal. If we put another lab rat in the box with our first rat, and then shock them both, the rats will attack each other (Weiss, 1971). It's as if the rats are blaming each other for the shock.

9.5.2 The Role of Attribution in Anger

Often, we behave just like our friends the rats. We look around for who is to blame for our uncomfortable feelings and sensations without being consciously aware of what we are doing. Yet even more problematic, paradoxically, those with whom we feel most comfortable are the most likely targets of our direct aggression. The old saying "you always hurt the ones you love" is really true. Don't get us wrong. We also get angry with people with whom we are not close or comfortable, but we are more likely to express our anger towards them indirectly. This is particularly true if they are in a position of authority over you. So instead of telling your boss how angry you feel, you might just complain to your friends at lunch. Then when you go home at the end of the day and your spouse or significant other does something even mildly annoying, you are ready to bite his head off.

But physiological arousal, in and of itself, does not produce your emotions. *It is how you label this arousal that determines what you feel.* This point was driven home in a classic experiment (Schacter & Singer, 1962) which changed how psychologists viewed emotions. In this study the researchers injected subjects with adrenalin, which can cause powerful arousal reactions, but told them that they were only getting a vitamin shot. The subjects were then exposed to a confederate (e.g. actor) who supposedly received the same injection, but who then behaved in either an angry or euphoric fashion. Subjects exposed to the angry confederate became angry, and those exposed to the euphoric stooge became happy. However, subjects injected with a placebo and also exposed to the same confederates did not have any strong emotional reactions. Schacter, in formulating his **Attribution theory**, concluded that emotion is much more than a physiological event. If humans are faced with physiological arousal of unknown origin, they will search their environment for an appropriate explanation or label for this arousal.

Thus, emotions are created by your evaluation of your internal and external environment. The subjects in Schacter's study attributed their arousal to either anger or elation depending on what appeared to be the case in the environment. If exposed to an angry confederate they interpreted their own arousal as anger and therefore reported being mad. In a similar vein, Berkowitz & Turner (1974) were able to elicit angry behavior from subjects merely by telling them that they were angry. In this study subjects were exposed to the mildly provoking behavior of two confederates and then given false feedback about their arousal levels. How the subjects subsequently behaved toward the actors was directly tied to the level of feedback they received—to how angry they thought they were based solely on inaccurate feedback.

This tendency to attribute the source of your uncomfortable feelings to an external agent further aggravates the problem because "putting it out there" lowers your control. If you perceive that you are not in control in a particular situation, then you are being reactive. And as we mentioned in Chapter 2, we feel we are in control when we believe we have a choice. Well, the fact is that whether or not you get angry or stay angry is really *always* your choice. Being able to recognize this gives you control. You see, it is not the event out there that causes you to flare; it is your interpretation of the situation which ultimately leads you to be, or not to be, angry.

The fact that we have choice as to whether we feel anger, or any feeling for that matter, is the reason why two people can be faced with the same situation yet respond in ways that are completely different. For instance, imagine that you are driving in your car and someone cuts you off, almost causing an accident. The common response is to react with immediate anger and to grumble or even scream at the inconsiderate driver who dared to intrude on your sacred vehicular space. You tell yourself, or him, what an idiot he is, perhaps questioning how he ever obtained a driver's license. The incident may even become an indictment of all the drivers in your city, none of which are as skilled as you. Meanwhile you are stewing in your own juices and continuing to aggravate yourself. You are well on the way to experiencing road rage.

Can you see how the meaning you gave this situation led to your angry response? Is it possible that another meaning, that also explains the other driver's behavior, could lead to a different response? What if, instead of assuming incompetence or inconsideration on the part of the other driver, you said to yourself, "poor guy, he must have a lot on his mind. I wonder what is going wrong for him?" Undoubtedly, were you to ask yourself these questions, your response to the same event would be quite different. Once again we are reminded of Covey's motto, "the way you see the problem is the problem." Not surprisingly, the solution invariably lies in changing the way you view the situation.

9.5.3 Anger and the Type A Personality

But you might be sitting there saying, "Why should I change? I have a right to be angry!" The truth is, you are correct. You do have a right to be angry, but are you happy with the results? Persistent or frequent anger has serious deleterious effects on your emotional and physical well-being, as well as on your ability to be effective. There is no doubt that anger and resentment damage your health. A convincing example of this comes from what we have learned about the **Type A personality**. In the 1970s, cardiologists Meyer Friedman and Ray Rosenman noticed that their patients tended to share certain personality characteristics. They called this cluster of behavioral traits the "Type A personality." Type A individuals tend to be very hard-driving, achievement-oriented, compulsive, overly concerned with time pressure and easy to anger, as compared to **Type B** individuals who are laid back, easygoing, and less concerned with time. A strong relationship was discovered between the Type A orientation and cardiac problems. But later research revealed that the only aspect of Type A behavior that was really related to heart disease was the "hostility" component. That is, one could be hard-driving and compulsive without incurring a greater risk of heart disease if hostility was not present. In one study (Barefoot, Dalhstrom, & Williams, 1983), conducted with physicians who are typically a very Type A group, 250 doctors were administered a hostility scale. Twenty-five years later the mortality rate of the high hostility scorers was several times higher. This has led health psychologists to conclude that of all human emotions, hostility is the deadliest. Anger is particularly harmful to your health when it is repressed or when it is turned back onto yourself. But inappropriate expression of anger towards others is also dangerous to your physical well-being as well as your interpersonal relationships. Hostility that is characterized by brooding resentment, suspicion and frequent angry outbursts is extremely damaging to your health (Smith, 1992). Take a moment to fill out the Hostility Scale to help determine if anger and hostility are a problem for you.

The fact that anger is a risk factor for heart attacks is well-documented. Anger sets off a physiological mechanism that makes your heart beat faster, your blood pressure rise, your coronary arteries constrict, and your blood get stickier. A study of more than 1,000 patients at Mount Zion Medical Center who had survived heart attacks found that those who had counseling to reduce their anger, aggression and hostility had half the rate of recurring heart attacks as those who received no such help dealing with anger (Friedman, Powell, & Thoresen, 1987).

Hostility Scale

Answer the following questions true or false.

_____ I often get annoyed at checkout cashiers or the people in front of me when I'm waiting in line at the supermarket or other stores.

_____ I usually keep an eye on the people I work or live with to make sure they're doing what they should.

_____ I often wonder how extremely fat people can have so little respect for themselves.

_____ Most people will take advantage of you if you let them.

_____ The habits of friends or family members often annoy me.

_____ When I'm stuck in traffic, I often start breathing faster and my heart pounds.

_____ When I'm annoyed with people, I always let them know about it.

_____ If someone wrongs me, I'll get even.

_____ I usually try to have the last word in an argument.

_____ At least once a week, I feel like yelling or even hitting someone.

If you answered "true" to five or more of these questions, you may qualify as excessively hostile.

9.5.4 Catharsis Is Not Always the Answer

There is a mistaken belief that a good way to release anger is to immediately vent it. George Bach, (1968) in his seminal book *The Intimate Enemy*, describes this as the **Vesuvius effect** when you explode like a volcano. Often after such a cathartic expression you do feel better, as if a load has been lifted off your shoulders. While this might work if you are alone in your room hitting your pillow, can you imagine just letting go with your boss? It is safe to say that it probably wouldn't be the most effective strategy. In addition, research indicates that such expressions tend to reinforce the anger, making you quicker to anger in the future. In one such study (Ebbesen & colleagues, 1975), 100 frustrated employees recently laid off by an aerospace company were divided into two groups. One group was given an opportunity to vent their anger toward the company via questioning designed to elicit hostility, while the other group discussed neutral topics. Both groups then filled out a questionnaire assessing their attitudes toward their former employer. Those allowed to vent expressed significantly more anger towards the company. Likewise, Bushman (2002) allowed subjects who had been angered to beat up a punching bag while ruminating about the person who had provoked them. When given a chance for revenge later on these subjects became even more aggressive. Bushman concluded, "Venting to reduce anger is like using gasoline to put out a fire."

This is similar to the earlier conclusion Diane Tice (1993) reached that giving vent to anger typically fails to dispel it and often only intensifies it. She found that it was far more effective for individuals to first cool down and then later, in a constructive, assertive fashion attempt to settle the conflict. Thus, psychologists no longer recommend the catharsis approach espoused by Freud because, in many instances, acting angrily can lead to further anger and perhaps even aggression. The situation in the Middle East between Israel and the Palestinians is the perfect example of this. Both sides justify escalating violence with their "eye for an eye, tooth for a tooth" philosophy. The bloodshed may not end until everyone left alive on both sides is both blind and in need of dentures.

9.5.5 Learning to Control Anger

Is anger always bad for you? Actually, the answer is no. Anger is a normal human reaction. It becomes problematic when it is chronic, persistent and unresolved. There are, in fact, instances when anger can be useful. Anger can be helpful for mobilizing your energy so that you can take appropriate action. If you were never able to get angry you might become so complacent that you would never seek to resolve issues in your life.

The task is not to always prevent anger, but to learn how to move through it efficiently and effectively. We often tell our students that "the only way out is through." You need to be aware of your anger and rather than getting mired in it, recognize it as a signal that something is amiss and must be addressed. Then you can use the energy it creates to mobilize you to take appropriate action. Many other authors and psychologists recommend various systems and methods for avoiding, controlling and redirecting anger. In his book, *The Trusting Heart: Great News about Type A Behavior*, Redford Williams (1989) lists a series of strategies for reducing your hostility level. It is likely that you will find these strategies to be familiar, combining methods outlined in previous as well as upcoming chapters, the only difference being that anger management is the focus. This list represents a good summary of ways to combat hostility.

- Become self-aware. Adopt the witnessing stance and monitor the self-talk which fuels your anger.

- Interrupt angry thoughts. A method called **thought stopping** is very useful here. To use this strategy, wear a rubber band on your wrist and snap it whenever you become aware of engaging in hostile, irrational self-talk. The mild pain you experience from the snap should help interrupt your negative thought patterns and provide an opportunity for you to use cognitive restructuring techniques.

- Cultivate empathy by stepping into the shoes of the other.

- Learn to laugh at yourself. Don't take yourself so seriously. Pay careful attention to the upcoming section on reframing.

- Practice the active relaxation techniques you have learned. Counting to ten before you respond and/or practicing diaphragmatic breathing can help you calm yourself and prepare to respond appropriately instead of impulsively to anger.

- Improve your listening skills. The next chapter will help you in this regard.

- Take the risk to trust others.

- Practice the art of forgiving others. The final section in this chapter will assist you in your personal journey of forgiveness.

Zillman (1989) recommends two main strategies for defusing anger. The first method basically involves using cognitive restructuring and reframing techniques to challenge anger-provoking thoughts, in order to facilitate a reevaluation of the original interpretation that triggered anger in the first place. However, he points out that timing is absolutely crucial in this process. The earlier in the anger sequence this occurs, the more likely it is to be useful for defusing or reducing anger. He refers to a "window of opportunity" for this to work. If anger has already escalated to the point of rage, efforts to think rationally often will not work because of what he terms a state of "cognitive incapacitation," where individuals literally cannot think straight because they are so blinded by rage. Can you ever recall a situation when you were beyond rational thinking because you were so enraged?

Zillman also advises that you pursue a "cooling off period" to defuse anger, that you allow yourself to cool down physiologically by seeking out a setting devoid of further triggers for anger. There are various ways to promote cooling off. Engaging in physical exercise such as walking, jogging, or lifting weights can be very useful because it works off the physical tension built up in fight/flight arousal, and can provide time for you to reflect on the situation and engage in rational thinking. Likewise, involvement in active relaxation techniques such as breathing exercises or progressive muscle relaxation is an excellent way to facilitate cooling off. Or it could be as simple as getting some space from another person during an argument to prevent an unproductive escalation of hostilities. In general, Zillman stresses that distraction is vital to allow for cool down. Many of these activities allow for distraction as well as direct tension reduction. Zillman further emphasizes that this cooling down period will backfire if that time is used to pursue a train of anger-inducing thoughts, for in that case the anger will continue to build rather than dissipate. The power of distraction is that it can derail an angry train of thought. Diane Tice surveyed strategies people use for handling anger, and found most people do find distractions such as watching TV, movies or reading useful in interfering with angry thoughts. But interestingly, she found that common indulgences such as shopping and eating proved to be ineffective distractions, as individuals tended to stew in angry thoughts while engaging in these pursuits (Tice & Baumeister, 1993).

9.5.6 Reframing Revisited

To quote Daniel Goleman:

> The train of angry thoughts that stokes anger is also potentially the key to one of
> the most powerful ways to defuse anger: undermining the convictions that are
> fueling the anger in the first place. The longer we ruminate about what has made
> us angry, the more 'good reasons' and self justifications for being angry we can
> invent. Brooding fuels anger's flames. But seeing things differently douses those
> flames. Tice found that reframing a situation more positively was one of the most
> potent ways to put anger to rest. (1995, p. 60)

We totally agree with Goleman's view. The most effective way of beginning
to use anger rather than be used up by it is to remember to consider the frame
through which you are viewing the particular situation. Take a couple of deep
diaphragmatic breaths and then shift your attention to your muscles, particularly
those muscles in your shoulders, neck and jaw. Take a moment to relax these.
Then assume the witness/observer stance. Look at the situation from the outside. Ask yourself, "How can I look at this differently?" Reframing is a powerful
method for dealing effectively with anger. We would like to offer you a couple of
reframes we have found particularly useful for working through anger.

LOOK FOR COMEDY   One approach involves viewing your life as a sitcom in
progress. It asks that you think of yourself as a comedy writer of your own life.
In almost all situations an element of humor or absurdity can be found if you
look at it from a different perspective. Seeing the humor inherent in a situation
effectively defuses much of the anger. Think for a moment, if you were an objective, uninvolved bystander witnessing your situation, is there any aspect of your
circumstance that could be seen as humorous? Who is your favorite stand-up
comedian? If that comic was observing what was happening to you, what pithy
or funny remarks would she make about you or your dilemma? You can probably remember times when you witnessed an event where a friend, colleague, or
relative became angry, while you had a hard time keeping a straight face because
you could see the absurdity in the situation. You can do this with yourself as well.
As a matter of fact, almost any situation will seem funny when you are looking
back at it after the passage of time. Realize that you have the choice to imagine
that time has already passed when you are involved in your particular dramas.

THE "GRAND DRAMA" VIEWPOINT   Or, yet another useful reframe involves
looking at your situation from a frame of reference where you view your life as
an unfolding drama for the benefit and entertainment of a higher being. And why
not? People who believe in a higher power may consider that their life is a gift
from God, and how they live their life is their gift to God. Seligman (2002) notes
the relationship between emotional equilibrium and having a spiritual dimension
in your life.

A CHAPTER IN YOUR LIFE   A related reframe is to consider that your life is a novel in progress, and what is happening to you at any moment can make for a fascinating chapter in the book that is your life. How can you write this chapter taking into account what you will ultimately learn from the experience? We find that any of these perspectives will help to get you unstuck from the anger of the moment. If none of these appeal to you, can you think of others that would serve you better? Take some time to reflect on this now.

VIEWING CRITICISM AS FEEDBACK   One of the things that often triggers your anger is criticism. It goes without saying that no one really likes to be criticized. But some individuals handle criticism better than others. Why is it that some people seem to take negative feedback in stride and even appear to benefit from it, while others are overwhelmed with anger and self-doubt? Again the answer lies in the meaning attributed to the criticism. One main reason is that negative feedback is viewed as a statement about your self-worth rather than an observation about your behavior. When viewed this way criticism tends to remind you of your inadequacies.

However, if you are able to adopt the reframe that it is not you but your actions that are being critiqued, it becomes easier to consider the possibility that there is validity to the complaint. You no longer need to feel as though there is something wrong with you, that you are a bad or worthless person, rather you need to focus your attention on the appropriateness, effectiveness or worthiness of a particular behavior.

You need to recognize that in any situation where you receive criticism, three possibilities exist: (1) your behavior is definitely out of line and the other person's complaint is valid; (2) your behavior is questionable but the criticism is also a reflection of biases or shortcomings of the critic; or (3) your behavior is fine and it is the critic who has the problem. There is an old saying, "criticism reflects the critic," which is very applicable here. It is important to take a good look at your behavior, but how you respond will depend on which possibility you decide best fits the situation. If you decide that your behavior has been inappropriate, you must be careful not to fall into the trap of taking this as evidence that you should feel guilty about it. This trap is avoided by remembering to look differently at your mistakes. As previously discussed, you *can* decide to view mistakes as feedback, important information which helps to train you in how to do things properly. It is when you realize that your mistakes are invaluable teachers that you will cease to repeat them.

CASE STUDY 1: ROAD RAGE   Sally is a high-powered executive who works downtown in a major metropolitan area. She enjoys the excitement and cultural amenities of the big city, but she prefers to live in a more rural atmosphere, so she purchased a home on the outskirts of the suburbs in an area that still feels like country. The price of this is that she has a very long commute, in rush hour traffic, to and from her job. On a good day it takes her 45 minutes to get to the office, and most days it takes over an hour to reach work. She hates the drive, but she is very satisfied with her job, and has no desire to move closer to work and lose the country environment she cherishes. Lately Sally has found herself frequently engulfed in road rage, getting furious at bad drivers or inconsiderate motorists who cut her off. She found herself screaming in her car, leaning on the horn unnecessarily long, making obscene hand gestures to other motorists, and then feeling agitated throughout the drive and even after she reached her destination. She was very concerned about her feelings and her behavior. She feared that she might enrage strangers with her offensive gestures, who might then attempt to retaliate in some fashion. Mostly she was upset about the holdover agitation she felt even after getting out of the car. Her blood pressure was up and she was getting frequent tension headaches during her drive home which lingered all night.

Assisting Sally to work through road rage to achieve road peace first involved helping her to recognize that she had a choice whether or not to respond with anger to difficult driving situations. She was encouraged to identify the underlying assumptions fueling her anger. She believed that she had no control in the situation; after all, she couldn't stop lousy drivers from making driving mistakes, going too slow, or cutting her off. But the thought that triggered the bulk of her anger was her assumption that "they got away with it," while putting her in danger in the process.

Sally was able to overcome her road rage by being willing to shift her thinking. She began to acknowledge that, while she certainly had absolutely no control over the driving behavior or competency of other motorists, she always had control over how she chose to respond to any given driving situation. She then searched for a way to *reframe* the trigger assumption: bad drivers get away with it. She recognized that if a given driver was really that unskilled, then it was just a matter of time before that person was either ticketed by police or hospitalized from a traffic accident. The next time she witnessed a bad driver, she fantasized that he got a speeding ticket later that day. She further realized that if a person wasn't an incompetent driver but just inconsiderate, then this inconsideration would catch up with him in other areas of life, particularly in interpersonal relationships. A person who always puts his needs above others rarely can sustain lasting relationships. So the next day, when a dapper businessman in a new Mercedes cut her off and almost ran her off the road, Sally imagined that he returned home that night and discovered that his wife had left him for being so insensitive.

Sally was amazed at how adopting these alternative perspectives, these reframes, and engaging in these fantasies defused her anger. Remembering to breathe slowly from the diaphragm when the driving got tense helped her to keep her mind open to new perspectives, rather than engaging in knee jerk reactions of rage. She also began using her time in the car more constructively. She began listening to books on tape and podcasts, rather than complaining that she didn't have time to read. Using her time more productively lowered her stress level, and reduced her feeling that she was wasting two hours a day in the car. The *distraction value* of this was such that she stopped spending time searching for bad drivers or driving errors as she had before. Within two weeks of adopting this change in perspective Sally was free of road rage. As a byproduct, her headaches decreased in frequency and severity and her blood pressure stabilized.

CASE STUDY 2: WORKPLACE ANGER   Carlos had been working at his sales job for a mid-sized manufacturing company for two years and had enjoyed phenomenal success. He had quadrupled his earnings in that time due to his high sales figures and he was the top salesman in the company. His forte was in developing new accounts and generating increased orders from existing customers. Rather than enjoy his success, Carlos became even more driven and began having inappropriate temper outbursts at work when other workers did not meet his expectations. He became enraged when other workers made minor errors which delayed the processing of orders for his customers. He would often yell at these co-workers and insult them. What upset him the most was what he perceived as the meddling behavior of the sales manager, his immediate boss. When his boss would attempt to assist him by helping with paperwork, Carlos took offense. He assumed that his boss was implying that he couldn't handle it by himself. Mostly he was worried about getting fired because of his temper outbursts or because he was disliked. He feared that the bosses wanted to fire him so they could hire someone else at a much lower salary level. He knew he had to deal with the situation when his boss took him aside and told him that he needed to work on his attitude. Carlos was having problems sleeping at night and relaxing on the weekends with his family because he was so caught up in anger and worry.

Carlos was encouraged to use diaphragmatic breathing, and wait ten minutes before responding to any mistakes made by co-workers or perceived slights by his superiors, so he would have time to *cool down*. Using cognitive restructuring he confronted his irrational expectation that people should always be perfect and never make mistakes. He was encouraged to identify the other assumptions that were underlying his anger. The first assumption was that he was soon to be fired despite his success. To find a reframe to combat this, he was encouraged to think of everything his company had to lose by firing him. He quickly realized that the company stood to lose a lot of money and business if he was let go, even if they did hire a lower paid replacement. He had to admit that it would be a very foolish move for his employers to fire him, even if they did find him to be a "pain in the butt." The second assumption involved his belief that his boss' efforts to help him with paperwork implied that he was not competent. When reflecting upon alternate explanations for his boss' behavior, Carlos realized that when his boss helped with paperwork it freed him up to do that which he did best. Therefore, assistance from his boss could help both Carlos and the company increase earnings.

When Carlos returned to work he practiced breathing techniques and taking a ten minute breather to walk around the office if hassles arose. Using the guidelines in Chapter 10 for practicing assertive as opposed to aggressive behavior, he approached his co-workers diplomatically and calmly. When his boss came to assist with his paperwork, rather than resenting it and glaring at him as he had done previously, he thanked him. Within a week he and his boss were on much better terms. They had a heart-to-heart talk, and his boss confirmed that he wanted to help to enable Carlos to focus solely on selling. Carlos suggested a brainstorming meeting between the sales and shipping departments to foster improved communication and problem-solving to expedite timely shipment of orders. At the meeting Carlos practiced empathic listening and began to understand why his co-workers made many of the errors. This meeting was very productive, and as a result numerous suggestions were made to help fix the existing problems. Carlos acknowledged that mistakes would still occur, but he was hopeful that the frequency could be significantly reduced by implementing the ideas offered at the meeting. Lastly, Carlos kept reminding himself that he was a very valuable employee who had control over whether he was fired by how he chose to behave in the workplace. Several weeks later his bosses took him aside and praised his work and the improvement in his attitude. From the discussion it was abundantly clear to him that he was, indeed, a very valuable employee with a secure job. Within two weeks he began to enjoy going to work again. His sleep normalized and he began to relax and have fun on his weekends.

Positive Psychology Exercise
Developing Your Own Plan to Defuse Anger

Take a moment and think about a situation or a person that often triggers your anger. Notice that we did not say something or someone who makes you angry—no one can make you angry, for whether you respond with anger is always your choice. Now, take a few moments to practice diaphragmatic breathing, and consciously release the tension from your muscles to better prepare you to deal with the stress of these thoughts. If it is a situation that you are thinking about, what alternate perspective or reframe can you create to help you view things differently? Are you harboring any irrational ideas which contribute to your anger and could be challenged? Spend a few minutes pondering the situation from this new frame of reference. What happens to your anger? Do you find it diminishing or perhaps even fading entirely? If you have been thinking about a person who often triggers your anger, make your best attempt to put yourself in the shoes of that individual. What feelings or motivations might that person have that led them to behave in ways that anger you? This does not mean that you have to agree with that person or condone her behavior, the only requirement is that you spend some time viewing the world from her eyes. Do you notice that it is harder to generate anger when you understand where someone else is coming from, even if you don't agree with them? Does that person's point of view have any validity, given that person's experiences or beliefs? Now that you have likely diminished your anger by thinking differently, are there any other alternative behaviors you could adopt that might help you cope? For example, would being more assertive help you to deal better with the person or situation? If your answer is yes, pay special attention to the next chapter.

9.5.7 Could Anger Have an Upside?

Earlier in this chapter we mentioned that anger is not always bad for you. A paradigm shift of sorts is now developing among many psychologists, brain scientists, and social/evolutionary biologists who question the long-standing view that anger is a negative and destructive state to be suppressed. They claim that there is an upside to this emotion as it is often necessary to mobilize you for action. According to Rodgers (2014) anger can potentially fuel optimism, leadership, creativity and problem-solving by focusing us in highly specific, goal-driven ways. Furthermore, when *wielded responsibly*, anger can actually inhibit aggression!

Our capacity to get angry is a product of natural selection. Our Stone Age ancestors, at times, needed to display anger to survive (the fight part of the fight/flight reaction), whether to fend off a dangerous predator or a hostile tribe declaring war, and as a result those who reacted with anger and then survived passed this capacity on to later generations. Thus it makes sense that even newborn babies are born ready to be angry and loudly express their needs.

Interestingly, when we *express anger appropriately*, our level of cortisol, the stress hormone, diminishes. This was demonstrated by Lerner (2001) who found that when subjects were experimentally induced into a state of righteous indignation, their *constructive expression of anger* decreased their cortisol levels. This implies that expression of anger can actually help us calm down and address a problem head on rather than run from it. The key is to find constructive ways to work through your angry feelings (i.e. assertiveness, exercise, active relaxation practice, mindfulness meditation) rather than destructive ways (physical or verbal aggression, passive-aggression). If you blow up and behave aggressively, you may feel better in the short run due to the adrenaline release, but this is fake relief, short-lived and almost always guaranteed to increase your stress in the long run. In addition, you become more likely to get in the habit of blowing up. Hence the familiar situation of the short-tempered boss who habitually barks insults and threats to employees, but quickly relaxes and acts like everything is just fine. Meanwhile the subdued staff is fantasizing about quitting and nursing their hatred for their boss. As a result, productivity often falls and the boss is avoided. On the other hand, total withdrawal is not the answer either. If you just walk away and ruminate about your feelings regarding the situation, you are stewing in your anger. However, walking away *temporarily* when enraged to calm and distract yourself (by for example, focusing on slowing your breathing) before developing a plan for a constructive response is adaptive.

Although anger was traditionally considered a negative and harmful emotion, recent findings in neuroscience conflict with this view. Therefore, neuroscientists are now characterizing emotions not as negative or positive, but rather by the motivational directions they inspire, that is, whether they propel us toward approach behaviors to achieve our goals or stimulate avoidance and withdrawal behaviors. According to Lerner (2001), "research will provide evidence . . . that the most adaptive and resilient individuals have highly flexible response systems. They are neither chronically angry nor chronically calm." Anger can be good for you as long as you keep the flame low and don't allow your amygdala to hijack your prefrontal cortex. The bottom line is that anger that is chronic, unresolved and suppressed is definitely toxic for you. Unmodulated catharsis or unrestrained expression of anger is often even more toxic, first to others and then back to you in terms of the unintended consequences. What is typically called for is a modulated, assertive response after you have calmed yourself which will further lower your stress. The next chapter will provide you with a very useful framework for assertiveness.

Questions

1. An emotional hijacking occurs when the _____ triggers the fight/flight response, which bypasses the _____ inhibiting its ability to process information rationally.

   A. hippocampus; amygdala

   B. amygdala; prefrontal cortex

   C. amygdala; cerebellum

   D. cortex; mirror neurons

2. Which aspect of the Type A personality is associated with a higher risk for heart attacks?

   A. achievement orientation

   B. compulsivity

   C. being laid back

   D. anger

3. Which of the following is useful for controlling anger?

   A. dwelling on criticism

   B. engaging in the Vesuvius effect

   C. hyperventilation

   D. adopting a cooling off period

9.6 Forgiveness

Define the process of forgiveness.

Since anger and resentment are damaging to your health and can undermine your effectiveness with others, then clearly, the ability to forgive and let go of past hurts and disappointments is a desirable goal. Let's be clear about what forgiveness is and is not. **Forgiveness** is not necessarily forgetting what happened, thereby placing yourself again in a situation where you could be mistreated. It is certainly not about condoning behavior you find offensive or hurtful. It is the process of letting go of the energy invested in past hurts or disappointments so that you can free that energy for more productive, growth-oriented activities. The decision to forgive stems from the realization that anger and resentment have a damaging effect on you. There is an old Chinese saying, "Before embarking on a mission of revenge, dig two graves." We wonder if you or anyone you know has ever said, "I don't get mad, I get even!" As cool as that statement might sound, you must realize the eventual toll such an approach will take on you.

Although forgiveness begins with a decision to do so, it is important to remember that it is a process. As such, it takes time and a willingness to go through the particular emotions involved, be it hurt, anger, or even depression. The problem develops when you get stuck in this process because of righteous indignation. Do not get caught in the trap of believing that you can only begin to forgive when an apology is offered or amends made. When and how you forgive is totally up to you, whatever the circumstances.

It is vitally important that you realize that forgiveness is a healing process that takes time, and will ebb and flow. Particularly if you have been hurt in a deep and profound way (either physically or emotionally), it is likely that your journey toward forgiveness will proceed through a series of steps that won't necessarily flow in a linear progression. You may move forward unevenly, and may even temporarily backtrack at times as you ultimately move forward. Sidney and Susan Simon (1990), in their book *Forgiveness: How to Make Peace with Your Past and Get on with Your Life*, describe six stages that provide an excellent description of the path to forgiveness. The stages are summarized as follows:

1. DENIAL

   Shortly after you have been hurt, you may find that you attempt to minimize the impact or importance of what happened to you, and suppress your feelings as part of the denying.

2. SELF-BLAME

   Your early attempts to make sense of what happened to you often involve the assumption that somehow you were to blame. If only you had done something different—perhaps if you had been less trusting, you could have avoided being hurt. Your self-esteem is often negatively affected by such self-recriminations.

3. VICTIM

   After you stop blaming yourself, you realize that you did not deserve the hurt you received, that you were, at best, treated unfairly and, at worst, victimized. But this recognition often leads to self-pity, emotional upset, misdirected anger, and other destructive emotions. While it is certainly necessary to pass through this stage, it is also vital not to become mired in it or you risk getting stuck in the victim role.

4. INDIGNATION

   To mobilize yourself out of the victim role, you will likely need to marshal a sense of righteous indignation about what happened to you, directed towards those responsible for your hurt. Anger towards those who hurt you and even the world at large may prevail, and thoughts of revenge may be prominent.

5. SURVIVOR

As your anger begins to wane, you will recognize that although you were hurt and did not deserve such, you survived. Your painful past experience may have robbed you in many ways, but may also have bolstered your strength and coping resources. Your compassion, empathy, and sense of humor begin to return as your obsession with your emotional pain begins to subside. You begin to recognize that you did the best that you could do in a difficult situation. As a result, your self-concept shifts from one of victim to survivor.

6. INTEGRATION

In this last stage, when forgiveness has really begun to take hold, you start to acknowledge that those who hurt you may have been playing out patterns of hurt or victimization from their own lives. You realize that just as you are much more than a victim, those who hurt you are more than just perpetrators. You begin to let go of the emotional energy involved in nursing hate, anger, bitterness, grudges, and/or revenge fantasies, which frees up your energy to focus on living your life fully. You are able to put your past in perspective, without forgetting it, recognize lessons learned from your hurt, and ultimately let go of unnecessary emotional baggage.

There have been at least eight studies in the domain of Positive Psychology measuring the effects of forgiveness on the emotional health of the forgivers. In one well-designed study, Thoresen and his colleagues (2001) found that forgiveness led to lower stress levels, less anger, increased optimism and improved health. Their results also showed that the greater the extent of forgiveness, the larger the improvements in emotional and physical well-being. The research of Michael McCullough (2001) indicates that the more you develop empathy, the more you are able to forgive. VanOyen Witvliet and her colleagues (2001) examined the physiological responses of college undergraduates as they imagined responding to their real life offenders in forgiving and unforgiving ways. The forgiving imagery emphasized developing empathy for the humanity of the offender. The results were very consistent with the Thoresen study. During forgiveness visualizations the participants experienced less stress, more positive emotions, less negative emotions, and a greater sense of personal control.

One method for freeing yourself up to forgive involves creating a forgiveness journal which puts the emphasis on the development of empathy. Robert Enright (2001), in his book *Forgiveness is a Choice*, reminds us that just about everyone has to live with a painful memory from someone who hurt us, oftentimes someone close to us, someone we trusted. He recommends that you attempt to tell the story of the person who hurt you in order to create an empathic state of mind. He provides suggested questions to address in your journal such as . . .

1. What was life like for the person who hurt you when that individual was growing up? Describe elements of that person's life that may have set the stage for the hurtful behavior. Be careful not to confuse forgiving with excusing.

2. At the time you were hurt, what was life like for that person?

3. Tell the story of your relationship with this person in a broader sense than the hurtful behavior or incident. What was the rest of your relationship with that person like?

4. How might that person be worse off now as a result of what was done to you?

5. Apart from how that person hurt you, what is this person like in other ways? Remember that you do not have to resume a relationship with this person even if he or she has other admirable qualities.

6. Has there been any change in your view of this person in any way as a result of this exercise?

Keeping a forgiveness journal or answering questions such as those posed above can help you develop empathy. This can allow you to move through the healing stages of forgiveness and reach the integration stage more quickly. While you need to go through the stages, you do not want to be mired in them for decades. If you find yourself stuck in the process and are in a good deal of emotional pain, consider consulting a professional therapist who can assist you in moving through your own process of healing.

ASSERTIVENESS   Some situations that anger you certainly call for some type of response beyond letting go of your anger. Many times you will need to respond to individuals who have angered you so as to rectify the situation or prevent future occurrences of whatever is provoking your hostility. This is best accomplished by dealing diplomatically and assertively with the other person or persons rather than passively avoiding conflict, and allowing your resentment to build and take a toll on you, or responding aggressively where you risk alienating others, making the situation worse and later being ashamed of yourself. A comprehensive treatment of effective and responsible assertive behavior is included in the next chapter.

Questions

1. Which of the following statements applies to the process of forgiveness?

    A. Forgiveness is an all or none experience which does not follow any particular stages.

    B. Forgiveness is as much for you as for the other person.

    C. Empathy is irrelevant for forgiveness.

    D. In order to forgive, you must forget.

2. Forgiveness is facilitated through the development of _____.

   A. a plan for revenge

   B. a Type B personality

   C. empathy

   D. repression

3. All of the following are stages in the process of forgiveness except _____.

   A. self-blame

   B. victim

   C. survivor

   D. emotional hijacking

Summary

This chapter emphasized the role of **emotional intelligence** (EQ) in effectiveness, pointing out that it is typically more important than IQ for success. EQ consists of self-awareness, emotional self-control, perceptiveness about others, and the ability to self-motivate along with skill in handling relationships. To facilitate the further development of your skills in these five EQ areas, this chapter provided guidelines for handling conflict in relationships, developing empathy, understanding and managing anger, along with learning how to forgive.

With regard to handling relationships, the role of **interdependence** for close relationships was featured as well as outlining the importance of having a win-win mindset. The concept of the **emotional bank account** was introduced for building trust and facilitating **win-win outcomes**. The importance of **empathy**, of being able to step into the shoes of the other, was stressed. Blocks to empathy were elucidated followed by suggestions about what you can do to become more empathic in your daily life.

The nature of anger was thoroughly explored including the physiology of anger, theories explaining the individual differences in anger expression along with a myriad of useful tips and techniques for managing anger constructively rather than destructively. Lastly, the importance of **forgiveness** was covered, including what forgiveness is, is not, and its benefits. The stages of forgiveness were reviewed along with guidelines for how to move through this difficult process.

Key Terms

Amygdala	Co-dependency	Emotional Hijacking
Attribution Theory	Emotional Bank Account	EQ
Catharsis	Emotional Intelligence	Empathy

Forgiveness
Frustration-Aggression
   Hypothesis
Interdependence
Lose-Lose Outcomes
Lose-Win Outcomes

Mirror Neurons
Prefrontal Cortex
Road Rage
Synergy
Thought Stopping
Type A personality

Type B personality
Vesuvius Effect
Win-Lose Outcomes
Win-Win or No Deal
Win-Win Outcomes

Shared Writing

Of all the tips, techniques, and suggestions offered in this chapter for dealing effectively with anger, which one would be most useful for you in the future? Write about a past or current situation which angered you and how you handled it. Write about how using a tip from this chapter may have been more useful to you for managing your emotions during that experience.

Chapter 9 Questions

1. Skill in understanding yourself and reading the emotional reactions of others is an important component in _____.

  a. problem solving

  b. emotional intelligence

  c. cognitive intelligence

  d. making money

2. According to Covey, to go for a win-win outcome you need both _____ and _____.

  a. cunning; communication

  b. communication; competition

  c. consideration; courage

  d. commitment; challenge

3. In order to really understand and appreciate another person's point of view, you need to _____.

  a. forgive and forget

  b. employ a cooling down period

  c. be co-dependent

  d. step into their shoes

4. Unrestrained expression of anger has been termed the _____ effect.

  a. Vesuvius

  b. Donald Trump

  c. Hijacking

  d. Marshmallow

5. Catharsis _____ the immediate venting of anger _____.

  a. is typically not a reliable nor effective way of reducing anger

  b. is recommended by experts for dispelling your anger

  c. is typical of the Type B personality

  d. is not related to emotional hijackings

6. _____ individuals tend to be very hard driving, achievement oriented, compulsive, overly concerned with time pressure, and easy to anger, as compared to _____ individuals who are laid back, easygoing, and less concerned with time.

a. Type C; Type D

b. Type B; Type A

c. Type A; Type B

d. Type B; Type EQ

7. Cognitive restructuring techniques are more effective if used _____ in the anger sequence.

a. early

b. late

c. midway

d. at any point

8. Which of the following statements applies to reducing anger?

a. Physical exercise will not defuse anger

b. Anger is always bad for you.

c. You always have a choice whether to be angry.

d. Reframing is useless for defusing anger.

9. Which of the following statements applies to interpersonal effectiveness?

a. Independence is always superior to interdependence.

b. In order to be interdependent, you must be co-dependent.

c. You need to prove to other people that your way is the right way.

d. It is not always possible to get a win-win outcome.

10. Which of the following applies to anger?

a. Playing violent video games has no affect on aggression for anyone.

b. Venting your anger will always reliably reduce it.

c. When we express anger in constructive ways, our level of cortisol, a stress hormone, decreases.

d. Recent findings in neuroscience reveal that anger is always bad for you.

Chapter 10
Building Effective Communication Skills

After reading this chapter, you should be able to:

10.1 Explain the importance of effective listening and common obstacles to being a good listener.

10.2 Identify the various elements of effective listening.

10.3 Recognize and appropriately interpret nonverbal signals.

10.4 Define the characteristics and benefits of assertiveness in communication.

10.5 Explain how the elements of the four-step framework can best be put into practice.

10.6 Describe the ways in which you may communicate assertiveness nonverbally.

The ancient Greeks had an enlightening philosophy regarding communication which was reflected in three sequentially arranged words: Ethos, Pathos and Logos. The first, **Ethos**, refers to your personal credibility, your trustworthiness, the faith people have in your integrity. Without this, the rest of your message is lost. It would be very difficult for someone to accept what you say if you are not considered to be a reliable source. **Pathos** refers to your empathic side. It means that you are capable of perceiving and attuning yourself with the emotional content of another person's communication, and that you have the ability to help the other person see that you do understand them. Without this your message is also lost.

does not believe that you understand them, then how can you consider their best interests? **Logos** is the logical, reasoning aspect of your communication when you are attempting to convey your needs or impart information.

The sequence of these is very important: First Ethos, then Pathos, then Logos. Most people tend to go straight for the Logos, the left brain logic, in communicating. That is, they immediately resort to their logic and their desire to meet their own needs without first taking the Ethos and the Pathos into consideration. But it is far more effective to do this in reverse. You must first be seen as trustworthy, and then be seen as able to empathize, before you can have a chance of getting your needs met or persuading someone to acknowledge your point of view. This is a paradigm shift for most people, particularly in a culture like ours that teaches you to speak your mind and say what you mean.

Previous chapters have dealt in depth with developing and communicating your ethos, your character. When we ask students in our classes and participants in our training sessions what represents high character, qualities such as honesty, integrity, genuineness, loyalty, fairness, self-control, discretion, humility, modesty and trustworthiness are commonly cited as typical of individuals with high character. Sound familiar? It all goes back to developing your signature strengths and virtues. You can't expect to automatically be trusted simply because you say you are trustworthy. You need to demonstrate that you are someone who can be trusted. Likewise, you don't gain a person's trust just because you are a really nice person who is well liked and charming. After all, a good criminal can do that! In fact, the best criminals do it fantastically! That is what con men are, right? They get your confidence. They are likeable. They give you the illusion of integrity. Genuinely high ethos is something that has to build up over time. There are many ways to do this. It could involve focusing on win-win outcomes or on making sincere deposits in the emotional bank account of another. For example, it could involve keeping a secret told to you in confidence by a friend, even though it would be in your best interest to reveal that secret to others. Instead, you put friendship and the privacy of your friend ahead of an opportunity for personal gain, a big deposit in the emotional bank account of another as well as a sign of integrity.

10.1 Pathos: Developing Empathy by Enhancing Listening Skills

Explain the importance of effective listening and common obstacles to being a good listener.

The second component of effective communication (pathos) refers to our ability to step into the shoes of the other. By far, the most effective way to do this is to be a good listener. This section will teach you a method of listening that will greatly enhance your ability to understand and empathize with another individual. But let us begin with a more general discussion about communication.

Communication can be most simply defined as the transfer of information among individuals. What are the means by which human beings communicate? Basically, we share information with each other in one of four ways: (1) speaking, (2) writing, (3) reading, and (4) listening. These are obviously not abilities which are inborn, but skills you learn and develop through experience. However, most of us have not received an equal amount of instruction in all these areas. From infancy you began the process of learning to speak, both in terms of mastering the words and the particular gestures characteristic of your language. As a young child your parents and other caregivers would repeat words and sounds and encourage you to mimic them. Later in school, you likely received more formal training in how to speak appropriately. Over the years you expanded your vocabulary and learned proper grammar. In fact, most colleges currently include a speech class as one of the general educational requirements. Similarly, your education in reading may have begun even before you attended school if your parents read to you. By the time you reached your school years you were taught how to translate the symbols on the page into meaningful sounds and words. Throughout your school career you took formal classes in reading, learning to refine your skills in this area. Your training in writing also began at an early age, from first scribbling your own name, to printing simple words, until you finally mastered cursive writing sometime in elementary school. Throughout your educational career you were exposed to numerous courses in writing, often called English classes, including multiple required courses in college.

Yet how many of you have ever received formal instruction in listening? If you are like most people, the answer to this question is that you have spent virtually no time or very minimal time actively learning how to listen. You might remember your parents saying, "shut up and listen," or your teachers admonishing you to stop talking to your classmates and listen to the lecture. But listening involves so much more than just being quiet.

10.1.1 Listening vs. Hearing

It is important to realize the difference between listening and hearing. If we were able to emerge from these pages and stand before you clapping loudly, you would surely be able to hear the sound of the palms of two hands forcefully colliding against each other, unless of course you had a severely disturbed hearing apparatus. Hearing, you see, is automatic. It can occur passively. It is very possible to hear what someone says, but not really listen to it. Your auditory membranes process the sound waves, but your brain could be oblivious to the message or meanings being transmitted.

Listening, on the other hand, is much more active. It is something you consciously choose to do. It cannot occur without your effort, your attention, and your concentration. Really listening requires a proactive decision to do so, followed by internal and external behaviors aimed at maximizing the probability of receiving an accurate message. Yet despite our inadequate training in this area, a study conducted with college students found that the majority of their time, up to 53%, was spent in listening activities (Barker, Edwards, & colleagues, 1981). This same study revealed that students spent approximately 14% of their communicating time writing, 16% reading, and 17% speaking. Another study (Wolvin & Coakley, 1991) showed that employees of major Fortune 500 corporations spend about 60% of their workday listening to others. It is very ironic that the communication skill we use the most is the one for which we are least prepared.

10.1.2 The Epidemic of Poor Listening

Communication is very much a two way street. It does not matter how well you speak if no one is there to listen. Studies of the listening ability of thousands of subjects reveal that most people fail to listen well (Atwater, 1986). Some of this is tied to memory. Research indicates that after hearing a ten minute presentation, the average person understands and retains only about half of what was said. After two days another one-half of the information is forgotten. Thus, you can expect to remember approximately one-forth of what you heard someone say two days before.

We have even more disquieting news about how poorly most of us listen. How well do you think college students listen? Not very well according to Paul Cameron, a professor at Wayne State University (cited in Adler & Towne, 1993), who assessed the thoughts of students in his introductory psychology class at random intervals during his lecture. Much to Professor Cameron's dismay the vast majority of his students were not necessarily listening to him. He found that 20% of his students, both male and female, were enjoying erotic thoughts! Another 20% were reminiscing about something. Only 20% were actually paying attention to his lesson, and of those only 12% were really actively listening and thinking about the lecture material. The other students were busy daydreaming, yearning for lunch, worrying, or surprisingly, thinking about religion. Now perhaps Professor Cameron was a boring lecturer, but it is much more likely that his students' sexual fantasies were just more compelling than anything taught in class.

To add to the problem, when attempting to improve communication skills, many people overlook the importance of strengthening listening ability (Chiasson and Hayes, 1993). Although most of us agree that listening is important, the overemphasis on speaking skills and the under-emphasis on receiving skills cause many to fail to recognize the vital nature of effective listening. This is not surprising. Our society stresses the value of speaking your mind, of being able to clearly state your position, feelings or needs. Think about it. When you picture an effective individual, don't you imagine someone who is not afraid to say what they think? Yet, as Covey (1991) observed, individuals who are interpersonally effective "seek first to understand, then to be understood." When your first emphasis is on truly comprehending and appreciating the other's paradigm or frame, you are building rapport. When people really feel understood, they are much more likely to develop trust in you. No wonder listening is a skill that is essential to making and keeping relationships. It involves making a commitment to understanding how other people feel, how they see their world, getting a sense of their particular map. It is about making the attempt to see the world through their eyes. Listening is arguably the most important deposit you can make into the emotional bank account you hold with someone. It is a compliment to others because when you truly listen it directly implies that you care about what is happening to them, that their life and experiences are important enough that you will pay attention to them. It is a way in which you can join in their world.

How well do you listen? Fill out the following questionnaire as straightforwardly as possible to assess your listening ability. This inventory lists behaviors involved in good and bad listening. Using the scale, objectively rate how you typically behave by checking the appropriate response. Don't feel bad if your score is not what you want it to be. Most people are not good listeners for reasons explained in the next section. This inventory may help you identify some listening behaviors you can begin working on to improve your listening skills.

Listening Questionnaire

1. Making eye contact with the person who is speaking.

Never	Seldom	Sometimes	Often	Always
1	2	3	4	5

2. Judging the subject as uninteresting.

Never	Seldom	Sometimes	Often	Always
5	4	3	2	1

3. Letting personal feeling and thoughts of prejudice interfere.

Never	Seldom	Sometimes	Often	Always
5	4	3	2	1

4. Keeping an open mind about the speaker's ideas.

Never	Seldom	Sometimes	Often	Always
1	2	3	4	5

5. Faking attention.

Never	Seldom	Sometimes	Often	Always
5	4	3	2	1

6. Listening just for the facts.

Never	Seldom	Sometimes	Often	Always
5	4	3	2	1

7. Resisting internal and external distractions.

Never	Seldom	Sometimes	Often	Always
1	2	3	4	5

8. Judging the speaker's delivery.

Never	Seldom	Sometimes	Often	Always
5	4	3	2	1

9. Using your thinking speed to reflect on the message.

Never	Seldom	Sometimes	Often	Always
1	2	3	4	5

10. Interrupting the speaker or jumping to conclusions.

Never	Seldom	Sometimes	Often	Always
5	4	3	2	1

Add up your score from all ten questions. Your score can be interpreted as follows:

25 or below: You need to work on your listening skills. Your difficulties in this area may be causing problems in your interpersonal relationships. Pay careful attention to the guidelines in this chapter and you can improve significantly in this area.

26 to 35: You are an average listener. With more attention to the fundamentals explained in this chapter, you should be able to improve your skills dramatically.

36 to 45: You are a good listener. Follow the suggestions outlined in this chapter and you can become an excellent listener.

46 to 50: You are an excellent listener. Keep it up. This chapter should help you refine your skills even further.

10.1.3 Barriers to Effective Listening

As mentioned earlier, true listening is much more than just being quiet while someone else is talking. In *Messages: The Communication Skills Book* the authors (McKay, Davis, & Fanning, 1983) point out that true listening requires that you have at least one of the four following intentions in mind.

1. To understand someone.
2. To enjoy someone.
3. To learn something.
4. To give help or solace.

So real listening does not occur unless you have at least one of the intentions stated above, and you act on it by paying attention and concentrating on what the other person is saying. According to McKay and his colleagues, pseudo or fake listening occurs when some other intention is being satisfied. There are many reasons why you may fail to listen. You may not feel like putting in the effort required to listen. Or you may avoid listening because someone is saying something that you don't want to hear or that threatens you, so you manage to block it out, either by not hearing it in the first place (selective attention) or forgetting it immediately (repression). Or you may listen poorly because you never learned how to listen effectively. Unfortunately, people sometimes pretend to listen when they really are not, and many pseudo-listeners are adept at appearing attentive. This may even be true for you, for each of us is guilty of occasionally acting as if we are listening when our attention is elsewhere. We may look at the person, nod our head in encouragement as if we agree with what the person is saying, even murmur "Mm-hmm" occasionally, but if asked to repeat or explain what was being said, we would be at a total loss.

When you are **pseudolistening** you are pretending to listen; your intention is not to listen but to meet some other need, such as:

1. Pretending to listen to make people think you're interested in them so that you will be liked.

2. Being vigilant to watch for signs of potential rejection.

3. Listening for one specific bit of information and ignoring everything else.

4. Focusing on your rebuttal or the next thing you want to say rather than on anything the person is saying.

5. Pretending to listen so someone will listen to you.

6. Listening to uncover someone's vulnerabilities or weakness in order to gain an advantage.

7. Looking only for the weak points in the speaker's line of reasoning so you can get ammunition for your counterattack, or to try to win an argument.

8. Checking only to see how the speaker is reacting to make sure you produce the desired effect.

9. Half-listening because that is what a nice person would do in the same situation.

10. Feigning listening because you don't know how to get away without hurting someone's feelings or offending them. Or your willingness to listen falters because the other person is boring you, and you are unsure how to make a graceful exit. In other words, you pretend to listen to be polite.

Even when it is your sincere intention to listen, there are factors which interfere with your ability to do so. These can be external, like the other person may overload you with information, or speak so quickly that you cannot process it all at once. Sometimes there are so many distractions in the surrounding environment, such as loud background noise, that it is hard to pay careful attention even when you want to do so. But the most common reasons are internal. You may be preoccupied, so caught up in your own thoughts, fantasies, or emotions that you cannot give sufficient attention to the other person. What follows are the most common barriers to effective listening:

1. **Judging**—Our natural tendency to judge, to define things as good or bad, cool or uncool, can be an enormous barrier to effective communication. Pre-judging someone in a negative way influences your ability to listen. Negative labels have tremendous power. For example, quickly labeling someone as stupid or crazy makes it highly unlikely that you will pay much attention to what that person has to say. When you are judgmental, other people are put on the defensive and typically turned off.

2. **Mind Reading**—Rather than paying attention to what the person is really saying you are busy operating on the basis of your assumptions about what the person is thinking and saying. Once in a while, if you are very perceptive, your efforts at mind reading may be on target, but for the most part

mind reading usually leads to miscommunications and misunderstandings. Remember the old joke, "When you assume you make an ass out of you and me" (ass/u/me).

3. **Stereotyping**—When you operate on the basis of your widespread generalizations about a person based on group membership or some physical characteristic, rather than getting to know that person for who he or she is, you are setting the stage for poor listening and distorted communications.

4. **Interrupting**—Frequent or needless interruptions disrupt communication and interfere with the flow of the conversation. When a speaker is interrupted repeatedly she will often become distracted, lose her train of thought, and feel frustrated. And if you are the one chronically interrupting, you are obviously attending more to what you want to say than to what is being said. Giving the other the time and space to talk is more than being polite, it is the essence of true listening. And the other person owes you the same respect. Interruptions are more likely to be made by persons in positions of authority over you like parents, teachers, or bosses. And men tend to interrupt more than women, particularly in male-female conversations.

5. **Comparing**—You are listening for the purpose of seeing how you measure up to the other person, drawing comparisons and contrasts in your head. The end result is that you are so busy feeling either inferior or superior that minimal attention is given to the speaker.

6. **Advising**—You put yourself in the role of the problem-solver and put your attention on searching for the right advice for the speaker. In the meantime, you don't hear what is most important, how the speaker is feeling and, consequently, you fail to acknowledge these emotions. Of course, there are many times when people will ask for your advice. In this instance we are referring to the tendency to take on that role even when your advice has not been solicited. Sometimes all the speaker wants is an opportunity to vent, to have someone listen sympathetically, and she is not looking to have the problem solved at that moment. This is a common occurrence in male-female conversations. Oftentimes women just want to be listened to, while men feel a compulsion to solve the problem rather than empathize. (See the next chapter for more on gender differences in communication.)

7. **Rehearsing**—You are busy concentrating on and reviewing what you want to say next which detracts from your ability to listen to the speaker.

8. **Stage-Hogging**—Stage hogs, also called conversational narcissists, listen with the primary intent of changing the focus of the conversation back onto them. At every opportunity they shift the topic back to what happened to them and their feelings.

9. **Filtering**—This occurs when you only listen to what you want to hear and ignore or forget the rest.

10. **Dueling**—You are so invested in arguing and debating, perhaps to show off your verbal or intellectual prowess or just to prove you are right, that you

fail to listen to any valid points made by the speaker. You argue for the sake of the argument.

11. **Derailing**—You keep changing the subject or making jokes to create detours in the conversation. This prevents the discussion from reaching any closure. The speaker may end up very annoyed with you.

12. **Daydreaming**—This occurs when something the person has said triggers off a chain of private associations, and before you know it you are attending to your fantasy and not the speaker. This is more likely to happen if you are bored or anxious. Be aware that this often ends up communicating that you do not value what the speaker has to say.

13. **Placating**—You are so invested in being "nice" or "polite" that you agree with everything the speaker says, either ignoring your true opinions or feelings, or pretending that you feel differently.

14. **Hidden Agendas**—When you enter a conversation with special interests or needs that are not evident on the surface and about which you are not forthcoming, the resulting communication is often distorted. It becomes difficult to really listen because you are looking for openings to further your agenda.

15. **Overreacting**—In this case you allow yourself to get caught up in emotion over a word or words that you find offensive or insulting, and your emotional reaction prevents you from hearing or being open to the main message being conveyed.

Questions

1. The communication skill we need to use the most is _____.
   A. talking
   B. listening
   C. writing
   D. reading

2. _____ refers to your integrity, _____ to your empathy, and _____ to your logic.
   A. Ethos; pathos; logos
   B. Logos; ethos; pathos
   C. Pathos; logos; ethos
   D. Ethos; logos; pathos

3. All of the following are barriers to effective listening except _____.
   A. mind-reading
   B. interrupting
   C. stage-hogging
   D. asking questions

10.2 The Building Blocks of Effective Listening

Identify the various elements of effective listening.

We have been given two ears but a single mouth,
in order that we may hear more and talk less.

Zeno of Citium

Now that you have learned the myriad ways that all humans, including you and the authors, fail to really listen to one another, it is time to introduce you to powerful methods of listening designed to facilitate your ability to understand and establish rapport with others which, ultimately, will improve your interpersonal relationships. This involves mastering the art of active listening.

10.2.1 Active Listening

Active listening, also called **reflective listening**, is a process of giving the speaker nonjudgmental responses as a way of checking the accuracy of what you have heard, and whether you fully understand the message the speaker is attempting to convey. Psychologists, clinical social workers, and marriage counselors, who are professional listeners, have long practiced this type of listening as a way of truly understanding and helping troubled individuals. It has become apparent that everyone could benefit from learning how to listen in this fashion to facilitate effective communication. Pay careful attention to these elements for active listening. If you make a sincere attempt to practice and incorporate these we guarantee that your listening skills will improve dramatically. Reflective listening has three essential components which are typically used in conjunction with one another, but will be presented separately for purposes of explanation.

1. PARAPHRASING   This involves stating in your own words what you think someone has just said. This gives the speaker the opportunity to find out if you have really understood the meaning of the communication. In the event that you have misunderstood, partially misunderstood, or missed an important point, the speaker can then clarify matters so that your understanding more nearly matches the intended message. It is important to paraphrase in your own words so that you do not fall prey to "parroting." **Paraphrasing** involves highlighting the main points of the speaker's message, rather than getting mired in exhaustive repetition or minor details. This technique is ideal for establishing rapport and really making the other person feel like you have heard him or her. Paraphrasing usually begins with phrases such as:

"It sounds like you are saying..."

"As I understand you..."

"What I hear you saying is..."

"You mean..."

"Correct me if I'm wrong, but are you saying...?"

"You think..."

"From your point of view..."

If the speaker's message is long or complicated it is best to summarize in your own words your understanding of the communication. Summarizing helps you to tie the various parts of the conversation into a meaningful whole. It lets the speaker know that you have heard the overall message and that you haven't just focused on one salient point. The use of summarization is especially useful when you are trying to resolve differences, defuse an argument, or problem solve. Summarizing responses could start with:

"Summing up what you've said..."

"Your main points, as I understand you, are..."

"Recapping what you have been saying..."

2. CLARIFYING   When you **clarify** you are basically asking questions to facilitate your understanding of the speaker's message, to get background information, additional relevant facts, or to fill in gaps in the narrative. This enables you to get the big picture. It is important to ask for clarification in the context of what the speaker thought and felt, from his or her relevant personal history. Of course, there is no right or wrong way to ask a question, as long as it is phrased in a non-judgmental way, and the tenor of the query will depend on the message being questioned. But some common clarification questions include:

"What do you mean?"

"I'm confused, could you clarify that?"

"Could you repeat that?"

"How did it happen?"

3. FEEDBACK   This involves sharing your reactions to what you have heard the speaker say. There are three rules for giving **feedback.** It should be:

1. Immediate

2. Honest

3. Supportive

For example, if your gut reaction is that the speaker has left something out of the message you could say, "I get the feeling that there's something you are not telling me." This invites the speaker to open up more if this is the case, to disagree if you are in error, and to feel as though you care enough to want to hear the whole story. If you had responded with non-supportive comments such as "You're holding out on me," or "You're lying," you would likely only elicit defensiveness on the part of the speaker.

Feedback can also involve sharing whether you agree or disagree with the speaker, particularly if the speaker is looking for your opinion. Imagine a scenario where a friend recounts to you a story of a foolish thing he has done, and he is asking you to confirm or deny this. A supportive but honest remark might be, "I think there is a real possibility that you did make a mistake." If you had responded with judgmental comments like, "You've been a total fool," or "You are such an idiot," this would only serve to hurt his feelings and make him think twice about sharing his weaknesses with you ever again.

10.2.2 Empathic Listening

This type of listening goes further than reflective listening because it involves putting yourself in the shoes of the other, as discussed in the previous chapter. Reik (1972) refers to this as "listening with the third ear," where you listen not just to the words but to the meanings behind the words such as to what the speaker is feeling and thinking. When you listen empathically you do your best to literally get inside of the other person's frame of reference, to attempt to see the world through his eyes, to understand his particular paradigm, and to understand how he feels. Perhaps, to go even a step further, to feel his or her pain. One requirement for **empathic listening** is that you recognize that everyone is trying to survive the best that they can. Here many of your reflective comments are focused on the feeling or emotional tone of the speaker's message, gleaned from the speaker's words and your reading of the speaker's body language. That is, you paraphrase and reflect or mirror back the speaker's feelings, attitudes and emotions. Reflective comments that focus on feelings could begin with phrases such as:

"I sense you are feeling..."

"You feel...(angry, sad, frustrated, etc.)"

"Do you feel...?"

"It appears that you feel..."

"You seem really...(sad, hurt, angry, etc.)"

Empathic listening is a powerful tool for enabling you to get accurate data from which to understand another person. Instead of projecting your own assumptions and feelings based on your personal history and making interpretations, you are getting in touch with the reality inside another person's head and heart. Empathic listening generates deposits in the emotional bank account. That is, because you are taking the time to really listen and understand, by virtue of this process you become supportive. When you listen empathically you are communicating, "I value you," and this, in and of itself, is one of the most important emotional bank account deposits you can possibly make.

When you first practice active or empathic listening it may feel somewhat artificial or phony, like you are talking in a way that is unnatural for you. Remember that the acquisition of any new skill usually feels awkward in the initial learning stages. Do you recall how awkward you felt when you were first learning to drive a car? But over time and with practice, driving became automatic and second nature to you. The same is true with reflective or empathic listening. With

The Global Perspective
Recognizing Our Basic Humanity

"At its simplest, empathy means feeling the same thing that another person is feeling; at its most sophisticated, it's understanding his entire life situation" (Glass, 2001). In order to be compassionate, it is often necessary that we question our initial judgmental perspective and look beneath the surface, genuinely seeking to understand what it must be like to be that other person. Too often, we insist on holding on to a paradigm that describes the other as evil, crazy, fanatic, brainwashed, retarded, or otherwise deranged and totally different from us. What if instead, we choose to assume that we are all just struggling humans trying to survive? That underneath our diversity is the fact that we are all human beings, and as Robert C. Roberts (1982) points out, our vulnerability to suffering, weakness, and death are things we have in common with absolutely every human being. These undeniable similarities give us the opportunity for fellowship with anyone who crosses our path. As global citizens, to truly foster compassion we need to believe that kinship extends beyond our immediate family, group, and country, to every member of the human race.

This is not to imply that coming to such awareness is easy, particularly when the other appears to be oblivious to that fact himself. Yet, it is essential to the development of empathy and true understanding. Consider the case of Mohammad Sidique Khan, a 30-year-old Briton of Pakistani ancestry and lifetime resident of the English city of Leeds. Khan was one of the four suicide attackers who bombed London's transit system on July 7, 2005. On that day, 56 people were killed in the attacks on three subway trains and a double-decker bus. There is no question that such waste of human life is wrong. It is hard to imagine the suffering of the victims and their surviving families, as well as the nation itself. Such acts deny our interconnectedness. It would be easy, if justifiable, to dismiss Khan and others like him as madmen or merely brainwashed puppets. But what if instead, we attempt to step into his shoes? What if we, out of a belief in our common humanity, really tried to imagine seeing the world through his eyes? What could have driven Khan to such desperation that he would willingly give up his life to deliver his message? It turns out that in a videotape recorded by Khan an undetermined amount of time prior to the attacks, we have a small chance to do that. Addressing himself to the Westerners, Khan said, "Until we feel security, you will be our targets. Until you will stop the bombing, gassing, imprisonment and torture of my people, we will not stop this fight." He said Westerners had failed to heed previous warnings, and that "therefore we will talk to you in a language that you understand. Our words are dead until we give them life with our blood." He went on to accuse Western civilians for the terror attacks against them (Miami Herald, September 3, 2005).

Why does he feel oppressed by us? What is it that we are allegedly doing? How are we attacking them? What bombings, gassing, torturing is he talking about? Do we share some responsibility for aggression in the world? Do they really just want to be left alone, to be separate? Can such disconnectedness be tolerated in a shrinking world or is our interconnectedness unavoidable? Can all of us come to the table to decide how we want the world to be?

time and practice it will come more naturally to you. The rewards of being a good listener will make the effort you put into developing this skill well worth it. It can be very gratifying to be told, "Thank you so much for listening to me."

Positive Psychology Exercise

Empathic Listening

Consider this story. For years you have been close friends with a woman, Maria, who has a habit of getting involved with men who treat her poorly. She had a rough childhood. Her father abandoned the family when she was a child, and her mother was so busy working to support Maria and her siblings that she had very little time for them while Maria was growing up. Maria has been involved with a man, Donald, who is an alcoholic. Although he treats her adequately when sober, when drunk he becomes verbally abusive and on one occasion he was physically abusive to her. She forgave him. Recently Maria lost her job, and when Donald invited her to live with him she jumped at the chance because she was broke. Late one night Maria knocks on your door, distraught and weeping. Her lower lip is swollen and bloody and her arm is bruised. She explains, "Donald came home drunk and flew into a rage because the apartment wasn't spotless. He said if that if I am at home and not working, the least I could do was clean up. I tried to explain to him that I was feeling sick today so I rested, but he wouldn't listen. He started screaming at me, calling me awful names, and then he grabbed my arm really hard and punched me in the mouth. I'm so afraid to go home, but I'm even more afraid to leave him. I can't make it on my own. It was my fault. I drove him to this. I should have cleaned up today and I didn't. I don't know what to do! But I don't have any choice; I have to go home to Donald."

Think about this event. Now take a few moments and rewrite the episode from the point of view of this woman. Before you give any consideration to how you might advise her to deal with this situation, imagine you are her, seeing the world through her eyes, walking in her shoes, and write down the thoughts, feelings and conscious experiences you have as Maria during the situation described above. In other words, try to experience the incidents just as Maria did. The goal here is not to condone Maria's decision to stay in abusive relationships, but to try to understand and empathize with her from her point of view. If you do want to have an impact on her future decision-making, empathizing with her first will help pave the way. If you are *unable* to put yourself in Maria's shoes you may have written something like this:

> What is wrong with Maria? How can she let herself be abused like that? If she had any sense at all she'd leave him immediately and never speak to him again. But she is obviously too stupid to do that. She's obviously very insecure and she clings to him because she is too cowardly to stand on her own two feet. She was abandoned by her father so she is trying to win the love of another man who is "no good" to compensate.

Here you were not putting yourself in Maria's shoes.
1. You were evaluating—she is stupid.
2. You were analyzing—she is insecure and cowardly.
3. You were explaining—she is trying to compensate for paternal abandonment.

10.2.3 Listening with Openness

It is very difficult to listen, to really hear what another person is telling you, if you are busy finding fault with the speaker or his or her words. When you adopt a judgmental stance you filter information and focus on whatever seems false, silly, or foolish, meanwhile ignoring any valid points or expressions of feeling.

Nearly everyone has trouble listening openly at least some of the time, particularly when the speaker is saying something antithetical to your point of view, or that contradicts your beliefs. Why is this? Because all of us, at least to some extent, fear being wrong. Your opinions and beliefs are closely tied to your self-esteem. You may equate being wrong with being stupid, bad or worthless. And it can be very threatening to witness your sacred cows being chopped into bits. How different the world would be if everyone could view their beliefs and opinions as temporary hypotheses, held until disproved or modified. The resulting openness to other paradigms or contradictory information would be a major step forward in interpersonal and international relations.

Adopting an accepting attitude is critical for creating a favorable climate for communication. Acceptance does not mean that you automatically agree with what the speaker is saying, or that you condone improper behavior. Acceptance refers to maintaining a basic attitude of positive regard towards the speaker, regardless of whether you agree with his or her words or behaviors. When people feel accepted it is much easier for them to be honest and open with you, and to put more stock in what you have to say. Adopting a judgmental stance puts others on the defensive and practically ensures that they will be very guarded in what they say and reveal to you.

Positive Psychology Exercise

Listening with Openness

In order to practice listening with openness, deliberately choose to listen to a radio or TV talk personality who espouses a view contrary to your own, be it political, religious, or moral. Take the time to listen with openness and find just one statement you can agree with, or fact that shouldn't be ignored. The point here is not to give up or forsake your whole philosophy on life, but to recognize common ground and the fact that even individuals with views diametrically opposed to yours will, from time to time, make points you consider valid.

10.2.4 Listening with Awareness

This involves listening with your eyes as well as your ears by paying as much attention to **nonverbal behavior** and voice tones as the words themselves. A good listener listens to and watches for more than the speaker's words. Attending to this dimension will give you valuable insights beyond the words and greatly enhance your ability to listen empathically.

In particular, pay attention to whether there is congruence, a match, between the speaker's body language, actions/nonverbal behaviors, and spoken words. Does the person's tone of voice, emphasis, facial expression, posture, and body movements fit the content of his or her communication? For example, if a speaker nods his or her head while saying no, or the reverse, subtly shaking the head no when agreeing to something, then obviously the person has ambivalent feelings. Or for a more extreme example, let's say someone tells you that his mother has just died, but meanwhile he is grinning and leaning back comfortably with his

The Global Perspective
The Global Ear

As you learned in Chapter 1, your paradigms about the world influence how you interpret your reality and even what you believe is truth. Most of us learn about past or current events in the world from TV news, the local newspaper, or school. If you are a news junkie then perhaps you surf the blogosphere or listen to talk radio to pick up news items or commentary. We assume that our media reports the truth. And indeed they do, but it is the truth from their perspective. The media plays a vital watchdog role in our society, but it is important to note that most popular media outlets (newspapers, TV channels, periodicals, radio stations) have, over the last twenty years, been increasingly taken over by powerful corporate conglomerates, and as such, they are not nearly as independent as they once were. As a result we are getting increasingly homogenized news accounts with less intensive investigative reporting, as the news has become more ratings-driven than concerned with discerning the facts. In addition, to some extent we are all brainwashed by the media who are now increasingly beholden to the corporate interests who own them.

If you take the time to look into news reports from other cultures or countries, you might find that often the same events are presented from very different perspectives. For example, reports from European news outlets, such as the BBC, often differ from U.S. broadcasts. Not surprisingly, the Al Jazeera TV network typically presents a very different take on events in the Middle East than U.S. TV networks. Even within the U.S. in these polarized times, different cable news outlets will present radically divergent perspectives on current affairs and emphasize vastly different events as exemplified by the gulf between FOX News and MSNBC or CNN. It has gotten to the point where each accuses the other of promulgating "fake news." Is anyone lying or is this just a function of how different perspectives affect reporting of supposedly objective "facts"? As a global citizen it is important to listen with openness to the views and perspectives of those in other cultures, even if you disagree. A refusal to even consider the views of others keeps you in the dark. Usually, common ground can be found when you are open-minded enough to listen. In our quest to improve worldwide relations and establish a lasting peace, a refusal to listen makes you a part of the problem rather than part of the solution. Take the risk and read or watch the news or commentary from other cultures. If you have friends who are recent arrivals from other countries, ask them how various world situations are perceived in their culture of origin. Open your global ears. Read or watch the news or commentary from other cultures. If you have friends who are recent arrivals from other countries, ask them how various world situations are perceived in their culture of origin. What do you learn from these experiences?

---

legs propped up on his desk. In this case you are receiving mixed signals, also referred to as **double messages**. There is no congruence between his words and his actions, thus the message is very confusing.

If the person's body language, facial expression, tone of voice and words don't match, your job as a listener is to clarify and give feedback about the discrepancy so as to deduce what the speaker is really feeling, or what is really going on. If you ignore the incongruity, you are settling for an incomplete or confusing message. It is important for you to realize that incongruity does not necessarily negate the veracity or sincerity of the spoken words. Resist the temptation to over-interpret nonverbal behavior. There typically are many potential explanations for incongruent body language. For example, in the case that someone smiles when telling you how sad he is that his mother has died, you should not necessarily assume that the person is secretly thrilled about the death. Sometimes people smile out of embarrassment over intense emotions, or as a way of distancing themselves from strong feelings. Similarly, if someone fails to keep eye contact when telling you she cares about you, does that necessarily mean that she is lying? Can you think of other reasons why she would behave in such a manner? For example, consider cultural differences in maintaining eye contact. Or think about the role of shyness in a person's ability to maintain eye contact. Remember, truly effective communicators always seek to clarify the message, without assuming that they already know the meaning of the message.

Questions

1. Reflective listening involves _____ what you have heard the speaker say so he/she can let you know if you have understood.

   A. questioning

   B. paraphrasing

   C. challenging

   D. ignoring

2. _____ listening focuses on reflecting back feelings and attempting to truly understand the other person's frame of reference.

   A. Empathic

   B. Reflective

   C. Emotive

   D. Pathos

3. Reflective listening includes all of the following components except_____.

   A. paraphrasing

   B. clarifying

   C. judging

   D. giving feedback

10.3 Understanding Nonverbal Behavior

Recognize and appropriately interpret nonverbal signals.

One of the main reasons why we are sometimes confused by what people say is because so much of what is being expressed is nonverbal. It has been estimated that only 7% of the emotional meaning of a face-to-face communication is conveyed by the words alone! That is a staggering figure. Up to 93% of meaning is communicated nonverbally (Mehrabian, 1971). It has been estimated that 38% of the emotional impact of our words is communicated by the vocal aspects of the message. This is referred to as **paralanguage**, which is a term given to how something is said rather that what is said. This includes characteristics such as the tone and pitch of voice, vocal inflections, emphasis on certain words, and the length and frequency of pauses. The other 55% of meaning is conveyed by facial expressions, bodily movements and gestures, duration of eye contact, and posture (Mehrabian, 1989). The reason why it is so important to pay close attention to nonverbal signals is that much of nonverbal behavior is unintentional and nonconscious, thereby revealing deep, underlying feelings or attitudes. A good listener attends to paralanguage, to those clues in voice tone, changes in pitch and tempo, and how quickly someone speaks. When anxious or excited, people tend to talk faster, but when depressed, grief-stricken, or overtired, speech generally is slower than normal.

Facial expressions are especially revealing, particularly the mouth and the lips. Smirking usually accompanies sarcasm. While in deep thought many people purse their lips, but when tense they may bite their lower lip. Most people recognize how revealing their faces are and may try to mask their emotions by putting on a face, such as smiling to hide anger. To a trained observer such forced expressions seem strained or put on, but an untrained eye could be fooled. The eyes have often been referred to as the "windows to the soul" because of what they can reveal. Our eyes are a good barometer of our level of social comfort. Avoidance of eye contact often reflects shyness, guilt or disinterest. Maintaining good eye contact communicates openness, interest and comfort. In addition, we tend to nonconsciously perceive pupil dilation as an indication of sexual attraction or interest. Too much eye contact, like staring, can reflect aggressiveness or erotic interests.

Body postures, bodily movements and gestures also reveal volumes about attitudes. If someone leans toward you it usually indicates interest and involvement in what you are saying, but if that person leans back it may reflect disinterest or a desire to get away. When people feel threatened there is a tendency to cross their arms over their body, a response known as body armoring. We get clues as to whether a person likes us or not by reading nonverbal cues. The kinds of nonverbal behaviors which can denote that someone likes you include smiling, head nodding, touching you, gesturing freely, raising the eyebrows, moving closer to you, and facing you squarely. On the other hand, body language that indicates dislike could include frowning, yawning, moving away, standing obliquely from you, shaking one's head and self-grooming actions (Kleinke, 1986).

Another important aspect of nonverbal communication is expressed through touch and the distance with which we choose to stand when interacting with others, referred to as **personal space**. Touching is perhaps the most intimate kind of physical closeness, which communicates different meanings depending on who does the touching and under what circumstances. Touch can reflect affection, sexual interest, dominance, caring, and sometimes aggression. The message that touch conveys will depend on how gentle or rough the touch, the length of the contact, whether it occurs in an appropriate context, whether it is a friend or a stranger doing the touching, and whether it is from the same or opposite sex. In an acceptable context, touch usually is well received. Touching behavior can also be an indicator of status and dominance. A higher status individual often feels free to touch a lower status person, but the reverse rarely happens. In addition, cultural factors play an important role because touching is considered more acceptable in some cultures than in others. For example, Latinos are much more comfortable with touching than say, the British. Cultural factors also play a focal role in acceptable distances for personal space. Intimate distance (0 to 18 inches away from the body) is reserved for family members, lovers, and very close friends. Personal distance (1 to 4 feet) is the space we earmark for conversations with friends and coworkers. Social distance (4 to 10 feet) is used for impersonal business and casual conversations. Public distance (10 feet and beyond) is reserved for speaking to a group. Carrying on personal or private business at such a distance would likely be considered very inappropriate, cold and aloof. Significant ethnic differences are apparent in the amount of personal space needed for comfortable interpersonal interactions. Americans, Germans and the English like more distance while Arabs, Greeks, Latin Americans, and the French prefer to interact at closer distances. Touching or standing too close to another person too soon can be perceived as an invasion of personal space.

The distance from which we stand from others when interacting can be very revealing about the nature of the relationship. One study demonstrated that couples in troubled marriages stood or sat significantly farther away from each other during conversations than those who were happily married (Crane, Dollahite, Griffin, & Taylor, 1987). A skilled marital counselor can learn volumes about a new couple presenting for marital therapy just by noting how far they sit from one another in the waiting room prior to their first appointment.

What about when an individual's words and overt behaviors do not match, even when words and nonverbal behaviors appear to be in sync? For example, let's consider a situation where someone appears to sincerely express interest in having a relationship with you, but continually makes excuses why he or she cannot spend any time with you. Or a situation where someone insists that engaging in a certain activity is very important to him, yet when the time comes to follow through he consistently fails to show up or do anything that is required. Oftentimes we are faced with dilemmas such as these, where people are giving very mixed messages between their words and their behaviors. As in the case with non-matching verbal and nonverbal cues, your job is to point out the discrepancy and ask for clarification. Follow the guidelines for the *Perception Check* explained later in this chapter for a method to get such clarification. If you have already done this and the discrepancy persists despite your best efforts, then the best rule of thumb, in general, is to believe the overt actions over the words.

10.3.1 The Rules for Effective Nonverbal Communication

Learning to accurately read nonverbal signals will greatly improve your ability to be perceptive and responsive to other people. As an added bonus, picking up on nonverbal cues will assist you in knowing when to adjust your own behavior. For example, if you are doing or saying something that offends or hurts another person, you can modify your behavior before the situation gets out of hand, as it might if you are oblivious to your impact on others. To summarize, we have synthesized this information into what we call the five rules for effective nonverbal communication:

Rule 1   Maintain good eye contact but be careful not to stare at others.

Rule 2   Use your body language appropriately to communicate interest in another, if that is your intent. Face the person squarely, lean forward, smile, gesture freely, keep your arms open, and nod your head at the appropriate times.

Rule 3   Speak clearly, fairly rapidly, and modulate your tone of voice and vocal inflections to keep your speech interesting.

Rule 4   Use the power of touch appropriately. Touch can be a potent tool for establishing rapport, but be careful. Strangers typically do not want or expect to be touched. Men often are not comfortable being touched by other men, except for close friends.

Rule 5   Respect the personal space of other people. Be sensitive to the cultural differences in what is perceived as an acceptable amount of personal space.

The subject of body language is fascinating and complicated, but a more in-depth discussion of this is beyond the scope of this chapter. If you are interested in learning more about nonverbal cues and how to accurately read them some suggested readings include:

Body Language   By Julius Fast
Manwatching   By Desmond Morris

10.3.2 Nonverbal Behavior for Effective Listening

Just as you the listener will be attuned to the body language of the speaker to help pick up feelings or underlying attitudes, the speaker will also react to the nonverbal aspects of how you listen. Certain nonverbal behaviors associated with good listening skills include:

1. Maintaining good eye contact

2. Leaning forward slightly

3. Nodding or saying, *"Uh huh,"* to let the speaker know that you are listening and to continue.

4. Keeping your arms open

5. Mirror the speaker

Remember that in order to establish high pathos, it is not enough to just deeply understand the other's experience. You have to enable the other person to feel that you do, indeed, "get him."

Questions

1. When our verbal behavior is not congruent with our nonverbal behavior, this is referred to as _____.

   A. paralanguage

   B. body armoring

   C. double messages

   D. false impressions

2. _____ refers to how something is said rather than the content of the words.

   A. Pathos

   B. Emotional intelligence

   C. Lying

   D. Paralanguage

3. Voice tone, facial expressions, and body postures are all examples of _____.

   A. verbal behaviors

   B. nonverbal behaviors

   C. body armoring

   D. paralanguage

10.4 Logos: Effective Communication—Developing Assertive Skills

Define the characteristics and benefits of assertiveness in communication.

Once you have established ethos and pathos, then and only then is it time to focus on logos. Effective communicators are adept at listening, but also skilled at expressing their own needs and desires. As mentioned earlier, effective communication is a two way street. It isn't enough to be a great listener if you cannot express yourself effectively in return. Oftentimes, the type of verbal expression that is hardest to master is the art of being appropriately and effectively **assertive**. Consider the following scenarios which may resemble situations that you or someone you know has had to face. These scenes were derived from stressful situations presented by participants in our Assertiveness Training workshops.

Scenario 1

You are a full-time student and also employed part-time to cover your expenses. A close friend of yours lost his job and was broke. Since you had some savings you offered to lend him several hundred dollars to meet his bills until he could find employment. He enthusiastically accepted your offer, and promised to pay you back as soon as he got a new job. A few weeks later he landed a job but made no mention about repaying the loan. You waited a few weeks for him to get paid and caught up with bills. A month passed and still no word from him on loan repayment. Then he invited you over to his home to see the brand new flat screen TV he just bought. You are feeling angry and thinking he may have taken advantage of your generosity by buying a luxury item before paying you back. Meanwhile, your car breaks down and without savings you are now in debt for the repair.

Scenario 2

You have developed a reputation at your company for being an excellent worker. As a result of your competence your boss keeps adding to your responsibilities. Although your workload has increased significantly, your boss has not offered you a raise. In order to keep up with your rising workload you have to work overtime several times a week. Since you are a salaried employee you do not get paid for overtime. You are growing increasingly resentful and stressed out. You worry constantly about keeping up with your work, but you are afraid to turn down new assignments and disappoint your boss.

Scenario 3

You have a long-standing friendship with someone whom you often get together with on the weekends. However, your friend has a habit of frequently canceling plans with you at the last minute, sometimes with good reason and other times not. You have been very understanding about this, and have not wanted to complain for fear of jeopardizing the relationship. It is Saturday night and you have special plans with this friend. You are all dressed and ready to leave when your phone rings and, once again, your friend cancels out. You feel very angry and disappointed.

Scenario 4

You are a legal secretary working for a high-powered attorney in a large law firm. Your boss, Mr. Reynolds, has a habit of strolling into work midmorning and wasting time until the afternoon when he goes into high gear and is quite productive. But because of his delays in getting down to work, paperwork that needs to be finished and filed that day is often not completed by the end of the workday at 5.00 p.m. You routinely work overtime for up to one full hour on almost a daily basis in order to complete paperwork that must be filed that day. Although this is inconvenient, the extra money you earn from overtime pay comes in handy and makes it worth your while. One day the firm's top managers announce that due to dwindling profits, all overtime work and pay will be indefinitely suspended. Your boss is not in agreement with this new policy, but has no power to change the mandate. You are very worried that you will be put in the uncomfortable position of having to work overtime for free in order to complete necessary tasks.

10.4.1 Assertiveness Defined

The scenarios described above represent the kinds of difficult situations that we all confront periodically. What these situations have in common is that they call for an assertive response. Whether you are a student, employee, employer, friend, or parent, situations will arise where you will need to assert yourself in order to deal with the situation. Assertion involves standing up for your personal rights and expressing ideas, needs, feelings and beliefs in direct, honest and appropriate ways without violating the rights of other people (Lange & Jakubowski, 1976). When you are assertive you can accept compliments and take criticisms. You can negotiate for what you need, disagree with another, and ask for clarification when you don't understand. You can set limits when necessary, and you are able to say "No."

The basic message you are communicating when you are assertive is: *This is what I think. This is what I feel. This is how I view the situation.* This message expresses who you are and is said without dominating, humiliating or degrading the other person. Assertion involves respect for others, but not deference. Deference is acting in a subservient manner as though the other person is right or better simply because they are older, more powerful, experienced, knowledgeable or in an authority position over you. When you express yourself in ways that are self-effacing, appeasing, or overly apologetic you are showing deference. Two types of respect are intimately involved in assertion: (1) respect for yourself, that is, expressing your needs and defending your rights; and (2) respect for the rights and needs of the other.

Assertive self-expression is a hallmark of effective communication skills. It is a prerequisite for satisfying interpersonal relationships. Being assertive will not give you an iron clad guarantee of having things go your way, but you maximize your chances of success while minimizing the chance of alienating others. Assertiveness contributes to interpersonal effectiveness, higher self-esteem, lower levels of stress, and more satisfying relationships (Davis, Eshelman, & McKay, 1988). Take a moment to fill out the following inventory (Rathus, 1973) to assess your level of assertiveness. In a nutshell, do you stand up for your rights or do you wimp out?

The Rathus Assertiveness Schedule (RAS)

Do You Assert Yourself or Wimp Out?

Indicate how well each item describes you by using the following scale:

3 = very much like me   −1 = slightly unlike me
2 = rather like me   −2 = rather unlike me
1 = slightly like me   −3 = very much unlike

_____ 1. Most people seem to be more aggressive and assertive than I am.*

_____ 2. I have hesitated to make or accept dates because of "shyness."*

_____ 3. When the food served at a restaurant is not done to my satisfaction, I complain about it to the waiter or waitress.

_____ 4. I am careful to avoid hurting other people's feelings, even when I feel that I have been injured.*

_____ 5. If a salesperson has gone to considerable trouble to show me merchandise that is not quite suitable, I have a difficult time saying, "No."*

_____ 6. When I am asked to do something, I insist upon knowing why.

_____ 7. At times, I look for a good, vigorous argument.

_____ 8. I strive to get ahead as well as most people in my position.

_____ 9. To be honest, people often take advantage of me.*

_____ 10. I enjoy starting conversations with new acquaintances and strangers.

_____ 11. I often don't know what to say to people who are sexually attractive to me.*

_____ 12. I will hesitate to make phone calls to business establishments and institutions. *

_____ 13. I would rather apply for a job or admission to a college by writing letters than by going through with a personal interview.*

_____ 14. I find it embarrassing to return merchandise.*

_____ 15. If a close and respected relative were annoying me, I would smother my feelings rather than express my annoyance.*

_____ 16. I have avoided asking questions for fear of sounding stupid.*

_____ 17. During an argument I am sometimes afraid that I will get so upset that I will shake all over.*

_____ 18. If a famed and respected lecturer makes a comment which I think is incorrect, I will have the audience hear my point of view as well.

_____ 19. I avoid arguing over prices with clerks and salespeople.*

_____ 20. When I have done something important or worthwhile, I manage to let others know about it.

_____ 21. I am open and frank about my feelings.

_____ 22. If someone has been spreading false and bad stories about me, I see him or her as soon as possible and "have a talk" about it.

_____ 23. I often have a hard time saying, "No."*

_____ 24. I tend to bottle up my emotions rather than make a scene.*

_____ 25. I complain about poor service in a restaurant and elsewhere.

(Continued)

_____ 26. When I am given a compliment, I sometimes just don't know what to say.*

_____ 27. If a couple near me in a theater or at a lecture were conversing rather loudly, I would ask them to be quiet or take their conversation elsewhere.

_____ 28. Anyone attempting to push ahead of me in a line is in for a good battle.

_____ 29. I am quick to express an opinion.

_____ 30. There are times when I just can't say anything.*

Scoring: For those items followed by an asterisk (*), change the signs (plus to minus, minus to plus). For example, if the response to an asterisked item was 2 it would then become −2. Then add up all the scores of the 30 items. Scores on this survey can vary from +90 to −90. The following table will show you how your score compares to those of 764 college women and 637 men from 35 college campuses across the U.S. For example, if you are a woman with a score of 26, your score exceeded 80% of the women in the sample, indicating that you are a very assertive person. If you are a man and you scored a 6, this is in the 40th percentile, a bit below average, which may indicate that you could benefit from becoming more assertive.

Percentiles for Scores on the RAS					
Women's Scores	Percentile	Men's Scores	Women's Scores	Percentile	Men's Scores
55	99	65	6	45	8
48	97	54	2	40	6
45	95	48	−1	35	3
37	90	40	−4	30	1
31	85	33	−8	25	3
26	80	30	−13	20	−7
23	75	26	−17	15	−11
19	70	24	−24	10	−15
17	65	19	−34	5	−24
14	60	17	−39	3	−30
11	55	15	−48	1	−41
8	50	11			

10.4.2 Differentiating Assertiveness from Passivity and Aggression

Non-assertion, also called **passivity**, involves violating your own rights by failing to express honest feelings, needs, thoughts and beliefs and consequently permitting others to potentially take advantage of you. It also involves expressing your thoughts and feelings in such an apologetic, diffident, or self-effacing manner that others can easily disregard you and/or your message. Nonassertion shows a lack of respect for your own needs. It can also imply a subtle lack of respect for the other person's ability to handle disappointments, to shoulder some responsibility, or to handle his or her own problems. The goal of passivity is to appease others and to avoid conflict at any cost. And often there is a high price to pay for routinely avoiding conflict. Part of the price paid for passivity is that it renders you ineffective.

Aggression involves directly standing up for your personal rights and expressing thoughts, feelings, needs and beliefs in ways which can be dishonest, usually inappropriate or intimidating, and always violates the rights of other people. The usual goal of aggression is domination and winning by intimidation, forcing the other person to lose, or at the very least, to lose face. Winning is assured by humiliating, degrading, belittling, or overpowering others so they become weaker and less able to express and defend their needs and rights. You need not get physical in order to be aggressive. Individuals who are aggressive directly compromise their effectiveness by alienating others.

We can think of assertiveness, passivity and aggression as being on a continuum with assertiveness, representing the effective midpoint between aggression and nonassertion. It represents a balance of respecting the rights of others while also respecting your own rights. It represents the effective middle ground of diplomacy between the deference and self-effacement characteristic of passivity, and the intimidation and bullying characteristic of aggressiveness. Put simply, when you are assertive you can set up a win-win situation. When passive you create a lose-win scenario and, obviously, when you are aggressive you produce a win-lose situation.

There is another ineffective option to assertiveness, and that is what we refer to as **passive-aggression,** which may sound like a contradiction in terms, but represents a form of behavior which we have all, at one time or another, demonstrated. Passive-aggressiveness is an indirect form of aggressiveness where we literally get back at someone, not by what we directly do or say, but by what we fail to do or say. The classic example is when you give someone the silent treatment when you are angry at him or her. This cold shoulder approach allows you to get back at the person by what you fail to do, that is, talk and be friendly. Or for another example, take the case of a formerly dedicated employee who feels that his boss is too demanding and eventually adopts an "I don't care attitude," deliberately working slowly and finding excuses to take time off work.

10.4.3 Negative Consequences of Non-assertion

Failure to handle situations in an assertive fashion can have very negative consequences for you and your personal and business relationships. In the short run, a passive stance helps you avoid anxiety-producing conflicts. However, in the long run, if you are frequently passive you will feel a growing loss of self-esteem and an increasing sense of resentment or anger. This increases your stress level which can lead to anxiety, depression and/or psychosomatic difficulties such as headaches, ulcers, or hypertension. On the other hand, handling situations in an aggressive manner also works in the short run because you may achieve a temporary emotional release and get your needs met through intimidation. But in the long run, the negative consequences of aggressiveness are obvious. Highly aggressive behavior at work may ultimately cost you promotions or even your job. If you are the boss, bullying your employees, supervisees, or co-workers leads to poor interpersonal relationships and literally invites passive-aggressive retaliation on the part of your colleagues. For example, a tyrannical boss may find that his subordinates react to his aggressive, authoritarian stance with work slow-downs, deliberate mistakes, property damage, theft, or backbiting. In your personal life, aggression can lead to failed relationships, high blood pressure, fights and even trouble with the law. People who are frequently aggressive eventually feel deeply misunderstood, unloved and unlovable because they fail to recognize the impact of their behavior on others and how such alienation is inevitable.

10.4.4 Benefits of Assertion

Being assertive maximizes the likelihood that your needs and the needs of others will be met, therefore increasing your effectiveness. It will definitely lower your personal level of stress and help ward off illness. One of the greatest benefits of assertiveness is that it will typically increase your self-respect and sense of self-efficacy, as well as garner respect from others. Numerous research studies support these conclusions. Galassi, Galassi, & Fulkerson (1984) reviewed the research on the effectiveness of assertive behavior as compared with either aggressive or passive behaviors for accomplishing the desired results, along with the impact of those differing styles. They concluded that an assertive approach is more likely to elicit compliance, greater respect, and sympathy, along with generating far less resentment or dislike than an aggressive approach. Although a passive approach is generally viewed by others as pleasant and friendly, it is far less likely to achieve compliance. In one study (Linehan, Brown, Neilson, Olney, & McFall, 1980), the effects of assertive responses were compared to the end results of flattery, fibbing, passivity and indirectness. Needless to say, the assertive responses won the day and were by far the most effective.

10.4.5 Why People Fail to Behave Assertively

There are many reasons and not all will apply to you. Ponder those reasons that are relevant for you and be aware of the misconceptions that often underlie your line of reasoning.

- Fear of loss of approval from others or of getting an angry response.
- Failing to distinguish between assertiveness and aggression. That is, mistaking assertiveness for aggression. This is a particular problem for women in

our culture who are given so many double messages, who are encouraged to be strong and outspoken and then vilified for being bitchy or masculine.

- Mistaking non-assertion for politeness or consideration. How can you learn to differentiate non-assertion from graciousness or politeness? A good rule of thumb is to listen to your body. Certain body signals will cue you when your response changes from politeness to non-assertion. Tension and discomfort will arise that typically are not present when you are being polite. If you are confused as to whether to assert yourself or whether to keep quiet and "be polite," you need to ask yourself the following questions:

  Am I likely to bring this up later?

  Will my relationship with this person suffer or change if I keep silent?

  Is there a hidden expectation present?

  Will I feel used because I have unexpressed expectations about reciprocity that may go unfulfilled?

- Mistaking passivity for being helpful because agreeing to do things you really don't want to do might help another person. In genuine helping, you eventually make yourself obsolete. In rescuing, you end up feeling used or taken advantage of by someone with an expectation that you will always be there to bail him out.

- Aggression is often an outgrowth of feelings of powerlessness, where a person believes that he will be controlled too easily by others unless he behaves aggressively. Here there is a tendency to behave aggressively as an overreaction to past emotional experiences.

- A maladaptive belief that aggression is justified and the only way to get through to other people.

- Aggression also often results from feelings of anger or hurt that have built up to a boiling point, leading to an explosion. If the situation had been dealt with assertively in the first place, the aggressive episode could have been prevented.

- Failure to accept your personal rights. It is hard to be assertive if you do not believe you have the right to express your reactions, take care of your needs and stand up for yourself. Some people not only feel that they shouldn't express their needs, but think they should not even have them in the first place.

The foundation of improving your assertive skills involves understanding and believing that you have certain rights as an individual and that it is not only okay, but healthy and useful to yourself and others to stand up for your rights. Individuals who are appropriately assertive and self-confident have internalized the following tenets (Lange & Jakubowski, 1976), as listed in the Assertive Bill of Rights:

The Assertive Bill of Rights

1. I have the right as a human being to have needs, and my needs are as important as the needs of others. I have the right to ask (not demand) that other people respond to my needs.

2. I have the right as a human being to have feelings and form opinions. Furthermore, I have the right to express these in ways that respect the feelings and opinions of others.

3. I have the right to expect respect from other people. It is incumbent upon me to also display the same respect for others. Respecting others does not mean that I allow them to take advantage of me or disregard my needs.

4. I have the right to choose whether, in a particular situation, I want to or can reasonably meet other people's needs or expectations.

5. I have the right to say "No."

6. If I frequently compromise my needs or sacrifice my rights, I am teaching others to take advantage of me.

7. If I live my life in such a way as to always avoid conflict or the possibility of hurting someone under any circumstances, I will end up hurting myself and others in the long run. It is only through the honest and timely expression of needs, feelings, reactions and thoughts that I can ultimately develop satisfying interpersonal relationships. When I am assertive everyone will benefit in the long run.

8. If I stand up for myself while simultaneously showing respect for others, I will gain self-respect as well as the respect of others.

9. By being assertive with others and explaining how their behavior affects me, I am giving them the opportunity to change their behavior and respecting their right to know where they stand with me.

10. I do not have the right to demean, intimidate, or manipulate other people into meeting my needs. I do have the right to ask, however, and to attempt to persuade while respecting their right to refuse.

10.4.6 The Power of "NO"

Central to your ability to be assertive is your willingness and ability to, at times, just say "No." To quote Judith Sills from her 2013 article on *The Power of No*:

> Wielded wisely, No is an instrument of integrity and a shield against exploitation. It often takes courage to say. It is hard to receive. But setting limits sets us free . . . No is both the tool and the barrier by which we establish and maintain the distinct perimeter of the self. No says, "This is who I am; this is what I value; this is what I will not do; this is how I will choose to act." (ppg. 53–54)

Many people are legitimately confused about when it is appropriate and/or healthy to say "No." Where should we draw the line between selfishness and a healthy self-interest? Adam Grant (2013), author of *Give and Take,* reminds us that saying "No" is one of the most important skills a people pleaser can develop. He emphasizes the importance of setting limits and saying "No" in maintaining a healthy work/life balance. "Without that ability, work will cannibalize your life," warns Grant. Sills (2013) recommends that you say "No" in the following situations:

1. When it keeps you true to your core values and principles.

2. When others attempt to take advantage of you, exploit you, or abuse you in any way.

3. When it is important to focus on your own goals rather than spend your time helping others reach their goals.

4. When you have to muster the courage to change course or make a difficult life decision.

Questions

1. Expressing your anger towards someone indirectly, by what you fail to do, is called _____.

    A. passivity

    B. aggression

    C. passive-aggression

    D. assertiveness

2. Assertiveness can be defined as _____.

    A. insisting that your way is the right way

    B. sacrificing your rights and needs for the sake of the rights and needs of others

    C. standing up for your rights and needs while disregarding the rights and needs of others

    D. standing up for your rights and needs without violating the rights and needs of others

3. Expressing your thoughts and feelings in such an apologetic or timid manner so that others can easily disregard your message is characteristic of

    _____.

    A. passive-aggressiveness

    B. passivity

    C. pathos

    D. logos

10.5 A Useful Framework for Assertive Behavior

Explain how the elements of the four-step framework can best be put into practice.

When learning to become more assertive or to polish your assertive skills, it can be very useful to have a framework or steps to follow in order to know how to construct a potentially effective assertive response. This applies on the job or in your personal life. A useful method known as "I Language" assertion, based upon the work of Thomas Gordon (1970), was developed to provide such a framework. In "I Language" assertion it is important that whenever possible, your language should include **"I" statements.** These statements refer to what you have observed, witnessed, or felt, so that you are taking responsibility for your feelings, experience and observations. This is in contrast to **"you" statements**, which typically involve pointing the finger at another person. What follows is a four-step framework that you should find helpful, especially at those times when you may not be sure how to proceed, for you can always fall back on these steps. This framework is not the gospel; you don't always have to follow this format, and this is not the only effective way to proceed. But nonetheless, this is still a very useful summary of how to construct an assertive response.

10.5.1 The Four-Step Framework

STEP ONE: THE PROBLEM BEHAVIOR The first step is to identify the problem behavior. It is important to keep your language to specific discussions of observable behaviors; do not address personality characteristics. For example, it is much more effective to say, "I am aware that you have not completed several reports that were due," rather than, "lately you have been so lazy!" The first sentence is merely a description of behavior or lack of behavior you observed, whereas the second sentence includes value judgments. If you make value judgments or comment on personality characteristics, particularly in a derogatory fashion, you are just likely to anger the other person, even if your description is totally accurate. You stand a greater chance of resolving the issue and getting the other person to listen to you if you limit your descriptions to observable behavior. If you merely tell someone he is "an idiot," it only demeans him and gives absolutely no information about what he did or did not do behaviorally to have merited that insult. Throughout the assertive steps, remember to use I statements that express your feelings without evaluating or blaming others. Just beginning your sentence with "I" is not enough. The focus of your statements needs to be on your feelings and your reactions, along with a statement connecting this to the specific observable behaviors of the other person. Recognize that there is a big difference between saying, "I feel hurt when you say _____," rather than, "You hurt me." Or contrast the blaming statement, "You are so mean to me," with the clarity of this message, "I feel angry when you break your promises."

STEP TWO: EFFECTS   Next you identify what effects the problem behavior has on you. There are two types of effects. The first refers to the difficulties or inconvenience that the problem behavior causes for you, and the second refers to emotions you have about the problem behavior such as anger, confusion, hurt, or disappointment. In some cases only difficulties are involved, in others only feelings, and in some instances both occur. When both are involved you can opt to only mention the difficulties and keep the feelings to yourself, such as in situations where you are dealing with strangers or peripheral acquaintances. This can also apply in a business situation, where it might be far more appropriate to deal with the problem behavior at hand than to express personal feelings.

STEP THREE: ALTERNATIVES TO THE PROBLEM BEHAVIOR   The third step involves specifying alternatives to the problem behavior. What is it that you would like the other person to do instead of or in addition to the problem behavior? You may think that this should be obvious and you don't need to spell it out, but many times, just because it is obvious to you what the person ought to be doing, it may not be obvious to him or her. Other people are not mind readers. If you are going to give feedback, give it fully and let others know clearly and diplomatically about your expectations. Once you have elucidated your expectations and have some inclination from the other person that she is receptive, you need to ask for a commitment for change. Do not be afraid to ask a person to commit to behaving differently. If she verbally agrees to change then she is more likely to follow through.

STEP FOUR: CONSEQUENCES (OPTIONAL)   It is very important to note that this last step is optional. Here you identify the consequences of the problem behavior if it persists. Basically, you are saying what will happen if the person does not stop the problem behavior. It is not always appropriate or possible to specify consequences, and that is why this step is optional. Sometimes the situation only calls for you to express how you feel about something and specifying consequences would be overkill. At other times it may be more strategic to wait to specify consequences and determine whether there is a need for escalation later on if the person refuses to change or acknowledge that there is a problem. Never specify a consequence that you are not thoroughly willing or able to follow through with, for then you run the risk that the other person will call your bluff and your credibility and clout will be damaged. If there are no consequences you can readily state and follow up on, then skip this step entirely.

10.5.2 Fine-Tuning the Assertive Steps

When asserting yourself, it is often very helpful to incorporate a style known as **empathic assertion**. Empathic assertion involves a statement reflecting pathos before starting with logos. Here you convey sensitivity to the other person over and above expressing your feelings or needs. When it is possible to proceed in this fashion, it is often highly effective because it helps to establish rapport and minimize defensiveness on the part of the other. It involves making a statement, usually in the first step, that conveys recognition of the other person's situation or feelings followed by another statement where you stand up for your rights and suggest other alternatives. It requires that you put yourself in the shoes of the other, and let him know that you have at least some understanding of his situation or feelings, but you still have your own needs to take into consideration.

Likewise, there are times when your initial efforts to be assertive are discounted and you will need to escalate. **Escalating assertiveness** describes a situation where you start with a minimal assertive response and, for whatever reason, it does not work. At this point, you do not back down but rather become increasingly firm and escalate without becoming aggressive. It is here that you may opt to include step four, the "consequences," because the other person has not responded appropriately to less firm statements on your part. Here you can gradually increase from a request to a demand. Or when someone is asking something of you, increase from stating a preference of "no" to an outright refusal. Or it could represent switching from an empathic assertive approach to a more firm, straightforward approach.

In the course of asserting yourself there are a variety of tactics others will often use to derail you before you get your point across. The most common tactic involves the other person interrupting you to tell their side of the story. Do not allow this. Firmly speak up and say, "Excuse me; I'd like to finish what I am saying." If they persist with interruptions, escalate and say, "Please stop interrupting me. I will give you plenty of time to reply, but now I would appreciate it if you would let me finish." Another side-tracking tactic is deflecting. Here a person responds to your assertion by bringing up things from the past, often irrelevant, that you have done to aggravate him. The best way to handle this is not to take the bait. Refuse to let the conversation be drawn in another direction, even if the complaint is valid. If it is valid you should promise to deal with it after your issue is resolved or thoroughly discussed. For example, you could say, "That is not relevant. If you want we can discuss that after we get through this."

10.5.3 Using the Four-Step Framework

If we return to the scenarios at the beginning of this section, we can construct assertive responses using the four-step framework and "I" statements. Study the following examples.

SCENARIO 1

> **Step One.** "Several months ago, when you were in a financial jam, I lent you $300. I was glad to help out. Over a month ago you got a new job but so far you have not paid back anything towards the loan. I recall that you had promised to pay me back as soon as you got a job. It has been over a month since you got hired at your new job."

Step Two. "I am feeling angry and disappointed that you chose to buy a new TV before paying me back. Right now I'm in debt because I had to pay to fix my car."

Step Three. "I would appreciate it if you could pay me back as soon as possible. If you cannot pay it back now, could you pay it in two or three installments? Can I have a commitment from you to pay back at least $100, if not the whole amount, by the end of this week?"

Step Four. "I am concerned that if this persists it will hurt our friendship."

SCENARIO 2

Step One. "I have been with this company for four years now and I'm pleased that you are happy with the quality of my work. Over the last few months, at your request, I have greatly increased my workload. In order to finish I have to work overtime and/or bring work home for which I do not get paid because I am salaried. And I have not gotten a salary raise in two years."

Step Two. "Given all the extra work I have taken on, I am easily doing the work of two employees. Although I have been willing to do the extra work, I do not feel I am being adequately compensated for the work I am doing."

Step Three. "I truly feel I deserve at least a 10% raise. My taking on extra work, over and above my job description, saves you from hiring someone else full- or part-time. I deserve to get some of that savings to you back in terms of increasing my salary. Can I receive a raise at this time?"

Note: If this should fail and the boss refuses, then escalate and include step four.

Step Four (option 1). "If you can't raise my salary at this time then I have no choice but to refuse to take on any more extra work. My job description does not indicate that I am responsible for those tasks."

Step Four (option 2). *This option is designed to use your leverage as a highly valued worker to persuade your boss to give you a raise.* "If you can't raise my salary at this time, I may have to begin searching for a new job. If I am going to be doing work at this level, then I deserve to be paid for my efforts. I know I can make significantly more money at other companies. My preference would be to stay here, but I may have no choice if you cannot raise my salary. By the way, keep in mind that if I have to leave, you may need to hire two people to handle my workload. So I believe it is in everyone's best interest for you to give me a raise."

SCENARIO 3

Step One. (Empathic assertion) "We have been friends for many years, and over this time there have been many times when you have canceled your plans with me, often at the last moment. I understand that sometimes things have come up for you that were out of your control, and you had to change our plans. But this has happened so often that I now feel I must speak up."

Step Two. "When you cancel out at the last minute it leaves me stranded because it is usually too late for me to make other plans, like tonight. And I feel irritated and disappointed, like I can't count on you. I fear our friendship will suffer."

Step Three. "I would greatly appreciate it if you could give me more advance notice when you are unable to keep our plans."

Step Four. (optional) "If you cannot commit to this then I may decide not to make plans with you again."

SCENARIO 4

Step One. "Mr. Reynolds, it is very important that we discuss the new rule about working overtime. (Empathic Assertion) I know that you had nothing to do with the new rules. But this is creating a problem for both of us. You usually don't come to the office until mid-morning and don't really get down to business until the afternoon. As a result, I have to stay overtime almost daily to get all the paperwork finished and filed on time."

Step Two. "If I do not stay late then important papers may not be filed on time. Our clients and your reputation will suffer, and I will feel as though I am not doing a good job. I am concerned that I will be put in the difficult position of having to work overtime for free which I feel is unfair to me. Working overtime takes away from my time with my family and makes it hard for me to keep up with my other responsibilities. I was willing to do it when I could earn a significant amount of extra money."

Step Three. "But I have some ideas about how we can resolve our mutual dilemma. First of all, you could agree to pay me out of your own pocket for overtime work and then I will be glad to continue as before. If that is not acceptable to you then we need to work together on time management. You need to come to the office by 9:00 a.m. and use your morning time more productively. If you are able to get the paperwork to me earlier in the day, then I will have no difficulty completing and filing all necessary papers by 5:00 p.m. I am willing to meet with you early each morning to help you organize your time more efficiently. We have to do something different because clearly we cannot continue functioning the same way. Which of these alternatives would you prefer?" *When asserting yourself with individuals in authority over you, it can be very effective to offer several options and ask them to pick one. That way they retain the illusion of control because they get to choose, and will often admire your ingenuity in developing solutions.*

Step Four. "I am not willing to work overtime on a regular basis unless I am compensated for my time. I may have to leave the office at closing time without completing important papers."

10.5.4 Tips for Saying No

Oftentimes the most difficult assertive response involves saying, "No," particularly to a friend or loved one. Sills (2013) offers the following suggestions for saying "No" in ways that help soften the potential blow or disappointment of others when you refuse.

1. Instead of responding with an automatic "Yes" that you may later regret, substitute that with, "I'll think about it." This prepares the other that you may decline while giving you time to weigh your options thoroughly.

2. Use soft language. Phrases such as the following say "No" but with tact and diplomacy:

   "I'd rather not" or "I'd prefer not to"

   "That sounds great, but I'm afraid I can't make it."

   "Let's agree to disagree."

3. Maintain a calm demeanor so your "No" does not convey anger.

4. Mention your commitment to others such as referring to the fact that your pre-existing obligations to others prevent you from agreeing to the request.

5. Rehearse your response in your mind beforehand, if possible.

Effective individuals are also adept at communicating in many situations, not all of which require an assertive response. There is an offshoot of the assertive response which has been called the **Perception Check** (Adler & Towne, 1993). This involves situations where there is not a need to assert yourself, per se, but when you are confused about the behavior of another and you want to check out what is really happening. A classic example, one that all of us have experienced at some point in our lives, is a situation where someone you care about is acting differently towards you, perhaps uncommunicative or standoffish. You don't have a clue as to what is going on. Is the person angry with you? Is the person upset, and if so, is that person upset for reasons that have absolutely nothing to do with you? The perception check is a useful, caring method for finding out and answering questions like those above.

An effective perception check is a three-step method with similarities to the four-step assertiveness framework, but with several fundamental differences. Here your aim is to be empathic, to elicit an honest response, and to listen to truly understand what is going on with the other person. First, identify what you have noticed about the other person by referring to observable behaviors or the absence of behaviors typical for that person, using "I" statements whenever possible. Secondly, give two possible alternatives or interpretations about what the person's behavior might mean or might be about. Lastly, ask for clarification. Statements which specify consequences or desired alternative behaviors have no place in the perception check. Of course, you do not always have to follow these steps, but if you are unsure how to proceed then this guideline will come in handy.

Questions

1. Which of the following is an effective "I" statement if your goal is to resolve a relationship problem?

    A. "I feel that you are selfish and uncaring."

    B. "I think you are a total slob and feel like you are trying to take advantage of me by leaving your stuff around for me to clean up."

    C. "I feel frustrated that you often change the subject when I try to express my concerns."

    D. "You are making me so angry."

2. When attempting to assert yourself, an effective message would start with

    _____.

    A. specifying consequences

    B. specifying alternatives

    C. apologizing for bringing the matter up in the first place

    D. identifying and describing the problem behavior using "I" statements

3. Which of the steps of the four-step assertive framework is optional?

    A. specifying the problem behavior

    B. identifying effects of the problem behavior

    C. laying out consequences if the problem behavior continues

    D. specifying alternatives to the problem behavior

10.6 Nonverbal Aspects of Assertiveness

Describe the ways in which you may communicate assertiveness nonverbally.

How you say what you say is just as important as what you say. That is, the body language you display has a profound effect on how your words will be interpreted and on the responses you will get. No matter how well crafted your assertive response may be or how appropriate your words, if your nonverbal behaviors are not congruent with your verbal communication you can totally sabotage your message, and greatly reduce the likelihood of getting the reaction you seek. If your nonverbal behaviors reflect passivity, deference, self-effacement, timidity, or lack of confidence you will undermine your message and invite others to discount your words. On the other hand, if your words are assertive and appropriate, but your demeanor is intimidating or aggressive it will also detract from your message.

Other people will respond with fear or resentment rather than accommodation. Effective communicators are congruent in words and body language.

Basically, you want to present a demeanor that is consistent with assertiveness. You want to put forth a bearing that is neither timid nor aggressive, but rather one that is forthright, confident, and matter-of-fact. In western culture one of the most effective ways to present a confident demeanor is to maintain eye contact. When you look directly into someone's eyes while talking to them it conveys confidence, self-assurance, and that you mean what you say. A passive stance usually involves minimal eye contact or looking down, which conveys lack of confidence or uncertainty about your position. An aggressive stance often involves staring a person down, which is not what we mean when we suggest making eye contact. Sometimes it is hard to maintain eye contact, particularly if you have trouble with being assertive, because it may make you uncomfortable. Despite this, we encourage you to train yourself to do so for several reasons: (1) it will make your assertive responses more effective, and (2) keeping eye contact gets a lot easier once you practice doing it.

Posture is also important when delivering an assertive response. You can maximize your effectiveness if you stand up straight, face the person squarely, and lean forward slightly. This conveys a sense of confidence. Likewise, if you are sitting down it is useful to lean forward slightly. Leaning back conveys fear or lack of confidence. People tend to lean back and look down when they are unsure of themselves or afraid. Obviously, getting too close to someone or getting in their face is an aggressive posture that you would want to avoid. It is always wise to respect the personal space of other people.

What you do with your arms reveals a lot about your internal state. For example, have you ever seen two people sitting across from each other in a restaurant, both with their arms folded across their body? Even though you might not overhear the content of their conversation, you can usually tell, just from their arm postures, that they are either arguing or annoyed with each other. How do you know this? Recall from the section on nonverbal communication earlier in this chapter that arms crossed over the body is a "body armoring" response, a nonconscious way to protect or hug yourself when feeling threatened. When threatened, most people will immediately adopt this posture nonconsciously. Thus, it is very important not to cross your arms over your body or you will convey that you feel intimidated by the encounter. Rather, make a point to leave your arms open. Open arms communicates that you are confident, comfortable and that you mean what you say. Incidentally, when on the receiving end of feedback, continue to maintain the open arm posture. In this way you will come across as non-defensive and open to feedback, qualities that are respected by others.

Also, allow yourself to gesture freely while asserting yourself. People tend to gesture and use their arms when they are comfortable. When you gesture you communicate comfort and confidence, therefore people are much more likely to take you seriously. But there is one gesture we recommend that you definitely avoid: pointing at someone. People hate it when you point at them like a scolding parent or an angry schoolteacher. They will tune you out and resist you if you resort to finger pointing.

Perhaps the most important nonverbal aspect of assertiveness is your tone of voice. So much is conveyed by the volume, pitch and rhythm of your voice. Avoid shouting which is perceived as aggressive. Also avoid being so soft-spoken that you come off as timid. It is best to speak in a firm, consistent voice tone where you pause for emphasis, and also emphasize key words by slowing down your voice tempo and increasing your volume slightly. Do not talk fast or swallow your words when asserting yourself. It may be useful to talk a little slower, particularly if you are a fast talker, and a little louder than usual for emphasis. Table 10.1 summarizes the differences between assertive vs. passive or aggressive communication styles.

TABLE 10.1 Differentiating Communication Styles

	PASSIVE	ASSERTIVE	AGGRESSIVE
Verbal Behaviors	Apologetic Indirect statements Rambling Not saying what you really mean Giving up easily	Direct statements Honest expression of feelings Describing objective behavior "I" statements Straightforward Good listener Talking slowly Emphasize key words	Accusations, threats Insults, put-downs Blaming "You" statements Sarcasm Failure to listen Manipulative comments
Nonverbal Behaviors	Incongruencies Poor eye contact Soft, timid voice Looking down Fidgeting Leaning back Slumped posture	Actions congruent with words Good eye contact Firm, calm voice Assured manner Gesturing Leaning forward Erect posture Open arms Face person squarely	Staring Yelling, shouting Loud, hostile voice tone Arms crossed over body Finger pointing Getting too close Clenched fists Breaking things
You Are	Scared, anxious Helpless Manipulated Ignored Resentful	Confident Effective Respectful Valued Relieved	Angry, full of rage Indignant Misunderstood Controlling Guilty
Others Feel	Frustrated Puzzled Unsure of your needs	Respected Valued	Intimidated Alienated Angry, resentful Humiliated, hurt Defensive
End Results	Stress Depression Low self-esteem Helplessness Failure to solve problem Resentment Lost opportunities Health problems	Problem solving Healthy self-esteem Self-respect Respect of others Satisfaction Good relationships Less stress Improved health	Interpersonal stress Guilt, remorse Low self-esteem Loss of self-respect Loss of respect from others Passive-Aggressive responses Frustration Failure to solve problems Broken relationships Loneliness Hostility from others Potential legal problems

The Global Perspective
Cross-Cultural Body Language

As you have learned, nonverbal communication is extremely important in any interaction with others. We tend to attribute more meaning to nonverbal aspects of communication and rely on nonverbal cues, especially when verbal messages are unclear or ambiguous. Since nonverbal behavior arises from our "cultural common sense," that is, our ideas about what is appropriate, normal, and effective (LeBaron, 2003), we interpret gestures, posture, silence, spatial relations, emotional expression, touch, physical appearance, and other nonverbal cues differently, depending on the part of the world in which we live. No wonder the importance of nonverbal communication becomes greatly multiplied when dealing with the varied cultures of our globe!

There are elements of nonverbal communication that are consistent across various cultures. Research has demonstrated that the emotions of enjoyment, anger, fear, sadness, and surprise are expressed in a very similar manner around the world. However, there are dramatic differences with regard to which emotions are appropriate to display in various cultures and by whom. For example, in many parts of the United States, it is more socially acceptable for women to display fear, but not anger, and for men to show anger, but not fear (Okun, Fried, and Okun, 1999).

Facial expressions can also lead to differing interpretations depending on the part of the world in which you live and the culture that predominates. In China and Japan, for instance, a facial expression that would signify happiness in other places may actually express anger or masked sadness, both of which would be inappropriate to express overtly. It is not difficult to see how these differences in interpretation may lead to confusion or conflict. Imagine that a Japanese woman is attempting to explain that the reason she had to cancel the previous meeting was due to a death in the family. She would likely do so with a smile on her face, based on her cultural belief that it is not appropriate to inflict the pain of grieving upon others. Her Western listeners, who understand smiles to mean friendliness and happiness, might interpret her behavior as cold or heartless. In addition, different norms regarding the appropriate degree of assertiveness in communicating can add to cultural misunderstandings. For example, most white Americans typically consider raised voices to be a sign that a fight has begun. In contrast, many African-American, Jewish, Italian, and Cuban Americans often feel that an increase in volume is a sign of an exciting conversation among friends.

Another nonverbal behavior, which varies greatly across cultures, is what is called proxemics, or the ways of relating to space. Very different ideas exist in different parts of the world about what constitutes polite space for conversations and negotiations. North Americans tend to prefer a large amount of personal space. This is likely because they are surrounded by it in their homes and countryside. Europeans, on the other hand, tend to stand closer to each other when talking, perhaps because they are accustomed to smaller personal spaces. An interesting study comparing North American and French children on a beach revealed that the French children tended to stay in a relatively small space near their parents, while U.S. children roamed up and down a large area of the beach (Okun, Fried, and Okun, 1999). The problem with our different ways of relating to space is the interpretations and judgments that we make regarding them. If Europeans are used to sitting or standing very close when they are talking to each other, they are likely to interpret the Americans' attempt to create more space as clear evidence of their coldness, condescension, or lack of interest. Conversely, an American who is accustomed to more personal space may perceive attempts to get closer as pushy, disrespectful, or aggressive.

Anthropologists Avruch and Black (1993) have noted that, when faced by an interaction that we don't understand, people tend to interpret the others involved as "abnormal," "weird," or "wrong." As global citizens, it is vital that we learn to control the human

(Continued)

tendency to translate "different from me" into "less than me." Such a paradigm does not engender trust or communication. It is important to remember the insight of a Maricopa Community College student in response to his participation in a collaborative project with a student in China: "I am happy to have met someone just like me, and yet nothing like me."

The key to effective cross-cultural communication is to begin with the assumption that there is a significant possibility that cultural differences are causing communication problems. Then, be willing to be patient and forgiving, rather than hostile and aggressive, should problems develop. You should always respond slowly and carefully in cross-cultural exchanges, not jumping to the conclusion that you know what is being thought and said. If things seem to be going badly, stop or slow down and think: What could be going on here? Is it possible that I misinterpreted what they said, or they misunderstood me? Am I misreading their non-verbal behavior or vice versa? Describe some of the key elements in effective cross-cultural communications.

10.6.1 Asserting Yourself with Aggressive People

It can be difficult and stressful to have to deal with aggressive, unreasonable, or nasty individuals, whether in your personal life or at your workplace. When dealing with such people it is common to feel as if you have no control, and to become angry and aggressive yourself. The following pointers should prove useful for handling encounters with aggressive people.

- Make ample use of empathic assertion. Try paraphrasing what you have heard the person say or commenting on the feelings expressed in their demeanor. For example, simple comments such as: "You sound like you are feeling very angry," or, "This is obviously very upsetting for you," can help an angry person to feel understood, and in some cases can help defuse their anger. It is also helpful to ask questions to get the person to clarify the problem and work towards a solution.

- Keep your focus. Aggressive interactions, particularly with people you know well, often get sidetracked from the original issue with laundry lists of everything else that is a problem. Work to bring the focus back to the issue at hand. Use phrases such as, "We've gotten off the subject. You were talking to me about..."

- Postpone the discussion until cooler heads prevail. If you and/or the other person are enraged, and neither of you will cool off soon, it may be wise to suggest discussing the matter later when both of you have calmed down. If the other person refuses to delay, explain that you need time to think about the issue and make a definite appointment to discuss it as soon as possible.

- Try the **broken record technique**. In an ordinary situation calling for an assertive response, the broken record technique could come off as obnoxious. But when dealing with an aggressive person who refuses to listen to your assertive response and who fails to respond to your efforts at escalation, this technique can come in handy to reinforce your request. Basically it involves repeating your request over and over, like a broken record, even if the other person is arguing, or ranting and raving. You just calmly continue to state your request, even during their protestations. It often involves being willing to interrupt. All parents have had to rely on this method at times when dealing with resistance or disobedience from children.

Questions

1. Which nonverbal behavior reflects passivity?
   - **A.** leaning back
   - **B.** leaning forward
   - **C.** finger pointing
   - **D.** good eye contact

2. Which nonverbal behavior would accompany an effective assertive response?
   - **A.** finger pointing
   - **B.** looking down
   - **C.** open arms
   - **D.** leaning back

3. Which nonverbal behavior would undermine an effective assertive response?
   - **A.** facing the person squarely
   - **B.** poor eye contact
   - **C.** erect posture
   - **D.** firm, calm voice

Summary

This chapter approached the subject of communication from the standpoint of the ancient Greek philosophy of **ethos, pathos,** and then **logos**. Ethos refers to your character (which we explored in- depth in previous chapters); pathos refers to your empathy and logos to your logic. To develop pathos, it is essential to have effective receptive communication skills, that is, the ability to really listen properly. The fact that there is an epidemic of poor listening was highlighted. The blocks to effective listening, many of which apply to each and every one of us, were reviewed. The process of **reflective listening**, a powerful method for really hearing and understanding the communications of another was described in detail. This was bolstered by an in-depth discussion of the meaning of various **nonverbal behaviors**, as up to 93% of the meaning in any face-to-face communication is conveyed nonverbally.

Effective communicators are adept at listening but also skilled at expressing their own needs and desires while respecting the needs and rights of others. This is the essence of the assertive response. To this end, one key aspect of expressing your logos is developing appropriate, responsible **assertive** skills. Assertiveness was differentiated from **aggression** and **passivity** while the benefits of assertion along with the negative consequences of non-assertion were explained. This chapter presented a useful four-step framework for constructing and conveying an assertive response with practical scenarios to illustrate the process. Lastly, the nonverbal aspects of passivity, assertion and aggression were reviewed to complete the template of how to develop effective assertive skills.

We urge you to practice using the four-step framework the next time you find yourself in a situation that calls for an assertive response, whether this happens in your personal life or on the job. These principles apply to all situations calling for effective assertiveness. Pay careful attention to how you feel after you assert yourself. Although you might experience some fight/flight activation as you initially engage in assertive behavior, the resulting relief and surge in self-confidence you are likely to experience afterwards will go a long way towards enhancing your perceived self-efficacy, boosting your self-esteem, and lowering your stress level.

Positive Psychology Exercise

1. We can virtually guarantee you that sometime in the next few weeks a situation will arise where you will feel the need to assert yourself, to express your needs, to say "No," or to check out a discrepancy you observe in the behavior of a friend or significant other. The situation may be as mundane as asking for a refund on damaged merchandise, or asking the noisy people behind you in the movie theater to be quiet. Whatever the situation may be, practice using the four step framework and see the difference it will make. Some people find it useful to rehearse the four steps in their mind prior to beginning the assertion, provided, of course, that you have the time to do so.

Key Terms

Active Listening
Aggression
Assertion
Broken Record Technique
Clarifying
Double Messages
Empathic Assertion
Empathic Listening

Escalating Assertiveness
Ethos
Feedback
"I" Statements
Logos
Nonverbal Behavior
Paralanguage
Paraphrasing

Passive-Aggression
Passivity
Pathos
Perception Check
Personal Space
Pseudo Listening
Reflective Listening
"You" Statements

Shared Writing

Which of the blocks to effective listening applies to you? Write about how you can become mindful of how and when you fail to listen well and what you can do to become a better listener.

Chapter 10 Questions

1. After two days, the average person remembers ____ of a conversation.

    A. 0%

    B. 25%

    C. 50%

    D. 100%

2. When you listen only to what you want to hear and ignore the rest, you are _____.

    A. derailing

    B. dueling

    C. filtering

    D. placating

3. Which of the following applies to effective listening?

    A. Listening happens automatically without any conscious effort on your part.

    B. It is important to be judgmental so people know where you stand.

    C. Good listeners don't ask questions, they just keep quiet.

    D. Good listeners are careful not to interrupt needlessly.

4. When you are listening with the primary goal of turning the conversation back to be about you, this is _____.

    A. rehearsing

    B. stage-hogging

    C. dueling

    D. comparing

5. What differentiates listening with awareness from reflective listening?

    A. judging the other

    B. stepping into the shoes of the other

    C. paraphrasing

    D. paying close attention to nonverbal behavior as well as words

6. Cultural factors play a big part in the _____ favored by each culture.

    A. single messages

    B. personal space

    C. double messages

    D. logos but not ethos

7. Which of the following applies to passivity?

    A. A common reason for failure to be assertive is mistaking passivity for politeness or consideration.

    B. The broken record technique is often used by passive individuals.

    C. Passivity is healthier for you in the long run than assertiveness.

    D. Only selfish people say "No."

8. If your initial efforts to be assertive are discounted, you will need to utilize _____.

    A. aggression

    B. passive-aggression

    C. escalating assertiveness

    D. the perception check

9. Empathic assertion _____.

   A. involves expressing yourself with a lot of emotion

   B. involves making a statement that emphasizes and describes your feelings

   C. involves making a statement that recognizes the other person's feelings and situation

   D. is a way to clarify yourself

10. It can be useful to use the perception check when _____.

   A. you are dealing with an aggressive person

   B. you are confused about the behavior of another and want to check out what is really going on

   C. you need to engage in escalating assertiveness

   D. the other person's verbal and nonverbal behaviors are consistent

Chapter 11
Establishing Positive Relationships

Learning Objectives

After reading this chapter, you should be able to:

11.1 Describe the key aspects of effective conversation and rapport building.

11.2 Explain how good friendships are built and maintained.

11.3 Explain the importance of attachment in both caregiving and romantic relationships.

11.4 Describe the ingredients in Sternberg's triangular theory of love.

11.5 Explain the behavioral and physiological aspects of creating and maintaining relationships.

11.6 Recognize some of the arguments for and against cohabitation.

11.7 Identify contributing elements of a successful marital relationship.

11.8 Recognize differences in the communication styles of men and women.

11.9 Describe the benefits of altruism.

In its totality, positive psychology is about all that makes for optimal human flourishing, and it goes without saying that what is of paramount importance to this is good relationships. In this context, we want to refer you back to the section in

Chapter 8 which discusses the two questions of utmost importance at the end of anyone's life. To reiterate, those questions are:

WAS I LOVED?

DID I LOVE WELL?

According to two current leading love researchers, Harry Reis and Shelly Gable (2003), even across different cultures and age groups, it is likely that having good relationships with other people is the single most important source of life satisfaction and emotional well-being for most individuals. In the same vein, positive psychology was characterized by one its founders, Christopher Peterson, as about "other people." For this reason Seligman (2011) included positive relationships as one of the core elements of PERMA. He asserts that "other people are the best antidote to the downs of life and the single most reliable up." This just underscores the lessons from Chapter 7 that good friends, harmonious relations with family, and healthy marriages promote happiness in ways that wealth, possessions, beauty and fame consistently fail to provide. Veroff, Douvan, & Kukla (1981) report that people, when asked to describe a very negative life event, invariably tell of the loss of an important relationship, either through death or break-up. Indeed, relationship problems are one of the most common reasons that individuals begin psychotherapy (Pinsker, Nepps, Redfield, & Winston, 1985).

11.1 How to Be a Good Conversationalist

Describe the key aspects of effective conversation and rapport building.

In order for relationships to develop and thrive, whether these ties are friendships, romances, or acquaintanceships, you need to utilize and fine tune your social skills. In the previous chapter we discussed the art of listening along with the importance of learning to read and understand nonverbal behaviors, and we also offered a framework for allowing you to express your needs and concerns in an assertive fashion. Recognize that initiating and growing relationships involves knowing how to engage in conversation and establish rapport with other people. Ultimately, effective communication is a two-way street. It requires good listening skills *and* good conversational skills. The foundation of successful interpersonal relationships, whether in your personal life or the workplace, depends on your ability to communicate your thoughts, feelings, concerns and needs. But just as hearing and listening are not necessarily the same thing, talking and communicating are not always the same. True communication only occurs if the speaker clearly expresses and the listener attends to and understands the message being conveyed.

People who are popular and well-liked typically are adept at making conversation. But being a good conversationalist is much more than just talking a lot.

We have all had the experience of being in the presence of someone who talked on and on, but bored us to death or made us uncomfortable with sustained self-absorption. Fontana (1990) offers these tips for expressing yourself effectively in conversations:

1. **Keep your message interesting.** Avoid rattling on incessantly about minor details, unless you know for sure that the listener sincerely wants to hear this trivia. Pay attention to nonverbal cues to discern whether the listener is getting bored and adjust your speech accordingly. If the listener starts to fidget, change the subject or ask a question.

2. **Show your sense of humor.** This doesn't mean you have to tell jokes or be a stand-up comedian. Allow yourself to make humorous or witty remarks when appropriate, and by all means, demonstrate that you have the capacity to poke fun or laugh at yourself. This puts others at ease by showing that you don't take yourself too seriously.

3. **Show an interest in the other person.** Refrain from being nosy, but do ask questions to draw the other person out. Most people will enjoy talking about themselves if given a chance, so you will make a good impression if you show a genuine interest in another person. Open ended questions, rather than yes or no questions, make for better conversation.

4. **Avoid monopolizing the conversation.** Avoid interrupting the other person.

5. **Stay focused on the topic at hand.** While everyone occasionally goes off on tangents, and sometimes this helps keep the conversation interesting, resist the urge to ramble without completing your main point.

6. **Offer sincere compliments when appropriate.** Everyone loves positive feedback.

7. **Refrain from engaging in annoying mannerisms** such as fidgeting or using irritating expressions, such as punctuating your statements with "you know" or "whatever."

8. **Engage in open, confident, non-verbal behaviors.** Face the person squarely, lean forward, stand upright, maintain good eye contact, keep your arms open and avoid shifting your weight from leg to leg which might appear as if you want to get away as soon as possible.

9. **Talk fairly rapidly, but not too rapidly.** A quick speech rate conveys enthusiasm, intelligence, confidence or expertise. If you notice signs of impatience in your listener, or if people are often finishing your sentences for you, this is a good tip-off that you are talking too slowly and need to pick up the tempo.

10. **Avoid controversy.** If this is an initial encounter and your goal is to make a good first impression then, according to Mary Mitchell (1998), refrain from discussing controversial topics such as religion or politics. Jokes are fine but avoid those that are vulgar or possibly could be perceived as prejudicial. Also, no one wants to hear about your health problems at a first meeting. Save the constipation stories for your loved ones!

Lastly, don't be afraid of small talk. While small talk is often dismissed as superficial or unimportant, nothing could be further from the truth. This idle chitchat or, "how's the weather" banter often serves as the ice breaker or lead-in to more meaningful encounters. Bernardo Carducci (1999) reminds us that just about every romance, or friendship or business deal begins with small talk when people first meet each other.

11.1.1 Building Rapport

There is yet another more sophisticated aspect of being a good conversationalist which has to do with being able to develop **rapport** with another person. Two people are said to have a good rapport when they are comfortable with one another and can get on the same wavelength, either emotionally, intellectually or both. To the extent that you can develop a good rapport with someone, you will increase the probability that you can put that person at ease and/or develop a friendship. Rapport building is affected by many variables. For example, it is often easier to establish a connection with someone if you share similar interests, backgrounds, values, or ways of thinking or expressing yourselves, the pull for "birds of a feather to flock together." Recent research (Chistakis & Fowler, 2014) supports this conclusively by demonstrating that friends have more DNA in common with each other than with strangers. Friends often display as much DNA in common as do fourth cousins. This is a function of the fact that we tend to choose friends who are more similar to ourselves which allows rapport to build naturally.

Likewise, if you are engaged in an activity together, like working on a project for a class or at work, this can help lay the groundwork for rapport. Psychologists have long known that **propinquity**, that is, having frequent contact with a person because you live close by or work nearby at the same workplace, is a big factor in who we develop as friends. But just being around a person a lot is no guarantee of friendship; propinquity only provides ample opportunity to develop rapport.

So how do you go about trying to establish rapport with another, be it a stranger or an acquaintance you would like to know better? To a great extent, developing rapport is about putting someone at ease by mirroring their nonverbal and verbal behavior. What does this mean? It requires that you be willing to be flexible in your presentation of self. This does not mean you need to be phony, but rather you need to mirror back those aspects of that person's behavior that you feel comfortable with. For example, if the person is very down to earth, feel free to let your hair down, but if the person is rather formal and uses a lot of big words, trot out your best vocabulary. If the person talks very fast, speed up your rate of speech. Likewise, if the person talks slowly, speak in a more languid way to mirror him or her. If the person gestures frequently, do the same, but if she is rather stiff, hold back on your gestures. Why does this work? Because most of us are more comfortable with people we perceive as being like us. Mirroring is one way of accomplishing this. Used in conjunction with empathic listening you will have the skills necessary to establish relationships. Charismatic and well-liked individuals do this mirroring automatically.

11.1.2 Overcoming Shyness

Some of you might react to these suggestions by saying, "I can't do this; I'm just too shy." Indeed, shyness is a fairly common problem reported by many people. Some people are shy in general, even with people they know well, while for others shyness is an issue mostly with strangers or in unfamiliar situations with new people. According to experts on shyness, Phillip Zimbardo and Lyn Henderson (2008), up to 40% of adults in the U.S. experience shyness during their lifetimes, from mild to severe. In addition, they claim that up to 13% of the U.S. population may have severe shyness, referred to as social anxiety disorder. There is clear evidence of a genetic component to shyness. Research has demonstrated that some infants show higher levels of stranger anxiety than others (Kagan, 1994). However, if you recall from previous discussions of the genetic loading on personality variables, at best only 40 – 50% of shyness can be attributed to genetic factors. The other 50% depends on your learning history and the choices you make. In other words, you can learn how to overcome shyness.

According to Bernardo Carducci, founder of the Shyness Research Institute and author of *Shyness: A Bold New Approach* (1999), there are three primary aspects of shyness:

1. **Excessive Self-Consciousness**—being overly aware of yourself in social situations, which leads to social anxiety

2. **Excessive Negative Self-Evaluation**—having low self-esteem, viewing yourself in a negative light

3. **Excessive Negative Self-Preoccupation**—paying way too much attention to all of the things you imagine you are doing wrong around other people

In general, overcoming shyness is about slowly desensitizing yourself to talking with people. This is accomplished by learning to relax, gradually exposing yourself to progressively more challenging social situations, and practicing social skills such as those previously discussed. The good news is that the more you practice, the better you get. On the other hand, being a loner, talking only to a select few people you know well, or avoiding situations with new people prevents you from having opportunities for growth and practicing social skills, and ultimately serves to reinforce your shyness. The following tips and suggestions are invaluable for overcoming social anxiety. You are now already familiar with many of these steps which have been discussed in previous chapters.

STEPS TO OVERCOMING SHYNESS

- **Understand your shyness** by recognizing the three factors previously mentioned and convert your self-consciousness into self-awareness.

- **Utilize cognitive restructuring** to challenge the negative thoughts or negative self-statements that reinforce your anxiety in social situations. Recognize that the world is not focusing primarily on you, as most people are too busy worrying about themselves.

- **Learn to accept yourself.** Remember that the most important relationship you have is with yourself.

- **Find and enhance your signature strengths and virtues.** How do your strengths give you an advantage? For example, being a quiet person allows you to be a better listener, which gives you a natural advantage for making and keeping friends.

- **Embrace your differences.** Be okay with being different. Trying to conform and be just like everyone else is exhausting.

- **Remember to remember to breathe** slowly from your diaphragm to calm yourself if you feel anxious in a social situation.

- **Release stress and tension though the practice of regular physical exercise.** Regular aerobic exercise will improve your mood, self-confidence, and self-esteem.

- **Use Visualization.** Imagine yourself conversing freely and confidently with others.

- **Practice thinking optimistically.** This will enhance your self-confidence.

- **Practice Social Skills.** Like any other skill, social skills can be cultivated through practice and real life experience. Practice in your head using visualization, or you can role play with a trusted friend.

- **Put the focus on other people instead of on yourself.** Ask open ended questions of others.

- **Practice being in uncomfortable situations.** Desensitize yourself by placing yourself in situations and gradually building up your tolerance. Start by going into social situations that are less intimidating and work your way up to more challenging encounters over time.

- **Know what settings bring out the best in you and begin there.** Going to bars and clubs is not the ideal setting for everyone.

- **Focus on the present moment.** Remember that when you are anxious you are either thinking about the past or the future. Bring yourself back to the here and now.

- **Do not leave an uncomfortable situation.** Turn the anxiety provoking situation into an opportunity for personal growth and introspection. Ask yourself, "What caused me to feel this way?" And more importantly, "Is there an alternate explanation for what is happening?" Although the desire to "escape" may be strong, it would be counterproductive because even though it decreases your anxiety in the short-term, leaving the scene rewards and increases your shyness in the long-term. It is very important to break this cycle of avoidance. Keep in mind that even the most popular individuals feel insecure and awkward at times.

- **Give up being perfect.** Do you tend to set unrealistic expectations for yourself by comparing yourself to TV celebrities, or people you idolize? If so, knock it off! Those "perfect" people you use for comparison are human as well. They make mistakes, do stupid things, say foolish things, and have bad breath in the morning just like you. You just don't hear about it or see it. Focus on excellence instead of perfection.

- **Accept rejection.** Into every life some rejection will flow. Accept that you too will experience some rejection in your life, and so will everyone else. It will not kill you. In fact, learning to cope with it is an important part of learning to deal effectively with life. To help you handle rejection consider the following tips:
  - Don't take it personally. It just wasn't meant to be. Not only was it not the best fit for you, it might even be a blessing in disguise.
  - Find the lesson. In every disappointment there is an important lesson to be learned and the potential for you to improve and gain insight into yourself. Nothing is lost if knowledge is gained.
  - Move on. When you throw a pity party, you are staying stuck. Self-pity never changed anything. Pick yourself up, dust yourself off, and try again and again and again. It will pay off.
- **Record your successes.** Keep a record or journal of your success. Visualize and remember those breakthroughs to help build your confidence prior to facing a social situation. Pull out your journal and read it when you need to remind yourself of your progress.

Questions

1. Which of the following is recommended for excelling at the art of conversation?
   A. Talk about yourself primarily.
   B. Go off on a lot of tangents.
   C. Show a sincere interest in the other person and what they have to say.
   D. Talk as fast as you can and avoid pausing so you will not be interrupted.

2. Really good conversationalists know how to _____.
   A. impress others
   B. establish rapport
   C. talk about themselves at length
   D. ingratiate themselves with a lot of insincere flattery

3. Which of the following is recommended for overcoming shyness?
   A. Avoid uncomfortable social situations.
   B. Remember to breathe.
   C. Focus on the past.
   D. Accept and take to heart all criticism without examining whether it has any validity.

11.2 Friendship

Explain how good friendships are built and maintained.

> *All other relationships and connections in this life are empty if friendship is not at the back of them to strengthen them. The relationship between mother and daughter, father and son, brother and sister, husband and wife, teacher and pupil, all these connections need a spirit behind them; and this spirit is the spirit of friendship.*
>
> Hazrat Inayat Khan from *In An Eastern Rose Garden*

In Chapter 8 we noted that when people reach the end of their lives they seldom wish that they had spent more time at the office. But when they look back at what gave their lives meaning, they invariably rate their close relationships as most important to that pursuit even if they have had remarkable career achievements (Bolt, 2004). Relationships are what make life worth living. Our happiness depends upon them. According to Peterson's (2006) summary of the research on friendship, feelings of well-being and life satisfaction are strongly associated with having high quality friendships.

As we look more carefully at friendships and the social support they provide, we realize that friendships do a lot more than keep us from being lonely on a Saturday night. It is literally a matter of life and death. Study after study links friendship and social support with health. For instance, a summary by David Myers (2004) noted the following:

- Leukemia patients who reported having strong social support had almost triple the two-year survival rate of patients who were more isolated.

- Heart attack recurrence was practically doubled in the six months after an initial attack when people were living alone. Over a five-year period, 50% of heart disease patients who lived alone died. Those who were married or had a close friend had an 84% survival rate.

- Studies consistently confirm a reduction in stress hormones, lowered blood pressure, and improvement in cardiovascular functioning when patients have a network of social support.

No one is entirely sure exactly how friends help us stay healthy. It may simply be that their presence is relaxing and reassuring and helps reduce the fight or flight response thereby promoting relaxation. We know that this boosts immune functioning. For many people, and especially for women, talking with a friend about a problem is a primary strategy for reducing stress. However, it may also be that friends encourage us to maintain healthier habits around eating, drinking, and smoking. Of course, this assumes that your friends have healthy habits. It is fairly common knowledge that some friends need to be left behind when people are attempting to cope with issues surrounding addiction.

It is also worth noting that being socially rejected by others not only impacts that individual but also affects those around him or her. One may literally become a less productive member of society and, in the extreme, may go on a murderous rampage as we witness periodically on the evening news. Bolt (2004) quotes Roy Baumeister at the 2002 APA convention summarizing this notion:

> *A great deal of psychological functioning is predicated on belonging to the group and enjoying the benefits, both direct and indirect, of that belongingness. Social exclusion undermines the basis for these sacrifices- it ceases to be worth it. The whole purpose of controlling yourself, behaving appropriately and making sacrifices is defeated. And so behavior may become impulsive, chaotic, selfish, disorganized and even destructive. (p. 184)*

The Global Perspective
Everything is Interconnected or How Wolves Change Rivers

We live in a world of relationships. Nothing in the Universe stands alone. As a result, all we do and all we fail to do have consequences which affect not only ourselves, but everyone and everything around us. Just as a pebble dropped in a still pool will create ripples across the entirety of its surface, our actions or inactions reverberate across time and space. We might delude ourselves into thinking that we are so insignificant that that there is little possibility that our behavior might lead to far reaching unintended outcomes, but it appears that, indeed, small differences can yield widely diverging results given sufficient time. Take as an example the following transcript reproduced from a video documenting the dramatic changes which have occurred in Yellowstone National Park since the reintroduction of the wolves. Thanks to the government's predator control program during the first decades of the twentieth century, wolves had been effectively eliminated from Yellowstone. But after years of persistent campaigns by conservationists, park managers, and biologists to bring the Gray Wolf (Canis lupus) back to what had once been its home, wolves returned after an absence of over seventy years. One of the most exciting scientific findings of the past half century has been the discovery of widespread trophic cascades. A trophic cascade is an ecological process which starts at the top of the food chain and tumbles all the way down to the bottom. And the classic example is what happened in the Yellowstone National Park in the United States when wolves were reintroduced in 1995. Now, we all know that wolves kill various species of animals, but perhaps we are slightly less aware that they give life to many others.

Before the wolves turned up—they'd been absent for seventy years—the number of deer, because there was nothing to hunt them, had built up in Yellowstone National Park. Despite efforts by humans to control them, they'd managed to reduce much of the vegetation there to almost nothing. They'd just grazed it away. But as soon as the wolves arrived, even though they were few in number, they started to have the most remarkable effects. First, of course, they killed some of the deer, but that wasn't the major thing. Much more significantly, they radically changed the behavior of the deer. The deer started avoiding certain parts of the park, particularly the places where they could be trapped most easily, particularly the valleys and the gorges and immediately those places started to regenerate. In some areas the height of the trees quintupled in just six years. Bare valley sights quickly became forests of Aspen and Willow and Cottonwood. And as soon as that happened, the birds

(Continued)

started moving in. The number of song birds and migratory birds started to increase greatly. The number of beavers started to increase because beavers like to eat the trees and beavers like wolves are ecosystem engineers, they create niches for other species. And the dams they built in the rivers provided habitat for otters and muskrats and ducks and fish and reptiles and amphibians. The wolves killed coyotes and as a result of that the number of rabbits and mice began to rise, which meant more hawks, more weasels, more foxes, more badgers. Ravens, and bald eagles came down to feed on the carrion that the wolves had left. Bears benefitted too, and their population began to rise as well, partly also because there were more berries growing on the regenerating shrubs. And the bears reinforced the impact of the wolves by killing some of the calves of the deer.

But here is where it gets really interesting. The wolves changed the behavior of the rivers. They began to meander less, there was less erosion, the channels narrowed, more pools formed, more riffle sections, all of which was great for wildlife habitats. The rivers changed in response to the wolves. And the reason was that the regenerating forest stabilized the banks so that they collapsed less often, so that the rivers became more fixed in their course. Similarly, by driving the deer out of some places and the vegetation recovering on the valley sides, there was less soil erosion, because the vegetation stabilized that as well. So the wolves, small in number transformed not just the ecosystem of the Yellowstone National Park, this huge area of land, but also its physical geography. (How Wolves Change Rivers, You Tube video at Sustainable Man as narrated by George Monbiot. To view visit http://www.youtube.com/watch?v5ysa50BhXz-Q#t). Describe some of the ways in which the reintroduction of wolves to Yellowstone National Park had a broader effect than originally predicted.

11.2.1 What Constitutes Friendship?

Beverly Fehr (1996) defined friendship as a "voluntary, personal relationship, typically providing intimacy and assistance, in which two parties like one another and seek out each other's company." Bolt (2004) notes that this definition highlights what seem to be the two critical dimensions of friendship, sharing and caring. Sharing and caring move us past liking and acquaintance, toward the deeper realm of friendship. Bolt noted that individuals who lack the opportunity to share their problems with a confidant experience more anxiety, depression, and physical symptoms. True caring between friends goes beyond exchanging support and favors. While a relationship is probably doomed to failure when there is no mutual give and take, true friends give their support and assistance without worrying about being repaid as soon as possible.

11.2.2 Creating Friendships

Friendships don't just happen. Like most other things of value they require committed effort. To a great extent we have already detailed the skill groups that are needed to form friendships. We would suggest that you revisit the section on creating win-win relationships in Chapter 9 with particular attention paid to the emotional bank account. Friendship is built upon trust and making regular deposits in the emotional bank account is the surest way to build that foundation. To enhance your friendships, we offer you what Bolt (2004) referred to as the "universal rules of friendship." The research reviewed suggests that the following thirteen rules provide excellent guidelines if you wish to have the joy of true friendship in your life.

1. Volunteer help in a time of need.
2. Respect the friend's privacy.
3. Keep confidences.
4. Trust and confide in each other.
5. Stand up for the person in their absence.
6. Don't criticize each other in public.
7. Show emotional support.
8. Strive to make him/her happy while in each other's company.
9. Don't be jealous or critical of a friend's other relationships.
10. Be tolerant of each other's friends.
11. Share news of success with the other.
12. Don't nag.
13. Seek to repay debts and favors and compliments.

Although we typically equate intimacy with a sexual relationship, this is not a requirement. "Intimacy is what you share with another human being who truly 'gets' you." (Phillips, 2017) Friendships provide as much opportunity for intimacy as romantic relationships. That's why people who begin as friends often end up as lovers, and why when a romance falls apart, we seek out our close friends for support and advice.

Intimacy begins when we self-disclose something meaningful to another person. When that is reciprocated a friendship ensues. But there are risks in opening-up. Is the other trustworthy? Does the other truly want to hear what we have to say? As a result, the preliminary stages of intimacy are often cautious. Social Penetration Theory (Altman & Taylor, 1973) posits that to build intimacy with a prospective friend or romantic interest, we begin with exploration, sharing impersonal or superficial tidbits to gauge how the other reacts. If the other is sufficiently responsive, then we feel safe to disclose even more. True intimacy takes time to grow. The process of opening-up to another and truly revealing yourself takes courage and patience, both of which are necessary to build sufficient trust to let defenses down. Genuine intimacy creates a bond where two people feel connected and understood with or without any sexual contact. This is what we crave when we are sad, stressed, or sick and need comfort and emotional support, while conversely it is also what we seek out to share our joys and successes, to celebrate with those who we trust are happy for us. As previously mentioned, this kind of social support is vital to our emotional and physical health.

But what if intimacy is imbalanced in an important relationship, if your friend is reluctant to open-up even if you have been more forthcoming? This does not necessarily mean you should ditch this friend. Lisa Phillips (2017) offers some tips on how to bring balance to a lopsided relationship or subtly encourage a reticent friend to open-up more. She suggests the following:

1. Be patient and make sure to reinforce (with praise and support) any attempt by the other to be more forthcoming.

2. Seek out other confidants or companions. No one friend can fulfill all your intimacy needs, accompany you everywhere, or share all your interests.

3. Avoid direct eye contact with a reticent friend. Spend time side-by-side instead, which may be less intimidating for a friend struggling with shyness or fear of self-disclosure.

4. Ask questions to draw your friend out. Make ample use of the Perception Check explained in Chapter 10.

5. Be compassionate. Use reflective listening and empathic listening. Do not offer advice unless it is requested.

Questions

1. Which of the following would be in contradiction to the "universal rules of friendship"?
   A. Put your own desires first.
   B. Keep confidences
   C. Show emotional support.
   D. Volunteer help in a time of need.

2. Having high quality friends and social support _____.
   A. is overrated
   B. is associated with physical and emotional health
   C. adds to your stress level
   D. is out of your control

3. _____ provide as much opportunity for intimacy as do romantic relationships
   A. Friendships
   B. Penpals
   C. Social media relationships
   D. Acquaintanceships

11.3 Attachment

Explain the importance of attachment in both caregiving and romantic relationships.

The concept of **attachment** has become important to understanding close emotional bonds, particularly those between family members and romantic partners.

It would be fair to say that attachment begins at the moment of birth and represents the emotional linkage that forms between a child and its caregivers, typically mom and dad, and allows for bonding over time (Ainsworth, Bell, & Stayton, 1992). A helpless newborn will only survive if an adult is willing, ready and able to meet its basic needs. So at birth a newborn's vital first questions concern whether he or she can count on his or her caregivers to be available, responsive, and responsible.

If caregivers fail to be appropriately available it can have a lasting impact on later behavior, as was initially documented by the British psychiatrist John Bowlby (1951), who introduced **attachment theory**. In 1950 Bowlby was assigned by the World Health Organization (WHO) to check on the mental health of children orphaned by World War II. What Bowlby discovered was that children raised in orphanages, even if clean and well fed, often developed pathological behaviors such as depression or head banging because they were profoundly emotionally neglected. That is, they had no opportunities to form warm, continuous relationships with a caring, adult caregiver. These children were basically just warehoused. Many of these orphans failed to thrive physically, and some even died from a lack of love. Bowlby's 1951 report revolutionized how children were treated at orphanages from that point forward. Bowlby spent the next twenty years studying how children form emotional bonds, and over the course of three volumes (1969, 1973, 1980) he elucidated his theory of attachment whereby he posited that humans are born with an innate predisposition to bond with an adult caregiver. Attachment evolved to ensure the survival of the species and operates via behaviors designed to regulate and indulge an infant's desire to be in close proximity to its primary caregiver. That is, an infant will continually monitor the whereabouts of the primary caregiver. If that caregiver is close by, the infant will be content and will play comfortably. If the caregiver moves away the child will become upset and all attention will be redirected towards regaining close proximity with the primary caregiver. And, according to Bowlby (1979), this attachment system does not disappear after diapers are shed; it operates throughout the lifespan of all individuals but is manifested in different ways.

Since that time Bowlby's theory has been refined and updated and several variations on the theme exist. The most elegant variation was introduced by Hazan and Shaver (1994) who explained that the question of whether a caregiver could be counted on to be available and responsive had three potential answers: yes, no, and maybe. They described three types of caregivers depending on which of the three answers they would give:

1. **Warm/Responsive**—Warm, loving, knows when to be supportive and when to back off, can be counted on to be there, reliable, trustworthy

2. **Cold/Rejecting**—Cold, distant, rejecting, not very responsive, very self-centered, child not a very high priority-often gives off message that child is a burden or a bother

3. **Ambivalent/Inconsistent**—Warm one minute and cold the next, loving and rejecting, unpredictable, has own agenda, does not always put child's needs first, loves child but does not always show it in the best possible way

11.3.1 Attachment Styles

All children are born with an inherent tendency or desire to bond. All children also have their own individual temperament, which combines with the level of responsiveness of the caregiver. This creates an interaction which leads to three distinct attachment styles as demonstrated by the behavior of young children in the Strange Situation Test (Ainsworth, 1973). In this experimental situation the behavior of one-year-old children is observed in a playroom that is unfamiliar to them while in the presence of their mother, after their mother leaves the room, and when a stranger enters the room prior to the return of their mother. This laboratory situation is designed to provide a wealth of information on how young children handle different separation situations. These three distinct patterns of attachment are observed:

1. **SECURE**—Young children with warm, responsive caregivers typically display secure attachments. While in the lab playroom with their moms they are comfortable exploring the unfamiliar environment. If mom leaves, the child becomes upset but then upon mom's return the child runs to her, is comforted, then calms down and resumes playing. Approximately 60% of North American infants displayed this pattern according to Hazan and Shaver (1994).

2. **AVOIDANT**—Young children with cold, rejecting caregivers display avoidant attachment. These kids don't cry when mom leaves the room nor do they seek her out when she returns. They ignore her as she may have ignored the child. They do not cling to mom like the securely attached young child. These children are just as unresponsive to strangers as to their mothers, preferring to focus on their toys. Approximately 25% of North American infants show this attachment pattern.

3. **ANXIOUS**—Young children who have experienced inconsistent and ambivalent parenting display anxious attachment. In the strange environment they are fearful and cling to mom and cry when she leaves the room, but at her return they are either indifferent or angry. Their inconsistent approach to mom mirrors her own inconsistency in parenting. These children are reluctant to explore their environments. They are hard to comfort and often cry even after being picked up. This style is displayed by approximately 15% of North American infants and is the rarest of the three patterns.

A later theoretical formulation put forth by Main and Solomon in 1986 identified a fourth attachment style.

4. **DISORGANIZED**—This is characterized by parental behavior that was frightening or traumatic (i.e. abusive) to the child or, at best, parental behavior that was profoundly neglectful or blind to the child's needs. This attachment style is also characterized by the passing on of anxiety ridden or disorganized behaviors to the child from the highly dysfunctional parent (Solomon & George, 1999).

11.3.2 Benefits of Secure Attachment

Children with a secure attachment history seem to fare better in a wide variety of social situations (Peterson, 2006) such as:

- Having more friends – being more popular (Sroufe, 1983)

- Less likely to be bullies or victims (Troy & Sroufe, 1987)

- More socially skilled (Pierrehumbert, Iannotti, Cumming, & Zahn-Waxler, 1989)

- Adapt better to school (Sroufe, Fox, & Pancake, 1983)

- More assertive with parents (Lyons-Ruth, 1991)

- Greater likelihood of good relationships (Peterson, 2006)

- Become more appealing to their caregivers and other people (Snyder & Lopez, 2007)

11.3.3 Attachment Styles in Romantic Relationships

What is really interesting about all of this is that attachment style isn't something that just describes how you interacted with your mom, or dad, or whoever was your primary caretaker when you were a baby or a teenager. It isn't a phenomenon that only affects the tenor of your relationships as a young child. The fact is that adult love relationships tend to mirror early infant attachments (Myers, 2002).

Your early care-giving experiences affect your expectations and view of the social world around you, whether you realize it or not. Our expectations revolve around questions such as, "Are people to be trusted?" Or, "Am I lovable or worthy of being loved?" The answers to these questions are rooted in your early, not consciously remembered experiences. And those answers will shape how you approach your close relationships, as it will affect two important components of your ability to relate: (1) your level of comfort with closeness (intimacy); and (2) your degree of anxiety or expectation of abandonment.

Think of your childhood attachment style as a paradigm you hold about what to expect from the world regarding relationships with a significant other. If you were fortunate to be raised by warm and responsive parents/caregivers, you likely have a secure mindset and view the world as typically safe, and others as reliable and trustworthy until proven otherwise. If you were raised by cold/rejecting parents, you likely hold negative and insecure schemas, and may expect rejection from others. You may feel uncomfortable with closeness as you probably experienced minimal intimacy with caregivers when young. You may feel more comfortable avoiding intimacy. If you experienced inconsistent parenting, then it is likely that you expect the world to be a very unpredictable place, and you anticipate rejection at every turn.

So it is not at all surprising that attachment styles established in infancy spill over in how adults conduct themselves in the context of romantic relationships with significant others. Cindy Hazan and Phillip Shaver (1987) had the insight that the three attachment types associated with children towards their caregivers could be utilized to describe how adults approached their intimate relationships. The four distinct styles can be described as follows:

1. **SECURE** adults are comfortable with getting close to others and are not overly concerned about either being abandoned or becoming too dependent on their significant other. Intimacy comes easily for secure adults whose relationships are characterized by trust, friendship, and the happiness that often flows as a result. Secure adults turn to others for comfort and support and are willing to be supportive to others. In marriage, secure adults are better able to accept their partners in spite of their faults and their relationships tend to be healthier and more long lasting.

2. **AVOIDANT** adults consistently find ways to keep emotional distance in their relationships with significant others. They tend to put less energy into maintaining relationships and are more likely to leave them. Some are fearful of or uncomfortable with closeness and intimacy while others are just dismissive of closeness and value independence and self-sufficiency over all else. Avoidant adults tend to withdraw when distressed rather than reaching out for comfort from loved ones. Their relationships often have emotional highs and lows, and they are prone to brief sexual encounters without emotional involvement.

3. **ANXIOUS** adults become obsessive when in love. Due to problems with trust and insecurity due their unpredictable upbringing, these individuals constantly expect to be rejected. These adults are often jealous, overly possessive, demand constant reassurance and reciprocity, and typically want more closeness than their partners are willing or able to give. Their relationships are often marked with instability, fraught with multiple break-ups and emotional angry outbursts. Such individuals can sometimes elicit self-fulfilling prophecies, that is, they are so afraid of abandonment that they literally drive their partners to leave them.

4. **DISORGANIZED** adults manifest chaotic, insensitive, explosive and even abusive behaviors. They crave security yet are unable to trust given their traumatic backgrounds.

Attachment Style Inventory

Fill out this inventory adapted from Levine & Heller (2014) to determine your dominant attachment style. Indicate the degree to which the following statements apply to you. When considering your answer think about your relationship history as a whole rather than just one relationship. How do you generally behave when in a relationship? Please answer all questions to get an accurate picture. Assign the following numeric values to these possible answers.

Strongly Agree	Agree	Neither Agree nor Disagree	Disagree	Strongly Disagree
5	4	3	2	1

1. It makes me nervous when my partner gets too close.

  | 5 | 4 | 3 | 2 | 1 |

2. I often worry that my partner will stop loving me.

  | 5 | 4 | 3 | 2 | 1 |

3. An argument with my partner doesn't usually cause me to question our entire relationship.

  | 5 | 4 | 3 | 2 | 1 |

4. When I show my partner how I feel, I fear s/he will not feel the same about me.

  | 5 | 4 | 3 | 2 | 1 |

5. I find it difficult to emotionally support my partner when s/he is feeling down.

  | 5 | 4 | 3 | 2 | 1 |

6. I don't feel the need to act out much in my romantic relationships.

  | 5 | 4 | 3 | 2 | 1 |

7. I fear that once someone get to know the real me, s/he won't like who I am.

  | 5 | 4 | 3 | 2 | 1 |

8. My independence is more important to me than my relationships.

  | 5 | 4 | 3 | 2 | 1 |

9. When my partner is upset I naturally know how to help him or her calm down.

  | 5 | 4 | 3 | 2 | 1 |

10. When I'm not involved in a relationship I feel somewhat anxious and incomplete.

  | 5 | 4 | 3 | 2 | 1 |

11. I hate feeling that other people depend on me.

  | 5 | 4 | 3 | 2 | 1 |

12. Sometimes people see me as boring because I create little drama in relationships.

  | 5 | 4 | 3 | 2 | 1 |

13. I miss my partner when we're apart but when we're together I feel the need to escape.

  | 5 | 4 | 3 | 2 | 1 |

14. I do not have difficulty expressing my needs and wants to my partner.

  | 5 | 4 | 3 | 2 | 1 |

15. If someone I'm dating begins to act cold and distant I'll worry that I've done something wrong.

  | 5 | 4 | 3 | 2 | 1 |

16. I bounce back quickly after a breakup. It's weird how I can just put someone out of my mind.

  | 5 | 4 | 3 | 2 | 1 |

17. I worry that if my partner leaves me I might never find someone else.

  | 5 | 4 | 3 | 2 | 1 |

18. If someone I've been dating begins to act cold and distant I will wonder what's happened but I won't assume it is about me until I know that for a fact.

  | 5 | 4 | 3 | 2 | 1 |

Scoring: Add up the values attached to the answers to each question in the following three columns. The highest score represents your predominant attachment style.

Column 1: Questions 3, 6, 9, 12, 14, and 18.   Total Secure Attachment Score _____

Column 2: Questions 1, 5, 8, 11, 13, and 16.   Total Avoidant Attachment Score _____

Column 3: Questions 2, 4, 7, 10, 15, and 17.   Total Anxious Attachment Score _____

BENEFITS OF SECURE ATTACHMENT IN ADULT RELATIONSHIPS:

- Less likely to divorce (Hazan & Shaver, 1987)
- Higher levels of compromise (Pistole, 1989)
- Lower rates of domestic violence and abuse (Dutton, Saunders, Starzomski, & Bartholomew, 1994)
- Better able to handle stress (Mikulincer, Florian, & Weller, 1993)
- More supportive of each other in joint problem solving tasks (Kobak & Hazen, 1991)
- More likely to practice safe sex practices (Brennan & Shaver, 1995)

11.3.4 Can Attachment Style Change?

By now you have an indication of which attachment style best describes you both in terms of your relationship with your parents and in your current love life. If you have a secure attachment, then this bodes well for the future of your relationships. But if you fall into one of the other two categories, are you forever stuck in relationship hell? Fortunately, the answer is no. Avoidant or anxious attachment styles can shift to a more secure attachment (Bolt, 2004). Understanding your attachment style and how it affects your behavior and expectations in relationships is the place to start. Using the cognitive restructuring techniques you have learned, you can begin to challenge any irrational thoughts that lead to maladaptive behaviors on your part, such as irrational jealousy or refusing to communicate with your partner by withdrawing.

Attachment patterns do not have to remain fixed. Bowlby (1988) argued that corrective relationship experiences foster more secure attachments. He postulated that since the purpose of attachment in the first place is to attain security, then change is more likely to occur in the direction of secure rather than insecure attachment. That is, we are more likely to pursue relationships that offer more as opposed to less security, than that to which we have become accustomed. Secure relationships are typically much more stable than either avoidant or anxious attachments.

11.3.5 Other Factors Affecting Attachment

There are three other components that strongly affect the strength and quality of attachment: closeness, care and commitment. Close physical proximity is a necessary component that allows both healthy infant and adult attachments to develop. These attachments have different primal motives, of course; for infants it is security, while for adults typically sexual attraction is at the core of an unfolding romantic attachment. But in both types of relationships the importance of physical touch is vital to emotional bonding, and close physical contact allows for this to occur.

The second important component for attachment to occur is a sense of safety that is mediated by care. Attachment grows best when there is easily accessed comfort and emotional support, whether from parent to child or between consenting adults. In this vein, it is interesting to note that research indicates that sensitivity and caring towards a significant other is a much better predictor of the strength of a relationship over the long-term than passionate sexual attraction (Kotler, 1985).

Security is derived from an environment of care, but that is only half of the story. The other half has to do with commitment. Children need to know that they can rely on caregivers who are consistently available, supportive, and committed to them in order to go forward into the world and meet the inevitable challenges of growing up. An adult in a stable, committed relationship is often better prepared to face the world of work and responsibility in a confident fashion. According to Hazan & Shaver (1994), commitment is the glue that ultimately holds relationships together over the long haul, ensuring security. But while commitment to children comes naturally for most parents, commitment in adult relationships is much trickier, requiring decisions and proactive behavior. Ultimately, closeness, care and commitment create an environment conducive to the development of attachment and even for love to grow.

11.3.6 Epigenetics: The Effect of Parenting Styles on Later Adjustment

Our friends in the animal kingdom have provided us with some tantalizing clues regarding the potential long-term, positive effects of loving early maternal care on genetic expression. While this animal research was not tied directly to attachment styles, it still points to hopeful possibilities for our species as well, if we extrapolate the results to humans.

Francis & colleagues (1999) demonstrated that the effects of calm, supportive mothering could be passed down through generations and influence genetic expression. They placed newborn rat pups, born to easily stressed rat mothers, with calm mothers who then reared the pups. Those adopted pups then grew up to be calm, and later were nurturing to their own offspring. Cameron & colleagues (2005), who also worked with rats, similarly observed that warm and nurturing behaviors of adopted mother rats led to healthy shifts in the pup's endocrine response to stress, thereby affecting gene expression for pups genetically predisposed to be anxious.

For examples closer to human parenting, we have the work of Suomi (1999) with rhesus monkeys. In this study, genetically over reactive baby monkeys, born from anxious mothers, were reared by calm, supportive, adoptive mother monkeys for their first six months of life. As a result, the babies calmed down. It appeared that the beneficial environmental effects of healthy early parenting reversed genetic predispositions towards anxiety or over reactivity to stress. Furthermore, these same monkeys raised by the nurturing moms were calm and supportive when raising their own children. This appears to demonstrate that the early rearing environment does influence and may even reverse the genetic expression of personality traits or temperament.

Questions

1. _____ begins at birth, represents the emotional linkage between an infant and its caregivers, and allows for bonding to take place over time.

   A. Love

   B. Attachment

   C. Co-dependence

   D. Co-parenting

2. Young children who have experienced inconsistent and ambivalent parenting display _____ attachment.

   A. secure

   B. avoidant

   C. disorganized

   D. anxious

3. _____ adults manifest chaotic, insensitive, and even abusive behaviors in relationships.

   A. Disorganized

   B. Avoidant

   C. Anxious

   D. Secure

11.4 Exploring the Meaning of Love

Describe the ingredients in Sternberg's triangular theory of love.

We think of love, sing of love, and say love makes the world go "round." Certainly for many people, love is the most important thing in their lives. We use the term "love" to describe everything from the food we eat ("I love pizza!") to objects ("I love that chair!") to deep enduring feelings we have for a cherished other human. We talk about love as if it is a single, uniform phenomenon, yet there are differing types of love. Robert Sternberg (1987) describes eight types of loving as part of his triangular theory of love. They include:

1. Non-love

2. Liking

3. Infatuated love (both strong emotional and sexual attraction)

4. Empty love (devoid of emotional involvement and physical attraction)

5. Romantic love (physically and emotionally bonded)

6. Companionate love
7. Fatuous love (instant attraction, passion and early short lived commitment)
8. Consummate love (passionate, intimate, and committed relationship)

Acknowledging these many types of love helps you realize that not all love is the same. The motives, thoughts, feelings, and behaviors attached to specific types of relationships can help you be aware of what type of "love" you may be seeking and/or experiencing. This can enhance your self-awareness and thoughtfulness about your caring connections with other people.

11.4.1 The Triangle Theory of Love

Sternberg (1987) describes the recipe for love as having three main ingredients: intimacy, passion, and commitment. **Intimacy** includes those feelings and behaviors that promote a sense of closeness, bondedness, and connectedness. Sternberg writes that intimacy includes at least ten elements:

1. Desiring to promote the welfare of the loved one.
2. Experiencing happiness with the loved one.
3. Holding the loved one in high regard.
4. Being able to count on the loved one in times of need.
5. Having mutual understanding with the loved one.
6. Sharing oneself and one's possessions with the loved one.
7. Receiving emotional support from the loved one.
8. Giving emotional support to the loved one.
9. Communicating intimately with the loved one.
10. Valuing the loved one.

Passion is primarily an expression of desires and needs such as self-esteem, nurturance, affiliation, dominance, submission, and sexual fulfillment. How strongly and which needs emerge depends on the person, situations and the kind of loving relationship. Passion and intimacy often interact with each other and fuel one another. Most people associate passion with sexual experiences, but it can be a part of any of the various needs one is feeling such as those listed above.

Commitment has two parts. The first part is a decision to love that person and the second is a commitment to maintain that love. This ingredient in a love relationship is especially important when (notice we didn't say "if") the couple gets into conflict. It is important to understand what the commitment means to each partner, although it can change over the course of the relationship. For example, in a marriage, does it mean commitment for life or commitment until the marriage isn't working?

Reexamining Sternberg's types of love, look at the connection between the type of love and the three ingredients of intimacy, passion and commitment in Table 11.1.

TABLE 11.1 Taxonomy of Kinds of Love

Kinds of Love	Intimacy	Passion	Commitment
Nonlove	−	−	−
Liking	+	−	−
Infatuated Love	−	+	−
Empty Love	−	−	+
Romantic Love	+	+	−
Companionate Love	+	−	+
Fatuous Love	−	+	+
Consummate Love	+	+	+

Note: + = component present;− = component absent. These kinds of love represent idealized cases based on the triangular theory. Most loving relationships will fit between categories, because the components of love occur in varying degrees, rather than being simply present or absent. (Sternberg, 1987, p. 51)

From this table you will note that Liking involves intimacy alone, Infatuated Love has passion alone, Empty Love has only commitment, Romantic Love integrates intimacy and passion, Companionate Love includes intimacy and commitment, Fatuous Love blends passion and commitment, but the ideal kind of loving relationship, Consummate Love, includes all three ingredients of intimacy, passion, and commitment. It is this latter type of love that most of us aspire to and some achieve. It is important, however, to remember that even if you accomplish consummate love, relationships are dynamic entities. Therefore, to make that ideal love last it is important that you and your partner build a strong emotional bank account, and that both of you proactively nurture the positive relationship you enjoy.

Nonlove lacks any of the three components. There is no passion, no intimacy, no commitment. For example, suppose you have a neighbor who lives a few houses down the block. You know her name, you recognize her, and sometimes you exchange a wave in passing or even have some brief spoken exchanges. There really is no relationship. This type of impersonal interaction is generally what we experience with people we see infrequently at work, in public, and with our other acquaintances.

Liking includes feelings we might have for our friends that we have known for years. When one experiences intimacy alone, we have liking, the type of platonic love that involves our friends. This is not, as Sternberg cautions, a casual non-important relationship, but rather a true friendship that does include a sense of connection, closeness and caring for the person. Liking, however does not include passion or commitment.

Infatuated Love involves only passion. Jamal first saw Maria at the gym and was smitten! He couldn't stop thinking about her and began getting up a half hour early to get to the gym just to be near her. He was overcome by his attraction toward her, and finally got up the nerve to talk to her. He asked her out for coffee after the workout, but she informed him that she was married. He had to back off, and in a short while he got over her. He no longer caught himself staring at her, and one day he realized that she had stopped coming to the gym.

This "love at first sight" is sudden, and can turn into an obsession about the other person. Being infatuated with someone results in a high state of passionate arousal but does not include either intimacy or commitment. In the case of Jamal, he did not even know Maria when he became fixated on her. As is usually the case in this type of love, it came upon him very suddenly, and was dispelled rather quickly when it did not lead to anything more. In infatuated love, the beloved becomes idealized rather than viewed realistically. Actually getting to know the person often leads to unpleasant surprises when he or she turns out not to be that prince or princess the obsessed person has imagined. This often leads to a swift termination. Likewise, the realization that there is no hope for this relationship to occur often leads to an abrupt end. Another concern is that the obsession could become very awkward for the recipient of such fixation. Infatuated love often comes across as a self-centered love, where personal needs rather than a true feeling of love are behind the pursuit of the beloved.

Empty Love is just as the term suggests—vacant. Many long-term marriages exist in such a barren environment and become *marriages of convenience*. Take for example the story of Rebecca and Stephen. They are an older couple who married years ago and raised children who moved to other cities. Theirs was a traditional marriage where Stephen was the bread-winner and Rebecca, who never worked, was the homemaker. They had fallen into a predictable routine with minimal one-on-one interaction. But each person did their part in the unwritten bargain to keep their lives going. Empty love has commitment as its only component. There is no passion; there is no intimacy. Why do they stay together? They stay because they find the arrangement convenient for survival, and may have insecurities about "making it" in the world on their own.

In many cases this is the state of long lasting marriages that began with a spark of passion, and had intimacy early on, which later faded. The couples seem resigned to this emotional emptiness. Sternberg points out that empty love, as in any type of love, can be one-sided where one partner still feels closeness and bonded to the other, but such is not reciprocated. Arnold Lazarus (1985) notes that when a long-term marriage devolves into empty love, it is difficult if not impossible to resurrect the old feelings of passion or intimacy that once existed.

Romantic Love combines intimacy with passion. Take into account the situation with Latoya and Dwayne. They met at a university summer program for advanced juniors in high school that introduced them to college course work. Their relationship started off friendly, but quickly advanced to a deep sense of love. They were inseparable during the six week program. But they lived across town and attended different high schools. They also had ambitious study and career plans for their lives. They recognized they were young with exciting futures ahead, and were both reluctant to commit to a permanent relationship, although they professed love for each other. Each got accepted to excellent colleges, but hers was on the east coast and he went to a university in California. Neither partner felt much certainty that their relationship would last through such separation. During their freshman year they saw each other occasionally, but eventually the relationship ended.

This is the typical pattern of romantic love where commitment is not included in the mix of intimacy and passion that provides the strong emotional attraction and friendship during the relationship. Although often the couple realizes they are not ready for a commitment, this does not seem to deter the relationship as they perceive commitment as something to think about down the road. A summer romance, like the one described here, is often highly exciting for the short-term with no real chance for continuing once the summer ends. Romantic love is often portrayed in classic literary works or popular movies about passionate couples who become true soul mates, only to have the relationship end such as in Romeo and Juliet. Although Elaine Hatfield and G. William Walster (1981) believe that there is no difference between romantic love and infatuation, Sternberg (1988) views the two as dissimilar noting that although some infatuations never progress beyond that stage, others do as the physical attraction leads to a realization that there is more to relationship beyond emotional chemistry. Furthermore, romantic love may not start off as infatuation, but evolve from a strong friendship that eventually grows into a fervent passion.

Companionate Love is a type that can endure throughout long-term relationships and marriages, but is lacking passion. It is comprised of intimacy which enables the partners to know each other extremely well, along with commitment to stick together through good times and bad as best friends. Millie and Miguel were married for more than two decades. They were certain that they were each other's best friend and were there for each other through major life crises. They were comfortable with each other and felt trust, security, and confidence in the strength of their commitment. Although they both realized that they were not now or maybe never were wildly passionate lovers, they were happy together and enjoyed each other's company.

Most romantic relationships, if they last long enough, do eventually shift into a companionate bond. Passion that may have existed in the early stage transitions into a strong commitment that keeps the relationship intact. However, one of the partners may still long for romance. This can lead to affairs outside the marriage which the roaming partner may rationalize is actually helping to keep the marriage in place. Or that partner may eventually leave the marriage to seek romance in a new love cycle.

Fatuous Love is similar to infatuation, but it has one difference. The couple not only feels a sudden intense passion, but they move rapidly to commitment. Take for example, Emily and Carlos. They met when both attended the same convention in Las Vegas. Instantly they were mutually attracted. Emily had broken her engagement a few months before, and Carlos' former girlfriend had recently called off their relationship. Certain they were meant for each other, they had a passionate fling that led to an elopement within a month. Shortly thereafter they began discovering aspects about each other that they were unaware of prior to the wedding. Needless to say, heartache turned into more heartbreak when their new marriage collapsed.

Typically those in fatuous love are those who are on the rebound from a failed relationship and have a strong need to be loved. They marry after knowing their partner for only a brief time. When they begin finding out about each other, imagine the surprises that emerge! Such marriages are usually a disaster and short lived. This is the type of romance and marriage often written about in tabloids from the Hollywood scene. Fatuous love is missing the intimacy that, over time, enables each person to learn about the other. Also, since the commitment is not there long enough to be well established, many fatuous love stories end in an early break-up.

Consummate Love is that glorious love for which most people yearn. This delightful type of love has it all—passion, intimacy and commitment. This composition is illustrated in the case of Jolinda and Juan. Admired as a model couple by their friends and family, they felt close and connected to each other and had great sex together even after twelve years of marriage. They seemed to read each other's minds and know each other so well they could predict each other's thoughts and behaviors. They had their ups and downs, as all couples do, but both remained enchanted with the relationship and had an extremely high regard for the other.

Consummate love is a complete love that results when all three components of Sternberg's triangular theory are present. Consummate love is not easy to attain, but even more difficult to maintain. We don't look for or expect to find consummate love in all our relationships. In fact, this type of love is often reserved only for that special love of one's life, a love that means the most to us and one we want to be as complete, complimentary, and as close to perfect as possible.

Think about the relationships you have with others in your life. Upon which of the ingredients of love are those connections built? Are you satisfied with that? If not, what changes could you make to achieve the kind of relationship you want?

Questions

1. Consummate love involves all three vital ingredients of _____.
    A. love, sex, and shared values
    B. honesty, fidelity, and rapport
    C. intimacy, passion, and commitment
    D. intimacy, compatibility, commitment

2. _____ love involves only passion.
    A. Fatuous
    B. Infatuated
    C. Consummate
    D. Romantic

3. Fatuous love involves _____.

    A. infatuation without commitment

    B. being catfished

    C. when someone pretends to be in love with you based on a hidden agenda

    D. sudden passion and a rush to commitment

11.5 The Chemistry of Love

Explain the behavioral and physiological aspects of creating and maintaining relationships.

Remember falling in love? When we ask our students in class to recollect, they invariably offer descriptions such as "beyond exciting," "lost my appetite," "couldn't sleep," "had butterflies in my stomach," "was obsessed," "thought about the person 24/7," "everything they did was wonderful," "wanted to be with them all the time." In contrast, when we ask them what it was like staying in love, the responses change to less dramatic adjectives such as "felt really comfortable," "felt secure," "thought of my lover as a best friend," "could share things easily," "saw my partner's faults, but it was okay." Most of us recognize that enduring love does inevitably change to an attachment phase that is deeper, yet much less exciting than the initial infatuation.

According to Helen Fisher (2004), an evolutionary anthropologist and research professor at Rutgers University, the experience of love can be best understood as a biological drive that is orchestrated by neurotransmitters and hormones. These **biochemicals** have evolved as a means of assuring the continuation of the species. The bliss we feel when we first fall in love is the result of significantly elevated levels of **dopamine** and **norepinephrine**, which cause, among other things, sleeplessness, lack of appetite, exhilaration, and single-mindedness. Add to this a decrease in serotonin, and no wonder you become so obsessed with the object of your affection! Fischer likens the effects when we are in the throes of passion to an addiction. And, indeed, as it turns out, these are the same brain chemicals released when you use cocaine. So whether from cocaine or Maria in Apartment 3, the elevated levels of norepinephrine and dopamine electrify the reward system in the brain.

Using f MRI technology, on both American and Japanese subjects of all ages, Fisher discovered that when someone falls in love, the parts of the brain that light up and become active are part of the reward system of the brain. One of them is the ventral tegmental area, a tiny part in the midbrain that makes dopamine and pumps it around the brain. This dopamine leads your prefrontal cortex (the thinking part of your brain) to feel more intense ecstasy, and increased motivation to make sure that your lover, or the drug, is there to give you more reward. That is probably responsible for the well documented *Romeo and Juliet effect*, the fact that when there are external barriers to a relationship, you try harder and you love harder.

Yet this "awe" brought about by norepinephrine and dopamine must eventually subside, as the levels of the neurochemicals themselves decrease. Truth be told, regardless of the generating source, you could not survive the elevated levels of the neourohormones. As the relationship becomes less novel, other neurochemicals begin to replace them, namely, **vasopressin** in men, and **oxytocin** in women. These are hormones that lead to long lasting attachment. They are called satisfaction hormones, because they do give a sense of calm and peace and security and often a cosmic sense of union. These "cuddle chemicals," released primarily during sex, facilitate the bond needed to raise children together.

So why is knowing this important? What practical application does it have? It turns out that the chemicals that give you the "high" get released in novel situations. It is the newness of an experience which prompts dopamine, with its intoxicating properties, to flood our synapses. In other words, new and varied stimuli can be sufficiently arousing to recapture what was initially so exciting about your mate. Not surprisingly, several studies have shown that couples who share exciting experiences report more relationship satisfaction, as well as romance, than do couples with more mundane habits. Endless routine, while perhaps comforting and stress reducing, can be the death of a relationship.

> When two people are under the influence of the most violent, most insane, most delusive, and most transient of passions, they are required to swear that they will remain in that excited, abnormal and exhausting condition until death do them part.
>
> George Bernard Shaw

11.5.1 Building Intimacy and Strong Relationships Over Time

One important lesson to remember is that in any long-term relationship, infatuation and sexual passion will eventually wear off because so much of it is based on novelty. After you have known someone and spent a lot of time with that person over several years (or in some cases several months), the novelty will eventually dissipate and the faults in your beloved's character will inevitably surface. In good relationships the infatuation is replaced with a deeper attachment not based solely on novelty. Intense passion can sometimes be stretched out for longer time periods in cases of long distance relationships, where you see your beloved infrequently so novelty takes longer to wear off, or in affairs where there is a danger and naughtiness factor that adds to the excitement and limits how much time a couple can spend with one another. But the bottom line is that the initial passionate infatuation is always time limited even in the best of relationships. Understanding this and knowing that it is normal helps foster realistic expectations for relationships. Epstein (2010) offers ten useful tips, based on intimacy research, about how to maintain love including:

1. **Arousal.** Research (Dutton & Aron, 1974) demonstrates that people tend to emotionally bond when aroused, like in situations involving adventures, stimulating exercise, or exposure to real or potential danger.

2. **Proximity.** When two people deliberately and consciously allow each other to invade their personal space, feelings of intimacy often result.

3. **Similarity.** Despite the cliché that "opposites attract," people typically pair off with others who are similar to themselves in important ways (Ariely and colleagues, 2007) or who are perceived to be similar (Tidwell and colleagues. 2012).

4. **Humor.** Lauer and Lauer (1986) found that in long-term happy relationships the partners made each other laugh a lot.

5. **Novelty.** Couples can help keep excitement alive in long-term relationships by avoiding endless routine and making an effort to engage in interesting and stimulating activities together whenever possible, to bring novelty back into the relationship.

6. **Vulnerability.** Allowing yourself to be vulnerable, which typically involves consciously lowering your inhibitions, facilitates bonding.

7. **Self-Disclosure.** People tend to bond when they confide in one another or share secrets, most likely because this involves allowing oneself to be vulnerable (Sprecher, 2014).

8. **Kindness, Accommodation and Forgiveness.** It is far easier to bond to someone who is kind, sensitive and thoughtful, especially when that person goes out of their way to accommodate your needs by deliberately changing his or her behavior. Forgiveness can also facilitate bonding as it requires a certain level of vulnerability.

9. **Touch and Sexuality.** Even simple non-invasive touch (i.e. a back rub) can generate positive feelings and closeness. Sexuality enables people to feel closer emotionally, especially for women. An important caveat, be careful to not confuse sexual attraction with love. You cannot truly love someone until you know them well and are past the infatuation stage which can blind you to the shortcomings of another or areas of major incompatibility.

10. **Commitment.** An essential element in building a long lasting love is commitment. When commitment is tenuous in long-term unions, it can lead to misinterpretation of a partners' behavior in a more negative direction.

What about what psychologists have called the intimacy-desire paradox, the concept that the greater the intimacy between partners, the less their sexual desire for each other? Given that newness and novelty are sexually arousing, does closeness and intimacy always attenuate sexual desire? Based on their research, Birnbaum, Reis, and colleagues (2016) claim that this intimacy-desire paradox does not necessarily hold true under all conditions. Their results point to the conclusion that whether intimacy decreases sexual desire depends on the context. "Responsiveness ignites desire by conveying the message that a partner is valued and worth pursuing. Sex is then seen as promoting an already cherished relationship," according to Birnbaum.

These researchers conducted three sequential experiments designed to determine whether partner responsiveness and intimacy-building behaviors could reawaken sexual desire within committed long-term relationships. For these studies, responsiveness was defined as behaviors that indicate sincere appreciation and support for a partner and a willingness to invest effort into the relationship. Responsive behaviors included listening and conveying understanding, communicating feelings of affection, and making the partner feel respected and valued. Not surprisingly, the results of the first study showed that, for women, sexual desire was greater while interacting with a responsive partner compared to an unresponsive partner. For men, the level of partner responsiveness was not associated with desire level. In the second study, the more often one partner displayed responsive behaviors, the more desire was reported by the other partner. In the third study, partners were asked to keep a daily diary for six weeks chronicling their sexual desire levels and their perceptions of their partner's responsiveness. Sexual desire for a partner was shown to be heightened when partners were perceived as responsive, but this effect was stronger for women. (Hint for men reading this book – responsive behaviors appear to have a subtle aphrodisiac effect on women. This is not an earthshaking finding. Women have been saying as much for millennia.)

In general, for many individuals (especially women) experiencing an intimate connection while feeling understood and valued is an essential element for sexuality to flourish. Therefore, it may not be the familiarity with each other that causes sexual desire to diminish, but rather the decline in unpredictability and novelty which are known to trigger a dopamine release and corresponding boost in libido. However, for some couples, intimacy and emotional validation go hand in hand with sexual desire and satisfaction. According to sexual satisfaction researcher David Frederick (based on the results from his 2016 study with Janet Lever and colleagues), "There are many ways intimacy and passion can become intertwined." Furthermore, his colleague Dr. Janet Lever states, "It was encouraging to learn that more than one third of the couples keep passion alive, even after a decade or two together. That won't happen on auto pilot: these couples made a conscious effort to ward off routinization of sex."

Questions

1. When we first fall in love, we experience elevated levels of brain chemicals such as _____.
   A. oxytocin and vasopressin
   B. serotonin and tryptophan
   C. dopamine and norepinephrine
   D. insulin and adrenaline

2. One of the primary factors triggering the release of the biochemicals of infatuation is _____.

    A. novelty

    B. attachment

    C. libido

    D. anxiety

3. A highly recommended way to relive the chemical high in long-term relationships is to _____.

    A. practice reflective listening

    B. argue

    C. give compliments

    D. do new and exciting things

11.6 Cohabitation

Recognize some of the arguments for and against cohabitation.

More than ever before couples are choosing to live together in loving and sexual relationships without getting married. This pattern is referred to as **cohabitation**, and data from Census 2000 revealed a 71% increase in the number of unmarried partners who lived together between 1990 and 2000 (U.S. Bureau of the Census, 2001). At present more than 5 million people in the United States are cohabitating. With over half of all women aged 25 to 39 having cohabitated at some point in their lives, living together in such an arrangement appears to have become the norm, rather than the exception. A generation or two ago, people who lived together were referred to as "living in sin." Be assured this was meant not in humor, but as a criticism. Witness the fact that until around 1970, cohabitation was illegal in all 50 states (Economist, 1999)! In contrast today, more than half of the Fortune 500 companies provide "domestic partner benefits" to both homosexual and heterosexual cohabiters (Miller & Solot, 1999).

Why do people cohabitate rather than marry? There are obviously multiple reasons, which include really getting to know a partner and their habits and character, wanting to see if they are compatible, saving money by living together, and feeling like they are not ready to marry yet (Poponoe & Whitehead, 2001). Interestingly, the cohabitation rate in the United States, which is about 5%, is low compared to the rate in other countries, such as Sweden and Norway, where 12% of heterosexual couples cohabit (Renzetti & Curren, 1998).

But are cohabitations successful? Do cohabitating couples have a higher rate of success if they marry later than do married couples who did not live together first? A study of 3,300 adults found that couples who live together before marriage are 46% more likely to divorce than those who did not (Labi, 1999). At first glance, this data might seem to indicate that cohabitating is, indeed, harmful to the longevity of the marriage and some conservative groups have alleged just that, calling it the "cohabitation effect." However, if you apply critical thinking you become aware that reaching such a conclusion about causality is definitely premature. Remember the difference between causation and correlation discussed in earlier chapters. There seem to be other factors that contribute to the difference, rather that the fact that the couple is cohabitating. For instance, couples who cohabitate tend to be less traditionally religious and more likely to believe in divorce when a marriage is not working. Whereas, couples who do not live together prior to marriage are likely to be more religious and less accepting of divorce (Miller & Solot, 1999). Thus, the causal factors are just as likely to be religion and attitude towards divorce, rather than whether or not they cohabitated. Another factor is that, on average, married couples have higher incomes than couples who live together outside of marriage. Given that financial problems are the most common factor associated with divorce, what we are actually seeing could be the effect of wealth and not cohabitation. Yet another possible factor is the age difference between cohabitating couples and married couples, as couples who choose to live together tend to be younger and the older the couple the less likely the divorce (Popenoe & Whitehead (2001).

So the answer to the question initially posed regarding the effectiveness of cohabitation is that we really don't know. Perhaps more importantly, the emphasis should be on the commitment between two people and the quality of the relationship, rather than whether or not they signed a marriage license.

Questions

1. When couples choose to live together prior to marriage, this is referred to as _____.

    A. blasphemy

    B. cohabitation

    C. arranged marriage

    D. polygamy

2. Cohabitation prior to marriage _____.

    A. has become the norm

    B. is still rare

    C. interferes with compatibility

    D. destroys relationships

3. Are couples who cohabitate prior to marriage more likely to divorce later on?

   A. Yes.

   B. No.

   C. It is unclear from the data.

   D. Yes, but only if they are religious.

11.7 Marriage

Identify contributing elements of a successful marital relationship.

By far, more adults marry than never marry, and the vast majority of individuals spend most of their lives within a marital relationship. Even today, the majority of young people say they are planning to marry at some point in their lives (Thornton & Young-DeMarco, 2001). In Western culture, romantic love and sexual attraction have become the basis for marriage. This has not always been the case, and it still is not in other cultures around the globe where marriages are arranged by the parents on the basis of age and social status. The partners in these couplings are expected to build their union and learn to love each other after marriage. It is surprising to most of us to note that a study comparing the levels of marital satisfaction between arranged marriages and those who married by choice demonstrated no significant difference between the two (Myers, Madathil, & Tingle, 2005)! Why? Perhaps because love is as much a decision as it is a condition.

Regardless of how the original pairing took place, maintaining satisfaction in the relationship over a long period of time takes attention, work, and commitment. Commitment in a relationship is often demonstrated by the decision to marry. Yet it is important to mention that many couples have long-term committed relationships, either heterosexual or homosexual, that do not involve marriage. Nonetheless, 93% of Americans say that a happy marriage is one of their most important life goals (Gallagher & Waite, 2000).

11.7.1 Factors Contributing to Long-Term Marital Satisfaction

So what are some of the factors that contribute to enduring satisfaction in relationships? One of these appears to be a sense of equality between the partners, particularly about decision making. Another is a genuine appreciation for one another and an attempt to understand the other's point of view. Also important is the ability to face conflict and disagreement early on, along with a willingness to work on the relationship by using effective communication (Byers, 2005).

John Gottman (1994), a renowned marital therapist, described four factors that were associated with long-term loving relationships. The first of these were positive memories about the beginning of the relationship. One of the authors, a practicing psychologist with a specialty in marital therapy, became aware of this fact early in his career. As part of the initial interview with couples, he asked each member of the pair if they remembered when they first fell in love. He noticed a better prognosis for resolving the issues they brought to psychotherapy when both partners were able to recall the loving feeling. A second factor involved similar levels of emotional expression between the partners. That is, it was okay when both partners were either very demonstrative or, conversely, more inhibited. Problems arose when there were very strong differences in styles of emotional expression, either with positive or negative emotions. The third factor outlined by Gottman and already previously mentioned was early confrontation of complaints and differences. When couples confronted each other constructively about disagreements early in their relationship, rather than sweeping them under the rug, the likelihood of continued satisfaction in the long run increased. Interestingly, Gottman did not find an absence of conflicts as predictive of marital happiness and fulfillment; rather it was how they handled such conflicts. Gottman's (1994) research indicated that the most effective partners in intimate relationships were able to avoid what he termed the *"Four Horsemen of the Apocalypse"* which are *criticism, contempt, defensiveness and stonewalling*. Defensiveness refers the inability to acknowledge or take responsibility for your behavior (i.e. blaming others for your behavior; refusing to listen to feedback and making excuses). Stonewalling occurs when you are evasive and/or refuse to discuss important issues or reveal yourself. Contempt refers to an attitude wherein you show no respect for another thereby communicating that you feel that person is below you. Of these four, contempt is often the most toxic and predictive of relationship termination.

Lastly, and perhaps most controversial in the field at the time, was Gottman's report that for marriages to be happy and fulfilling, there needed to exist a 5 to 1 ratio between positive and negative interactions. This ratio, referred to as the "**Losada ratio**" was discovered by Marcel Losada, who originally studied flourishing in business environments (Losada, 1999; Losada & Heaphy, 2004). His research determined that when there was better than a 2.9 : 1 ratio of positive to negative statements among employees within an organization, that business flourished economically. Gottman (1993) derived the same results when analyzing the weekend conversations of married couples. Below the 2.9 : 1 ratio couples were on the road to divorce, with the average Losada ratio at the time of divorce down to 1.5 : 1. A 5 : 1 Losada ratio, that is, five positive statements to every negative statement, between spouses predicts a healthy and loving marriage.

The fact is that maintaining frequent positive interactions is crucial to continued satisfaction in a relationship. It does appear that it is the little things that count. When a partner tells another, "You don't love me anymore," what it most likely means is "You are not doing the many little things you used to do that I interpreted as meaning you loved me." Once again, continuing to make deposits into the emotional bank account emerges as critical to the success of a marriage or any other relationship. And it appears that not allowing the account to go into deficit is not enough. Instead, for a relationship to flourish there needs to be a reserve of funds. In a latter study, Gottman found that the quality of the friendship with one's spouse is the most important factor in marital satisfaction for both men and women (Gottman & Silver, 2000).

An earlier study where 351 married couples were asked why their marriages have lasted found that marriages seem to last longest when both partners have a positive attitude toward the marriage, view their partner as a best friend, and like their partner as a person. Qualities that individuals particularly liked in their partner were being caring and giving, having integrity, and having a sense of humor. It was not that these couples were not aware of flaws in their partners; it was that they felt that the positive qualities far exceeded the negative ones. They preferred shared activities as opposed to separate ones and they also believed marriage to be a long-term commitment (Lauer, Lauer, & Kerr, 1990).

A review of the literature on marital satisfaction by Karney & Bradbury (1995) concluded that successful marriages that remain strong over the long haul often exhibit certain other characteristics. These included parents of both spouses having had successful, happy marriages, spouses with similar attitudes, interests, and personality styles, an adequate and steady income for the couple, satisfaction for both the partners regarding their sexual sharing (the quality was much more important than the frequency), and the woman having not been pregnant when the couple married.

In yet another study in which the investigators asked a sample of 560 women and men to judge the relative importance of a number of varying ingredients to the continued success of a relationship, the following elements were judged as most important to high-quality relationships (Sprecher, Metts, Burleson, Hatfield, & Thompson, 1995):

- Companionship: Sharing mutual interests and enjoying many activities together.
- Sexual expression: Spontaneity and variety in sexual sharing and feeling sexually attractive to one's partner.
- Supportive communication: Open and honest communication and a willingness to talk about difficult issues and concerns.

But why worry so much about making relationships last? With the divorce rate hovering around 50%, why not just accept that maybe, as some argue, we are not meant to be together "until death do us part?" One reason, as we have discussed earlier, is that researchers have consistently found that marriage positively affects a person's health and general level of happiness. People who are married tend to be healthier, happier, and enjoy longer lives than either single, widowed, or divorced individuals of similar ages (Zheng & Hart, 2002). Marriage, it seems, makes us more resistant and resilient to the impact of a number of possible traumatic events, such as losing our job, retiring, or becoming significantly ill. Suicide rates for single men are twice as high as those of married men. Similarly, single men experience more psychological problems, such as depression and nightmares (Faludi, 1991). While initially, these benefits seemed to apply more to men, the last few years have evidenced a trend whereby the physical and mental health benefits of marriage apply equally to both men and women (Simon, 2002).

11.7.2 Absent Presence: Technoference in Relationships

The technological rise of hand-held mobile devices, particularly smartphones, has expanded and enhanced our cultural and social world, but is simultaneously degrading our intimate personal relationships. Over the last decade more and more couples and relationship counselors report that technoference, the intrusion of cell phones, social media messages and other hand-held devices, is taking a toll on relationships. In a review article Marano & Streiber (2016) describe statistics showing that 70% of young married women report that important face-to-face conversations were completely cut off when a partner became distracted by a cell phone or desire to send a text. According to a 2014 Pew Research survey, 42% of participants in a serious relationship in the age range of 18 to 29 reported that their partners were often distracted by a mobile device. For couples of all age ranges, 25% claimed that cell phone usage was interfering with ongoing interactions. To make matters even worse, a study (Misra and colleagues, 2014) demonstrated that the mere presence of a smart phone (just as a nearby background object not in use) inhibited private conversations as partners appeared less willing to disclose their feelings or listen and try to understand each other.

This recent phenomenon appears to be growing. One of the authors, who regularly conducts couple and marital counseling sessions, has noticed an ongoing increase in couples reporting significant communication problems while "feeling neglected" due to one or both partners being overly involved with their smartphones, whether texting, surfing for information, trolling Facebook, online shopping, or just playing games while ignoring the significant other. Furthermore, the tendency to attempt to have meaningful discussions by text or worse yet, argue via text, leads to even more misunderstandings and miscommunications. Recall the lessons from Chapter 10 on non-verbal behavior indicating that 93% of the meaning of any message is not conveyed by the words. Where does that leave you when you are trying to discuss a serious issue by text with only 7% of the necessary information needed to truly understand each other? This author routinely gave homework assignments instructing couples to: (1) put away their phones when spending quality time together; and (2) use text messaging only to convey necessary, mundane information (e.g. What's your ETA?) and never to discuss anything consequential or serious.

If you stop and think about it, it is often in those unstructured, relaxed moments couples spend together (like riding in a car or walking the dog) that there is often the greatest potential to build closeness and a sense of connection. According to Marano & Streiber (2016), "Each of these deceptively minor interludes is an opportunity for couples to replenish a reservoir of positive feelings that dispose them kindly to each other when they hit problems." In other words, these are the times when it is easiest to make deposits in that all-important emotional bank account you carry with your significant other. But if your nose is regularly buried in your phone or your thumbs are busy texting, your partner fades into the background, neglected and ignored. Many people are so busy checking their devices they are oblivious to their partner's needs or bids for attention and connection. Next time you are in a restaurant, take a moment to look around. Notice how many couples are sitting across from each other, each staring at their phone instead of attending to each other. When you see that, you will know those are couples who already have issues (and are avoiding each other by focusing on their phones) or will soon develop problems due to **technoference**.

Przybylski & Weinstein (2012) reported that smartphones also create a barrier to establishing new relationships. In their study, pairs of strangers were assigned to discuss either impersonal or personal topics. According to these researchers, the presence of a smartphone, even if out of the visual field, inhibited the development of interpersonal closeness and trust reducing the extent to which individuals felt understanding and empathy from their partner. This was especially true under conditions where the pair was asked to discuss something personal that would require self-disclosure. The researchers further hypothesized that this inhibiting effect happens on a subconscious level.

Why would mobile devices nonconsciously inhibit intimacy? Misra (2016) posits that smartphones lead to a fragmenting of human consciousness and attention. Smartphones give off environmental cues offering enticing tidbits of information about other people, events, interests, breaking news, etc. which distracts from the person right in front of us. The upshot is that we feel less connected to a face-to-face partner thus less inclined to be open. What follows is a lower depth and quality of interaction in the presence of smartphones. Over time our habitual use of these devices diminishes our capacity for rapport and empathy. If you are physically present with your partner but frequently lured away by your mobile device, you have **absent presence** (Gergen, 2002). Most of us typically expect our close friends or significant other to be interested and involved when we are together. The closer partners are, the more entrenched this expectation, leading to greater disappointment if a device becomes a third party in a relationship.

Aagaard (2015) studied the effects of technoference on relationships among students ages 16 to 20. He found that the primary effect was an attitude of indifference associated with the ongoing presence of technology. He concluded that technoference misaligns partners emotionally, which leads to communications characterized by poor eye contact, delayed responses, and flat affect. Missing were the easy rhythms of rapport and humor that flow within healthy relationships where partners focus on and respond to each other rather than zero in on a screen in their hand.

Is technoference taking a toll on any of the important relationships in your life? Are you often absent present, distracted by your smartphone or iPad, while with people you care about? Have you recently felt neglected by a significant other who was too busy texting to really pay attention to what you have to say? If the answer to any of these questions is yes, what do you plan to do about it before the relationship withers away? You have a choice about your behavior, about how much time you want to devote to your device at the expense of your spouse, lover, friend, or cherished relative. And if the one who is absent present is your partner or friend, you can choose to use the assertive skills you gained from Chapter 10 to identify the problem and ask for what you need. Think about it. What's more important; the most recent Facebook post, or that game of Candy Crush, or your relationships?

11.7.3 Improving Marital Communication— Active and Constructive Responding

One of the goals of positive psychology is to teach individuals how to improve the quality of their relationships. The following discussion, while geared towards improving marital communication, is applicable to any relationship with a significant other or friend. Learning to engage in **active, constructive responding** will enhance your Losada ratio with others, thereby enabling you to improve troubled relationships and turn good relationships into great ones.

According to Pileggi (2010), how couples respond to each other over good news may matter more to their relationships than how they support each other during the tough times. Shelly Gable (2006) surmises that although working as a team to deal with problems is vital to a relationship, this will not necessarily enable a couple to find enjoyment in each others' company. It is also vitally important for a couple to be able to feel and share joy with one another. Our significant others often come to us to share news about their accomplishments, successes, as well as a myriad of other positive or interesting things that happen to them. According to Gable, how we respond to these communications can either build the relationship or undermine it. Barbara Frederickson (1998) reminds us that sharing positive emotions enables us to connect more closely with our partner as it helps break down barriers and creates stronger emotional attachments. In general, there are four basic ways of responding to your significant other when they approach you with good news (Gable & colleagues, 2004; 2006), summarized as follows:

Active & Constructive: Acknowledging what the speaker has said, asking questions, offering praise, excitement and optimistic expectations, sharing the good feelings and supporting the positive emotions of the other.

Passive & Constructive: An unemotional reaction, giving polite but subdued acknowledgement to the speaker with minimal enthusiasm or follow-up questions.

Passive & Destructive: Ignoring what the speaker is telling you, shrugging it off as if it has no importance and/or changing the subject quickly.

Active & Destructive: Immediately pointing out all the potential pitfalls about what the speaker has told you, complaining about the effects of the news on you, expressions of pessimism or negative emotions about the news, failure to express congratulations or offer any enthusiasm.

To flesh this out, review the example of these four possible responses to the following scenario: Your significant other comes home from work and informs you s/he just got a "terrific performance review" which should positively impact the size of the year-end bonus.

Active & Constructive: "That's wonderful! I'm so glad your boss is finally appreciating how hard you work and the quality of your work. I am so proud of you! You deserve a big bonus and I'm sure you will get it. Tell me all about your review. What compliments did you get and from whom?" *Nonverbal behavior*: Displays of positive emotion, good eye contact, smiles, laughs, hugs if appropriate.

Passive & Constructive: "That's nice. It's about time." *Nonverbal behavior:* No follow up questions, minimal emotions like it is no big deal or unimportant, a demeanor equivalent to being told some neutral information about the weather.

Passive & Destructive: "OK, now what we need to think about is what to cook for dinner." *Nonverbal behavior*: Disinterest, minimal eye contact, no questions or comments, changing the subject to a neutral, unrelated topic.

Active & Destructive: "I'll bet you use that as an excuse to work longer hours than you are now, and then what happens to me? I'll be stuck doing even more stuff at home alone while you are busy getting your ego propped up at work. I hope you are happy. By the way, don't get your hopes up. Your boss is way too cheap to give you a bonus." *Nonverbal behavior*: Anger, sarcasm, glaring, passive-aggressive looking away or walking away. No questions or praise.

Which one of these attitudes would you like to come home to? That's a no brainer! If you put yourself in the shoes of the person coming home with good news, it is very easy to see how the active and constructive response would build good feelings and rapport in your relationship. The other three options would either lead to disappointment on your part or even anger and resentment if your significant other chose an active, destructive reply. Using active and constructive responding allows you to make deposits in the emotional bank account you hold with your significant others.

Remember that positive emotions are contagious. Allow yourself to be infused with the joyous emotions of the other and then give the gift of returning it. The more you do this with a spouse or significant other, the better your Losada ratio, and the better the relationship. In addition, engaging in active and constructive responding will draw people to you. They will like you more and want to talk to you. Everyone likes someone who shows a sincere interest in them combined with a willingness to acknowledge and celebrate their successes.

Positive Psychology Exercise

Practice Active and Constructive Responding

The next time a friend, relative, co-worker or especially your spouse tells you about something good that happened to them, go out of your way to reply in an active and constructive fashion. Ask them all about it and show enthusiasm. Pay attention to their response and to how you feel.

THE IMPORTANCE OF PROVIDING EMOTIONAL SUPPORT What about when your partner comes home with negative news, particularly involving work related complaints or stressors? Providing emotional support to a spouse or significant other is just as important as responding constructively to good news. Emotionally supportive partners improve the quality of their relationships with an extra added benefit: this helps your partner cope better with workplace stress. Consider the following unpublished study conducted in 2011 by Wayne Hochwarter, professor at the Florida International University college of Business (as reported in the Miami Herald on 2/15/2012). In this study 400 working couples in both blue and white collar professions were surveyed to determine how couples handle it when both experience daily workplace stress. Partners who did not feel that they received adequate emotional support at home returned to work even more distressed. When mutual positive spousal support was present, these couples reported the following as compared to the non-supportive couples:

- 33% more positive relationships with co-workers
- 33% more satisfaction with time spent with spouse
- 20% higher level of career satisfaction
- 25% less fatigue
- 25% higher ability to concentrate at work

Clearly, it is important to be there for your partner, to be available as a sounding board, a shoulder to cry on, or just to be willing to listen to the other vent. Partners can also help their significant other to problem solve or reframe workplace issues. In Hochwarter's study, there were differences between men and women in the type of supportive behaviors they desired. Both genders wanted their partner to understand the unique demands and stressors of their particular job or work environment. However, the women wanted empathic responses from their men, and to be cut slack on household chores when they were overworked. In general, what men wanted from their significant others was affection, expressions of appreciation and opportunities to have some time alone. This brings us to the very interesting topic of how gender influences communication styles and patterns between men and women.

Questions

1. A Losada ratio of 5:1 positive to negative interactions in a marriage predicts
   _____.

   A. divorce

   B. conflict

   C. a healthy and lasting relationship

   D. getting bored with each other

2. Of all the negative attitudes displayed in marriage, _____ is the most toxic and predictive of divorce.

   A. criticism

   B. contempt

   C. defensiveness

   D. stonewalling

3. The best way to reply to your significant other when s/he tells you something positive that has happened to her/him is to use _____ and _____ responding.

   A. active; constructive

   B. passive; constructive

   C. passive; destructive

   D. active; destructive

11.8 Communication Styles—Do Men and Women Speak a Different Language?

Recognize differences in the communication styles of men and women.

Most of us have a wealth of experience from our own history of relationships to recognize that one of the most important factors affecting the longevity and quality of relationships is communication. Have you ever experienced difficulties communicating with the opposite sex? Did it ever feel like you were speaking a different language? Most of us have had the experience of looking back at an argument with a heterosexual partner and wondering what we were actually fighting about. Research supports the fact that conversations among men and women are, indeed, more difficult than same-sex groups (Athenstaedt, Haas, & Schwab, 2004; Edwards & Hamilton, 2004).

11.8.1 Genderlects: Report Talk vs. Rapport Talk

Deborah Tannen (1990, 1994), a professor of linguistics at Georgetown University, has done extensive research on the different communication patterns between men and women. She contends that while not necessarily speaking a different language, it is as if we are speaking different dialects of the language. She refers to these conflicting dialects as **genderlects.** A word of caution here, please be aware that the patterns we will discuss are generalizations and do not necessarily apply to every individual man or woman. Remember that at our core, we are far more similar than we are different (Hyde, 2005).

Men's and women's genderlects stem from different paradigms each appears to hold about the world. Men tend to perceive the world and their relationship with others as hierarchical. A hierarchy is much like a ladder, with each man posed on one of its rungs. They must struggle to either move up the ladder or at least maintain their position. Women, on the other hand, are more likely to view the world as a series of interactions and interconnections. Their goal is to remain connected and avoid isolation. Studies have revealed that women tend to use more rapport-talk, aimed at establishing connections and relationships, while men favor report-talk, which imparts knowledge (Eckstein & Goldman, 2001).

Tannen (1990) studied videotapes of individuals from a variety of age groups talking to members of their own gender. As she watched children communicate and interact with each other in same-sex playgroups, she became aware that girls habitually faced each other squarely when talking, maintained good eye contact, and seemed to enjoy conversing with one another. Girls were also more likely to play in small groups, or even in pairs. Winning or losing in their play was not as important as maintaining intimacy and a sense of community. This is clearly demonstrated when girls play house. They wanted to get along with their friends so that everyone could have a turn. On the other hand, boys appeared to use speech as a way to express dominance in groups which were hierarchically organized and everyone knew their place in the hierarchy. Their main focus seemed to be on directing and winning. Their play groups tended to have a leader who would tell everyone what to do. Interactions among the boys reflected attempts to vie for attention and deflect the challenges of other boys in order to remain the center of attention. They often jockeyed for position by telling jokes, showing off, or claiming they were the best at things. When boys and girls encountered conflict, both wanted to get their own way, but their methods were starkly different. Boys tended to rely on insistence and threats of physical violence, while girls usually tried to avoid confrontation and arrive at a compromise.

Differences in communication style between adult men and women are rooted in this apparent fact that they have grown up in different sociolinguistic subcultures and have learned different communication rules and assumptions (Maccoby, 1998; Maltz & Borker, 1982). These rules follow them through life and become problematic when as adolescents, they begin to communicate in mixed-sex groups with the same rules they used to communicate with their same-sexed peers.

STATUS VS. SUPPORT   For men, conversation is often about getting and maintaining the upper hand and preventing others from pushing them around. For women, talking is frequently a way to exchange confirmation and support. Tannen offers an example from her own life which amply demonstrates this difference. Tannen and her husband are both following academic careers, doing research and teaching in higher education. Because such vocations most often require a job setting at a university, for a period of their lives they lived a few hours away from each other. Tannen noticed that whenever she and her husband were at a gathering and someone would comment on how difficult it must have been to live apart, her husband's typical retort was something like, "Oh, it's not so bad. We see each other every weekend and because we are academics, we have summers off. With transportation as easy at it is these days, it's not really a big burden." He would interpret the comment as an attack on the quality of their marriage, and thereby his status, and seek to defend it. She on the other hand, would respond more with something like, "It is really difficult. I miss him so much at nights during the week. And the packing and unpacking can get really old quickly." For her the communication was about support, about empathizing with how hard it must be for Tannen and her husband. Given these different paradigms, no wonder we often hear women tell their opposite sex partners, "Why do you have to be so aggressive?" and men respond with, "Why do you have to be so talkative?"

INDEPENDENCE VS. INTIMACY   Because women think in terms of being close and giving and receiving support, very often, their goal is to achieve and preserve intimacy. In contrast, men, given their concern with status, instead value being perceived as independent. A personal example that occurred to one of the male authors provides a perfect illustration. The couple had been married about a year when an old graduate school friend of the husband called him to tell him he would be visiting Miami for the weekend to help his father move to an assisted living facility. He would be done with his responsibilities by Friday evening and rather than return to New York, wondered if he could come and spend a couple of nights at the couple's home. The husband had not seen his friend for years so his natural response was, "Sure, it will be great! That way you can also meet my new wife." Imagine his surprise when he got home and announced the good news.

"Why didn't you call me?" his wife hurtfully inquired.

"Why, do you have a problem with it? Are we doing something this weekend?" he asked.

"Well no, but we should make these decisions together," she tried explaining.

"But that would seem like I have to ask your permission! I would have had no problems calling him back and canceling if we had something else planned," he pleaded.

Clearly the man was concerned about checking in with his wife, because in his mind it would imply a lack of independence. His wife, on the other hand, placed in a similar situation would love to call her husband and check in because it would signify the level of closeness that they possessed. "See how close we are, we check with each other for everything!"

ADVICE VS. UNDERSTANDING One of the hallmarks of independence is the ability to come up with solutions to problems with which we are presented. Typically, when someone approaches a man to talk about a problem, his general tendency is to provide advice, to offer a solution. In contrast, for intimacy to be achieved it is important to really understand the other person's experience. It follows that more often than not, when a woman complains about something, she is not necessarily looking for an answer to a problem, but rather to feel understood. Tannen (1990) provides a wonderful example in her book *You Just Don't Understand* about a woman who had a benign lump removed from her breast. She hesitantly shared with her husband her discomfort with the scar and the change in her breast's shape. He quickly responded with the solution. *"You can always have plastic surgery."* His wife was hurt and accused him of being insensitive for feeling that she should again go under the knife just because he didn't like the scar. Her husband was hurt and puzzled. "I don't care about the scar," he retorted. "It doesn't bother me at all." To which his wife replied, "Then why are you telling me to have plastic surgery?" She was not looking for solutions; she was looking for emotional support.

INFORMATION VS. FEELINGS Generally for men, conversations are vehicles with which to impart information. Not surprisingly, research shows that, in opposition to popular belief, men tend to talk more than women in public situations. They are likely to ask the first question, ask more questions, and engage in monologues for a longer time than women do. They are also much more prone to interrupt others (Moore & Davidson, 2000). In contrast, women speak much more at home than their heterosexual partners. They talk about their feelings and problems and see the discussion as a way to work on them. Men often perceive the communication as just wallowing in complaints. For women, not being told about something such as personal feelings or troubles seems like a rejection from their partner. They value the intimacy involved in sharing secrets and worries, whereas men are more likely to feel vulnerable doing so. Consider how this is manifested in the different ways men and women manage stress. In response to stress, men tend to isolate, to withdraw; they are likely to want to unplug and perhaps just watch TV. Women are more prone to lean towards what has been called the "tend and befriend" response. The tendency toward making sure the environment is in order and then talk. For women, conversing will lead to a decrease in the fight/flight response, yet for men it will likely cause an increase. No wonder women often complain that their husbands never share what goes on at work! When her husband responds with "nothing" to his wife's request about what happened that day, he is thinking there is no new information to report and besides he wants to get away from it, not relive it. To his wife he is not sharing his feelings and his day, which will decrease her understanding of her partner and thereby lead to less intimacy between them.

ORDERS VS. PROPOSALS Women often begin statements with words such as "Let's" or "Why don't we," as in statements like "Let's park over here" or

"Why don't we stop for coffee?" Such statements are meant as suggestions, not demands, intended to begin a negotiation about what the couple will do next. This style of speaking is aimed at getting others to do what they want, but by first winning agreement. Men, because of the hierarchical nature of their world do not want to feel dominated or like they are in a one-down position. Not surprisingly, they frequently resist being told what to do. They are likely to interpret the woman's communication as a veiled command and become resentful of it. It is interesting to note that when stating an opinion, women, but not men, often end their statements with tag questions, such as "It's really dreary today, isn't it?" or "That's a great suggestion, isn't it?" These tag questions appear aimed at initiating discussion and decreasing the chances of disagreement. For similar reasons, women tend to use disclaimers, as in "Maybe I'm wrong, but . . ." and question statements, such as "Am I wrong? as well as hedge words like "kind of" or "sort of" (Carroll, 2007).

CONFLICT VS. COMPROMISE   Because of their goal of preserving harmony and remaining connected, women often attempt to prevent confrontation by refusing to openly oppose what others want. While a win/win attitude is clearly helpful, sometimes it's a lot more useful for a woman to assert herself, even if doing so might lead to conflict. In fact, one of the factors associated with successful long-term relationships according to John Gottman (2000) is early confrontation of complaints and differences. This is not to suggest that habitually opposing others is a recipe for success. Clearly, a balance between seeking to compromise with a willingness to face conflict when necessary would have the greatest chance of success.

11.8.2 Applying Your Understanding of Gender Differences in Communication

Okay, so there are differences in the way men and women communicate. Now that you know this, what good is it? Tannen asserts that the first step in improving communication between the sexes is being aware of and accepting that there are gender differences in communication styles. It is not a question of one style being better or worse or more right or wrong than the other. When we understand the differences and the dissimilar paradigms from which they stem, we can question our own interpretation of an interaction and arrive at solutions to difficult or seemingly irresolvable problems or predicaments. So when a man says, "I'm tired; I don't want to talk; I just want to watch TV or something," rather than taking that as a personal rejection, his female partner might realize he is just stressed and wants get away from anything that reminds him of it. Or when a woman says she wants to talk, her mate might remember that she is not asking for her problem to be solved, just for him to listen. He might then let go of being Mr. Fix-it, and practice some of the skills and principles discussed in Chapter 10 on empathic listening.

There have been some criticisms of Tannen's genderlect theory. For one, Tannen believes gender differences are based on biological sex. A different model argues that the stylistic differences are found more on the basis of gender roles than biological sex (Edwards & Hamilton, 2004). According to this theory, men who are higher in nurturance exhibit more cooperative speech, while women low in nurturance evidence more dominance speech. Additionally, most studies on gender differences in communication have used primarily young subjects who were middle-class and well educated Americans. It is questionable whether these differences are true of other cultures. For example, none of these differences in communication were found when Chinese men and women were studied (Mortenson, 2002). Perhaps this again reflects the different goals between individualistic societies and collectivist cultures.

Questions

1. The conflicting dialects used by men and women are called _____ by Tannen.

   A. Mars and Venus

   B. gender bias

   C. his and hers

   D. genderlects

2. Women's communication primarily reflects _____.

   A. maintaining their status

   B. showing their independence

   C. a show of dominance

   D. increasing intimacy

3. Men's communication primarily reflects _____.

   A. maintaining their status

   B. increasing intimacy

   C. providing support

   D. expressing their feelings

11.9 Altruism

Describe the benefits of altruism.

The early Greeks described three types of love: Eros, Philo, and Agape. **Eros**, from which the word "erotic" comes, is the "love at first sight" experience that sparks quickly with intense feelings but is not long lasting, often vanishing as quickly as it began. That is what was referred to as Infatuation by Sternberg and discussed earlier in this chapter. **Philo** is the reciprocal type of mutual brotherly love. It is based on friendship between two people and has an "I'll love you as long as you love me" connection. It is based on give and take where two people benefit from each other. This equates to Sternberg's conception of Companionate Love. **Agape** Love is that which is given without any expectation of return. It is selfless love like the love a mother has for her child or that we show for those in need. This is the type of love that leads to the self-sacrificing caring for others we call **altruism.**

So let us return to a theme we have been exploring from the very first pages of this book, the value of stepping into another's shoes and feeling as if you are that person. The best relationships are built around our capacity for empathy, as well as our willingness to give freely and forgive gracefully. The data is clear. When you give help or service, you get something in return even if you don't expect it. Adults involved in giving service experience improvements on all measures of happiness and well-being. The elderly experience improved health and longer life from their participation in volunteer work (Brown, Nesse, Vinokur, & Smith, 2003). Seligman (2002) found that college students discovered service to be more gratifying than pleasurable activities, the so-called "do good, feel good" effect. It is obviously good for those who receive the kindness and if the recipient of the kindness is happier as a result then they will tend to be kinder and more helpful themselves (Isen, 1972). Most interestingly, it is even good for those who observe an act of kindness, like seeing someone helping a lost child find their parents. As you witness an act of kindness or a loving gesture, neurochemicals, such as oxytocin, are released and literally give you that heartwarming feeling in your chest that makes you feel more open, loving and trusting (Haidt, 2006).

An evolutionary argument can also be made for altruism. Darwin theorized that if a group of unrelated individuals out survives or out propagates a competing group, its' gene pool will multiply. Therefore, it follows that cooperation within that group would enhance survival. Cooperation is possible because of human hive emotions such as love, forgiveness, gratitude and empathy – the foundation of altruism. Cacioppo & Patrick (2008) remind us that we humans are not an impressive physical species in terms of strength, speed or natural weapons. Our competitive advantage comes from our ability to work together, plan, reason and problem solve to achieve goals. A group that displays such cooperation and altruism is more likely to survive to pass on its genes.

But altruism is the willingness to act in another's interest even if there is no apparent reward or benefit for doing so. The truly altruistic person is motivated by the prospect of improving someone else's situation. Considering the paragraph above, it has been suggested that this type of motivation for behavior is nonexistent. In other words, no one does anything without some sort of benefit, however subtle, flowing back to them. But as we noted in Chapter 9 in our discussion of empathy, people seem to be willing to sacrifice for others for no other reason than reducing another's suffering. This has been confirmed in over 25 studies (Batson, Ahmad, Lishner, and Tsang, 2005).

Ultimately, is this really so surprising? Perhaps it is only to scientists who need experimental data to be convinced. In the annals of human history we have always been captivated by the capacity of the sage or saint to sacrifice for the benefit of another completely unknown to them. For example, in the Christian tradition we see Jesus speaking up to prevent a woman from being stoned to death. In this incident, he even educates the murderous crowd giving them a lesson in empathy. He points out that those who wish to punish this woman are no different than her when he says, "Let he who is without sin cast the first stone." Indeed, the central premise of Christianity itself is that Christians are saved because Jesus died for their sins. Matthieu Ricard (2006) in *Happiness* shares this story from the Buddhist tradition.

> Dola Jigme Kalsang was a Tibetan sage of the nineteenth century. One day while on pilgrimage to China, he came to the central square of a small town where a crowd had gathered. As he approached, he found that a thief was about to be put to death in a particularly cruel fashion: he was to be made to straddle an iron horse that had been heated to red-hot. Dola Jigme pushed his way through the crowd and proclaimed, "I am the thief!" A great silence fell; the presiding mandarin turned impassively to the newcomer and asked, "Are you ready to assume the consequences of what you have just told us?" Dola Jigme nodded. He died on the horse and the thief was spared. (p. 207)

We are equally fascinated by the hero or parent who willingly gives their life so that another life or lives can be saved. What is happening when this happens? More importantly, what questions does it pose for all of us who seek to lead a life worth living, and want to experience a sense of well-being, what the Greeks called eudemonia. In other words, how does this knowledge inform our most deeply held values?

The essential insight of the mystic is the realization that all of life is unified. There is no real distinction between us and the objects of our perception. Through various practices, mystics work to see through the illusion or perspective that we are separate from the people and things around us. This is how it is written in the Upanishads, the earliest recorded sacred writings.

> Who sees all beings in his own Self, and his own Self in all beings, loses all fear... When a sage sees this great Unity and his Self has become all beings, what delusion and what sorrow can ever be near him?

> Isa Upanishad, verses 6–7

All religions have capitalized on this notion of all the members being part of a single body. Thus, when we are exhorted to follow the Golden Rule and treat others as we would like to be treated, what we are actually doing is recognizing ourselves in the other and helping us because we really are not separate at all.

Science can give us insight into how this mystical consciousness arises in the body. Jonathan Haidt (2006) in his book, *The Happiness Hypothesis*, summarizes some of the most fascinating data in psychology in regard to various religious practices. The method most common among the various religious traditions for accessing the state of unitive or cosmic consciousness is meditation. Modern technology allows us to look into the brain and see exactly what happens when meditators report being in this mystical state. As it turns out, two areas in the parietal lobes of the brain experience a drastic reduction in activity. These areas are responsible for your orientation in space. In other words, they keep track of the boundaries of your body and where you perceive your body to be in space. When these areas are deprived of this information regarding the edges of your body and where you are in space, they continue to try to locate you. As a result of this you begin to feel expanded out into space with no boundaries. You lose the limited sense of yourself and, in Haidt's own words, "feel(s) merged with something vast, something larger than the self." You have in Buddhist terms become empty of the sense of the self but full of everything else, experiencing unitive or mystical consciousness. The emotional state which accompanies this is usually a feeling of unconditional love for all things.

These states can also be accessed by groups who participate in meditative or rhythmic activities such as drumming, chanting, or even marching. The result is an extraordinary bonding among the members of the group. This identification with the group can be so intense that group members are willing to do anything including sacrificing their lives to protect the group. In a real sense, at this moment of ultimate sacrifice, the individual may have the sense that they are not really dying because the group they are so identified with goes on. There is a part of being human that is very much like being part of a hive.

Sadly, while this breeds tremendous cohesion within groups, it also can lead to branding anyone outside the group as evil. We need look no further than national and international politics, hostilities between religious factions all claiming to serve God, or the tragic lessons of Nazi Germany where an entire country was brought together for what were ultimately evil ends. Can we begin to take seriously the notion of global citizenship; where we do our best to affirm life for ever greater numbers of people and animals and the plants that support them?

So, science shows us what happens in the brain and body when we perceive unitive consciousness. But, is this just an illusion or is it something real upon which you should base your relationships? Perhaps that is the wrong question. Remember, since this is a book about optimal functioning, the better question would be to ask, "Does it help to enhance the quality of your life and relationships?" We feel secure in saying that your world and our world will be a better place if you seek to fulfill your capacity to be altruistic. Consider this final word on happiness and relationships from Jonathan Haidt:

> *Happiness is not something that you can find, acquire, or achieve directly. You have to get the conditions right and then wait. Some of those conditions are within you. . . . Other conditions require relationships to things beyond you. Just as plants need sun, water, and good soil to thrive, people need love, work, and a connection to something larger. It is worth striving to get the right relationships*

*between yourself and others, between yourself and your work, and between your-
self and something larger than yourself. If you get these relationships right, a
sense of purpose and meaning will emerge.*

The Happiness Hypothesis (p. 283–9)

Questions

1. _____ refers to an altruistic love given without any expectation of
   return.

   A. Eros

   B. Philo

   C. Dildo

   D. Agape

2. Altruism _____.

   A. serves an evolutionary function

   B. does not really exist

   C. works best when you expect something in return

   D. is not related to empathy

3. Philo refers to _____.

   A. A love of philosophy

   B. Infatuation

   C. Brotherly love

   D. Altruistic acts

Summary

This chapter dealt with many aspects of the R in PERMA, that of relationships.
Beginning with areas of communication vital to relationship development, tips
for becoming a good conversationalist and establishing rapport were outlined.
A primer including suggestions for overcoming shyness was included. This was
followed by an exploration of the importance of friendship to our physical health
and emotional well-being, along with guidelines on how to make and keep good
friendships.

A thorough overview of attachment theory and attachment styles in children
was presented along with an explanation of how childhood attachment patterns
convert to adult attachment styles in romantic relationships. Sternberg's Triangle
Theory of Love was detailed demonstrating how different combinations of the
presence or lack of intimacy, passion, and commitment lead to different kinds of

love. The biochemistry of love was explored along with advice on how to keep relationships strong, vital, and intimate over time, stressing the importance of having realistic expectations about the longevity of sexual passion.

The factors leading to marital satisfaction and dissatisfaction were examined and suggestions for improving marital communication (active and constructive responding) were offered for maximizing your Losada ratio (the ratio of positive to negative interactions within a relationship). The four toxic attitudes to avoid (criticism, contempt, defensiveness, and stonewalling) to keep a relationship healthy were discussed. The genderlects proposed by Deborah Tannen, those differences in communication styles between men and women, were dissected in great detail with advice on how to improve cross-gender communication. Lastly, the concept of altruism (agape love) was explained.

Positive Psychology Exercise

1. Think of an unexpected kind thing to do for someone, be it a stranger, friend or significant other, and go do it! Pay attention to what happens to your mood.

Key Terms

Absent Presence
Active and Constructive
    Responding
Altruism
Agape
Attachment
Attachment Theory
Biochemicals
Cohabitation
Commitment
Companionate Love

Consummate Love
Dopamine
Empty Love
Eros
Fatuous Love
Genderlects
Infatuated Love
Intimacy
Liking
Losada Ratio
Nonlove

Norepinephrine
Oxytocin
Passion
Philo
Propinquity
Rapport
Romantic Love
Technoference
Vasopressin

Shared Writing

Think of a past relationship and determine where it fits within the Triangle theory of love. Write about why you categorized it as you did. What did you learn from this relationship in relation to insights you may have gleaned from this chapter regarding what makes for a healthy or unhealthy relationship?

Chapter 11 Questions

1. Which of the following is essential to making and keeping friendships?

   A. Make deposits in the emotional bank account.

   B. Withhold emotional support.

   C. Gossip about the person behind their back.

   D. Disregard the friend's privacy.

2. Which of the following recent developments is interfering with the quality of relationships?

   A. the influence of fake news

   B. technoference leading to absent presence

   C. online dating

   D. binge watching TV

3. Shyness is _____.

   A. a very rare problem

   B. caused by excessive negative self-preoccupation

   C. impossible to overcome

   D. exacerbated by being in the here and now

4. Which of the following is useful for overcoming shyness?

   A. defensive pessimism

   B. avoiding social situations

   C. using cognitive restructuring to challenge negative self-statements

   D. focusing on the past and the future

5. _____ attachment can result from being raised by abusive, highly dysfunctional parents.

   A. Anxious

   B. Disorganized

   C. Avoidant

   D. Secure

6. Children raised by cold, rejecting caregivers typically display _____ attachment.

   A. secure

   B. anxious

   C. disorganized

   D. avoidant

7. Intimacy and commitment without passion leads to _____.

   A. empty love

   B. fatuous love

   C. consummate love

   D. companionate love

8. According to Gottman, the four dangerous attitudes to avoid in intimate relationships are _____, _____, _____, and _____.

   A. anger; sadness; jealousy; contempt

   B. criticism; contempt; defensiveness; stonewalling

   C. jealousy; stonewalling; revulsion; indifference

   D. defensiveness; anger; indifference; revulsion

9. Men favor _____ while women favor _____.

   A. criticism; praise

   B. understanding; advice

   C. report talk; rapport talk

   D. feelings; information

10. The type of love that leads to the self-sacrificing caring for others we call altruism is:

    A. Eros

    B. Philo

    C. Agape

    D. Porno

Section Three

Occupational Effectiveness

To truly flourish and be effective, we must live a life of meaning and purpose. Often this involves our job, our career, or our volunteer activities, as one does not need to receive a paycheck to do meaningful work. Becoming effective in our personal and interpersonal lives will better prepare us for occupational success. But carrying effectiveness over into the workplace also entails educating ourselves about the unique challenges inherent in such an environment. Every workplace has requirements, both in general and specific to each setting, even if we work from home. The following three chapters will help us better understand the ever-changing workplace environment, how to decide our career path, how to look for and secure a job, but most importantly, how to keep our jobs by comprehending how to apply emotional intelligence in the workplace situation while handling the potential demands or problems characteristic of our jobs.

Chapter 12: Knowing the Workplace
Chapter 13: Designing Your Own Career
Chapter 14: Applying Positive Psychology at Work

Chapter 12
Knowing the Workplace

Learning Objectives

After reading this chapter, you should be able to:

12.1 Identify current trends in the workforce.

12.2 Explain the effects of increasing global interdependence on the skills required to participate in the world economy.

12.3 Recognize the career areas likely to experience the largest amount of growth in the coming years.

12.4 Define styles of leadership and their differing effects on the workplace.

12.5 Describe how performance reviews can help you identify areas of strength and need for improvement.

12.6 Identify ways to recognize and effectively manage stress in the workplace.

Do you remember when you started college? You had to get yourself registered for classes. The campus was full of buildings that housed, among other things, classrooms . . . and you had to find the rooms where your classes would be held. You had to figure out where the bookstore and cafeteria were. You were probably not able to function comfortably or effectively until you knew your way around. It also helped to learn specific terms used by other students to describe things related to college life. Understanding what "credits" are and how they relate to completing a degree was also useful information. Once you became familiar with the college environment, things made more sense. You could move around, make choices and decisions and figure things out a lot easier.

Likewise, when you first enter your work life, you can find yourself in a similar situation. To function better in the career world, you need to know some of the basics. Consider what is going on around you, what you will be experiencing, and the behaviors expected of you professionally and personally. Knowing these basics helps you anticipate things, adapt more easily and in general be more effective in your career oriented behavior. This attained sophistication regarding your new surroundings will make you more confident in your decision-making processes and work habits, thus enhancing the quality of your work. Even if you are a more seasoned worker with years of work experience before returning to college, you still have to orient to a new college experience and/or the possibility of a new work environment as your professional career changes.

The average worker has typically worked eight hours a day, five days a week, 50 of the 52 weeks in a year. That's most of your year right there! Add to that the trend in technology where workers are expected to be available 24/7 which is even more consuming. When you consider that you may work thirty or more years of your adult life, it becomes clear that the most of your life is spent in your career. Get the picture? And what if your career is not rewarding? How many people do you know or hear about who hate their work? You don't want to be one of them, right? It is probably not a coincidence that most heart attacks occur at 9:00 a.m. on Monday mornings! Could this be related to work? So there's something to be said about getting some basic information about the dynamic environment in which we fulfill our career aspirations. So let's find out what's happening in the world of work.

12.1 Occupational Trends

Identify current trends in the workforce.

One trend that is obvious to everyone is that the workplace is constantly evolving. Alvin Toffler (1971), a sociologist, pointed out decades ago that change was changing. The rate of change itself is accelerating, speeding up like a boulder rolling down a mountainside. Unlike the lives our parents or grandparents lived, things now are changing so fast it is mind-boggling! We have moved from an agriculture-based economy to a manufacturing economy to a service economy. Now we are in an information economy. Add to all of that the influence of portable computers, electronic notebooks, smart phones, social networking sites, all representing profound changes.

For those of you younger than thirty, it may be difficult for you to imagine what life was like before computers. Computers have changed the way things happen in so many arenas. To name a few, consider business, government, education, communications, and automobile operations. We depend on computers to operate practically everything in life. What would happen if the computers suddenly stopped? At the turn of the century in 2000, there was great concern about computers and Y2K. Experts pondered the potential chaos and disaster that could result from failed computers. Fortunately, Y2K was a false alarm. Now, since 9/11, there is concern that chaos could be caused by cyberattacks on computer systems which could greatly damage our economy. Since computers are so important to keeping things running, there is a new term for these experts in information and communications technology. We call them **gold collar workers**.

It is estimated that well over 80% of the world's technological advances have occurred in the last hundred years. Technology feeds on itself—one breakthrough leads to a host of other advances which then spur on even more developments. This cycle is never ending and will keep accelerating. Additionally the Internet has changed the way we do everything from shopping to research to communicating. This is related to the ongoing information explosion. There was more information produced in the 30 years from 1965 to 1995 than had accumulated in the entire previous history of civilization, in the roughly 5000 year period spanning 3000 B.C. through 1965! A study conducted at the University of California at Berkeley found that five exabytes of information was produced in 2002. An exabyte is equal to a billion gigabytes or approximately 500,000 times the amount of data in the Library of Congress' print collection. These researchers estimate that the amount of available information is doubling every three years (Lyman and Varian, 2003). This information is available to us instantaneously, not only from the Internet, but TV, and satellites or on our handheld communication device. The more we learn and discover, the more we must change or risk falling more and more behind.

Other changes are happening today. These include such things as increased diversity in the workforce, global competition and interdependence, and new organizational patterns in the workplace. Other factors influencing change are uncertainty following the terrorist attacks of 9/11, unemployment/underemployment, and major instability in the economy, the blending of work and non-work in employees' lifestyles, and how one views work security.

12.1.1 Increased Diversity

One of the changes we see in society is the increasing diversity in the workforce. Unlike previous decades where white males dominated the workforce, the Bureau of Labor Statistics projects that those entering the workforce include greater representation of diverse groups and older workers. Minorities, which comprised about one third of the U.S. population in 2011, are projected to become the majority in the workforce in 2039. By 2023, minorities will comprise more than half of all children (U.S. Census Bureau News, May 17, 2012). Minority representation in major counties shows that more than 11 percent of the nation's counties have more than 50 percent minority population, with Miami Dade County, Florida having the highest proportion at 82 percent until surpassed by Maverick, Texas which has 92 percent.

Hispanics have become the largest minority group in the United States at 16.7 percent in 2011. Although there are high concentrations of Hispanics in several states, this population is dispersed throughout the nation. More than half of all immigrants coming here in 2000 were from Latin America. Within the Hispanic population are subgroups with cultural and socioeconomic differences. Asian Americans, with their many subgroups, are a smaller total number, but comprise a fast growing ethnic group in the United States. African American and Native American growth rates are higher than the growth rate for Non-Hispanic Caucasians which expected to drop from 68 percent in 2012 to 43 percent by 2060. The portion of our population made up of persons born outside the United States is 12.9% (U.S. Census Bureau, 2010).

We see the rising numbers and influence of women who comprised 58.1% of our civilian labor force in 2011 (Bureau of Labor Statistics, 2013). Such diversity means a variety of ethnic, social, and cultural customs and attitudes among workers who co-exist in the same workplace. Additionally, more disabled workers, who comprise the fastest growing minority group in the workforce, are broadening the scope of workplace differences. The potential for misunderstandings and conflict is obvious. Learning to interact positively with people of varied backgrounds, cultures and characteristics brings a growing challenge.

Often we are unaware of our prejudicial attitudes or behaviors. When describing a group of people involved in an activity, how many times do we hear someone refer to a particular person in the group as "this Black guy" when no one else's skin color is mentioned. It is irrelevant in any case; is it not? Why is this person's skin color singled out? Why isn't he just referred to as "a guy" as the others were? And what goes on in the minds of those who heard that man so described. What stereotypes do we carry around relating to African Americans? Hispanics? Women? Asians? Persons with disabilities? Working harmoniously with a variety of people whose personalities and attitudes are formed from environments different from the one we know, requires that we have an open mind. We must be willing to respect differences and to learn about and appreciate a broad array of perceptions and behaviors in the workplace. Remember empathic listening? The extent to which we can understand what it is like to be in that person's shoes impacts our sensitivity and level of respect. Further, if we learn to value and appreciate diversity for creating a richness that surpasses homogeneity, it increases our chances for success in our careers. Remember, not only the workforce, but the clients, customers, patients, or students you count on for your work are also diverse. Relating effectively with a mix of people is necessary for success.

In addition to the diverse groups mentioned above, another source of diversity in the workplace is the growing age gap found among present day workers. Workers are living longer and working longer. Life expectancy for the U.S. population reached 78.37 in 2013 (Bureau of Labor Statistics, 2013). Eighty percent of baby boomers say they plan to work at least part-time during their retirement (MarksJarvis, November 13, 2007). DeCenzo (1997) breaks age groups into three separate eras: (1) those born pre-1946; (2) those born between 1946–1964; and

(3) those born after 1964. He labels these groups and summarizes some of the differences in the following chart:

	Mature Workers Born pre-1946	Baby Boomers born 1946–1964	Baby Busters/ Generation X Born after 1964
Value Most	Family	Careers/Money	Personal Gratification
Want from Job	Security	Advancement	Control own destiny
Ideal Vacation	Trip to town of ancestors	Disneyland	Deserted Caribbean island

The differences in these generations' values and attitudes are obvious. The **mature workers** lived during or close to the time of the Great Depression. In that era resources were scarce, unemployment abounded, and people learned to be exceedingly frugal to survive. It makes sense that this group desires security from their jobs. This group likes to watch TV news magazine shows like *60 Minutes*. They do not want to be caught unaware like in the stock market crash of 1929 or Pearl Harbor in 1941.

The **baby boomers** evolved in a great era of building, including the evolution of the space program, the rapid advancement of technological innovation such as TV and other communications networks. These post-World War II babies had a more plentiful life than their parents. They came to see careers as central to their lives and value advancement and the money it brings. Many workers of this era are "workaholics."

The **baby busters** or **Generation X** group born after 1964 are seeking personal gratification and want work to allow them the freedom to pursue their own interests. They are looked upon as selfish and intolerant by the older two age groups.

More recent studies have reported on the group following the Generation Xers. This group is referred to as **Generation Y**, representing individuals born between approximately 1977 to 2000. There are about 70 million who comprise 26% of the U.S. population. These group members grew up in an era of prosperity, expanding technology, and are more ethnically diverse than any previous generations. They are expected to outnumber the large number of baby boomers that made up that generation. Gen Y individuals, also referred to as "**Millennials**" or "Net Generation," have grown up with computers and are astute in computer use; the majority have computers and internet access. They are less cynical, more optimistic, self-confident, and expect to be better off financially than their parents. They are the most educationally oriented generation in history, recognizing that education is the key to their success. "They are more open and tolerant as products of biracial and multicultural marriages, and rail against sexism and homophobia. They are the best hope we've had so far for a more open, tolerant society" (Tulgan and Martin, 2001). They are socially conscious and are spurring a trend of volunteerism with a concern for the environment, poverty, health status, the elderly and other community problems or issues. They want their careers to offer them meaningful roles at work where they feel they are making a contribution. They want to be a part of a very motivated work team and develop an open-minded workplace. They have high monetary and personal goals. Their self-confidence has prepared them to make the moves necessary from one job to another to fulfill their goals.

So what is the generation after Generation Y? You guessed it, **Generation Z**. This group was born from 2000 to the present. They are also called Generation M for multitasking, or the Net Generation or Generation 9/11. They are highly connected as they have been exposed throughout to technologies such as the World Wide Web, smart phones and texting, tablet computers, YouTube and other social media. They are therefore called "digital natives" and, unlike their predecessors, they have never known a world without these technologies. Generation Z are known for quickly gathering, organizing, and storing information on-line leading to the term *digital curation*. They are also very open in sharing their ideas and perspectives on an assortment of media, topics, and products.

How do you imagine these diverse groups might interact together in the same workplace? What types of conflicts can you envision? Have you had any experiences with this issue in your work history? And don't forget that clients and customers being served are reflecting the generational diversity, too.

12.1.2 Changes in Organizational Structure

In addition to working in a global economy, another continuing trend is businesses seeking more economical practices to improve profits. We see changes occurring both among and within organizations. In the corporate world, we see businesses grouping together, merging with each other, buying out others and otherwise combining forces. We see companies going bankrupt or being swallowed up in takeovers, resulting in long standing firms going out of business. Another business issue is that of the gap in earnings between corporate executives and workers, as well as concerns regarding ethical practices within corporations.

The national and international economic downturn beginning in 2007 brought major layoffs in all types of businesses. Real estate sales came to a standstill, banks were struggling to survive, the stock market and home values plummeted, retail sales dropped, and automobile manufacturers reduced production and staffing. In 2008 health care was eventually the only industry hiring workers. Companies in the U. S. and in Europe closed down for extended periods during the holiday season that December. The U.S. economy has slowly rebounded since then.

One continuing trend is **downsizing**, which was used extensively in the economic downturn of the late 2000s. This of course brings major organizational change within a company. The process of downsizing means doing more with less as positions are cut from the payroll to reduce costs. Once the workforce within the company is leaner, companies begin to expect workers to cross-train, meaning learning the work of another employee. For instance, we see respiratory therapists and nurses cross-training in hospitals; we see financial aid and registration clerks cross-training on a college campus.

Further, technology is being implemented to increase efficiency and minimize the need for personnel. Personnel costs, by the way, are the most expensive items in the budget. Robots or computers are also being used to replace humans in doing tasks. Increasingly, automation serves as the greatest threat to many jobs, particularly blue collar vocations such as cashiers, toll booth operators and even truck drivers with the advent of self-driving vehicles.

This "reduction in the workforce" has led to two categories of workers: (1) full time or **core workers**; and (2) part-time or **contingent workers** (DeCenzo, 1997). Historically we have expected that most people would be "core" workers. However, since change is so commonplace in organizations, the best way to be prepared for changing personnel needs is to hire people for projects or short-term temporary work. Then when there are seasonal changes, changing needs for expertise, or different priorities and projects, there is no need to retain them. Tourism companies, hospitals, colleges, and a host of other businesses use these hiring practices. Full-time workers usually have benefits not offered to part timers and full-time employees have more job stability. Part-time workers may receive higher salaries, but generally do not receive health insurance, retirement packages, and other benefits.

The advantages to working full time includes the security of a paycheck, job stability, position or rank, and benefits, such as paid vacations, retirement packages, sick leave and others. The advantages of being a contingent worker include flexibility in work schedule, extended time off, possibly higher salary and opportunity to change work environments frequently. With the increased use of technology, workers are "connected" electronically to their work through cell phones, cyber cafes, and the like. This is having implications for the nature of the work day or work week. As mentioned earlier, there is an increasing expectation among managers that their employees will be available 24/7 to solve problems that could impact profits. This is causing a blurring between work and non-work time. The portability of technology has a growing number of workers working at home, telecommuting, and trouble-shooting from remote locales.

The self-confidence, technological expertise, interest in continued learning, and optimism of the Generation Y and Z groups has produced self-reliant, competent, flexible individuals who are better able to deal with the changes in organizational structure than their older counterparts. Continuing change has been a greater part of their lives and they not only cope, but *seek* new challenges and opportunities for career fulfillment.

Questions

1. Sociologist Alvin Toffler pointed out many decades ago that change itself is

   _____.

   A. constant

   B. changing

   C. a myth

   D. retroactive

2. It is estimated that well over 80% of the world's technological advances have occurred in the last _____ years.

    A. 10

    B. 50

    C. 25

    D. 100

3. People born between approximately 1977 and 2000 are referred to as "Millennials," also known as _____.

    A. Generation Z

    B. Generation X

    C. Generation Y

    D. the Lost Generation

12.2 Global Interdependence

Explain the effects of increasing global interdependence on the skills required to participate in the world economy.

People say we live in a shrinking world. Yet, we know the earth hasn't actually shrunk (except, perhaps for melting ice caps!). Today, interacting with people around the world has become so easy and accessible. The marketplace is no longer just *our* community, *our* state, or even *our* country. We are intermixed in many ways. Not only is travel easier and more accessible, but people are more mobile, living and working in different parts of the world. Communicating with someone on the other side of the globe is only a computer and e-dress away. It is even being said that we have moved from an information economy to a global information economy. More and more countries are finding new groups of people in their presence, and diversity is an issue on every continent. So called "American" cars today are built from car parts made all over the world. Businesses begun in one country now operate everywhere. If we made a note of it, we would probably discover that we have an "international" day most every day, using household items, tools, medicines and foods from other countries as part of our routine. Some countries earn more than half their income from exports. In fact, what began hundreds of years ago as trading between countries has evolved into the workplace becoming the whole earth.

To succeed in this global community, it is imperative that one has a respect for diversity and appreciation of culture. Consideration for political values, moral patterns, as well as social and economic conditions is also necessary. To get a sense of the increasing worldwide influence on our lives, it is useful to examine what is happening with **outsourcing**.

We have all dialed a technical support number with a computer problem, and had the call answered by a representative residing in India and speaking with a British accent. When this occurred, you had just experienced "outsourcing." Now when you call your local hospital, airline, or other business or service establishment, you are likely to be experiencing outsourcing also. Outsourcing refers to the *source* of the production being *outside*. The "outside" may be out of the company, the city, the state, the nation or the continent.

Outsourcing is not a new idea. In fact, in many ways outsourcing is an extension of the contingent workers discussed above. These workers are not employees of the company, but work for a separate company who contracts to do the work from another place, perhaps from anywhere around the globe. Historically in the United States, lower-paid laborers from other countries have been used to build railroads, to cut sugar cane, and to harvest other crops. More recently nurses have been recruited from abroad to fill the gap of labor shortages in that field. For years manufacturing has been using inexpensive labor from overseas to make clothing and other items. Increasingly, lesser-paid workers are still being used, but no longer do they have to leave their homes and take up residence in a new culture. We all wear articles with labels that read "Made in China," or Russia, Indonesia, Poland, to name a few countries. Business services, however, do not have "made in" labels. Therefore, we may be unaware that as a customer in the U.S., we are being served by someone on the other side of the earth. American companies are increasingly contracting with businesses located elsewhere to provide the work from there.

However, outsourcing is a two way street. Many American companies are the vendors for other national or international businesses outsourcing manufacturing, computer technology, and other services. There is increasing competition for American providers as other companies around the world are getting into outsourcing. The complementary term **insourcing** refers to workers in one country locally providing labor for companies owned outside of their country. For example, American workers are employed here for a European or Asian company. A report by the U.S. Chamber of Commerce (2004) found that direct foreign investment now exceeds $487 billion and supports 6.4 million jobs in the United States. Consider, for instance, the automobile industry where large numbers of Americans are working here at home for Honda, Toyota, and Nissan, all foreign owned companies. It is estimated that some 150,000 jobs have been insourced from Mexico to the U.S. (Fraser, 2004). Insourcing is increasing in the U.S. as China and other companies are raising their costs. Also, many American companies are bringing their manufacturing and services back to this country.

What *is* new is the growth of outsourcing to include not only manufacturing labor, but information technology and services of all kinds. Thomas Friedman, *New York Times* columnist and author who visited Bangalore, India (the Silicon Valley of India) in 2004, points out that all sorts of U.S. jobs can be outsourced. He notes that "we visited . . . everything from radiological labs that are reading the x-rays done by big American hospitals to accounting firms that are now using Indian CPAs to do your taxes, to cartoons and game companies that now have Indian artists drawing for American games . . . (News Hour with Jim Lehrer, 2004). In addition to manufacturing being outsourced and technical support teams for computer companies, we have workers on outsourcing contracts for all sorts of services. These include selling credit cards; making airline reservations and tracing lost luggage; handling purchasing, human resources tasks, customer relations, and on-line ordering; processing banking operations; transcribing medical records and radiologists reading x-rays; as well as a variety of call centers in many fields. One begins to wonder what job could not be outsourced and therefore done at a lesser cost to a company or organization?

In the case of **offshoring** (i.e., outsourcing to another country), comparing salary differences requires a look at the economics of outsourcing for both countries involved. It is rather obvious why companies in America are seeking to outsource all sorts of work to lower labor costs. Traditionally in America not only salaries, but benefits such as vacation time, sick leave, insurances, employment taxes and the like contribute to the high cost of labor. Total costs for personnel are the major expense of nearly all service companies and organizations, often running well over 90% of the total budget. Imagine the increased earnings of businesses that can greatly reduce their personnel costs by contracting for outsourced labor. This leads to lowering the costs for consumers and improving their own companies. Catherine Mann (2004) reports that, based on price reductions from global sourcing, the U.S. Gross Domestic Product (GDP) in 2004 was $230 billion more than it would have been, or the equivalent of each working person in the United States making $2000 more that year.

Although the cost of labor in India and other countries is much less than in the United States, these same salaries are an increase for the workers in these countries. For example as Friedman notes, previously many young college graduates in India who were not engineers could never get jobs there paying $200 to $300 a month, which is the beginning pay for a call center employee. Obviously such low starting salaries would be impossible in the United States, thus the cost savings for the businesses that outsource. At the same time, the salaries and ultimately the standard of living increases for the workers and their country's economy is increased accordingly.

Outsourcing is not only expanding to all sorts of work categories, but is also spreading all over the globe. India started as the major nation to take in outsourced American work, and interestingly enough is now outsourcing some of their contract work to other countries. The *New York Times* (September 25, 2007) reported that Infosys, an Indian Company of 75,000 employees is opening offices in numerous countries around the world such as Mexico, the Czech Republic, Thailand and China, and in low-cost regions of the United States. The global interdependence that outsourcing has forged is seen in the example of an American bank needing a computer system to handle loans for Hispanic customers using Infosys, an Indian vendor (7000 miles away), to supply it with Mexican engineers working 150 miles south of the U.S. border. Although India has been the prime country involved in outsourcing, many other countries are scrambling to get into the act. Ireland has been active for several years in contracting commitments. Russia, who has had a surplus of scientists and engineers from the Cold War, is engaging these professionals for contracted scientific and computer systems work. Hungary and Mexico are vying for contracts with U.S. companies. Growth has been seen not just in countries seeking contracted work, but in the number of countries who are now also outsourcing their labor. Friedman described accent classes he visited in India where not only the American accent was being taught, but also British and Canadian accents to accommodate call center clients from the United Kingdom and Canada.

This increased interconnection in trading work within and among countries of the world reflects a growing global interdependence which has contributed to the global economic issues of recent years. The impact of outsourcing raises implications for the level of education or re-education needed for 21st century workers. When your job disappears, it's not just a matter of finding similar work at another firm . . . it has broader implications for change. The questions for you to keep in mind are: "How will this influence my career experience as I enter or continue in the labor market? What does it mean for my educational requirements and employment patterns? How can I be most effective in my career where the workplace has become the whole world?"

The Global Perspective
Is Outsourcing a Blessing or a Curse?

Since outsourcing now involves countries all over the world interacting in the trade of goods and services, what are the economic, political, and social impacts of this global interdependence? Is outsourcing a blessing for enhancing and sustaining our world, or is it a curse? The debate has been intense in the United States.

Those who are against outsourcing include many labor unions, industry associations, and of course displaced workers who are infuriated. Researchers estimate the total number of American jobs outsourced will reach 3.3 million or more by 2015 (McCarthy, 2002). Brainard and Litan (2004) report that up to 14 million Americans work in occupations that could reasonably be considered "at risk."

A most outspoken critic of outsourcing is Lou Dobbs, former anchor and managing editor of CNN's Lou Dobbs Tonight. He contends that U.S. corporations are sending American jobs overseas so rapidly that this country's economy is facing a crisis of historic proportions (NOW, 2004). Dobbs (2004) believes that corporate America controls the politicians through campaign funding and lobbying, and controls the media through which most of us get our information, including the Congress. This is why he suggests, that trade laws and agreements, as well as government reports and agencies support outsourcing as good for our economy, when in reality it is seriously hurting the middle class. Is outsourcing increasing the gap between the "haves" and the "have nots" within America? Are we now a government "by the corporations" rather than "by the people"?

Finance Professor Rory L. Terry (2004) also argues against outsourcing, stating that we are not inherently

(Continued)

superior to our foreign competitors in creativity and innovation as some suggest. He points to the many international students enrolled in our most difficult degree programs at prestigious universities, and our low rank in mathematics and science education. He also notes that many of our highest paying jobs can be exported such as doctors, accountants, engineers, computer programmers, architects, and scientists.

There are other advantages to companies from outsourcing beyond the low cost of labor such as no labor unions, no Social Security or Medicare benefit payments, no unemployment taxes, no health benefits for workers, no child labor laws, no safety or environmental protection costs or restrictions, no worker retirement benefits or pension costs. But what does this mean for off shore workers doing the jobs? In addition to working conditions, what is the impact on the environment if there are no safety nor environmental protection measures? Is offshoring negatively impacting the health and safety of workers and the environment?

Terry (2004) and others enumerate social costs in the U.S. from outsourcing that are paid for by the people . . . not by the corporations. Beyond the loss of jobs, he points out the costs of a reduced tax base, high unemployment costs, pricey government retraining programs, loss of national sovereignty, more expensive raw materials, not to mention the social problems of higher rates of child abuse, spousal abuse, alcoholism, bankruptcy, divorce and the like as unemployment climbs. What does this do to our standard of living? Are we allowing corporate profits to diminish our quality of life?

Although there are many against outsourcing, there are those who see it very positively. As many point out, all socio-economic changes cause a shift in the jobs available. Indeed, the advent of the automobile put those who worked making saddles, horseshoes, and tackle for horses out of work. Likewise, the coming of the computer put typewriter companies out of business. Changes always create temporary losses, but lead to increased gains in new jobs being created. In fact, each year there are thousands of jobs lost and new ones created as processes and technology change. This is known as "churning" of jobs as they shift and has been going on for centuries. Proponents of outsourcing point out such patterns of replacement are natural in an economy and not any different today than in past history.

Fraser (2004) sees outsourcing as a win-win opportunity, giving us more goods and services at a lower cost. It raises the standard of living for everyone with huge benefits to low-income people and seniors living on fixed incomes. Equally positive is "in sourcing" and the estimated total of 6.4 million insourced jobs brought to the U.S. Fraser also points out that "this global synergy improves freedom and opportunity across the world by helping to eradicate poverty in the poorest countries" (2004).

An IT industry study reports that outsourcing in fact creates jobs (CNN/Money, 2004). This study indicates that offshoring lowers costs, inflation, and interest rates while it increases productivity. This in turn boosts business and consumer spending and increases our economy. These benefits are projected to produce a total of 317,000 net new jobs through 2008.

The increase in the U.S. economy as well as in the receiving countries implies outsourcing is reducing the gap between the "haves" in the U.S. and the "have nots" in less developed countries. Though the wages paid are low by American standards, they are an increase for the workers there. Does this not help those workers and the global economy? A government official in India reported their economy increasing at a remarkable 8% per year. He also touted their educational preparedness with more than 18 million graduates a year, more than a million of them in engineering. His area now has 15 universities, 1500 IT companies, and 180,000 workers in IT that are expected to rise to 500,000 (Gowda, 2005). Isn't what outsourcing has done for India possible elsewhere? These are some of the arguments for and against outsourcing. What would a global citizen think, feel, and do about outsourcing? How might outsourcing affect your decisions about your career? Looking at the broader picture, how can we ensure that outsourcing is a plus for our globe?

Questions

1. When the source of production or a provided service resides outside of a parent company's city, state, or nation, it is called _____.

    A. downsizing

    B. insourcing

    C. outsourcing

    D. exportation

2. Outsourcing production or services specifically to another country is called _____.

    A. decentralization

    B. offshoring

    C. insourcing

    D. reconfiguring

3. Outsourcing and offshoring teach us that the workplace in the 21st century has become _____.

    A. nonexistent

    B. vastly smaller

    C. a matter of local politics

    D. the whole world

12.3 Occupations in Demand

Recognize the career areas likely to experience the largest amount of growth in the coming years.

With an ever expanding, aging and more and more diverse population we will have a changing mix of goods and services being demanded. Workers' skills will have to change to meet these changing requirements. Employers will continue increasing the use of technological developments and revised business practices to enhance their production at lower costs. The fastest growing occupations will be those that require more education and training. However, there is also an increase in the number of occupations that involve short-term training. It is an important issue to be aware of what "hot" new jobs or steady old ones are in demand. For example, suppose you wanted to be a blacksmith. These workers make the metal shoes that horses wear. That dream would have been easy to fulfill a hundred years ago, when horses were used for transportation, but today you will find very limited opportunities.

What careers related to specific post secondary education are projected to have the fastest growth in the decade from 2012–2022? The ten fastest growing occupations are listed here in descending order:

- Industrial-organizational psychologists
- Personal care aides
- Home health aides
- Insulation Workers
- Interpreters and translators
- Diagnostic medical sonographers
- Occupational therapy assistants
- Genetic counselors
- Physical Therapist's Assistant and Aides.
- Skin care specialists

What occupations are projected to have the largest increase in employment over the 2012 to 2022 period? The ten highest growing categories are listed below in descending order:

- Office and administrative support
- Sales and related occupations
- Food preparation and serving related
- Education, training and library occupations
- Transportation and material moving
- Management occupations
- Healthcare practitioners and technical occupations
- Production occupations
- Business and financial operations
- Construction and extraction occupations

Although this information is current for the latest report from the Bureau of Labor Statistics, at the time of this printing, it is important to note that unanticipated events such as terrorist attacks, widespread hurricane disaster, collapse of mortgage businesses, failures of banks and investment companies, and major stock market losses can greatly impact the economy and therefore the resultant employment and unemployment patterns. For example, costs to industries for increased security, insurance, shipping and delays at borders were estimated to be as high as $150 billion just for the year following the September 11th attack on the World Trade Center (Bernasek, 2002). Therefore you as the reader are encouraged to secure the most recent data and projections that can be found on the Bureau of Labor Statistics website at http://stats.bls.gov. This site has a large volume of information, employment related topics, recent news releases and monthly updates.

Questions

1. One of the fastest growing occupations projected between 2012 and 2022 is _____.

   A. dentists

   B. railyard workers

   C. industrial-organizational psychologists

   D. miners

2. One of the largest growing categories of employment—those projected to have the largest increase in employment—from 2012 to 2022 is _____.

   A. aerospace engineering

   B. professional athletics

   C. farm equipment maintenance

   D. office and administrative support

3. The fastest growing occupations will be those that require _____.

   A. manual labor

   B. more education and training

   C. reduced cognitive capacity

   D. an Associate of Arts (AA) degree

12.4 Leadership in the Workplace

Define styles of leadership and their differing effects on the workplace.

In small businesses or offices as well as large organizations, there is a "climate" that reflects the personalities of the people there, especially the person or persons in charge. This may vary from place to place depending on such things as the nature of the work, the type of organization, but especially important is the style of leadership provided by those with administrative responsibility. The setting may be very structured and formal, or it may be loose and casual, depending on the type of work and the size of the organization. For example, if you work in a small automotive repair shop with a single owner/operator, you may have few employees and a casual climate. If you work for the county court system, you may have hundreds of employees in specialized jobs. There may be strict job expectations, highly structured procedures, policies, and a great deal of formal documentation.

In every work setting, the type of organization is summed up in the basic mission or purpose that the organization exists to achieve. The more the members of the organization understand and agree with the mission, the more likely people will work as a team to accomplish the purpose. However, there are other things besides the purpose that affects how employees work together.

A major consideration is the leadership style demonstrated in the work environment. Think of the leaders you have known in organizations or jobs. What differences in behavior styles have you noticed displayed by the people who are in charge? Obviously, in any work setting you are going to be affected by the leadership operating in the environment. So let's take a look at leadership. Let's consider what it means. Then, let's examine variations in style that produce differing results. Finally, let's ask about the possibility of leadership in your future.

12.4.1 What Is Leadership?

There are endless definitions, but they all seem to come down to the idea that **leadership** means influencing people to think and/or act a certain way. Leadership implies there is a goal or desired outcome, and that communication is used to guide members of a group to accomplish that goal or achieve that outcome.

Many people use the words "**leader**" and "**manager**" to mean the same thing, but many researchers and writers distinguish between these terms. In general, the main difference between a leader and a manager is that the leader is concerned with people. The leader focuses on the attitudes, reactions, motivations and the behaviors people exhibit toward accomplishing the mission of the organization. Leaders also usually have a broad long-range vision of where the company is headed. Managers, on the other hand, are more concerned with the details of the tasks to be accomplished in a work group. They keep the operations going smoothly. Their focus is directed on day-to-day processes. Some distinctions between leadership and **management** are summarized as follows:

Management	Leadership
Appointed to role	Emerge from group
Formal authority	May have no formal authority
Efficiency	Effectiveness
Systems	Innovation
Controls	Creativity
Policies	Adaptability
Procedures	Flexibility
Structure	Vision
Look to bottom line	Look to horizon
Reward and punish	Inspire

Warren Bennis (1989) illustrates the difference in function between a manager and a leader as follows:

Manager	Leader
Is a copy	Is an original
Asks how and when?	Asks what and why?
Accepts the status quo	Challenges the status quo
Is the good classic soldier	Is his or her own person
Does things right	Does the right thing

The role of a manager and leader may exist in the same person in an organization but often do not. Managers may or may not be leaders; leaders may or may not have management skills. Some people consider leadership a part of management; others see leadership and management as very different functions. What do you think?

12.4.2 Variations and Outcomes

Early on we talked about how reality is all in your head, and how perceptions influence how you think, react, and behave. Douglas McGregor (1960) stated that leader behavior is a function of how a leader perceives workers. McGregor determined two general ways leaders might see reality. In what he called **Theory X**, the leader views workers as people who dislike work, have to be closely supervised or pushed because they are basically lazy, irresponsible, or self-centered with little concern for the organization. However, McGregor's **Theory Y** leaders see workers as people who consider work as a pleasurable, natural part of life. They are internally motivated to be productive, accomplish goals, and are willing to learn and accept responsibility. These people are looked upon as creative and capable of contributing ideas to the organization.

Leadership styles can be categorized in three major categories: (1) autocratic; (2) democratic; and (3) laissez faire. They fall on the continuum from the *power* being concentrated in a single person (**autocratic**), concentrated on the group and its leader (**democratic**), or to the group operating rather independently from the leader (**laissez faire**). The relationship of the leader to the group is visually depicted in the figure on the next page:

In the *autocratic* style, the information flows from the leader to the group in a one-way direction. The leader is like a dictator who makes the decisions and maintains control. Workers are told what to do and how to do it. Workers are expected to adopt a submissive relationship to the leader. Some autocratic leaders are "benevolent dictators" who make decisions with the interests of employees in mind and are supportive of employees. But there is no gathering of information from employees in determining decisions.

In the *democratic* style, also called participative style, the leader embraces employee involvement in decision-making and gathers opinions, information,

Figure 12.1

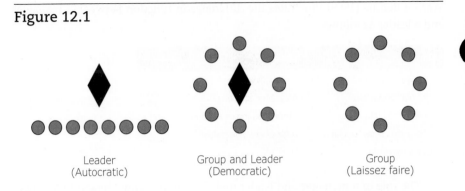

Leader	Group and Leader	Group
(Autocratic)	(Democratic)	(Laissez faire)

suggestions and preferences from employees. The participative leader may or may not actually implement the employee's recommendations, but at least considers the employee input in arriving at a decision. If the decision of the leader were different from the group, the democratic leader usually explains his or her rationale for the decision and indicates how the employee opinions played into the outcome. Democratic leaders believe that valuing employee input allows workers to feel more a part of the process and therefore keeps them more committed. This typically is the case. For the best results with the democratic style, the group needs to have an appropriate amount of interest in common with the leader, and the necessary knowledge and skills to contribute significantly to the decision making process.

The *laissez faire* style of leadership places the power for decision making within the group. The leader is more of a liaison between the work group and outsiders and secures needed resources for the group to meet its goals. **Empowerment** is a term heard frequently in discussions of work settings; this means providing the group with the authority to make decisions as a group. Of the three leadership styles, the laissez faire approach imparts the most power to the group.

Is there one best style of leadership? Not really. It all depends on the context in which the leadership occurs. There are times when an autocratic approach is most definitely the best way. Consider this . . . What if a fire broke out in your classroom? You would not want your professor to say, (while the room is filling up with smoke!) "Now students . . . let's brainstorm together and discuss ideas about how we should respond to this fire alarm." Clearly autocratic orders given to vacate the room are the most efficient and appropriate response.

Laissez faire leadership works best when the work group is highly knowledgeable about their work and highly motivated toward the goals of the organization. Physicians doing research in a laboratory, for example, probably need very little direction to do a good job. Professors in a college are rarely told by their deans how to teach a course. Having the freedom to work independently has traditionally been reserved for the highly educated and knowledgeable professions. Currently in the workplace there is a trend for self-managed teams operating without a traditional boss or supervisor. Rather, the responsibility for planning, organizing, and overseeing work is carried out by the team members. Large American companies with fifty or more employees have half of their employees working in self-managed or problem-solving teams (Boyett and Snyder, 1998). Goleman (1995) quotes Shoshana Zuboff, a Harvard Business School psychologist who noted that

> *Corporations have gone through a radical revolution within this century, and with this has come a corresponding transformation of the emotional landscape. There was a long period of managerial domination of the corporate hierarchy when the manipulative, jungle-fighter boss was rewarded. But that rigid hierarchy started breaking down in the 1980s under the twin pressures of globalization and information technology. The jungle fighter symbolizes where the corporation has been; the virtuoso in interpersonal skills is the corporate future. (p. 149)*

Although democratic leadership provides the best balance of power by involving more people in the decision making process, there are times when a more autocratic or laissez faire approach may be the most appropriate. Leadership doesn't occur in a vacuum; therefore the context of the situation helps determine the best method to follow.

Numerous researchers have referred to this "it depends on the situation" idea as contingency leadership, situational leadership, or contextual leadership. In fact, it is suggested that the truly effective leader can vary his or her style to match the needs of the situation at hand. In this case the leader should consider not only the situation, but also the type of followers and the leader's own preferred style. These are qualities embedded in what Daniel Goleman calls *emotional intelligence* (1995). When people are anxious or upset, they cannot focus, remember, or make good decisions. As Goleman states, "leadership is not domination, but the art of persuading people to work toward a common goal." For our own careers, recognition of our core feelings about what we do and what changes might make us more satisfied is basic to our own emotional intelligence and therefore our success. Goleman (1995) suggested three applications of emotional intelligence in the workplace: (1) being able to air grievances as helpful critiques; (2) creating an atmosphere in which diversity is valued rather than a source of friction; and (3) networking effectively. As discussed earlier, these skills are reflected in the characteristics of Generation Y individuals now entering the workplace in huge numbers.

12.4.3 Leadership from a Positive Psychology Perspective

Transformational Leadership, a style of leading first introduced by James MacGregor Burns (1978) in his dealing with political leadership provides a complementary fit with a Positive Psychology approach to organization in the workplace. According to Burns, transformational leadership involves engagement with others in such a way that leaders and followers elevate each other to higher levels of motivation and morality. They share the same purpose. Transformational leaders offer a purpose that transcends short-term goals and focuses on higher level intrinsic needs. This results in followers identifying with the leader. Bass (1985, 1998) enumerates four components of transformational leadership. These are:

1. **Idealized influence.** This is similar in some ways to charisma. It involves behaviors that leaders exhibit because they *choose* to do the right thing. They do this because of their commitment to their own character strengths, integrity and actions, as well as commitment to their followers. Employees respect leaders that make such choices as reflected in their behavior. Seeing this makes them likely to trust their leader and have positive perceptions of interpersonal fairness. Such leadership is also referred to as "authentic leadership" (Avolio, Griffith, Wernsing and Walumbwa, 2010).

2. **Inspirational motivation.** Leaders convey a vision that is appealing to the employees regarding their workplace and working patterns, leading to optimism toward future goals, and reflecting the meaning of their work. Meaning is, of course, one of the five PERMA components. This is shown when leaders inspire their followers to be their very best and to achieve greater levels than the followers themselves ever thought possible. Such leaders convince employees that they can break through perceived barriers to high accomplishments. Leaders instill in their employees a sense of self-efficacy and confidence.

3. **Intellectual stimulation.** Leaders do not offer all the answers. Rather they encourage their employees to challenge assumptions, respect their ability to think for themselves, and to question long held perspectives and practices. This leads employees to become more confident and ultimately strengthens their perceived effectiveness.

4. **Individualized consideration.** Leaders exhibit this by demonstrating that they care about their employees' development, and physical and psychological safety. Behaviors such as mentoring, listening empathically, showing concern, and being compassionate in dealing individually with employees express their individualized consideration. They are particularly sensitive when employees are having a difficult time. Such behavior fosters a positive interpersonal relationship with each employee (Bass, 1985, 1998; Sivanathan, Arnold, Turner and Barling, 2004).

Transformational leadership is positive in its approach, focused on what can go right in an organization as a workgroup. Seligman (2011) would refer to such institutions as positive institutions where leaders and employees share a common vision and goals for the group. Through mutual teamwork and synergy while carrying out the work of the organization, they stimulate and elevate each other to achieve higher levels of optimal functioning and well-being. All employees and the leader work hard to produce a high level of accomplishment (another of the PERMA components) and celebrate together their mutual success. When all members of the work group are on the same page, working as a team to accomplish mutual goals, the resulting environment leads to individual well-being, enhanced productivity, high job satisfaction and positive institutions. It is a win-win for all involved! Colonel Mark A. Homrig, U.S. Airforce, (2001, December 21), writing about transformational leadership, closes his discussion with an excerpt from an Army officer in Afghanistan on whose body a diary was found that compared the U.S. with fighting the Russians.

> *He noted that when you take out the Russian leader, the units stop and mill about, not sure of what to do next. But he added that when you take out a U.S. leader, somebody always and quickly takes his place and with no loss of momentum. A squad leader goes down, it may be a private that steps up to the plate before they can iron out the new chain of command. And the . . . thing is that the private knows what . . . he is doing. (p. 7)*

Colonel Homrig closes, "When leader and led values are in sync, followers don't have to be supervised; they will know what to do when the time comes, and isn't that the goal of good leadership?"

12.4.4 Is Leadership in My Future?

Are you already a leader? Are leaders born or made? There are ideas and research supporting both sides. Perhaps you can develop leadership skills just like any other abilities you acquire with work and practice, like how to drive a car, how to write a paragraph, or how to play a musical instrument. Some research has suggested that there may be some inborn traits that characterize an effective leader such as emotional stability, dominance, enthusiasm, conscientiousness, social boldness, being somewhat emotionally detached, self-assured and compulsive. Whether evolving from nature or nurture, to be effective as a leader, people need to have skills in several areas. Specifically, there is a need for: (1) technical knowledge related to the area of work; (2) interpersonal effectiveness; and (3) critical thinking skills.

Management consultants Frigon and Jackson (1996) suggest that successful leaders should be able to do the following:

1. Share power and authority
2. Build mutual trust and respect
3. Use team building, problem solving and process analysis
4. View all tasks as cooperative undertakings
5. Decentralize decision making
6. Avoid finger pointing
7. Believe that everyone has good ideas
8. Chase fear out of the workplace
9. Cooperate with organized labor
10. Recognize that this is a long-term commitment

Dubrin (1999) lists the following behaviors and skills of an effective leader:

1. Develop appropriate self-confidence (not too weak; not too confident)
2. Practice strong ethics

3. Develop partnerships with people (emphasize power sharing)

4. Help group members reach goals and achieve satisfaction

5. Make expectations known

6. Set high expectations

7. Give frequent feedback on performance

8. Manage a crisis effectively

9. Cultivate a strong customer orientation

10. Ask the right questions

Many executives hiring personnel look for people who are high in academic skills, when what they really need are leaders who have strong emotional intelligence. The Hay Group did a study revealing that leaders that displayed strength in eight or more of non-cognitive competencies developed highly motivating, top performing work places. But leaders of this caliber are rare, with only 18% of executives attaining this level. Seventy-five percent of leaders who displayed only three or fewer strengths in people skills created negative workplace climates where workers felt apathetic or disinterested (Druskat, V., Batista-Foguet, J., and Wolff, S., 2011).

Daniel Goleman (2013) describes a study by Accenture that interviewed 100 CEOs about the skills needed to run a company successfully. From this, the varying responses evolved into a list of 14 abilities. No one could have them all, but one stood out as a major competence . . . *self-awareness*, a major component of EQ. Effective leaders need to assess their own strengths and weaknesses and then to surround themselves with a team of staff whose strengths complement the leader. Self-awareness is the first place to begin when thinking about your career. This is a skill with many positive uses for a leader or for an effective worker. Goleman further notes that having empathy in balance with other abilities promotes better employee performance. The leader should not have low empathy nor an overabundance but a balance. Leaders also need to be motivated to mentor and advise employees. He suggests that this means:

- Articulating an authentic vision of overall direction that energizes others even as it sets clear expectations.

- Coaching, based on listening to what people want from their life, career and current job. Paying attention to people's feelings and needs, and showing concern.

- Listening to advice and expertise; being collaborative and making decisions by consensus when appropriate.

- Celebrating wins, laughing, knowing that having a good time together is not a waste of time but a way to build emotional capital.

Gardner (2002) noted that the advantages of leadership include financial and status rewards as well as a sense of satisfaction from successfully leading a group to a common goal. On the down side, leaders must invest a huge amount of time and energy and may be the brunt of criticism from others who may question his or her motives and integrity. He notes that leaders typically have a strong desire to use power over others or a strong need to accomplish great things. Other characteristics of a leader are ambition and the ability and willingness to work extremely hard. Kirkpatrick and Locke (1991) enumerate the following leadership traits:

1. Drive
2. Honesty and Integrity
3. Self-confidence
4. Creativity
5. Expertise
6. Cognitive ability
7. Leadership motivation
8. Flexibility

Flexibility may well be the single most important one of these traits which enables leaders to recognize the most appropriate approach or actions to take in a given situation.

Gender differences continue to be seen regarding leadership. Few women hold leadership positions in government; as of 2017, only 32 of the Fortune 500 major corporations have a woman heading the company. The idea of a woman, the nurturer, as a corporate head has not been the traditional thinking in American society. However, as Jean Lipman-Blumen (1992) points out, the concept of female leadership is no longer an oxymoron. Considering global interdependence, the trends toward team driven work patterns in corporations, and the technologically networked world, the traditional leadership of the past based on competitive, controlling, aggressive, self-reliant individualists is not well suited for the world ahead. What she calls "connective leadership," an integrative model of leadership that creatively revitalizes individualism incorporating the female perspective, sees the world as a system of interconnected uniquely important parts, rather than as independent, competitive, isolated and unequal entities. This is better suited to the current environment.

The leaders of the 21st Century must demonstrate the essential elements for optimal functioning enumerated throughout this text. These include knowing how to reframe and be flexible, being proactive, self-confident, able to master stress in the midst of constant change, maintaining a high level of wellness, thinking ahead as a visionary, and managing oneself for accomplishment. Further, leaders for this century must be emotionally intelligent, be good at listening to and expressing thoughts and feelings, and be knowledgeable about workplace trends and how to thrive in career endeavors.

As you prepare for your future and your contributions as a leader in the workplace, keep this in mind. A good place to continue developing your skills in the areas listed above is in your role right now as a student in your college career. You are a potential leader in your classes, in your peer groups, on your campus, in your jobs at this moment.

As a Chinese philosopher stated in the 6th century B.C.:

> *To lead people, walk beside them . . .*
> *As for the best leaders, the people do not*
> *Notice their existence.*
> *The next best, the people honor and praise.*
> *The next, the people fear;*
> *And the next, the people hate . . .*
> *When the best leader's work is done the*
> *People say,*
> *"We did it ourselves!"*

—Lao-tsu

Questions

1. _____ means influencing people to think and/or act in a certain way.

    A. Coercion

    B. Leadership

    C. Partnership

    D. Servitude

2. Participative leadership is also known as a _____ style of leadership.

    A. bureaucratic

    B. laissez-faire

    C. autocratic

    D. democratic

3. A transformational leader is someone who _____.

    A. has an unusual amount of influence on followers and can elevate them to higher levels of motivation and morality

    B. can argue persuasively for a position and convince a work team to adopt that position

    C. has the ability to consistently meet task-leadership goals

    D. fosters a cold, impersonal relationship with his or her employees

12.5 Performance Evaluations

Describe how performance reviews can help you identify areas of strength and need for improvement.

Many of us have a reaction when the term "performance rating" comes up. It certainly gets our attention—like when a teacher says, "This is going to be on the test"—and we start writing down this now *important* information! We may have been taught that we should not be judgmental about other people and most of us get a little anxious about someone officially "judging" us. Of course our reaction to the idea of having our work performance evaluated in writing depends on many things. First, our level of self-esteem comes into play. Secondly, our reaction is based on how we perceive our job performance. Additionally, the level of trust we have for the evaluator and the process also impacts our reaction.

In our careers, we can count on there being a formal evaluation process that documents our work performance. **Performance reviews** in a large organization may be more formal than in a small business. The process is usually done at least once annually, with shorter periods involved during a probationary period. Performance appraisal is used in all kinds of organizations to make decisions about employees. These decisions could include getting a raise or promotion, identifying a need for training or development, or even being terminated. Performance evaluations are something you need to be aware of when you first start a new position. It is vital that you create a vision of yourself as you want to be in this new position. This provides the basis for setting your goals to achieve that vision.

12.5.1 Why Are Performance Reviews Important?

Basically, performance reviews are formal methods for giving you written feedback about how well you are doing in your job, identifying your strengths and weaknesses. If you need to improve or need more training in some aspect of your work, identifying this is the first step to enhancing your performance. The "documenting" part of the process is important to the organization and to you. This begins a permanent part of your personnel file and "follows" you throughout your work history at this organization, and perhaps beyond! It is important, not only to the organization, but to you as a record of your work. Suppose you have a work history encompassing years of excellent work. Then you encounter a supervisor who may have inappropriate or capricious reasons for wanting to terminate you. Your *documented* history of excellence becomes your basis for challenging this.

12.5.2 The Review Process

Ideally, the performance evaluation process is a joint activity that involves your supervisor and you. The expectations for the work that is being evaluated should have been established in the beginning. Goal setting with your supervisor is the first step. If formal goal setting is not a part of the review process, then a set of standards, job description, or written expectations should be the *a priori* (or before the fact) basis for rating your work behavior. It's pretty hard to know if you are performing well if it's not clear what you're supposed to be doing. Some specific expectations communicated before you begin the evaluation period should become the basis for comparison or rating of your work.

DeCenzo (1997) describes the performance appraisal process as including the following steps:

1. Performance standards for your job are established by the organization.
2. You and your supervisor set measurable goals.
3. Your performance is evaluated using some type of evaluation form.
4. Your performance is compared to the pre-established measurable goals. (You may be asked to evaluate yourself.)
5. You and your supervisor discuss the formal appraisal.
6. Your performance is "rewarded" or corrective action taken.

You wouldn't be satisfied if you sat in a class for a whole semester and didn't get any feedback on your progress until you got your final grade. Likewise, you wouldn't want to work for a whole year without any feedback on your progress. There's a saying that "no news is good news" meaning if something were wrong, you'd hear about it. That is not a good rule to apply in your work evaluation. If you have not received any indications from your supervisor regarding the level of your performance, remember that you are in charge of your success. . . . ASK! You might say to your manager, "I've been working here for about two months now, and I wanted to ask you about how you think I am doing? If you have a few minutes to share your feedback, I would really appreciate it." Feedback should be a continuous year-long process that gets documented in the annual performance review. There really shouldn't be any surprises for you or your supervisor if there has been communication throughout the year.

What your performance is judged by may include individual goals that you and your supervisor have set. If not, there may be a list of expectations that appear on the standard company evaluation form. The format for the written document may also vary. It could be essay, or short answer, or checking a rating form. The categories of description of your performance may vary. Some have only two ratings, satisfactory and unsatisfactory. Others may have a broader range of ratings such as Outstanding, Above Expectations, Met Expectations, Below Expectations, Unsatisfactory (this sounds like an A,B,C . . . grading situation, doesn't it!)

Although ideally, the final judgment of your performance will involve input from both your supervisor and you, the supervisor has the final word in rating your performance. Many appraisal systems allow for the employee to register differing opinions in writing. This does not change the supervisor's official rating of you as an employee or the copy of that in your file. However, the employee's rebuttal may become a part of the documentation for that evaluation.

The annual evaluation should be a quiet, private, un-rushed meeting between the supervisor and the employee. This may be one of the few times or even the only time that you and your supervisor have a one-on-one discussion of this significance. It is an opportunity to confirm mutually known information and discuss information about work that is new to either the supervisor or the employee. For example, an employee may share that he is taking a college course related to work of which the supervisor was not aware. Likewise, the supervisor may know of resources to help an employee that was previously unknown. It may also be a time to discuss goals for the next evaluation period. Some people report that their formal work appraisal is just a quick going over of a checklist. This may leave the impression that such sessions and the documents are not really that important. Don't be misled. It still goes in your personnel file as a formal record of your year's work. Look over the document carefully and discuss any points you think are inaccurate or incomplete. Use all the skills learned earlier in this book to assertively communicate any areas of concern with your supervisor.

12.5.3 How Can I Use the Performance Review?

You should keep a file of your performance reviews for several reasons. First, they comprise a record of your work performance over time from which you can find patterns in your behavior. This is extremely significant information for your career development. You may note that more than one supervisor has commented upon an area of strength. You may also see a pattern of observations about areas in which you need to improve. This can be useful in helping you identify your strengths as well as those areas that need development.

Secondly, your compilation of performance reviews serves as a reality check regarding your own self-awareness and self-assessment. It is helpful to receive feedback from others about what you excel in, even if you already feel you are skilled in the area. It confirms for you aspects that increase or affirm your strengths. Although it may "sting" momentarily, it is also an opportunity to discover places where you need improvement.

A third reason for hanging on to your performance reviews is that it provides you with information that you may want to use to update your resume every year. Even though you do not expect to be "job hunting" every year, the process of updating your resume when the information is fresh will keep you ready should the need or the opportunity present itself. Performance rating forms are found in many and varied forms. Some are open ended for supervisor comments; some have specific topics and ratings. Items taken from an actual performance rating form are shown below. These are only sample items and not a complete employee evaluation form.

Purpose:	To assist in accurately appraising employees, to improve performance, to enhance the supervisor/employee relationship, to improve the motivational climate, and to serve as a useful tool in the growth and development of employees.
Instructions:	1. Evaluate employee's work performance for the evaluation period under your supervision (refrain from basing judgments on recent events or isolated incidents). Do not allow personal feelings or personalities to govern your evaluation.
	2. Check the appropriate rating that best describes the employee's performance; Check ALL categories.
	3. After the employee signs this evaluation, no changes may be made without the employee's knowledge.

QUALITY OF WORK Consider standard of workmanship, accuracy, neatness, skill and thoroughness of work accomplished.

Makes frequent errors. Needs improvement.	Makes recurrent errors. Needs improvement.	Usually accurate.	Is almost always accurate.	Is exact and precise.

QUANTITY OF WORK Consider use of time, ability to meet schedules, and productivity levels expected of this position.

Does not meet minimum requirements.	Does just enough to get by.	Volume of work is satisfactory.	Very industrious, more than required.	Superior work and production.

JOB KNOWLEDGE Knowledge concerning work duties which an individual should have to accomplish a satisfactory job performance rating.

Poorly informed, lacks work experience.	Lacks knowledge of some phases of work.	Moderately informed. Good potential.	Understands all phases of work.	Has complete mastery of all phases of assigned work.

ATTITUDE Consider cooperation with supervisor, co-workers and other groups with whom this employee associates in accomplishing his/her work.

Problems in working with others in office/ outside contacts.	Occasionally has problems in working with others.	No problem working with others.	Cooperative, tolerant, able to work with others to accomplish tasks.	Exceptional; effective in personal relations at all levels.

If you were designing a performance rating form, what descriptors or strengths of character do you think you would want to include? From the items on the form above, which, if any, do you think are not clear, or not appropriate?

12.5.4 Policies and Procedures—The Rules of the Game

Another area that matters in knowing the workplace is being familiar with policies and procedures. Imagine that you are driving in city traffic and there are no traffic signs, no traffic lights, and no stop signs. Everyone is driving however and wherever he or she wants. Some people are on the left side of the street; some are driving on the right side. What a mess . . . total chaos! It's pretty obvious, we need some "rules of the game" to bring direction and order to driving (in fact, it's hard enough *with* rules!).

Suppose you enroll in a college course and there is no course syllabus. This leaves the student with no explanation of what the course is about, requirements and expectations, or the grading policy. How secure would you feel? How would you be able to predict what is going to happen? See the point? We really DO want rules! It helps us know what to expect and how to succeed.

When we look at it this way, it is easy to see that we need some level of conformity. It helps groups of people accomplish their mission. There is a need for structure and organization. We really do need to know the "rules of the game."

In order to bring consistency and order to the workplace, companies have rules that are usually called "Policies and Procedures." These explain how things are supposed to work. The **policies** describe the general guidelines or rules for governing activity; the **procedures** tied to them indicate how these guidelines are to be carried out in actual task activities. Jeannette Lannon (2007) distinguishes the differences between policies and procedures as:

POLICIES

- Global in nature
- Do not change often
- Broad terms and requirements
- Explains what and why
- Approved by the board

PROCEDURES

- Specific actions are identified
- Continually improved upon
- Detailed description of activities
- Explains how, when, and who
- Enforced by management

12.5.5 Policies and Procedures—Written and Unwritten

Policies and procedures are documented in some written volume and/or available through an on-line network. The length, detail and formal presentation of the rules can be voluminous or brief. At the College where three of the authors are employed, there traditionally were two huge volumes, one for policies and a second for procedures. Fortunately, all these policies and procedures are now accessible to employees on-line for ready reference.

Usually a handbook and/or a formal orientation session will serve to highlight the policies and procedures that are relevant for specific employees. These explain such policies as work hours, benefits, safety issues, absenteeism, and disciplinary procedures. It is important to read your employee handbook and keep it for future referral. If you violate a policy or procedure you weren't aware of, but you've been given the information in writing . . . well, you can see how this could affect you at the workplace.

In addition to the formal written company or organization policies and procedures, there are endless "unwritten" practices, norms, ways of doing things that are not written down anywhere, but like so many social conventions in life, that are known and followed by the majority of workers. In society, for example, if we walk into a restaurant and all the tables are empty except for only one person sitting at one of the tables, we would not walk over to that table and sit next to that person. In fact, we would probably select a seat that is some distance from that other customer. This is an example of a social convention regarding selecting seating in a public place. This "rule" of behavior is probably not written down in an etiquette book anywhere, but it is one that most people learn with experience. So how do you, as a new employee get the scoop on these workplace practices that are not recorded anywhere? The answer is to find a mentor.

A **mentor** is a senior or experienced employee who serves to assist a new employee through advising, role modeling, explaining normative behavior, introducing contacts, and generally being available to answer questions and give support. Several studies have examined the effect of having a mentor and found that employees with mentors tended to make more money at a younger age and were more likely to follow a career plan than those employees without a mentor (Gomez-Majia, Balkin, and Cardy, 1995) Many companies and organizations have formalized mentoring programs where a new employee is assigned a mentor to help him or her integrate into the workplace. Such mentoring programs should have specific goals, clear role definition of the mentor and the protégé, training for mentors, and should encourage the new employee's independence and self-reliance (Newby and Heide, 1992). If you are not assigned a mentor when joining an organization, it is important to seek out a mentor, preferably an experienced employee who appears to be successful. Professional and trade associations are another area where mentoring from experts in the field is available. Not only educational aspects are valuable from such associations, but the social connections and networking opportunities are important to members (Dansky, 1996). The Social Security Administration (SSA) of the U. S., which is a huge bureaucracy, instituted a mentoring system to shepherd new employees through entry-level training. It has been a plus for both the new and the seasoned employees doing the mentoring. The SSA jumped from number 21 into the top 10 in 2007, ranking number 7 in the "Best Places to Work in the Federal Government" study. They attribute the jump and improved service to the implementation of a mentoring program. (Walker, April 30, 2007)

12.5.6 Advantages of Policies and Procedures

Since we like to be in charge of our lives, sometimes rules and regulations seem confining or controlling and even something to be ignored. But, in the workplace we need to recognize there are some advantages to having clearly spelled out rules. Some of the advantages include:

1. Clear understanding of expectations and responsibilities
2. Understanding of consequences of behavior
3. Predictability of the work environment
4. Security of knowing how to succeed
5. Fairness and equity in rules applying to all employees

6. Continuity and consistency of services throughout your organization

7. Enabling employees to direct themselves rather than management micro-managing staff

If you are unfamiliar with the "rules of the game" and have not received any information as a new employee, you should find out information by asking and by seeking a mentor. Develop your own "employee handbook" as you collect information if you receive little or no orientation to a new position.

Questions

1. A formal, written appraisal of an employee's work performance is called a
   _____.

   A. work analysis
   B. leadership memo
   C. quality control
   D. performance evaluation

2. The first step in the performance appraisal process is _____.

   A. performance standards for a given job are established by the organization
   B. performance is either rewarded or corrective action is taken
   C. performance is compared to a supervisor's idea of how the organization should improve
   D. rating an employee using standards established during the performance appraisal

3. The "rules of the game" in a workplace are called _____ and
   _____.

   A. expectancies; actualities
   B. policies; procedures
   C. ideals; realities
   D. Theory X; Theory Y

12.6 Stress in the Workplace

Identify ways to recognize and effectively manage stress in the workplace.

The mechanics of stress were addressed stress earlier in this text in Chapters 5 and 6 to facilitate your understanding of its effects. Further, we learned methods for keeping stress at levels that allow us to remain in charge of ourselves. Recognizing the potential for stress on the job is essential to knowing the workplace, therefore a few more words on the topic are in order.

There are some things that are a given. One is that the stimulation from events in most any workplace today sets the stage for a stress epidemic. The potential is there. A second given is that one of two things will happen. You will either:

(1) Succumb to stress at work and suffer the consequences of physical, psychological, and spiritual drain, or

(2) Master stress at work and keep your body, mind, and spirit balanced and productive in meeting your goals and enjoying the rewards.

To help you in the process of discovering how you are experiencing your workplace, the following Workplace Stress Test may provide insight and stir your thoughts on the matter. Take a moment to complete this exercise. Perhaps ask a co-worker or friend to complete it, too. Then talk it over and be sure to include ideas for bringing things into physical and psychological equilibrium. Draw on earlier lessons about stress mastery from Chapters 5 and 6 if your Workplace Stress score is moderate to high.

Workplace Stress Test

If your score is 35 to 55 you are moderately stressed.
If your score is 55 or more you are definitely stressed.

1 = Never   2 = Rarely   3 = Some of the time   4 = All of the time

	1	2	3	4
1. I feel tired at work even with adequate sleep.	1	2	3	4
2. I feel frustrated in carrying out my responsibilities at work.	1	2	3	4
3. I am moody, irritable, or impatient over small problems.	1	2	3	4
4. I want to withdraw from the constant demands on my time and energy.	1	2	3	4
5. I feel negative, futile, or depressed about work.	1	2	3	4
6. My decision-making ability is less than usual because of work.	1	2	3	4
7. I think that I am not as efficient at work as I should be.	1	2	3	4
8. I feel physically, emotionally, or spiritually depleted.	1	2	3	4
9. The quality of my work is less than it should be.	1	2	3	4
10. My resistance to illness is lowered because of my work.	1	2	3	4
11. My interest in doing fun activities is lowered because of work.	1	2	3	4
12. I feel uncaring about the problems and needs of my co-workers, customers, clients, patients, etc., at work.	1	2	3	4
13. Communication with my co-workers, friends, or family seems strained.	1	2	3	4
14. I am forgetful.	1	2	3	4
15. I have difficulty concentrating on my job.	1	2	3	4
16. I am easily bored with my job.	1	2	3	4
17. I feel a sense of dissatisfaction with my job—that there's something wrong or missing.	1	2	3	4
18. When I ask myself why I get up and go to work, the only answer that occurs to me is "I have to."	1	2	3	4

An important aspect of dealing with workplace stress involves the issue of **pacing**. Work environments may be super busy, or slow and laid back. You may not be able to control the pace of your workplace atmosphere, but you surely can control yourself, right? The whole notion of "pacing yourself" on the job to lower stress is a good idea, but only if you pace yourself in the right way. Pacing yourself properly can enhance productivity and lower stress. Pacing yourself wisely is not a matter of slowing down, but rather using strategic planning for structuring your time. Here are some pacing tips that will enable you to recharge your batteries, revitalize yourself and ultimately be more productive and creative.

12.6.1 Tips for Pacing Yourself

- Pay attention to your natural body rhythms to determine at what times you function at your best. Are you a morning or a night person? When possible, schedule your most difficult tasks for your peak performance hours. Try to avoid tackling difficult or exhausting projects during that part of the day when your energy is at its lowest.

- Shift between pleasant and unpleasant tasks. After finishing a difficult piece of work, shift to something mindless, easy and/or pleasant.

- Allow some time each day, even when you are swamped with work, for pleasurable work tasks, even if they are not highly productive.

- Use your breaks and lunches to relax. Do not work over lunch unless it is absolutely essential.

- Take mini-breaks for three to five minutes throughout the day to de-stress and balance yourself. Talk to a co-worker, have a refreshing drink.

- Choose leisure activities that balance the unique stresses in your line of work. For example, if you deal with people's complaints all day long then choose solitary, peaceful pursuits, or if you are cooped up in a windowless office all day then choose outdoor activities. If you work alone make sure your leisure time includes social activities with friends.

- Take vacations. Carefully consider the length and type of vacation you plan in order to balance work stresses. If your work is very sedentary, plan an active vacation. If your work is physically exhausting, plan a vacation where you allow a good amount of time for just kicking back and relaxing. If you work alone and feel lonely, visit friends or family or vacation with others.

- If possible take a break during your workday to exercise, do relaxation practices, or run an errand. We have discussed the importance of stretching your muscles for decreasing stress and physical strain. Take a moment several times during the day to stretch one or more of those muscle groups when you feel tense or fatigued.

Questions

1. One way to deal with stress in the workplace is to _____.

    A. take on greater responsibilities

    B. pace yourself

    C. double-check your own work and the work of your teammates

    D. sleep less and work more

2. Stimulation from events in most any workplace sets the stage for _____.

    A. exploitation of the workforce

    B. underachievement

    C. spiritual enlightenment

    D. a stress epidemic

3. Paying attention to your natural body rhythms can allow you to _____.

    A. schedule your most difficult tasks for your peak performance hours

    B. call in sick to work when necessary

    C. form more effective work teams

    D. adopt a leadership position in your organization

Summary

In this chapter we have been examining aspects of the work environment that are important for you to recognize, anticipate, and confront. We have prepared you with strategies to enable you to "move around" with ease. We have looked at trends in the world of work such as accelerating change, new organizational patterns, global interdependence, diversity, and leadership styles. We have reviewed some of the administrative realities of the workplace such as policies, procedures and performance evaluations. These topics were presented to give an overview of what to expect in today's workplace. We have closed with added suggestions on how to master the stress that looms in the work environment. Having looked at the workplace, you are now ready to move on to examining your role in this milieu as you create it for yourself.

Positive Psychology Exercises

1. Pick three people in your life (present or past) that represent each of these three major styles of leadership: autocratic, democratic and laissez faire. How did you respond to each of these leaders? If you are or were a leader, which type would you aspire to be most of the time?

2. Design a performance appraisal form for a job you have done or are now doing. Consider the main areas of work. Imagine that you are the owner of the company or the chief operating officer (CEO) of the organization. What would be most important to the organization?

3. If you were a transformational leader, list six things you would be sure to do to make your workplace a positive one that promotes optimal productivity and optimal functioning for you and each employee.

4. Visualize a work environment that takes place in a positive institution. List the elements or events that reflect positivity and support well-being.

Key Terms

Autocratic	Idealized Influence	Millennials
Baby Boomers	Individualized Consideration	Offshoring
Baby Busters	Insourcing	Outsourcing
Contingent Workers	Inspirational Motivation	Pacing
Core Workers	Intellectual Stimulation	Performance Review
Democratic	Laissez Faire	Policy
Downsizing	Leader	Procedure
Empowerment	Leadership	Theory X
Generation X	Management	Theory Y
Generation Y	Manager	Transformational Leadership
Generation Z	Mature Workers	
Gold Collar Worker	Mentor	

Shared Writing

Describe three strategies you could use to reduce stress in the workplace. What makes these strategies effective?

Chapter 12 Questions

1. What term is used to describe experts in information and communication technology?

   A. Green collar workers

   B. Blue collar workers

   C. White collar workers

   D. Gold collar workers

2. _____ have become the largest minority group in the United States.

   A. Asian-Americans

   B. Hispanics

   C. African-Americans

   D. Native-Americans

3. A _____ asks how and when, whereas a _____ asks what and why.

   A. manager; leader

   B. follower; bystander

   C. leader; manager

   D. visionary; reactionary

4. Ingo Larsen sees his workers as people who dislike work and who are basically lazy and irresponsible. What theory of leadership does Ingo endorse?

   A. Theory Y

   B. Theory X

   C. Theory Z

   D. Omega theory

5. The _____ style of leadership places the power of decision making within the group.

   A. demagogic

   B. democratic

   C. autocratic

   D. laissez-faire

6. The general guidelines or rules for governing activity in the workplace are called _____.

   A. procedures

   B. policies

   C. indicators

   D. mission statements

7. A senior employee who assists a new employee through advising, role modeling, and offering support is called a _____.

   A. consigliere

   B. manager

   C. rectifier

   D. mentor

8. Policies and procedures in a given workplace are usually contained in _____.

   A. an employee handbook

   B. a leader's secure files

   C. weekly memos to managers

   D. the oral history of the organization

9. Rudy checks his email, holds office hours, and signs a daily stack of forms during his lunch break. Rudy appears not to be very good at _____ during his work day.

   A. leading others

   B. completing tasks

   C. pacing himself

   D. following procedures

10. One strategy for pacing yourself at work is to _____.

    A. shift between pleasant and unpleasant tasks

    B. arrive earlier and stay later in the workplace

    C. sleep less and work more

    D. multitask and assume greater responsibilities

Chapter 13
Designing Your Own Career

Learning Objectives

After reading this chapter, you should be able to:

13.1 Relate different theories of vocational behavior to your understanding of your own strengths and interests.

13.2 Identify various ways to gather information about different careers and act on career choices.

13.3 Recognize the important elements of applying for, acquiring, and maintaining employment.

Suppose you were going to build a house. You would have a lot invested in your home, right? And you wouldn't want a house just "put together" on a whim. No, you'd want an architectural drawing carefully planned showing the details of the whole project. The house plan would be based on information about your needs, limits, and preferences. Houses are a lot like careers . . . a lot is invested and you may live in them a long time. Yet, in your educational experience we'll bet that you have not (in a decade or more of schooling) had a meaningful experience of learning about occupations, how to choose one, how to plan your work life, or how to achieve career success. Career education is just not a priority for our K–12 school curriculum. For a decision and an area of our lives that we spend so much time in, and that has such an impact on our lives, it is extremely important to select a career as an informed choice rather than in a casual way or by default.

13.1 Theories About Career Choices

Relate different theories of vocational behavior to your understanding of your own strengths and interests.

Many psychologists have studied and developed theories about career choice. Some presented theories saying we move through stages from childhood fantasies of career toward more realistic ideas. There are some people who determined as a child they wanted to be in a certain profession and remained committed to that goal through their life career. In contrast, there are many students who know they want a college degree, but they're not sure in what area or how this relates to their career life after college. Some students have decided on a career, but may actually know very little about what is required to enter that profession, or what life in that career means in terms of day-to-day activities or demands, salary, availability, work locations or the like.

Psychologist John Holland (1985) developed a theory regarding vocational behavior that considers six basic personality orientations. He described the six types as:

1. **Realistic**—These people apply scientific principles in things that they do. They may have mechanical abilities; they like doing or making things. Examples of occupations in this category would be pilot, electrician, engineer, or construction worker.

2. **Investigative**—People in this group like abstract thinking, discovering new knowledge, testing hypotheses, solving problems. Examples of workers in this category would be a research scientist such as a physicist, chemist, medical researcher, college or university professor.

3. **Conventional**—People in this category enjoy working in structured situations. They are usually very self-disciplined, orderly, like organizing and can work comfortably at routine, repetitive tasks. Occupations in this area include clerical worker, accountant, bank teller, data entry or billing clerk.

4. **Enterprising**—This group includes people who are persuasive, like to influence other people, are risk-takers, and enjoy business ventures. Sales managers, real estate brokers, and business owners would fall in this category.

5. **Social**—Individuals with this orientation like to work with people especially in helping relationships. Occupations in this area would include social worker, counselor, teacher, and health care worker.

6. **Artistic**—This group includes people who are creative, imaginative, emotional, and who hold unconventional perspectives which they like to express in artistic forms such as painting, sculpting, music, writing, and dance.

Holland noted that everyone has some of all these inclinations, but we could rank order them in terms of preferences for ourselves. Review these six types and place them in order from the most to least preferred orientation as you see yourself. Completing an interest inventory such as the Strong Interest Inventory can help you in determining the preferred order of these orientations for you. Occupations that combine your top two or three of Holland's orientations may be the ones that best fit your personality.

Anne Roe (1972), another psychologist and occupational theorist, identified an array of variables that relate to vocational behavior. She sees these components interacting for each of us and changing in importance as we move through our career development. The elements she discusses include the following:

State of the economy—the general state of things . . . war, peace, inflation, recession, labor markets and employment rates, trends for specific businesses, expansion or failures of specific business areas.

Family Background—Family origin, culture, socio-economic circumstances, values, educational levels, aspirations and expectations.

Chance—Unexpected events such as running into someone who knows of a position that just became open, being "in the right place at the right time." One's reaction to the chance event, however, is not a matter of chance! Also, many so-called "chance" events are not really random . . . they are influenced by the person's behavior. (Refer back to the Section on luck in Chapter 2.)

Marital Situation—If not married, nor aspiring to be, the effect of this variable will be different than for someone married. Particularly with two partners having careers in today's world, the degree of willingness to re-locate to accommodate a partner's promotion, the concern for care of children, and the amount of time available for family life all affect careers.

Physical—Refers to physical capacities, not only appearance and strength, but additionally sensory and perceptual capacities

Intellectual—Cognitive abilities of a general nature as well as special abilities of all sorts. The more recent ideas of multiple intelligences relates here.

Temperament and Personality—Natural or acquired patterns of behaviors, preferences, styles, ways of taking in and responding to stimuli in the environment.

Interests and Values—What activities, environments, and events capture our attention and liking? What values are basic to our lives? What is most important to us?

Learning and Education—What we know from general education and experience.

Acquired Skills—Special skills and techniques learned through organized training.

Roe suggested that the further from the average that any of these variables may be at any given time, the more significance that element will have in influencing career behavior. For example, in time of economic extremes—war, depression—the *economy* becomes a large factor; if a physical handicap develops then *physical* becomes a looming factor. The advantage of Roe's theory is that it goes beyond the individual in looking at career decisions and planning to family issues and other environmental realities. Since none of us operates in isolation, this is a reminder that our careers occur in the social context of which we are a part.

Consider the variables from Roe's theory of vocational behavior. What insights can you gain about yourself in relation to the factors listed above?

13.1.1 Focusing on Strengths—Applying Positive Psychology in Your Career

A relevant philosophy about personal satisfaction and professional development has been inspired by Buckingham and Clifton, both from the Gallup Organization, based on hundreds of thousands of case studies and careful analysis. In their book, *Now, Discover Your Strengths* (2001), these authors say most organizations are built on two flawed assumptions: (1) that each person can learn to be competent in almost anything; and (2) that each person's greatest room for growth is in his or her areas of greatest weakness. Instead, they contend, the best managers in corporations and organizations assume that: (1) each person's talents are enduring and unique; and (2) the greatest room for growth is in areas of greatest strength. They note that training and development in companies that focus on "improving weaknesses" are doing damage control . . . not development. A *strength* is defined as "a consistent, near perfect performance in an activity." From over two million interviews, these authors extracted 34 themes that in combination help capture the unique themes in each person's life. Questions they would ask a person include: "What are your strengths?" How can you capitalize on them?" "What are your most powerful combinations?" "Where do they take you?" "What one, two or three things can you do better than 10,000 other people?" These writers affirm the notion that instead our strengths and **talents** are what we must develop and let shine, instead of focusing on our weaknesses. They provide numerous case examples from anonymous individuals in the world of work as well as some famous people like Tiger Woods and Bill Gates. Tiger Woods learned to maximize his ability to drive a golf ball, rather than focusing on his weakness in getting out of sand traps. Gates was not talented in running a business, so he found a partner who specialized in this. This allowed Gates to focus on his talent and strengths in software development and to excel.

In this new philosophy of career decisions and development, some of Buckingham and Clifton's 34 specific themes will become apparent in a combination that helps capture the unique themes in each person. Among these, the five most dominate themes form a cluster they would call one's "signature theme." This signature theme is then related to career areas. Three principles of living a life of strength include: (1) being able to do consistently, over and over the same work happily and successfully; (2) not needing strength in every aspect of a role to excel; and (3) that you will excel only by maximizing your strengths, never by "fixing" your weaknesses. These authors have developed an inventory called the *StrengthsFinder*, an online questionnaire that yields your five dominant themes. To use this resource, one must purchase their book to obtain an identification number for access to this inventory. Talents are considered to be any recurring pattern of thought, feeling or behavior that can be productively applied. Reviewing the physiology of the brain in early development, these writers note that recurring patterns evolve from early years. Since the brain retains connections that are related to these evolving talents and discards neural connections not being used, it is not possible to switch to a new design of talents after a certain age. Therefore, our talents are enduring qualities that must be developed if we are to excel in the workplace.

Seligman (2002) also writes about strengths and the importance of capitalizing on them. We have discussed his six core virtues that comprise good character which are acted out through what Seligman terms *signature strengths.* We have reviewed the 24 of them as they relate specifically to the six virtues. He makes a point of differentiating between a "talent" and a "strength," considering talent to be an innate, non-moral, and relatively fixed phenomenon that you either have or you don't. Strengths, on the other hand, are acquired, moral, and open to further development. You can develop a strength by your own will by first deciding to acquire it and then working to develop it. Seligman states that building strengths and virtues and using them on a day-to-day basis is about making proactive choices. He suggests beginning by determining which strengths you own and can use, and that this process of discovery can inspire your creativity and desire to lead the good life. To help you determine your strengths, you can use the results of the Signature Strengths Survey in Chapter 3 or complete the full version of Seligman's Values-In-Action Strengths Survey, online at www.authentichappiness.org. You are encouraged to do this to gather important information about yourself that will help you in determining your own career area. Keep in mind, however, that Seligman believes that to be a virtuous person, one displays, by acts of will, all or most of the six core virtues by exhibiting at least one of the related strengths.

The positive tone of these philosophies are similar to the work of researchers who have studied professional reward and satisfaction in the workplace, discovering a connection between: (1) people who are passionate about their work and find it fulfilling; and (2) the success of the companies for whom they work. As more and more workers become passionately engaged, (remember the "E" in PERMA) the company's productivity increases. It is important to discover your natural talents and strengths and to develop them for use in your career life. Centering on building our strengths rather than worrying about "weaknesses" is a relieving thought for many of us!

13.1.2 Self-Assessment

Whether it is deciding on a specific career, deciding where to complete your studies for that line of work, or determining your goals and long-range objectives for your professional life, the place to begin is looking at yourself. Self-awareness is the first step. How well do you know yourself? How can you find out about yourself? Where do you begin?

Looking inward at ourselves is referred to as **introspection**, which is the process of discovering what is going on inside ourselves and noticing patterns in our behaviors, feelings, and attitudes. It is an interesting journey, one we are

The Global Perspective
Strengths and Virtues Embraced Worldwide

In his research on the nature of happiness, Martin Seligman resurrected the idea of *character* into the field of psychology. He considered the development of character an important aspect of leading a happier, more effective life. He and his colleagues began a search through the literature of all major religions and philosophical traditions. These included Aristotle and Plato, Aquinas and Augustine, the Old Testament and the Talmud, Confucius, Buddha, Lao-Tze, the Koran and many others. They were amazed to find the same six core virtues emerging over centuries, from all over the earth, and from all of the over two hundred volumes they reviewed. The virtues that these diverse cultures and religions agreed upon were: (1) wisdom and knowledge; (2) courage; (3) love and humanity; (4) justice; (5) temperance; and (6) spirituality and transcendence.

Since it is difficult to scientifically measure such abstract characteristics, Seligman studied observable behaviors reflecting these traits. He calls these behavior clusters "strengths." For example, the core virtue of justice includes duty, acting in accordance with requirements of one's position, social custom, law or religion. But how *duty* might be shown behaviorally may differ from one culture to another. For instance, consider Joe, a manager in a U.S. restaurant, whose boss assigns him the task of implementing a new procedure on order taking. He thinks about how he might carry out this task using his individual skills and talents to meet his needs and do the job well. He generates some ideas and then asks for some time with the boss to discuss his ideas. Joe is exhibiting the individualistic tradition of problem solving in American culture. Across the globe, in a restaurant in Japan, Tanaka is a manager whose boss gives her the same assignment to implement a new procedure on order taking. She nods when receiving the task assignment and proceeds, without questioning her boss, to complete the job. She is concerned about the best way to complete the task to everyone's satisfaction. In Japan, there is strong collectivist tradition which focuses on the group as a whole and workers are motivated to maintain *wa* (harmony). She is representing that tradition in her approach. Both

Tanaka and Joe are serious about being responsible for their assignment; they are each demonstrating the strength of *duty*, but the approach is slightly different, following cultural traditions. Seligman (2002) and his researchers purposely sought to identify traits that were consistent across the globe. As Seligman stated, " . . . I want my formulation of the good life to apply just as well to Japanese and to Iranians as to Americans."

Another illustration of the overlap of these virtues is seen in an exhibit in the Smithsonian National Museum of the American Indian. Although this group was not among those studied by Seligman, the key values of this culture are very similar to those same six core virtues. The museum display describes the story of the "Seven Grandfathers" from Native American folklore portraying seven specific virtues that together represent good character. These include: (1) honesty, (2) love, (3) courage, (4) trust, (5) wisdom, (6) humility, and (7) respect. Through storytelling of a legend about a young brave who confronted the grandfathers in a dream, this oral tradition taught character development in the tribes.

Why were Seligman's virtues found nearly everywhere? Because they represent traits that are basic and universal to a world that is fit for human habitation. Proof of this comes from considering the kind of world we would have without these virtues. Imagine the opposites of the six virtues: (1) stupidity and ignorance; (2) fear and withdrawal; (3) hate and egoism; (4) unfairness and inequality; (5) volatility; and (6) isolation and self-centeredness. Think of how such core patterns of behavior would play out in a world with a fragile environment and scarce resources such as water and energy.

Since a large part of how we all function in the world is in terms of our career, it is important to consider the link between your strengths and your life's work. Seligman makes a clear connection between tapping into your personal strengths and virtues for choosing a career. The research shows that above a certain basic standard of living, money does not buy happiness. It is more effective to choose a career that capitalizes on your personal strengths, as this leads not only to your own happiness, but to the ideals of global citizenship.

Seligman makes a clear connection between tapping into your personal strengths and virtues for choosing a career. Based on this, what kind of career do you think would be right for you? What are some of your personal strengths and virtues that would serve you well in the career you've selected?

---

often too busy and too caught up in the day-to-day demands to do. Introspection takes time, quietness, reflection.

You might be wondering, "So how do I 'introspect' myself?" Well, you could stand before a mirror and have a conversation with yourself. Ask yourself questions about what you think is important in life, your personality characteristics, your interests, dislikes, and on and on. Earlier in the text we discussed the *witnessing stance* where you psychologically step outside yourself and view yourself as a witness, attempting, as much as anyone can, to be objective. Some other approaches to self-awareness include writing, getting feedback, completing assessment instruments, and portfolio development.

WRITING   Whenever we are trying to figure out what we think and feel, writing can be a helpful tool. Writing your thoughts down often allows them to crystallize while you discover your own ideas. Writing diaries or journals of various types can help you to expose patterns in your life. Keeping a career related journal where you capture information about yourself related to your work life might be a useful way to enhance your self-awareness.

Nancy Anderson (2004), a professional career counselor and author, uses writing as a major part of her work with clients. She suggests you write an autobiography starting with your grandparents and describe the beliefs of each grandparent about money, work, sex, gender, religion and love. If you don't know, ask your parents or a relative. Pay attention especially to the grandparent of the same gender as you. Next describe how your parents were brought up by their parents. Anderson urges journaling how your parents met, their marriage, children, then focus on you—your birth, early care-taking, preschool, socialization, elementary and secondary schooling, and so forth to your life today. Anderson recognizes that such a writing project may take a long while and may produce fears for you. She discusses six basic fears—fear of poverty, criticism, illness, losing love, old age, and death and encourages you to examine them, determining which of them affects you most. The purpose of writing this autobiography is to understand your past—then let it go. This and other writing projects such as your personal mission statement can lead to a greater awareness of who you are and how you got there. Writing helps you sort out your thinking, find insights, as well as helping you discover your feelings and values.

FEEDBACK   Gathering feedback from other people is another way to learn about yourself. What kinds of impressions, personality quirks, strengths, hang-ups, and habits others observe about you is useful . . . and sometimes surprising. You can gather information from others informally and verbally by asking them what they see you doing, how they would characterize your personality, what they see as your strengths and weaknesses. Many times getting unsolicited feedback is a part of our interaction with others. Our bosses, teachers, co-workers, and friends give us feedback regularly by their comments to us, their requests of us, the referrals they make to us, suggestions they give us, or questions they ask us. Sometimes their relationship with us requires written feedback of a more formal nature. Work supervisors and teachers evaluate us regularly and their feedback of our behavior is documented in our personnel file or the grade roll. Reviewing such feedback may expand your awareness of self.

ASSESSMENT INSTRUMENTS   Many inventories, surveys, and rating scales exist for helping people to assess themselves. Many of these assessment tools are available through campus career counseling centers, testing centers or through faculty. Popular inventories include the Strong Interest Inventory, COPS-P and the Myers-Briggs Type Indicator. The Strong Interest Inventory asks questions about your preferences and provides a profile of your interest patterns. This inventory has integrated the Holland theory of six orientations into the interpretation of the interest information.

The COPS-P Interest Inventory provides interest scores referencing the COP-System Career Clusters. With a focus on professional occupations, the COPS-P can be used to explore college majors, help college students conquer career indecision and assist adult professionals with career issues. The inventory heightens self-awareness while providing access to the most current occupational information available. The Myers-Briggs Type Indicator (MBTI) is a personality instrument built on Jungian theory of human behavior. It is one of the most researched instruments in existence. This inventory yields a personality type (one of 16 possibilities) which helps you see the way you take in and process information and your style of decision-making. The MBTI yields your *type* based on your preference for (1) focusing more on the world of people or of ideas, (2) perceiving through intuition or sensing, (3) making decisions based on thinking or feeling, and (4) structuring tasks for completion or seeking new possibilities. Although we all use both options in each of the four dimensions, we lean toward using our preference. Each of the possible 16 MBTI *types* offers equal strengths for ways of functioning optimally.

The National Career Development Association maintains a website (http:ncda.org) that lists and sells books for career planning. Readers are encouraged to visit this site and others to explore ways to gain assistance in self-assessment.

Other written information is available by reviewing your performance on aptitude or achievement testing. In high school, what was your profile of scores on the achievement tests you took? Did you take the SAT or ACT examinations? Are there other tests you have taken such as course placement tests? If you are considering post graduate studies, how did you perform on the GRE, or LSAT (if applying to law school) or the MCAT (for medical school)? Your patterns of scores on these tests are another piece of information to plug into the "Who am I?" equation.

ONLINE ASSESSMENT OPPORTUNITIES   In addition to published inventories and surveys, as mentioned above, there are numerous websites that contain self-assessment inventories or surveys that can be answered online. Many of these ask that you complete questions which are then analyzed and feedback given you as to the "fit" for certain career groups. Robert Reardon, Program Director of the Career Center at Florida State University, is a test author and researcher who considers test validity, reliability, standardization procedures, theory base and quality of work areas to be concerned about when using online assessments (Hansen, 2002). Richard Bolles (2001, 2002) author of a career classic book, *What Color is Your Parachute* lists seven rules about taking career tests as follows:

1. There is no test that everyone loves.
2. There is no one test that always gives better results than others.
3. No test should necessarily be assumed to be accurate.
4. You should take several tests, rather than just one.
5. Always let your intuition be your guide.
6. Don't let tests make you forget that you are absolutely unique on the face of the earth—as your fingerprints attest.
7. You are never finished with a test until you've done some good hard thinking about yourself.

The Florida Academic Counseling and Tracking for Students organization and the Florida Department of Education have partnered to provide students with the internet version of Florida eChoices, a career exploration and information system from Careerware. The site is https:www.flchoices.org. This program allows students and adults to assess and identify interests and match those interests with occupations within Florida. The site http://ss.flvc.org also has extensive databases of occupations, colleges, universities and graduate schools. This site includes career planning assistance, helps individuals assess their work related values, interests, and skills as well as help in searching for related occupations and college majors. This highly researched and comprehensive program is updated regularly and provides students and adults with a realistic view of the best educational and career options for future success.

PORTFOLIO DEVELOPMENT   Artists have used portfolios—examples of their achievement—for years to apply for positions, to seek entrance into educational programs, to sell their work and ideas to others. A portfolio is a collection of representative samples of what you have done. Some school programs have expanded portfolios to English classes and other subjects where the portfolio becomes a collection of papers written and work completed to document learning. Keeping a job or career portfolio wherein you collect evidence of your accomplishments can help you write an annual self-assessment of your work, and can help document reasons you might make requests for such things as a promotion or a raise. Such a notebook of information is most useful when you begin writing or updating your resume. The Florida eChoices site http://www.flchoices.org can help you in preparing your portfolio.

PUTTING IT ALL TOGETHER   You may decide to use Holland's theory to rank personality orientations for yourself. You can use Roe's ideas to determine what you know about physical characteristics, personality patterns, family background, values, intellectual skills, interests, and the like. You may try writing or gathering feedback from people and assessment instruments. Through online assessments you can determine patterns in your values, interests, and skills. By whatever means you employ, it is important in self-assessment to determine the answers to questions like: "What do I *value* in life?" "What's more important—money or family—or something else?" "What are my *personality* characteristics?" "Am I an introvert or extrovert, organized or unstructured, quiet or talkative, dominant or submissive, emotional or not, rely on thinking or feelings to make decisions, a leader or a follower, assertive, creative, modest, tenacious, versatile, efficient, conservative, humorous, ambitious?" "What are my *skills* and talents?" "What are my *strengths*?" "Am I best at thinking, talking, creating, fixing, analyzing, learning, organizing, explaining, helping, writing, problem solving, or leading?" "Who Am I?" The more I can understand myself, the better prepared I am to determine the career path I plan to take.

13.1.3 Occupational Information

After completing your self-assessment, the next step is to gather information about careers that relate to your own personality, interests, values and aspirations. Instead of focusing on one specific career, it is helpful to look at information about **career families** such as technology, health and human services, research, business, marketing, or categories of work environments such as corporations, government, educational institutions, and hospitals. The *Dictionary of Occupational Titles* (DOT) classifies jobs by the focus on concern for people, for data, or for things. This is an example of a broad grouping of tasks and interest. Which of these three categories interests you most?

Questions

1. The psychologist who developed six basic personality orientations was
   _____.

   A. Elton French

   B. P. D. Morehouse

   C. John Holland

   D. J. B. Rhine

2. People with a/an _____ orientation enjoy working in structured situations and prefer orderly, routine tasks.

   A. conventional

   B. investigative

   C. artistic

   D. enterprising

3. The process of looking inward at ourselves is referred to as _____.

   A. intrusion

   B. introspection

   C. self-absorption

   D. reality monitoring

13.2 Finding Information About Careers

Identify various ways to gather information about different careers and act on career choices.

There are several sources you may want to tap to find information about careers. One place you do *not* want to get your information is from television programs that portray stories of people in specific fields. The real world may not be nearly as exciting as a TV series in the field of police work, law, hospitals, crime scene investigation or other work settings. Furthermore, a TV show probably will not portray the profession realistically. Consider the difference between the activities of policemen shown on a particular TV series and some of the actual footage of police work in real localities.

13.2.1 Sources

There are several ways of finding information about occupations such as the nature of the work, the necessary preparation, work environment, employment outlook, and salaries.

USING BOOKS   In addition to the DOT mentioned above, the *Occupational Outlook Handbook* is an excellent source of information about careers. *Careers Encyclopedia* is another book resource. There are also many books on specific career areas. Most major book stores have a career section which contains books for specific careers and occupational areas. Many sources for information are found online such as the *Occupational Outlook Handbook*.

USING ONLINE RESOURCES   There are several ways the computer can be an excellent resource for finding information. One advantage to computer sources is that they can be updated more quickly than book sources and therefore may be more current. Online searches can enable you to find statistics and information especially through the Bureau of Labor Statistics (website: stats.bls.gov). Many other career related sites can be found by searching on specific key words. Popular sites for students seeking career help include the following:

Monster—*www.monster.com*

CareerBuilder—*www.careerbuilder.com*

Quintessential Careers—*https://www.livecareer.com/quintessential*

Jobhunters—*www.jobhuntersbible.com*

JobsWeb—*http://www.jobsweb.com/*

LinkedIn—*www.linkedin.com*

Readers are encouraged to explore search engines with key words such as *career planning, career decisions, career development* and the like to find other online sources.

CAMPUS CAREER CENTERS   One of the best and most helpful things you could do for yourself is to visit the Career Center or Career Advisors at your Campus Advisement Office. These resource centers have tons of information from a multitude of sources. Further they usually have an array of software programs designed to help you gather information. You can get help in how to use online programs to assist you in career planning. Career counselors are available to guide you in sorting out the information you have gathered about yourself and occupations. They will help you in making a career decision and evaluating your decision.

PROFESSIONAL ASSOCIATIONS AND ORGANIZATIONS   Another good source of information can be found by tapping into websites for professional organizations and associations. Search engines can lead you to a variety of occupational groups that have information about their own professions designed for prospective students in those fields. If you go to www.quintcareers.com/professional_organizations and scroll down, you can find several sites for finding numerous associations. For example, the American Society of Information Science and Technology lists conferences, displays news articles about the field, and has an online journal of the organization as well as other career resources. The National Education Association, at www.nea.org has a variety of resources in the teaching field. It contains news articles, information for teachers, and special information for students. Likewise the American Psychological Association at www.apa.org lists scholarships available in psychology, articles regarding careers in the field, and links to related APA sites such as www.psyccareers.com. APA offers a printable brochure about the field of psychology for prospective students in the field.

INTERVIEW   An excellent way to find out about the real picture of the day-to-day activities of an occupation is to interview a person or persons within the career. Determine and compile a list of questions you want answered before you arrange a meeting. At the beginning of the interview, be sure to ask those individuals how they feel about their work. Remember if they are negative about their employment, they will probably give more negative answers to your questions. Try to sort out how much of their information is filtered through a generally pessimistic lens. Conversely, if they enjoy their work, you can find out why they say this . . . again remember that an optimistic person will enjoy anything more. So be sure to ask questions about facts, hours, details . . . not just opinions.

GAINING FIRST-HAND EXPERIENCE—INTERN OR VOLUNTEER   Any type of opportunity to spend time at a work site is even better than an interview. Not only can you actually view the day-to-day work activities of individuals involved in that occupation, but you can get a broader picture of the work environment. You can get a feel for the skills required to do the tasks, the pace of operations, organizational patterns, team versus individual work, and generalization versus specialization in activities.

If you are unable to find a formal "internship" program, you may be able to arrange to be an observer, shadow a worker for a period of time, or be a volunteer in the organization. In order to get your foot into the door for potential future hiring, you could volunteer to work for free for a specified time period with the understanding that you would be hired later if the organization is impressed with your work. Another avenue for finding placement in a work setting to experience the environment is through Service Learning assignments in college classes whereby students put in volunteer hours at businesses and community organizations. Another opportunity for learning about careers while earning college credit is through cooperative education courses. In cooperative education courses, students are placed in a business or organization with the opportunity to learn and gain college credits while volunteering their time. All of these methods for first-hand experience not only add to your knowledge, but also could be added to a resume when you seek your first position in your chosen profession.

No matter what sources of information you investigate, it is necessary to gather information about any careers you may be considering. If you have acquired a lot of information about yourself in your Self-Assessment, it is equally important to find out as much as possible about potential careers. These two areas of information prepare you for deciding or confirming a career choice or a career change and preparing you for designing your career life.

13.2.2 Making the Decision

Psychologists have studied the "decision-making" processes people use to determine choices. It seems safe to say that day-to-day decisions like what to eat for breakfast, what to wear, or where to study on campus are easily made in routine ways. However, when a more significant and complex decision like where to attend college, whether to get married, *and what career to choose* has to be made, more sophisticated methods may be called for. Researchers have identified different patterns for making complex decisions that include several variables. Most suggest that a better decision is made by use of a systematic method of comparing important factors against the alternate choices.

A planned method of making a decision requires committing thoughts on paper. It could be a simple plus or negative column for given alternatives. Or it could involve a more elaborate process such as making a table on a page listing one or several factors involved in a decision. For example, suppose Maria has completed her self-assessment and determined her areas of strength, interests, personality patterns, and these results point to three possible careers she is considering. Suppose now she considers her values regarding what is most or least important to her. She determines that salary is less important than considerations such as growth opportunities, work schedule, and "fit" with personality. To accommodate this she decides to give each factor a weighted value from 1 (lowest) to 3 (highest). She then gives a rating to each choice from one to three (low to high) regarding how she rates this career on that criterion. So she makes a matrix comparing factors with the three choices as follows:

Factors	Factor Value	Career A Law	Career B Nursing	Career C Teaching
Opportunity for professional growth	(3)	2	2	2
Work schedule	(3)	1	2	3
Location	(2)	1	2	3
Size of organization	(2)	2	2	3
Benefits	(3)	2	1	3
"Fit" with personality	(3)	3	1	3
Core position availability	(2)	2	3	2
Flexibility for horizontal moves	(2)	2	3	3
Advancement	(2)	3	2	2
Salary	(1)	3	2	2

Because the factors are not equal in her value system, Maria decides to multiply the factor value times the rating for each career choice. Then by adding the products for each career, a total is found for each of the three choices. In this case, the teaching career option clearly has the most weight and stands out as the best choice.

Factors	Factor Value	Career A Law	Career B Nursing	Career C Teaching
Opportunity for professional growth	(3)	2 = 6	2 = 6	2 = 6
Work schedule	(3)	1 = 3	2 = 6	3 = 9
Location	(2)	1 = 2	2 = 4	3 = 6
Size of organization	(2)	2 = 4	2 = 4	3 = 6
Benefits	(3)	2 = 6	1 = 3	3 = 9
"Fit" with personality	(3)	3 = 9	1 = 3	3 = 9
Core position availability	(2)	2 = 4	3 = 6	2 = 4
Flexibility for horizontal moves	(2)	2 = 4	3 = 6	3 = 6
Advancement	(2)	3 = 6	2 = 4	2 = 4
Salary	(1)	3 = 3	2 = 2	2 = 2
		47	44	61

This may seem like an involved way of trying to make a decision, but considering the importance and the consequences of a career choice, it is worth the effort. If you use the Florida CHOICES online program, it will automatically integrate your work values as a factor into the decision-making process and determine the outstanding choice.

Whether you determined your decision the "long way" per above or through a software program, a final step in decision-making is to reflect upon, review, and as time goes on re-affirm your decision. It is always a good idea after you make a major decision to look within yourself, through **introspection**, and ask yourself how you feel about the decision. In this age of rapid change and with new experiences, it may be that your decisions will have to be revised or changed as you move along. Coming back to re-evaluate the decision is, in any case, a helpful last step.

13.2.3 Setting Goals

After deciding on a career to pursue, the next step is to set specific *goals* to move you along from where you are now to entering that field and onward to planning your career path. Again, this is the time to incorporate the ideas we discussed earlier (see Chapter 8) about creating a vision. Your career development vision embodies the goals for your career path. As you now envision yourself in the career you have chosen, What do you see yourself doing? What is your role? What added responsibilities have you taken on? How have you grown in the profession? What you see in your vision is the basis for your long-term goals.

Since it is difficult to nail down every detail of what you want your life to be at the other end of your career, you may want to be more specific with goals to get yourself from here to entering the profession. Where are you right now in your educational process? What short-range goals do you want to achieve in the next two years? In the next five years? What is the next step for your educational process? And bringing your goal setting even closer, what are the implications for your goals right now and your plans for next semester? Or this semester, for that matter!

Again, this means getting information. You may need to collect data from colleges and universities where you will possibly complete your education to enter your chosen profession. It is a good idea to review the course requirements for the completion of your degree and your reaction to taking these courses. Hopefully, you will feel eager to study the requirements of your chosen career. If you review the curriculum and discover that the list of courses really turns you off, maybe you need to revisit your decision. This doesn't mean that the advanced study will be easy, but, at the very least, the topics should be areas you are interested in learning about.

When you have determined your goals, you are ready to begin a written career plan. Huge numbers of small businesses fail every year. When examining why this occurs, one variable that seems to make a difference is the *business plan*. Most failed businesses have a poorly thought out business plan, or none at all. If you are more or less a spontaneous person and "planning" makes you uncomfortable, then you need work harder than others to develop your plan in writing. In a sense, isn't your career the "business" of your life? The better you plan based on information, the more likely it is that you will succeed.

A **career plan** should include your basic mission or goal, your long range requirements, your current skills, interests and experiences, and your short-term goals. A sample career plan is as follows:

CAREER GOAL   To become a licensed registered nurse. To provide assessment, care planning, implementation of nursing intervention, and evaluation of results with hospitalized patients.

Long-range, general abilities and requirements:

- At lease a bachelor's degree in nursing
- Ability to work as part of a health care team
- Knowledge of the scientific method
- Critical thinking skills
- Capacity for record keeping
- Teaching skills
- Skills in writing care plans
- Knowledge of chemistry, anatomy and physiology, and microbiology
- License from state Board of Professional Regulations

Current skills, interests, and experiences:

- Summer employment with home health company
- High school science courses
- Experience working within a team (summer employment, school organizations, course projects)
- High school writing courses (four years of English, technical writing)
- Top 10% in high school class
- Problem solving ability and organizational skills
- Interest in helping others

Short-term, specific goals to make your dreams a reality:

- Complete current college semester
- Good test scores
- Acceptance to a university with a good nursing program
- Keep grades up to meet requirements for nursing school
- Continue work experience or part-time employment in local hospital
- Participate in campus organizations for nursing students

- Earn a bachelor's degree
- Consider graduate school
- Improve assessment and planning skills through courses to enhance these skills
- Determine areas of content for preparing for board examination

(Adapted from Adventures in Education, Planning a Career, Texas Guaranteed Student Loan Corporation, 1998)

Questions

1. The *"DOT"* as a source of career information stands for _____, published by the federal government.
   A. *Development of Theories*
   B. *Dictionary of Occupational Titles*
   C. *Designing Our Tomorrows*
   D. *Death or Taxes*

2. In addition to interviews and internships, an excellent first place to look for career information and job listings is on the _____.
   A. covers of matchbooks
   B. public transportation system
   C. bulletin board in the local Post Office
   D. Internet

3. A _____ should include your basic mission or goal, your long-range requirements, and your short-term goals.
   A. career plan
   B. life statement
   C. testament
   D. eulogy

13.3 Getting the Job

Recognize the important elements of applying for, acquiring, and maintaining employment.

There are many important sources you can turn to for assistance in seeking employment. The campus career center has materials that will help you. Your college may have recruitment days/weeks, job fairs and special programs for job seekers. Additionally, there is an abundance of help online for open positions and tips on resume writing, search ideas, and such. Some of these are listed above. Your career service center staff will help you find these and other sites if you need help.

Also, a number of business and industry directories are found in your campus library. The librarian will help you locate and use career related directories. Contacting the human resources department of these companies will provide information on job postings. Another helpful library resource is the collection of professional journals. These are published by organizations for the profession and often contain employment advertising. Emailing or calling the headquarters office of the organization may yield additional resources for listings of employment opportunities. Other methods to use include:

1. Using the internet—http://jobhuntersbible.com and many other sites have invaluable information on where to find job openings, how to make contacts, and website information for professional organizations.

2. Developing a network of contacts—professional, family, work associates, faculty members, friends, former employers, religious or other community groups.

13.3.1 Preparing Your Resume

Again, there are many publications that can be helpful in your campus career center, in the campus or public library and in large bookstores. Further, going online is an excellent way to find tips for developing your **resume** and viewing sample resumes. The best plan regarding your resume is to customize your resume for each specific position opening for which you are applying. In today's world of technology, among large companies the first "screener" of your resume may very well be a scanner, not a person. Scanners can be programmed to read and sort out specific key words (also called buzz words) in a resume that relate to the specific position. Resumes not containing those key words are never read by a person. There are various ways to organize your resume including: (1) chronological order beginning with your most recent position or job; or (2) function or task accomplishments; or (3) targeting your information for a specific position, thereby creating a customized single resume.

The chronological order format is the one most employers prefer even though it is rather traditional. The second style, function or task accomplishments, usually identifies a general area under which examples of achievements are listed. For example:

PROGRAM DEVELOPMENT

— Developed new employee orientation program

— Implemented weekly seminars for improvement ideas

— Wrote materials for personal finance program for employees

The third, and preferred, way of organizing is the targeted format which tailors the resume to fit a specific position or job opening. Here the information presented is not of a general nature. Instead it includes only those items that are related to the job opening. This type of resume focuses on the match between you and the requirements of the position.

Resumes are to be brief, usually only one page. Items to be included are:

1. *Who You Are*—Full name (highlighted or large type), full address, email address, and phone numbers with area code. Be sure you can be contacted through the information given in this section.

2. *Job Objective or Goal*—This is optimal here, but could be in cover letter instead.

3. *Education*—Other educational activities such as organizations, offices held, internship or co-op experiences, scholarships, and the like may be included here.

4. *Experience and Achievements*—List in reverse chronological sequence. Don't just list title; explain responsibilities of the job in brief.

5. *References*—Three or four actual references may be given (be sure to check with the person first), or you can say "References are available upon request."

6. As a guideline, use action verbs in writing such as "managed, coordinated, developed, wrote, designed, evaluated, organized and prepared."

Following is a sample resume:

Maria Student
245 College Street
Anywhere, Virginia 24609
(480) 394-5575
mstudent@compugo.com

OBJECTIVE
A challenging position in marketing and sales management

EDUCATION
Bachelor of Business Administration, Marketing Major
Wilson University, Atlanta, Georgia

Co-op Student in Sales Director's Office
Mainstream Manufacturing Company, Atlanta, Georgia

RELATED EXPERIENCE

Sales Representative

- Full-time temporary in summers; part-time during academic year, General Warehouse Products, Atlanta, Georgia
- Handled general sales and specialized in computer related products
- Learned sales protocol, account follow-up, and packaging
- Served as back-up to sales manager in his absence

Co-op Intern

- Assigned to assist sales director, Mainstream Manufacturing Company, Atlanta, Georgia
- Coordinated sales representatives schedules
- Monitored sales records
- Developed and presented in-service training sessions
- Received award from sales representatives for contributions as an intern

Service in University Student Business Leaders Association

- Member for three years
- Chairperson, Charity Drive Project, raised $5,000 through projects
- Recording Secretary, maintained minutes, records, agendas
- President, senior year. Developed orientation program for high school students, computerized financial and historical records systems, led development of a video program for business students

Professional Characteristics

- Highly motivated, organized
- Excellent writing, oral and presentation skills
- Positive attitude, broad perspective in planning and problem solving
- Enthusiastic and energetic
- Eager to learn, grow and develop professionally

13.3.2 Writing Your Cover Letter

Your **cover letter** is an original business letter that complements your resume. The purpose of this letter is to get the employer to read your resume. Most organizations post job openings online and prefer digital communication, therefore you will likely be applying online, first filling out the specific job application and attaching your cover letter and resume. If there is not a specific job posting, then design your cover letter as a **letter of inquiry**. *The letter should be brief, one page, and to the point.* It should be emailed to a specific person. If you are unsure who to address it to, then email or call the Human Resources Department or a receptionist and ask for the correct spelling of the name and email address of the person to whom you should direct your materials.

1. Your first paragraph is to stimulate interest . . . to indicate why you are writing, how you found out about this company, and what position you are seeking.

2. Your second paragraph (and third, if there is one) should make clear what you have to offer the company. You should point out how your skills, knowledge and experience match those listed in the job posting and/or how your skills fit with the company.

3. Your last paragraph is designed to get a response from the employer. Indicate in this closing paragraph when and how you will contact the employer to follow up.

Following is a sample cover letter:

Maria Student
245 College Street
Anywhere, Virginia 24609

Today's date

Joshua Barker, Manager
Sales Division
BCD Corporation
2420 N. W. Major Boulevard
Atlanta, Georgia 30319

Dear Mr. Barker:

I am writing to apply for the sales manager position as advertised at LinkedIn.com. I see in this position an opportunity to use my knowledge and skills in salesmanship and my organizational skills in management.

The attached resume included details my education and related experience. I will receive my degree in marketing with an emphasis in management from Wilson University in April. I have worked during summers and part-time in the academic year at General Warehouse Products as a sales representative. At the University I was a co-op student in the sales director's office at the Mainstream Manufacturing Company in Atlanta. As president of the Student Business Leaders Association on campus, I enhanced my leadership and organizational skills through several service projects we achieved. I am highly motivated, energetic and hard working.

I would appreciate an opportunity to meet with you personally to discuss my qualifications and your organization's needs. I will call your office next week to inquire regarding an appointment.

Sincerely,

Your full name

Enclosure

When your cover letter is successful, the employer will read your resume. When your resume is successful, you will be selected for an interview. Now let's think of some pointers for the actual meeting with a prospective employer.

13.3.3 Preparing for the Job Interview

How you compose your application letter, fill out an application, present your qualifications in your resume, and handle yourself on the telephone are all important, but the *single most* significant factor in the selection process is how you conduct yourself in your employment interview. One survey (Byham, 1997) revealed that 80% of respondents in a national study didn't consider interview preparation as important as having a positive attitude. Yet, recruiters and interviewers for companies report that such preparation is one of the most important factors in persuading an employer to consider an applicant for a position. You can be a happy, smiling, easy-going, perfectly positive person in the interview, but corporate interviewers indicate that if it is apparent you have not prepared for this event, you can *positively* count yourself out of the running!

The goal of your interview, that you must have firmly tattooed in your brain, is to get an offer for a position. The interview is the prime opportunity for you to communicate what you can do for the company or organization. Your job is to make clear to the employer how your skills, knowledge, experience, motivation, and work habits match what is needed in the desired position. As the saying goes, remember, "You never get a second chance to make a first impression!"

Preparation for your interview means doing your homework—gathering information, anticipating your response to questions, devising your own questions, and rehearsing your introductions. Think through and practice giving an overview of who you are and your qualifications. You should prep for an interview with just as much enthusiasm, intensity and interest as you would for a final exam.

It is necessary to gather information about the organization or company and the position. What you should know:

a. What is the nature and purpose of the organization?

b. Who are the key leaders in the company?

c. How small or large is the organization? Number of employees? Amount of sales? Number of clients served?

d. In what other locations do branches exist?

e. What is the organizational pattern for the company?

f. Who are the major competitors for this product or service?

g. What is the organization's reputation?

h. What information about this company has been in the news?

i. What are the requirements of the position you are seeking?

j. What does the job description include as responsibilities of the job?

k. Why is the position you are seeking available?

Where you can find the information:

Corporate Directories, Annual Reports, publications circulated within and publicly by the organization, the company's home webpage, Chambers of Commerce, newspaper articles, and magazine and trade journal articles and advertisements. You can also call the company as ask questions, request brochures, and inquire about other publications or video presentations designed to provide information about the organization. Study all aspects of the job description if you are seeking a specific job that is posted for applications. In learning about the company, determine the vocabulary used to describe customers, products, services and processes; in other words, learn the "lingo" of the culture.

13.3.4 The Five C's to Keep in Mind

There are several reminders that need to be stored in your head as you prepare for your interview. Five specific pointers to remember are the five Cs. These are as follows:

1. **Challenged**—Feel the spirit of challenge as you face the task of selling yourself to an employer. Recognize that this is important, but that you can do this . . . and do it well!

2. **Communicative**—This is the time to put forth all of the skills you have learned from this text on interpersonal effectiveness. Be sure you are listening to understand, that you clearly know what is being asked. Don't answer before you have a moment to gather your thoughts and organize your answer. Then when you have thought it out, answer clearly and concisely.

3. **Candid**—Be honest and direct and you will come across as the trustworthy, genuine person that you are.

4. **Comfortable**—Be relaxed and at ease. If you are tense and anxious, you could make interviewers tense (a situation you don't want!). Be yourself. Don't try to put on a show or be something you are not. Imagine if you were hired yet someone other than you got the job??? That is, imagine what a mess you create if you project yourself as someone you are not and they hire that impersonator! Your troubles would just be beginning!!

5. **Confident**—Never make a clear negative statement about yourself. This applies even if an interviewer directly asks you, "What do you see as your weakness?" That is, do *not* put yourself down! Find a way to respond that doesn't make you look compromised. For example, you might say, "Some people consider me overly concerned with facts, but others will tell you I am extremely thorough and that if I report something, you can count on it being on the money!" Or "because I am so meticulous and conscientious, I have to guard against being a workaholic." In both cases you are describing an alleged weakness and framing it as a characteristic that would make for a good employee. Your phraseology is extremely important. Consider the difference between how these two responses could be perceived . . . "I am out of

work" compared to "I am in transition in my career." When asked about your academic career contrast "My G.P.A. was 2.0" to "I experienced a variety of opportunities in college from which I learned. In addition to my coursework, I learned about teamwork, persistence and leadership as part of the baseball team, and I organized the Career Forum sponsored by the student government association."

13.3.5 The Actual Interview Process

The following nine steps describe the stages of the job interview, followed by a summary of tips regarding what to do and not to do during the interview process.

1. Introductions—Introduce yourself in a friendly and courteous way. Pay close attention and remember information given as you meet your interviewer, both verbal and non-verbal information.

2. Wait to be invited to be seated.

3. Listen, respond, and ask your questions in the exchange of the interview.

4. Mentally note any follow-up requests such as supplying references or transcripts.

5. Sense when the interview is drawing to a close.

6. Clarify with the interviewer the next steps in the process.

7. Summarize your pleasure at the interview experience, what you will do as the next step, and state succinctly your enthusiasm and qualifications for the job.

8. Thank the interviewer as you prepare to leave.

9. Follow up with a written (handwritten or typed) letter of thank you.

Tips to Keep in Mind

DOs	DON'Ts
Your homework . . . gather information	Appear uninformed regarding the organization
Rehearse . . . practice orally	Talk too much
Prepare questions you might ask	Pretend to be listening
Dress a level above the job you are seeking	Interrupt the interviewer
Arrive on time	Put yourself down
Have a firm handshake	Be arrogant
LISTEN	Be rude
Show interest	Question about salary early in the interview—do it at the end, if at all
Be nice	
Be yourself	Be an Extremist . . . moderation is the key . . . in dress and ideas or attitudes
Think what it's like to be in the interviewer's shoes	
Ask your questions	Have a telephone interview if you can avoid it
Think before responding	Be vague or indirect
Maintain eye contact most of the time	Be negative
Thank the interviewer when you leave	
Send a written follow-up expressing your appreciation and interest in the position	

13.3.6 After Leaving the Interview

Although you may feel a sense of relief and accomplishment after the interview, before you call a friend to get together to celebrate, force yourself to sit with a pad and pencil to review and jot notes about the interview. What did the interviewer ask you? Where were you more uncertain about your responses? Where did you shine? What did the interviewer say or do that gave you clues as to how you were doing in the interview? Were there areas of knowledge where you wish you had had more information?

Capture in writing as much as you can about the experience before you even leave the area. You will remember the most about the experience right after it happened. Even an hour later, your recollection will be less complete. This is hard to make yourself do, but can be very significant for preparation for a second interview . . . either at this company or at another. You have proven your ability to write a cover letter, resume and secure an interview! After you have rendered your experience to writing, pat yourself on the back!

13.3.7 Keeping Your Job

In preparing your resume, in your conduct during your interview and especially in the process of maintaining your position, it is important to think through and have clearly in your mind the ways that you add value to the establishment for which you are working. When you actually get the job . . . you think, "Whew! I did it, I got the job." But the needed energy for the task is not over; it is just starting. You have conveyed your *potential* value added to this organization, now you have to prove it. This is where the rubber hits the road, so to speak. Especially in times of downsizing, what you can contribute to the bottom line of your company or organization is paramount. You did a lot of work to understand your assets, your skills, your strengths of character that you bring to this workgroup. You prepared for and made your career decision, wrote your resume, and interviewed successfully. All this effort will help build your skills in assuring that you are contributing considerably to your workplace. A valued employee is more likely to be a continuing and positively progressing employee. Loza (2009) offers the following tips for keeping your job:

- **Show value**—if you are not adding value, there is little reason to keep you
- **Stay current**—staying up to date in your field increases your employer's options
- **Network internally**—you can find out about opportunities in other departments
- **Sell your organization or department**—be an advocate for your place of work
- **Sell yourself**—adding value is good; having others *know* you add value is better

- **Show a good attitude**—nobody wants a whiner or complainer around
- **Assess your role**—determine your strengths that can help your company
- **Show flexibility**—show willingness to be used in ways that benefit your company
- **Build respect**—for your abilities and for yourself as a person; do the right things
- **Have a plan**—apply these tips; have a plan for the worst case scenario

Questions

1. What are the five Cs to remember in an interview?
   A. Cuddle, chuckle, cajole, cheer, click
   B. Commit, control, confront, chastise, condemn
   C. Challenged, communicative, candid, comfortable, confident
   D. Complex, contemplate, charisma, conjoin, convey

2. After leaving a job interview, you should follow up with a _____ thanking the interviewer.
   A. written letter
   B. warm hug
   C. fist bump
   D. high five

3. One of the most important behaviors for keeping your job is adding _____ to your company.
   A. extra work
   B. value
   C. frustration
   D. cleanliness

Summary

In this chapter we have reviewed the process of planning your own career and making it happen. We examined Holland's six personality orientations and how these relate to career fit. We considered the variables that Roe believes influence our career success. We investigated the power to excel by discovering and enhancing our strengths. We noted the importance of discovering and building your strengths. We described ways you can gain information about your interests, personality characteristics, values, and skills. We explored the ways to find information about careers in order to analyze the connection between the nature of the work and your own "human nature." We reviewed methods for decision-making that allowed for value differences for specific factors. We discussed goal setting and development of a career plan. We looked at the steps in getting the job, preparing your resume, cover letter and the interview process. We emphasized the importance of adding value to your company, and shared other ways to help you keep your job. Whether you are preparing to enter a profession for the first time, or if you have years of experience in the professional world, the real value of all of this is you putting it to work when designing your own career!

Positive Psychology Exercises

1. Take Seligman's Positive Psychology Values-in-Action survey to identify your signature strengths.
2. Complete the *Self-Directed Search* or *Strong Interest Inventory* and list three occupations that fit your orientation and that appeal to you.
3. Discuss your career goal or tentative goal with a friend using the factors in Anne Roe's vocational theory.
4. Develop a career plan using the sample in the chapter as a guide.
5. Keep a self-assessment journal, recording new insights and information as you gather it.

Key Terms

Added Value	Enterprising	Realistic
Artistic	Introspection	Resume
Career Families	Investigative	Social
Career Plan	Letter of Inquiry	Talent
Conventional	Personality	Values
Cover Letter		

Shared Writing

What are some of your signature strengths? List a few and explain how these strengths might be an asset in a particular career area.

Chapter 13 Questions

1. Burt is high in mechanical ability, and likes making things and doing things. He has considered a career as an electrician, plumber, or carpenter. Burt's personality orientation related to work is most likely _____.

   A. investigative

   B. enterprising

   C. realistic

   D. social

2. Millicent is pursuing a career as a social worker because she really likes to help people in need and she feels she's skilled at doing so. Millicent's personality orientation related to work is _____.

   A. social

   B. artistic

   C. realistic

   D. conventional

3. The psychologist who looks at marital situation as a factor in career decision is _____.

   A. Lavinia Dock

   B. Anne Roe

   C. Mary Phelps Jacob

   D. Carly Haufe

4. The Myers-Briggs Type Indicator (MBTI), COPS-P, and Strong Interest Inventory are all examples of _____ that can help a person identify her or his employment interests.

   A. interviewing techniques

   B. major theories

   C. performance appraisals

   D. assessment instruments

5. A government agency that compiles trends, averages, and other information related to occupations is the _____.

   A. Institute for Peace and Prosperity (IPP)

   B. Bureau of Labor Statistics (BLS)

   C. Risk Management Agency (RMA)

   D. Citizens' Council on Comptroller Policies (CCCP)

6. Barry has compiled a list of questions he wants to ask the local butcher in the hopes of identifying whether he, himself, might want to pursue a career in butchery one day. Barry is using the _____ technique to gather information about occupational options.

   A. interview

   B. self-assessment

   C. introspective

   D. personality profile

7. Which of these would be a long-range general ability a person might have in her or his career plan?

   A. Donate food to the homeless this season.

   B. Get good test scores.

   C. Complete the current college semester.

   D. Acquire knowledge of the scientific method.

8. A résumé should be _____ page(s).

   A. one

   B. three

   C. five

   D. seven

9. A letter that responds to a specific position that's open is referred to as a letter of
_____.

A. application

B. inquiry

C. intent

D. coverage

10. The goal of your interview is to
_____.

A. get an offer for a position

B. play hard to get

C. negotiate a top salary

D. make a new friend

Chapter 14

Applying Positive Psychology at Work

 Learning Objectives

After reading this chapter, you should be able to:

14.1 Identify the eight competencies of emotionally intelligent individuals.

14.2 Describe specific ways in which understanding yourself will help you better understand others.

14.3 Explain why understanding your own needs helps you to behave in ways that allow you to achieve your goals.

14.4 Identify the different skills needed to effectively work with others.

14.5 Explain why identifying your strengths and changing your behavior to incorporate these strengths will have a positive effect on your development.

14.6 Identify strategies for resolving common problems in the workplace.

14.7 Explain how proactivity and personal responsibility influence your effectiveness in the workplace.

14.8 Define the concept of flow and its relationship to motivation.

Positive Psychology—the science and study of flourishing, of psychological strengths and positive emotions—brings great promise for achieving pleasure and fulfillment in the workplace. Through the development and use of strengths, such as creativity, open-mindedness, integrity, interpersonal skills, leadership, hope, and enthusiasm, we are able to enhance production, fulfillment and the satisfaction that we enjoy in our work life (Seligman, 2002, 2011). Strengths that are vital to a positive work life are emotional and social intelligence (Goleman, 1998, 2006), which are related to our ability to work effectively with others. When you have these skills, you are known as being **people smart**.

In the 1600s the poet John Donne wrote, "no man is an island . . . ." He was right. We all have to deal with people. No matter what type of career you may be in, whether you are a computer programmer, sales manager, engineer, artist, physical therapist, teacher, or other, you will be doing your work in the company of other people. Some occupations have a great deal of contact with other people; some involve minimal interaction, but *all* jobs involve working in a social context of some sort. Aristotle said centuries ago that humans are social animals. So it makes sense that to be successful and excel on the job, you will also have to be people smart. Research shows that the reason most people are fired from their jobs is not because they lack the technical skills and knowledge to do the job, but because they cannot get along with other people, their bosses, co-workers, clients, customers, patients, students, whomever their position requires they serve. The increasing use of work teams to complete projects in the workplace further emphasizes this skill.

Is there someone you know who is really "smart" when it comes to taking a test, spewing out dates and knowledge, answering questions with the most obscure facts? They might win a million with their final answers, *but* how well do they do on the job, working in a populated environment? Do they have a working knowledge of how to interact effectively with people?

14.1 What Does It Mean to Be People Smart?

Identify the eight competencies of emotionally intelligent individuals.

When we think of being "smart" we think of having a high IQ, which supposedly refers to being very intelligent in terms of cognitive skills. However, what we have traditionally referred to as IQ tests primarily measure skills in language and analytic/mathematics problem solving. Thus, our concept of "intelligence" centers around thinking skills involving memory, logic, organizing ideas and the like. Howard Gardner (1983) challenged this traditional concept of intelligence when he proposed his theory of multiple intelligences. He described eight different types of human intelligence. The two of import here are the personal ones, **intrapersonal** and **interpersonal intelligences**. These speak to our ability to be aware of our inner selves and to connect effectively in working with other people.

Daniel Goleman (1995), discussed earlier, notes the significance of knowing yourself as a part of emotional intelligence. For him, self-awareness is an ongoing attention to one's internal states that can be at best a non-judgmental consciousness of feelings, or at a minimum, recognition of what is happening emotionally rather than "being immersed and lost in it." Goleman discusses the anatomy of our brain and cerebral emotional centers that are involved in normal functioning. He relates a story of a man who, because of brain surgery for a tumor, lost the normal neural connections in his brain between his cognitive and emotional centers, which left his thinking devoid of emotional connections. This disability in his emotional functioning led to severe problems for this individual. He lost his job as a corporate lawyer; his wife left him; he couldn't handle his financial affairs; and he was even unable to make simple decisions. This illustrates how important our emotions are to function normally. Goleman points out that even in usual day-to-day activity, a person who is annoyed by a rude encounter in the early part of the day, but unaware of his feelings, is likely to continue for hours afterward snapping at other people and making curt responses for no good reason. As Goleman explains, once this person brings the feelings from the initial rude morning encounter into his awareness, he can then evaluate things anew. This allows him to change his frame and his behavior positively toward others. Thus, Goleman illustrates the importance of our being able to feel our emotions and to be aware of them as a basis for behaving with emotional intelligence.

Silberman and Hansburg (2000) state that individuals who are people smart exhibit the following competencies:

1. **Understanding People**—listening actively, empathically, clarifying, reading and interpreting beyond words to non-verbal cues and messages, and able to read other people's styles and motives in order to work with them effectively.

2. **Expressing Yourself Clearly**—knowing how to get your message across by reading the verbal and non-verbal responses of those with whom you are communicating and responding appropriately.

3. **Asserting Your Needs**—being your own person, having and establishing limits, and being straightforward with your wishes.

4. **Exchanging Feedback**—giving feedback easily and diplomatically as well as seeking feedback from others in a non-defensive fashion.

5. **Influencing Others**—being able to motivate others to action, able to connect with others, discover their needs, knowing how to defuse or reduce resistance and make persuasive appeals.

6. **Resolving Conflict**—able to use the above mentioned skills to get the main issue out in the open, able to figure out the needs and concerns of all involved, and to suggest creative solutions.

7. **Being a Team Player**—accepting the challenge to work with others by complementing their styles, coordinating the efforts of team members without being bossy, and building consensus.

8. **Shifting Gears**—understanding differences in people, able to make changes in one's own behavior, willing to try new and different things, able to reframe, and knowing how to handle the risk of change.

There are meaningful rewards for developing these skills. When you understand someone else, you are appreciated; when you explain yourself clearly, you are understood; when you assert yourself, you are respected; when you exchange feedback, you are enlightened; when you influence others positively, you are valued; when you resolve conflict effectively, you are trusted; when you collaborate with teammates, you are prized; when you shift gears, your relationships are renewed (Silberman and Hansburg, 2000).

These competencies described by Silberman and Hansburg echo the ideas of Goleman regarding emotional intelligence. Do these eight competencies ring any bells related to the steps you've been learning throughout this text about being a more effective person? Hopefully, you are mentally connecting the ways in which reframing, being proactive, listening and expressive skills all play out in the workplace.

Questions

1. If I am able to understand myself and appreciate my feelings, Howard Gardner would say this is _____ intelligence.
   A. componential
   B. interpersonal
   C. intrapersonal
   D. esoteric

2. Being your own person, having and establishing limits, and being straightforward with your wishes are all aspects of _____.
   A. exchanging feedback
   B. asserting your needs
   C. resolving conflict
   D. shifting gears

3. Part of "shifting gears" when showing "people smarts" is _____.
   A. giving feedback diplomatically
   B. being able to motivate others to action
   C. understanding differences in people
   D. listening actively

14.2 Understanding Yourself

Describe specific ways in which understanding yourself will help you better understand others.

The aged admonitions from Socrates and Shakespeare to know and be true to yourself are filled with wisdom. Just as you probably can't really love someone fully if you don't love yourself first, you obviously need to understand yourself before you can become astute in knowing others. So let's start with some questions to think about.

14.2.1 What Do You Want the Outcome to Be?

Whether you are talking about your career, your marriage or family, your grades for this semester, or your tennis swing, you have to have a vision of the desired result. As we discussed previously, athletes training for Olympic feats work with trainers to visualize their success. The more specific and clear the image in your mind, the more likely you are to achieve it. If you don't have a goal in mind, it's like going on a trip with no destination. How do you know if you're getting closer? How would you know when you're there? How *can* you know, if you don't even know where you're going? Have you ever tried to do a class project when you didn't understand the assignment? How can you know if you're doing a good job, if you don't have a clue what you are trying to accomplish? Or why you're doing this thing in the first place?

Goal setting is the answer to these mysteries. If you have a clear goal that you are trying to achieve, it gives you direction and focus. This helps you to know if you are staying on track, moving in the right direction, and how well you are doing.

Imagine yourself ten years down the road. What do you see for your life? For your career life? Family life? If you said you wanted to be a successful lawyer, for example, and you simultaneously desired to be a very involved parent with your two children, then how is that going to work? Lawyers spend an incredible amount of time at their jobs, especially in the first decade or so of their work. How are you going to do this and still manage to spend time with your children? Suppose you want to make a lot of money in a career in demand. So you decide to be a computer engineer. But, what you really enjoy are outdoor sports and participating in mountain bike races with your significant other. How are you going to work those long hours and be on call at all hours when systems problems occur, yet spend a long vacation biking in France or finding time to travel for races out of town? Is there a way to reconcile competing goals?

As you can see, setting a goal leads you to the next steps of planning how you are going to accomplish this. Employers in companies and organizations report that the best performing employees are those who consistently set goals for themselves. Research over the years has confirmed that college students who complete their degrees, compared to those who drop out, are more likely to have begun their studies with a specific major and career goal in mind. It makes it a lot easier to do your assignments, prepare for tests, get yourself to those early classes and such when you know *why* you are doing these things.

Goals are usually classified into two categories . . . long-term and short-term. We have many short-term goals everyday. Sometimes, just getting through the day is one of your short-term goals! Turning your thoughts toward what you want the outcome to be is an important first step. Daily goals might be in the form of a *To Do* list. For important matters related to career, family, or health issues the goals will be longer-term. Clarifying your goals helps provide the direction, like a lighthouse blinking a steady reminder of the course ahead. Keep a file, folder, a notebook or journal in which you discuss and record your goals, both long and short-term. We all talk to ourselves anyway, so begin a written dialogue with yourself about the outcome you desire. Also, refer back to your personal mission statement for guidance.

14.2.2 What Is Your Personality Like?

This second question will also help you be smarter about who you are. We use the word "personality" in everyday speech. We might say, "Oh, she has such an outgoing personality." What do we mean when we use that term? **Personality** refers to our characteristic patterns of behavior including our thoughts and emotions. In other words, even though we have lots of thoughts and feelings, and behave in all kinds of ways, we have consistency in certain ways of behaving. It is like a theme or refrain in a musical piece that comes back to repeat itself.

Each individual has his own collection of unique behavioral quirks. You and your brothers and sisters (if you have any) may have some behavioral characteristics that are alike, but the whole package of how you and your siblings each behave is different. So we each have our own personality scheme. Most researchers agree that this pattern of behaviors is formed in our early years and we probably cannot make major changes in our behavior patterns. Even though we may not be able to move from being a perfectionist to the opposite extreme of tolerating or even liking disorder, we can learn how our perfectionist pattern helps and hinders us. It is unlikely that an extrovert would change and become an introvert. But again, an extrovert can recognize how his outgoing nature is an asset or a liability and change his behavior accordingly.

In trying to develop an awareness and understanding of your personality, there are many sources or methods you could use. Numerous personality assessment instruments have been developed by theorists to determine personality patterns. One of the most popular instruments is the Myers-Briggs Type Indicator.

Without visiting a psychologist for psychological assessment, you already have a handle on some of your patterns of behavior. You sense whether or not you are decisive, bright, shy, disorganized, out-going, competitive, calm, sad, suspicious, or quiet, for example. So besides formal psychological evaluation, you can utilize introspection, the process of looking inside yourself, to discern your personality patterns.

14.2.3 How Can You Get and Use Feedback?

You can determine information about your personality by gathering feedback from others who know you well and have seen you behave over time. Ask them to describe you. Another place where written and verbal feedback is available is in learning settings. You have been getting teachers' comments about your behavior and work patterns for years in the form of anecdotal comments and in formal grading or rating systems. Think back over your report cards and other school experiences to see what patterns are evident in your behavior. Think of your interactions with your friends. How did they describe you or react to you when you were in school?

14.2.4 How Can You Keep a Balance?

Sometimes, the very thing at which you are best, if taken to extreme, becomes your downfall. For example, if you are really good at persuasion, that can lead to a successful career in law, sales, business, or politics. However, it can begin to create the opposite affect if you carry your strength too far by behaving in ways that are seen as dominant, insensitive, pushy, or overbearing. So the secret is to know your personality and find a healthy balance. This means recognizing how your personality patterns help and hinder you. Learning to use your personality traits to maximize your effectiveness and monitor and manage them when they become ineffective is a key to success.

Positive Psychology Exercise

The Upside and Downside of Your Strengths

Through thinking about yourself, reviewing and gathering feedback, and perhaps completing a personality survey, determine five adjectives that describe your personality. Decide how they are strengths and how they could be weaknesses. Keep them in mind, and use them well!

Questions

1. To determine direction and focus, it is helpful to _____.

   A. do what society tells you to do

   B. obey others

   C. stick with tried and true behavior

   D. set goals

2. Characteristic patterns of behavior, including thoughts and emotions, are a definition of _____.

   A. intelligence

   B. personality

   C. motivation

   D. vitality

3. One key to success is recognizing how your personality patterns both _____ and _____ you.

   A. define; describe

   B. help; hinder

   C. shape; mold

   D. restrict; free

14.3 How Personal Needs Drive Behavior

Explain why understanding your own needs helps you to behave in ways that allow you to achieve your goals.

Understanding your needs is another important key to behaving in ways that move you closer to achieving your goals. You might have heard people commenting about someone's behavior by saying, "Oh, she just needs to be with people" or "he needs to always be at the top of the class," or "he always wants to be in charge." These three comments reflect the work of David McClelland (1961) who pioneered research which described and explained what drives people to behave in certain patterns. He called the first need alluded to above, the need for **affiliation**, to be in social settings, connected to other people. The second comment above describes someone McClelland would say has a need for achievement, always striving to be at the top, to accomplish a lot, to exhibit high levels of performance. The third description portrays what McClelland called the need for power. We all have some of these needs, but if you were to rank your needs from the highest to the middle to the lowest, how would you order them? Do you see examples of this ranking reflected in your behavior? In any of your role models? What about your parents?

Another psychologist who studied needs and developed a theory was Abraham Maslow (1970). Maslow spent much of his life examining what was right with people instead of what is wrong. He was interested in determining the characteristics of extremely psychologically healthy people, extraordinary people who made a difference in this world. From his research he developed a

Figure 14.1 Maslow's Hierarchy of Needs

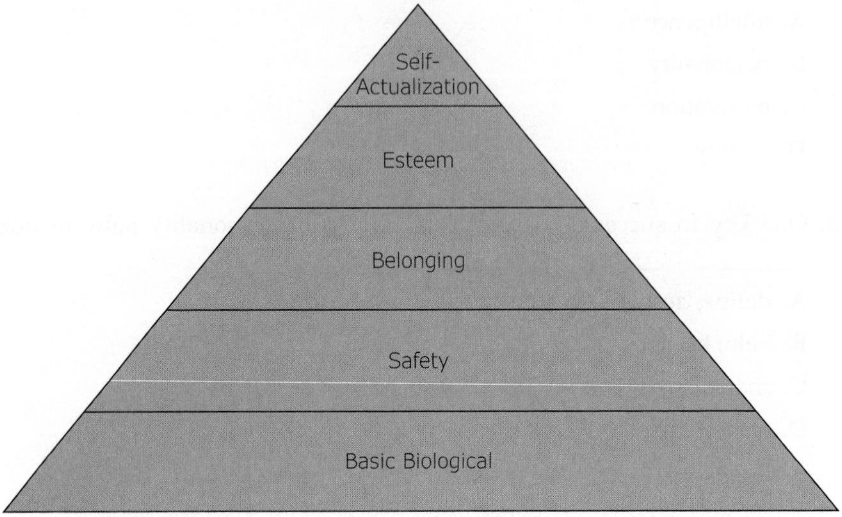

hierarchy of needs that are depicted in pyramid form, since each level presumes the lower level(s) of needs is/are already met. His hierarchy is as follows:

Maslow explained that our initial requirements were biological needs for sustaining life, such as air, water, food, and sex. When these are satisfied, the next level of need that emerges is for safety which causes us to behave in ways to feel secure and safe. This would include shelter from the elements, and in today's world might include locks, alarms systems and bars on our windows! When safety concerns are met, Maslow said we then experience desires for connection to other people, a craving for affiliation, belonging, and social interaction. Then esteem necessities would emerge and we would behave in ways to meet those. The highest level in Maslow's hierarchy is **self-actualization** needs. These are of the highest order and include concern for things like *the good, the true, and the beautiful*. People who are aspiring to be self-actualizing are experiencing a high level of fulfillment in their lives. As Maslow said, they are actualizing, or bringing to reality, the potential we all have as humans for the good life. However, Maslow said that most people never fully reach this highest level. He described the characteristics of self-actualized people as:

Being practical and realistic in problem solving
Accepting of themselves and other people
Being genuine, natural and spontaneous
Having a need for privacy
Being independent, self-reliant
Having **peak experiences**, moments of exhilaration and ecstasy
Identifying with and respecting all humankind

Following strongly held values and ethics

Maintaining deep, close relationships with a small number of people

Demonstrating a broad, non-hostile sense of humor

Being innovative and creative

Being individualistic and resisting conformity

Appreciating the natural and social environment

The extent to which you can identify with your needs, be they for achievement, social connections, for power, for safety, and so forth, the more you can understand why you may be behaving in a certain way. Needs can be conscious or nonconscious. The idea of needs explains what motivates our behavior. This is why public schools have instituted breakfast programs for students. Administrators have recognized that if kids are hungry, they aren't going to care much about learning that $1 + 1 = 2$.

A good way to get in touch with what needs *are* operating in your life is to take an inventory of how and where you spend your time. What are you investing your efforts and energies doing? The theory suggests that the answer to this question informs you about your true **motivation**. It's not a question of are you motivated or not motivated. It is a question of what needs are you motivated (and therefore behaving) to meet? What is the focus of your motivation?

We can learn a huge lesson from the advertisement industry in our country. Massive amounts of money are spent on advertising, and for what purpose? No, it's not to make us buy a product or service. It is for us to be convinced that we need it; then *we* take care of the buying part, sometimes even if we can't afford it! And look what a great success the advertisement industry has had. Think of all the things we are convinced we need in order to live such as smart phones, huge flat screen TVs, laptops, tablets and faster wireless service.

If we are rationally convinced that a specific degree, occupation, or lifestyle are what we need, we will behave in ways to make it happen. So this brings us back to our goals. If we set goals and then find ourselves not motivated to do the things we must to achieve those goals . . . perhaps we *need* to work on our needs! If we can convince ourselves, like the advertisers, that we need what those goals will bring, then we will behave to achieve those goals. This cycle of behavior starts with awareness of our need pattern that is presently operating and convincing ourselves to make changes in our priorities, to see our goals as *necessary*. This will bring us to the power of commitment. Can you think of something in your life, perhaps not necessarily easy to achieve, that you decided you *were* going to do? You didn't say, "Maybe I'll do this," or "I'll try to do this." Instead, you said, "I *am* going to do this." Notice that whatever obstacle you had to overcome to do this thing, you figured out a way to handle it? And remember how good it felt when you could say, "Yessssss . . . I did it!"

If you convince yourself you **need** to meet that goal, you are lighting the flame of commitment which fires you into action. The intensity of this kind of energy is amazing. And you are on your way to achieving your goal, meeting your new need!

The first step to reaching success is awareness . . . then commitment . . . then comes change. Become aware of what needs are driving your behavior. Think of how can you work with those needs, using them to maximize your success, override them with newly determined needs, or stop and satisfy them, then move on.

14.3.1 Triggers for Positive and Negative Behaviors

One of the smartest things you can do to learn about yourself is to become aware of your **triggers**. Triggers set you off, either in a positive way—energized to behave in ways to be effective, or in a negative way—aroused to act out your emotions and attitudes in ways that are destructive, to others and/or yourself. In the medical world they speak of "triggers" that set off physical problems, like allergies or migraine headaches and admonish patients to become aware of trigger situations and avoid them. On the positive side, health care givers encourage the presence of positive trigger situations like aromatherapy, massage, meditation, deep breathing and the like that activate calming behaviors and reduce stress.

Our triggers come from somewhere. Are we born with them? No way. The specific events or incidents or words or situations that initiate our predictable responses are learned associations. We probably learned them early in our lives, perhaps long before we really remember the original incidents. These incidents involved pleasant or unpleasant consequences in our earlier times and those same feelings get generated today, even though the circumstances are different. Triggers can stir feelings that are happy, delightful, and positive as well as feelings that are sad, uncomfortable, and negative. The key is to identify the triggers that set off negative responses, avoid and monitor them, and seek out those triggers that spark our joyous feelings.

The steps for managing negative trigger situations in your life are:

1. Be aware of what sets off the reaction, your unique set of triggers.
2. Monitor the situation.
3. Use cognitive restructuring to explore the logic of the situation.
4. Determine alternative responses that you can employ to minimize or avoid self-destructive behaviors and the consequences of such.

In the case of positive emotions, become aware of the triggers that initiate them. Then deliberately gravitate to situations that expose you to those triggers that enhance your happiness. Handling your personality patterns is important in moving toward achieving your goals and meeting your needs. The extent to which you become proficient in using triggers to your advantage, the more personally effective you will be. You will be people smart about yourself. You will also be better prepared to engage in understanding the behaviors of others. The following exercise will help you identify your triggers.

Positive Psychology Exercise

Identifying Triggers

If you think about common feelings you can identify behavioral responses, that is, how you react when feeling this emotion. You can also identify what happened just before the feeling became evident. This probably triggered the emotion. For example, if you think of a time when you felt *anger*, you can also identify your behavioral response. You can also identify what triggered the emotion and determine if this is a common antecedent to angry feelings, and complete the following form that lists numerous common feelings. This will give you insight about specific triggers and behaviors that you may want to revisit and alter. Now consider the following set of emotions and fill in the blanks for examples of patterns in your behavior:

FEELING	BEHAVIORAL RESPONSE	TRIGGERED BY
Anger		
Sadness		
Anxiety		
Power		
Compulsion		
Joy		
Calm		
Amused		
Alive		
Happy		
Warmth		
Love		
Exhilaration		

14.3.2 The Impact of Technology on Emotional Intelligence

Daniel Goleman (2013) raises some interesting questions about the impact of the growing use of digital means for human connection. He states that today's children are growing up "more attuned to machines and less to people than has ever been true in human history." He notes that "the social and emotional circuitry of a child's brain learns from contact and conversation with everyone it encounters over the course of a day. These interactions mold brain circuitry; the fewer hours spent with people—and the more spent staring at a digitized screen—portents deficits," so says Goleman. For example, Delouche and colleagues (2010) studied the value of DVDs designed to help babies learn vocabulary words. Their findings were very clear that infants learn from adults, not videos. In their study the children who learned the words directly from their parents (without the DVD) learned significantly better than the control group exposed to DVDs.

Currently, the workplace is teeming with situations requiring our capacity to connect effectively with others, that is, to be people smart. The ability to relate effectively with others is an essential characteristic for success in the workplace. It will be very interesting to see how the cohort of children growing up in this technological age, referred to as digital *natives*, will differ from previous generations based on their reliance on electronic communication. However, it will be many years before these children will be entering adulthood and the business world. Who knows what the workplace will be like then, especially considering that the digitalization of our lives with the plethora of available electronic devices is a fairly recent phenomenon. It will be fascinating to watch how this plays out in the future. We can only hope that technoference does not result in absent presence becoming the norm in the workplace of tomorrow.

Questions

1. Bartleby has a strong desire to stay connected to other people and be in social settings. Bartleby is high in _____.

   A. need for power

   B. need for affiliation

   C. need for control

   D. need for achievement

2. Abraham Maslow developed a _____ to describe different types of motives in daily life.

   A. hierarchy of needs

   B. taxonomy of motivations

   C. dictionary of wants

   D. compendium of goal states

3. Something that sets you off, in either a positive or a negative way, is called a _____.

   A. need

   B. motivation

   C. trigger

   D. supernormal sign stimulus

14.4 Understanding Others

Identify the different skills needed to effectively work with others.

In addition to understanding yourself, your career success also hinges on your being able to understand and interact effectively with other people. In fact you must *first* understand yourself in order to understand others. This is reinforced by the findings of Tania Singer (2009), a director and researcher of empathy and self-awareness at the Brain Science Institute in Leipzig, Germany. Based on her research findings in this area, she agrees that you have to understand your own feelings to be able to understand those of others. Hiring and firing data shows the importance of working effectively with others. Research on ratings of top performers consistently ranks interpersonal skills, emotional intelligence, and political skills as being more important than mental ability or intelligence (Goleman, 1998; Ferris, 1999; Kaplan and Kaiser, 2010).

In other words, no matter how traditionally *smart* you may be, it is your *people smarts* that carry the most weight in achieving *excellence* in your performance ratings. Such ratings are the basis for decisions about retention, promotion, advancement and growth opportunities in employment settings. There are many

Figure 14.2

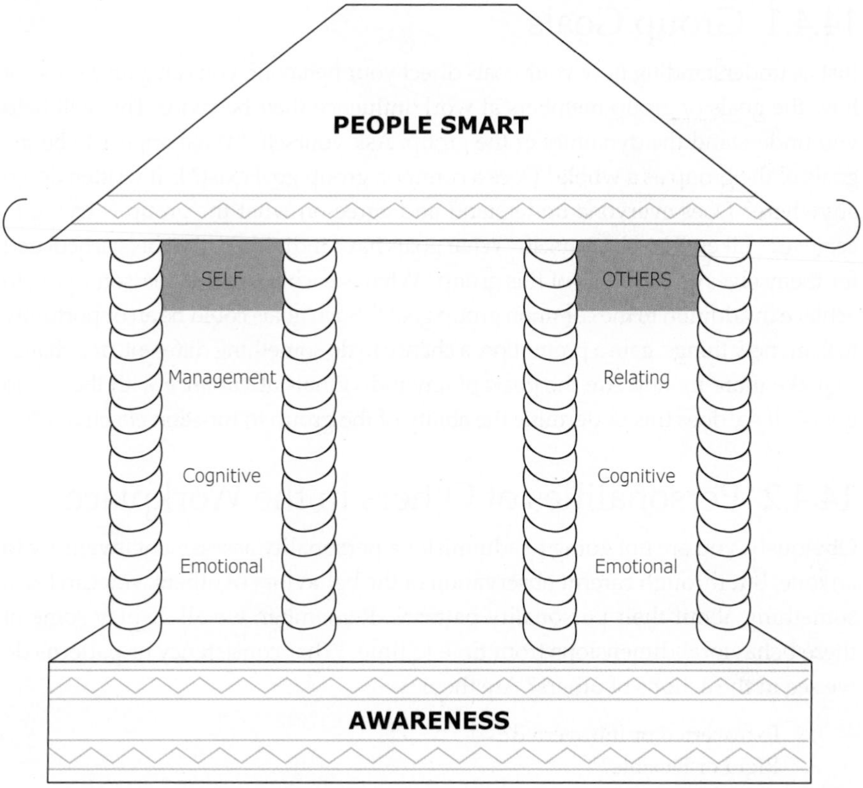

parallels between managing yourself and working well with others in sensing, analyzing, and behaving effectively in your work setting. These can be seen in the following model that is called the *People Smart Pagoda*. In building any structure, you have to start from the ground up. The same is true in building your skills in working with people.

Awareness—of yourself and of others—stands as a foundation upon which to build skills for self-management and skills for connecting effectively with the other people in your work environment. We've discussed methods for becoming more aware of yourself. We looked at how introspection and feedback help you gather information to better understand your goals, needs, personality and situational triggers. In the same way we can develop a sharper awareness of others in our environment by examining these same factors in your co-workers.

To begin, you can carefully observe those around you. This means tuning in all your senses to gather information about them. Not only do you need to listen as intently as you can to the messages of others, but you must also observe the non-verbal messages being sent. In listening empathically, you attempt to understand what it is like to be in another person's skin. This enables you to gain insights into why that person is behaving as she does. In other words, the best way to understand the personalities, needs, goals, and behavioral triggers of others is to be a keen observer of cues and a sensitive and empathic listener.

14.4.1 Group Goals

Just as understanding how your goals direct your behavior, you can gain a sense of how the goals of group members at work influence their behavior. This will help you understand the dynamics of the group. Ask yourself, "What appear to be the goals of the group as a whole? Does a common group goal exist? Is it written down anywhere? Does everyone understand and agree on what the group is trying to achieve?" Likewise, ask yourself, "What goals have individual members articulated for themselves as members of this group? What is each individual person trying to achieve in addition to the common group goal?" Such goals could be an opportunity to learn new things, gain a promotion, a chance to do something different, or a chance to make more money. Are the goals of any individuals at variance with the group goals? If so, does this undermine the ability of the group to function effectively?

14.4.2 Personalities of Others in the Workplace

Obviously, you are not going to administer a personality assessment inventory to anyone, but through careful observation of the behaviors of others, you can learn something about their personality patterns. Remember, we all display some of these behavioral dimensions from time to time. What consistency or patterns do we see in the actions of others? Are they:

> Extroverted or Introverted?
> Rigid or Flexible?
> Organized or Free Flowing?

Happy or Sad?
Stable or Moody?
Secure or Insecure?
Decisive or Wishy-Washy?
Conservative or Liberal?
Confident or Uncertain?
Energetic or Laid Back?
Positive or Negative?

You become more competent in "reading" others' behavior from a process that simulates the method scientists use to find out new information. It begins with experience in being a detective of sorts in a work group. First you observe carefully, trying to gather evidence of actions, comments, and body language that give you a hunch about that person. Then "test out" your hunch or hypothesis about that person's personality by future observations, even predicting what that person will do and discovering whether you are either: (1) right (maybe this **is** a pattern); or (2) you're wrong (mistaken impression, start over). We do this sort of thing at some level each time we meet a new person and form impressions. Usually we are not aware we are doing this. But if we work consciously at being a better observer of behavior, both verbal and non-verbal, this can help us develop expertise in "psyching" out people in our work environment.

When we get a better sense of the personality patterns of those we work with, we are better able to understand their behavior. This allows us to think and choose approaches that are more effective in dealing with each specific person. For example, in working with a person who has "dominance" as part of their personality, when making suggestions for change at work, you might make a special effort to express your suggestion in a way that doesn't threaten that person's perceived authority. Compare the two approaches here:

SCENE 1

Roger: "Hi Steve, how's it going?"

Steve: "Pretty busy. Hey Roger, I thought I told you to be here at 7:30. It's almost 7:45. We're going to be slammed with customers today."

Roger: "Well, instead of you always making up the schedule like we are just robots, why don't you let us pick when we want to come in. I'm not a morning person. If we did the scheduling a different way, maybe things would go better."

Steve: "I am the manager, and don't *you* forget it! I know how we need to staff this place! Now get busy!"

SCENE 2

Roger: "Hi Steve, how's it going?

Steve: "Pretty busy. Hey Roger, I thought I told you to be here at 7:30. It's almost 7:45. We're going to be slammed with customers today."

Roger: "Sorry I got here late. Listen, I was thinking about how I am late sometimes, and I know you have a handle on what would work and what wouldn't.

I was wondering what you might think of this idea I had about scheduling. When things are less busy, maybe we could talk and I could share my ideas to see what you think about them. Okay?"

Steve: "That sounds okay for later. Right now we have to get going."

Roger: "Right, we'll talk later. Thanks for listening. I'd better hustle."

In the first scene, Roger does two things that annoy Steve. First he tries to put the blame on Steve, his manager, for his being late. This means he is not being *proactive*. Secondly, he is attacking Steve's competence and authority regarding the staff scheduling. Especially if he knows that Steve has a dominant personality, can you see what a mistake this is? The first scene will probably continue to go "down hill" from there.

In the second scene, Roger takes responsibility for his lateness. He recognizes that Steve has a need to be in control, and acknowledges his "competence" in knowing what will work or not before Roger indicates he has some thoughts about scheduling. He asks, doesn't tell, Steve about sharing his idea. He is also sensitive to the reality that there is a lot of work to do as the place is busy and he has contributed to the stress with his tardiness. He doesn't expect the workplace to come to a halt now so he can discuss his idea. He does, however, plant a seed . . . that he wants to share an idea, and he solicits some agreement from Steve to listen later. Wisely, he doesn't press for a specific time given the obvious need to pitch in and get to work. He can come back to Steve's agreement to talk at another less busy time and try to set up a specific time for discussion.

Roger achieves his goals in this situation by being aware of Steve's personality, as well as being proactive. With practice, you get better and better at observing and analyzing how the exchange between people moves back and forth. You can pinpoint the specific comments and emotional expressions that shift the content and the tone of the interaction. Knowing something about how the parties involved "tick" can help you anticipate their behavior.

14.4.3 Needs of Others in the Workplace

Closely related to "personality," the needs that are operating at a given time will motivate a person to act one way or another. Just as you gain an understanding of your own needs and how that causes you to behave to meet those needs, the same is going on for your co-workers. Using Maslow's hierarchy or McClelland's theory of needs, you can gain an awareness of patterns of behavior that reflect the needs of those around you.

To the extent that you can sense the needs of others, you can be a part of meeting those while also meeting your own needs. In the example above with Roger and Steve, the need for power was operating in both parties. Steve, being very dominant, needed to maintain control. Roger, desiring to have some power in giving input to decision-making, wanted to share his idea. In scene 2 we could see both of these needs being met. It would appear that Roger also had a need for affiliation that was stronger than his need for power, as he addressed the issue differently in scene 2, designed to avoid alienating Steve. Roger's behavior in scene 2 paved the way for a possible win-win outcome, but in scene 1, Roger was obviously pushing for a win-lose outcome that could only further hamper their working relationship.

14.4.4 Social and Cultural Conventions

If we are to understand behavior exchanges we must be aware of the influences of culture, ethnicity, age, gender and other social or cultural aspects that shape our behavior and that of others. The increasing diversity of the workplace and global interdependence challenges us to expand our knowledge in this area. To the extent that we can recognize the context from which a person comes, we can appreciate our differences rather than being threatened by them. These skills and attitudes are also part of what makes for a global citizen, and promotes awareness of and empathy for others.

The Global Perspective
How are Global Citizens "People Smart"?

Global citizens are "people smart" in effectively extending their connections to others way beyond those in their inner circles. They operate within a frame of openness and a willingness to identify with all of humanity. If we observe global citizens as they relate to others, we will see the following attitudes and behaviors exhibited:

- Accepting responsibility for global citizenship
- Being comfortable with differences
- Relating with empathy to those within cultures different than their own
- Reading about international events
- Listening effectively
- Believing they are empowered to make a difference
- Communicating with non-English speakers
- Recognizing that today's challenges cannot be solved by the same kind of thinking and actions that created them
- Understanding the impact of culture on our lives, and its effect on attitudes and behaviors
- Acknowledging that one's own culture, religion, and values are not universally shared

- Speaking at least one language other than their native tongue
- Appreciating different groupings in America's own multicultural structure
- Volunteering in service programs (local, national, and international)
- Working effectively in diverse teams
- Motivated by love rather than fear
- Regarding all people of the world as important
- Tolerating ambiguity
- Articulating human differences and similarities
- Exercising moral leadership
- Having respect for human dignity
- Behaving ethically
- Conserving environmental resources

Which of the above attitudes and behaviors relate to your strengths? Which ones might you work on in your quest to be a global citizen? Which one do you want to work on first? How can developing these competencies enhance your being "people smart" in the workplace?

An awareness of social conventions regarding **idioms**, expressions or sayings, in a culture is important to our understanding of others. If we take everything said in its literal meaning we may be confused and uninformed. If someone refers to a person as "a nut," someone unfamiliar with that idiom might be confused, wondering "a walnut, an almond? I don't get it!"

Further, the general rules of courtesy and custom, sometimes called etiquette, are important to understand lest we unknowingly offend someone by behavior that could be construed as rude, as we discussed earlier. Discomfort might be caused when different customs are practiced in the workplace.

14.4.5 Triggers for Positive and Negative Behaviors in Others

Just as we discussed emotional intelligence as helping us recognize triggers that set off our own emotions and behaviors, it is helpful to be able to identify triggers that can set off, or annoy, other people. Being aware of what makes others *tick* can not only help you avoid *ticking them off*, but can assist in contributing to their positive thoughts, feelings and behaviors. Behaviorist theories hold that all behavior is conditioned as a result of the environmental contingencies. This would suggest that we *can* influence those around us to behave positively. Gaining an understanding of what events initiate what responses, perhaps we can help our bosses, co-workers, and customers act positively. This, in turn, becomes a reward for us.

Questions

1. What is the common foundation upon which to build skills for self-management and for connecting effectively with other people in the workplace?

   A. Awareness

   B. Desire

   C. Craving

   D. Understanding

2. Operating much as a detective might, the first step toward successfully "reading" others is to make _____.

   A. careful observations of their behaviors

   B. amends for past wrongdoings and grievances

   C. friends with their loved ones

   D. detailed hypotheses about the causes of their behaviors

3. Expressions or sayings in a culture are called _____.

    A. idioms

    B. norms

    C. conventions

    D. static symbols

14.5 Using Your Strengths as You Develop in the Workplace

Explain why identifying your strengths and changing your behavior to incorporate these strengths will have a positive effect on your development.

One of the aspects of Positive Psychology is the focus on strengths rather than weaknesses. Some managers, administrators, educators, and others in leadership roles around the world are leading with their employee's talents in mind. However, they are in the minority in the United States, United Kingdom, Canada, France, Japan, and China, all countries where a Gallup study was conducted (Hodges and Clifton, 2004).

Clifton and Hodges distinguish between the terms strength, talent and theme, pointing out that a strength is the ability to provide consistent, near-perfect performance in a given activity. The process of building a strength involves three steps: (1) identifying dominant themes of talent; (2) discovering specific talents; and (3) refining them with knowledge and skills. Talent naturally exists within you, while skills and knowledge must be acquired.

Individuals who go through identifying talents and integrating them into their frames, then change their behavior to match their talents, report increased satisfaction and production, in other words, optimal functioning, as a result of focusing on what they do best. The StrengthsFinder web-based assessment (at *http://www.strengthsfinder.com*) can assist individuals in working through these stages and represent more than three decades of study of success in more than 30 countries.

Neuroscience explains that between the ages of three and fifteen, the human brain organizes itself by strengthening the synaptic connections used often, while seldom used connections diminish over time. Harry Chugani, professor of pediatrics, neurology and radiology notes that regarding synaptic connections in the brain, "Roads with the most traffic get widened. The ones rarely used fall into disrepair." (Coffman & Gonzalez-Molina, 2002). After age fifteen, the pattern of synaptic connections becomes predominately stable. Therefore, the greatest payoff in development is to focus on your strengths and talents, where the synaptic connections are already robust.

14.5.1 Positive Outcomes of Strength-Based Development

Data from follow-up surveys of people who completed strengths assessment shows that strength-based development is related to positive outcomes. In a study conducted by Hodges and Clifton (2004), respondents reported that learning about strengths helped them make better life choices, resulted in greater productivity, and increased their self-confidence.

In the workplace, strengths-based development was incorporated into the Toyota North American Parts Center California with 400 employees on 54 work teams. Workers were assessed and given feedback on their strengths, while managers were trained in the use of strengths. A session was held to move employees from focusing on their own strengths to exploring the strengths of their team members in order to optimize their team relationships and performance. This effort resulted in a per-person increase in productivity of 6%. In this project two teams received a more intensive strengths-based development program and achieved a productivity increase of 9% in only six months (Connelly, 2002).

Employee engagement is tied to such performance outcomes as customer satisfaction, productivity, and employee turnover (Harter, Schmidt, and Hayes, 2002). A survey item that has a strong conceptual relationship to a focus on strengths is "opportunity to do what I do best." This same item is strongly linked to success, and is defined as above median workplace performance. A meta-analysis of more than 300,000 employees in 51 companies indicates that when employees believed there was ample opportunity to do what they do best, this corresponded to a 38% higher probability of greater productivity and 44% higher probability of improved customer loyalty and employee retention (Harter and Schmidt, 2002).

A study compared 65 organizations using interventions to strengthen employee engagement to a control group of 61 companies without such interventions. The organizations utilizing interventions registered higher employee engagement from year one to two and even more when followed for three years (Clifton and Harter, 2003). Following a strengths-based and employee engagement intervention program at St. Lucie Medical Center in Florida, employee turnover dropped 50% and engagement scores rose to the top quarter in the study's database. Patient satisfaction jumped by 160%.

Not only is engagement significant, but workers are concerned with meaningfulness. More than one set of workers are seeking meaning from their work. The Baby Boomers are ageing into their 60s in huge droves and are beginning to think more about meaning and purpose than about money in their rewards for working. Interestingly enough, younger groups such as Generation Y students are also focusing more on the meaning of work than the money earned. This is evidenced by Daniel Pink (2009) who describes Generation Y students who were studying for their MBA at Harvard Business School. These students noted that as the economy was plunging in 2009, business people were seen as the core of the problems and were portrayed as villains in this situation. A group of second-year students made a plan. They drew up a pledge resembling the Hippocratic Oath (in medicine) for graduates of the business school to sign. It was not intended as a legal document, but as a code of conduct that leans more toward "purpose maximization" than "profit maximization." The 500 word oath begins "As a manager, my purpose is to serve the greater good by bringing people and resources together to create value that no single individual can create alone." It also says "I will safeguard the interests of my shareholders, co-workers, customers and the society in which we operate." Words such as "purpose, greater good, sustainable" that are part of this oath are seldom heard in business classes. In spite of that, in just a few weeks nearly one quarter of the graduating class had signed the pledge. As Pink shares, one student from the group that wrote this oath said, "My hope is that at our 25th reunion, our class will not be known for how much money we made or how much money we gave back to the school, but for how the world was a better place as a result of our leadership."

These findings show that focusing on strengths is a powerful way to increase your positive feelings, thoughts and behaviors in the workplace. It also has implications for the development of positive psychological and organizational behavior, in other words, positive institutions, in which to carry out your work. Focusing on strengths can also increase hope, subjective well-being, and confidence. As noted above, strength-based organizations and companies yield rich returns in **P**ositive emotions, **E**ngagement, and **M**eaning for workers as they enhance their **A**ccomplishments, all PERMA components of an optimally functioning individual.

14.5.2 Positive Institutions

Building **positive institutions** has been a pillar of positive psychology since its inception, and refers to studying strengths that foster better communities. Creating family and school environments that help children flourish, identifying and building workplaces that support satisfaction and high productivity while generating communities that promote civic engagement are goals of positive psychology. Characteristics of positive institutions have been identified by numerous researchers to include:

- Exhibiting transparency, authenticity, open honesty
- Having, knowing, and achieving the mission
- Working constructively to deal with conflict and adversity
- Performing in a growth mode
- Modeling a positive role by the CEO
- Considering the whole as greater than the sum of the parts
- Empowering people to have greater decision latitude

- Having a strong sense of purpose that is shared across the organization
- Looking forward
- Emphasizing getting better
- Focusing on strengths-based approach
- Treating people as individuals with individual strengths

The Global Perspective
Bright Green, Deep Green, or Green Yet Unseen

In his latest book, *1493*, Charles Mann discusses the impact of the "discovery" of the new world by Christopher Columbus. Most of us know it as a tale of genocide and devastation of indigenous populations. However, it is a much more complex story of the impact of introducing new plants and animals into an existing ecosystem, and the unintended and unforeseen consequences that followed around the entire planet. For example, the Americas did not have any animals such as cows, horses, goats and sheep. Pigs, chickens, ducks and the parasite that causes malaria were also absent. The genocide of the native peoples of the Americas was enabled by the diseases brought by these explorers, who for millennia had been living in close quarters with these animals. Smallpox, measles, influenzas, and malaria were unknown in the Americas. Up to 90% of native peoples were killed by these diseases. In many respects the European explorers didn't destroy the wilderness; they created it with the loss of the peoples who had been tending the land.

As we have noted earlier, there is little quarrel with the notion that with seven billion people on the planet, we are in the middle of another major disruption of Earth's systems with no certainty whatsoever what the outcome will be in terms of the survival of our own or other species. We are, however, perhaps the only species that knows consciously that something is happening and that are able to take action. Consider two schools of thought that suggest what we might do.

The *deep green movement* generally believes that humans must return to a simpler way of life that involves voluntarily reducing population and decentralizing food and energy production and distribution. They maintain that large cities, factory farming, and huge centralized power production as seen in the most developed countries in the world are altering the climate and poisoning Earth and the life on it. On the extreme ends of this movement some envision the destruction of dams and

returning to life without electricity. While many may envy and aspire to gain the material advantages of modernity, they are ultimately unsustainable. Further, they add that these technological developments have separated us from a meaningful connection with Earth and the life on it. In fact, they come from a misunderstanding of our place in the story of the universe. On the body of Gaia, humans have become the moral equivalent of a cancer interested only in its own growth while unaware of destroying the body, the source of its life.

The *bright green movement* responds that we cannot turn back the hands of the clock and return to a time of small family farms. They agree that our technological reach has left no place on the planet unpolluted and that our numbers are too large; but they also would maintain that what we need is a kind of forward escape using technology to create a better designed future. The problems we face are problems we have created. We have been driven solely by profit and a false economy that did not take into account the cost of the consequences of poorly designed manufacturing, farming, and energy production. Well-designed cities, farms, and production processes would account for the inevitable waste that they generate. Prior to production they would determine how every single by-product could be recycled. Their mantra is *waste equals food*. If a material cannot be safely discarded and reabsorbed into the environment, it must be captured and reused in industrial cycles. Anything that does not fit these criteria must be phased out of use as soon as possible (McDonough and Braungart, 2002).

Both of these movements believe the other is naïve. Deep green for instance states that cities are inherently unsustainable and have always had to plunder the countryside around them to survive. "Where do you get the food, the energy, the water? Where does the shit go? . . . we can[not] have an industrial culture and also wild nature" (Jensen, 2011). Bright green would argue that kind of thinking is a failure of imagination. Properly designed cities can in fact provide food, energy, and recycling of waste without polluting their surroundings. They also note that women who move to cities begin to have fewer children and that this may be an approach to helping reduce population.

We have no choice but to choose and choose again. Where do you stand? How can you find out more about both positions? Can you choose even knowing that all decisions are made on the basis of insufficient information and there, indeed, may be unintended consequences?

Greenberg (2007) considers two additional characteristics that are central to positive institutions: *meaning* and *recognition*. Pratt and Ashford (2003) analyzed the distinctions between meaning *at work* and meaning *in work*. Meaning that comes from one's work involves identifying and applying strengths and re-crafting one's job. Meaning *at work* includes contributing to the greater good in some way. The growing implementation of positive organizational programs and applied research to determine results is being referred to as *positive organizational scholarship (POS)*. Examples include Seligman's (2011) description of the Comprehensive Soldier Fitness program, a strength-based positive approach the U.S. Army has employed to the training of troops. Results showed greater resilience, less frequent post-traumatic-stress-disorder (PTSD), and lower depression related to combat experiences. Positive institutional programs have been developed for use in schools. One example is School-Wide Positive Behavior Support (SWPBS) with the goal of facilitating the academic achievement and healthy, prosocial development of children and youth in environments that are safe and conducive to learning (Sprague and Horner, 2006). Studies examining the effectiveness of SWPBS in schools have shown reductions in disciplinary office visits, vandalism, aggression, delinquency, and alcohol and drug use. Praise is an important component of the program for reinforcing positive behavior. Likewise, in the workplace, Greenberg (2007) found that managers who gave frequent recognition and encouragement had employees who were more optimistic and engaged, and produced better results, helping to facilitate the P, E, and A of PERMA!

Positive institutions have potential for improving the well-being of their participants, whether it is a family, a school, an army, or a workplace. Finding positive functioning at any stage, age or setting is exciting, considering, as Seligman (2011) speculates, that positivity could spread beyond the community to the nation and the world. The end result is enhanced resiliency for the individuals involved.

Questions

1. Which of the following is one of the steps in the process of building a strength?

    A. Identifying dominant themes of talent

    B. Feeling good about yourself

    C. Completing a job interest inventory

    D. Asking others to identify strengths they think you have

2. Workers are concerned with both _____ and _____ in the workplace.

   A. engagement; meaningfulness

   B. pay equity; salary increases

   C. current goals; past goals

   D. discipline; rigor

3. Two characteristics that are central to positive institutions are _____ and _____.

   A. meaning; recognition

   B. stress; strain

   C. abundance; disbursement

   D. future orientation; past orientation

14.6 Overcoming Problems in the Workplace

Identify strategies for resolving common problems in the workplace.

As you think about enjoying your work and functioning at an optimal level of motivation, it is important to come back to the reality that problems are inevitable on any job if you work there long enough. Being informed about some of these potential problems and ways to cope with them can help you proactively prevent or lessen the intensity of these situations. Let us examine some of the more common problems found in most work settings.

14.6.1 Beware of Polarization

Being people smart as you interact with co-workers, clients, supervisors, or others, it is important that you remember the lessons of reframing to avoid falling into the trap of **polarization**. Deborah Tannen in her book *The Argument Culture* (1998) makes the case that many aspects of life in Western cultures such as the U.S. are couched in a debate of two opposing views. This is seen in the political arena in our country where there is a war of sorts between those on the *left* and those on the *right*. Both groups refuse to listen to each other or to consider that there are other points of view beside just those two. Likewise, in employment settings factions can develop and view the situation with an *us vs. them* mentality. Tannen believes that framing information into an argument between two sides focuses on the conflict, which in the process fails to integrate ideas and address the broader picture. Most issues have more than just two alternatives; yet, journalism, the media, politics and even education have conditioned us to be more interested when there is a fight, a conflict, a debate. The result of this is that many Americans embrace the belief that a debate always produces better information, when in many cases it may actually limit being fully informed. Tannen suggests that to move from debate to dialogue, it is important to remember that those in our work setting who disagree are still members of the same community. She lists rules of engagement to remember, which are:

- Don't demonize colleagues with whom you disagree
- Don't affront their deepest moral commitments
- Talk less of rights, which are nonnegotiable, and more of needs, wants,
- Leave some issues out
- Engage in a dialogue of convictions. Don't be *so* reasonable and conciliatory that you lose touch with a core of belief you feel passionately about

Tannen notes that Asian cultures emphasize harmony and seek methods of inquiry that focus more on assimilating ideas and exploring the relations among them than on opposing ideas and fighting over them. The Chinese approach to **yin** and **yang** depicts integration where each is dynamic and changing. Rather than the dualism of debate, yin is always present in yang and changing into yang and vice versa.

Being empathetic towards a co-worker who holds a different view provides you with an opportunity to "try on" a new perspective. This, in turn, may broaden your own thinking and help you discover commonalities with your colleague, an unlikely outcome if you just completely shut out the other's view. Remember that war is a lose-lose situation, even in a war of ideas or words.

14.6.2 How to Resolve Conflict—A Model for Conflict Resolution

Many authors have put forth useful guidelines for **conflict resolution**. What follows is our synthesis of several systems which we have broken down into seven major steps. In theory, this format is designed to be used in more formalized situations, but can be applied for any need to resolve conflict.

In reality the steps may not flow as smoothly as presented here. You may find it necessary to switch back and forth between steps if snags develop in the process, or if you encounter resistance on the part of the either side. But in any event, it is important not to skip any of the steps. They all build upon one another. You can't have a building without a foundation, and you can't have a fourth floor without a third floor.

STEP ONE: ACKNOWLEDGE/IDENTIFY THE PROBLEM OR CONFLICT TO YOURSELF.   Don't run away from the conflict or attempt to avoid it with a premature resolution like immediately giving in, or insisting on your way. Admit that there is a problem, and recognize that some conflict is an unavoidable part of life, particularly among people who live or work together. What is important is how it is handled. But you also need to recognize that the problem causing the conflict belongs to you. Why? Because you are the one who is dissatisfied; you are the one who therefore needs to "own" the problem as yours. This is not the same as saying that it is all your fault, or that you are to blame, but rather that it is your problem because it causes discontent for you. Recognizing this important fact will make a difference when the time comes to approach the other party involved. Instead of ranting or raving or being judgmental, it can help if you state your concerns in a descriptive fashion, which will likely be more accurate and objective, while minimizing the possibility of eliciting a defensive reaction from the other party. Part of acknowledging what the problem is for you is to enable you to identify the unmet needs resulting from this problem or conflict.

STEP TWO: AGREE ON A DATE AND A PROCEDURE. It may be pointless to try to resolve a conflict unless all parties are prepared to do so and have set aside the time to do so. Fights often ensue because one party confronts another who isn't ready at that moment to deal with the issue at hand. It is very useful to set aside a time beforehand to deal with the issues. Request that a meeting time be set up at a mutually agreeable time and date with adequate time allotted. Decide the appropriate place where the meeting should take place. When negotiations may take place over several meetings, it may be wise to alternate locations since most people feel more comfortable on their home turf, or to have the meeting in a neutral location. Another important procedural issue involves who will attend the meeting. If more than two parties are involved in the dispute, agree beforehand on who can and should be included in the meeting.

STEP THREE: DESCRIBE YOUR PROBLEM AND YOUR NEEDS. Even though your position may be different or in conflict with that of the other party, that does not mean that you do not have some shared or compatible interests. If you didn't have some shared interests you probably would not be sitting at the bargaining table to begin with.

Describing your position has several aspects to it. The first aspect involves stating your position and your needs clearly and forthrightly. Follow the guidelines for assertive responses, which will allow you to present your side effectively. To present your position effectively, it is important to do your homework. By this we mean plan what you intend to say. Feel free to use prepared statements, even charts or tables of figures if appropriate to highlight the salient points of your position.

After stating your wants and needs it is then often strategically useful to define the conflict in terms of a mutual problem to be solved, building on the notion of shared interests. This "we are in this together" approach helps to tap the motivation of all involved parties to cooperate in reaching a win-win outcome. Endeavor to consider the situation or the conflict separately from the personalities involved. It helps if you are willing to be at least somewhat flexible in your position, and that you enter the negotiations with the mind set that both you and the other party are basically reasonable people who want to reach a fair resolution to a problem in which you both have legitimate interests. Notice that we never refer to the other person or persons as your "opponent" or "adversary," but rather simply as the other party. This helps to foster a climate where a win-win outcome has a chance.

Recognize that you begin creating a climate for either cooperation or contention from the moment the negotiations begin. To create a cooperative atmosphere, begin the meeting with ice-breaker conversation. In prolonged negotiations, it can be useful to have meals together so as to promote an opportunity to view each other as people, apart from the conflict, and build rapport.

It is also very important that you manage your emotions appropriately. If you did not have strong emotions regarding the issue at hand, it is unlikely that you would be going through a complicated process like conflict resolution. It is important to control your anger for it will not serve you well in this process. Direct expression or indulgence of anger may cause the other party to become defensive and dig in their heels. Anger will cloud your ability to think rationally and flexibly in your own best interest. Avoid giving ultimatums. We advise you to exert your positive power by being assertive. Positive power thrives on a willingness to believe that the problem can be solved and a commitment to remain with the process.

Once you have presented your position you need to check whether the other party has understood what you said and what you meant. Given that this may be an emotionally charged situation, it is certainly possible that there have been some miscommunications or misunderstandings. Before proceeding, make sure that the other party has fully understood your point of view, not that they need to necessarily agree with you at this point in the process, but at least that they comprehend your message, what you want, what you need, and why. Ask the other party to state their understanding of your position. If they have misunderstood some aspect of it, then take this opportunity to correct their misconceptions.

STEP FOUR: SERIOUSLY CONSIDER THE OTHER PARTY'S POINT OF VIEW   Let the other party express their point of view and give it serious consideration. Do your best to step into their shoes and see the situation or conflict from their eyes. Remember the value of being willing to give up being right. Just as you asked the other party to share their understanding and interpretation of your position, do the same and share your understanding of their point of view. Give them the opportunity to clarify their position or correct any misunderstandings you may have about where they stand and why.

Equalize the amount of time for both parties to present their side. The other party has just as much right as you to get their needs met and find satisfaction. First, if you expect them to cooperate in meeting your needs, it is reasonable to expect that you will behave in a fair fashion. Secondly, it is essential if you want to achieve a win-win outcome, or any solutions for that matter. If the other side has difficulty expressing themselves, then ask questions to draw them out and help them to clarify their position. In some situations, it may be appropriate to ask about the feelings and experiences that led to their current position. The more you understand them and the more they understand about you, the more likely you can arrive at a win-win solution.

STEP FIVE: EXPLORE POSSIBLE SOLUTIONS   Generate as many potential solutions as possible and later evaluate them to decide which one best meets everyone's needs. Adopt the attitude that there are may be more than one solution that is mutually satisfying. The advice of McKay, Davis and Fanning (1983), from their book *Messages: The Communication Skills Book*, is especially relevant here. They enjoin you to . . .

> *Get rid of the notion that there is only one best way to divide up the pie, that the pie is only so big, and that you absolutely must get the biggest piece. These are all self-defeating ideas. There are actually several good ways to cut up a pie. You may even find a way to make the pie bigger. And ending up with the biggest piece isn't always ideal, especially if you antagonize people and end up getting your pie in the face. (p. 152)*

It may be very important to do homework beforehand to determine what is fair, especially in a business negotiation or some type of deal involving merchandise and/or money. Tracking down precedents or benchmarks will help you generate proposals that are reasonable.

Brainstorming involves the uninhibited offering of ideas and suggestion by all members of a group. All interested parties should be encouraged to participate. All suggestions, no matter how outlandish or unrealistic, should be listed on a blackboard or large writing pad without judgment. Do not, at this stage, criticize, praise, or in any other way evaluate the suggestions. Just list them all, no matter how ridiculous or unworkable any might be. Generate as many ideas as possible for further exploration. Remember that even a seemingly crazy idea may lead to another great idea. Try to come up with as long a list as possible, the more and the wilder the better. Approach the problem from every angle. Try to go beyond the 9 dots. To facilitate this process try looking at the problem through the eyes of imaginary experts. How would a judge solve the problem, or a cop, or a psychologist or a school principal? What about your mother, or your brother? How would a banker, or a priest, minister or rabbi attempt to resolve this issue? Oftentimes shifting to the mind set of another can free you of your blinders and help you see possibilities that had eluded you beforehand. This last suggestion is especially helpful if you are stuck brainstorming all by yourself.

While brainstorming, also consider time honored methods for resolving issues or forging compromises. The classic way of dividing disputed assets or property is splitting it down the middle, if possible. In buying or selling the equivalent solution is to split the difference. Consider the ways you could soften aspects of your position that are not critical to you in order to make your proposal more palatable to the other party. Permanent changes can be proposed as temporary ones to see how they will work out. Major changes can be done in steps. Unconditional demands can be made contingent upon something important to the other party.

STEP SIX: EVALUATE AND NEGOTIATE   Set a reasonable deadline that is agreeable to all parties involved, otherwise negotiations could go on forever. Many people become willing to budge when they see the deadline approaching. Of course you can always extend the deadline if necessary, but having one in place helps to move things along.

Begin to evaluate each option. Some will be easily identified as unworkable or unrealistic and quickly discarded. At first glance, some will be acceptable to one side but totally unacceptable to the other side. Discuss these using the guidelines for clear communication and effective listening, and eliminate those that will never, under any circumstances, be considered by one side or other. At this point the list should be whittled down to those solutions which are potentially acceptable to each side.

At this point, if you have communicated your position effectively and been a good listener, you should have developed an improved working relationship with the other side. State the options that you favor as proposals. Approach the proposal slowly and describe your favored solution in detail. Then move on to your second or third choice, if such exist. Listen to the option or options favored by the other side. This creates a cycle of proposal/counter proposal that may be repeated several times, including discussions and time-outs to consider various propositions. Discuss the difficulties you each have with the proposals. As proposals and counter proposals evolve, it is likely that their terms will keep moving ever closer together. Look for the overlap between your proposal and that of the other party. What adjustments can be made to make the proposals more aligned with one another? Keep in mind what needs to happen to generate a win-win solution, based on your needs and your knowledge of the needs of the other party. By offering choices, being flexible, and open to new information, you create a cooperative climate that makes this type of back and forth negotiation possible. Do not offer your proposal as an ultimatum for that is guaranteed to fail.

While this negotiation is ongoing, if you sense that the other party is in an agreeable frame of mind, this is the time to present a "**yesable proposal**." A "yesable proposal" is an aspect of your position that, if stated as a direct question, it would be easy for the other side to answer yes. For example, if you are negotiating for a pay raise, you could ask whether such a raise would be forthcoming if you agreed to increased productivity on your part. If you know that improved productivity is important to your boss, then you are offering to meet his/her needs in exchange for what you want (a win-win solution).

If a win-win solution is just not possible despite all your best efforts, then you need to begin to negotiate a compromise. Even in this case the process of working toward win-win has not been in vain. You likely have, as a result of this process, forged a better working relationship with the other party. The resulting atmosphere of goodwill may prevent future conflicts or may help in solving further dilemmas down the road.

To reach an agreement, of course there must be consensus. It is usually quite clear when this has been achieved when only two people are negotiating, but if there are more than two participants, especially if the issues at hand are important, it may be best to take a more formal vote. Usually a hand vote will suffice, but in a business negotiation involving many individuals it may be useful to do a confidential written vote to minimize group pressures and allow each party to vote freely.

Herb Cohen, in his book *You Can Negotiate Anything* (1980), recommends that you write what he terms a memorandum of agreement, intent, or understanding, detailing all aspects of the agreement. This written record is there to remind all parties of the exact nature of the agreement you have reached. All parties should sign it. It can prevent misunderstandings later on if one party insists that the agreement was different from your memory of such. It also builds on the fact that people are more likely to follow through after they have entered into a more formalized, signed arrangement. This memorandum should be written in straightforward, common-sense language. In a more formal negotiating situation such as collective bargaining, such agreements need to be written in legal language and may need to be composed by an attorney.

STEP SEVEN: ENACT THE SOLUTION AND FOLLOW-UP Develop a plan regarding what is to be done, when, where, and who is responsible for what. It helps to include this information in the written agreement. It is also useful to begin implementing the plan as soon as possible to avoid the resistance or suspicions that delays could arouse.

Until you have enacted the plan and given it some time to see how it is working, you cannot reasonably evaluate whether the solution has worked. As you close your negotiations decide when and how to evaluate the plan. How long to wait and how to conduct the evaluation process depends on the nature of the plan and how complicated it is. After a reasonable amount of time has passed to test the viability of the solution, have another meeting and discuss the results of the follow-up evaluation. If there are difficulties with implementation, then brainstorm how to adjust or modify the plan. If it is a total failure, you may need to scrap it and start from scratch.

14.6.3 Substance Abuse

Millions of people on this earth are dependent on alcohol and other drugs. The cost of this in the workplace is seen in behaviors such as shoddy quality of work, low productivity, inconsistent performance, bizarre behaviors, absenteeism, and problems relating to others. In addition, there is often a lack of interest in work as well as a lack of concentration that adds to carelessness. This, in turn, adds to health hazards in the workplace such as the 40% of on-the-job injuries and about half of all work-related deaths that occur because of alcohol or drug abuse (Dubrin, 1999, DeCenzo, 1997).

Many larger companies maintain employee assistance programs where help with **substance abuse** and other personal problems is provided. In the case of alcohol or drug abuse there are hospital-based rehabilitation programs that help with overcoming addiction. Also there are self-help twelve step groups such as Alcoholics Anonymous and Narcotics Anonymous that are available to people who want to overcome their addictions. Twelve step programs help individuals with substance abuse problems to develop a support network of people to aid in recovery and maintenance of sobriety.

14.6.4 Lack of Advancement

Another common workplace problem involves not being considered for promotions for which you have aspirations. Studies have shown that having a **mentor** in the work setting is significant for success. A mentor is an experienced worker who takes a new worker "under his or her wing" to promote understanding of such realities as: (1) how things work in the environment; (2) the accepted norms for behavior; (3) who key people are in the organization; and (4) how one can get ahead. One problem for female workers is that, especially in certain business and professional settings, there are few if any mentors available. It is important to seek out experienced workers that might serve as mentors when you begin your career.

Another strategy for moving up in the organization is to discuss your aspirations with your supervisor, especially when you meet for your annual performance appraisal. Obviously, this assumes you have rapport with your supervisor and that your work evaluations have been positive. Your supervisor has information or can point you in the right direction regarding position postings, availability, and educational/experience requirements for these positions. The human resource or personnel office is another source of information and guidance for exploring ways to move ahead in your organization.

Demonstrating your commitment and motivation for meeting the organization's goals is of paramount importance if you have aspirations for advancement. In your career, if you wish to make a move, you need information about the positions in which you are interested. You need to know what is required for that job and then demonstrate that you have the desired skills and knowledge. In today's terms, what we bring to an organization is referred to as our "added value." We need to know that what we do, in fact, adds value to a company or organization, and be thoughtful in making this known effectively as we seek advancement. Companies are beginning to recognize that employees who truly add the most value to the organization are those who are engaged in their work (an element of positive psychology) and enjoy what they do. These companies are seeking to increase opportunities for intrinsic (or internal) rather than extrinsic (or external) rewards (Hay Group, 2001).

Your people smarts and leadership skills are important since these assets are especially crucial for positions that involve managing others. Inquire with the training department (if there is one in your company) for ways to secure assistance in enhancing your skills in this area if needed.

Be aware that moving up in your own department or area may be more difficult than seeking a position in a new section or division of the organization.

Sometimes, making a move up means making a move out . . . not only out of the department, but out of the company or organization to another employer.

Remember the power of persistence. Gather as much information and feedback as you can if you have been passed over for promotions. Try to identify your goals for preparing yourself for the position you want, and most importantly don't give up.

14.6.5 Burnout

Another potential problem in the workplace is **burnout**. This is a collection of physical, emotional and mental reactions that reflect exhaustion. Burnout is the result of constant and re-occurring emotional pressures in the workplace and/or at home. It can also be caused by poor management of yourself in time, feeling unable or unequal to do a job, an overwhelming workload, inability to adapt to change, lack of adequate supervision from a manager, and an inability to meet deadlines. Burnout sufferers tend to disengage from their work and may withdraw from the people around them. Production suffers. The burnt out person develops a negative self-concept and negative attitudes toward work and the workplace. The person is drained and may appear apathetic, angry, withdrawn, or lazy. Physical symptoms such as headaches, chest pains, gastrointestinal problems and back pains may occur.

Burnout can happen to anyone who is experiencing too many pressures with too little support, but it is especially found among the helping professions such as health care, social work, law enforcement, and education. Persons feeling burnout may view themselves as a failure. They may be in positions where they give and give to others, but lack a source of support for their own needs. Burnout can result in people behaving as if they are powerless to turn things around (i.e. learned helplessness). They may behave like victims and begin blaming others, further compromising their relationships with co-workers.

Burnout is often found among persons who are perfectionists, idealists, or workaholics. They may start their work with great enthusiasm, very intense energy and highly positive attitudes. They are usually high achievers. Eventually they push themselves beyond their own limits and things begin to break down, leading to burnout.

14.6.6 Difficult People

If you work long enough, undoubtedly you will find yourself dealing with some difficult people. Developing skills in conflict resolution, assertiveness, and listening empathically will enable you to find ways to deal effectively with challenging individuals. Maintaining your own calm in these cases is half the battle and enables you to create a plan for confronting the situation as early as possible. If you are unsuccessful in your efforts, consider seeking assistance from a third party who might act as a mediator. Be alert; don't allow yourself to slip into denial. The problem doesn't go away, and could get worse.

14.6.7 Sexual Harassment

Sexual harassment has been around for years. Business law professors Roberts and Mann (1996) examined the extent of sexual harassment in the workplace. They described a 1976 poll found where 9 out of 10 women reported that they had been subjected to unwanted sexual advances at work. A Federal Government survey found that 42 percent of women and 15 percent of men reported some sexual harassment at work. A Federal Government study for the years 1985–87 estimated government costs from the effects of sexual harassment at $267 million.

In 1992, Anita Hill (1997) accused Supreme Court nominee Clarence Thomas of sexual harassment. This case was highly publicized and the following year, the number of sexual harassment cases increased dramatically as attention crystallized on this problem.

Sexual harassment is defined by the U.S. Equal Employment Opportunity Commission (March 4, 2008) as "unwelcome sexual advances, requests for sexual favors, and other verbal or physical conduct of a sexual nature constitute sexual harassment when this conduct explicitly or implicitly affects an individual's employment, unreasonably interferes with an individual's work performance, or creates an intimidating, hostile, or offensive work environment." In 2007, the EEOC resolved 11,592 charges of sexual harassment and recovered $49.9 million in monetary benefits (not including monetary benefits from litigation). There are two conditions which qualify as sexual harassment: (1) **quid pro quo**, which involves getting something for giving something, such as a person in authority demanding sexual favors to keep a job benefit; (2) **hostile environment** involves a situation where (a) a co-worker or supervisor engages in unwanted sex-based behavior which renders the workplace intimidating, or hostile, or (b) the purpose is to unreasonably interfere with work performance. Hostile environment cases are more controversial since there may be so many perceptions of "intimidating" or "offensive." A company is liable if they are informed of sexual harassment and ignore it. However, a company may be held liable even if they did not know about the sexual harassment. The safest bet for a company is to have a clear policy and to be sure all employees are aware of the rules.

The advent of the MeToo movement in late 2017 has generated much greater awareness about issues of sexual abuse, sexual misconduct and sexual harassment in the workplace. At the same time this has provided a safe space for many women to speak out about past abuse, along with empowering women to be assertive in the present in dealing with harassment in today's workplace. Hopefully, this movement will also help sensitize men to the need to be more mindful of the rights and needs of women to be treated respectfully on the job.

DeCenzo (1997) summarizes ideas for protecting yourself from sexual harassment as follows:

1. Know the organization's policy on sexual harassment.
2. Let the offending individual know you're irritated by his or her behavior.
3. Document such events.
4. If the offensive behavior is repeated, complain to someone in authority.
5. Keep records of your work.
6. Seek help from an attorney if you're not satisfied with what the organization is doing or has done.
7. Keep your spirits high.

14.6.8 Discrimination

Since the Civil Rights movement began over thirty years ago we have become more sensitive to the need to treat all people equally. We are aware of concern for discrimination based on race or gender, but there is a broader range of areas that fall under the Equal Employment Opportunity (EEO) guidelines. The following factors are the official bases for EEO **discrimination**:

Race	National Origin
Color	Sex
Religion	Sexual Orientation
Disability	Reprisal
Age	

Color discrimination occurs in situations where members of the same race are treated differently because of the color of their skin or because of the shades of brown skinned persons. National origin refers to ancestors or country of origin. **Reprisal** refers to disciplinary action for raising an allegation of discrimination.

Age discrimination involves decisions being made about employees based on their age, usually affecting older workers. Steinhauser (1998, 1999) notes that in 1994 the median age of workers was 38 years old. In 2005 the median age was 41. According to AARP, nearly one-in-three U.S. workers will be over 50 by the year 2012 (CareerBuilder.com, February 7, 2008). Between 1996 and 1998 American companies paid out over $200 million in fines for age discrimination. This amount does not include legal fees. First Union Corporation, a large bank, agreed to pay $58.5 million to 239 of its former employees who sued for age discrimination. Steinhauser says this is just the "tip of the iceberg," and notes that jury verdicts are historically higher in age discrimination than those based on race, gender or disability. In recent years with downsizing and massive layoffs, the courts have made it much harder to win an age discrimination case, and if you lose, you may be blackballed as a trouble maker when seeking other employment.

If you are experiencing workplace discrimination falling within any of the above categories, it is important to seek the guidance of the human resources representative at your place of employment in charge of EEO compliance.

Being aware of these potential problems and/or issues in the workplace and having strategies to prevent or deal with them increases the probability of having a positive workplace experience. Especially since we spend so much of our adult life at work, it is critical that our workweek include positive emotions and fulfillment. In fact, we should have enjoyment.

Questions

1. _____ can result in an "us versus them" mentality.
   - **A.** Type III thinking
   - **B.** Self-actualization
   - **C.** Polarization
   - **D.** Cooperation

2. What is the first step in conflict resolution?
   - **A.** Describe your own needs to your interaction partner.
   - **B.** Identify the problem or conflict.
   - **C.** Seriously consider the other party's point of view.
   - **D.** Negotiate a settlement.

3. The uninhibited offering of ideas and suggestions by all members of a group is called _____.
   - **A.** validated discussion
   - **B.** positivity
   - **C.** parallel processing
   - **D.** brainstorming

14.7 Making Work Fun

Explain how proactivity and personal responsibility influence your effectiveness in the workplace.

Once upon a time there were two people sleeping in their own houses. At 6:30 a.m. alarm clocks sounded in both homes. In both bedrooms an arm stretched over to the alarm clock to find the button. And that was the end of the similarity.

GEORGE hit the snooze alarm and dozed off for a few more minutes. When the alarm sounded again, he thought, "Oh, darn, it's Monday morning already." George dragged himself out of bed and stumbled toward the kitchen to find the coffee pot. "Why does it have to be Monday?" he moaned. Eventually he grabbed a donut with his coffee, got himself dressed and dashed out thinking, "I'm going to be late again . . . oh well, who cares?"

At work, George frowned as he entered the office. "Man, it is too hot in here. Why do they keep this office so hot?" He passed a couple of co-workers who greeted him smiling. "What's with them?" he thought. "What's there to be so happy about?" He sat at his desk and stared blankly at the pile of papers on his desk. "I'll never get this all done. This is too much." For a moment he put his head down on his desk, but lifted it up and started taking the papers off the pile, to begin work.

At noontime, George decided he had to stay in and work. So he ordered a quick sandwich and brought it back to the office to eat while working over lunch. "I'm so far behind, I'll never catch up," he mumbled as the clock struck one.

In the afternoon, George kept looking at the clock. "It's moving so slowly," he muttered. "When will this day end?"

HARRY turned off the alarm and hopped out of bed to stretch. "What a sleep; boy, I slept like a rock," he thought. He dressed eagerly and ate breakfast while reading the newspaper. Then he rose slowly and eagerly headed for the door. "What a nice day," he thought as he headed out into the morning sun. "Not a cloud in that blue sky . . . nice way to start."

At work, Harry smiled and greeted his co-workers. "How was your weekend?" he asked the fellow at the next desk, remembering that this guy was meeting his girlfriend's parents over the weekend. He settled in at his desk and reviewed his calendar. Next, he began organizing his day by making a "To Do" list. Then he launched into reviewing a report for the scheduled afternoon meeting. He mused, "This is a well done report."

At noontime, Harry left the office to meet his friend from college for lunch. He strolled down the block to the sidewalk café they agreed on. "Couldn't have picked a better day to enjoy eating outside," he thought.

In the afternoon, Harry, report and notes in hand, entered the meeting thinking, "This'll be a challenge!"

Which of these two would you rather be? If these guys worked for Snow White, we might have Grumpy George and Happy Harry. How are their attitudes different? How are they approaching their work? Which one is making work fun?

Given how much of our lives are invested in our work, and how closely the quality of our lives is linked to our work gratification, it's something to think about. Earlier we discussed how important your career choice is to your happiness. The best occupational arrangement is when your work reflects your passions, that which you love to do. This is usually something that you do very well. It is like a positive cycle. Those things we like, we prefer to do. Since we prefer them, we do them more often. Doing them more often makes us more proficient, so we like them even more. Think of your history. What subjects did you like the best in elementary school? Did that continue into high school? Is there some connection between that subject and the career choice you've considered or decided upon? A study by British behavioral scientists (Lonier, 1994) found a connection between desires in youth and success in adult life. In this longitudinal study, fifty people were followed from age 7 to age 35 (a total of 28 years). The findings showed that nearly all of the subjects wound up in a professional area related to their interests during ages 7 to 14. Most strayed from these interests after childhood, but those adults who were successful returned to their childhood dreams by the age of 35. For some it was as a hobby or leisure time activity. This suggests that we re-visit our early years and look for patterns in our interests. If you have years of working experience, what have been your likes and dislikes in these experiences? Terri Levine (2002), marketing expert, author, and professional coach for people exploring work issues, suggests a "looking back exercise" where you find a quiet place to think and ask yourself questions and write down your answers. Ask questions such as "What were the activities that gave you pleasure? What jobs or volunteer activities did you really like in your teen years? How did you feel about doing the job or activity?" She relates case studies where by doing this "looking back exercise," adults seeking a career change discovered their real enthusiasm. Do you know what really engages your excitement? Are you following your passion?

Additional factors that matter for work enjoyment include autonomy, opportunities for growth and learning, and positive triggers that keep you feeling good. Also significant is the ability to cope with problems in the workplace and resolve them in a way that doesn't compromise your values and ethics. Being informed regarding potential issues can help you prevent problems or minimize their impact.

14.7.1 Taking Charge

When you think about going to work, who are you really working for? Are you working for a company or organization? A boss? Your landlord? The auto insurance company? Or are you working for yourself? By this we don't necessarily mean that you are self-employed but that you are an employed self. Confusing? Well, look at it this way. Your whole being is involved in your career. If you change jobs, *you* are the thing that stays intact while moving to a new position. You need to see yourself as somewhat of an entrepreneur in the workplace. More and more today, workers in all types of fields are recognizing that the stability of a life long position or even several years in the same company is unlikely to happen. As one study points out, before 1990 an unspoken contract existed between employer and employee. That was, "You commit to working here for the long-term and we will offer you job security, good pay and promotions." However, economic recession, re-engineering, and downsizing caused a breach in that contract. Now there is a new mindset among young people beginning their careers since 1990. They do not expect life-time employment with a single employer. They consider personal fulfillment in their work a birthright, and to find it they will take different options. They work as free agents or even become self-employed to find fulfillment (Hay Group, 2000). In reality, we are all self-employed. You need to sense that you are in charge of you, and that the skills and talents you possess are valuable to the organization.

Being proactive and taking responsibility for yourself is an important step to personal effectiveness. Likewise, applying this habit in your work life will contribute to your autonomy, your being in control. Remember the discussion of stress hardiness attitudes. Control was the first one. If problems occur, you are the one to do something about the impact these problems have on you. If there is something you want or desire to achieve, you are the one to make that happen. Remember we referred to this as having an internal locus of control. If you are not in control of your life then who is? Do you want others controlling you or do you want to take charge of your life?

Being at the helm in your life leads to a sense of hope. This is an emotion that is tied to optimism. If not this, what is the alternative? Hopelessness, helplessness and despair. Who wants that in life? A German study (Lundberg, 1980) examined subjects faced with a task of increasing pressure. Subjects with the highest hope of success produced brain chemicals that enabled them to keep functioning at a high level of effectiveness. Further, they did not produce levels of cortisol, a chemical which is harmful to our bodies and is typically released during stress. In contrast, subjects in this study who were motivated by fear of failure had very high cortisol levels. This finding reinforces the old self-fulfilling prophecy that "what I believe will happen, will happen." In this study, those with an "I can do this" attitude of self-efficacy stayed more calm, focused and productive. This is where the ideas and strategies for mastering stress come in handy. Keep in mind the old adage: "Can't never did anything."

Optimism is also related to persistence. This is an important key to career success. You may know about former basketball star, Michael Jordan, who holds numerous records in the National Basketball Association (NBA) including being named as most valuable player in the NBA finals six times. He was told by his school coach one year that he wasn't good enough to play on his high school team. Now think about it. He could have given up, given away his basketball, and quit. But he was using the other two C's of stress hardiness attitudes. He had commitment to his goal and he saw this as a challenge, not a defeat. Do you suppose Michael Jordan has made or missed most of the basketball shots he's tried? Of course, he has missed more. Look at the lesson in persistence he exemplifies.

When things don't go our way, when difficult things happen, when we make mistakes, we have the opportunity to learn. Mistakes are a blessing in disguise. Think about it. When you leave a test you have taken, which questions are you pondering in your mind? Probably not the ones you got right, but the one's you missed. This spurs you to figure things out. A workshop speaker once shared an expression that has relevance here:

Winners lose more than losers,

but they're winners because they stay in the game.

Remember this and choose to be a winner, to be the master of your life, and take charge!

Questions

1. Who should be in charge of you in the workplace?
   - **A.** Your coworkers
   - **B.** Your boss
   - **C.** You
   - **D.** Your mom

2. An important step toward personal effectiveness is being _____.
   - **A.** proactive
   - **B.** reactive
   - **C.** retired
   - **D.** programmatic

3. Optimism tends to be related to _____.
   - **A.** failure
   - **B.** persistence
   - **C.** insecurity
   - **D.** utility

14.8 Intrinsic and Extrinsic Motivation

Define the concept of flow and its relationship to motivation.

The source of your motivation can be **intrinsic** (internal) or **extrinsic** (external). We have experience with both throughout our lives in interactions with our parents, friends, teachers, and bosses.

The two types of motivation are contrasted as follows:

Intrinsic	Extrinsic
Comes from within	Comes from external world
Incites passion	Helps set goals
Makes you feel good	Heightens expectation
Rewards you while you work	Rewards you outside of work, afterward

Examples of intrinsic motivation would include mastery, self-esteem, the joy from accomplishment, pleasure while doing the task, and intensive engagement in the work. Examples of extrinsic motivation would include money, grades, candy, and praise. A family trying to promote learning in their child might give him money for each "A" he brings home on his report card. The child makes the connection between "As" and money. As he gets older, he may avoid subjects in which he thinks he might not get an "A." What's happened? Perhaps, getting good grades has become more important than learning. Hopefully, some learning occurred in the classes in which he got the "As", but what about the subjects he avoided in high school? When grades become the extrinsic reward we are seeking, it influences our behavior. For example, you might put off studying a subject, then cram for an exam just to get a high grade. You may pass the course but not retain much information. In contrast, what about a situation when a person wants the knowledge? She may not even take a course. She may search the internet, peruse a book, a video, attend a demonstration, or ask questions to learn what she wants to know. There is no grade because the knowledge is the thing! And she feels the reward *while* she is learning.

How does this show up in the workplace? Managers and supervisors try to "motivate" people to work hard and do a good job. Often they use rewards such as money, time off, or public recognition to manipulate workers into working hard. In many places we have seen an "Employee of the Month" plaque hanging on the wall with the name and picture of a worker being displayed.

14.8.1 Flow

Mihalyi Csikszentmihalyi, former chair of the University of Chicago Department of Psychology, now at Claremont Graduate University and Director of the Quality of Life Research Center has for over 30 years been studying the lives of thousands of people seeking to find what makes people satisfied, fulfilled, and happy. As described in Chapter 7, he has described the concept of **flow**, a state in which people find their work exhilarating and in which they perform at their best no matter what type of work they do. Flow occurs when our skills are fully engaged and we feel ourselves stretching to meet challenges. We become lost in our work and so fully engaged that we lose all concept of time. In this state our work seems to run smoothly, effortlessly, with adaptability. The flow itself is a pleasure. In studying flow this researcher discovered that workers, on average, were in this state about half the time while on the job, and about 20 percent of time during leisure time.

In contrast, workers reported the most common emotional state during leisure was apathy (Goleman, 1998). Csikszentmihalyi (pronounced chick-sent-me-high-ee) found that most people live at two extremes. They are (1) stressed by work or obligations, or (2) they are bored by spending their leisure time on activities that were passive. He states that people can live enhanced, happier lives by learning new skills and increasing the challenges they face each day (Chamberlain, 1998). He has found that a typical day is full of anxiety and boredom; however "flow experiences provide the flashes of intense living against this dull background" (Csikszentmihalyi, 1990). Flow as an optimal experience is characterized by:

- a sense of playfulness
- a feeling of being in control
- concentration and highly focused attention
- mental enjoyment of activity for its own sake
- a distorted sense of time
- a match between the challenge at hand and one's skills

People experience more flow from what they do on their jobs than from leisure activities such as watching television. It seems that TV's main virtue is that is occupies the mind without demands. Flow is hard to achieve without effort. Flow is not "wasting time." Those who learn to control inner experience will be able to determine the quality of their lives, which Csikszentmihalyi (1993) says is as close as any of us can get to being happy. He outlines the pathway to flow as follows:

1. **Make it a Game** – Consider tasks as games, with rules, objectives, challenges to be overcome and with rewards.
2. **Have a Powerful Goal** – As you play the game, think often of the overriding social, intellectual or spiritual purpose that drives your efforts.
3. **Focus** – Let all distractions, those within or without, go. Center all your attention on the game.
4. **Surrender to the Process** – Just let go. Don't try or strain to achieve your objective. Let it happen and enjoy the process of work.
5. **Experience Ecstasy** – (the feeling, not the drug!) This is the natural results of the previous four steps. It will hit you suddenly, by surprise. There is no mistaking it. This is a "natural high."
6. **Create Peak Productivity** – Your ecstatic state opens reservoirs of resourcefulness, creativity and energy. Productivity and quality of work shoot through the roof (1990).

What this researcher determined after many years examining the concept of flow is that happiness is not something that just happens. It does not arise from luck or random chance. It is not something that money can buy or power command. It doesn't depend on external events, but instead, how we interpret them.

Happiness, Csikszentmihalyi writes, is a condition that must be prepared for, cultivated, and defended privately by each individual. It is in learning to control our inner selves that we create the merit of life's experience. Indeed our happiness comes not from the outer world around us, but from what we experience within. It comes from intrinsic, not extrinsic payoffs.

Although all work settings have extrinsic rewards such as positive performance reviews, promotions, and bonuses, Goleman (1998) also considers the most powerful motivators as those that are internal, not external. He points out that both *motivation* and *emotion* come from the same Latin root meaning "to move." The internal feelings we experience while working on a task are more intense than rewards being offered by others. Holahan and Sears (1995) surveyed 1,528 men and women at the end of their business or professional careers who were asked what were their greatest sources of satisfaction. The results indicated that the top three were: (1) creative challenge of the work; (2) stimulation of the work; and (3) the chance to keep learning. The next three in order were: (1) pride in accomplishments; (2) friendships at work; and (3) assisting or teaching other workers. Further down the list came status and even lower than that came the financial rewards. The indications from research are that what we are feeling about our work is much more significant than the external "carrots" that may be held out to us. Knowing this, it makes lots of sense to tune in once more to our self-awareness and discover our feelings. We know how high-spirited our mood is when we are doing what we love to do.

14.8.2 Your Frame Determines Your Work Orientation

Writers describe three different frames about work: a job, a career, and a calling. We do a **job** to pay bills. Collecting a paycheck on a regular basis is the prime motivator for you to show up and do your work. When you no longer need the paycheck or your wages get lowered or stopped, you leave the job. A **career** is something into which you invest much more of yourself. It usually requires more educational preparation than a job. It is something you stay with over an extended period of your life. You have more of your identity tied up with your career. A career offers more than just a paycheck. There are opportunities for advancement that mean more money, status and power. However, when you reach your highest position, you may not be able to advance further and begin to lose interest. You no longer feel so invested in this career. You may start looking elsewhere for satisfaction and reward. Seligman (2002) contrasts these levels of work with a third level, a **calling**, which he describes as a passionate commitment to work for its own sake. We often think of people in helping professions as having a "calling," especially those in religious work. People with a calling view their work as contributing to the greater good, to something larger and find their work fulfilling in its own right, without concern for money or advancement. They may accept a position without even knowing what the salary pays.

Historically, positions with a calling included prestigious workers such as rabbis, priests, or other clergy, Supreme Court Justices, physicians, and scientific researchers. Seligman points out that new research now shows that any job can become a calling, and any calling can become a job. For example, a physician who only cares about money and not about his patients has a job. Conversely, a garbage collector who sees his work as making the environment cleaner has a calling. It is possible to reframe any job into a calling by identifying the far-reaching impact your work has on others and the environment. In this way you are shifting from being extrinsically motivated to intrinsically motivated in your work.

Think of how a receptionist can have a calling. What about a grocery store cashier? What type of frame would elevate this work to a calling? How does reframing these positions impact the motivation for the person doing the work? If you are employed, how do you frame your own work?

The Global Perspective
Happiness and Meaning in Work

Do global citizens have more fun? Are they happier? Do they experience a deeper sense of meaning in their work? As we examine the link between the behaviors of global citizens and the essence of fun, satisfaction and meaning, we will see that the answer to these questions is a resounding "Yes!"

Let's explore "fun" first. Most of us have a clear sense of what it feels like to have fun and we know it involves positive feelings. Having "fun" at work, however, doesn't mean that we walk around giggling all day, being frivolous about our work. Rather, it means we are feeling optimistic and positive a lot more than we feel pessimistic and negative. So how is fun connected to global citizenship? Global citizens relate comfortably to all kinds of people, far beyond the circle of those from their own culture. They relate to people with respect and regard them as important, and work effectively with diverse teams. Basically, they are motivated by love not fear. These behaviors mean that they experience other people in a positive, joyous way rather than in a suspicious or frightened way. In the final analysis, we can see that global citizens are able to positively engage with a wide variety of people, increasing their opportunities for fun.

When we look at "happiness," it is important to distinguish between a transient burst of joy that can come from things like a funny movie, a good grade on a quiz, recognition at work, in contrast to what Seligman (2002) calls *enduring* happiness, a lasting and general sense which impacts your life. In studying happiness nationally and internationally, he found that once the standard of living gets above meeting basic needs, the correlation between wealth and satisfaction with life disappears. In other words, you cannot buy happiness. Seligman (2002) states that "by activating an expansive, tolerant, and creative mindset, positive feelings maximize the social, intellectual and physical benefits that will accrue". If we look at the behaviors of a global citizen, we note they have an expansive mindset shown by relating with empathy to those of differing cultures, acknowledging that their views and values are not universally shared, and that they are able to tolerate ambiguity. Using these traits, global citizens will accrue the benefits of enduring happiness, not only in the workplace, but additionally, in their lives.

Examining the broader aspect of *meaning* in our work life, remember our discussion of *flow* wherein a person is fully engaged in an activity.

(Continued)

Csikszentmihaly (1990) calls these experiences "the enjoyments" and they are *not* momentary pleasures. They can be of the mind, or social, or from a physical activity but include the following aspects: a challenging task; requiring skill; concentration; clear goals; getting immediate feedback; deep, effortless involvement; a sense of control; lack of a sense of self; and the stopping of time. Unlike engaging in pleasures which lead to biological satiation, when we are in flow we are being proactive—investing—growing psychologically for our future. People who use their signature strengths are more likely to experience flow in their day-to-day lives. People who are good listeners, who read about international events, who are bilingual, who recognize that a new mode of thinking is necessary to solve today's challenges (all characteristics of a global citizen), are less likely to spend their lives passively. Instead, they are more likely to engage in activities that facilitate growth leading to lasting gratification and a deeper sense of meaning.

Is it possible that human lives can have a noble purpose? Is it possible that our lives have meaning that goes beyond the meaning we create for ourselves? These are questions Seligman pondered when considering that biological evolution in humans has perhaps powered our species to grow from being savage, to barbarian, to civilized. Seligman (2002) says a meaningful life is "one that joins with something larger than we are—and the larger that something is, the more meaning our lives have". We have choices and the possibility to contribute not only to our own, but to all of humankind's continuing growth. Seligman describes the good life as one where deriving happiness is the result of using your signature strengths every day to forward knowledge, power, or goodness. A life that does this is filled with meaning. Those who accept responsibility for global citizenship believe they are empowered to make a difference, behave ethically, exercise moral leadership and will undoubtedly find increased satisfaction and meaning in their careers. What do you think: Is it possible that our lives have meaning that goes beyond the meaning we create for ourselves? How might a sense of satisfaction and meaning in our careers contribute to the overall growth of humankind?

Questions

1. Taffi works hard at her job each day because she values the sense of accomplishment that results from a job well done. Taffi seems to be motivated by _____ factors.

   A. reprisal

   B. extrinsic

   C. external

   D. intrinsic

2. Bitsy works hard at her job each day because the harder she works, the more she gets paid, and she really likes getting paid. Bitsy seems to be motivated by _____ factors.

   A. intrinsic

   B. extrinsic

   C. internal

   D. prosaic

3. The state in which people find their work exhilarating and they perform at their best has been described as _____.

   A. optimization

   B. flow

   C. necessitation

   D. homeostasis

Summary

In this chapter we have discussed ways for applying the principles of positive psychology to your life in the workplace. We examined the need for and the how to of being *people smart*. We have emphasized the importance of being an astute observer and developing your strengths related to people skills. We began recognizing how important it is to know yourself, your goals, personality, needs and behavioral triggers. This means having a sense of awareness about your own emotions, thoughts and behaviors. It also means using your cognitive self in concert with your emotional self in order to manage yourself for success.

When you turned to knowing about others, you discovered that the process is parallel to that for yourself. You also need to know about the goals, personality, needs and triggers that guide not only your behavior but the behavior of others. The social conventions of courtesy, etiquette and other social/cultural norms are important, as well. If you seek to achieve career success, knowing your job and having the required work training and skills is a necessary, but not sufficient condition. To really reach excellence in your work performance, you must also be people smart!

We also looked at issues related to experiencing your work as pleasurable. We reviewed those aspects that reside primarily in your power, like taking charge and seeking intrinsic motivation. We described exciting new findings regarding the personally rewarding feelings of "flow." We also discussed potential problems you may encounter in the workplace including substance abuse, conflict resolution, lack of advancement, burnout, sexual harassment and discrimination.

Bearing in mind your work and career effectiveness, it is important that you know the workplace, spend time designing or re-designing your career, and sharpen your people skills. Start with an "I can" attitude. Stay aware of what's happening to you . . . not only your work and your thoughts, but your feelings. Work with the strength of social intelligence. If you realize things are not right, take charge and work to change the things you can. Determine goals to revitalize yourself in your current position, or determine a goal for changing positions. Remember, *you are in charge of your life and your happiness in the workplace.*

Positive Psychology Exercises

1. Grab a piece of paper and let's do some free writing. Jot down the things that come to mind regarding your career. What do you want to accomplish in your career? How long with this take? Who are the other people who figure into the equation such as spouse, children, co-workers, clients, or boss? After you have listed about five different things you want to achieve through your career. Ask yourself what these successes look like? Imagine yourself ten years from now . . . what will your life be like?

2. In your self-discovery journaling, write down three to five areas where you invest most of your time. This will reveal to you something about your motivations and the needs that are operating in your life.

3. Identify someone you consider to be "people smart." Observe their behavior carefully and how their interactions are effective. Do you see any patterns?

4. List three intrinsic and three extrinsic motivators operating in your life right now.

5. Think of three separate times you were in "flow" while doing a task. What were you doing in each situation?

6. Write three possible questions you might ask your supervisor to determine the degree to which she values positivity in her management role.

Key Terms

Affiliation

Brainstorming

Burnout

Calling

Career

Conflict Resolution

Discrimination

Extrinsic Motivation

Flow

Hierarchy of Needs

Hostile Environment

Idioms

Interpersonal Intelligence

Intrapersonal Intelligence

Intrinsic Motivation

Job

Mentor

Motivation

Needs

Peak Experiences

People Smart

Personality

Polarization

Positive Institution(s)

Quid Pro Quo

Reprisal

Self-actualization

Sexual Harassment

Substance Abuse

Triggers

Yesable Proposal

Yin/Yang

Shared Writing

Describe the steps of conflict resolution in the workplace as they apply to a particular scenario from your personal experience.

Chapter 14 Questions

1. According to Howard Gardner's theory of multiple intelligences, the ability to connect effectively in working with other people is called _____.

   A. intrapsychic awareness

   B. intrapersonal intelligence

   C. interpersonal intelligence

   D. extraordinary perception

2. Goals are usually divided into _____ and _____ categories.

   A. long-term; short-term

   B. achievable; unrealistic

   C. self-focused; other-focused

   D. intrapsychic; extrapsychic

3. Nunzio is always striving to be at the top of whatever he does, to accomplish a lot, and to exhibit high levels of performance. Nunzio is high in _____.

   A. need for power

   B. need for achievement

   C. need for affiliation

   D. need for belongingness

4. A person who realizes her or his potential and has peak experiences, is self-reliant, centered in values and ethics, and identifies with all human beings, is someone who is _____.

   A. high in need for power

   B. high in need for affiliation

   C. high in need for achievement

   D. self-actualized

5. At the base of Maslow's hierarchy of needs are _____ needs.

   A. esteem

   B. basic biological

   C. belongingness

   D. safety

6. The best way to understand the personalities, needs, goals, and behavioral triggers of others is to be _____.

   A. intrusive in their work lives

   B. in a leadership position

   C. remote and detached from other people

   D. a keen observer of cues

7. Understanding coworkers' _____ contributes to understanding the dynamics of the group itself.

   A. group goals

   B. private histories

   C. economic backgrounds

   D. childhoods

8. _____ is the term used to describe physical, mental, and emotional reactions that reflect exhaustion.

   A. Degeneration

   B. Extinction

   C. Burnout

   D. Fatigue

9. Agnetha is told by her boss that the only way she'll ever get a promotion is if she agrees to have sex with him. This type of sexual harassment is called _____.

    A. ipso facto

    B. hostile work environment

    C. in vino veritas

    D. quid pro quo

10. A passionate commitment to work for its own sake is a/an _____.

    A. job

    B. calling

    C. career

    D. avocation

Glossary

absent presence   occurs when you are physically present with your partner but frequently distracted or lured away by your mobile device.

accomplishment   is achievement.

ACT   is an acronym for Acceptance and Commitment Techniques.

active and constructive responding   is a way of interacting in a positive and supportive way with your partner when he/she brings you good news.

active listening   a process of reflecting back (paraphrasing) to the speaker nonjudgmental responses as a way of checking accuracy of what we have heard, and whether we fully understand the message the speaker is attempting to communicate.

active relaxation   involves a variety of techniques for becoming aware of your body and your physiological reactions so that you may consciously reduce your level of arousal.

added value   the specific and/ or unique contributions you offer to your place of employment through your knowledge, skills or work accomplishments.

aerobic exercise   is exercise that conditions your cardiovascular system.

affiliation   refers to need to be in social situations and connected to other people.

agape   an early Greek term for a selfless love that is given without any expectation of return.

aggression   occurs when thoughts, feelings, needs, and beliefs are expressed in ways which can be dishonest, usually inappropriate or intimidating, and always violate the rights of other people.

altruism   self-sacrificing caring for others.

ambiguous figures   images capable of being perceived in more than one way depending on one's frame of reference such as optical illusions.

amygdala   a center in our primitive brain responsible for anger and other emotional outbursts, can produce a "emotional hijacking" when it perceives what it thinks is an emergency and bypasses the neocortex.

appreciative inquiry   a method for establishing positive goals whereby you inquire as to what is right about a situation and ask how more of it can be created, in stark contrast to the typical tendency to ask what is wrong and how to fix it.

artistic   people who are creative, imaginative, emotional, and who hold unconventional perspectives which they like to express in artistic forms such as painting, sculpting, music, writing, and dance.

assertion   a communication process through which we stand up for our personal rights and express ideas, needs, feelings, and beliefs in direct, honest, and appropriate ways without violating the rights of other people.

attachment   having an emotional bond of affection, loyalty, or fond regard.

attachment theory   John Bowlby's theory regarding how children attach or not attach to an adult caregiver, which affects how they will thrive and may influence lifelong patterns of attachment in later adult relationships.

attitude of gratitude   involves noticing, appreciating, and being thankful for the people, events, and even the small benefits of your life.

attribution theory   a theory of emotion which states that if humans are faced with physiological arousal of unknown origin, they will search their environment for an appropriate explanation or label for this arousal.

auditory   our hearing, represented in sounds, words, and language.

authentic happiness   refers to Martin Seligman's definition of happiness as something more akin to life satisfaction or contentment encompassing living a meaningful life, utilizing your skills and talents while living your life with purpose and as part of a community.

authoritarian parenting   a restrictive, punitive style of parenting focusing on following rules and assuming that the child is incompetent.

authoritative parenting   parents who are involved, warm, and nurturing while at the same time setting meaningful limits and controls for the child.

autocratic   power is concentrated in a single person.

autogenic training   involves talking oneself into deep relaxation by repeating certain phrases *over* and *over* while focusing your attention on a particular muscle group or physiological response.

autonomic nervous system   part of the peripheral nervous system that acts independently of conscious control and coordinates such involuntary processes as respiration, digestion, and heart rate. It is composed of the sympathetic (arousal) and parasympathetic (calming) branches.

awareness   recognizing your current state of health or consciousness.

baby boomers   born between 1946–1964, Post World War 11 babies who came to see careers as the central part of their lives.

baby busters or generation X   born after 1964 who seek personal gratification and want work to allow them freedom to pursue their own interests.

beginner's mind   to see things with the wonder of a child seeing things for the first time.

behaviorism   a deterministic theory of personality that states that humans are a product of our conditioning, learning histories, and our current reinforcement schedules.

biochemicals   substances related to living organisms and life processes.

body wisdom   knowledge of how your body affects your thoughts.

brain reserve   an increase in the connections between neurons believed to help the brain become more resistant to age-related or disease-related damage.

brainstorming   the uninhibited offering of ideas and suggestion by all members of a group.

broaden and build   theory explains the wide ranging, beneficial effects of positive emotions which let us know that we are safe, there by enabling us to engage in activities geared for the future which push our adaptation in ways than enhance our abilities.

broken record technique   is a technique used with an aggressive person when escalating assertiveness does not work. It involves repeating our request over and over, like a broken record, even if the other person is arguing, or ranting and raving.

bruxism   teeth grinding at night.

burnout   collection of physical, emotional and mental reactions that reflect exhaustion and are the result of constant or re-occurring emotional pressures.

calling   a passionate commitment to work for its own sake; such work contributes to the greater good, to something larger than self and is fulfilling in its own right without concern for money or advancement.

career   employment with opportunities for advancement, status, power and money that often is a major part of a person's identity.

career families   grouping together of specific careers with similar work requirements and personnel training and/or characteristics in a broader category such as technology, health care, business.

career plan   a written planning document that outlines your basic goal, your long-range requirements, current skills, interests and experiences, strengths, and your short-term goals.

catastrophizing   giving oneself the message that a situation is too awful or overwhelming to bear or that the worst is about to happen.

catharsis   Freud's theory that venting or acting out anger had beneficial effects. Current research contradicts this theory.

challenge   the ability to focus on the opportunities that problems present rather than the dangers.

character   the development of virtues and their corresponding signature strengths.

clarifying   a process of asking questions to facilitate our understanding of the speaker's message, to get background information, additional relevant facts, or to fill in the narrative.

co-dependency   the relationship that ensues when two individuals depend on each other because deep inside they feel they could not survive on their own.

cognitive distortions   the tendency to look for verification to support your existing opinions.

cognitive restructuring   a powerful strategy for refuting irrational beliefs and changing your self-talk.

Cognitive-behaviorism   a branch of psychology postulating that the study of humans should not focus solely on overt behavior but must include our covert behavior, the thoughts and self-talk that precede our behavior.

cohabitation   living together in a loving and sexual relationship.

collective unconscious   a storehouse of experience to which we are all connected.

commitment   believing that what you do is of value and importance.

commitment in relationships   decision to love that person and to maintain that love.

companionate love   has commitment and intimacy without passion: a marriage of best friends.

concordance rate   the probability that twins display the same trait or characteristic.

conditional positive regard   occurs when a parent judges a child's value and delivers their love based on the acceptability of the child's behavior at the moment.

conditions of worth   when an individual thinks they are worthwhile or lovable only if they behave in certain ways or meet certain standards.

conflict resolution   achieving consensus and a written agreement to a problem or issue where the parties were in conflict and holding opposing views.

connection   considered an additional stress hardiness attitude; having meaningful connections to others is a crucial factor in resilience to stress.

consummate love a complete type of love that involves passion, intimacy and commitment.

contingent workers part-time workers.

control the belief that one is in control of their life rather than the stressors being in control, recognizing that ultimately you always have control over how you choose to respond.

conventional people who enjoy working in structured situations, are self-disciplined, orderly, and like organizing and work comfortably at routine tasks. Sample occupations would be accountant, clerical worker, data entry or billing clerk, bank teller.

core workers full time workers.

correlation a reliable association between any two variables; the greater the degree of relationship the higher the correlation. Correlation does not guarantee causation.

cortisol stress hormone released by adrenal glands linked to hypertension, atherosclerosis, heart disease, weight gain, and immune system suppression.

cover letter an original business letter that you compose that complements your resume, the purpose of which is to get the employer to read your resume.

deep processing a study technique involving thinking about what you just read and imagining how you can connect it to your life.

defensive pessimism a strategy that anticipates a negative outcome and then takes steps to avoid that outcome.

defer gratification the ability to wait for reinforcements until a later time which represents the opposite of low frustration tolerance.

defusion (in ACT) is an acceptance strategy rather than control strategy utilizing a wide variety of techniques designed to help reduce the power of unwanted or negative thoughts, emotions or images.

delusional thinking believing in ideas that are not reality based like those involving fears of persecution which persist even in the face of clear cut evidence to the contrary.

democratic power concentrated on the group and its leader.

determinism a belief in cause and effect relationships and by implication the absence of free will in human affairs.

diaphragmatic breathing an active relaxation technique involving slow, deep, rhythmic breaths that originate in the diaphragm as opposed to the thorax or upper chest.

differential relaxation the ability to contract only those muscles that are necessary to accomplish the task at hand, while keeping all other muscles relaxed.

discrimination treating a person differently because of race, color, religion, disability, age, national origin, gender, or sexual orientation.

dispositional pessimism a strategy of negative thinking in general, based on thoughts about the past, leading to negative expectations about the future.

distress negative stress.

distributed processing accounts for the fact that your brain constructs images even when no information is coming to your eyes, merely by firing a network.

dopamine a neurotransmitter in the brain that is essential for normal nerve activity and involved in the experience of pleasure.

double message when in a communication there is incongruence between the verbal aspects and the nonverbal aspects of a message.

downsizing cutting positions to do more with less and save costs.

Duchenne smile a full-face smile where not only your mouth turns up, but the corners of your eyes crinkle, as well. That is, you smile with your eyes as well as your mouth.

duration neglect the fact that the length of an experience influences how we interpret the positive or negative impact of experiences.

elaborative rehearsal a study technique involving paraphrasing material you study, taking this information and putting in your own words as if you were teaching it to another. It is very effective for facilitating memory and recall.

emotional bank account an emotional account we hold with each other by virtue of being in a relationship. We make withdrawals from and deposits into this bank account based on our behaviors and attitudes toward the other.

emotional hijacking occurs when the amygdala bypasses the neocortex and we respond impulsively and explosively with anger.

emotional intelligence involves a cluster of skills including being perceptive about the feelings and motivations of others as well as yourself, being able to motivate yourself and persevere in the face of frustration, the ability to delay gratification, to control your emotions and impulses, and to empathize with others.

emotion-focused coping attempting to deal with a stressor by moderating one's own emotional response to the stressor.

empathic assertion a very effective type of assertion in which the speaker begins by making a statement that conveys recognition of the other person's situation or feelings followed by another statement where the speaker stands up for their personal rights and suggests other alternatives.

empathic listening   a listening process involving putting ourselves in the shoes of the other, seeing the world through their eyes, understanding their particular paradigm and how they feel.

empathy   an other oriented emotional response elicited by and congruent with the perceived welfare of someone else involving the ability to imagine how the world looks through the eyes of another.

empowerment   providing the group with the authority to make decisions.

empty love   empty love for another that has only commitment, but lacks passion and intimacy.

endorphins   the body's naturally produced pain killers.

engagement   occurs when we are involved in gratifying activities, where we often lose track of time and our skills are matched to the challenges allowing us to tap into our strengths. This sets the stage for flow.

enterprising   people who are persuasive, like to influence other people, are risk-takers and enjoy business ventures. Sample occupations would be sales manager, real estate broker, and business owner.

epigenetics   examines the bridge between nature and nurture whereby your environment and your choices influence the expression of your genes and even the genetic code you pass to later generations.

EQ   emotional quotient reflecting your emotional intelligence.

eros   an early Greek term from which the word "erotic" comes referring to quick, intense feeling for another that does not last long.

escalating assertiveness   the change from a minimal assertive response to a more forceful one, when the former does not work. It may involve including consequences, changing to a demand, or giving an outright refusal.

ethos   the first of three sequentially arranged words in a Greek philosophy about communication. It refers to our personal credibility, our trustworthiness, and the faith people have in our integrity.

eudemonia   a complex concept which refers to being true to your inner self and increasing happiness by identifying your own signature strengths and virtues and then living your life in accordance with these.

eustress   positive stress.

executive functions   of the brain, located in the prefrontal cortex, include planning, judgment, focus, screening out distractions, organizing, using and integrating new information and inhibiting thoughts and actions.

exercise   a critical component of wellness; a natural outlet for built up physiological arousal that releases muscular tension allowing the body to return to equilibrium.

existentialism   a European philosophy focused on the nature of meaning and free will.

experiential avoidance   is a vicious cycle involving ongoing attempts to control, avoid, escape or banish unwanted or negative thoughts, feelings, memories or images, even when doing so becomes self-defeating, useless or costly.

explanatory style   a perspective one has in dealing with the world such as optimism or pessimism.

external locus of control   an individual's belief that they are a victim, buffeted and abused by external events over which they have no control.

extroversion   the ability of an individual to be outgoing and comfortable around other people.

extrinsic motivation   the urge to spend energy and effort for an external reward.

fatuous love   feelings similar to infatuation for another, but includes a rapid move to commitment.

feedback   a process of sharing our reactions to what we have heard the speaker say. It should be immediate, honest, and supportive.

fight/flight response   a survival mechanism present in humans and most animals that prepares us to deal with physical danger.

financial competence   refers to your ability to successfully manage your personal finances.

flexibility exercises   include exercises that maintain healthy joints, good posture, body alignment and the capacity to move the body in its potential for full range of motion.

flow   a state in which a person finds the challenge of a task to be equal to their skills whereby their abilities and interests are fully engaged. Often the person loses the concept of time and finds the involvement to be gratifying.

flourishing   refers to the primary goal of positive psychology which is to help individuals live a full and meaningful life commensurate with optimal human functioning.

forgiveness   the ability to let go of the negative energy attached to bad memories without necessarily forgetting what happened or allowing yourself to again be abused.

frames of reference   paradigms to enable us to organize and understand our world, our perceptions, our experiences.

free will   the ability of humans to ignore so-called determining factors and freely choose how and when to act.

frustration-aggression hypothesis early theory attempting to explain the root causes of anger and aggression. It focused on the role of frustration as a result of being blocked from reaching a goal as a primary factor.

functional fixedness becoming locked into thinking about using objects only in the most conventional or familiar ways.

fusion (in ACT) represents is the melding of a thought with an event as if they are one in the same and acting as if the thought is reality.

genderlects Deborah Tannen's term for ways men and women use the same language to communicate different meanings when talking with each other.

general adaptation syndrome (GAS) a three-stage process (alarm, resistance, exhaustion) that describes how stress related symptoms and illnesses emerge in the body.

Generation X or the "baby busters" were born after 1964 and before 1977 who are seeking personal gratification and want work to allow them the freedom to pursue their own interests.

Generation Y born between 1977 to 2000. Also referred to as "Millennials" or "Net Generation," they have grown up with computers and the majority have computers and internet access. They are more open and tolerant than previous generations.

Generation Z people born in 1990's to present who have been exposed to information technologies their whole life and are referred to as "digital natives."

global citizen is an individual who places emphasis on individual choice, in a collective setting, for the greater good.

glucocorticoids stress hormones known to weaken immune functioning leading to an increased susceptibility to diseases.

gold collar workers are experts in information and communications technology – IT experts.

grit the combination of exceptional passion and perseverance to achieve a goal.

gustatory our sense of taste represented by various flavors.

hallucinations seeing, hearing, or feeling things that aren't really there.

hatha yoga a branch of Yoga that emphasizes physical postures and stretches that incorporate breath control and focused, meditative concentration.

hedonic capacity the ability of an individual to experience positive emotions based on both genetics as well as environment and learning histories.

hedonic treadmill the fact that we tend to inevitably adapt to fortunate circumstances and take these for granted.

hedonism the pursuit of momentary pleasures.

hierarchy of needs Maslow's theory that needs arise in the following ascending order: biological, safety, belonging, esteem and self-actualization which he depicted in a pyramid form.

hippocampus a structure in the brain integral to the process of memory and new learning.

homeostasis the natural tendency of the body to maintain a balanced internal state in order to ensure physical survival.

hostile environment work situation where a co-worker or supervisor engages in intimidating actions and/or unwanted sex based behavior which renders the workplace intimidating or where the purpose is to interfere with work performance.

Humanism a theoretical orientation positing that our personalities and our behavior are not so much a product of our conditioning and conditions but of our choices in response to them; developed by Maslow and Rogers.

hyperventilation a rapid, shallow type of over breathing, that reduces the level of carbon dioxide and calcium in the blood leading to physical symptoms including dizziness, numbness, and muscle tension.

"I" statement a statement involving what we have observed or felt, so that we are taking responsibility for our feelings, experience, and observation.

ideal self the person you feel you should be.

idealized influence similar to charisma which leaders exhibit because they are committed to their own and their follower's integrity and right actions. Employees respect and trust leaders and perceive the leader as fair.

idioms an expression of a specific language that is peculiar to itself and cannot be understood from the individual meanings of the words used to convey it.

implicit memory the neural storehouse for our expectations, attitudes, assumptions, fears, motivations, and moods below the level of conscious awareness.

individualized consideration leaders show caring for employees' development, and physical and psychology safety by exhibiting mentoring, listening empathically, and compassion for individuals especially when they are having a difficult time. This leads to a positive interpersonal relationship.

infatuated love feelings for another involving only passion.

inferiority complex describes an individual with chronically low self-esteem.

inflation is the rise of the costs of goods or services that, over time, erodes the value of your money or savings.

information overload having or gathering too much information which inhibits decision making.

insourcing   workers in one country locally providing labor for companies owned outside of their country.

inspirational motivation   leaders inspire their followers to do their very best and to achieve greater levels than followers thought possible; leaders instill in employees a sense of self-efficacy and confidence.

intellectual stimulation   leaders encourage employees to challenge assumptions, think for themselves, and question existing perspectives and practices which leads greater perceived effectiveness.

interdependence   the relationship that ensues when two or more independent individuals decide to come together to achieve a common goal.

internal locus of control   an individual's belief that they are responsible for the ultimate outcomes in their life; proactivity.

intrapersonal intelligence   ability to understand oneself, appreciate one's feelings and motivations thereby regulating one's life.

interpersonal intelligence   capacity for understanding intentions, motivations and desires of other people and thereby interact and work effectively with them.

interval training   consists of alternating bursts of speed or high intensity activity for a set amount of time or distance followed by a longer period of rest by either walking or jogging depending on your fitness level.

intimacy   feeling and behaviors that promote a sense of being close, bonded and connected.

intrinsic motivation   the urge to spend energy and effort for an internal reward.

introspection   looking inward at one's own thoughts, feelings, sensations; self-examination.

investigative   people who like abstract thinking, discovering new knowledge, solving problems. Sample occupations would be physicist, chemist, medical researcher, college or university professor.

job   employment to pay bills.

kinesthetic   our sense of touch represented by feelings and physical sensations.

laissez faire   group operates rather independently from leader.

leader   has long range vision of where organization is heading; focuses on people and their behaviors as exhibited toward accomplishing the mission of the business or organization.

leadership   influencing people to think and/or act in a certain way.

learned helplessness   the state of expecting that nothing you do will matter or affect your fate or an outcome based on your prior learning history.

letter of application   letter written to apply for a specific position that is open.

letter of inquiry   letter written to ask about whether or not there is a position available.

liking   feeling positive about another, such as feelings we may have about long-time friends.

locus of control   the nature of how an individual perceives their ability to control their response to life events; on a continuum from external to internal.

logos   the third of three sequentially arranged words in a Greek philosophy about communication. It refers to the logical, reasoning aspects of our character and our communication.

Losada ratio   refers to the ratio of positive to negative interactions in a relationship. Typically, the higher this ratio the healthier the relationship.

lose-lose   a paradigm of interpersonal interactions where neither of the participants get what they want and neither side is satisfied with the outcome.

lose-win outcome   an outcome where you lose and the other party wins.

low frustration tolerance   the inability or difficulty with accepting the fact that in order to receive future rewards you often need to undertake present discomfort.

malevolent attitude   the belief that one is surrounded by enemies; a belief that one is detestable and deserves to be treated poorly.

manager   concerned with the details of the tasks to be accomplished by the work group with focus on day-to-day processes, keeping the operations going smoothly.

management   refers to a group of managers tasked with keeping day to day operations functioning on a smooth and efficient fashion.

mantra   a meditative practice which involves the consistent repetition of a sound or phrase ultimately leading to a reduction in thought and focused awareness in the present moment.

mature workers   born pre-1946 and lived during or close to the time of the Great Depression in 1930's.

meditation   the ability to maintain a focused awareness in the present moment.

mentor   senior or experienced employee who serves to assist a new employee through advising, role modeling, explaining normative behavior, and available to answer questions and give support.

metacognition   becoming aware of your emotions

metamood   becoming aware of your emotions.

millennials   are the group born between 1977 and 2000 who have grown up with computers, have social media savviness and are typically more tolerant of multiculturalism.

mindfulness is the cultivation of awareness by practicing awareness.

mirror neurons a type of neuron which has the ability to fire in the exact pattern in order to execute the behavior that is being observed.

mnemonics techniques used to aid in memory which work by making material more meaningful by adding a structure, such as making it into a song or rhyme, or linking it with other entrenched memories like the letters of the alphabet.

modeling the ability of humans to learn how to do something, simply by observing others.

morphic resonance implies that all matter and living things are connected and affected by fields that influence not only their structure, but also their behaviors.

motivation the investment of energy and effort toward the meeting of some need or achieving a goal.

needs a perceived or unconscious requirement for a specific state or object which may generate behavior toward obtaining that essential reward.

negativity bias on an unconscious level, we are more sensitive and reactive to negative stimuli thus negative states are more readily converted into neural structures than positive states. In a nutshell, we learn faster from pain than pleasure.

neocortex the thinking brain or seat of higher reasoning and planning.

neural Darwinism the weakening of unused synaptic connections and the strengthening of the busiest connections.

neurogenesis the ability of the brain to grow new neurons which appears to happen most readily within the hippocampus.

neurons a specialized cell that conducts impulses through the nervous system.

neuroplasticity the capacity of the brain to change its internal structure by reorganizing neural pathways based on new experiences.

nonconscious mind the part of the mind containing aspects of our functioning of which we are totally unaware.

nonlove impersonal interaction with acquaintances that lacks passion, intimacy or commitment.

nonreflexive reality is a reality that we cannot influence by our thoughts, expectations or desires such as what happens with the weather.

nonverbal behavior refers to facial expressions, tone of voice, body posture, rate of speech, and eye contact which conveys most of the meaning in interpersonal communication.

norepinephrine a hormone, also referred to as adrenalin, which is secreted during the fight/flight response and functions as a vasoconstrictor.

nutrition the study of the impact of diet on health and wellness.

observational learning another name for modeling, more currently used in the literature.

offshoring outsourcing to another country.

olfactory refers to our sense of smell.

optimism bias the belief that the future will most likely be better than either the past or present.

optimism the attitude of perceiving and interpreting potential problems in way that gives them meaning and provides a sense of control; looking for reasons to be happy and satisfied with life.

outsourcing the source of the production is outside of the company, city, state, nation or continent.

oxytocin a hormone secreted by the pituitary gland that facilitates bonding between mother and child and for females in romantic relationships.

pacing using strategic planning for structuring your time to enhance productivity and lower stress.

paradigm a particular way of seeing or conceptualizing things. Also referred to as a perspective, schema, or frame.

paradigm shift a change in the overriding theoretical framework that governs a scientific discipline; a sudden or gradual change in how one perceives a situation.

paralanguage how something is said rather than what it is said. Includes characteristics such as the tone and pitch of voice, vocal inflections, emphasis on certain words, and the length and frequency of pauses.

paraphrasing stating in your own words what you think someone has said.

parasympathetic nervous system the branch of autonomic nervous system that allows your body to gradually calm down after the fight/flight response.

Pareto principle the 80/20 rule. It teaches that 80% of the benefit comes from doing 20% of the work.

passion the exuberant expression of desires and needs.

passive relaxation involves inactivity or passive activity such as watching TV which is not nearly as effective for lowering arousal as active relaxation techniques.

passive-aggression a communication process through which we indirectly express aggression, not by what we directly do or say, but by what we fail to do or say.

passivity a communication process through which we fail to express honest feelings, needs, thoughts, and beliefs, and consequently permit others to potentially take advantage of us.

pathological critic   a negative inner voice that attacks and judges you.

pathos   the second of three sequentially arranged words in a Greek philosophy about communication. It refers to our ability to perceive and attune ourselves with the emotional content of another person's communication.

peak experiences   moments of exhilaration and ecstasy.

peak-end theory   explains the fact that our recollections of pleasure are influenced by the intensity of the experience, as well as how it ended.

people smart   being aware of thoughts, feelings and behaviors of self and others and using these skills to enable positive and effective interactions with others. It also refers to emotional intelligence in the workplace.

perception   occurs when our brain interprets sensations and ascribes meaning to them.

perception check   is an offshoot of the assertive response where you are confused about the behavior of another and want to inquire about what is really happening with that person.

performance review   formal evaluation process that documents work performance.

permissive-indulgent parenting   parents who are involved and loving with their children but who fail to set limits or provide meaningful controls *over* their behavior.

permissive-indifferent parenting   refers to parenting that is not particularly harsh or punitive, but treats the child as if she is not particularly important; uninvolved in child's life.

personal space   the distance with which we choose to stand when interacting with others and the extent to which we are comfortable with being touched.

personality   a pattern of qualities, traits, character or behavior that is relatively stable for a person.

pessimism   the opposite of optimism; expectations that are negative.

philo   an early Greek term for mutual brotherly love such as friendship.

placebo effect   the phenomenon that occurs when an individual responds positively to a treatment or drug because of their expectations it will work rather than any actual effectiveness of the treatment or drug.

polarization   a concentration of groups, forces, or interests about conflicting or contrasting positions.

policies   general guidelines or rules for governing activity.

positive affectivity   another name for an individual's hedonic capacity.

positive emotions   a wide range of pleasant emotions in the past, present and future; being able to know what it is to be happy and to experience an enduring sense of well-being.

positive institutions   seek to improve the well-being of their participants whether in a family, school, community, governmental, workplace or other setting. Such institutions facilitate achievement of the organization's goals allowing the participants and the institution to reap positive rewards.

positive psychology   the study of the healthy aspects of human functioning that make us effective in our lives; the study of optimal human functioning.

post-traumatic growth   when individuals become more effective and stress resistant as a result of having endured trauma.

power nap   refreshing yourself by taking a short nap for an energy boost.

prediction errors   the discrepancy between what you expect and what can actually happen.

predictive coding   is a process your brain employs to protect you from being inundated with information processing whereby it makes forecasts about what it is seeing and changes these predictions only when it makes an error.

prefrontal cortex   area of the brain associated with higher reasoning and planning.

Premack principle   this principle states that if two behaviors differ in their likelihood of occurrence, the less likely behavior can be reinforced by using the more likely behavior as a reward.

proactivity   refers to taking the initiative, doing what is necessary and being response-able. It is a guiding paradigm of effective individuals.

proactive interference   the phenomenon in which old learning inhibits retention of new material.

problem-focused coping   problem focused attempts to deal with a stressor head-on to remove or diffuse its effects.

procedures   manner in which policies are to be carried out in actual task activities.

progess paradox   despite the fact that life has improved for most Americans in terms of standard of living and health, our self-reported happiness levels have not kept pace with the increase in health, wealth, and education.

procrastination   when important tasks or responsibilities are left undone or are completed in a careless manner because inadequate time was left to complete the task properly.

progressive relaxation   a systematic process of relaxing the body by first tensing and then releasing the tension in various muscles throughout the body.

propinquity   living or working near or close by another person.

pseudo listening   fake listening which does not include one of the necessary intentions for real listening: to understand someone, to enjoy someone, to learn something, or to give help or solace.

psychoanalytic theory   Sigmund Freud's deterministic theory of personality formation focused on the experiences of the first five to six years of growth.

psychological flexibility   represents (in ACT) the ability to be in the present moment, open to experience and able to do what matters; the ability to easily shift your frame of reference or to think out of the box.

psychoneuroimmunology   the study of the relationship between stress, our immune system and health outcomes in order to facilitate healing.

psychophysiological disorders   illnesses that are triggered and exacerbated by stress.

psychosomatic illness   when a physical disorder is affected or in some cases even caused by stress and/or emotional/psychological factors.

psychotic episode   loss of contact with conventional reality marked by hallucinations and delusional thinking.

qi gong   working with the breath and visual imagery to move energy through the body.

quid pro quo   getting something for giving something.

rapport   being on the same wavelength with another person emotionally, intellectually or both.

real self   the person you feel you actually are.

realistic   people who like doing and making things applying scientific principles. Sample occupations would be pilot, electrician, engineer, or construction worker.

reflective listening   another term for active listening.

reflexive reality   is reality that we can influence or even directly determine by virtue of our beliefs, perceptions and expectations (like a self-fulfilling prophecy).

reframing   the process of actively changing perspectives to create paradigm shifts.

representational system   method by which we encode information in our brain utilizing our five senses: visual, auditory, kinesthetic, gustatory, and olfactory.

reprisal   disciplinary action for raising an allegation of discrimination.

resilience   the ability to bounce back from severe trauma or loss. It can also be defined as the capacity to adapt successfully in the presence of risk and adversity.

resume   a concise personal history of your education, experience, and achievements to demonstrate that you are qualified for a job you seek.

retroactive interference   the phenomenon in which new learning interferes with previous learning.

road rage   irrational levels of anger while driving.

romantic love   feelings for another that combine intimacy and passion but lacks commitment.

savoring   the awareness of pleasure that comes from paying deliberate conscious attention to your experience of pleasure in the moment.

schema   an equivalent term for paradigm, a way of seeing things.

schizophrenia   a severe disorder of thought and emotions where individuals have difficulty differentiating traditional reality from their own internal fantasies and fears.

selective attention   the focusing of consciousness on a partial aspect of all we are capable of experiencing.

selective perception   the tendency to perceive that which we expect to be there.

self-control   the ability to defer gratification.

self-actualization   the achievement of Maslow's highest order of needs; experiencing extraordinarily high levels of fulfillment in one's life.

self-awareness   the ability to think about your own thoughts and notice your emotions and physiological processes.

self-concept   your paradigm about yourself reflected in how you might describe yourself.

self-efficacy   a perception of perceived competence. A combination of internal locus of control and proactivity.

self-esteem   a measure of how much you value yourself and feel useful and necessary in the world.

self-talk   the running commentary that goes on in your head during the course of the day.

self-worth   the degree to which you feel worthwhile as a human being within the standards of your culture.

sensation   the process of receiving stimuli from our surroundings.

serotonin   a neurotransmitter that when maintained at healthy levels helps you to stay relaxed, sleep well, and have less sensitivity to pain.

service learning   the combination of community service and classroom instruction with a focus on critical, reflective thinking as well as personal and civic responsibility.

sexual harassment   unwelcome sexual advances, requests for sexual favors and other verbal or physical conduct of a sexual nature, especially when it affects an individual's employment or interferes with an individual's work.

signature strengths   those behaviors and traits which characterize the presence of a virtue in an individual's character and which can be developed by exercising proactive choice; not the same as talents.

social   persons who like to work with people especially in helping relationships. Sample occupations would be social worker, counselor, teacher, and health care workers.

social support   having meaningful connections to others helps people resist stress.

spurious correlation   the human tendency to perceive a correlation or relationship between things that really does not exist.

SQ4R   a method for studying which consists of the following steps: survey, question, read, recite, review and reflect.

strength training   exercise that builds, strengthens, and maintains muscle capacity and balance.

stress   anything that requires an adaptive response on the part of the organism; anything that requires you to respond or to make a change or an adjustment.

stress hardiness   the ability to resist the negative effects of stress through exercising the attitudes of control, commitment, and challenge.

stress mastery   the weaving of stress reduction techniques into the fabric of your life in a way that adds time, increases awareness, and cultivates wisdom.

stress sensitization   the tendency to respond to stress in the same way that we respond to an allergy, that is, the body overreacts to minor stresses as if they were major ones.

substance abuse   excessive use of substances (usually alcohol or other drugs) that alter a person's mood and/or behavior and may lead to social, physical, emotional, and job-related problems.

SWOOP   is an acronym for Success, Wish, Outcome, Obstacle and Plan, a five-stage visualization technique derived from MCII for enhancing motivation and volition.

sympathetic nervous system   a branch of the autonomic nervous system that mobilizes your body for action via the fight/flight response.

synapse   the space between neurons where one neuron communicates with another.

synchronicity   refers to meaningful coincidences and also implies that events in our lives are connected in a way that is beyond our material measuring devices.

synergy   the result of interdependence, which is more than the individual contributions of the participants.

tai chi   a meditative practice that consists of a slow series of movements coordinated with the breath; a moving meditation.

talent   any recurring pattern of thought, feeling or behavior that can be productively applied and can be developed into a strength.

technoference   refers to the intrusion of cell phones, social media messages and other hand-held devices on the quality of relationships and interpersonal communication.

test anxiety   involves being so anxious or phobic about taking a test that it can interfere with test performance.

testwiseness   developing test sophistication. It involves learning strategies for guessing that can help increase the likelihood of picking the right answer, particularly on multiple choice exams.

theory X   leader views workers as people who dislike work and have to be closely supervised.

theory Y   leader views workers as people who like their work, are motivated, and are productive, and willing to learn.

thought stopping   a technique used to interrupt unwanted thoughts by snapping a rubber band worn on the wrist to interrupt angry, obsessive or irrational thoughts and using the pain as a reminder to utilize cognitive restructuring.

time affluence   refers to being rich in free time and is associated with lower stress and higher levels of well-being.

traits   a psychological characteristic exemplified by consistent behaviors across time, place, and situations.

transformational leadership   engagement between leader and others that elevates each other to higher levels of motivation and morality; share common purposes and focuses on high level intrinsic needs; followers identify with the leader.

transpersonal psychology   school of psychology which explores the overlap between the realms of psychology and spirituality.

triggers   an event that initiates or sets off another event.

Type A personality   individuals who tend to be very hard driving, achievement oriented, compulsive, overly concerned with time pressure and easy to anger.

Type B personality   individuals who are laid back, easygoing, and less concerned with time.

unconditional positive regard   occurs when a parent demonstrates acceptance of a child as having intrinsic merit regardless of their behavior at the moment.

unconscious mind   the part of the mind containing aspects of our functioning of which we are totally unaware. Also referred to as the nonconscious mind.

undoing   theory which proposes that positive emotions can literally function as an antidote to undo the physiological effects of negative emotions.

values   a core principle, standard or quality considered desirable.

vasopressin   a hormone secreted by the posterior lobe of the pituitary gland, which for men facilitates bonding in romantic relationships.

Vesuvius effect   a cathartic expression of anger where the individual explodes just like a volcano.

virtues   strengths that are valued in every culture, valued in their own right, and are changeable by choice and exercise of will.

vision quest   a search for, or recognition of an aspect of your destiny that will aid you in deciding how to *move* forward with your life.

visual   our vision represented in mental pictures.

visualization   a time-honored method of deliberately using imagery, visual or otherwise, to alter your feelings, your behavior, and even your physiology.

volition   the skills and know-how to follow through and complete a plan of action.

warrior's stance   the ability to maintain a relaxed and balanced posture with an alert focus of attention on the present moment.

well-being = happiness + meaning: a state of health and life satisfaction combined with a sense of purpose.

wellness   well-being as an integration of the mind, body, and spirit; encompasses many components of human functioning such as relationships, exercise, nutrition, spirituality, and stress mastery.

win-lose   a paradigm of interpersonal interactions where the goal is to compete and maximize your gains without regard to the other participants.

win-win   a paradigm of interpersonal interactions where the goal is to find a solution that satisfies the needs of everyone involved beyond mere compromise.

win-win or no deal   a paradigm of interpersonal interactions where the parties agree that if they cannot find a solution that is mutually beneficial then there is no deal.

wishstorming   basically brainstorming about what you would wish for if you had an unlimited supply of wishes.

witnessing stance   the ability to stand apart from ourselves to view ourselves from the outside.

yesable proposal   an aspect of your position, that, if stated as a direct question, it would be easy for the other side to answer yes.

yin/yang   in East Asian thought, the two complementary forces or principles that make up all aspects and phenomena of life. Yin is female; yang is male.

"you" statement   a statement which typically involves pointing the finger at, that is blaming another person.

References

Aagaard, J. (2015). Mobile devices, interaction and distraction: A qualitative exploration of absent presence. *AI & Society*. DOI: 10.1007/S00146-015-0638-Z

Aaron, A., Norman, C., Aaron E., McKenna, C., & Heyman, R. (2000). Couples shared participation in novel and arousing activities and experienced relationship quality. *Journal of Personality and Social Psychology, 78*, 273–283.

Abascal, J. R., Brucato, L., & Brucato, D. (2001). *Stress Mastery: The Art of Coping Gracefully*. Upper Saddle River, N.J.: Prentice Hall Press.

Abel, E. & Kruger, M. (2010). Smile intensity in photographs predicts longevity. *Psychological Science, 20*, 1–3.

Abramson, L., Alloy, L., Hankin, B., Clements, C., Zhu, L., & Hogan, M. 2000). Optimistic cognitive style and invulnerability to depression. In J. Gillham (Ed.), *The Science of Optimism and Hope* (pp. 75–98). Philadelphia, PA: Templeton Foundation Press.

Abramson, M., Seligman, M., & Teasdale, J. (1978). Learned Helplessness in Humans: Critique and Reformulation. *Journal of Abnormal Psychology, 87*, 49–74.

Achtenberg, J. (1985). *Imagery in Healing*. Boston: New Science Library.

Ader, R. & Cohen, N. (1975). Behaviorally conditioned immunosuppression. *Psychosomatic Medicine, 37* (4), 333–340.

Ader, R. & Cohen, N. (1982). Behaviorally conditioned immunosuppression and murine systemic lupus erythematosus. *Science, 2315* (4539), 1534–1536.

Adler, A. (1928). *Understanding Human Nature*. London: Allen & Unwin.

Adler, R. & Towne, N. (1993). *Looking Out/Looking In*. San Diego, CA.: Harcourt Brace Jovanovich.

Adriaanse, M., Oettingen, G., Gollwitzer, P., Hennes, P., de Ridder, D., & De Wit, J. (2010). When planning is not enough: Fighting unhealthy snacking habits by mental contrasting with implementation intentions (MCII). *European Journal of Social Psychology, 40*(7), 1277–1293.

Ainsworth, M. (1973). The development of infant-mother attachment. In B.M. Caldwell & H.N. Ricciuti (Eds.), *Review of Child Development Research* (Vol. 3, pp. 1–94). Chicago, IL: University of Chicago Press.

Ainsworth, M., Bell, S., & Stayton, D. (1992). Infant-mother attachment and social development: "Socialization" as a product of reciprocal responsiveness to signals. In M. Woodhead, R. Carr, & P. Light (Eds.), *Becoming a Person* (pp. 30–55). London: Routledge.

Aknin, L., Norton, M., & Dunn, E. (2009). From Wealth to Well-Being? Money Matters but less than People Think. *Journal of Positive Psychology*, No. 6. 523–527.

Album, M. (1997). *Tuesdays with Morrie*. New York: Doubleday.

Alberti, R. & Emmons, M. (1974). *Your Perfect Right*. California: Impact Press.

Alexander, C., Swanson, G., Rainforth, M., Carlilse, T., Todd, C., & Oates, R. (1993). Effects of the Transcendental Meditation Program on Stress Reduction, Health, and Employee Development: A Prospective Study in two Occupational Settings. *Anxiety, Stress and Coping, 6*, 245–262.

Allred, K.D., & Smith, T.W. (1989). The Hardy Personality: Cognitive and Physiological Responses to Evaluative Threat. *Journal of Personality and Social Psychology, 56*, 257–266.

Allsoe, K., Hundrup, V., Thomsen, J., & Olser, M. (2010). Psychosocial Work Environment and Risk of Ischemic Heart Disease in Women: The Danish Nurse Cohort Study. *Occupational and Environmental Medicine, 67*, 503–531.

Altman, I. & Taylor, D. (1973). *Social Penetration: The Development of Interpersonal Relationships.* Oxford, England: Holt, Rinehart & Winston.

American Institute of Stress (AIS). *http://www .stress.org/job.htm.*

American Psychological Association (APA). (2007) Stress in America Survey. *http://www.apa.org/ release/stressproblem.html*

American Psychological Association (APA). (2017) Stress in America Survey. *http://www.apa.org/ release/stressproblem.html*

Anderson, N. (2004). *Work with Passion: How to Do What You Love for a Living.* Novato, CA.: New World Library.

Anderson, R., & Radley, J. (2014). Aging and HPA status predict Prefrontal Deficits. *Journal of Neuroscience.* 34(25) 8387–8397.

Anderson, S. M. (1998). *Service Learning: A National Strategy for Youth Development.* Position paper issued by the Task Force on Education Policy. Washington, D. C. Institute for Communitarian Policy Studies, George Washington University.

Anderson, C., Shibuya, A., Ihori, N., Swing, E., Bushman, B., Sakamoto, A., Rothstein, H., & Saleem, M. (2010). Violent Video Game Effects on Aggression, Empathy and Prosocial Behavior in Eastern and Western countries: A meta-analytic review. *Psychological Bulletin,* 13(6), 151–173.

Andreas, C., & Andreas, S. (1989). *Heart of Mind: Engaging your Inner Power to Change with Neuro-Linguistic Programming.* Moab, Utah: Real People Press.

Andreas, G., Tennat, C., Hewsen, D., & Schonell, M. (1979). The Relation of Social Factors to Physical and Psychiatric Illness. *American Journal of Epidemiology,* 109, 186–204.

Antonucci, T., & Jackson, J. (1983). Physical health and self-esteem. *Family Community Health,* 6 (2), 1–9.

Ardell, D. (1975, April). Meet John Travis, Doctor of Well-Being. *Prevention Magazine.*

Ardell, D. (1986). *High Level Wellness.* Berkeley: Ten Speed Press.

Argyle, M. (1987) *The Psychology of Happiness.* London: Methuen.

Argyle, M. (1987) *The Psychology of Happiness (2nd Ed.).* East Sussex, England: Routledge.

Ariely, D. (2008). *Predictably Irrational.* New York: Harper Collins

Ariely, D., Norton, M., & Frost, J. (2007). Less is More: The Lure of Ambiguity or why Familiarity breeds Contempt. *Journal of Personality and Social Psychology,* Vol 92. No.1 97–105.

Aspinwall, L. C., Taylor, S. E. (1992). Modeling Cognitive Adaptation: A Longitudinal Investigation of the Impact of Individual Differences and Coping on College Adjustment and Performance. *Journal of Personality and Social Psychology,* 63, 989–1063.

Astin, A. W., & Sax, L. J. (1998). How Undergraduates are Affected by Service Participation. *Journal of College Student Development.* 39(3), 251–263.

Astin, A. W., Vogelgesang, L. J., Ikeda, E. K., & Yee, J. A. (2000). How Service Learning affects Students. Los Angeles: UCLA Higher Education Research Institute. *ERIC Ed.* No. 445, 577.

Atlas, L. & Wager, T. (2012). How Expectations Shape Pain. *NeuroScience Letters.* Vol. 520. No. 2 140–148.

Athenstaedt, U., Haas, E., & Schwab, S. (2004). *Gender Role Self-Concept and Gender-Typed Communication-Behavior in Mixed Sex and Same Sex Dyads.* Netherlands: Springer.

Atkinson, B. (Jan/Feb, 2014). The Great Deception-We're less in control than we think. *The Psychotherapy Networker,* Vol. 38, No. 1, 27–33/50–51.

Atwater, E. (1986). *Human Relations.* New York: Prentice Hall.

Auerbach, S. M., & Grambling, S. E. (1998). *Stress Management: Psychological Foundations.* Upper Saddle River, N.J.: Prentice Hall

Auerbach, S. M., Martelli, M., & Mercuri, L. G. (1983). Anxiety Information, Interpersonal Impacts and Adjustment to a Stressful Health Care Situation. *Journal of Personality and Social Psychology,* 44, 1284–1296.

Averill, J. R. (1983). Studies on Anger and Aggression: Implications for Theories of Emotion. *American Psychologist, 38, 1145–1160.*

Avolio, B., Jakari, G., Wernsing, T. & Walumbwa, F. (2010). What is Authentic Leadership Development? In Linley, P.A., Harrington, S. & Garcia, N. (Eds.), *Oxford Handbook of Positive Psychology and Work.* (pp 39–51). New York: Oxford University Press, Inc.

Avruch, K. & Black, P. W. (1993). Conflict Resolution in Inter-cultural settings. In Sandole, D. & Van der Merwe, H. (Eds.). *Conflict Resolution Theory and Practice: Integration and Application.* (pp. 131–145). Manchester: Manchester University Press

Bach, G., & Wyden, P. (1968). *The Intimate Enemy.* New York: Avon.

Bandler, R., & Grinder, J. (1975). *The Structure of Magic I.* Palo Alto, California: Science and Behavior Books.

Bandura, A. (1965). Influence of model's reinforcement contingencies on the acquisition of imitative behaviors. *Journal of Personality and Social Psychology,* 1, 589–595.

Bandura, A. (1977). Self-Efficacy: Toward a theory of behavioral change. *Psychological Review*, 84, 191–215.

Bandura, A. (1986). *Social Foundations of Thought and Action.* New York: Prentice Hall.

Bandura, A. (1997). *Self-Efficacy: The Exercise of Control. New York: Freeman.*

Banks, P., Present, D. & Steiner, P. (1983). *The Chrohn's Disease and Ulcerative Colitis Fact Book.* New York, New York: Simon & Schuster.

Banyon Partners. (2011). 2011 in Review: The Market. *Quarterly Outlook.*

Barefoot, J. R., Dahlstrom, W. G., & Williams, R. B. (1983). Hostility, CHD Incidence and Total Mortality: A 25 Year Follow-up Study of 255 Physicians. *Psychosomatic Medicine, 45, 559–563.*

Barker, L., Edwards, R., Gaines, C., Gladney, K., & Holley, F. (1981) An Investigation of Proportional Time Spent in Various Activities by College Students. *Journal of Applied Communication Research,* 8, 101–109.

Barkow, J. (1997). Happiness in evolutionary perspective. In N.L. Segal, G.E. Weisfeld, & C.C. Weisfeld (Eds.), *Uniting Psychology and Biology:*

Integrating Perspectives on Human Development (pp. 397–418). Washington, D.C.: American Psychological Association.

Barnett T. P. (March, 2003). The Pentagon's New Map- War and Peace in the 21st Century. *Esquire,* Vol. 139, Issue 3.

Bass, B.M. (1998). *Transformational Leadership: Industrial, Military and Educational Impact.* Mahwah, New Jersey: Lawrence Erlbaum.

Batson, C. D. (1991). *The Altruism Question: Toward a Social-Psychological Answer.* Hillsdale, New Jersey: Lawrence Erlbaum Publishers.

Batson, C., Ahmed, N., Lishner, D., & Tsang, J. (2005). Empathy and altruism. In C.R. Snyder & S.J. Lopez (Eds.) *Handbook of Positive Psychology.* (pp. 485–498). New York: Oxford University Press.

Batson, C., Duncan, B., Ackerman, P., Buckley, T., & Birch, K. (1981). Is empathic emotion a source of altruistic motivation? *Journal of Personality and Social Psychology,* 40, 290–302.

Baumeister, R. F. (1996). Should Schools Try to Boost Self-Esteem? Beware the Dark Side. *American Educator,* 20, 14–19.

Baumeister, R. F. (August, 2000). Psychology of evil and violence. *Paper presented at the 110th Annual Convention of the American Psychological Association,* Chicago, IL.

Baumeister, R., Campbell, J., Krueger, J., & Vohs, K. (2003). Does High Self-Esteem Cause Better Performance, Interpersonal Success, Happiness or Healthier Lifestyles? *Psychological Science in the Public Interest.* Vol.4 No.1. 1–44.

Baumeister, R., Gailliot, M., DeWall, C., & Oaten, M. (2006). Self-Regulation and Personality: How interventions increase regulatory success, and how depletion moderates the effects of traits on behavior. *Journal of Personality,* 74, 1773–1801.

Baumeister, R., Vohs, K., & Tice, D. (2007). The strength model of self-control. *Current Directions in Psychological Science,* 16, 351–355.

Baumrind, D. (1991). Effective Parenting during the Early Adolescent Transition. In Cowen, P. & Hetherington, E. (Eds.). *Advances in Family Research.* (pp. 28–31), Vol. 2, Hillsdale, N. J.: Lawrence Erlbaum Associates.

Beck, A. (1970). Cognitive Therapy: Nature and Relation to Behavior Therapy. *Behavior Therapy,* 1, 84–200.

Beck, A. (1979). *Cognitive Therapy and Emotional Disorders.* New York: New American Library.

Becklen, R. & Cervone, D. (1983). Selective looking and the noticing of unexpected events. *Memory and Cognition,* 11, 601–608.

Benjamin, L.T., Cavell, T.A., & Shallenberger, W.R. (1987). Staying with Initial Answers on Objective Tests: Is It a Myth? In M.E. Ware & R. J. Millard (Eds.). *Handbook on Student Development: Advising, Career Development and Field Placement.* (pp. 45–52), Hillsdale, N. J.: Lawrence Erlbaum Associates..

Bennis, W. G. (1989). *On Becoming a Leader.* Reading, PA.: Addison Wesley.

Benson, H. (1976). *The Relaxation Response.* New York: Avon Books.

Benson, H. (1979). *The Mind-Body Effect.* New York: Simon & Schuster.

Benson, H. (1985). *Beyond the Relaxation Response.* Berkeley, California: Berkeley Books.

Benson, H. (1997). *Timeless Healing: The Power and Biology of Belief.* New York: Simon & Schuster.

Benson, H. (2000). *The Relaxation Response.* New York: Bantam Books.

Bergeman, C., Chipuer, H., Plomin, R., Pederson, N., McClearn, G., & Nesselroade, J. (1993). Genetic and environmental effects on openness to experience, agreeableness, and conscientiousness.: An adoption/twin study. *Journal of Personality,* 61, 159–179.

Berk, I. S., Tan, S. A., Nehlsen-Cannarella, S. L, Napier, B. J., Lee, J. W., Hubbard, R. W. Lewis, J. E., Eby, W. C., & Fry, W. F. (1988). Humor Associated Laughter Decreases Cortisol and Increases Spontaneous Lymphocyte Blastogenesis. *Clinical Research,* 36, 435A

Bernasek, A. (Feb., 2002). The Friction Economy. American Business Just Got the Bill for the Terrorist Attacks: $ 151 Billion a Year. *Fortune,* 145, 104.

Bernstein, R. & Edwards, T. (2008, August, 14th). An older and more diverse nation by Midcentury. *U.S Census Bureau News. http://www.census.gov/*

Press-release/www/eleaes/aschides/population/012496 .html

Berns, G., Chappelow, J., Zink, C., Pagnoni, G., Martin-Skurski, M. & Richards, J. (2005). Neurobiological correlates of social conformity and independence during mental rotation. *Biological Psychiatry,* 58, No. 3.

Berns, G. (2010). *Iconoclast.* Boston, MA: Harvard Business Press.

Birnbaum, G., Reis, H., Mizrahi, M., Kanat-Maymon, Y., Sass, O., & Granovski-Milner, C. (2016). Intimately connected: The importance of partner responsiveness for experiencing sexual desire. *Journal of Personality and Social Psychology,* 111(4), 530–546.

Black, S. & Bevan, S. (1992). At the movies with Buss and Durkee: A natural experiment on film violence. *Aggressive Behavior* 18, 37–45.

Bolles, R. (2002). Free On-line Tests Dealing with Careers. *http://www.JobHuntersBible.com.*

Bolles, R. (2006). What Color is Your Parachute? Berkeley, CA.: Ten Speed Press.

Bolles, R. (2014). *What Color is Your Parachute? 2015 Edition.* Berkeley, CA.: Ten Speed Press.

Bolt, M. (2004). *Pursuing Human Strengths: A Positive Psychology Guide.* New York: Worth Publishers.

Bonner, R. L., & Rich, A. R. (1991). Predicting Vulnerability to Hopelessness: A Longitudinal Analysis. *The Journal of Nervous and Mental Disease,* 179, 129–32.

Bourne, E. J. (1990). *The Anxiety and Phobia Workbook.* Oakland, CA.: New Harbinger Publications.

Bowlby, J. (1951). *Maternal Care and Mental Health.* Geneva, Switzerland: World Health Organization

Bowlby, J. (1969). *Attachment and Loss: Vol I. Attachment.* New York: Basic Books.

Bowlby, J. (1973) *Attachment and Loss: Vol. 2. Separation: Anxiety and Anger.* New York: Basic Books.

Bowlby, J. (1980) *Attachment and Loss: Vol. 3. Loss, Sadness and Depression.* New York: Basic Books.

Bowlby, J. (1988) *A Secure Base: Parent-Child Attachment and Healthy Human Development.* New York: Basic Books.

Boyett, J. H., & Snyder, D. P. (1998). Twenty-First Century Workplace Trends. *On the Horizon*. 6 (2), 4–9.

Boyke, J., Driemeyer, J., Gaser, C., Buchel, C. & May, A. (2008). Induced brain structure changes in the elderly. *The Journal of Neuroscience*, 28(28), 7031–7035.

Brainard, L., & Litan, R. E. (April, 2004). *"Offshoring" Service Jobs: Bane or Boom and What to Do?* Brookings Institution Policy Brief, No. 132.

Breathnach, S. B. (1995). *Simple Abundance: A Daybook of Comfort and Joy*. New York: Warner Books.

Brehm, B. (1998). *Stress Management. Increasing Your Stress Resistance*. New York: Longman.

Brennan, K. & Shaver, P. (1995). Dimensions of adult attachment, affect regulation, and romantic relationship functioning. *Personality and Social Psychology Bulletin*, 23, 23–31.

Breslow, L. (1983). The Potential of Health Promotion. In D. Mechanic (Ed.). *Handbook of Health, Health Care and the Health Professions*. New York: Free Press.

Brickman, P. & Campbell, D. (1971). Hedonic relativism and planning the good society. In M.H. Appley (Ed.), *Adaptation-level Theory* (pp. 287–305). New York: Academic Press.

Brickman, P., Coates, D., & Janoff-Bulman, J. R. (1978). Lottery Winners and Accident Victims: Is Happiness Relative? *Journal of Personality and Social Psychology*, 36, 917–927.

Brockner, J., & Guare, J. (1983). Improving the Performance of Low Self-Esteem Individuals: An Attributional Approach. *Academy of Managerial Psychology*, 26, 642–656.

Brosnan, S. & deWaal, F. (2003). Monkeys reject unequal pay, *Nature*, 425, 297–299.

Brown, J. D. (1998). *The Self*. New York: McGraw-Hill.

Brown, J. D. (2007). *The Self*. New York: Psychology Press.

Brown, J. P. (1991). Staying Fit and Staying Well: Physical Fitness as a Moderator of Life Stress. *Journal of Personality and Social Psychology*, 60, 555–561.

Brown, S. L., Nesse, R. M., Vinokur, A. D., & Smith, D. M. (2003). Providing Social Support May be more Beneficial than Receiving it: Results from a Prospective Study of Mortality. *Psychological Science*, 14, 320–327.

Bruhn, J. & Wolf, S. (1979). *The Roseta Story*. Norman, OK: University of Oklahoma Press.

Bruhn, J. & Wolf, S. (1993). *The Power of Clan: The Influence of Human Relationships in Heart Disease*. New Brunswick, N.J.: Transaction Publishers.

Bruner, J., & Postman, L. (1949). On the Perception of Incongruity: A Problem. *Journal of Personality*, 18, 206–233.

Brunwasser, S. & Gillham, J. (2008). *A Meta-Analytic Review of the Penn Resiliency Programme* (paper presented at the Society for Prevention Research), San Francisco, CA. May, 2008.

Bryant, F. (2003). Savoring Beliefs Inventory (SBI): A Scale for measuring beliefs about savoring. *Journal of Mental Health*, 12, 175–196.

Bryant, F. (2006). The *Process of Savoring: A New Model of Positive Experience*. Mahwah, N.J.: Erlbaum

Bryant, F. B., Veroff, J. *Savoring: A Process Model for Positive Psychology*. Unpublished manuscript.

Brydon, L, Magid, K., & Steptoe, A. (2006). Platelets, coronary heart disease, and stress. *Brain, Behavior and Immunity*, 20, 113–119.

Buchanan, G., Gardenswartz, C., & Seligman, M. (1999). Physical health following a cognitive behavioral intervention. *Prevention and Treatment*, 2.

Buckingham, M., & Clifton, D. (2001). *Now, Discover Your Strengths*. New York: The Free Press.

Buettner, D. (2017, Nov.). The world happiest places. *National Geographic*, 30–59.

Buettner, D. (2017). *Blue Zones of Happiness*. Washington, D.C.: National Geographic Partners.

Burger, J. M. (2004). *Personality* (6th Ed.). Belmont, CA.: Wadsworth/Thomson Publishers.

Buscaglia, L. (1982). *Love*. New York: Ballantine Books.

Bushman, B. (2002). Does Venting Anger Feed or Extinguish the Flame? Catharsis, Rumination, Distraction, Anger and Aggressive Responding. *Personality and Social Psychology Bulletin*, 28, 724–731.

Bushman, B. & Phillips, C. (2001). If the television program bleeds, memory for the advertisement recedes. *Current Directions in Psychological Science,* 2, 43–47.

Byham, W. (1999). *Landing the Job You Want.* New York: Crown Publishing Group.

Byers, E. S. (2005). Relationship satisfaction and sexual satisfaction: A longitudinal study of individuals in long-term relationships. *Journal of Sex Research,* 42(2), 113–118.

Cacioppo, J., Hawkley, L., Crawford, L., Ernst, J., Burleson, R., Kowalewski, W., Kowalewski, E., Van Cauter, E., & Berntson, G. (2002). Loneliness and Health: Potential Mechanisms. *Psychosomatic Medicine,* 64, 407–417.

Cacioppo, J. & Patrick, W. (2008). *Loneliness: Human Nature and the Need for Social Connection.* New York: W.W. Norton.

Callahan, C., Mchorney, C., & Murrow, C., Eds. (2003). Determinants of Successful Aging: Developing an Integrated Research Agenda for the 21st Century. *Annals of Internal Medicine,* 139(8)

Campbell, J. (1959). *Masks of God: Creative Mythology.* New York: The Viking Press.

Campbell, J. (1988). Joseph Campbell and The Power of Myth with Bill Moyers. *A production of Apostrophe S. Productions in association with Public Affairs Television Inc. and Alvin H. Perlmutter, Inc.* Audio CD version, (2001) St. Paul, Minnesota: HighBridge Co.

Cameron, N., Champagne, F., Parent, C., Fish, E., Ozaki-Kurada, K., & Meany, M. (2005). The programming of individual differences in defensive responses and reproductive strategies in the rat through variations in maternal care. *NeuroScience and Biobehavioral Reviews,* 29, 843–865.

Canfield, J., & Hansen, M. (1995). *The Aladdin Factor.* New York: The Berkeley Publishing Group.

Cannon, T., Kaprio, J., Lonnquist, J., Huttunen, M., & Koskenvuo, M. (1998). The Genetic Epidemiology of Schizophrenia in a Finnish Twin Cohort. *Archives of General Psychiatry,* 55, 67–754.

Cantor, J. (1999). Review of the book Children and media violence. *Journal of International Communication* , 6(1). *http://www.mnstate.edu/gunarat/jicreviews6-1.htm*

Cantor, J. (2009). *Conquer CyberOverload: Get more Done, Boost your Creativity and Reduce Stress.* Cyber Outlook Press.

Capaldi, D. & Patterson, G. (1996). Can violent offenders be distinguished from frequent offenders? Predictions from childhood to adolescence. *Journal of Research in Crime and Delinquency,* 33, 206–231.

Carducci, B. (1999). The Pocket Guide to Making Successful Small Talk. New York: Mass Market Publishing.

Carducci, B. (1999). *Shyness; A Bold New Approach.* New York: Harper Collins

Carpi, J. (Jan./Feb., 1996). Stress...Its Worse Than You Think. *Psychology Today,* 34–76.

Carter, T., & Gilovich, T. (2012). "I am What I do, Not What I Have:" The Differential Centrality of Experiential and Material Purchases to the Self. *Journal of Personality and Social Psychology.* 102 No. 2. 210–215.

Carvalha, A., Del Bel Cury, A., & Garcia, R. (2008). Prevalence of bruxism and emotional stress and the association between them in Brazilian police officers. *Brazilian Oral Research.* Vol. 22., No. 1

Carver, C. S., & Gaines, J. G. (1987). Optimism, Pessimism and Postpartum Depression. *Cognitive Therapy and Research,*11, 449–462.

Carver, C. S., Pozo, C., Harris, S.D., Noriega, V., Scheier, M. E., & Robinson, D. S.. (1993). How Coping Mediates the Effect of Optimism on Distress: A Study of Women with Early Stage Breast Cancer. *Journal of Personality and Social Psychology,* 65, 375–390.

Carver, C. S., & Scheier, M. E. (1999). Optimism. In C. R. Snyder (Ed.). *Coping: The Psychology of What Works.* (pp. 182–204). New York: Oxford University Press.

Castenada, C. (1998). *The Teachings of Don Juan: A Yaqui Way of Knowledge.* California: University of California Press.

Castenada, C. (1991). *Journey to Ixtlan: The Lessons of Don Juan.* New York: Simon & Schuster.

Chamber of Commerce of the U. S. (2004, April). *Special Report: Jobs, Trade, Sourcing and the Future of the American Workforce. http://www.uschamber .com/media/pdfs/outsourcing/pdf.*

Chamberlain, J. (July, 1998). Reaching Flow to Optimize Work and Play, *APA Monitor Online www.apa.org/monitor*. Washington, D.C.: American Psychological Association, Vol 29, No. 7.

Chang, E. (1996a). Evidence for the cultural specificity of pessimism in Asians vs. Caucasians: A test of a general negativity hypothesis. *Personality and Individual Differences*, 21, 819–822.

Chang, E. (2001a). A look at the coping strategies and styles of Asian Americans: Similar and different? In C.R. Snyder (Ed.). *Coping with Stress: Effective People and Processes* (pp. 222–239). New York: Oxford University Press.

Chetty, A., Friedman, K., Taravoch-Lahn, E., Kirby, E & colleagues. (2014). Stress and Glucocorticoids promote oliogodendrogenesis in the adult hippocampus. *Molecular Psychiatry. Doi:10.1038/mp2013.190*

Chiasson, C., & Hayes, L. (1993). The Effects of Subtle Differences between Listeners and Speakers on the Referential Speech of College Freshmen. *The Psychological Record*, 43, 13–24.

Chiu, A., Chon, S., & Kimball, A. (2003). Changes in the severity of acne vulgaris as affected by examination stress. *Archives of Dermatology*, Vol. 139, No. 7, 897–900.

Chopra, D. (1993). *Ageless Body, Timeless Mid: The Quantamal Alternative to Growing Old*. New York: Harmony Books.

Christakis, M. & Fowler, J. (2008). Dynamic spread of happiness in a large social network: Longitudinal analysis over 20 years in the Framington Heart Study. *British Medical Journal online*.

Christakis, M. & Fowler, J. (2014). Genome Wide Analysis reveals Genetic Similarities among Friends: Study finds truth to "friends are the family you choose." Science Daily, July 2014. www.Sciencedaily.com/releases/2014/07/14071415313htm>

Clark, D. & Watson, D. (1999). Temperament: A new paradigm for trait psychology. In L.A. Perwin & O.P. John (Eds.) *Handbook of Personality* (2nd Ed., pp. 399–423). New York: Guilford Press.

Clifton, D., & Harter, J. (2003). Strengths investment. In K.S. Cameron, J. E. Dalton, & R. E. Quinn (Eds.). *Positive Organizational Scholarship* (pp. 111–121). San Francisco, CA.: Barrett-Koehler.

Cohen, H. (1980). *You Can Negotiate Anything*. New York: Bantam Books

Cohen, S., Alper, C., Doyle, W., Treanor, J., & Turner, R. (2006). Positive emotional style predicts resistance to illness after experimental exposure to rhinovirus or influenza A virus. *Psychosomatic Medicine,* 68, 809–815.

Cohen, S., Doyle, W., Skoner, D., Rubin, B., Gualtney, J. (1997). Social Ties and Susceptibility to the Common Cold. *Journal of the American Medical Association,* 277. 1940–1944.

Cohen, S., Doyle, W., Turner, R., Alper, C., & Skoner, D. (2003). Emotional style and susceptibility to the common cold. *Psychosomatic Medicine,* 65, 652–657.

Cohen, S., & Edwards, J. (1989). Personality Characteristics as Moderators of the Relationship Between Stress and Disorder. In Neufeld, R. (Ed.). *Advances in the Investigation of Psychological Stress.* New York: Wiley and Sons.

Cohen, S., Frank, E., Doyle, W., Skoner, D., Rubin, B., & Gualtney, J. (1998). Types of stressors that increase susceptibility to the common cold in adults. *Health Psychology,* 17, 214–223.

Cohen, S., Tyrell, D., & Smith, A. (1991). Psychological stress and susceptibility to the common cold. *New England Journal of Medicine,* 325, 606–612.

Cohen, S., Tyrell, D., & Smith, A. (1993). Life events, perceived stress, negative affect and susceptibility to the common cold. *Journal of Personality and Social Psychology,* 64, 131–140.

Cohen, S., & Wills, T. A. (1985). Stress, Social Support and the Buffering Hypothesis. *Psychological Bulletin,* 98, 310–357.

Connelly, J. (2002). All together now. *Gallup Managerial Journal*, 2(1), 13–18.

Contrada, R. (1989). Type A behaviors, Personality Hardiness and Cardiovascular Responses to Stress. *Journal of Personality and Social Psychology,* 57. 895–903.

Coopersmith, S. (1967). *Antecedents of Self-Esteem.* San Francisco, CA.: Freeman Press

Coue', E. (1922). *Self-Mastery Through Conscious Auto-Suggestion*. London: Allen & Unwin.

Covey, S. (1991). *The Seven Habits of Highly Effective People*. New York: Simon & Schuster.

Covey, S., Merrill, A., & Merrill, R. (1994). *First Things First*. New York: Simon & Schuster.

Cousins, N. (1981). *Anatomy of An Illness as Perceived by the Patient*. New York: Bantam Books.

Cousins, N. (1983) *The Healing Heart*. New York: Norton Books.

Cozolino, L. (2014). *The Neuroscience of Human Relationships: Attachment and the Developing Social Brain*. New York, New York: W.W. Norton and Co.

Crane, D. R., Dollahit, D. C., Griffin, W., & Taylor, V. L. (1987). Diagnosing Relationships with Spatial Distance: An Empirical Test of a Clinical Principle. *Journal of Marital and Family Therapy*, 13, 307–318.

Crocker, J., & Carnavale, J., (Sept/Oct, 2013). Letting Go of Self-Esteem. *Scientific American Mind*. 27–33.

Crocker, J., Luhtanen, R. & Bouvrette, S. (2001). *Contingencies of Self Worth in College Students: Predicting Freshman Year Activities*. Unpublished manuscript, University of Michigan, Ann Arbor, Michigan.

Crocker, J. & Wolfe, C. T. (2001). Contingencies of Self-Worth. *Psychological Review*, 108, 593–623.

Csikszentmihalyi, M. (1990). *Flow: The Psychology of Optimal Experience*. New York: Harper & Row.

Csikszentmihalyi, M. (1993). *The Evolving Self: A Psychology for the Third Millennium*. New York: Harper Collins Publishers.

Cutuli, J., Chaplin, T., Gillham, J., Reivich, K. & Seligman, M. (2006). Preventing co-occuring depression symptoms in adolescents with conduct problems: The Penn Resiliency Program. *New York Academy of Science*, 1094, 282–286.

Daloz, L., Keen, C., Keen, J., & Parks, S. (1997). *Common Fire: Lives of Commitment in a Complex World*. New York: Beacon Press.

Danner, D., Snowden, D., & Friesen, W. (2001). Positive Emotions in Early Life and Longevity: Findings from the Nun Study. *Journal of Personality and Social Psychology*, 80, 804–813.

Dansky, K. H. (1996). The Effect of Group Mentoring on Career Outcomes. *Group and Organizational Management*. 21, 5–21.

David, C., & Kistner, J. (2006). Do positive self-perceptions have a dark side? *Journal of Abnormal Child Psychology*.

Davidson, R., & Kabat-Zinn, J. (2003). Alterations in brain and mind function produced by mindfulness meditation. *Psychosomatic Medicine*, 65, 564–570.

Davis, M. (1980). A multidimensional approach to individual differences in empathy. *Catalog of Selected Documents in Psychology*, 10, 85.

Davis, M., Eshelman, E.R., & McKay, M. (1988). *The Relaxation and Stress Reduction Workbook*. Oakland, California: New Harbinger Publications.

Dawes, R. M. (1994). *House of Cards: Psychology and Psychotherapy Built on Myth*. New York: Free Press.

DeCenzo, D. (1997). *Human Relations: Personal and Professional Development*. Upper Saddle River, N.J.: Prentice Hall.

Deci, E. L. (1995). *Why We Do What We Do: The Dynamics of Personal Autonomy*. New York: Putnam Books.

Deci, E. L. & Ryan, R. M. (1995). Human Autonomy: The Basis for True Self Esteem. In M. H. Kemis (Ed.), *Efficacy, Agency and Self Esteem* (pp 31–49). New York: Plenum.

Deci, E. L. & Ryan, R. M. (2000). The "what" and "why" of goal pursuits. Human needs and the self determination of behavior. *Psychological Inquiry*, 11, 227–268.

Deffenbacher, J. L., Oeting, E. R., & Lynch, R. S. (1994). Development of a Driving Anger Scale. *Psychological Reports*, 74, 83–91.

Dekoven, B. (2001). *Discover the Fun of Work*. Washington, D. C.: Greater Washington Society of Association Executives. *http://www.gwsae.org*.

Deinzer, R., Kleineidam, C., Stiller-Winkler, R., Idel, H., & Bachg, D. (2000) Prolonged reduction of salivary immunoglobulin A (slgA) after a major academic exam. *International Journal of Psychophysiology*, Vol. 37, No. 3, 219–232.

DeLoache, J., Choing, C., Sherman, K., Islam, N., Vanderborght, M., & Troseth, G. (2010). Do

Babies Learn from Baby Media? *Psychological Science*, 21, 1570–1574.

Dickerson, S., Gable, S., Irwin, M., Aziz, N., & Kemeny, M. (2009). Social-evaluative threat and proinflammatory cytokine regulation: An experimental laboratory investigation. *Psychological Science*, 20, 1237–1243.

Diener, E. (1984). Subjective well-being. *Psychological Bulletin*, 95(3), 542–575.

Diener, E., Ng, W., Harter, J., & Arora, R. (2010). Wealth and Happiness across the World: Material prosperity predates life evaluation; whereas psychosocial prosperity predicts positive feeling. *Journal of Personality and Social Psychology*, 99, No. 1, 52–61.

Dement, W., & Vaughan, C. (1999). *The Promise of Sleep: A Pioneer in Sleep Medicine Explores the Vital Connection Between Health, Happiness and a Good Night's Sleep.* California: Harcourt Press.

Diamond, J. (2005). *Collapse: How Societies Choose to Fail or Succeed.* New York, N. Y.: Penguin Group.

DiClemente, C., Fairhurst, S., & Piotrowski, N. (1995). Self-Efficacy and addictive behaviors. In J.E. Maddux (Ed.) *Self-Efficacy, Adaptation and Adjustment: Theory, Research and Application* (pp. 109–142). New York: Plenum.

Dillon, K., Baker, K., & Minchoff, B. (1985). Positive Emotional States and the Enhancement of the Immune System. *International Journal of Psychiatry.* Med 15: 13–18.

DiMarco, C. *(1997). Career* Transitions: A Journey of Survival and Growth. Scottsdale, Arizona: Gorsuch Scarisbrick Publishers.

Dobbs, L. (2004). *Exporting America: 'Why Corporate Greed is Shipping American Jobs Overseas.* New York, N. Y.: Warner Books.

Dollard, J., Miller, N. E., Doob, L. W., Mowrer, O. H., & Sears, R. R. (1939). *Frustration and Aggression.* New Haven, CT: Yale University Press.

Donne, J. (1995). *Poems and Prose.* New York: A.A. Knopf: Distributed by Random House.

Dorin, J. (2017). How to Keep the Passion Alive. *Scientific American Mind.* March/April,. 17.

Dossey, L. (1989). *Recovering the Soul.* New York: Random House.

Doyle, W., Gentile, D. & Cohen, S. (2006). Emotional style, nasal cytokines and illness expression after experimental rhinovirus exposure. *Brain, Behavior and Immunity*, 20, 175–181.

Draganski, B., Gaser, C., Kempermann, G., Kuhn, H., Winkler, J., Buchel, C., & May, A. (2006). Temporal and spatial dynamics of brain structure changes during extensive learning. *The Journal of Neuroscience*, 26 (23), 6314–6317.

Druskat, V., Bastista-Foguet, J., & Wolff, S. (2011). The Influence of Team Leader Competencies on the Emergence of Emotionally Competent Team Norms. *Paper presented at the Annual Academy of Management Conference,* San Antonio, Texas, August, 2011.

Dubrin, A. (1999). *Human Relations: Personal and Professional Development*, 5th Ed. Upper Saddle River, N.J.: Prentice Hall.

Duckworth, A., Grant, H., Loew, B., Oettingen, G., & Gollwitzer, P. (2011). Self-regulation strategies improve self-discipline in adolescents: Benefits of mental contrasting and implementation intentions. *Educational Psychology: An International Journal of Experimental Educational Psychology*, 31(1), 17–26.

Duckworth, A., Peterson, C., Matthews, M. & Kelly, D. (2007). Grit: Perseverance and passion for long term goals. *Journal of Personality and Social Psychology.* Vol. 92, No. 6 , 1087–1101.

Dunn, E., Aknin, L. & Norton, M. (2008). Spending money on others promotes happiness. *Science*, 319, 1687–1688.

Dunn, E. & Norton, M. (2012). *Happy Money: The Science of Smarter Spending.* New York: Simon & Schuster.

Dunn, H. L. (1961). *High Level Wellness.* Arlington, Virginia: R.W. Beatty.

Dusek, J., Out, H., Wohlwheter, A., Mang, B., Zerbini, L, Joseph, M., Benson, H. & Libermann, T. (2008). Genomic counter-stress changes induced by the relaxation response. PloS One3 e2576.

Dutton, D., & Aron, P. (1974). Some evidence for heightened sexual attraction under conditions of high anxiety. *Journal of Personality and Social Psychology*, 30, 510–517.

Dutton, D., Saunders, K., Starzomski, A., & Bartholomew, K. (1994) Intimacy-anger and insecure attachment as precursors of abuse in intimate relationships. *Journal of Applied Social Psychology, 24,* 1367–1386.

Dutton, J. & Glynn, M. (2009). Positive Organizational Scholarship. In Barling, J. & Cooper, C. (Eds.). *The Sage Handbook of Organizational Behavior* (pp. 693–712). Vol. 1, Micro Approaches. Los Angeles, CA: Sage.

Dweck, C. S. (1999). *Self-Theories: Their Role in Motivation, Personality and Development.* Philadelphia: Psychology Press.

East, S. & Tinker, B. (Oct. 9, 2015). How to think straight in the age of information overload. *CNN Health: Vital Signs. http://www.cnn.com*

Easterbrook, G. (2003). *The Progress Paradox: How Life Gets Better while People Feel Worse.* New York: Random House.

Ebbesen, E., Duncan, B., & Konecni, V. (1975). Effects of content of verbal aggression on future verbal aggression: A field experiment. *Journal of Experimental Social Psychology, 11,* 192–204.

Eckstein, D., & Goldman, A. (2001). The couple's gender-based communication questionnaire (CGCQ). *The Family Journal: Counseling and Therapy for Couples and Families, 10,* 1, 101–108.

Edwards, R., & Hamilton, M. (2004). You need to understand my gender role: An empirical test of Tannen's model of gender and communication. *Sex Roles, 50* (7–8), 491–504.

Ehrenreich, B. (2009). *Bright Sided: How the Relentless Promotion of Positive Thinking has Undermined America.* New York: Holt.

Elias, M. (November, 11, 2002). A generous spirit may yield generous life span. *USA Today.* p. 4A

Elkind, M. (2004). Diagnosis and classification of primary headache disorders. In: *Standards of Care for Headache Diagnosis and Treatment* (pp. 4–18). Chicago, IL: National Headache Foundation.

Elliot, W. (2001). Cyclic and circadian variations in cardiovascular events. *American Journal of Hypertension, 14,* 291–295.

Ellis, A. (1975). *A New Guide to Rational Living.* California: Wilshire Books.

Ellis, A., & Harper, R. (1961). *A Guide to Rational Living.* California: Wilshire Books.

Ellis, A., & Knaus, W. J. (1977). *Overcoming Procrastination.* New York: Signet, New American Library.

Emler, N. (2001). *Self-Esteem: The costs and causes of low self worth.* York, PA: York Publishing Services.

Emmons, R. A., & McCullough, M. E. (2003). Counting Blessings vs. Burdens: An Experimental Investigation of Gratitude and Subjective Well-Being in Daily Life. *Journal of Personality and Social Psychology, 84,* 377–389.

Enright, R. D. (2001). *Forgiveness is a Choice: A Step by Step Process for Resolving Anger and Restoring Hope.* Washington, D. C.: American Psychological Association.

Epstein, R. (2011). How to best fight stress: Measuring and ranking relevant competencies. Presented at the annual meeting of the Western Psychological Association, Los Angeles, CA, April 2011.

Epstein, S. (1992). Coping Ability, Negative Self-Evaluation, and Overgeneralization: Experiment and Theory. *Journal of Personality and Social Psychology, 62,* 826–836.

Ericsson, K. & Ward, P. (2007). Capturing the naturally occurring superior performance of experts in the laboratory. *Current Directions in Psychological Science, 16,* 346–350.

Estrada, C., Isen, A., & Young, M. (1997). Positive affect facilitates integration of information and decreases anchoring in reasoning among physicians. *Organizational Behavior and Human Decision Processes, 72,* 117–135.

Eyler, J., Giles, D., & Braxton, J. (1997). The Impact of Service Learning on College Students. *Michigan Journal of Community Service Learning, 4,* 5–15.

Faludi, S. (1991). *Backlash: The undeclared war against American women.* New York: Crown.

Fanning, P. (1988). *Visualization for Change.* Oakland, CA.: New Harbinger Publications.

Farah, M. J. (2000). The neural bases of mental imagery. In M.S. Gazzaniga (Ed.), *The Cognitive Neurosciences* (2nd. Ed., pp. 965–974). Cambridge, MA: MIT Press.

Fast, J. (1970). *Body Language*. New York: M. Evans & Co.

Feather, D. T. (1991). Human values, global self-esteem and belief in a just world. *Journal of Personality, 59*, 83–107.

Fehr, B. (1996). *Friendship Processes*. Thousand Oaks, CA: Sage Publications.

Feldner, M., Zvolensky, M., Eifert, G. & Spira, A. (2003). Emotional avoidance: An experimental test of individual differences and response suppression using biological challenge. *Behavior Research and Therapy, 41*(4), 403–411.

Felsman, J. K., & Vaillant, G. E. (1987). Resilient Children as Adults: A 40 Year Study. In Anderson, F. J. & Cohler, B. J. (Eds.) *The Invulnerable Child*. New York: Guilford Press.

Fensterheim, H., & Baer, J. (1975). *Don't Say Yes When You Want to Say No*. New York: David McKay.

Ferris, G. (June, 1999). *Political Skill at Work*. Champaign, ILl.: University of Illinois News Bureau.

Fibel, B., & Hale, W. (1978). The generalized expectancy for success scale –A new measure. *Journal of Consulting and Clinical Psychology, 46*, 924–931.

Fincham, F. (2000). Optimism and the family. In J. Gillham (Ed.), *The Science of Optimism and Hope* (pp. 271–298). Philadelphia, PA: Templeton Foundation Press.

Finkel, D., & McGue, M. (1997). Sex differences in nonadditivity of the multidimensional personality questionnaire scales. *Journal of Personality and Social Psychology, 72*, 929–938.

Finzi, E., & Wasserman, E. (2006). Treatment of depression with botulinum toxin A: A case series. *Dermatological Surgery, 32*, 645–650.

Fisher, H. (2004). *Why we Love: The Nature and Chemistry of Romantic Love*. New York: Henry Holt.

Fitzgerald, T. E., Tennen, H., Affleck, G., & Pransky, G. S. (1993). The Relative Importance of Dispositional Optimism and Control Appraisals in Quality of Life after Coronary Artery Bypass Surgery. *Journal of Behavioral Medicine, 16*, 375–390.

Fleming, J., & Courtney, B. (1984). The Dimensionality of Self-Esteem: II Hierarchical Facet Model for Revised Measurement Scales. *Journal of Personality and Social Psychology, 46*, 404–421.

Flett, T. K., Blankstein, K. R., Hewitt, P. L., & Koledin, S. (1992). Components of Perfectionism and Procrastination in College Students. *Social Behavior and Personality, 20*, 85–94.

Fontana, D. (1990). *Social Skills at Work*. Leicester, England: British Psychological Society.

Fordyce, M. (1977). Development of a program to increase personal happiness. *Journal of Counseling Psychology, 24*, 511–520.

Fordyce, M. (1983). A program to increase happiness: Further studies. *Journal of Counseling Psychology 30*, 483–498.

Francis, D., Diorio, L., Liu, D. & Meany, M. (1999). Nongenomic transmission across generations of maternal behavior and stress responses in the rat. *Science, 286*, 1155–1158.

Frankl, V. (1959). *Man's Search for Meaning*. New York: Pocket Books.

Fraser, A. A. (2004, March 10). *What's Really Happening with Jobs and Outsourcing?* Heritage Foundation Lecture # 827 (delivered to Employers Association in Peoria, Illinois.) *www.heritage.org/Research/Labor/h/827.cfm*.

Frederick, D., Lever, J., Gillespie, J. & Garcia, J. (2016). What keeps passion alive? Sexual satisfaction is associated with sexual communication, mood setting, sexual variety, oral sex, orgasm and sex frequency in a national U.S. study. *The Journal of Sex Research, 1*. DOI: 10.1080/00224499.2015.1137854.

Fredrickson, B. (1998). What good are positive emotions? *Review of General Psychology, 2*, 300–319.

Fredrickson, B. (2000). Cultivating positive emotions to optimize health and well-being. *Prevention and Treatment, 3*. http://journals.apa.org/prevention.

Fredrickson, B., & Branigan, C. (2005). Positive emotions broaden the scope of attention and thought-action repertoires. *Cognition and Emotion, 19*, 313–332.

Fredrickson, B. & Losada, M. (2005). Positive affect and the complex dynamics of human flourishing. *American Psychologist*, 60, 678–681.

Fredrickson, B., Mancuso, R, Branigan, C., & Tugade, M. (2000). The undoing effects of positive emotions. *Motivation and Emotion*, 24, 237–258.

Freedberg, S. (Nov, 17th, 1996). Mounting Cost of White Collar Stress. *Miami Herald*, 1B.

Freidman, M.. & Rosenman, R. H. (1974). *Type A Behavior and Your Heart*. New York: Knopf.

Freud, S. (1924). *A General Introduction to Psychoanalysis*. London: Boni & Liveright.

Frey, B., Benesch, C., & Stutzer, A. (2007). Does TV make us happy? Journal of Economic Psychology, 28, 283–313.

Friedman, M., Powell, L., & Thoresen, C. (1987). Effect of discontinuing Type A behavior counseling on Type A behavior and cardiac recurrence rate of post myocardiac infarction. *American Heart Journal*, 114, 483–490.

Frigon, N., & Jackson, H. (1996). *The Leader: Developing the Skills and Qualities You Need to Lead Effectively*. New York: Amacom Books.

Frijda, N. (1994). Emotions are functional, most of the time. In. P. Ekman & R. Davidson (Eds.) *The Nature of Emotion: Fundamental Questions* (pp. 112–122). New York: Oxford University Press.

Fuller, B. (1970). *Operating Manual for Spaceship Earth*. New York: Pocket Books.

Gable, S., Gonzaga, G. & Strachman, A. (2006). Will you be there for me when things go right? Supportive responses to positive events disclosures. *Journal of Personality and Social Psychology*, 89, 904–917.

Gable, S., Reis, H., Impett, E., & Asher, E. (2004). What do you do when things go right? The intrapersonal and interpersonal benefits of sharing good events. *Journal of Personality and Social Psychology*, 87, 228–245.

Galassi, J. P., Galassi, M. D., & Fulkerson, K. (1984). Assertion Training in Theory and Practice: An Update. In C. M. Franks (Ed.). *New Developments in Behavior Therapy: From Research to Clinical Application*. (pp. 319–376). New York: Haworth Press.

Gallagher, M., & Waite, L. (2000). *The Case for Marriage*. New York: Doubleday.

Gallo, W., Teng, H., Falbu, T., Kasl, S., Krumholz, H., & Bradley, E. (2006). The impact of late career job loss on myocardial infarction and stroke: A 10 year follow-up using the Health and Retirement Survey. *Occupational and Environmental Medicine*, 63, 683–687.

Gardiner, J., Gawlik, B. & Richardson-Klavehn, A. (1994). Maintenance rehearsal affects knowing, not remembering; Elaborative rehearsal affects remembering, not knowing. *Psychonomic Bulletin and Review*, 1, 107–110.

Gardner, H. (1983). *Frames of Mind: The Theory of Multiple Intelligences*. New York: Basic Books.

Gardner, H. (1993). *Multiple Intelligences: The Theory in Practice.*. New York: Basic Books.

Gardner, H. (1999). *Intelligence Reframed: Multiple Intelligences for the 21st Century*. New York: Basic Books.

Gardner, H., & Hatch, T. (1989). Multiple Intelligences Go To School. *Educational Researcher*, 18, 8–9.

Gardner, R. (2002). *Psychology Applied to Everyday Life*. U. S. A.: Wadsworth/Thomson Learning, Inc.

Garfield, C. (1984). *Peak Performance*. Los Angeles, CA.: Houghton Mifflin & Co.

Gaser, C., & Schlang, G. (2003). Brain structures differ between musicians and non-musicians. *Journal of Neuroscience*, 23(27), 9240–9245.

Gawain, S. (1978). *Creative Visualization*. California: Whatever Publishing

Geers, A., Helfer, S., Kosbab, K., Weiland, R., & Landry, S. (2005). Reconsidering the role of personality in placebo effects: Dispositional optimism, situational expectations annd the placebo response. *Journal of Psychosomatic Research*, Vol. 58, Issue 2, 121–127.

Gergen, K. (2002). The challenge of absent presence. In Katz, J.E. & Aarkhus, M.A. (Eds.). *Perpetual Contact: Mobile Communication, Private Talk and Public Performance*. Cambridge: Cambridge University Press. 227–241.

Gilbert, D. (2006). *Stumbling on Happiness*. New York: Knopf

Gilbert, D., Pinel, E., Wilson, T., Blumberg, S., & Wheatley, T. (1998). Immune neglect: A source of durability bias in affective forecasting. *Journal of Personality and Social Psychology*, 75, 617–638.

Gillham, J., Hamilton, J. Freres, D., Patton, K. & Gallop, R. (2006). Preventing depression among early adolescents in the primary care setting: A randomized controlled study of the Penn Resiliency Program. *Journal of Abnormal Child Psychology*, 34, 203–219.

Gillham, J., Reivich, K., Jaycox, L & Seligman, M. (1993). Prevention of depressive symptoms in schoolchildren: Two year follow-up. *Psychological Science*, 6, 343–351.

Giltay, E, Gelenijnse, J, Zitman, F., Hoekstra, T. & Schouten, E. (2004). Dispositional optimism, and all-cause and cardiovascular mortality in a prospective cohort of elderly Dutch men and women. *Archives of General Psychiatry*, 61, 1126–1135.

Giridharadas, A. (2007, September, 25th). Outsourcing Work, So India is Exporting Jobs. *New York Times. http://www.nytimes .com/2007/09/25/business/worldbusiness/25outsource .html?-r=1*

Gladwell, M. (2008). *Outliers: The Story of Success.* New York: Little, Brown & Co.

Glass, P. (June-July, 2001). Nurturing Empathy. *Parenting Magazine.* p. 72.

Gleick, J. (1987). *Chaos – Making a New Science.* New York: Penguin Books.

Gold, S. (2017). How to be a Better Organizer. *Scientific American Mind* (March/April). 18.

Goleman, D. (1977). *The Varieties of the Meditative Experience.* New York: E. P. Dutton.

Goleman, D. (1988). *The Meditative Mind.* New York. Penguin Books.

Goleman, D. (1995). *Emotional Intelligence.* New York, N. Y.: Bantam Books.

Goleman, D. (1998). *Working with Emotional Intelligence.* New York, N.Y.: Bantam Books.

Goleman, D. (2006). *Social Intelligence: The New Science of Human Relationships.* New York, New York: Bantam Dell.

Goleman, D. (2013). *Focus: The Hidden Driver of Excellence.* New York, N.Y.: Harper Collins.

Gollwitzer, P. M. (1999). Implementation Intentions. *American Psychologist*, 54, 493–503.

Gollwitzer, P., Oettingen, G., Kirby, T., & Duckworth, A. (2011). Mental contrasting facilitates academic performance in school children. *Motivation and Emotion*, 35, 403–412.

Gomez-Mejia, L. R., Balkin, D, & Cardy, R. (1995). *Managing Human Resources.* Upper Saddle River, N.J.: Prentice Hall.

Goodman, C. (2012). Support at Home Good for Career. *The Miami Herald.* (2/15/2012), 5–6.

Goodman, D. (1974). *Emotional Well-Being Through Rational Behavior Training.* Springfield, IL.: Charles C. Thomas.

Gordan, T. (1970). *Parent Effectiveness Training.* New York: Peter H. Wyden.

Gore, S. (1978). The Effect of Social Support in Moderating the Health Consequences of Unemployment. *Journal of Health and Social Behavior*, 19, 157–165.

Gottesmann, I. (1991). *Schizophrenia Genesis: The Origins of Madness.* New York: W. H. Freeman.

Gottlieb, K., & Robinson, G. (2002). *A Practical Guide for Integrating Civic Responsibility into the Curriculum.* Washington, D. C.: Community College Press.

Gottman, J.M. (1993). The roles of conflict engagement, escalation and avoidance in marital interaction: A longitudinal view of five types of couples. *Journal of Consulting and Clinical Psychology*, 61, 6–15.

Gottman, J. M. (1994). *Why Marriages Succeed or Fail.* New York: Simon & Schuster.

Gottman, J. M. (2000). *Seven Principles for Making Marriages Work,* New York: Three Rivers Press.

Gottman, J., & Silver, N. (2000). *The Seven Principles for Making Marriages Work.* New York: Crown Publishers.

Gowda, S. (2005). Offshoring in India. *Offshoring-Process, Pain or Profit.* Report of a workshop held at the London School of Business.

Gradanski, B., Gaser, C., Busch, V., Schuierer, G., Bogdahn, U. & May, A. (2004). Neuroplasticity: Changes in grey matter induced by training. *Nature*, 427, 311–312.

Gramling, S. E., & Auerbach, S. M. (1998). *Stress Management Workbook: Techniques and Self-Assessment Procedures.* Englewood Cliffs, N. J.: Prentice Hall.

Grant, A. (2013). *Give and Take: A Revolutionary Approach to Success.* New York: Viking Press.

Greenberg, M. (2007). Positive Psychology and Institutions: Highlights from a Panel Discussion. *Positive Psychology News Daily. http://positivepsychologynews.com.*

Grof, S. (1985). *Beyond the Brain.* Albany, New York: State University of New York Press.

Grof, S. (1988). *The Adventure of Self Discovery.* Albany, New York: State University of New York Press.

Gura, T. (December, 2008). I'll Do It Tomorrow. *Scientific American Mind,* 27–33.

Gura, T. (March/April, 2013). When Pretending is the Remedy. *Scientific American Mind,* 34–39.

Haidt, J. (2006). *The Happiness Hypothesis.* Cambridge, MA: Basic Books.

Hamburg, D. (1994). *Today's Children: Creating a Future for a Generation in Crisis.* New York: Time Books.

Hammond, S. A. (1998). *The Thin Book of Appreciative Inquiry.* Thin Book Publishing.

Hansen, K. (2002). *Online Career Assessments: Helpful Tools of Self-Discovery.* Deland, FL.: Quintessential Careers. *http://www.quintcareers.com.*

Hansen, M., Jones, R. & Tocchini, K. (2017). Shinrin-yoku (forest bathing) and nature therapy: A state of the art review. *International Journal of Environmental Research in Public Health,* 14(8), piiE851. DOI:10.3390/iserph14080851

Hanson, R. (2013). *Hardwiring Happiness: The New Brain Science of Contentment, Calm and Confidence.* New York: Harmony Books/Random House.

Hanson, R. (Jan./Feb., 2014). The Next Big Step. *The Psychotherapy Networker,* Vol 38, No. 1, 18–25/48.

Harbaugh, W., Mayr, U. & Burghart, B. (2007). Neural responses to taxation and voluntary giving reveal motives for charitable donations. *Science,* 316, 1622–1625.

Harker, L., & Keltner, D. (2001). Expressions of positive emotion in women's college yearbook pictures and their relationships to personality and life outcomes across adulthood. *Journal of Personality and Social Psychology,* 80, 112–124.

Harris, R. (2009). *ACT Made Simple.* Oakland, CA.: New Harbinger.

Harris, R. (2011). *The Happiness Trap: How to Stop Struggling and Start Living.* Boston, MA: Trumpeter.

Harris, T. (1967). *I'm OK, You're OK: A Practical Guide to Transactional Analysis.* New York: Avon Books.

Harter, J., & Schmidt, F. (2002). *Employee engagement, satisfaction and business-unit level outcomes: Meta-analysis.* Princeton, N.J.: The Gallup Organization.

Harter, J., Schmidt, F., & Hayes, T. (2002). Business-unit level relationship between employee satisfaction, employee engagement, and business outcomes: A meta-analysis. *Journal of Applied Psychology,* 877, 268–279.

Hartmann, T. (1998). *The Last Hours of Ancient Sunlight.* New York, N. Y.: Three Rivers Press.

Haskins, R. & Sawhill, I. (2009). *Creating an Opportunity Society.* Washington, D.C.:Brookings Institution Press.

Harvard Medical School. (April, 2002). The Mind and the Immune System – Part I. *The Harvard Mental Health Letter,* Vol. 18, No. 10, 1–3.

Harvard University. *Check Out Policy.* Harvard Botanical Library. Cambridge, Mass.: Harvard University.

Hayes, S.; Strosohl, K. & Wilson, K. (1999). *Acceptance and Commitment Therapy: An Experiential Approach to Behavior Change.* New York: Guilford Press.

Hazan, C., & Shaver, P. (1987). Romantic love conceptualized as an attachment process. *Journal of Personality and Social Psychology,* 52, 511–524.

Hazan, C., & Shaver, P. (1994). Attachment as an organizational framework for research on close relationships. *Psychological Inquiry,* 5, 1–22.

Heine, S., Lehman, D., Markus, H., & Kitayama, S. (1999). Is there a universal need for positive self-regard? *Psychological Review,* 106, 766–794.

Hellman, C., Budd, M., Borysenko, J., McClelland, D., & Benson, H. (1990). The study of the effectiveness of two group behavior medicine interventions for patients with psychosomatic complaints. *Behavioral Medicine*, 16, 165–173.

Helson, R. (1967). Personality characteristics and developmental history of creative college women. *Genetic Psychology Monographs*, 76, 205–256.

Hewitt, J. R., (2005). The social construction of self-esteem. In C. R. Snyder & S. J. Lopez (Eds.) *Handbook of Positive Psychology* (pp. 135–147). New York: Oxford University Press.

Higbee, K. L. (1988). *Your Memory: How It Works and How to Improve It*. (2nd Ed.). New York: Prentice Hall Press.

Hill, A. (1997). *Speaking Truth to Power*. New York: Doubleday.

Hinder, S. (1998). Time for a New Role. *Mail Tribune*. Medford, Oregon.

Holahan, C., & Sears, R., (1995). *The Gifted Group in Later Maturity*. Palo Alto, CA: Stanford University Press.

Holland, J. (1985). *Making Vocational Choices: A Theory of Vocational Personalities and Work Environment*, 2nd. Ed., Upper Saddle River, N.J.: Prentice-Hall.

Holmes, D. S., & Roth, D. L. (1988). Effects of Aerobic Exercise Training and Relaxation Training on Cardiovascular Activity during Psychological Stress. *Journal of Psychosomatic Research*, 32, 469–474.

Holmes, T. H., & Rahe, R. H. (1967). The Social Readjustment Rating Scale. *Journal of Psychosomatic Research*, 11, 213–218.

Holt, P., Fine, M. J., & Tollefson, N. (1987). Mediating Stress: Survival of the Hardy. *Psychology in the Schools*, 24, 51–58.

Holt-Lunstad, J., Smith, T., & Layton, J. (2010). Social relationships and mortality risk: A meta-analytic review. *PlosMedicine* 7(7)@100316 http://t.coltngr9Y6RA6 PLOSMedicine

Holzel, B., Ulrich, O., Gard, T., Hempel, H., Lueygandt, M., Morgen, K., & Vaitl, D. (2008). Investigations of Mindfulness Meditation Practitioners with voxel based morphometry. *Social, Cognitive and Affective Neuroscience*, 3, 55–61.

Horney, K. (1956). The Search for Glory. In Moustakas, C. (Ed.) *Self-Exploration and Personal Growth*. (pp. 86–91). New York: Harper Colophan Books.

Horrigan, M. W. (2004, February). Employment projections to 2012: Concepts and Context. *Monthly Labor Review*, Bureau of Labor Statistics.

Houston, J. (1987). *The Search for the Beloved*. New York: Tarcher/Putnam Books.

Huppert, F. & So, T. (2009). What percentage of people in Europe are flourishing and what characterizes them. *www.isgols2009.institutodeglinnocenti .it/Content_en/Huppert.pdf*.

Huta, V., Park, N., Peterson, C., & Seligman, M. (2005). Pursuing pleasure versus eudemonia: Links with different aspects of well-being. *Unpublished manuscript*, McGill University, Montreal, Canada.

Hyde, J. S. (2005). The gender similarities hypothesis. *American Psychologist*, 60(6), 581–592.

Inglehart, R., Foa, R., Peterson, C., & Wetzel, C. (2008). Development, Freedom and Rising Happiness: A Global Perspective (1981–2007). *Perspectives in Psychological Science*, Vol. 3, No. 4, 264–285.

Ingraham, C. (Dec. 16, 2017). Study shows income redistribution from the poor to the rich. *Miami Herald*.

Isen, A. (1991). The Influence of Positive Affect on Clinical Problem Solving. *Medical Decision Making*. (July-Sept.).

Iyengar, S. (2010). *The Art of Choosing*. New York, New York: Grand Central Publishing.

IT World.com. (2005). *Study: Europe Overtakes U.S. in Big Outsourcing Deals. ITWorld.com/ Man/2701/050114outsourcing/*

Jacobson, E. (1929, 1974). *Progressive Relaxation*. Chicago: The University of Chicago Press, Midway Reprint.

Jaksic, N., Aukst-Margetic, B., & Jakovljevic, M. (2013). Does personality play a relevant role in the placebo effect? Psychiatria Danubina, Vol. 25, No.1, 17–23.

James, P., Hart, J.; Banay, R. & Laden, F. (2016). Exposure to greenness and mortality in a nationwide prospective cohort study of women. *Environmental Heath Perspectives*, 124. DOI:10.1289/ehp.1510363

Janes, L., & Olson, J. (2000). Jeer pressures: The behavioral effects of observing ridicule of others. *Personality and Social Psychology Bulletin*, 26(4), 474–485.

Jensen, D. (2011). Bright Green Realtity Check. *Orion*, Nov-Dec., 12–13.

Johannessen, K., Oettingen, G., & Mayer, D. (2012). Mental contrasting of a dieting wish improves self-reported health behaviour. *Psychology & Health*, 27(sup2), 43–58.

Johnson, L. (2008). *Handouts from the Brief Therapy Center.* Salt Lake City, UT: Head Acre Books

Jorason, D., & Lietman, R. (1994). *The McNeil National Pain Study.* New York: Louis Harris & Associates.

Jung, C. (1972). *Synchronicity – An Acausal Connecting Principle.* London: Routledge.

Jung, C. (1981). *The Archetypes and the Collective Unconscious.* Princeton, N.J.: Princeton University Press.

Kabat-Zinn, J. (1990). *Full Catastrophe Living.* New York: Dell Publishing.

Kabat-Zinn, J. (1994). *Wherever You Go There You Are.* New York: Hyperion.

Kagen, J. (1994). *Galen's prophecy. Temperament in Human Nature.* New York: Basic Books.

Kahneman, D. (1999). Objective happiness. In D. Kahneman, E. Diener & N. Schwarz (Eds.) *Well-being: The Foundations of Hedonic Psychology* (pp. 3–25). New York: Russell Sage.

Kahneman, D., & Deaton, A. (2010). "High income improves evaluation of life but not emotional well-being." *Proceedings of the National Academy of Science of the U.S.A.*, 107, No. 38, 16489–16493.

Kalanit, G., Henson, R. & Martin, A. (2006). Repetition and the brain: Neural models of stimulus-specific effects. *Trends in Cognitive Sciences* Vol 10, No. 1, 14–23.

Kamen-Siegel, L., Rodin, J., Seligman, M. & Dwyer, J. (1991). Explanatory style and cell-mediated immunity in elderly men and women. *Health Psychology*, 10, 229–235.

Kanar, C. (1991). *The Confident Student.* Boston, Mass.: Houghton Mifflin Co.

Kaniel, R., Massey, C. & Robinson, D. (2010). The importance of being an optimist: Evidence from labor markets. *The Natinal Bureau of Economic Research.* NBER Working Paper #16328. *www.nber .org/papers/w16328.pdf*

Kaplan, R. & Kaiser, R. (2010). Toward a Positive Psychology for Leaders. In Linley, P., Harrington, S. & Garcea, N. (Eds.). *Oxford Handbook of Positive Psychology and Work.* (pp. 107–117). New York: Oxford University Press.

Kappes, A., Singmann, H., & Oettingen, G. (2012). Mental contrasting instigates goal pursuit by linking obstacles of reality with instrumental behavior. *Journal of Experimental Social Psychology*, 48(4), 811–818.

Karney, B., & Bradbury, T. (1995). The longitudinal course of marital quality and stability: A review of theory, method and research. *Psychological Review*, 118, 3–34.

Kashdan, T., & Biswas-Diener, R. (August, 2013). What Happy People do Differently. *Psychology Today*, 51–59.

Kashdan, T. & Steger, M. (2007). Curiosity and stable and dynamic pathways to wellness: Traits, states and everyday behaviors. *Motivation and Emotion*, 31, 159–173.

Kasser, T., & Ryan, R. M. (1993). A Dark Side of the American Dream: Correlates of Financial Success as a Central Life Aspiration. *Journal of Personality and Social Psychology*, 65, 410–422.

Kasser, T., & Ryan, R. M. (1996). Further Examining the American Dream: Differential Correlates of Intrinsic and Extrinsic Goals. *Personality and Social Psychology Bulletin*, 22, 280–286.

Kasser, T., & Sheldon, K. (2008). Time affluence as a path toward personal happiness and ethical business practice: Empirical evidence from psychological studies. *Journal of Business Ethics*, 84, No. 52, 243–255.

Keita, G., & Hurrell, J. (1994). Job *Stress in a Changing Workforce: Investigating Gender, Diversity and Family Issues.* Washington, D.C.: APA Books.

Kemeny, M. E., Gruenewald, T. L. (2000). Affect, Cognition, the Immune Sytsem and Health.

In Mayer, E. A. & Saper, J. (Eds.). *The Biological Basis for Mind Body Interactions: Progress in Brain Research Series.* (pp. 291–308). Amsterdam: Elsevier Science B.V.

Khan, H. I. In an Eastern Rose Garden. In *The Message Volumes Of Hazrat Inayat Khan. Vol. VII.*

Kirkpatrick, S., & Locke, E. (1991). Leadership: Do Traits Matter? *Academy of Management Executive.* 5 (2), 48–60.

Kleinke, C. L. (1986). *Meeting and Understanding People.* New York: W. H. Freeman & Co.

Kobak, R., & Hazan, C. (1991). Attachment in marriage: The effects of security and accuracy of working models. *Journal of Personality and Social Psychology,* 60, 861–869.

Koch, H. (1986). The management of chronic pain in office-based ambulatory care: *National Ambulatory Medical Care Survey,* No. 123, (DHHS Publication No. PHS 86–1250). Hyattsville, MO: U.S. Public Health Service.

Kobasa, S. C. (1979). Stressful Life Events, Personality and Health: An Inquiry into Hardiness. *Journal of Personality and Social Psychology,* 37, 1–11.

Kobasa, S. C. (1982). Commitment and Coping in Stress Resistance among Lawyers. *Journal of Personality and Social Psychology,* 42, 707–717.

Kobasa, S. C. (Sept., 1984). How much Stress Can You Survive? *American Health,* 64–71.

Kobasa, S. C., Maddi, S. R., & Puccetti, M. C. (1982). Personality and Exercise as Buffers in the Stress-Illness Relationship. *Journal of Behavioral Medicine,* 5, 391–404.

Kopp, S. (1972). *If You Meet the Buddha on the Road, Kill Him!* Palo Alto, CA.: Bantam Books/Science & Behavior Books.

Kosslyn, S., Thompson, W., Kim, I, & Alpert, N. (1995). Topographical representations of mental images in primary visual cortex. *Nature,* 6565, 496–498.

Larson, R. J., & Buss, D. M. (2002). *Personality Psychology: Domains of Knowledge about Human Nature.* New York: McGraw – Hill.

Lauer, J., & Lauer, R. (1986). *Till death Do Us Part.* New York: Haworth Press.

Lauer, R., Lauer, J., & Kerr, S. (1990). The long-term marriage: Perceptions of stability and satisfaction. *International Journal of Aging and Human Development,* 31(3), 189–195.

Lawler, K.A., & Smied, L.A. (1987). The Relationship of Stress, Type A behavior and Powerlessness to Physiological Responses in Female Clerical Workers. *Journal of Psychosomatic Research,* 31, 555–563.

Lazar, S., Kerr, C., Wasserman, R., Gray, J., Greve, D., Treadway, M., McGarvey, M., Quinn, B., Dusek, J., Benson, H., Rauch, S., Moore, C., & Fisch, B. (2005). Meditation experience is associated with increased cortical thickness. *Neuroreport,* 16, 1893–1897.

Lazarus, R. (1966). *Psychological Stress and the Coping Process.* New York: McGraw-Hill.

Lazarus, R. (1991). *Emotions and Adaptation.* New York: Oxford University Press.

Lazarus, R., & Folkman, S. (1984). *Stress Appraisal and Coping.* New York: Springer Publishing Co.

Leach, G. (2008). Stress Statistics. *www.hardcore .stressmanagement.com*

LeBaron, J. (July, 2003). *Beyond Intractability: A Free Knowledge Base on More Constructive Approaches to Destructive Conflict.* www/beyondintractibility.org.

LeDoux, J. (1993). Emotional Memory Systems in the Brain. *Behavioral Brain Research,* 58.

Lee, D., Sui, X. & Blair, S. (2009). Does physical activity ameliorate the health hazards of obesity? *British Journal of Sports Medicine,* 43, 49–51.

Lee, Y., & Seligman, M. (1997). Are Americans more optimistic than the Chinese? *Personality and Social Psychology Bulletin,* 23, 32–40.

Lefcourt, H. (2005). Humor. In C. R. Snyder & S .J. Lopez (Eds.) *Handbook of Positive Psychology* (pp. 619–631). New York: Oxford University Press.

Lefkowitz, M. M., Eron, L. D., Walder, L. O., & Huesmann, L. R. (1977). *Growing Up to be Violent: A Longitudinal Study of the Development of Aggression.* New York: Pergamon Press.

Lemish, D. (1998). Fighting against television violence: An Israeli case study. In U. Carlsson & C. von Feilitzen (Eds.) *Children and Media Violence.* Goteborg, Sweden: The UNESCO Int. Clearinghouse on Children and Media Violence.

Lenhart, A. & Duggan, M. (2014). Couples, the internet and social media. *Pew Research Center Report.*

Lerner, M. (1980). *The Belief in a Just World.* New York: Plenum.

Lerner, J. & Keltner, D. (2001). Fear, Anger and Risk. *Journal of Personality and Social Psychology,* Vol. 81, No. 1, 146–159.

Levenson, H. (1981). Differentiating among Internality, Powerful Others and Change. In H. M. Lefcourt (Ed.). *Research with the Locus of Control Construct* (Vol. I, pp. 1–63). New York: Academic Press.

Levine, T. (2000). *Work Yourself Happy: A Step-by-Step Guide to Creating Joy in Your Life and Work.* Buckingham, Pa: Lahaska Press.

Levitin, D. (2014). *The Organized Mind: Thinking Straight in the Age of Information Overload.* New York: Penguin Press

Linehan, M. D., Brown, S. H., Nielson, S. L., Olney, K. G., & McFall, R. M. (Nov., 1980). *The Effectiveness of Seven Styles of Assertion.* Paper presented at the Annual Convention of the Association for the Advancement of Behavior Therapy, New York.

Linley, P., Harrington, S. & Garcea, N. (2010). *Oxford Handbook of Positive Psychology and Work.* New York: Oxford University Press, Inc.

Lipman-Blumen, J. (1992). Connective Leadership: Female Leadership Styles in the 21st Century Workplace. *Sociological Perspectives.* Berkeley, CA.: University of California Press.

Loehr, J.E., & Migdow, J.A. (1986). *Take a Deep Breath.* New York: Villard Books.

Loftus, M. (2013). When Virtue Becomes Vice. *Psychology Today,* 52–56.

Long, B. C. (1984). Aerobic Conditioning and Stress Inoculation: A Comparison of Stress Management Interventions. *Cognitive Therapy and Research,* 8, 517–542.

Lonier, T. (1994). *Working Solo.* New York: Portico Press.

Lovelock, J. (1979). *Gaia: A New Look at Life.* Oxford: Oxford University Press.

Losada, M. (1999). The complex dynamics of high performance teams. *Mathematical and Computer Modeling,* 30, 179–192.

Losada, M. & Heaphy, E. (2004). The role of positivity and connectivity in the performance of business teams: A nonlinear dynamics model. *American Behavioral Scientist,* 47, 740–765.

Loza, J. (2009). *10 Ways to Keep your Job despite the tough economy. www.techrepurblic.com.*

Luders, E., Toga, A., Lepore, N., & Gaser, C. (2009). The underlying anatomical correlates of long term meditation: Larger hippocampal and frontal volumes of gray matter. *NeuroImage,* 45, 672–678.

Lundbergk U. (1980). Catecholamine and cortisol excretion under psychologically different laboratory conditions. In J. Usdin, T. Kvetnanski, & D. Kopin (Eds.), *Catecholamines and Stress: Recent Advances,* North Holland: Elsesvier.

Luthans, F. & Youssef, C. (2007). Positive Organizational Behavior in the Workplace: The Impact of Hope, Optimism and Resilience. *Journal of Management,* 33, 774–800.

Lykken, D., McGue, M., Tellegen, A., & Bouchard, T. (1992) Emergenesis: Genetic traits that may not run in families. *American Psychologist,* 47, 1565–1577.

Lyman, P. & Varian, H. (2003) How much Information? *http://www.sims.berkeley.edu/how-much.info-2003*

Lyons-Ruth, K. (1991). Rapprochement or approachment: Mahler's theory reconsidered from the vantage point of recent research on early attachment relationships. *Psychoanalytic Psychology,* 8, 1–23.

Lyubormirsky, S., King, L., & Diener, E. (2005). The benefits of frequent positive affect: Does happiness lead to success? *Psychological Bulletin,* 131, 803–855.

Lyubormirsky, S., Sheldon, K., & Schkade, D. (2005). Pursuing happiness: The architecture of sustainable change. *Review of General Psychology,* 9, 111–131.

Maccoby, E. (1998). *The Two Sexes: Growing up Apart, Coming Together.* Cambridge, Mass: Harvard Press.

Maccoby, E. & Martin, J. (1983). Socialization in the Context of the Family. In Munsen, P. (Ed.).

Handbook of Child Psychology. (pp. 28–41), 4th Ed., Vol. 4. Hillsdale, N. J.: Erlbaum.

Maddi, S., & Kobasa, S., (1984). *The Hardy Executive: Health Under Stress.* Homewood, IL: Dow Jones-Irwin.

Maddux, J. (1995). Self-efficacy Theory: An Introduction. In J.E. Maddux (Ed.). *Self-Efficacy, Adaptation and Adjustment: Theory, Research and Application* (pp. 3–36). New York: Plenum.

Maddux, J. (2005). Self-Efficacy: The power of believing that you can. In C. Snyder & S. Lopez (Eds.) *Handbook of Positive Psychology* (pp. 277–287). New York: Oxford University Press.

Maguire, E., Woollett, K., & Spiers, H. (2006). London taxi drivers and bus drivers: A structural MRI and neuropsychological analysis. *Hippocampus, 16*(12), 1091–1101.

Main, M. & Solomon, J. (1986). Discovery of an insecure-disorganized/disoriented attachment pattern: Procedures, findings and implications for the classification of behavior. In T.B. Brazelton & M. Yogman (Eds.) *Affective Development in Infancy.* 95–124. Norwood, N.J.: Ablex.

Maier, S. F., & Watkins, L. R. (1998). Cytokines for Psychologists: Implications of Bidirectional Immune-to-Brain Communication for Understanding Behavior, Mood and Cognition. *Psychological Review, 105*(1), 83–107.

Maier, S. F. & Seligman, M. E. (1976). Learned Helplessness: Theory and Evidence. *Journal of Experimental Psychology: General, 105,* 3–46.

Maltz, D., & Borker, R. (1982). A cultural approach to male-female miscommunication. In J. Gumperz (Ed.) *Language and Social Identity* (pp. 281–312). New York: Oxford University Press.

Mann, C. L. (2004). What outsourcing means for the U.S. IT workers and for the U.S. economy. *Communications of the ACM,* Vol 47, No. 7. *http://www.acmqueue.com.*

Manning, M. R., Williams, R.F., & Wolfe, D.M. (1988). Hardiness and the Relationship between Stressors and Outcomes. *Work and Stress, 2,* 205–216.

Marano, H. & Strieber, A. (2016). Love interruptus. *Psychology Today, 49*(4), 50–57.

MarksJarvis, G. (2007, November 13th). Baby boomers and retirement happiness. *Chicago Tribune.com. http://newsblog.chicagoTribune.com/marksjarvis-on-money/*

Maslow, A. (1968). *Toward a Psychology of Being.* 2nd Ed. New York: Van Nostrand Reinhold.

Maslow, A. (1970). *Motivation and Personality,* 2nd. Ed., New York: Harper & Row.

Masten, A. (2001). Ordinary Magic: Resilience process in development. *American Psychologist, 56,* 227–238.

Matheny, K., Aycock, D., Pugh, J., Curlette, W., & Cannella, K. (1986). Stress coping: A qualitative and quantitative synthesis with implications for treatment. *The Counseling Psychologist, 14,* 499–549.

Matthews, K. (2005). Psychological perspectives in the development of coronary heart disease. *American Psychologist, 60,* 783–796.

Matthews, K., Owens, J., Edmundowicz, D., Lee, L. & Kuller, L. (2006). Positive and negative attributes and risk for coronary and aortic calcification in healthy women. *Psychosomatic Medicine, 68,* 355–361.

Mattiasson, I., Lindgarde, F., Nilsson, J., & Theorell, T. (1990). Threat of unemployment and cardiovascular risk factors: Longitudinal study of quality of sleep and serum cholesterol concentrations in men threatened with redundancy. *British Medical Journal, 301,* 461–466.

McCann, I. L., & Holmes, D. S. (1984). Influence of Aerobic Exercise on Depression. *Journal of Personality and Social Psychology, 46,* 1142–1147.

McCarthy, J. (2002). *"3.3 Million Jobs go Offshore".* Cambridge: MA: Forrester Research, Inc.

McClain, L. (1987). Behavior During Examinations: A Comparison of "A", "C" and "F" Students. In M. E. Ware & R. J. Millard (Eds.). *Handbook on Student Development: Advising, Career Development and Field Placement.* (pp. 40–42). Hillsdale, N.J.: Lawrence Erlbaum Associates.

McClelland, D. (1961). *The Achieving Society.* New York: Van Nostrand.

McCraty, R. (2003). Influence of cardiac afferent input on heart-brain synchronization and cognitive performance. *International Journal of Psychophysiology, 45*, 72–73.

McCraty, R., & Atkinson, M. (2003). Psychophysiological coherence. Boulder Creek, CA: HeartMath Research Center, *Institute of HeartMath Publication No. 03–016.*

McCullough, M. E. (2001). Forgiving. In C. R. Snyder (Ed.). *Coping with Stress: Effective People and Processes.* (pp. 93–113). New York: Oxford University Press.

McDonough, W. & Braungart, M. (2002). *Cradle to Cradle.* New York: North Point Press.

McGilley, B. M., & Holmes, D. S. (1989). Aerobic Fitness Response to Psychological Stress. *Journal of Research on Personality, 22*, 129–139.

McGuigan, F.L. (1984). Progressive Relaxation: Origins, Principles and Clinical Applications. In Woolfolk, R.L., & Lehrer, P.M. (Eds.). *Principles and Practices of Stress Management.* New York: Guilford Press.

McGregor, D. (1960). *The Human Side of Enterprise.* New York: McGraw-Hill.

McKay, M., Davis, M., & Fanning, P. (1981). *Thoughts and Feelings: The Art of Cognitive Stress Intervention.* Oakland, California: New Harbinger Publications.

McKay, M., Davis, M., & Fanning, P. (1983). *Messages: The Communication Skills Book.* Oakland, CA: New Harbinger Publications.

McKay, M., & Fanning, P. (1987). *Self Esteem.* Oakland, CA: New Harbinger Publications.

Mechelli, A., Crinion, J., Noppeney, V, O'Doherty, J., & Ashburner, J. (2004). Structural plasticity in the bilingual brain. *Nature, 431.*

Meichenbaum;, D. (2012). *Roadmap to Resilience: A Guide for Military, Trauma Victims and Their Families.* Clearwater, Fl.: Institute Press.

Medina, J. (2008). *Brain Rules.* Seattle, WA: Pear Press.

Meehl, P. (1975). Hedonic capacity: Some conjectures. *Bulletin of the Menninger Clinic, 39*, 295–307.

Mehrabian, A. (1971). *Silent Messages.* Belmont, CA: Wadsworth.

Mehrabian, A. (Sept., 1989). Communication Without Words. *Psychology Today*, 53–55.

Miami-Dade College. *Classified Staff Evaluation Form.* Miami, FL : Department of Human Relations.

Miami-Dade College. *Policy Manual.* Miami, FL.

Miami-Dade College. *Procedures Manual.* Miami, FL.

Mikulincer, M., Florian, V., & Weller, A. (1993). Attachment styles, coping strategies, and post-traumatic psychological distress: The impact of the Gulf War in Israel. *Journal of Personality and Social Psychology, 64*, 817–826.

Miller, A. (April, 1988). Stress on the Job. *Newsweek Magazine*, 40–45.

Miller, G. & Blackwell, E. (2006). Turning up the heat: Inflammation as a mechanism linking chronic stress, depression and heart disease. *Current Directions in Psychological Science, 15*, 269–272.

Miller, G. & Chen, E. (2010). Harsh family climate in early life presages the emergence of a proinflammatory phenotype in adolesence. *Psychological Science, 21*, 848–856.

Miller, M., & Soldt, D. (1999). Organization for unmarried people condemns cohabitation report.

Millman, D. (1991). *Sacred Journey of the Peaceful Warrior.* Tiburn, CA: H. J. Kramer, Inc.

Mirsky, A., & Quinn, O. (1988). The Genain Quadruplets. *Schizophrenia Bulletin, 14*, 595–612.

Mischel., W., Ebbesen, E., $ Zeiss, A. (1972). Cognitive and attentional mechanisms in delay of gratification. *Journal of Personality and Social Psychology, 21*, 204–218.

Mischel, W. & Peake, P. K. (1990). Predicting Adolescent Cognitive and Self Regulatory Competencies from Preschool Delay of Gratification. *Developmental Psychology, 6*, 978–986.

Misra, S., Cheng, L., Genevic, J. & Yuan, M. (2014). The quality of in-person social interactions in the presence of mobile devices. *Environment and Behavior,* 48(2), 275–298.

Mochon, D., Norton, M. & Ariely, D. (2008). Getting off the hedonic treadmill one step at a time: The impact of regular religious practice and exercise on well-being. *Journal of Economic Psychology*, 29, No. 5, 632–647.

Monbiot, G. (2013). How Wolves Change Rivers. *You Tube video at Sustainable Man.* http://www.youtube.com/watch?v=ysa50BhXz-Q#t).

Moneta, G., & Csikszentmihalyi, M. (1991). The effect of perceived challenges and skills on the quality of subjective experience. *Journal of Personality*, 64, 275–310.

Moore, N., & Davidson, J. (2000). Communicating with new sex partners: College women and questions that make a difference. *Journal of Sex and Marital Therapy,* Vol 26., (3), 215–230.

Mori, K., & Mori, H. (2009). Another test of passive facial feedback hypothesis: When your face smiles, you feel happy. *Perceptual and Motor Skills*, 109, 1–3.

Morris, T., Spittle, M., & Watt, A. (2005). *Imagery in Sport.* Human Kinetics Publishers, Inc.

Mortenson, S. T. (2002). Sex, communication, values, and cultural values. *Communication Reports*, 15(1), 57–71.

Murphy, L. R. (1987). A Review of Organizational Stress Management Research: Methodological Considerations. In J. M. Ivancevich & D.C. Ganster (Eds.). *Job Stress: From Theory to Suggestions.* (pp. 215–227), New York: Haworth Press.

Myers, D. G. (1992). *The Pursuit of Happiness: Who is Happy and Why.* New York: William Morrow.

Myers, D. G. (1993). *The Pursuit of Happiness.* New York: Avon.

Myers, D. G. (2002) *Social Psychology* (7th Ed.). New York: McGraw Hill

Myers, D. G. (2004). *Psychology* (7th Ed.). New York: Worth Publishers.

Myers, D. G. (2013). *Psychology* (10th Ed.). New York: Worth Publishers.

Myers, D., & Diener, E. (1995). Who is happy? *Psychological Science*, 6, 10–19.

Myers, J., Madathil, J., & Tingle, L. (2005). Marriage satisfaction and wellness in India and the United States: A preliminary comparison of arranged marriages and marriages of choice. *Journal of Counseling and Development*, 83, 183–190.

Myers-Briggs, I. (1993). *Introduction to Type: A Guide to Understanding your Results on the Myers-Briggs Type Indicator.* Palo Alto, CA.: Consulting Psychologists Press.

Nakazawa, D. (2008). *The AutoImmune Epidemic.* New York: Simon & Schuster.

Neisser, V. (1979). The control of information pickup in selective looking . In A. D. Pick, (Ed.) Perception *and its Development: A Tribute to Eleanor J. Gibson* (pp. 201–219). New Jersey: Lawrence Erlbaum Associates

Newby, T., & Ashlyn, H. (1992). The Value of Mentoring. *Performance* Improvement Quarterly. Tallahassee, Fl.: The Learning Systems Institute, Florida State University, 54, 2–15.

National Ambulatory Medical Care Survey (2006), National Center for Health Statistics. *http://www.cdc.gov/nationalcenterforhealthstatistics*

National Institute on Alcohol Abuse an Alcoholism (NIAAA). *www.niaaa.nih.gov.*

National Institute of Mental Health (NIMH). *http://nimh.nih.gov/index.shtml.*

Newshour with Jim Lehrer. (March 9, 2004) *Terence Smith interviewing Thomas Friedman. http://www.pbs.org/newshour/bb/asia/jan-june04/friedman/03-09.html.*

Niven, D. (2002). *100 Simple Secrets of Successful People.* San Francisco, CA.: Harper Collins Publishers.

Nolen-Hoeksema, S. (2000) Growth and resilience among bereaved people. In J. Gillham (Ed.) *The Science of Optimism and Hope* (pp. 107–127). Philadelphia, PA: Templeton Foundation Press.

Norem, J. (2001). *The Positive Power of Negative Thinking: Using Defensive Pessimism to Harness Anxiety and Perform at Your Peak.* New York: Basic Books.

Norem, J., & Cantor, N. (1986). Defensive pessimism: "Harnessing" anxiety as motivation. *Journal of Personality and Social Psychology*, 51, 1208–1217.

NOW with Bill Moyers. (August 4, 2004). Interview with Lou Dobbs. *www.pbs.org/now/transcript/transcript334.*

Nowck, K. M. (1989). Coping Style, Cognitive Hardiness and Health Status. *Journal of Behavioral Medicine,* 12, 145–158.

Nuernberger, P. (1981). *Freedom from Stress: A Holistic Approach.* Pennsylvania: Himalayan Intl. Inst. of Yoga Science and Philosophy Publishers.

Oberman, L., Hubbard, E., McCleery, J., Altschuler, I., Ramachandran, V., & Pineda, J. (2006). EEG evidence for mirror neuron dysfunction in autism spectral disorders. *Cognitive Brain Research,* 24(2), 190–198.

Ochsner, K. (2002). Rethinking feelings: An fMRI study of the cognitive regulation of emotion. *Journal of Cognitive Neuroscience,* 14, 1215–1229.

Oettingen, G. (2014). *Rethinking Positive Thinking: Inside the New Science of Motivation.* New York: Penguin/Random House.

Oettingen, G., Mayer, D., & Thorpe, J. (2010). Self-regulation of commitment to reduce cigarette consumption: Mental contrasting of future with reality. *Psychology & Health,* 25(8), 961–977.

Okun, B. F., Fried, J., & Okun M. L. (1999). *Understanding Diversity: A Learning as Practice Primer.* Pacific Grove, CA.: Brooks/Cole Publishing.

O'Hanlon, B. (2007). *Pathways to Spirituality.* New York: W.W. Norton.

O'Leary, A., & Brown, S. (1995). Self-efficacy and the physiological stress response. In J.E. Maddux (Ed.). *Self-Efficacy, Adaptation and Adjustment: Theory, research and Application* (pp 227–248). New York: Plenum.

Orman, S. (2007). *Women and Money.* New York: Spielgel & Grau.

Orman, S. (2010). *Suze Orman's Action Plan: New Rules for New Times.* New York: Spiegel & Grau.

Ornish, D. (1972). *Dr. Dean Ornish's Program for Reversing Coronary Heart Disease without Drugs or Surgery.* New York: Ballantine Books.

Ornish, D. (1990). *Dr. Dean Ornish's Program for Reversing Heart Disease.* New York: Ballantine Books

Ornish, D. (Oct. 3, 2005) *Love is Real Medicine.* Newsweek Magazine., p. 56.

Osterkamp, L., & Press, A. (1988). *Stress? Find Your Balance.* Lawrence, Kansas: Preventive Measures, Inc.

Otto, M., Pollack, M., & Burlow, D. (2004). *Stopping Anxiety Medication (SAM): Pain Control therapy for Benzodiazepine Discontinuation.* New York: Oxford University Press.

Park, B., Tsunetsugu, Y., Kasetani, T., Kagawa, T., & Miyazaki, Y. (2010). The physiological effects of shinrin-yoku (taking in the forest atmosphere or forest bathing): Evidence from field experiments in 24 forests across Japan. *International Journal of Environment, Health and Preventive Medicine,* 15(1), 18–26.

Parker, R. (2002). Why Marraiges Last: A Discussion of the Literature. *Australian Insititue of Family Studies.* www.aifs.gov.au/institute/pubs/RP28.html.

Patel, C. (1984). Yogic therapy. In R.L. Woolfolk & P. M. Lehrer (Eds.). *Principles and Practice of Stress Management.* New York: Guilford Press.

Patel, D. (2002). *Workplace Forecast: A Strategic Outlook.* Alexandria, Va.: Society for Human Resource Management.

Pauk, W. (1997). *How to Study in College.* Boston: Houghton Mifflin.

Paul, A. (2011). The Uses and Abuses of Optimism and Pessimism. *Psychology Today,* (December), 56–63.

Pavlov, I. (1927/1960). *Conditioned Reflexes: An Investigation of the Physiological Activity of the Cerebral Cortex.* (G.V. Anvey, Translator). New York: Dover (Original translation published 1927**).**

Peavey, B. (1982). Biofeedback assisted relaxation: Effects on phagocytic immune function. *Doctoral dissertation,* North Texas State University, Denton, Texas.

Pelham, B., & Swann, W. (1989). From Self-Conceptions to Self Worth: On the Sources and Structure of Global Self-Esteem. *Journal of Personality and Social Psychology,* 57, 672–680.

Pelletier, K. (1984). *Healthy People in Unhealthy Places: Stress and Fitness at Work.* New York: Delacorte Press/Seymour Lawrence.

Peterson, C. (2000). The Future of Optimism. *American Psychologist,* 55(1), 44–55.

Peterson, C. (2006). *A Primer In Positive Psychology*. New York: Oxford University Press.

Peterson, C., & Barrett, L. (1987). Explanatory style and academic performance among university freshmen. *Journal of Personality and Social Psychology*, 53, 603–607.

Peterson, C., & deAvila, M. (1995). Optimistic explanatory style and the perception of health problems. *Journal of Clinical Psychology*, 51, 128–132.

Peterson, C., Maier, S., & Seligman, M. (1993). *Learned Helplessness: A Theory for the Age of Personal Control*. New York: Oxford University Press.

Peterson, C., & Park, C. (1998). Learned helplessness and explanatory style. In D. G. F.Barone, V. B. Van Hasselt & M. Herson (Eds.) *Advanced Personality* (pp. 287–310). New York: Plenum.

Peterson, C., Park, N., & Seligman, M. (2005b). Orientations to happiness and life satisfaction: The full life versus the empty life. *Journal of Happiness Studies*, 6, 25–41.

Peterson, C., Seligman, M., & Valliant, G. (1988). Pessimistic explanatory style is a risk factor for physical illness: A 35 year longitudinal study. *Journal of Personality and Social Psychology*, 55, 23–27.

Peterson, C., Seligman, M., Yurko, K., Martin, L., & Friedman, N. (1998). Catastrophizing and untimely death. *Psychological Science*, 9, 49–52.

Peterson, D. (1984). *Human Error Reduction and Safety Management*. Deer Park, New York: Alovey.

Petrovic, P. (2002). Placebo and opiod analgesia-imaging a shared neuronal network. *Science*, 295, 1737.

Phelps, S., & Austin, N. (1987). *The Assertive Woman*. California: Impact Publishers.

Phillips, L. (2017). Getting Close. *Psychology Today*, 44–53.

Pierrehumbert, B., Iannotti, R., Cummings, E., & Zahn-Waxler, C. (1989). Social functioning with mother and peers at 2 and 5 years: The influence of attachment. *International Journal of Behavioral Development*, 12, 85–100.

Piff, P., Stancato, D., Cote, S., Mendoza-Denton, R. & Keltner, D. (2012). Higher social class predicts increased unethical behavior. *Proceedings of the National Academy of Science, 109(11), 4086–4091*.

Pink, D., (2009) *Driven: The Surprising Truth about what Motivates Us*. New York: Riverside Books, Penguin Group, Inc.

Pistole, M. (1989). Attachment in adult romantic relationships: Style of conflict resolution and relationship satisfaction. *Journal of Social and Personal Relationships*, 6, 505–510.

Plomin, R., Owen, M., & McGuffin, P. (1994). The genetic basis of complex human behaviors. *Science*, 264, 1733–1739.

Popenol, D., & Whitehead, B. (2001). *The State of our Unions 2000: The Social Health of Marriage in America, The National Marriage Project*. Rutgers, the State University of New Jersey.

Powell, K. E., Spain, K. G., Christenson, G. M., & Mollenkamp, M. P. (1986). The Status of the 1990 Objective for Physical Illness and Exercise. *Public Health Reports*, 101, 15–21.

Pratt, M. & Ashford, B. (2003). Fostering meaningfulness in working and at work. In Cameron, K., Dutton, J. & Quinn, R. (Eds.) *Positive Organizational Scholarship: Foundations of a New Discipline* (pp. 309–327). San Francisco, CA: Berrett-Kohler Publishers.

Premack, D. (1959). Toward Empirical Behavior Laws I. Positive Reinforcement. *Psychological Review*, 66(4), 219–233.

Przybylski, A. & Weinstein, N. (2012). Can you connect with me now? How the presence of mobile communication technology influences face-to-face conversation quality. *Journal of Social and Personal Relationships*. DOI:10.1177/0265407512453827

Putnam, R. (2000). *Bowling Alone*. New York: Simon & Schuster.

Pychel, T. (2000). Don't delay. *http://blogs.psychology today.com/blog/don't-delay*

Radin, D. (1997). *The Conscious Universe*. New York, New York: Harper Collins.

Rajendran, R., & Kaliappan, K. (1990). Efficacy of behavioral programme in managing the academic stress and improving academic performance. *Journal of Personality and Clinical Studies*, 6, 193–196.

Ramachandran, V. (2000). Mirror neurons and imitation learning as the driving force behind the "great leap forward" in human evolution. *Edge, the third culture,* No. 69. *http://www.edge/org/3rd_culture/ramachandran/ramachandran_index.html.*

Ram Dass. (1990). *Journey Of Awakening-A Meditators Guidebook.* New York: Bantam Books.

Rasmussen, H., Scheier, M. & Greenhouse, J. (2009). Optimism and Physical Health: A Meta-Analytic Review. *Annals of Behavioral Medicine,* 37, 239–256.

Rathus, S. A. (1973). A 30-item schedule for assessing assertive behavior. *Behavior Therapy,* 4, 398–406.

Rathus, S., & Nevid, J. (1995). *Adjustment and Growth: The Challenges of Life* (6th Ed.) New York: Harcourt Brace.

Raymond, M., & Moser, R. (1995). Aviators at Risk. *Aviation, Space and Environmental Medicine,* 66, 35–39.

Reckmeyer, W. J. (July, 2005). *Developing Global Citizenship-Leadership for the 21st Century.* Salzburg, Austria Seminar: Community Colleges as Sites for Global Citizenship.

Reik, T. (1972). *Listening with the Third Ear.* New York: Pyramid Press.

Renzetti, C., & Curren, D. (1998). *Living Sociology.* Needham Heights, MA: Allyn & Bacon.

Rhodewalt, F., & Zone, J.B. (1989). Appraisal of Life Change, Depression and Illness in Hardy and Non-Hardy Women. *Journal of Personality and Social Psychology,* 56: 81–88.

Ricard, M. (2006). *Happiness.* New York, New York: Little, Brown & Co.

Richardson, A. (1969). *Mental Imagery.* New York: Springer – Verlag.

Rimland, B. (1982). The altruism paradox. *The Southern Psychologist,* 2(1), 8–9.

Rizzolatti, G., & Craighero, L. (2004). The mirror-neuron system. *Annual Review of Neuroscience,* 27, 169–192.

Robbins, A. (1986). *Unlimited Power.* New York: Ballantine Books.

Roberts, B., & Mann, R. (Winter, 1996). Sexual Harassment in the Workplace: A Primer. *Akron Law Review,* 29, 269.

Roberts, R. C. (1982). *Spirituality and Human Emotion.* Grand Rapids, MI: Eerdmans.

Robinson, F.R. (1970). *Effective Study (4th Ed.).* New York: Harper & Row Publishers.

Robinson, J., & Martin, S. (2008, December). Channeling unhappiness: In Good and Bad Economic times. *Social Indicators Research online.* University of Maryland. *http://www.newsdesk .umd.edu/mar/send.cfm?articleID+1798*

Roe, A. (1972). Perspectives on Vocational Development. Whiteley, J. & Resnikoff, A. (Eds.) *Perspectives on Vocational Development.* Washington, D.C.: American Personnel and Guidance Association.

Rogers, C. (1951). *Client-Centered Therapy: Its Current Practice, Implications and Theory.* Boston: Houghton Mifflin

Rogers, C. (1959). A Theory of Therapy, Personality and Interpersonal Relationships as Developed in the Client-Centered Framework. In Koch, S. (Ed.). *Psychology: A Study of a Science.* (pp. 33–51), Vol 3. New York: McGraw Hill.

Roper Starch Worldwide, Inc. (1999). *Baby Boomers Envision their Retirement.* Washington, D. C.: American Association of Retired Persons.

Roseman, M., Milette, K., Zhao, Y. & Thombs, B. (2010). Is optimism associated with physical health? A commentary on Rasmussen et. al. *Annals of Behavioral Medicine,* 39, 204–206.

Rosengren, A., Tibblin, G. & Wilhelmsen, L. (1991). Self perceived psychological stress and incidence of coronary artery disease in middle-aged men. *American Journal of Cardiology,* 68, 1171–1175.

Rosenzweig, E., & Gilovich, T. (2012). Buyers remorse or mixed opportunity? Differential regrets for material and experiential purchases. 102, No. 2 215–223.

Rossi, E. (1986). *The PsychoBiology of Mind-Body Healing.* New York: W. W. Norton & Co.

Roth, D. L., & Holmes, D. S. (1987). Influences of Aerobic Exercise Training and Relaxation Training on Physical and Psychological Health Following Stressful Life Events. *Psychosomatic Medicine,* 49, 355–365.

Roth, D., Weibe, D., Fillingian, R., & Shay, K. (1989). Life Events, Fitness, Hardiness and Health: A Simultaneous Analysis of Proposed Stress-Resistance Effects. *Journal of Personality and Social Psychology,* 57, 136–142.

Rotter, J. (1966). Generalized Expectancies for Internal vs. External Locus of Control of Reinforcement. *Psychological Monographs: General and Applied,* 80, (Whole No. 609).

Ruas, J., Orhan, F., Agudelo, L, Fermenia, T., Goiny, M., & Porsmyr-Palmerte, M. (2014). Skeletal muscle PGC 1a1 modulates kynurenine metabolism and mediates resilience to stress-induced depression. *Cell* 09/2014, 159(1), 33–45.

Ryan, R. M., & Deci, E. L. (2000). Self Determination Theory and the Facilitation of Intrinsic Motivation, Social Development, and Well Being. *American Psychologist,* 55, 68–78.

Ryff, C., & Singer, B. (1996). Psychological well-being: Meaning, measurement, and implications for psychotherapy research. *Psychotherapy and Psychosomatics,* 65, 14–23.

Sachs, B. (1991). Coping with stress. *Stress Medicine,* 7, 61–63.

Salovey, P., Mayer, J. D., & Caruso, D. (2002). The Positive Psychology of Emotional Intelligence. In C. R. Snyder & S. J. Lopez (Eds.). *Handbook of Positive Psychology.* (pp. 159–171). New York: Oxford University Press.

Sanfey, A. (2003). The neural basis of economic decision-making in the ultimatum game. *Science,* 300, 1755–1758.

Sanorajski, RT., Delaney, C., Durham, L., Ordy, J. M., Johnson, J. A., & Dunlop, W. P. (1985). Effect of Exercise on Longevity, Body Weight, Locomotor Performance and Passive Aggressive Memory of Mice. *Neurobiology of Aging,* 6, 17–24.

Sarason, B. R., Sarason, I. G., & Pierce, G. R. (Eds.). (1990). *Social Support: An Interactional View.* pp. 9–25. New York: Wiley

Sawka-Miller, K. & Miller, D. (2007). The Third Pillar: Linking positive psychology and school-wide positive behavior support. *School Psychology Forum: Research in Practice,* Vol. 2, Issue 1, 26–38.

Schacter, S., & Singer, J. (1962). Cognitive, Social and Physiological Determinants of Emotional State. *Psychological Review,* 69, 379–399.

Sharot, T. (2011). *The Optimism Bias. A Tour of the Irrationally Positive Brain.* New York: Panteon Books.

Sharot, T. (12/12/2012). Why We are Wired to Look on the Bright Side. The Optimism Bias I Video on *TED.Com.*

Scheier, M. F., & Carver, C. S. (1993). On the Power of Positive Thinking: The Benefits of Being Optimistic. *Current Directions in Psychological Science,* 2, 26–30.

Scheier, M. F., Carver, C. S., & Bridges, M. W. (1994). Distinguishing Optimism from Neuroticism (and Trait Anxiety, Self Mastery, and Self-Esteem): A Reevaluation of the Life Orientation Test. *Journal of Personality and Social Psychology,* 57, 1024–1040.

Schiraldi, G. (1993). *Building Self-esteem: A 125 day program.* Dubuque, IO: Kendall/Hunt.

Schneider, I., Smith, W., & Witcher, S. (1984). The relationship of mental imagery to white blood cell (neutrophil) function: Experimental studies of normal subjects. *Paper presented at the 36th Annual Scientific Meeting of the International Society for Clinical and Experimental Hypnosis,* San Antonio, Texas (10/25/84)

Schneider, S. L. (2001). In Search of Realistic Optimism: Meaning, Knowledge, and Warm Fuzziness. *American Psychologist,* 56, 250–263.

Scholz, J., Klein, M., Behrens, T. & Johansen-Berg, H. (2009). Training induces changing in white matter architecture. *Natural Neuroscience,* Vol. 12 (11), 1370–1371.

Schwartz, H.A., Eichstaedt, J., Kern, M., Dziurzynski, L, Agrawal, M., Park, G., Lakshmikanth, S., Jha, S., Seligman, M. & Unger, L. (2013) Characterizing Geographic Variation in Well-Being Using Tweets. *Association for the Advancement of AI. www.aai.org.*

Scott, D. (1980). *How to Put More Time in Your Life.* New York: Rawson, Wade Publishers.

Schroeder, D., Penner, L., Dovidio, J., & Piliavin, J. (1995). *The Psychology of Helping and Altruism.* New York: McGraw Hill.

Seaward, B. L. (1997). *Managing Stress*. Boston: Jones & Bartlett.

Segerstrom, F., & Miller, G. (2004) Psychological stress and the human immune system: A meta-analytic study of 30 years of inquiry. *Psychological Bulletin*, 104, 601–630.

Seligman, M. (1991). *Learned Optimism*. New York: Knopf.

Seligman, M. (1995). The effectiveness of psychotherapy: The consumer report study. *American Psychologist*, 50, 965–974.

Seligman, M. (1998b). *Learned Optimism: How to Change Your Mind and Your Life* 2nd Ed. New York: Pocket Books.

Seligman, M. (2002). *Authentic Happiness*. New York: Free Press.

Seligman, M. (2011). *Flourish*. New York: Free Press.

Seligman, M., Nolen-Hoeksema, S., Thornton, N., & Thornton, K. (1990). Explanatory style as a mechanism of disappointing athletic performance. *Psychological Science*, 1, 143–146.

Seligman, M., & Shulman, P. (1986). Explanatory Styles as a Predictor of Productivity and Quitting among Life Insurance Sales Agents. *Journal of Personality and Social Psychology*, 50, 832–838.

Seligman, M., Steen, T., Park, N., & Peterson, C. (2005). Positive Psychology progress. Empirical validation of interventions. *American Psychologist*, 60, 410–421.

Seligman, M., Reivich, K., Jaycox, L., & Gillham, J. (1995). *The Optimistic Child*. New York: Houghton Mifflin.

Selye, H. (1956). *The Stress of Life*. New York: McGraw Hill.

Selye, H. (1974). *Stress Without Distress*. New York: Dutton.

Selye, H. (1982). History and Present Status of the Stress Concept. In Goldberg, L. & Breznitz, S. (Eds.). *Handbook of Stress; Theoretical and Clinical Aspects*. New York: Free Press.

Shanahan, D., Bush, R., Gaston, K., Lin, J., Barber, E. & Fuller, R. (2016). Health benefits from nature experiences depend on dose. *Scientific Reports*. 6, 28551. DOI: 1038/srep28551

Sheppard, J.A., & Kashani, J.H. (1991). The Relationship of Hardiness, Gender and Stress to Health Outcomes in Adolescents. *Journal of Personality*, 59, 747–768.

Sheldrake, R. (1981). *A New Science of Life: The Hypothesis of Formative Causation*. London: Blond & Briggs.

Sheikh, A. (Ed.) (2005). *Healing Images: The Role of Imagination in Health*. Amityville, New York: Baywood Publishing Company.

Shemming, D. (2011). *Understanding Disorganized Attachment: Theory and Practice for Working with Children and Adults*. Philadelphia, PA: Kingsley Publishers.

Sherwood, B. (2009, February 2nd). What it takes to survive. *Newsweek Magazine*, 50–53.

Siebert, A. (1996). *The Survivor Personality*. Perigree Books, Berkley Publishing Group.

Siegel, B. (1986). *Love, Medicine and Miracles*. New York: Harper & Row.

Silberman, M, & Hansburg, F. (2000). *People Smart: Developing your Interpersonal Intelligence*. San Francisco, CA.: Berrett-Kochler Publishers.

Sills, J. (2013). The Power of No. *Psychology Today*, 53–61.

Simon, S. B., & Simon, S. (1990). *Forgiveness: How to Make Peace with Your Past and Get on with Your Life*. New York, N. Y.: Warner Books.

Simon, R. W. (2002). Revisiting the relationships among gender, martial status, and mental health. *American Journal of Sociology*, 107(4), 1065–1097.

Singer, T, Critchley, H., & Preuschoff, K. (2009). A Common Role of Insula in Feelings, Empathy and Uncertainty. *Trends in Cognitive Sciences*, 13(8), 334–340.

Simonton, O., Matthews-Simonton, S., & Creighton, J. (1978). *Getting Well Again*. New York: Bantam Books

Skinner, B. F. (1953). *Science and Human Behavior*. New York: MacMillan.

Slopen, N., Glynn, R., Buring, J., Albert, M. (2010). Job strain, job insecurity and incident cardiovascular disease in the Womens' Health Study. *Circulations*, Abstract 18520 Cir.ahajournals,org

Smith, M. (1975). *When I Say No, I Feel Guilty.* New York: The Dial Press.

Smith, T. W. (1992). Hostility and Health: Current Status of a Psychosomatic Hypothesis. *Health Psychology,* 11, 139–150.

Snyder, C. R., & Feldman, D. B. (2000). Hope for the Many: An Empowering Social Agenda. In C. R. Snyder (Ed.). *Handbook of Hope: Theory, Measures and Applications.* (pp. 389–412). San Diego, CA.: Academic Press.

Snyder, C., & Lopez, S. (Eds.), (2005). *Handbook of Positive Psychology.* New York: Oxford University Press.

Snyder, C., & Lopez, S. (2007). *Positive Psychology.* California: Sage Publications.

Solnick, S., & Hemenway, D. (1998). Is more always better?: A survey on positional concerns. *Journal of Economic Behavior and Organization,* 37(3), 373–383.

Solomon, J. & George, C. (1999). *Attachment Disorganization.* New York, New York: Guilford Press.

Sone, T., Nakaya, N., Ohmori, K., Shimozu, T., Higashiguchi, M. & Kakizaki, M. (2008). Sense of life worth living (ikigai) and mortality in Japan: Ohsaski study. *Psychosomatic Medicine,* 70, 709–715.

Sorbi, M., & Tellegen, B. (1986). Differential effects of training in relaxation and stress-coping in patients with migraine. *Headache,* 26, 473–481.

Soussignan, R. (2001). Duchenne smile, emotional experience, and autonomic reactivity: A test of the facial feedback hypothesis. Emotion, 2, 52–74.

Southwick, S., & Charney, M. (2012). *Resilience: The Science of Mastering Lifes Greatest Challenges.* Cambridge University Press.

Speisman, R. Kumar, D., Rani, A., Foster, T., & Ormerod, B. (2013). Daily exercise improves memory, stimulates hippcampul neurogenesis and modulates immune and neuroimmune cytokines in aging rats. *Brain Behavior Immunity,* 28, 25–43.

Spence, J. T. (1985). Achievement American style: The rewards and costs of individualism. *American Psychologist,* 40, 1287–1288.

Sprague, J. & Horner, R. (2006). School wide positive behavior supports. In Jamerson, S. & Furlong, M. (Eds.). *Handbook of School Violence and School Safety: From Research to Practice* (pp. 413–427). Mahwah, N. J.: Erlbaum.

Sprecher, S. (2014) Taking Turns: Reciprocal self-disclosure promotes liking in initial interactions. *Journal of Experimental Social Psychology.* http://www.academia.edu/33048221/takingturns

Sprecher, S., Metts, S., Burleson, B., Hatfield, E., & Thompson, A. (1995). Domains of excessive interaction in intimate relationships: Associations with satisfaction and commitment. *Family Relations,* 44, 203–210.

Sroufe, L. (1983). Infant-caregiver attachment and patterns of adaptation in preschool: The roots of maladaptation and competence. In M. Perlmutter (Ed.) *Minnesota Symposium in Child Psychology* (Vol. 16, pp. 41–81). Hillsdale, N.J.: Erlbaum.

Sroufe, L., Fox, N., & Pancake, V. (1983). Attachment and dependency in developmental perspective. *Child Development,* 54, 1615–1627.

State University System Board of Regents. *Policy Manual.* Atlanta: State of Georgia.

Steel, P. (2007). The nature of procrastination: A meta-analytic and theoretical review of quintessential self-regulatory failure. *Psychological Bulletin,* Vol. 133, No. 1, 65–94.

Steele, C. M. (1997). A Threat in the Air: How Stereotypes Shape Intellectual Identity and Performance. *American Psychologist,* 52, 613–629.

Steinhauser, S. (July, 1998). Age Bias: Is Your Corporate Culture in Need of an Overhaul? *H.R. Magazine,* 87–91.

Steinhauser, S. (Sept./Oct., 1999). Beyond Age Bias: Successfully Managing an Older Workforce. *Aging Today.*

Steptoe, A., Wardle, J. & Marmot, M. (2005). Positive affect and health related neuroendocrine, cardiovascular and inflammatory processes. *Proceedings of the National Academy of Sciences,* 102, 6508–6512.

Stewart, S. (October, 2002). The Worst of All Possible Worlds. *The University of Chicago Magazine,* Vol. 95, Issue 1.

Stotland, E. (1969). Exploratory investigations of empathy. In L. Berkowitz (Ed.) *Advances in Experimental Social Psychology* (Vol. 4, pp. 271–314). New York: Academic Press.

Strack, F., Martin, L., & Stepper, S. (1988). Inhibiting and facilitating conditions of the human smile: A nonobtrusive test of the facial feedback hypothesis. *Journal of Personality and Social Psychology*. Vol. 54, No. 5, 768–777.

Sui, X., Laditka, J., Hardin, J. & Blair, S. (2007). Estimated functional capacity predicts mortality in older adults. *Journal of the American Geriatric Society*, 55, 1940–1947.

Sullivan, H.S. (1953). *The Interpersonal Theory of Psychiatry*. New York: Norton.

Suomi, S.J. (1999). Attachment in Rhesus Monkeys. In J. Cassidy & P. Shaver (Eds). *Handbook of Attachment: Theory, Research and Clinical Applications* (pp. 181–197). New York: New York: Guilford Press.

Talbot, M. (1991). *The Holographic Universe*. New York, New York: HarperCollins Publishers.

Tafardi, R., & Swann, Jr., W. (1995). Self-liking and self-competence as dimensions of global self-esteem: Initial validation of a measure. *Journal of Personality Assessment*, 65(2), 332–342.

Tafardi, R., & Swann, Jr., W. (1996). Individualism-collectivism and global self-esteem. *Journal of Cross-Cultural Psychology*, 27(6), 651–672.

Tangney, J. P., & Baumeister, R. F. (2000). *High Self Control Predicts Good Adjustment, Less Pathology, Better Grades and Interpersonal Success*. Unpublished Manuscript. George Mason University, Fairfax, Va.

Tannen, D. (1990). *You Just Don't Understand: Women and Men in Conversation*. New York: Ballantine Books.

Tannen, D. (1994). *Talking from 9 to 5*. New York: William Morrow.

Tannen, D. (1998). *The Argument Culture*. New York, N.Y.: Random House.

Tart, C. (1986). *Waking Up*. Boston: Shambhala.

Taylor, S. E. (2000). Biobehavioral Responses to Stress in Females: Tend and Befriend, not Fight or Flight. *Psychological Review*, 107 (3), 411–429.

Taylor, S., & Brown, J. (1988). Illusion and well-being- a social psychological perspective on mental health. *Psychological Bulletin*, 103(2), 193–210.

Tellegen, A., Lykken, D., Bouchard, T., Wilcox, K., Segal, N., & Rich, S. (1988). Personality similarity in twins reared apart and together. *Journal of Personality and Social Psychology*, 54, 1031–1039.

Terry, R. L. (2004, March 12). Answers on Outsourcing. *CNN Money*. *www.money.cnn/2004/03/11/commentary*

Thoresen, C., Luskin F., & Harris, A. (1998). Science and Forgiveness Interventions: Reflections and Recommendations. In E. L. Worthington (Ed.). *Dimensions of Forgiveness: Psychological Research and Theological Perspectives*. Philadelphia, PA.: Templeton Foundation Press.

Thornton, A., & Young-DeMarco, L. (2001). Four decades in attitudes toward family issues in the U.S.. The 1960's to the 1990's. *Journal of Marriage and Family*, 63(4), 1009.

Tice, D., & Baumeister, R. (1993). *Handbook of Mental Control*. Vol. 5. In Wegner, D, & Pennebaker, J. (Eds.). Englewood Cliffs, N. J.: Prentice Hall Press.

Tice, D. & Baumeister, R. (1997). Longitudinal Study of Procrastination, Performance, Stress and Health: The Costs and Benefits of Dawdling. *Psychological Science*, 8, 454–458.

Tidwell, N., Eastwick, P., & Findle, E., (2013). Perceived, not actual similarity predicts initial attraction in a live romantic context: Evidence from the speed dating paradigm. *Personal Relationships vol. 20, Issue 2, 199–215*.

Tindle, H., Chang, Y., Kuller, L., Manson, J., Robinson, J., Rosal, M., Siegle, G. & Matthews, K. (2009). Optimism, clinical hostility and incident coronary heart disease and mortality in the Women's Health Initiative. *Circulation*, 118, 1145–1146.

Titchener, E. (1909) *Elementary Psychology of the Thought Processes*. New York: Macmillan.

Toffler, A. (1971). *Future Shock*. New York, N, Y.: Bantam Books.

Toffler, A. (1981). *The Third Wave*. New York, N. Y.: Bantam Books.

Tolle, E. (2005). *A New Earth: Awakening to Your Life's Purpose*. New York, N. Y.: Penguin Group.

Tough, P. (2012). *How Children Succeed: Grit, Curiosity and the Hidden Power of Character.* New York: New York: Houghton Mifflin/Harcourt Publishing.

Travis, J. (1981). *Wellness Workbook.* Berkeley, CA: Ten Speed Press.

Troy, M., & Sroufe, L. (1987). Victimization among preschoolers: Role of attachment relationship history. *Journal of American Academy of Child and Adolescent Psychiatry, 26,* 166–172.

Tugade, M., & Fredrickson, B. (2004). Resilient individuals use positive emotions to bounce back from negative emotional experiences. *Journal of Personality and Social Psychology, 86,* 320–333.

Uchino, B. (2006). Social Support and Health: A review of physiological processes potentially underlying links to disease outcomes. *Journal of Behavioral Medicine, 29,* 377–387.

Uhl, C. (2004). *Developing Ecological Consciousness: Path to a Sustainable World.* Boulder, Col.: Rowman & Littlefield Publishers.

Underwood. A., & Kalb, C. (June, 1999). STRESS. *Newsweek Magazine,* 56–63.

Unger, L., & Thumuluri, L. (1997). Trait empathy and continuous helping. *Journal of Social Behavior and Personality, 12,* 785–800.

U. S. Census Bureau. (2001). Unmarried Couples Increase. *Intel/Health. http://www.intel.health.com*

U. S. Census Bureau. (2010). Selected Social Characteristics in the United States. *American Fact Finder. http://factfinder2.census.gov/faces/tableservices/jsf/pages.*

U. S. Dept. of Labor. Bureau of Labor Statistics. (2000). Washington, D.C.: U.S. Government Printing Office. *www.state.bls.gov.com*

U. S. Dept. of Labor. Bureau of Labor Statistics (2011). Overview of the 2008–2009 projections. *Occupational Outlook Handbook.. www.bls.gov/oco/oco2003.htm*

U.S. Dept. Of Labor, Employment and Training Administration. (1991). *Dictionary of Occupational Titles.* Lanham, MD.: Bernan Press.

U.S. Dept. Of Labor. *Occupational Outlook Handbook* Washington, D. C.: U.S. Government Printing Office

U.S. Dept. Of Labor. (2014). *Occupational Outlook Handbook 2014-2015.* New York: Skyhorse Publishing.

U.S. Equal Employment Opportunity Commission. (April, 1997). *Technical Assistance Manual.* Washington D.C.: USEEOC Technical Assistance Program.

U. S. Surgeon General. (1979) Healthy People: The Surgeon General's Report on Health Promotion and Disease Prevention. *U. S. Dept. of Health, Education and Welfare (PHS) Publication No. 79-55071,* Washington, D. C.: U. S. Government Printing Office.

U.S. Surgeon General. (2008). *www.cdc.gov/nccdphp/sgr/index.htm* (1999).

Vaillant, G. E. (1977). *Adaptation to Life.* Boston, Mass.: Little, Brown Publishers.

Vaillant, G. E. (2003). *Aging Well: Surprising Guideposts to a Happier Life from the landmark Harvard Study of Adult Development.* New York: Little, Brown & Co.

VanBoven, L., & Gilovich, T. (2003). To Do or to Have? That is the Question. *Journal of Personality and Social Psychology, 85,* no. 6, 1193–1202.

Veenhoven, R. (Oct., 2006). *How do we Assess how Happy we are? Tenets, Implications and Tenability of Three Theories.* Paper presented at New Directions in the Study of Happiness conference. University of Notre Dame, South Bend, Indiana.

Vohs, K., Mead, N., & Goode, M. (2008). Merely activating the concept of money changes personal and interpersonal behavior. *Current Directions in Psychological Science.* 17, No. 3, 208–212.

Wager, T., Rilling, J., Smith, E., Sokolik, A., Casey, C., Davidson, R., Kosslyn, S., Rose, R., & Cohen, J. (2004). Placebo induced changes in fMRI in the anticipation and experience of pain. *Science, 303,* 1162–1167.

Walker, R. (2008). Mentoring helps SSA become a better workplace. *http://www.fcw.com/print/13-131news/102557-1.html*

Wallace, R. & Benson, H. (1972). The Physiology of Meditation. *Scientific American, 226,* 85–90.

Watson, D. (2000). *Mood and Temperament.* New York: Guilford Press.

Watson, D. (2005). Positive affectivity: The disposition to experience pleasurable emotional states. In C.R. Snyder & S.J. Lopez (Eds.) *Handbook of Positive Psychology* (pp. 106–119). New York: Oxford University Press.

Wegner, D., Erber, A. & Zanakos, S. (1998). Ironic processes in the mental control of mood and mood related thought. *Journal of Personality and Social Psychology,* 65(6), 1093–1104.

Weinstein, N. (1989). Optimistic biases about personal risks. *Science,* 246, 1232–1233.

Weiss, J. (1971). Effects of coping behavior in different warning signal conditions on stress pathology in rats. *Journal of Comparative and Physiological Psychology,* 77, 113.

Wenzloff, R. & Wegner, D. (2000). Thought suppression. *Annual Review of Psychology,* 51, 59–91.

White, A. (2007). A Global Projection of Subjective Well-Being: A Challenge to Positive Psychology? *Psychtalk,* 56, 17–20.

Wilber, K. (1979). *No Boundary.* Los Angeles: Center Publications.

Williams, J., Hogan, T., & Anderson, M. (1993). Positive states of mind and athletic injury risk. *Psychosomatic Medicine,* 55, 468–472.

Williams, R. (1989). *The Trusting Heart: Great News about Type A Behavior.* New York: Random House.

Wilson, T., Wheatley, T., Myers, J., Gilbert, D., & Assom., D. (2000). Focalism: A source of durability bias in affective forecasting. *Journal of Personality and Social Psychology,* 78, 821–836.

Winner, E. (2000). The origins and ends of giftedness. *American Psychologist,* 55(1), 159–169.

Wiseman, R. (2003). *The Luck Factor.* London, UK: Random House.

Witvliet, C. V., Ludwig, T., & Vander-Laan, K. (2001). Granting Forgiveness or Harboring Grudges: Implications for Emotion, Physiology and Health. *Psychological Science,* 121, 117–123.

Wolvin, A. & Coakley, C. (1991). A Survey of the Status of Listening Training in some Fortune 500 Corporations. *Communication Education,* 40, 152–164.

Yerkes, R. M., & Dodson, J. D. (1908). The Relation of Strength of Stimulus to Rapidity of Habit Formation. *Journal of Comparative and Neurological Psychology,* 18, 459–482.

Zillman, D. (1989). Mental Control of Angry Aggression. In Wegner, D., & Pennebaker, J. (Eds.). *Handbook of Mental Control.* Englewood Cliffs, N.J.: Prentice Hall Press.

Zimbardo, P., & Henderson, L. (2008). Shyness. *Encyclopedia of Mental Health.* San Diego, CA: Academic Press.

Zheng, W., & Hart, R. (2002). The effects of martial and nonmarital union transition on health. *Journal of Marriage and Family,* 64(2), 420–433.

Zullow, H., Oettingen, G., Peterson, C., & Seligman, M. (1988). Explanatory style and pessimism in the historical record: CAVing, LBJ, presidential candidates and east vs. west Berlin. *American Psychologist,* 673–682.

Zyfowsky, D. G. (1970). Fifteen needs and values. *Vocational Guidance Quarterly,* 18, 182.

_____ *Basis of EEO Discrimination.* Washington, D. C.: Equal Employment Opportunity Commission. *www.eeoc.gov.com.*

_____ (2001). Engage Employees and Boost Performance. *Working Paper.* Philadelphia, PA.: Hay Group.

_____ (1998). Planning a Career. *Adventures in Education,* Texas Guaranteed Loan Corporation.

_____ (1998). *Self-Directed Search.* Odessa, FL.: Psychological Assessment Resources, Inc. Website (@www.sdstest3.com).

_____ (1994). *Strong Vocational Interest Inventory.* Palo Alto, CA.: Consulting Psychologists Press.

_____ 2004, August). The Foreign Born Population in the United States: 2003. *Population Statistics, U.S. Census Bureau.*

_____ (2006, January 30th). The Future of Outsourcing. *http://www.businessweek.com/print/magazine/content/06_05/b3969401.htm?chang=gl*

_____ (2003, March). *Current Population Survey. U.S. Census Bureau http://census.gov/populaton/www/socdemo/foreign/cps2003.html*

_____ (2009). 12 Step Guide to Financial Success. *Mapping yourFuture.org.*

Credits

Index